get with the programming

Through the power of practice and immediate personalized feedback, MyProgrammingLab improves your performance.

PROBLEM SOLVING with C++

Eighth Edition

Eighth Edition

PROBLEM SOLVING with C++

Walter Savitch

UNIVERSITY OF CALIFORNIA, SAN DIEGO

CONTRIBUTOR

Kenrick Mock

UNIVERSITY OF ALASKA, ANCHORAGE

International Edition Contributions by

Arup Kumar Bhattacharjee

RCC INSTITUTE OF INFORMATION TECHNOLOGY, KOLKATA

Soumen Mukherjee

RCC INSTITUTE OF INFORMATION TECHNOLOGY, KOLKATA

Addison Wesley

Boston   Columbus   Indianapolis   New York   San Francisco   Upper Saddle River
Amsterdam   Cape Town   Dubai   London   Madrid   Milan   Munich   Paris   Montreal   Toronto
Delhi   Mexico City   São Paulo   Sydney   Hong Kong   Seoul   Singapore   Taipei   Tokyo

Editorial Director: *Marcia Horton*
Editor-in-Chief: *Michael Hirsch*
Acquisitions Editor: *Matt Goldstein*
Editorial Assistant: *Chelsea Bell*
Vice President, Marketing: *Patrice Jones*
Marketing Manager: *Yezan Alayan*
Marketing Coordinator: *Kathryn Ferranti*
Vice President, Production: *Vince O'Brien*
Managing Editor: *Jeff Holcomb*
Senior Production Project Manager: *Marilyn Lloyd*
Publisher, International Edition: *Angshuman Chakraborty*

Acquisitions Editor, International Edition: *Arunabha Deb*
Publishing Assistant, International Edition: *Shokhi Shah*
Senior Operations Supervisor: *Alan Fischer*
Operations Specialist: *Lisa McDowell*
Text Designer: *Sandra Rigney*
Cover Designer: *Central Covers*
Cover Image: *Aron Jungermann / Getty Images*
Media Editor: *Daniel Sandin*
Media Project Manager: *Wanda Rockwell*
Full-Service Vendor: *Nesbitt Graphics, Inc.*
Cover Printer: *Lehigh Phoenix Color*

Pearson Education Limited
Edinburgh Gate
Harlow
Essex CM20 2JE
England

and Associated Companies throughout the world

Visit us on the World Wide Web at:
www.pearsoninternationaleditions.com

© Pearson Education Limited 2012

ISBN 10: 0-273-75218-9
ISBN 13: 978-0-273-75218-9

British Library Cataloguing-in-Publication Data
A catalogue record for this book is available from the British Library

10 9 8 7 6 5 4 3 2 1
14 13 12 11 10

Typeset in Giovanni Std-Book by Nesbitt Graphics, Inc.
Printed and bound by Edwards Brothers in The United States of America

The publisher's policy is to use paper manufactured from sustainable forests.

Preface

This book is meant to be used in a first course in programming and computer science using the C++ language. It assumes no previous programming experience and no mathematics beyond high school algebra.

If you have used the previous edition of this book, you should read the following section that explains the changes to this eighth edition, the section explaining MyProgrammingLab, and then you can skip the rest of this preface. If you are new to this book, the rest of this preface will give you an overview of the book.

Changes to the Eighth Edition

This eighth edition presents the same programming philosophy as the seventh edition. All of the material from the seventh edition remains, but with the following enhancements:

- The material on stream classes used to introduce the concept of inheritance has been removed from Chapter 10. Instead, inheritance is introduced with the much simpler bank account example used throughout the chapter.
- Additional material on:
    scoping
    parameter passing
    random number generation
    dynamic arrays

has been added and the presentation has been reworked in several chapters.

- Twenty-five new programming projects have been added throughout the book and integrated into the existing projects at the end of each chapter.
- Fifteen new VideoNotes have been added to the book's Companion Website, for a total of fifty-four VideoNotes. These VideoNotes walk students through the process of both problem solving and coding to help reinforce key programming concepts. An icon appears in the margin of the book when a VideoNote is available regarding the topic covered in the text.

If you are an instructor already using the seventh edition, you can continue to teach your course almost without change.

Flexibility in Topic Ordering

This book was written to allow instructors wide latitude in reordering the material. To illustrate this flexibility, we suggest two alternative ways to order the topics. There is no loss of continuity when the book is read in either of these ways. To ensure this continuity when you rearrange material, you may need to move sections rather than entire chapters. However, only large sections in convenient locations are moved. To help customize a particular order for any class's needs, the end of this preface contains a dependency chart, and each chapter has a "Prerequisites" section that explains what material needs to be covered before each section in that chapter.

Reordering 1: Earlier Classes

To effectively design classes, a student needs some basic tools such as control structures and function definitions. This basic material is covered in Chapters 1 through 6. After completing Chapter 6, students can begin to write their own classes. One possible reordering of chapters that allows for such early coverage of classes is the following:

Basics: Chapters 1, 2, 3, 4, 5, and 6. This material covers all control structures, function definitions, and basic file I/O. Chapter 3, which covers additional control structures, could be deferred if you wish to cover classes as early as possible.

Classes and namespaces: Chapter 10, Sections 11.1 and 11.2 of Chapter 11, and Chapter 12. This material covers defining classes, friends, overloaded operators, and namespaces.

Arrays, strings and vectors: Chapters 7 and 8

Pointers and dynamic arrays: Chapter 9

Arrays in classes: Sections 11.3 and 11.4 of Chapter 11

Inheritance: Chapter 15

Recursion: Chapter 14 (Alternately, recursion may be moved to later in the course.)

Pointers and linked lists: Chapter 13

Any subset of the following chapters may also be used:

Exception handling: Chapter 16

Templates: Chapter 17

Standard Template Library: Chapter 18

Reordering 2: Classes Slightly Later but Still Early

This version covers all control structures and the basic material on arrays before doing classes, but classes are covered later than the previous ordering and slightly earlier than the default ordering.

Basics: Chapters 1, 2, 3, 4, 5, and 6. This material covers all control structures, function definitions, and the basic file I/O.

Arrays and strings: Chapter 7, Sections 8.1 and 8.2 of Chapter 8

Classes and namespaces: Chapter 10, Sections 11.1 and 11.2 of Chapter 11, and Chapter 12. This material covers defining classes, friends, overloaded operators, and namespaces.

Pointers and dynamic arrays: Chapter 9

Arrays in classes: Sections 11.3 and 11.4 of Chapter 11

Inheritance: Chapter 15

Recursion: Chapter 14. (Alternately, recursion may be moved to later in the course.)

Vectors: Chapter 8.3

Pointers and linked lists: Chapter 13

Any subset of the following chapters may also be used:

Exception handling: Chapter 16

Templates: Chapter 17

Standard Template Library: Chapter 18

Accessibility to Students

It is not enough for a book to present the right topics in the right order. It is not even enough for it to be clear and correct when read by an instructor or other experienced programmer. The material needs to be presented in a way that is accessible to beginning students. In this introductory textbook, I have endeavored to write in a way that students find clear and friendly. Reports from the many students who have used the earlier editions of this book confirm that this style makes the material clear and often even enjoyable to students.

ANSI/ISO C++ Standard

This edition is fully compatible with compilers that meet the latest ANSI/ISO C++ standard.

Advanced Topics

Many "advanced topics" are becoming part of a standard CS1 course. Even if they are not part of a course, it is good to have them available in the text as enrichment material. This book offers a number of advanced topics that can be integrated into a course or left as enrichment topics. It gives thorough coverage of C++ templates, inheritance (including virtual functions), exception handling, and the STL (Standard Template Library). Although this book uses libraries and teaches students the importance of libraries, it does not require any nonstandard libraries. This book uses only libraries that are provided with essentially all C++ implementations.

Dependency Chart

The dependency chart on the next page shows possible orderings of chapters and subsections. A line joining two boxes means that the upper box must be covered before the lower box. Any ordering that is consistent with this partial ordering can be read without loss of continuity. If a box contains a section number or numbers, then the box refers only to those sections and not to the entire chapter.

Summary Boxes

Each major point is summarized in a boxed section. These boxed sections are spread throughout each chapter.

Self-Test Exercises

Each chapter contains numerous Self-Test Exercises at strategic points. Complete answers for all the Self-Test Exercises are given at the end of each chapter.

VideoNote

VideoNotes

VideoNotes are Pearson's new visual tool designed for teaching students key programming concepts and techniques. These short step-by-step videos demonstrate how to solve problems from design through coding. VideoNotes allow for self-paced instruction with easy navigation including the ability to select, play, rewind, fast-forward, and stop within each VideoNote exercise.

myprogramminglab

Online Practice and Assessment with MyProgrammingLab

MyProgrammingLab helps students fully grasp the logic, semantics, and syntax of programming. Through practice exercises and immediate, personalized feedback, MyProgrammingLab improves the programming competence of beginning students who often struggle with the basic concepts and paradigms of popular high-level programming languages.

A self-study and homework tool, a MyProgrammingLab course consists of hundreds of small practice problems organized around the structure of this textbook. For students, the system automatically detects errors in the logic and syntax of their code submissions and offers targeted hints that enable students to figure out what went wrong—and why. For instructors, a comprehensive gradebook tracks correct and incorrect answers and stores the code inputted by students for review.

MyProgrammingLab is offered to users of this book in partnership with Turing's Craft, the makers of the CodeLab interactive programming exercise system. For a full demonstration, to see feedback from instructors and students, or to get started using MyProgrammingLab in your course, visit www.pearsoninternationaleditions.com/myprogramminglab.

DISPLAY P.1   Dependency Chart

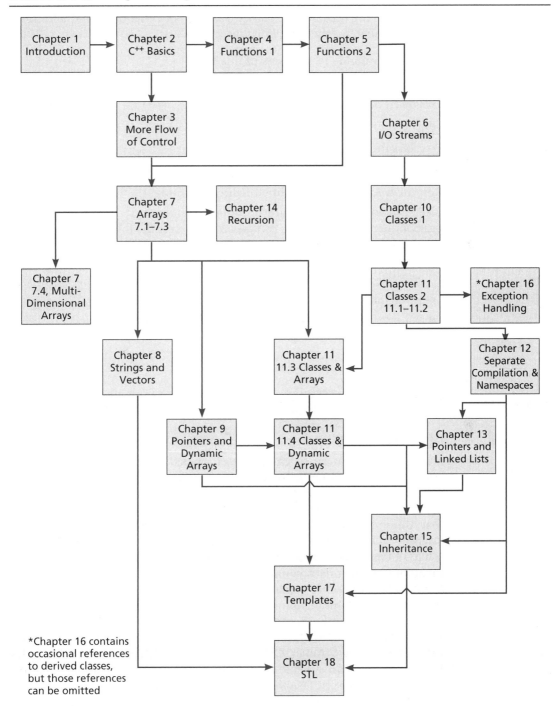

*Chapter 16 contains
occasional references
to derived classes,
but those references
can be omitted

Support Material

There is support material available to all users of this book and additional material available only to qualified instructors.

Materials Available to All Users of this Book

- Source Code from the book
- PowerPoint slides
- VideoNotes

To access these materials, go to:
www.pearsoninternationaleditions.com/savitch

Resources Available to Qualified Instructors Only

Visit Pearson Education's instructor resource center at pearsoninternationaleditions.com/savitch to access the following instructor resources:

- Instructor's Resource Guide—including chapter-by-chapter teaching hints, quiz questions with solutions, and solutions to many programming projects
- Test Bank and Test Generator
- PowerPoint Lectures—including programs and art from the text
- Lab Manual

Contact Us

Your comments, suggestions, questions, and corrections are always welcome. Please e-mail them to savitch.programming.cpp@gmail.com

Acknowledgments

Numerous individuals and groups have provided me with suggestions, discussions, and other help in preparing this textbook. Much of the first edition of this book was written while I was visiting the Computer Science Department at the University of Colorado in Boulder. The remainder of the writing on the first edition and the work on subsequent editions was done in the Computer Science and Engineering Department at the University of California, San Diego (UCSD). I am grateful to these institutions for providing a conducive environment for teaching this material and writing this book.

I extend a special thanks to all the individuals who have contributed critiques or programming projects for this or earlier editions and drafts of this book. In alphabetical order they are: Joseph Allen, Noah Aydin, Claire Bono, Richard Borie, Andrew Burt, Edward Carr, Karla Chaveau, Wei Lian Chen, Joel Cohen, Doug Cosman, Charles Dowling, Scot Drysdale, Joe Faletti, Alex Feldman, Sheila Foster, Paulo Franca, Len Garrett, Jerrold Grossman, Eitan M. Gurari, Andrew Haas, Dennis Heckman, Bob Holloway, Nisar Hundewale, Matt Johnson, Bruce Johnston, Larry Johnson, Thomas Judson, Huzefa Kagdi,

Paul J. Kaiser, Michael Keenan, Brian R. King, Paul Kube, Gilliean Lee, Barney MacCabe, Steve Mahaney, Michael Main, Walter A. Manrique, Anne Marchant, John Marsaglia, Nat Martin, Cynthia Martincic, Bob Matthews, Jesse Morehouse, Ethan Munson, Donald Needham, Dung Nguyen, Joseph D. Oldham, Jennifer Perkins, Jeff Roach, Carol Roberts, Ken Rockwood, John Russo, Amber Settle, Naomi Shapiro, Susanne Sherba, Michal Sramka, James Stepleton, Scott Strong, David Teague, Jeffrey Watson, Jerry Weltman, John J. Westman, and Linda F. Wilson.

I extend a special thanks to the many instructors who used early editions of this book. Their comments provided some of the most helpful reviewing that the book received.

Finally, I thank Kenrick Mock who implemented the changes in this edition. He had the almost impossible task of pleasing me, my editor, and his own sensibilities, and he did a superb job of it.

Walter Savitch

Brief Contents

Contents

Chapter 15 Inheritance 841

Chapter 16   Exception Handling   897

Chapter 17   Templates   929

Introduction to Computers and C++ Programming 1

The whole of the development and operation of analysis are now capable of being executed by machinery. . . . As soon as an Analytical Engine exists, it will necessarily guide the future course of science.

CHARLES BABBAGE (1792–1871)

INTRODUCTION

In this chapter we describe the basic components of a computer, as well as the basic technique for designing and writing a program. We then show you a sample C++ program and describe how it works.

1.1 COMPUTER SYSTEMS

A set of instructions for a computer to follow is called a program. The collection of programs used by a computer is referred to as the **software** for that computer. The actual physical machines that make up a computer installation are referred to as **hardware.** As we will see, the hardware for a computer is conceptually very simple. However, computers now come with a large array of software to aid in the task of programming. This software includes editors, translators, and managers of various sorts. The resulting environment is a complicated and powerful system. In this book we are concerned almost exclusively with software, but a brief overview of how the hardware is organized will be useful.

Hardware

There are three main classes of computers: *PCs, workstations,* and *mainframes.* A **PC (personal computer)** is a relatively small computer designed to be used by one person at a time. Most home computers are PCs, but PCs are also widely used in business, industry, and science. A **workstation** is essentially a larger and more powerful PC. You can think of it as an "industrial-strength" PC. A **mainframe** is an even larger computer that typically requires some support staff and generally is shared by more than one user. The distinctions between PCs, workstations, and mainframes are not precise, but the terms are commonly used and do convey some very general information about a computer.

A **network** consists of a number of computers connected so that they may share resources such as printers and may share information. A network might contain a number of workstations and one or more mainframes, as well as shared devices such as printers.

For our purposes in learning programming, it will not matter whether you are working on a PC, a mainframe, or a workstation. The basic configuration of the computer, as we will view it, is the same for all three types of computers.

The hardware for most computer systems is organized as shown in Display 1.1. The computer can be thought of as having five main components: the *input device(s)*, the *output device(s)*, the *processor* (also called the *CPU*, for *central processing unit*), the *main memory*, and the *secondary memory*. The processor, main memory, and secondary memory are normally housed in a single cabinet. The processor and main memory form the heart of a computer and can be thought of as an integrated unit. Other components connect to the main memory and operate under the direction of the processor. The arrows in Display 1.1 indicate the direction of information flow.

An **input device** is any device that allows a person to communicate information to the computer. Your primary input devices are likely to be a keyboard and a mouse.

An **output device** is anything that allows the computer to communicate information to you. The most common output device is a display screen, referred to as a *monitor*. Quite often, there is more than one output device. For example, in addition to the monitor, your computer probably is connected to a printer for producing output on paper. The keyboard and monitor are sometimes thought of as a single unit called a *terminal*.

DISPLAY 1.1   Main Components of a Computer

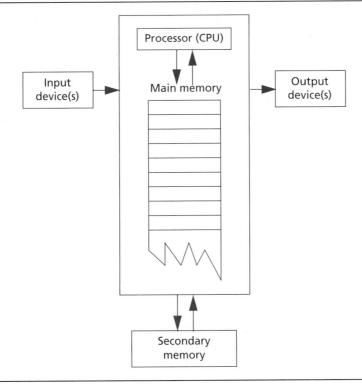

In order to store input and to have the equivalent of scratch paper for performing calculations, computers are provided with *memory*. The program that the computer executes is also stored in this memory. A computer has two forms of memory, called *main memory* and *secondary memory*. The program that is being executed is kept in main memory, and main memory is, as the name implies, the most important memory. **Main memory** consists of a long list of numbered locations called *memory locations*; the number of memory locations varies from one computer to another, ranging from a few thousand to many millions, and sometimes even into the billions. Each memory location contains a string of 0s and 1s. The contents of these locations can change. Hence, you can think of each memory location as a tiny blackboard on which the computer can write and erase. In most computers, all memory locations contain the same number of zero/one digits. A digit that can assume only the values 0 or 1 is called a **binary digit** or a **bit.** The memory locations in most computers contain eight bits (or some multiple of eight bits). An eight-bit portion of memory is called a **byte,** so we can refer to these numbered memory locations as *bytes*. To rephrase the situation, you can think of the computer's main memory as a long list of numbered memory locations called *bytes*. The number that identifies a byte is called its **address.** A data item, such as a number or a letter, can be stored in one of these bytes, and the address of the byte is then used to find the data item when it is needed.

If the computer needs to deal with a data item (such as a large number) that is too large to fit in a single byte, it will use several adjacent bytes to hold the data item. In this case, the entire chunk of memory that holds the data item is still called a **memory location.** The address of the first of the bytes that make up this memory location is used as the address for this larger memory location. Thus, as a practical matter, you can think of the computer's main memory as a long list of memory locations of *varying sizes*. The size of each of these locations is expressed in bytes and the address of the first byte is used as the address (name) of that memory location. Display 1.2 shows a picture of a hypothetical computer's main memory. The sizes of the memory locations are not fixed, but can change when a new program is run on the computer.

Bytes and Addresses

Main memory is divided into numbered locations called **bytes.** The number associated with a byte is called its **address.** A group of consecutive bytes is used as the location for a data item, such as a number or letter. The address of the first byte in the group is used as the address of this larger memory location.

The fact that the information in a computer's memory is represented as 0s and 1s need not be of great concern to you when programming in C++

DISPLAY 1.2   Memory Locations and Bytes

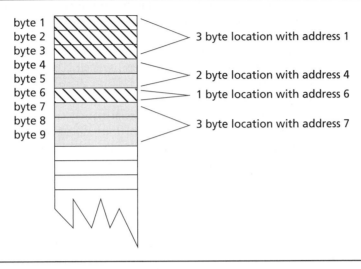

(or in most other programming languages). There is, however, one point about this use of 0s and 1s that will concern us as soon as we start to write programs. The computer needs to interpret these strings of 0s and 1s as numbers, letters, instructions, or other types of information. The computer performs these interpretations automatically according to certain coding schemes. A different code is used for each different type of item that is stored in the computer's memory: one code for letters, another for whole numbers, another for fractions, another for instructions, and so on. For example, in one commonly used set of codes, 01000001 is the code for the letter A and also for the number 65. In order to know what the string 01000001 in a particular location stands for, the computer must keep track of which code is currently being used for that location. Fortunately, the programmer seldom needs to be concerned with such codes and can safely reason as though the locations actually contained letters, numbers, or whatever is desired.

Why Eight?

A **byte** is a memory location that can hold eight bits. What is so special about eight? Why not ten bits? There are two reasons why eight is special. First, eight is a power of 2. (8 is 2^3.) Since computers use bits, which have only two possible values, powers of 2 are more convenient than powers of 10. Second, it turns out that eight bits (one byte) are required to code a single character (such as a letter or other keyboard symbol).

The memory we have been discussing up until now is the main memory. Without its main memory, a computer can do nothing. However, main memory is only used while the computer is actually following the instructions in a program. The computer also has another form of memory called *secondary memory* or *secondary storage*. (The words *memory* and *storage* are exact synonyms in this context.) **Secondary memory** is the memory that is used for keeping a permanent record of information after (and before) the computer is used. Some alternative terms that are commonly used to refer to secondary memory are *auxiliary memory*, *auxiliary storage*, *external memory*, and *external storage*.

Information in secondary storage is kept in units called **files,** which can be as large or as small as you like. A program, for example, is stored in a file in secondary storage and copied into main memory when the program is run. You can store a program, a letter, an inventory list, or any other unit of information in a file.

Several different kinds of secondary memory can be attached to a single computer. The most common forms of secondary memory are *hard disks, diskettes, CDs, DVDs,* and *removable flash memory drives.* (**Diskettes** are also sometimes referred to as *floppy disks.*) **CDs** (compact discs) used on computers are basically the same as those used to record and play music, while **DVDs** (digital video discs) are the same as those used to play videos. CDs and DVDs for computers can be read-only so that your computer can read, but cannot change, the data on the disc; CDs and DVDs for computers can also be read/write, which can have their data changed by the computer. **Hard disks** are fixed in place and are normally not removed from the disk drive. Diskettes and CDs can be easily removed from the disk drive and carried to another computer. Diskettes and CDs have the advantages of being inexpensive and portable, but hard disks hold more data and operate faster. **Flash drives** have largely replaced diskettes today and store data using a type of memory called flash memory. Unlike main memory, flash memory does not require power to maintain the information stored on the device. Other forms of secondary memory are also available, but this list covers most forms that you are likely to encounter.

Main memory is often referred to as **RAM** or **random access memory.** It is called *random access* because the computer can immediately access the data in any memory location. Secondary memory often requires **sequential access,** which means that the computer must look through all (or at least very many) memory locations until it finds the item it needs.

The **processor** (also known as the **central processing unit,** or **CPU**) is the "brain" of the computer. When a computer is advertised, the computer company tells you what *chip* it contains. The **chip** is the processor. The processor follows the instructions in a program and performs the calculations specified by the program. The processor is, however, a very simple brain. All it can do is follow a set of simple instructions provided by the programmer. Typical processor instructions say things like "Interpret the 0s and 1s as numbers, and then add the number in memory location 37 to the number in memory location 59, and put the answer in location 43," or "Read a letter of input, convert it to its code as a string of 0s and 1s, and place it in memory location 1298." The processor can add, subtract, multiply, and divide and can move things from one memory location to another. It can interpret strings of 0s and 1s as letters and send the letters to an output device. The processor also has some primitive ability to rearrange the order of instructions. Processor instructions vary somewhat from one computer to another. The processor of a modern computer can have as many as several hundred available instructions. However, these instructions are typically all about as simple as those we have just described.

Software

You do not normally talk directly to the computer, but communicate with it through an *operating system*. The **operating system** allocates the computer's resources to the different tasks that the computer must accomplish. The operating system is actually a program, but it is perhaps better to think of it as your chief servant. It is in charge of all your other servant programs, and it delivers your requests to them. If you want to run a program, you tell the operating system the name of the file that contains it, and the operating system runs the program. If you want to edit a file, you tell the operating system the name of the file and it starts up the editor to work on that file. To most users, the operating system is the computer. Most users never see the computer without its operating system. The names of some common operating systems are *UNIX*, *DOS*, *Linux*, *Windows*, *Mac OS*, *iOS*, and *Android*.

A **program** is a set of instructions for a computer to follow. As shown in Display 1.3, the input to a computer can be thought of as consisting of two parts, a program and some data. The computer follows the instructions in the program and in that way performs some process. The **data** is what we conceptualize as the input to the program. For example, if the program adds two numbers, then the two numbers are the data. In other words, the data is the input to the program, and both the program and the data are input to the computer (usually via the operating system). Whenever we give a computer

DISPLAY 1.3   **Simple View of Running a Program**

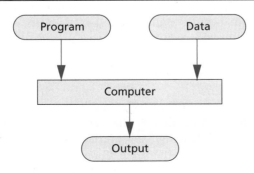

both a program to follow and some data for the program, we are said to be **running the program** on the data, and the computer is said to **execute the program** on the data. The word *data* also has a much more general meaning than the one we have just given it. In its most general sense, it means any information available to the computer. The word is commonly used in both the narrow sense and the more general sense.

High-Level Languages

There are many languages for writing programs. In this text we will discuss the C++ programming language and use it to write our programs. C++ is a high-level language, as are most of the other programming languages you are likely to have heard of, such as C, C#, Java, Python, PHP, Pascal, Visual Basic, FORTRAN, COBOL, Lisp, Scheme, and Ada. **High-level languages** resemble human languages in many ways. They are designed to be easy for human beings to write programs in and to be easy for human beings to read. A high-level language, such as C++, contains instructions that are much more complicated than the simple instructions a computer's processor (CPU) is capable of following.

The kind of language a computer can understand is called a **low-level language.** The exact details of low-level languages differ from one kind of computer to another. A typical low-level instruction might be the following:

```
ADD X Y Z
```

This instruction might mean "Add the number in the memory location called X to the number in the memory location called Y, and place the result in the memory location called Z." The above sample instruction is written in what is called **assembly language.** Although assembly language is almost the same as the language understood by the computer, it must undergo one simple translation before the computer can understand it. In order to get a computer to follow an assembly language instruction, the words need to be translated into strings of 0s and 1s. For example, the word ADD might translate to 0110, the X might translate to 1001, the Y to 1010, and the Z to 1011. The version of the instruction above that the computer ultimately follows would then be:

```
0110 1001 1010 1011
```

Assembly language instructions and their translation into 0s and 1s differ from machine to machine.

Programs written in the form of 0s and 1s are said to be written in **machine language,** because that is the version of the program that the computer (the machine) actually reads and follows. Assembly language and machine language are almost the same thing, and the distinction between them will not be important to us. The important distinction is that between machine language and high-level languages like C++: Any high-level language program must be translated into machine language before the computer can understand and follow the program.

Compilers

A program that translates a high-level language like C++ to a machine language is called a **compiler.** A compiler is thus a somewhat peculiar sort of program, in that its input or data is some other program, and its output is yet another program. To avoid confusion, the input program is usually called the **source program** or **source code,** and the translated version produced by the compiler is called the **object program** or **object code.** The word **code** is frequently used to mean a program or a part of a program, and this usage is particularly common when referring to object programs. Now, suppose you want to run a C++ program that you have written. In order to get the computer to follow your C++ instructions, proceed as follows. First, run the compiler using your C++ program as data. Notice that in this case, your C++ program is not being treated as a set of instructions. To the compiler, your C++ program is just a long string of characters. The output will be another long string of characters, which is the machine-language equivalent of your C++ program. Next, run this machine-language program on what we normally think of as the data for the C++ program. The output will be what we normally conceptualize as the output of the C++ program. The basic process is easier to visualize if you have two computers available, as diagrammed in Display 1.4. In reality, the entire process is accomplished by using one computer two times.

Compiler

A **compiler** is a program that translates a high-level language program, such as a C++ program, into a machine-language program that the computer can directly understand and execute.

The complete process of translating and running a C++ program is a bit more complicated than what we show in Display 1.4. Any C++ program you write will use some operations (such as input and output routines) that have already been programmed for you. These items that are already programmed for you (like input and output routines) are already compiled and have their object code waiting to be combined with your program's object code to produce a complete machine-language program that can be run on the computer. Another program, called a **linker,** combines the object code for these program pieces with the object code that the compiler produced from your C++ program. The interaction of the compiler and the linker are diagrammed in Display 1.5. In routine cases, many systems will do this linking for you automatically. Thus, you may not need to worry about linking in many cases.

Linking

The object code for your C++ program must be combined with the object code for routines (such as input and output routines) that your program uses. This process of combining object code is called `linking` and is done by a program called a `linker`. For simple programs, linking may be done for you automatically.

DISPLAY 1.4   Compiling and Running a C++ Program (Basic Outline)

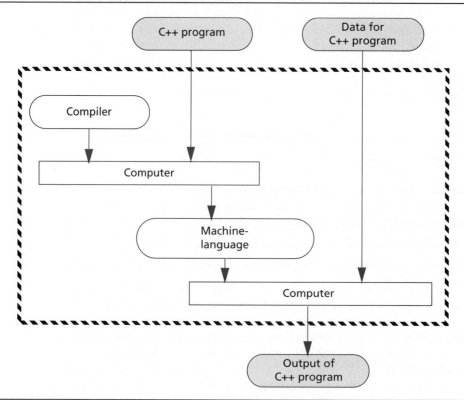

DISPLAY 1.5   Preparing a C++ Program for Running

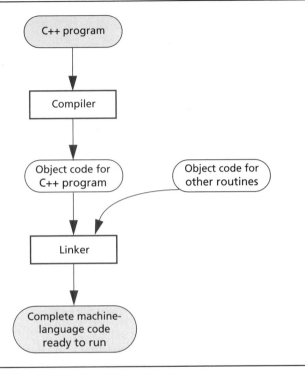

SELF-TEST EXERCISES

1. What are the five main components of a computer?

2. What would be the data for a program to add two numbers?

3. What would be the data for a program that assigns letter grades to students in a class?

4. What is the difference between a machine-language program and a high-level language program?

5. What is the role of a compiler?

6. What is a source program? What is an object program?

7. What is an operating system?

8. What purpose does the operating system serve?

9. Name the operating system that runs on the computer you use to prepare programs for this course.

10. What is linking?

11. Find out whether linking is done automatically by the compiler you use for this course.

1.2 PROGRAMMING AND PROBLEM-SOLVING

The Analytical Engine has no pretensions whatever to originate anything.
It can do whatever we know how to order it to perform. It can follow analysis;
but it has no power of anticipating any analytical relations or truths. Its prov-
ince is to assist us in making available what we are already acquainted with.

ADA AUGUSTA, *Countess of Lovelace (1815–1852)*

HISTORY NOTE Charles Babbage, Ada Augusta

The first truly programmable computer was designed by **Charles Babbage**, an English mathematician and physical scientist. Babbage began the project sometime before 1822 and worked on it for the rest of his life. Although he never completed the construction of his machine, the design was a conceptual milestone in the history of computing. Much of what we know about Charles Babbage and his computer design comes from the writings of his colleague **Ada Augusta**, the Countess of Lovelace and the daughter of the poet Byron. Ada Augusta is frequently given the title of the first computer programmer. Her comments, quoted in the opening of the next section, still apply to the process of solving problems on a computer. Computers are not magic and do not, at least as yet, have the ability to formulate sophisticated solutions to all the problems we encounter. Computers simply do what the programmer orders them to do. The solutions to problems are carried out by the computer, but the solutions are formulated by the programmer. Our discussion of computer programming begins with a discussion of how a programmer formulates these solutions.

In this section we describe some general principles that you can use to design and write programs. These principles are not particular to C++. They apply no matter what programming language you are using.

Algorithms

When learning your first programming language, it is easy to get the impression that the hard part of solving a problem on a computer is translating your ideas into the specific language that will be fed into the computer. This definitely is not the case. The most difficult part of solving a problem on a computer is discovering the method of solution. After you come up with a method of solution, it is routine to translate your method into the required language, be it C++ or some other programming language. It is therefore helpful to temporarily ignore the programming language and to concentrate instead on formulating the steps of the solution and writing them down in plain English, as if the instructions were to be given to a human being rather than a computer. A sequence of instructions expressed in this way is frequently referred to as an *algorithm*.

A sequence of precise instructions which leads to a solution is called an **algorithm.** Some approximately equivalent words are *recipe, method,*

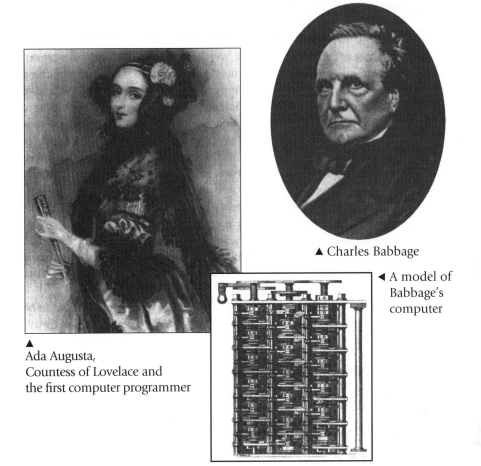

▲ Charles Babbage

◀ A model of
Babbage's
computer

▲
Ada Augusta,
Countess of Lovelace and
the first computer programmer

directions, *procedure*, and *routine*. The instructions may be expressed in a programming language or a human language. Our algorithms will be expressed in English and in the programming language C++. A computer program is simply an algorithm expressed in a language that a computer can understand. Thus, the term *algorithm* is more general than the term *program*. However, when we say that a sequence of instructions is an algorithm, we usually mean that the instructions are expressed in English, since if they were expressed in a programming language we would use the more specific term *program*. An example may help to clarify the concept.

Display 1.6 contains an algorithm expressed in English. The algorithm determines the number of times a specified name occurs on a list of names. If the list contains the winners of each of last season's football games and the name is that of your favorite team, then the algorithm determines how many games your team won. The algorithm is short and simple but is otherwise very typical of the algorithms with which we will be dealing.

DISPLAY 1.6 An Algorithm

`Algorithm that determines how many times a name occurs in a list of names:`

1.   `Get the list of names.`
2.   `Get the name being checked.`
3.   `Set a counter to zero.`
4.   `Do the following for each name on the list:`
      `Compare the name on the list to the name being checked,`
      `and if the names are the same, then add one to the counter.`
5.   `Announce that the answer is the number indicated by the counter.`

The instructions numbered 1 through 5 in our sample algorithm are meant to be carried out in the order they are listed. Unless otherwise specified, we will always assume that the instructions of an algorithm are carried out in the order in which they are given (written down). Most interesting algorithms do, however, specify some change of order, usually a repeating of some instruction again and again such as in instruction 4 of our sample algorithm.

The word *algorithm* has a long history. It derives from the name al-Khowarizmi, a ninth-century Persian mathematician and astronomer. He wrote a famous textbook on the manipulation of numbers and equations. The book was entitled *Kitab al-jabr w'almuqabala*, which can be translated as *Rules for Reuniting and Reducing*. The similar-sounding word *algebra* was derived from the Arabic word *al-jabr*, which appears in the title of the book and which is often translated as *reuniting* or *restoring*. The meanings of the words *algebra* and *algorithm* used to be much more intimately related than they are today. Indeed, until modern times, the word *algorithm* usually referred only to algebraic rules for solving numerical equations. Today, the word *algorithm* can be applied to a wide variety of kinds of instructions for manipulating symbolic as well as numeric data. The properties that qualify a set of instructions as an algorithm now are determined by the nature of the instructions rather than by the things manipulated by the instructions. To qualify as an algorithm, a set of instructions must completely and unambiguously specify the steps to be taken and the order in which they are taken. The person or machine carrying out the algorithm does exactly what the algorithm says, neither more nor less.

Algorithm

An `algorithm` is a sequence of precise instructions that leads to a solution.

Program Design

Designing a program is often a difficult task. There is no complete set of rules, no algorithm to tell you how to write programs. Program design is a creative process. Still, there is the outline of a plan to follow. The outline is given in diagrammatic form in Display 1.7. As indicated there, the entire program design process can be divided into two phases, the *problem-solving phase* and the *implementation phase*. The result of the **problem-solving phase** is an algorithm, expressed in English, for solving the problem. To produce a program in a programming language such as C++, the algorithm is translated into the programming language. Producing the final program from the algorithm is called the **implementation phase.**

The first step is to be certain that the task—what you want your program to do—is completely and precisely specified. Do not take this step lightly. If you do not know exactly what you want as the output of your program, you may be surprised at what your program produces. Be certain that you know what the input to the program will be and exactly what information is supposed to be in the output, as well as what form that information should be in. For example, if the program is a bank accounting program, you must know not only the interest rate but also whether interest is to be compounded annually, monthly, daily, or whatever. If the program is supposed to write poetry, you need to determine whether the poems can be in free verse or must be in iambic pentameter or some other meter.

Many novice programmers do not understand the need to design an algorithm before writing a program in a programming language, such as C++, and so they try to short-circuit the process by omitting the problem-solving phase entirely, or by reducing it to just the problem-definition part. This seems reasonable. Why not "go for the mark" and save time? The answer is that *it does not save time*! Experience has shown that the two-phase process will produce a correctly working program faster. The two-phase process simplifies the algorithm design phase by isolating it from the detailed rules of a programming language such as C++. The result is that the algorithm design process becomes much less intricate and much less prone to error. For even a modest-size program, it can represent the difference between a half day of careful work and several frustrating days of looking for mistakes in a poorly understood program.

The implementation phase is not a trivial step. There are details to be concerned about, and occasionally some of these details can be subtle, but it is much simpler than you might at first think. Once you become familiar with C++ or any other programming language, the translation of an algorithm from English into the programming language becomes a routine task.

As indicated in Display 1.7, testing takes place in both phases. Before the program is written, the algorithm is tested, and if the algorithm is found to be deficient, then the algorithm is redesigned. That desktop testing is performed by mentally going through the algorithm and executing the steps yourself.

DISPLAY 1.7   Program Design Process

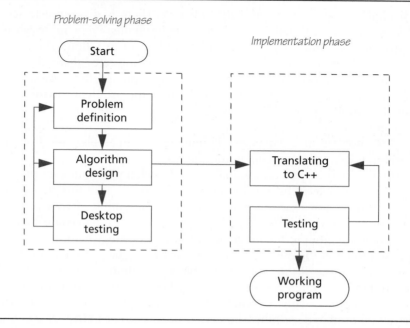

For large algorithms this will require a pencil and paper. The C++ program is tested by compiling it and running it on some sample input data. The compiler will give error messages for certain kinds of errors. To find other types of errors, you must somehow check to see whether the output is correct.

The process diagrammed in Display 1.7 is an idealized picture of the program design process. It is the basic picture you should have in mind, but reality is sometimes more complicated. In reality, mistakes and deficiencies are discovered at unexpected times, and you may have to back up and redo an earlier step. For example, as shown in Display 1.7, testing the algorithm might reveal that the definition of the problem was incomplete. In such a case you must back up and reformulate the definition. Occasionally, deficiencies in the definition or algorithm may not be observed until a program is tested. In that case you must back up and modify the problem definition or algorithm and all that follows them in the design process.

Object-Oriented Programming

The program design process that we outlined in the previous section represents a program as an algorithm (set of instructions) for manipulating some data. That is a correct view, but not always the most productive view. Modern programs are usually designed using a method known as *object-oriented programming,* or **OOP.** In OOP, a program is viewed as a collection of interacting objects. The methodology is easiest to understand when the program is a simulation program. For example, for a program to simulate a highway interchange, the objects might represent the automobiles and the lanes of the highway. Each object has algorithms that describe how it should behave in different situations. Programming in the OOP style consists of designing the objects and the algorithms they use. When programming in the OOP framework, the term *Algorithm design* in Display 1.7 would be replaced with the phrase *Designing the objects and their algorithms*.

The main characteristics of OOP are *encapsulation, inheritance,* and *polymorphism*. Encapsulation is usually described as a form of information hiding or abstraction. That description is correct, but perhaps an easier-to-understand characterization is to say that encapsulation is a form of simplification of the descriptions of objects. Inheritance has to do with writing reusable program code. Polymorphism refers to a way that a single name can have multiple meanings in the context of inheritance. Having made those statements, we must admit that they hold little meaning for readers who have not heard of OOP before. However, we will describe all these terms in detail later in this book. C++ accommodates OOP by providing **classes,** a kind of data type combining both data and algorithms.

The Software Life Cycle

Designers of large software systems, such as compilers and operating systems, divide the software development process into six phases collectively known as the **software life cycle.** The six phases of this life cycle are:

1. Analysis and specification of the task (problem definition)

2. Design of the software (object and algorithm design)

3. Implementation (coding)

4. Testing

5. Maintenance and evolution of the system

6. Obsolescence

We did not mention the last two phases in our discussion of program design because they take place after the program is finished and put into service. However, they should always be kept in mind. You will not be able to add improvements or corrections to your program unless you design it to be easy to read and easy to change. Designing programs so that they can be easily modified is an important topic that we will discuss in detail when we have developed a bit more background and a few more programming techniques. The meaning of obsolescence is obvious, but it is not always easy to accept. When a program is not working as it should and cannot be fixed with a reasonable amount of effort, it should be discarded and replaced with a completely new program.

SELF-TEST EXERCISES

12. An algorithm is approximately the same thing as a recipe, but some kinds of steps that would be allowed in a recipe are not allowed in an algorithm. Which steps in the following recipe would be allowed in an algorithm?

```
Place 2 teaspoons of sugar in mixing bowl.
Add 1 egg to mixing bowl.
Add 1 cup of milk to mixing bowl.
Add 1 ounce of rum, if you are not driving.
Add vanilla extract to taste.
Beat until smooth.
Pour into a pretty glass.
Sprinkle with nutmeg.
```

13. What is the first step you should take when creating a program?

14. The program design process can be divided into two main phases. What are they?

15. Explain why the problem-solving phase should not be slighted.

1.3 INTRODUCTION TO C++

Language is the only instrument of science . . .

SAMUEL JOHNSON (1709–1784)

In this section we introduce you to the C++ programming language, which is the programming language used in this book.

Origins of the C++ Language

The first thing that people notice about the C++ language is its unusual name. Is there a C programming language, you might ask? Is there a C– or a C– – language? Are there programming languages named A and B? The answer to most of these questions is no. But the general thrust of the questions is on the mark. There is a B programming language; it was not derived from a language called A, but from a language called BCPL. The C language was derived from the B language, and C++ was derived from the C language. Why are there two pluses in the name C++? As you will see in the next chapter, ++ is an operation in the C and C++ languages, so using ++ produces a nice pun. The languages BCPL and B do not concern us. They are earlier versions of the C programming language. We will start our description of the C++ programming language with a description of the C language.

The C programming language was developed by Dennis Ritchie of AT&T Bell Laboratories in the 1970s. It was first used for writing and maintaining the UNIX operating system. (Up until that time UNIX systems programs were written either in assembly language or in B, a language developed by Ken Thompson, who is the originator of UNIX.) C is a general-purpose language that can be used for writing any sort of program, but its success and popularity are closely tied to the UNIX operating system. If you wanted to maintain your UNIX system, you needed to use C. C and UNIX fit together so well that soon not just systems programs, but almost all commercial programs that ran under UNIX were written in the C language. C became so popular that versions of the language were written for other popular operating systems; its use is not limited to computers that use UNIX. However, despite its popularity, C is not without its shortcomings.

The C language is peculiar because it is a high-level language with many of the features of a low-level language. C is somewhere in between the two extremes of a very high level language and a low-level language, and therein lies both its strengths and its weaknesses. Like (low-level) assembly language, C language programs can directly manipulate the computer's memory. On the other hand, C has many features of a high-level language, which makes it easier to read and write than assembly language. This makes C an excellent choice for writing systems programs, but for other programs (and in some sense even for systems programs), C is not as easy to understand as other languages; also, it does not have as many automatic checks as some other high-level languages.

To overcome these and other shortcomings of C, Bjarne Stroustrup of AT&T Bell Laboratories developed C++ in the early 1980s. Stroustrup designed C++ to be a better C. Most of C is a subset of C++, and so most C programs are also C++ programs. (The reverse is not true; many C++ programs are definitely not C programs.) Unlike C, C++ has facilities to do *object-oriented programming*, which is a very powerful programming technique described earlier in this chapter.

A Sample C++ Program

Display 1.8 contains a simple C++ program and the screen display that might be generated when a *user* runs and interacts with this program. The person who runs a program is called the **user**. The output when the program is run is shown in the Sample Dialogue. The text typed in by the user is shown in color to distinguish it from the text output by the program. On the actual screen both texts would look alike. The source code for the program is shown in lines 1–22. The line numbers are shown only for reference. You would not type in the line numbers when entering the program. Keywords with a predefined meaning in C++ are shown in color. These keywords are discussed in Chapter 2. The person who writes the program is called the **programmer**. Do not confuse the roles of the user and the programmer. The user and the programmer might or might not be the same person. For example, if you write and then run a program, you are both the programmer and the user. With professionally produced programs, the programmer (or programmers) and the user are usually different persons.

DISPLAY 1.8   A Sample C++ Program

```
1      #include <iostream>
2      using namespace std;

3      int main( )
4      {
5          int number_of_pods, peas_per_pod, total_peas;

6          cout << "Press return after entering a number.\n";
7          cout << "Enter the number of pods:\n";

8          cin >> number_of_pods;

9          cout << "Enter the number of peas in a pod:\n";
10         cin >> peas_per_pod;
11         total_peas = number_of_pods * peas_per_pod;
12         cout << "If you have ";
13         cout << number_of_pods;
14         cout << " pea pods\n";
15         cout << "and ";
16         cout << peas_per_pod;
17         cout << " peas in each pod, then\n";
18         cout << "you have ";
19         cout << total_peas;
20         cout << " peas in all the pods.\n";

21         return 0;

22     }
```

Sample Dialogue

```
Press return after entering a number.
Enter the number of pods:
10
Enter the number of peas in a pod:
9
If you have 10 pea pods
and 9 peas in each pod, then
you have 90 peas in all the pods.
```

In the next chapter we will explain in detail all the C++ features you need to write programs like the one in Display 1.8, but to give you a feel for how a C++ program works, we will now provide a brief description of how this particular program works. If some of the details are a bit unclear, do not worry. In this section we just want to give you a feel for what a C++ program is.

The beginning and end of our sample program contain some details that need not concern us yet. The program begins with the following lines:

```
#include <iostream>
using namespace std;
int main()
{
```

For now we will consider these lines to be a rather complicated way of saying "The program starts here."

The program ends with the following two lines:

```
    return 0;
}
```

For a simple program, these two lines simply mean "The program ends here."

The lines in between these beginning and ending lines are the heart of the program. We will briefly describe these lines, starting with the following line:

```
int number_of_pods, peas_per_pod, total_peas;
```

This line is called a **variable declaration.** This variable declaration tells the computer that number_of_pods, peas_per_pod, and total_peas will be used as names for three *variables*. Variables will be explained more precisely in the next chapter, but it is easy to understand how they are used in this program. In this program the **variables** are used to name numbers. The word that starts this line, int, is an abbreviation for the word *integer* and it tells the computer that the numbers named by these variables will be integers. An **integer** is a whole number, like 1, 2, –1, –7, 0, 205, –103, and so forth.

The remaining lines are all instructions that tell the computer to do something. These instructions are called **statements** or **executable statements.** In this program each statement fits on exactly one line. That need not be true, but for very simple programs, statements are usually listed one per line.

Most of the statements begin with either the word cin or cout. These statements are input statements and output statements. The word cin, which is pronounced "see-in," is used for input. The statements that begin with cin tell the computer what to do when information is entered from the keyboard. The word cout, which is pronounced "see-out," is used for output, that is, for sending information from the program to the terminal screen. The letter c is there because the language is C++. The arrows, written << or >>, tell you the direction that data is moving. The arrows, << and >>, are called 'insert' and 'extract,' or 'put to' and 'get from,' respectively. For example, consider the line:

```
cout << "Press return after entering a number.\n";
```

This line may be read, 'put "Press...number.\n" to cout' or simply 'output "Press...number.\n"'. If you think of the word cout as a name for the screen (the output device), then the arrows tell the computer to send the string in quotes to the screen. As shown in the sample dialogue, this causes the text contained in the quotes to be written to the screen. The \n at the end of the quoted string tells the computer to start a new line after writing out the text. Similarly, the next line of the program also begins with cout, and that program line causes the following line of text to be written to the screen:

```
Enter the number of pods:
```

The next program line starts with the word cin, so it is an input statement. Let's look at that line:

```
cin >> number_of_pods;
```

This line may be read, 'get number_of_pods from cin' or simply 'input number_of_pods'.

If you think of the word cin as standing for the keyboard (the input device), then the arrows say that input should be sent from the keyboard to the variable number_of_pods. Look again at the sample dialogue. The next line shown has a 10 written in bold. We use bold to indicate something typed in at the keyboard. If you type in the number 10, then the 10 appears on the screen. If you then press the Return key (which is also sometimes called the *Enter key*), that makes the 10 available to the program. The statement which begins with cin tells the computer to send that input value of 10 to the variable number_of_pods. From that point on, number_of_pods has the value 10; when we see number_of_pods later in the program, we can think of it as standing for the number 10.

Consider the next two program lines:

```
cout << "Enter the number of peas in a pod:\n";
cin >> peas_per_pod;
```

These lines are similar to the previous two lines. The first sends a message to the screen asking for a number. When you type in a number at the keyboard and press the Return key, that number becomes the value of the variable peas_per_pod. In the sample dialogue, we assume that you type in the number 9. After you type in 9 and press the Return key, the value of the variable peas_per_pod becomes 9.

The next nonblank program line, shown below, does all the computation that is done in this simple program:

```
total_peas = number_of_pods * peas_per_pod;
```

The asterisk symbol, *, is used for multiplication in C++. So this statement says to multiply number_of_pods and peas_per_pod. In this case, 10 is multiplied by 9 to give a result of 90. The equal sign says that the variable total_peas should be made equal to this result of 90. This is a special use of the equal sign; its meaning here is different than in other mathematical contexts. It gives the variable on the left-hand side a (possibly new) value; in this case it makes 90 the value of total_peas.

The rest of the program is basically more of the same sort of output. Consider the next three nonblank lines:

```
cout << "If you have ";
cout << number_of_pods;
cout << " pea pods\n";
```

These are just three more output statements that work basically the same as the previous statements that begin with cout. The only thing that is new is the second of these three statements, which says to output the variable number_of_pods. When a variable is output, it is the value of the variable that is output. So this statement causes a 10 to be output. (Remember that in this sample run of the program, the variable number_of_pods was set to 10 by the user who ran the program.) Thus, the output produced by these three lines is:

```
If you have 10 pea pods
```

Notice that the output is all on one line. A new line is not begun until the special instruction \n is sent as output.

The rest of the program contains nothing new, and if you understand what we have discussed so far, you should be able to understand the rest of the program.

PITFALL   Using the Wrong Slash in \n

When you use a \n in a cout statement be sure that you use the **backslash,** which is written \. If you make a mistake and use /n rather than \n, the compiler will not give you an error message. Your program will run, but the output will look peculiar. ■

■ PROGRAMMING TIP   Input and Output Syntax

If you think of cin as a name for the keyboard or **in**put device and think of cout as a name for the screen or the **out**put device, then it is easy to remember the direction of the arrows >> and <<. They point in the direction that data moves. For example, consider the statement:

```
cin >> number_of_pods;
```

In the above statement, data moves from the keyboard to the variable number_of_pods, and so the arrow points from cin to the variable.

On the other hand, consider the output statement:

```
cout << number_of_pods;
```

In this statement the data moves from the variable number_of_pods to the screen, so the arrow points from the variable number_of_pods to cout. ■

Layout of a Simple C++ Program

The general form of a simple C++ program is shown in Display 1.9. As far as the compiler is concerned, the **line breaks** and **spacing** need not be as shown there and in our examples. The compiler will accept any reasonable pattern of line breaks and indentation. In fact, the compiler will even accept most unreasonable patterns of line breaks and indentation. However, a program should always be laid out so that it is easy to read. Placing the opening brace, {, on a line by itself and also placing the closing brace, }, on a line by itself will make these punctuations easy to find. Indenting each statement and placing each statement on a separate line makes it easy to see what the program instructions are. Later on, some of our statements will be too long to fit on one line and then we will use a slight variant of this pattern for indenting and line breaks. You should follow the pattern set by the examples in this book, or follow the pattern specified by your instructor if you are in a class.

In Display 1.8, the variable declarations are on the line that begins with the word int. As we will see in the next chapter, you need not place all your variable declarations at the beginning of your program, but that is a good default location for them. Unless you have a reason to place them somewhere else, place them at the start of your program as shown in Display 1.9 and in the sample program in Display 1.8. The **statements** are the instructions that are followed by the computer. In Display 1.8, the statements are the lines that begin with cout or cin and the one line that begins with total_peas followed by an equal sign. Statements are often called **executable statements.** We will use the terms *statement* and *executable statement* interchangeably. Notice that each of the statements we have seen ends with a semicolon. The semicolon in statements is used in more or less the same way that the period is used in English sentences; it marks the end of a statement.

DISPLAY 1.9   Layout of a Simple C++ Program

```
 1    #include <iostream>
 2    using namespace std;
 3
 4    int main()
 5    {
 6        Variable_Declarations
 7
 8        Statement_1
 9        Statement_2
10        ...
11        Statement_Last
12
13        return 0;
14    }
```

For now you can view the first few lines as a funny way to say "this is the beginning of the program." But we can explain them in a bit more detail. The first line

```
#include <iostream>
```

is called an `include` **directive.** It tells the compiler where to find information about certain items that are used in your program. In this case `iostream` is the name of a library that contains the definitions of the routines that handle input from the keyboard and output to the screen; `iostream` is a file that contains some basic information about this library. The linker program that we discussed earlier in this chapter combines the object code for the library `iostream` and the object code for the program you write. For the library `iostream` this will probably happen automatically on your system. You will eventually use other libraries as well, and when you use them, they will have to be named in directives at the start of your program. For other libraries, you may need to do more than just place an `include` directive in your program, but in order to use any library in your program, you will always need to at least place an `include` directive for that library in your program. Directives always begin with the symbol #. Some compilers require that directives have no spaces around the #, so it is always safest to place the # at the very start of the line and not include any space between the # and the word `include`.

The following line further explains the `include` directive that we just explained:

```
using namespace std;
```

This line says that the names defined in `iostream` are to be interpreted in the "standard way" (`std` is an abbreviation of *standard*). We will have more to say about this line a bit later in this book.

The third and fourth nonblank lines, shown next, simply say that the main part of the program starts here:

```
int main()
{
```

The correct term is *main function*, rather than *main part*, but the reason for that subtlety will not concern us until Chapter 4. The braces { and } mark the beginning and end of the main part of the program. They need not be on a line by themselves, but that is the way to make them easy to find and we will therefore always place each of them on a line by itself.

The next-to-last line

```
return 0;
```

says to "end the program when you get to here." This line need not be the last thing in the program, but in a very simple program it makes no sense to place it anywhere else. Some compilers will allow you to omit this line and will figure out that the program ends when there are no more statements to execute. However, other compilers will insist that you include this line, so it is best to get in the habit of including it, even if your compiler is happy without it. This line is called a **return statement** and is considered to be an executable statement because it tells the computer to do something; specifically, it tells the computer to end the program. The number 0 has no intuitive significance to us yet, but must be there; its meaning will become clear as you learn more about C++. Note that even though the `return` statement says to end the program, you still must add a closing brace, }, at the end of the main part of your program.

PITFALL   Putting a Space Before the `include` File Name

Be certain that you do not have any extra space between the < and the `iostream` file name (Display 1.9) or between the end of the file name and the closing >. The compiler `include` directive is not very smart: It will search for a file name that starts or ends with a space! The file name will not be found, producing an error that is quite difficult to locate. You should make this error deliberately in a small program, then compile it. Save the message that your compiler produces so you know what the error message means the next time you get that error message.   ■

Compiling and Running a C++ Program

VideoNote
Compiling and Running
a C++ Program

In the previous section you learned what would happen if you ran the C++ program shown in Display 1.8. But where is that program and how do you make it run?

You write a C++ program using a text editor in the same way that you write any other document—a term paper, a love letter, a shopping list, or whatever. The program is kept in a file just like any other document you prepare using a text editor. There are different text editors, and the details of how to use them will vary from one to another, so we cannot say too much more about your text editor. You should consult the documentation for your editor.

The way that you compile and run a C++ program also depends on the particular system you are using, so we will discuss these points in only a very general way. You need to learn how to give the commands to compile, link, and run a C++ program on your system. These commands can be found in the manuals for your system and by asking people who are already using C++ on your system. When you give the command to compile your program, this will produce a machine-language translation of your C++ program. This translated version is called the *object code* for your program. The object code must be linked (that is, combined) with the object code for routines (such as input and output routines) that are already written for you. It is likely that this linking will be done automatically, so you do not need to worry about linking. But on some systems, you may be required to make a separate call to the linker. Again, consult your manuals or a local expert. Finally, you give the command to run your program; how you give that command also depends on the system you are using, so check with the manuals or a local expert.

■ PROGRAMMING TIP   Getting Your Program to Run

Different compilers and different environments might require a slight variation in some details of how you set up a file with your C++ program. Obtain a copy of the program in Display 1.10. It is available for downloading over the Internet. (See the Preface for details.) Alternatively, *very carefully* type in the program yourself. Do not type in the line numbers. Compile the program. If you get an error message, check your typing, fix any typing mistakes, and recompile the file. Once the program compiles with no error messages, try running the program.

If you get the program to compile and run normally, you are all set. You do not need to do anything different from the examples shown in the book. If this program does not compile or does not run normally, then read on. In what follows we offer some hints for dealing with your C++ setup. Once you get this simple program to run normally, you will know what small changes to make to your C++ program files in order to get them to run on your system.

If your program seems to run, but you do not see the output line

        Testing 1, 2, 3

then, in all likelihood, the program probably did give that output, but it disappeared before you could see it. Try adding the following to the end of your program, just before the line `return 0;` these lines should stop your program to allow you to read the output.

DISPLAY 1.10   Testing Your C++ Setup

```
1     #include <iostream>
2     using namespace std;
3
4     int main( )
5     {
6         cout << "Testing 1, 2, 3\n";
7         return 0;
8     }
9
```

> *If you cannot compile and run this program, then see the programming tip entitled "Getting Your Program to Run." It suggests some things to do to get your C++ programs to run on your particular computer setup.*

Sample Dialogue

```
Testing 1, 2, 3
```

```
char letter;
cout << "Enter a letter to end the program:\n";
cin >> letter;
```

The part in braces should then read as follows:

```
cout << "Testing 1, 2, 3\n";
char letter;
cout << "Enter a letter to end the program:\n";
cin >> letter;
return 0;
```

For now you need not understand these added lines, but they will be clear to you by the end of Chapter 2.

If the program does not compile or run at all, then try changing

```
#include <iostream>
```

by adding .h to the end of iostream, so it reads as follows:

```
#include <iostream.h>
```

If your program requires iostream.h instead of iostream, then you have an old C++ compiler and should obtain a more recent compiler.

If your program still does not compile and run normally, try deleting

```
using namespace std;
```

If your program still does not compile and run, then check the documentation for your version of C++ to see if any more "directives" are needed for "console" input/output.

If all this fails, consult your instructor if you are in a course. If you are not in a course or you are not using the course computer, check the documentation for your C++ compiler or check with a friend who has a similar computer setup. The necessary change is undoubtedly very small and, once you find out what it is, very easy.

■ SELF-TEST EXERCISES

16. If the following statement were used in a C++ program, what would it cause to be written on the screen?

```
cout << "C++ is easy to understand.";
```

17. What is the meaning of \n as used in the following statement (which appears in Display 1.8)?

```
cout << "Enter the number of peas in a pod:\n";
```

18. What is the meaning of the following statement (which appears in Display 1.8)?

    ```
    cin >> peas_per_pod;
    ```

19. What is the meaning of the following statement (which appears in Display 1.8)?

    ```
    total_peas = number_of_pods * peas_per_pod;
    ```

20. What is the meaning of this directive?

    ```
    #include <iostream>
    ```

21. What, if anything, is wrong with the following #include directives?

    a. `#include <iostream >`
    b. `#include < iostream>`
    c. `#include <iostream>`

1.4 TESTING AND DEBUGGING

"And if you take one from three hundred and sixty-five, what remains?"

"Three hundred and sixty-four, of course."

Humpty Dumpty looked doubtful. "I'd rather see that done on paper," he said.

LEWIS CARROLL, *Through the Looking-Glass*

A mistake in a program is usually called a **bug,** and the process of eliminating bugs is called **debugging.** There is colorful history of how this term came into use. It occurred in the early days of computers, when computer hardware was extremely sensitive and occupied an entire room. Rear Admiral Grace Murray Hopper (1906–1992) was "the third programmer on the world's first large-scale digital computer." (Denise W. Gurer, "Pioneering women in computer science" CACM 38(1):45–54, January 1995.) While Hopper was working on the Harvard Mark I computer under the command of Harvard professor Howard H. Aiken, an unfortunate moth caused a relay to fail. Hopper and the other programmers taped the deceased moth in the logbook with the note "First actual case of bug being found." The logbook is currently on display at the Naval Museum in Dahlgren, Virginia. This was the first documented computer bug. Professor Aiken would come into the facility during a slack time and inquire if any numbers were being computed. The programmers would reply that they were debugging the computer. For more information about Admiral Hopper and other persons in computing, see Robert Slater, *Portraits in Silicon* (MIT Press, 1987). Today, a bug is a mistake in a program. In this section we describe the three main kinds of programming mistakes and give some hints on how to correct them.

Kinds of Program Errors

The compiler will catch certain kinds of mistakes and will write out an error message when it finds a mistake. It will detect what are called **syntax errors,** because they are, by and large, violation of the syntax (that is, the grammar rules) of the programming language, such as omitting a semicolon.

If the compiler discovers that your program contains a syntax error, it will tell you where the error is likely to be and what kind of error it is likely to be. When the compiler says your program contains a syntax error, you can be confident that it does. However, the compiler may be incorrect about either the location or the nature of the error. It does a better job of determining the location of an error, to within a line or two, than it does of determining the source of the error. This is because the compiler is guessing at what you meant to write down and can easily guess wrong. After all, the compiler cannot read your mind. Error messages subsequent to the first one have a higher likelihood of being incorrect with respect to either the location or the nature of the error. Again, this is because the compiler must guess your meaning. If the compiler's first guess was incorrect, this will affect its analysis of future mistakes, since the analysis will be based on a false assumption.

If your program contains something that is a direct violation of the syntax rules for your programming language, the compiler will give you an **error message.** However, sometimes the compiler will give you only a **warning message,** which indicates that you have done something that is not, technically speaking, a violation of the programming language syntax rules, but that is unusual enough to indicate a likely mistake. When you get a warning message, the compiler is saying, "Are you sure you mean this?" At this stage of your development, you should treat every warning as if it were an error until your instructor approves ignoring the warning.

There are certain kinds of errors that the computer system can detect only when a program is run. Appropriately enough, these are called **run-time errors.** Most computer systems will detect certain run-time errors and output an appropriate error message. Many run-time errors have to do with numeric calculations. For example, if the computer attempts to divide a number by zero, that is normally a run-time error.

If the compiler approved of your program and the program ran once with no run-time error messages, this does not guarantee that your program is correct. Remember, the compiler will only tell you if you wrote a syntactically (that is, grammatically) correct C++ program. It will not tell you whether the program does what you want it to do. Mistakes in the underlying algorithm or in translating the algorithm into the C++ language are called **logic errors.** For example, if you were to mistakenly use the addition sign + instead of the multiplication sign * in the program in Display 1.8, that would be a logic error. The program would compile and run normally but would give the wrong answer. If the compiler approves of your program and there are no run-time errors but the program does not perform properly, then undoubtedly your program contains a logic error. Logic errors are the hardest kind to diagnose, because the computer gives you no error messages to help find the error. It cannot reasonably be expected to give any error messages. For all the computer knows, you may have meant what you wrote.

PITFALL   Assuming Your Program Is Correct

In order to test a new program for logic errors, you should run the program on several representative data sets and check its performance on those inputs. If the program passes those tests, you can have more confidence in it, but this is still not an absolute guarantee that the program is correct. It still may not do what you want it to do when it is run on some other data. The only way to justify confidence in a program is to program carefully and so avoid most errors. ■

SELF-TEST EXERCISES

myprogramminglab

22. What are the three main kinds of program errors?

23. What kinds of errors are discovered by the compiler?

24. If you omit a punctuation symbol (such as a semicolon) from a program, an error is produced. What kind of error?

25. Omitting the final brace } from a program produces an error. What kind of error?

26. Suppose your program has a situation about which the compiler reports a warning. What should you do about it? Give the text's answer and your local answer if it is different from the text's. Identify your answers as the text's or as based on your local rules.

27. Suppose you write a program that is supposed to compute the interest on a bank account at a bank that computes interest on a daily basis, and suppose you incorrectly write your program so that it computes interest on an annual basis. What kind of program error is this?

CHAPTER SUMMARY

The collection of programs used by a computer is referred to as the **software** for that computer. The actual physical machines that make up a computer installation are referred to as **hardware.**

■ The five main components of a computer are the input device(s), the output device(s), the processor (CPU), the main memory, and the secondary memory.

- A computer has two kinds of memory: main memory and secondary memory. Main memory is used only while the program is running. Secondary memory is used to hold data that will stay in the computer before and/or after the program is run.

- A computer's main memory is divided into a series of numbered locations called **bytes**. The number associated with one of these bytes is called the **address** of the byte. Often, several of these bytes are grouped together to form a larger memory location. In that case, the address of the first byte is used as the address of this larger memory location.

- A **byte** consists of eight binary digits, each either zero or one. A digit that can only be zero or one is called a **bit.**

- A **compiler** is a program that translates a program written in a high-level language like C++ into a program written in the machine language that the computer can directly understand and execute.

- A sequence of precise instructions that leads to a solution is called an **algorithm.** Algorithms can be written in English or in a programming language, like C++. However, the word *algorithm* is usually used to mean a sequence of instructions written in English (or some other human language, such as Spanish or Arabic).

- Before writing a C++ program, you should design the algorithm (method of solution) that the program will use.

- Programming errors can be classified into three groups: syntax errors, run-time errors, and logic errors. The computer will usually tell you about errors in the first two categories. You must discover logic errors yourself.

- The individual instructions in a C++ program are called **statements.**

- A variable in a C++ program can be used to name a number. (Variables are explained more fully in the next chapter.)

- A statement in a C++ program that begins with cout << is an output statement, which tells the computer to output to the screen whatever follows the <<.

- A statement in a C++ program that begins with cin >> is an input statement.

Answers to Self-Test Exercises

1. The five main components of a computer are the input device(s), the output device(s), the processor (CPU), the main memory, and the secondary memory.

2. The two numbers to be added.

3. The grades for each student on each test and each assignment.

4. A machine-language program is a low-level language consisting of 0s and 1s that the computer can directly execute. A high-level language is written in a more English-like format and is translated by a compiler into a machine-language program that the computer can directly understand and execute.

5. A compiler translates a high-level language program into a machine-language program.

6. The high-level language program that is input to a compiler is called the source program. The translated machine-language program that is output by the compiler is called the object program.

7. An operating system is a program, or several cooperating programs, but is best thought of as the user's chief servant.

8. An operating system's purpose is to allocate the computer's resources to different tasks the computer must accomplish.

9. Among the possibilities are the Macintosh operating system Mac OS, Windows, VMS, Solaris, SunOS, UNIX (or perhaps one of the UNIX-like operating systems such as Linux). There are many others.

10. The object code for your C++ program must be combined with the object code for routines (such as input and output routines) that your program uses. This process of combining object code is called linking. For simple programs, this linking may be done for you automatically.

11. The answer varies, depending on the compiler you use. Most UNIX and UNIX-like compilers link automatically, as do the compilers in most integrated development environments for Windows and Macintosh operating systems.

12. The following instructions are too vague for use in an algorithm:

```
Add vanilla extract to taste.
Beat until smooth.
Pour into a pretty glass.
Sprinkle with nutmeg.
```

The notions of "to taste," "smooth," and "pretty" are not precise. The instruction "sprinkle" is too vague, since it does not specify how much nutmeg to sprinkle. The other instructions are reasonable to use in an algorithm.

13. The first step you should take when creating a program is to be certain that the task to be accomplished by the program is completely and precisely specified.

14. The problem-solving phase and the implementation phase.

15. Experience has shown that the two-phase process produces a correctly working program faster.

16. C++ is easy to understand.

17. The symbols \n tell the computer to start a new line in the output so that the next item output will be on the next line.

18. This statement tells the computer to read the next number that is typed in at the keyboard and to send that number to the variable named peas_per_pod.

19. This statement says to multiply the two numbers in the variables number_of_pods and peas_per_pod, and to place the result in the variable named total_peas.

20. The #include <iostream> directive tells the compiler to fetch the file iostream. This file contains declarations of cin, cout, the insertion (<<) and extraction (>>) operators for I/O (input and output). This enables correct linking of the object code from the iostream library with the I/O statements in the program.

21. a. The extra space after the iostream file name causes a *file-not-found* error message.
    b. The extra space before the iostream file name causes a *file-not-found* error message.
    c. This one is correct.

22. The three main kinds of program errors are syntax errors, run-time errors, and logic errors.

23. The compiler detects syntax errors. There are other errors that are not technically syntax errors that we are lumping with syntax errors. You will learn about these later.

24. A syntax error.

25. A syntax error.

26. The text states that you should take warnings as if they had been reported as errors. You should ask your instructor for the local rules on how to handle warnings.

27. A logic error.

PROGRAMMING PROJECTS

Visit www.myprogramminglab.com to complete many of these Programming Projects online and get instant feedback.   `myprogramminglab`

1. Using your text editor, enter (that is, type in) a C++ program that allows the user to enter the number of pens, pencils and erasers bought, and then outputs the total cost of all the items purchased. Assume that each pen costs 10 cents, each pencil costs 6 cents, and each eraser costs 4 cents. In the output, display the total cost as well as the cost incurred for each item purchased. Be certain to type the first line exactly as shown in Display 1.8.

2. Write a C++ program that first writes the statement `Welcome to the world of C++` to the screen, and then goes on to do the same things that the program in Display 1.8 does. You will only have to add one line to the program to make this happen. Recompile the changed program and run it. Then, to change the program even more, add one more line that will make the program write the statement `Have a good day` to the screen at the end of the program. Be certain to add the symbols \n to the last output statement so that it reads as follows:

   ```
   cout << " Have a good day\n";
   ```

   (Some systems require that final \n, and your system may be one of them.) Recompile and run the changed program.

3. Modify the C++ program that is shown in Display 1.8 by changing the multiplication sign * in the program to a division sign /. Compile the changed program and run it. Enter a 0 input for "number of peas in a pod." Notice the run-time error message that occurs because it is division by zero. Update the code so that if the denominator is zero, the program should issue a warning.

4. Modify the C++ program in Display 1.8. Change the multiplication sign * in your C++ program to a subtraction sign –. Recompile and run the changed program. Notice that the program compiles and runs perfectly fine, but the output is incorrect. That is because this modification is a logic error.

5. Write a C++ program that reads in two integers and then outputs both their sum and their product. One way to proceed is to start with the program in Display 1.8 and to then modify that program to produce the program for this project. Be certain to type the first line of your program exactly the same as the first line in Display 1.8. In particular, be sure that the first line begins at the left-hand end of the line with no space before or after the # symbol. Also, be certain to add the symbols \n to the last output statement in your program. For example, the last output statement might be the following:

```
cout << "This is the end of the program.\n";
```

(Some systems require that final \n, and your system may be one of these.)

VideoNote
Solution to Programming
Project 1.6

6. The purpose of this exercise is to produce a catalog of typical syntax errors and error messages that will be encountered by a beginner and to continue acquainting you with the programming environment. This exercise should leave you with a knowledge of what error to look for when given any of a number of common error messages.

Your instructor may have a program for you to use for this exercise. If not, you should use a program from one of the previous Programming Projects.

Deliberately introduce errors to the program, compile, record the error and the error message, fix the error, compile again (to be sure you have the program corrected), then introduce another error. Keep the catalog of errors and add program errors and messages to it as you continue through this course.

The sequence of suggested errors to introduce is:

a. Put an extra space between the < and the iostream file name.
b. Omit one of the < or > symbols in the include directive.
c. Omit the int from int main().
d. Omit or misspell the word main.
e. Omit one of the (); then omit both the ().
f. Continue in this fashion, deliberately misspelling identifiers (cout, cin, and so on). Omit one or both of the << in the cout statement; leave off the ending curly brace }.

7. Write a program that prints out "C S !" in large block letters inside a border of *s followed by two blank lines then the message Computer Science is Cool Stuff. The output should look as follows:

```
*************************************************************
              C C C              S S S S        ! !
            C       C           S         S      ! !
            C                   S                ! !
            C                   S                ! !
            C                   S S S S          ! !
            C                           S        ! !
            C                           S        ! !
            C       C           S         S      ! !
              C C C              S S S S        0 0

*************************************************************
          Computer Science is Cool Stuff!!!
```

8. Write a program that allows the user to enter a number of quarters, dimes, and nickels and then outputs the monetary value of the coins in cents. For example, if the user enters 2 for the number of quarters, 3 for the number of dimes, and 1 for the number of nickels, then the program should output that the coins are worth 85 cents.

9. Write a program that allows the user to enter a time in seconds and then outputs how far an object would drop if it is in freefall for that length of time. Assume that the object starts at rest, there is no friction or resistance from air, and there is a constant acceleration of 32 feet per second due to gravity. Use the equation:

$$\texttt{distance} = \frac{\texttt{acceleration x time}^{2}}{2}$$

You should first compute the product and then divide the result by 2 (The reason for this will be discussed later in the book).

10. Write a program that inputs a character from the keyboard and then outputs a large block letter "C" composed of that character. For example, if the user inputs the character "X," then the output should look as follows:

```
  X X X
 X     X
 X
 X
 X
 X
 X
 X     X
  X X X
```

C++ Basics 2

Don't imagine you know what a computer terminal is. A computer terminal is not some clunky old television with a typewriter in front of it. It is an interface where the mind and the body can connect with the universe and move bits of it about.

DOUGLAS ADAMS, *Mostly Harmless* (the fifth volume in *The Hitchhiker's Trilogy*)

INTRODUCTION

In this chapter we explain some additional sample C++ programs and present enough details of the C++ language to allow you to write simple C++ programs.

PREREQUISITES

In Chapter 1 we gave a brief description of one sample C++ program. (If you have not read the description of that program, you may find it helpful to do so before reading this chapter.)

2.1 VARIABLES AND ASSIGNMENTS

Once a person has understood the way variables are used in programming, he has understood the quintessence of programming.

E. W. DIJKSTRA, *Notes on Structured Programming*

Programs manipulate data such as numbers and letters. C++ and most other common programming languages use programming constructs known as *variables* to name and store data. Variables are at the very heart of a programming language like C++, so that is where we start our description of C++. We will use the program in Display 2.1 for our discussion and will explain all the items in that program. While the general idea of that program should be clear, some of the details are new and will require some explanation.

Variables

A C++ variable can hold a number or data of other types. For the moment, we will confine our attention to variables that hold only numbers. These variables are like small blackboards on which the numbers can be written. Just as the numbers written on a blackboard can be changed, so too can the number held by a C++ variable be changed. Unlike a blackboard that might possibly contain no number at all, a C++ variable is guaranteed to have some value in it, if only a garbage number left in the computer's memory by some previously run program. The number or other type of data held in a variable is called its **value**; that is, the value of a variable is the item written on the figurative blackboard. In the program in Display 2.1, `number_of_bars`, `one_weight`, and `total_weight` are variables. For example, when this program is run with the input shown in the sample dialogue, `number_of_bars` has its value set equal to the number 11 with the statement

```
cin >> number_of_bars;
```

Later, the value of the variable `number_of_bars` is changed to 12 when a second copy of the same statement is executed. We will discuss exactly how this happens a little later in this chapter.

Of course, variables are not blackboards. In programming languages, variables are implemented as memory locations. The compiler assigns a memory location (of the kind discussed in Chapter 1) to each variable name in the program. The value of the variable, in a coded form consisting of 0s and 1s, is kept in the memory location assigned to that variable. For example, the three variables in the program shown in Display 2.1 might be assigned the memory locations with addresses 1001, 1003, and 1007. The exact numbers will depend on your computer, your compiler, and a number of other factors. We do not know, or even care, what addresses the compiler will choose for the variables in our program. We can think as though the memory locations were actually labeled with the variable names.

DISPLAY 2.1   A C++ Program *(part 1 of 2)*

```
1     #include <iostream>
2     using namespace std;
3     int main( )
4     {
5         int number_of_bars;
6         double one_weight, total_weight;
7
8         cout << "Enter the number of candy bars in a package\n";
9         cout << "and the weight in ounces of one candy bar.\n";
10        cout << "Then press return.\n";
11        cin >> number_of_bars;
12        cin >> one_weight;
13
14        total_weight = one_weight * number_of_bars;
15
16        cout << number_of_bars << " candy bars\n";
17        cout << one_weight << " ounces each\n";
18        cout << "Total weight is " << total_weight << " ounces.\n";
19
20        cout << "Try another brand.\n";
21        cout << "Enter the number of candy bars in a package\n";
22        cout << "and the weight in ounces of one candy bar.\n";
```

(continued)

DISPLAY 2.1   A C++ Program *(part 2 of 2)*

```
23        cout << "Then press return.\n";
24        cin >> number_of_bars;
25        cin >> one_weight;
26
27        total_weight = one_weight * number_of_bars;
28
29        cout << number_of_bars << " candy bars\n";
30        cout << one_weight << " ounces each\n";
31        cout << "Total weight is " << total_weight << "  ounces.\n";
32
33        cout << "Perhaps an apple would be healthier.\n";
34
35        return 0;
36    }
```

Sample Dialogue

```
Enter the number of candy bars in a package and the weight in
ounces of one candy bar.
Then press return.
11 2.1
11 candy bars
2.1 ounces each
Total weight is 23.1 ounces.
Try another brand.
Enter the number of candy bars in a package and the weight in
ounces of one candy bar.
Then press return.
12 1.8
12 candy bars
1.8 ounces each
Total weight is 21.6 ounces.
Perhaps an apple would be healthier.
```

Names: Identifiers

The first thing you might notice about the names of the variables in our sample programs is that they are longer than the names normally used for variables in mathematics classes. To make your program easy to understand, you should always use meaningful names for variables. The name of a variable (or other item you might define in a program) is called an **identifier**.

Cannot Get Programs to Run?

If you cannot get your C++ programs to compile and run, read the Programming Tip in Chapter 1 entitled "Getting Your Program to Run." That section has tips for dealing with variations in C++ compilers and C++ environments.

An identifier must start with either a letter or the underscore symbol, and all the rest of the characters must be letters, digits, or the underscore symbol. For example, the following are all valid identifiers:

```
x x1 x_1 _abc ABC123z7 sum RATE count data2 Big_Bonus
```

All of the previously mentioned names are legal and would be accepted by the compiler, but the first five are poor choices for identifiers, since they are not descriptive of the identifier's use. None of the following are legal identifiers and all would be rejected by the compiler:

```
12 3X %change data-1 myfirst.c PROG.CPP
```

The first three are not allowed because they do not start with a letter or an underscore. The remaining three are not identifiers because they contain symbols other than letters, digits, and the underscore symbol.

C++ is a **case-sensitive** language; that is, it distinguishes between uppercase and lowercase letters in the spelling of identifiers. Hence the following are three distinct identifiers and could be used to name three distinct variables:

```
rate RATE Rate
```

However, it is not a good idea to use two such variants in the same program, since that might be confusing. Although it is not required by C++, variables are often spelled with all lowercase letters. The predefined identifiers, such as main, cin, cout, and so forth, must be spelled in all lowercase letters. We will see uses for identifiers spelled with uppercase letters later in this chapter.

A C++ identifier can be of any length, although some compilers will ignore all characters after some specified and typically large number of initial characters.

Identifiers

Identifiers are used as names for variables and other items in a C++ program. An identifier must start with either a letter or the underscore symbol, and the remaining characters must all be letters, digits, or the underscore symbol.

There is a special class of identifiers, called **keywords** or **reserved words,** that have a predefined meaning in C++ and that you cannot use as names for variables or anything else. In this book, keywords are written in a different type font like so: *int, double*. (And now you know why those words were written in a funny way.) A complete list of keywords is given in Appendix 1.

You may wonder why the other words that we defined as part of the C++ language are not on the list of keywords. What about words like cin and cout? The answer is that you are allowed to redefine these words, although it would be confusing to do so. These predefined words are not keywords; however, they are defined in libraries required by the C++ language standard. We will discuss libraries later in this book. For now, you need not worry about libraries. Needless to say, using a predefined identifier for anything other than its standard meaning can be confusing and dangerous, and thus should be avoided. The safest and easiest practice is to treat all predefined identifiers as if they were keywords.

Variable Declarations

Every variable in a C++ program must be *declared*. When you **declare** a variable you are telling the compiler—and, ultimately, the computer—what kind of data you will be storing in the variable. For example, the following two declarations from the program in Display 2.1 declare the three variables used in that program:

```
int number_of_bars;
double one_weight, total_weight;
```

When there is more than one variable in a declaration, the variables are separated by commas. Also, note that each declaration ends with a semicolon.

The word *int* in the first of these two declarations is an abbreviation of the word *integer*. (But in a C++ program you must use the abbreviated form *int*. Do not write out the entire word *integer*.) This line declares the identifier number_of_bars to be a variable of *type int*. This means that the value of number_of_bars must be a whole number, such as 1, 2, –1, 0, 37, or –288.

The word *double* in the second of these two lines declares the two identifiers one_weight and total_weight to be variables of type *double*. A variable of type *double* can hold numbers with a fractional part, such as 1.75 or –0.55. The kind of data that is held in a variable is called its **type** and the name for the type, such as *int* or *double*, is called a **type name.**

Every variable in a C++ program must be declared before the variable can be used. There are two natural places to declare a variable: either just before it is used or at the start of the main part of your program right after the lines

```
int main()
{
```

Do whatever makes your program clearer.

Variable Declarations

All variables must be declared before they are used. The syntax for
variable declarations is as follows:

SYNTAX

```
Type_Name Variable_Name_1, Variable_Name_2, ...;
```

EXAMPLES

```
int count, number_of_dragons, number_of_trolls;
double distance;
```

Variable declarations provide information the compiler needs in order
to implement the variables. Recall that the compiler implements variables as
memory locations and that the value of a variable is stored in the memory
location assigned to that variable. The value is coded as a string of 0s and 1s.
Different types of variables require different sizes of memory locations and
different methods for coding their values as a string of 0s and 1s. The computer
uses one code to encode integers as a string of 0s and 1s. It uses a different
code to encode numbers that have a fractional part. It uses yet another
code to encode letters as strings of 0s and 1s. The variable declaration tells
the compiler—and, ultimately, the computer—what size memory location to
use for the variable and which code to use when representing the variable's
value as a string of 0s and 1s.

Syntax

The **syntax** for a programming language (or any other kind of language)
is the set of grammar rules for that language. For example, when we talk
about the syntax for a variable declaration (as in the box labeled "Variable
Declarations"), we are talking about the rules for writing down a well-
formed variable declaration. If you follow all the syntax rules for C++, then
the compiler will accept your program. Of course, this only guarantees that
what you write is legal. It guarantees that your program will do something,
but it does not guarantee that your program will do what you want it to do.

Assignment Statements

The most direct way to change the value of a variable is to use an *assignment
statement*. An **assignment statement** is an order to the computer saying, "set

the value of this variable to what I have written down." The following line from the program in Display 2.1 is an example of an assignment statement:

```
total_weight = one_weight * number_of_bars;
```

This assignment statement tells the computer to set the value of total_weight equal to the number in the variable one_weight multiplied by the number in number_of_bars. (As we noted in Chapter 1, * is the sign used for multiplication in C++.)

An assignment statement always consists of a variable on the left-hand side of the equal sign and an expression on the right-hand side. An assignment statement ends with a semicolon. The expression on the right-hand side of the equal sign may be a variable, a number, or a more complicated expression made up of variables, numbers, and arithmetic operators such as * and +. An assignment statement instructs the computer to evaluate (that is, to compute the value of) the expression on the right-hand side of the equal sign and to set the value of the variable on the left-hand side equal to the value of that expression. A few more examples may help to clarify the way these assignment statements work.

You may use any arithmetic operator in place of the multiplication sign. The following, for example, is also a valid assignment statement:

```
total_weight = one_weight + number_of_bars;
```

This statement is just like the assignment statements in our sample program, except that it performs addition rather than multiplication. This statement changes the value of total_weight to the sum of the values of one_weight and number_of_bars. Of course, if you made this change in the program in Display 2.1, the program would give incorrect output, but it would still run.

In an assignment statement, the expression on the right-hand side of the equal sign can simply be another variable. The statement

```
total_weight = one_weight;
```

changes the value of the variable total_weight so that it is the same as that of the variable one_weight. If you were to use this in the program in Display 2.1, it would give out incorrectly low values for the total weight of a package (assuming there is more than one candy bar in a package), but it might make sense in some other program.

As another example, the following assignment statement changes the value of number_of_bars to 37:

```
number_of_bars = 37;
```

A number, like the 37 in this example, is called a **constant,** because unlike a variable, its value cannot change.

Since variables can change value over time and since the assignment operator is one vehicle for changing their values, there is an element of time involved in the meaning of an assignment statement. First, the expression on the right-hand side of the equal sign is evaluated. After that, the value of the variable on the left side of the equal sign is changed to the value that was obtained from that expression. This means that a variable can meaningfully occur on both sides of an assignment operator. For example, consider the assignment statement

```
number_of_bars = number_of_bars + 3;
```

This assignment statement may look strange at first. If you read it as an English sentence, it seems to say "the number_of_bars is equal to the number_of_bars plus three." It may seem to say that, but what it really says is "Make the *new* value of number_of_bars equal to the *old* value of number_of_bars plus three." The equal sign in C++ is not used the same way that it is used in English or in simple mathematics.

Assignment Statements

In an assignment statement, first the expression on the right-hand side of the equal sign is evaluated, and then the variable on the left-hand side of the equal sign is set equal to this value.

SYNTAX

Variable = Expression;

EXAMPLES

```
distance = rate * time;
count = count + 2;
```

PITFALL   Uninitialized Variables

A variable has no meaningful value until a program gives it one. For example, if the variable minimum_number has not been given a value either as the left-hand side of an assignment statement or by some other means (such as being given an input value with a cin statement), then the following is an error:

```
desired_number = minimum_number + 10;
```

This is because minimum_number has no meaningful value, so the entire expression on the right-hand side of the equal sign has no meaningful value. A variable like minimum_number that has not been given a value is said to be **uninitialized.** This situation is, in fact, worse than it would be if minimum_number had no value at all. An uninitialized variable, like minimum_number, will simply have some "garbage value." The value of an uninitialized variable is determined by whatever pattern of 0s and 1s was left in its memory location by the last program that used that portion of memory. Thus if the program is run twice, an uninitialized variable may receive a different value each time the program is run. Whenever a program gives different output on *exactly* the same input data and without *any* changes in the program itself, you should suspect an uninitialized variable.

One way to avoid an uninitialized variable is to initialize variables at the same time they are declared. This can be done by adding an equal sign and a value, as follows:

```
int minimum_number = 3;
```

This both declares `minimum_number` to be a variable of type `int` and sets the value of the variable `minimum_number` equal to 3. You can use a more complicated expression involving operations such as addition or multiplication when you initialize a variable inside the declaration in this way. However, a simple constant is what is most often used. You can initialize some, all, or none of the variables in a declaration that lists more than one variable. For example, the following declares three variables and initializes two of them:

```
double rate = 0.07, time, balance = 0.0;
```

C++ allows an alternative notation for initializing variables when they are declared. This alternative notation is illustrated by the following, which is equivalent to the preceding declaration:

```
double rate(0.07), time, balance(0.0);
```

Whether you initialize a variable when it is declared or at some later point in the program depends on the circumstances. Do whatever makes your program the easiest to understand. ■

Initializing Variables in Declarations

You can initialize a variable (that is, give it a value) at the time that you declare the variable.

SYNTAX

```
Type_Name Variable_Name_1 = Expression_for_Value_1,
          Variable_Name_2 = Expression_for_Value_2, . . .;
```

EXAMPLES

```
int count = 0, limit = 10, fudge_factor = 2;
double distance = 999.99;
```

ALTERNATIVE SYNTAX FOR INITIALIZING IN DECLARATIONS

```
Type_Name Variable_Name_1 (Expression_for_Value_1),
          Variable_Name_2 (Expression_for_Value_2),  . . .;
```

(continued)

EXAMPLES

```
int count(0), limit(10), fudge_factor(2);
double distance(999.99);
```

■ PROGRAMMING TIP   Use Meaningful Names

Variable names and other names in a program should at least hint at the meaning or use of the thing they are naming. It is much easier to understand a program if the variables have meaningful names. Contrast the following:

```
x = y * z;
```

with the more suggestive:

```
distance = speed * time;
```

The two statements accomplish the same thing, but the second is easier to understand.   ■

■ SELF-TEST EXERCISES   myprogramminglab

1. Give the declaration for two variables called `feet` and `inches`. Both variables are of type *int* and both are to be initialized to zero in the declaration. Use both initialization alternatives.

2. Give the declaration for two variables called `count` and `distance`. `count` is of type *int* and is initialized to zero. `distance` is of type *double* and is initialized to 1.5.

3. Give a C++ statement that will change the value of the variable `sum` to the sum of the values in the variables `n1` and `n2`. The variables are all of type *int*.

4. Give a C++ statement that will increase the value of the variable `length` by 8.3. The variable `length` is of type *double*.

5. Give a C++ statement that will change the value of the variable `product` to its old value multiplied by the value of the variable `n`. The variables are all of type *int*.

6. Write a program that contains statements that output the value of five or six variables that have been declared, but not initialized. Compile and run the program. What is the output? Explain.

7. Give good variable names for each of the following:
    a. A variable to hold the speed of an automobile
    b. A variable to hold the pay rate for an hourly employee
    c. A variable to hold the highest score in an exam

2.2 INPUT AND OUTPUT

Garbage in means garbage out.

PROGRAMMERS' SAYING

There are several different ways that a C++ program can perform input and output. We will describe what are called *streams*. An **input stream** is simply the stream of input that is being fed into the computer for the program to use. The word *stream* suggests that the program processes the input in the same way no matter where the input comes from. The intuition for the word *stream* is that the program sees only the stream of input and not the source of the stream, like a mountain stream whose water flows past you but whose source is unknown to you. In this section we will assume that the input comes from the keyboard. In Chapter 6 we will discuss how a program can read its input from a file; as you will see there, you can use the same kinds of input statements to read input from a file as those that you use for reading input from the keyboard. Similarly, an **output stream** is the stream of output generated by the program. In this section we will assume the output is going to a terminal screen; in Chapter 6 we will discuss output that goes to a file.

Output Using cout

The values of variables as well as strings of text may be output to the screen using cout. There may be any combination of variables and strings to be output. For example, consider the following line from the program in Display 2.1:

```
cout << number_of_bars << " candy bars\n";
```

This statement tells the computer to output two items: the value of the variable number_of_bars and the quoted string " candy bars\n". Notice that you do not need a separate copy of the word cout for each item output. You can simply list all the items to be output preceding each item to be output with the arrow symbols <<. The above single cout statement is equivalent to the following two cout statements:

```
cout << number_of_bars;
cout << " candy bars\n";
```

You can include arithmetic expressions in a cout statement as shown by the following example, where price and tax are variables:

```
cout << "The total cost is $" << (price + tax);
```

The parentheses around arithmetic expressions, like price + tax, are required by some compilers, so it is best to include them.

The symbol < is the same as the "less than" symbol. The two < symbols should be typed without any space between them. The arrow notation << is often called the **insertion operator.** The entire cout statement ends with a semicolon.

Whenever you have two cout statements in a row, you can combine them into a single long cout statement. For example, consider the following lines from Display 2.1:

```
cout << number_of_bars << " candy bars\n";
cout << one_weight << " ounces each\n";
```

These two statements can be rewritten as the single following statement, and the program will perform exactly the same:

```
cout << number_of_bars << " candy bars\n" << one_weight
     << " ounces each\n";
```

If you want to keep your program lines from running off the screen, you will have to place such a long cout statement on two or more lines. A better way to write the previous long cout statement is

```
cout << number_of_bars << " candy bars\n"
     << one_weight << " ounces each\n";
```

You should not break a quoted string across two lines, but otherwise you can start a new line anywhere you can insert a space. Any reasonable pattern of spaces and line breaks will be acceptable to the computer, but the previous example and the sample programs are good models to follow. A good policy is to use one cout for each group of output that is intuitively considered a unit. Notice that there is just one semicolon for each cout, even if the cout statement spans several lines.

Pay particular attention to the quoted strings that are output in the program in Display 2.1. Notice that the strings must be included in double quotes. The double quote symbol used is a single key on your keyboard; do not type two single quotes. Also, notice that the same double quote symbol is used at each end of the string; there are not separate left and right quote symbols.

Also, notice the spaces inside the quotes. The computer does not insert any extra space before or after the items output by a cout statement. That is why the quoted strings in the samples often start and/or end with a blank. The blanks keep the various strings and numbers from running together. If all you need is a space and there is no quoted string where you want to insert the space, then use a string that contains only a space, as in the following:

```
cout << first_number << " " << second_number;
```

As we noted in Chapter 1, \n tells the computer to start a new line of output. Unless you tell the computer to go to the next line, it will put all the output on the same line. Depending on how your screen is set up, this can produce anything from arbitrary line breaks to output that runs off the screen. Notice that the \n goes inside of the quotes. In C++, going to the next line is considered to be a special character (special symbol) and the way you spell this special character inside a quoted string is \n, with no space between the two symbols in \n. Although it is typed as two symbols, C++ considers \n to be a single character that is called the **new-line character.**

Include Directives and Namespaces

We have started all of our programs with the following two lines:

```
#include <iostream>
using namespace std;
```

These two lines make the library iostream available. This is the library that includes, among other things, the definitions of cin and cout. So if your program uses either cin or cout, you should have these two lines at the start of the file that contains your program.

The following line is known as an include **directive.** It "includes" the library iostream in your program so that you have cin and cout available:

```
#include <iostream>
```

The operators cin and cout are defined in a file named iostream and the above include directive is equivalent to copying that named file into your program. The second line is a bit more complicated to explain.

C++ divides names into **namespaces.** A namespace is a collection of names, such as the names cin and cout. A statement that specifies a namespace in the way illustrated by the following is called a *using* **directive.**

```
using namespace std;
```

This particular *using* directive says that your program is using the std ("standard") namespace. This means that the names you use will have the meaning defined for them in the std namespace. In this case, the important thing is that when names such as cin and cout were defined in iostream, their definitions said they were in the std namespace. So to use names like cin and cout, you need to tell the compiler you are using namespace std;.

That is all you need to know (for now) about namespaces, but a brief clarifying remark will remove some of the mystery that might surround the use of *namespace*. The reason that C++ has namespaces at all is because there are so many things to name. As a result, sometimes two or more items receive the same name; that is, a single name can get two different definitions. To eliminate these ambiguities, C++ divides items into collections so that no two items in the same collection (the same namespace) have the same name.

Note that a namespace is not simply a collection of names. It is a body of C++ code that specifies the meaning of some names, such as some definitions and/or declarations. The function of namespaces is to divide all the C++ name specifications into collections (called *namespaces*) such that each name in a namespace has only one specification (one "definition") in that namespace. A namespace divides up the names, but it takes a lot of C++ code along with the names.

What if you want to use two items in two different namespaces such that both items have the same name? It can be done and is not too complicated, but that is a topic for later in the book. For now, we do not need to do this.

Some versions of C++ use the following, older form of the `include` directive (without any `using namespace`):

```
#include <iostream.h>
```

If your programs do not compile or do not run with

```
#include <iostream>
using namespace std;
```

then try using the following line instead of the previous two lines:

```
#include <iostream.h>
```

If your program requires `iostream.h` instead of `iostream`, then you have an old C++ compiler and should obtain a more recent compiler.

Escape Sequences

The backslash, \, preceding a character tells the compiler that the character following the \ does not have the same meaning as the character appearing by itself. Such a sequence is called an **escape sequence.** The sequence is typed in as two characters with no space between the symbols. Several escape sequences are defined in C++.

If you want to put a \ or a " into a string constant, you must escape the ability of the " to terminate a string constant by using \", or the ability of the \ to escape, by using \\. The \\ tells the compiler you mean a real backslash, \, not an escape sequence backslash, and \" means a real quote, not a string constant end.

A stray \, say \z, in a string constant will on one compiler simply give back a z; on another it will produce an error. The ANSI Standard provides that the unspecified escape sequences have undefined behavior. This means a compiler can do anything its author finds convenient. The consequence is that code that uses undefined escape sequences is not portable. You should not use any escape sequences other than those provided. We list a few here.

```
new line          \n
horizontal tab    \t
alert             \a
backslash         \\
double quote      \"
```

If you wish to insert a blank line in the output, you can output the new-line character \n by itself:

```
cout << "\n";
```

Another way to output a blank line is to use endl, which means essentially the same thing as "\n". So you can also output a blank line as follows:

```
cout << endl;
```

Although "\n" and endl mean the same thing, they are used slightly differently; \n must always be inside of quotes and endl should not be placed in quotes.

A good rule for deciding whether to use \n or endl is the following: If you can include the \n at the end of a longer string, then use \n as in the following:

```
cout << "Fuel efficiency is "
     << mpg << " miles per gallon\n";
```

On the other hand, if the \n would appear by itself as the short string "\n", then use endl instead:

```
cout << "You entered " << number << endl;
```

Starting New Lines in Output

To start a new output line, you can include \n in a quoted string, as in the following example:

```
cout << "You have definitely won\n"
     << "one of the following prizes:\n";
```

Recall that \n is typed as two symbols with no space in between the two symbols.

Alternatively, you can start a new line by outputting endl. An equivalent way to write the above cout statement is as follows:

```
cout << "You have definitely won" << endl
     << "one of the following prizes:" << endl;
```

■ **PROGRAMMING TIP**   **End Each Program with a \n or endl**

It is a good idea to output a new-line instruction at the end of every program. If the last item to be output is a string, then include a \n at the end of the string; if not, output an endl as the last action in your program. This serves two purposes. Some compilers will not output the last line of your program unless you include a new-line instruction at the end. On other systems, your program may work fine without this final new-line instruction, but the next program that is run will have its first line of output mixed with the last line of the previous program. Even if neither of these problems occurs on your system, putting a new-line instruction at the end will make your programs more portable. ■

Formatting for Numbers with a Decimal Point

When the computer outputs a value of type *double*, the format may not be what you would like. For example, the following simple `cout` statement can produce any of a wide range of outputs:

```
cout << "The price is $" << price << endl;
```

If `price` has the value 78.5, the output might be

```
The price is $78.500000
```

or it might be

```
The price is $78.5
```

or it might be output in the following notation (which we will explain in Section 2.3):

```
The price is $7.850000e01
```

But it is extremely unlikely that the output will be the following, even though this is the format that makes the most sense:

```
The price is $78.50
```

To ensure that the output is in the form you want, your program should contain some sort of instructions that tell the computer how to output the numbers.

There is a "magic formula" that you can insert in your program to cause numbers that contain a decimal point, such as numbers of type *double*, to be output in everyday notation with the exact number of digits after the decimal point that you specify. If you want two digits after the decimal point, use the following magic formula:

```
cout.setf(ios::fixed);
cout.setf(ios::showpoint);
cout.precision(2);
```

If you insert the preceding three statements in your program, then any `cout` statement that follows these three statements will output values of type *double* in ordinary notation, with exactly two digits after the decimal point. For example, suppose the following `cout` statement appears somewhere after this magic formula and suppose the value of `price` is 78.5:

```
cout << "The price is $" << price << endl;
```

The output will then be as follows:

```
The price is $78.50
```

You may use any other nonnegative whole number in place of 2 to specify a different number of digits after the decimal point. You can even use a variable of type *int* in place of the 2. We will explain this magic formula in detail in Chapter 6. For now you should think of this magic formula as one long instruction that tells the computer how you want it to output numbers that contain a decimal point.

If you wish to change the number of digits after the decimal point so that different values in your program are output with different numbers of digits, you can repeat the magic formula with some other number in place of 2. However, when you repeat the magic formula, you only need to repeat the last line of the formula. If the magic formula has already occurred once in your program, then the following line will change the number of digits after the decimal point to 5 for all subsequent values of type *double* that are output:

```
cout.precision(5);
```

Input Using cin

You use cin for input more or less the same way you use cout for output. The syntax is similar, except that cin is used in place of cout and the arrows point in the opposite direction. For example, in the program in Display 2.1, the variables number_of_bars and one_weight were filled by the following cin statements (shown along with the cout statements that tell the user what to do):

Outputting Values of Type *double*

If you insert the following "magic formula" in your program, then all numbers of type *double* (or any other type that allows for digits after the decimal point) will be output in ordinary, everyday notation with two digits after the decimal point:

```
cout.setf(ios::fixed);
cout.setf(ios::showpoint);
cout.precision(2);
```

You can use any other nonnegative whole number in place of the 2 to specify a different number of digits after the decimal point. You can even use a variable of type *int* in place of the 2.

```
cout << "Enter the number of candy bars in a package\n";
cout << "and the weight in ounces of one candy bar.\n";
cout << "Then press return.\n";
cin >> number_of_bars;
cin >> one_weight;
```

You can list more than one variable in a single `cin` statement. So the preceding lines could be rewritten to the following:

```
cout << "Enter the number of candy bars in a package\n";
cout << "and the weight in ounces of one candy bar.\n";
cout << "Then press return.\n";
cin >> number_of_bars >> one_weight;
```

If you prefer, the `cin` statement can be written on two lines as follows:

```
cin >> number_of_bars
    >> one_weight;
```

Notice that, as with the `cout` statement, there is just one semicolon for each occurrence of `cin`.

When a program reaches a `cin` statement, it waits for input to be entered from the keyboard. It sets the first variable equal to the first value typed at the keyboard, the second variable equal to the second value typed, and so forth. However, the program does not read the input until the user presses the Return key. This allows the user to backspace and correct mistakes when entering a line of input.

Numbers in the input must be separated by one or more spaces or by a line break. If, for instance, you want to enter the two numbers 12 and 5 and instead you enter the numbers without any space between them, then the computer will think you have entered the single number 125. When you use `cin` statements, the computer will skip over any number of blanks or line breaks until it finds the next input value. Thus, it does not matter whether input numbers are separated by one space or several spaces or even a line break.

---

cin Statements

A `cin` statement sets variables equal to values typed in at the keyboard.

SYNTAX

```
cin >> Variable_1 >> Variable_2 >> ... ;
```

EXAMPLE

```
cin >> number >> size;
cin >> time_to_go
    >> points_needed;
```

Designing Input and Output

Input and output, or, as it is often called, **I/O,** is the part of the program that the user sees, so the user will not be happy with a program unless the program has well-designed I/O.

When the computer executes a `cin` statement, it expects some data to be typed in at the keyboard. If none is typed in, the computer simply waits for it. The program must tell the user when to type in a number (or other data item). The computer will not automatically ask the user to enter data. That is why the sample programs contain output statements like the following:

```
cout << "Enter the number of candy bars in a package\n";
cout << "and the weight in ounces of one candy bar.\n";
cout << "Then press return.\n";
```

These output statements **prompt** the user to enter the input. Your programs should always prompt for input.

When entering input from a terminal, the input appears on the screen as it is typed in. Nonetheless, the program should always write out the input values some time before it ends. This is called **echoing the input,** and it serves as a check to see that the input was read in correctly. Just because the input looks good on the screen when it is typed in does not mean that it was read correctly by the computer. There could be an unnoticed typing mistake or other problem. Echoing input serves as a test of the integrity of the input data.

■ **PROGRAMMING TIP**   Line Breaks in I/O

It is possible to keep output and input on the same line, and sometimes it can produce a nicer interface for the user. If you simply omit a \n or endl at the end of the last prompt line, then the user's input will appear on the same line as the prompt. For example, suppose you use the following prompt and input statements:

```
cout << "Enter the cost per person: $";
cin >> cost_per_person;
```

When the cout statement is executed, the following will appear on the screen:

```
Enter the cost per person: $
```

When the user types in the input, it will appear on the same line, like this:

```
Enter the cost per person: $1.25
```

■

SELF-TEST EXERCISES

8. Give an output statement that will produce the following message on the screen:

   ```
   The answer to the question of
   Life, the Universe, and Everything is 42.
   ```

9. Give an input statement that will fill the variable the_number (of type *int*) with a number typed in at the keyboard. Precede the input statement with a prompt statement asking the user to enter a whole number.

10. What statements should you include in your program to ensure that, when a number of type *double* is output, it will be output in ordinary notation with three digits after the decimal point?

11. Write a complete C++ program that writes the phrase Hello world to the screen. The program does nothing else.

12. Write a complete C++ program that reads in two whole numbers and outputs their sum. Be sure to prompt for input, echo input, and label all output.

13. Give an output statement that produces the new-line character and a tab character.

14. Write a short program that declares and initializes *double* variables one, two, three, four, and five to the values 1.000, 1.414, 1.732, 2.000, and 2.236, respectively. Then write output statements to generate the following legend and table. Use the tab escape sequence \t to line up the columns. If you are unfamiliar with the tab character, you should experiment with it while doing this exercise. A tab works like a mechanical stop on a typewriter. A tab causes output to begin in a next column, usually a multiple of eight spaces away. Many editors and most word processors will have adjustable tab stops. Our output does not.

    The output should be:

    ```
    N   Square Root
    1   1.000
    2   1.414
    3   1.732
    4   2.000
    5   2.236
    ```

2.3 DATA TYPES AND EXPRESSIONS

They'll never be happy together. He's not her type.

OVERHEARD AT A COCKTAIL PARTY

The Types *int* and *double*

Conceptually, the numbers 2 and 2.0 are the same number. But C++ considers them to be of different types. The whole number 2 is of type *int*; the number 2.0 is of type *double*, because it contains a fraction part (even though the fraction is 0). Once again, the mathematics of computer programming is a bit different from what you may have learned in mathematics classes. Something about the practicalities of computers makes a computer's numbers differ from the abstract definitions of these numbers. The whole numbers in C++ behave as you would expect them to. The type *int* holds no surprises. But values of type *double* are more troublesome. Because it can store only a limited number of significant digits, the computer stores numbers of type *double* as approximate values. Numbers of type *int* are stored as exact values. The precision with which *double* values are stored varies from one computer to another, but you can expect them to be stored with 14 or more digits of accuracy. For most applications this is likely to be sufficient, though subtle problems can occur even in simple cases. Thus, if you know that the values in some variable will always be whole numbers in the range allowed by your computer, it is best to declare the variable to be of type *int*.

Number constants of type *double* are written differently from those of type *int*. Constants of type *int* must not contain a decimal point. Constants of type *double* may be written in either of two forms. The simple form for *double* constants is like the everyday way of writing decimal fractions. When

---

What Is Doubled?

Why is the type for numbers with a fraction part called *double*? Is there a type called "single" that is half as big? No, but something like that is true. Many programming languages traditionally used two types for numbers with a fractional part. One type used less storage and was very imprecise (that is, it did not allow very many significant digits). The second type used *double* the amount of storage and was therefore much more precise; it also allowed numbers that were larger (although programmers tend to care more about precision than about size). The kind of numbers that used twice as much storage were called

(continued)

> *double-precision* numbers; those that used less storage were called
> *single-precision*. Following this tradition, the type that (more or less)
> corresponds to this double-precision type was named *double* in C++.
> The type that corresponds to single-precision in C++ was called *float*.
> C++ also has a third type for numbers with a fractional part, which is
> called *long double*. These types are described in the subsection entitled
> "Other Number Types." However, we will rarely use the types *float* and
> *long double* in this book.

written in this form, a *double* constant must contain a decimal point. There is, however, one thing that constants of type *double* and constants of type *int* have in common: No number in C++ may contain a comma.

The more complicated notation for constants of type *double* is frequently called **scientific notation** or **floating-point notation** and is particularly handy for writing very large numbers and very small fractions. For instance,

3.67×10^{17}

which is the same as

367000000000000000.0

is best expressed in C++ by the constant 3.67e17. The number

5.89×10^{-6}

which is the same as

0.00000589

is best expressed in C++ by the constant 5.89e-6. The e stands for *exponent* and means "multiply by 10 to the power that follows."

This e **notation** is used because keyboards normally have no way to write exponents as superscripts. Think of the number after the e as telling you the direction and number of digits to move the decimal point. For example, to change 3.49e4 to a numeral without an e, you move the decimal point four places to the right to obtain 34900.0, which is another way of writing the same number. If the number after the e is negative, you move the decimal point the indicated number of spaces to the left, inserting extra zeros if need be. So, 3.49e-2 is the same as 0.0349.

The number before the e may contain a decimal point, although it is not required. However, the exponent after the e definitely must *not* contain a decimal point.

Since computers have size limitations on their memory, numbers are typically stored in a limited number of bytes (that is, a limited amount of storage). Hence, there is a limit to how large the magnitude of a number can be, and this limit is different for different number types. The largest allowable number of type *double* is always much larger than the largest allowable number of type *int*. Most current implementations of C++ will allow values of type *int* as large as 2,147,483,647 and values of type *double* up to about 10^{308}.

Other Number Types

C++ has other numeric types besides *int* and *double*. Some are described in Display 2.2. The various number types allow for different size numbers and for more or less precision (that is, more or fewer digits after the decimal point). In Display 2.2, the values given for memory used, size range, and precision are only one sample set of values, intended to give you a general feel for how the types differ. The values vary from one system to another and may be different on your system.

Although some of these other numeric types are spelled as two words, you declare variables of these other types just as you declare variables of types *int* and *double*. For example, the following declares one variable of type *long double*:

    long double big_number;

The type names *long* and *long int* are two names for the same type. Thus, the following two declarations are equivalent:

    long big_total;

and the equivalent

    long int big_total;

Of course, in any one program, you should use only one of the above two declarations for the variable big_total, but it does not matter which one you use. Also, remember that the type name *long* by itself means the same thing as *long int*, not the same thing as *long double*.

The types for whole numbers, such an *int* and similar types, are called **integer types**. The type for numbers with a decimal point—such as the type *double* and similar types—are called **floating-point types**. They are called *floating-point* because when the computer stores a number written in the usual way, like 392.123, it first converts the number to something like e notation, in this case something like 3.92123e2. When the computer performs this conversion, the decimal point *floats* (that is, moves) to a new position.

You should be aware that there are other numeric types in C++. However, in this book we will use only the types *int*, *double*, and occasionally *long*. For most simple applications, you should not need any types except *int* and *double*. However, if you are writing a program that uses very large whole numbers, then you might need to use the type *long*.

DISPLAY 2.2   Some Number Types

Type Name	Memory Used	Size Range	Precision
short (also called *short int*)	2 bytes	-32,768 to 32,767	(not applicable)
int	4 bytes	-2,147,483,648 to 2,147,483,647	(not applicable)
long (also called *long int*)	4 bytes	-2,147,483,648 to 2,147,483,647	(not applicable)
float	4 bytes	approximately 10^{-38} to 10^{38}	7 digits
double	8 bytes	approximately 10^{-308} to 10^{308}	15 digits
long double	10 bytes	approximately 10^{-4932} to 10^{4932}	19 digits

These are only sample values to give you a general idea of how the types differ. The values for any of these entries may be different on your system. Precision refers to the number of meaningful digits, including digits in front of the decimal point. The ranges for the types float, double, and long double are the ranges for positive numbers. Negative numbers have a similar range, but with a negative sign in front of each number.

The Type *char*

We do not want to give you the impression that computers and C++ are used only for numeric calculations, so we will introduce some nonnumeric types now, though eventually we will see other more complicated nonnumeric types. Values of the type *char*, which is short for *character*, are single symbols such as a letter, digit, or punctuation mark. Values of this type are frequently called *characters* in books and in conversation, but in a C++ program this type must always be spelled in the abbreviated fashion *char*. For example, the variables symbol and letter of type *char* are declared as follows:

```
char symbol, letter;
```

A variable of type *char* can hold any single character on the keyboard. So, for example, the variable symbol could hold an 'A' or a '+' or an 'a'. Note that uppercase and lowercase versions of a letter are considered different characters.

The text in double quotes that are output using cout are called *string* values. For example, the following, which occurs in the program in Display 2.1, is a string:

```
"Enter the number of candy bars in a package\n"
```

Be sure to notice that string constants are placed inside of double quotes, while constants of type *char* are placed inside of single quotes. The two kinds of quotes mean different things. In particular, 'A' and "A" mean different things. 'A' is a value of type *char* and can be stored in a variable of type *char*. "A" is a string of characters. The fact that the string happens to contain only one character does *not* make "A" a value of type *char*. Also notice that, for both strings and characters, the left and right quotes are the same.

The use of the type *char* is illustrated in the program shown in Display 2.3. Notice that the user types a space between the first and second initials. Yet the program skips over the blank and reads the letter B as the second input character. When you use cin to read input into a variable of type *char*, the computer skips over all blanks and line breaks until it gets to the first nonblank character and reads that nonblank character into the variable. It makes no difference whether there are blanks in the input or not. The program in Display 2.3 will give the same output whether the user types in a blank between initials, as shown in the sample dialogue, or the user types in the two initials without a blank, like so:

JB

The Type *bool*

The next type we discuss here is the type *bool*. This type was added to the C++ language by the ISO/ANSI (International Standards Organization/ American National Standards Organization) committee in 1998. Expressions of type *bool* are called *Boolean* after the English mathematician George Boole (1815–1864), who formulated rules for mathematical logic.

Boolean expressions evaluate to one of the two values, *true* or *false*. Boolean expressions are used in branching and looping statements that we study in Section 2.4. We will say more about Boolean expressions and the type *bool* in that section.

DISPLAY 2.3   The Type char *(part 1 of 2)*

```
1    #include <iostream>
2    using namespace std;
3    int main( )
4    {
5        char symbol1, symbol2, symbol3;

6        cout << "Enter two initials, without any periods:\n";
7        cin >> symbol1 >> symbol2;
8        cout << "The two initials are:\n";
9        cout << symbol1 << symbol2 << endl;
10       cout << "Once more with a space:\n";
```

(continued)

DISPLAY 2.3   The Type char *(part 2 of 2)*

```
11          symbol3 = ' ';
12          cout << symbol1 << symbol3 << symbol2 << endl;
13          cout << "That's all.";
14          return 0;
15      }
```

Sample Dialogue

```
Enter two initials, without any periods:
J B
The two initials are:
JB
Once more with a space:
J B
That's all.
```

Introduction to the Class string

Although C++ lacks a native data type to directly manipulate strings, there is a string class that may be used to process strings in a manner similar to the data types we have seen thus far. The distinction between a class and a native data type is discussed in Chapter 10. Further details about the string class are discussed in Chapter 8.

To use the string class we must first include the string library:

```
#include <string>
```

Your program must also contain the following line of code, normally placed at the start of the file:

```
using namespace std;
```

You declare variables of type string just as you declare variables of types *int* or *double*. For example, the following declares one variable of type string and stores the text "Monday" in it:

```
string day;
day = "Monday";
```

You may use cin and cout to read data into strings, as shown in Display 2.4. If you place the '+' symbol between two strings, then this operator concatenates the two strings together to create one longer string. For example, the code:

```
"Monday" + "Tuesday"
```

Results in the concatenated string of:

```
"MondayTuesday"
```

Note that a space is not automatically added between the strings. If you wanted a space between the two days, then a space must be added explicitly:

```
"Monday " + "Tuesday"
```

When you use `cin` to read input into a `string` variable, the computer only reads until it encounters a *whitespace* character. **Whitespace** characters are all the characters that are displayed as blank spaces on the screen, including the blank or space character, the tab character, and the new-line character `'\n'`. This means that you cannot input a string that contains spaces. This may sometimes cause errors, as indicated in Display 2.4, Sample Dialogue 2. In this case, the user intends to enter `"Mr. Bojangles"` as the name of the pet, but the string is only read up to `"Mr."` since the next character is a space. The `"Bojangles"` string is ignored by this program but would be read next if there was another `cin` statement. Chapter 8 describes a technique to input a string that may include spaces.

Type Compatibilities

As a general rule, you cannot store a value of one type in a variable of another type. For example, most compilers will object to the following:

```
int int_variable;
int_variable = 2.99;
```

The problem is a type mismatch. The constant `2.99` is of type *double* and the variable `int_variable` is of type *int*. Unfortunately, not all compilers will react the same way to the above assignment statement. Some will issue an error message, some will give only a warning message, and some compilers will not object at all. But even if the compiler does allow you to use this assignment, it will probably give `int_variable` the *int* value 2, not the value 3. Since you cannot count on your compiler accepting this assignment, you should not assign a *double* value to a variable of type *int*.

DISPLAY 2.4 The `string` Class *(part 1 of 2)*

```
1    #include <iostream>
2    #include <string>
3    using namespace std;
4    int main()
5    {
6        string middle_name, pet_name;
7        string alter_ego_name;
8
```

(continued)

DISPLAY 2.4   The string Class *(part 2 of 2)*

```
 9        cout << "Enter your middle name and the name of your pet.\n";
10        cin >> middle_name;
11        cin >> pet_name;
12
13        alter_ego_name = pet_name + " " + middle_name;
14
15        cout << "The name of your alter ego is ";
16        cout << alter_ego_name << "." << endl;
17
18        return 0;
19
20    }
```

Sample Dialogue 1

```
Enter your middle name and the name of your pet.
Parker Pippen
The name of your alter ego is Pippen Parker.
```

Sample Dialogue 2

```
Enter your middle name and the name of your pet.
Parker
Mr. Bojangles
The name of your alter ego is Mr. Bojangles Parker.
```

The same problem arises if you use a variable of type *double* instead of the constant 2.99. Most compilers will also object to the following:

```
int int_variable;
double double_variable;
double_variable = 2.00;
int_variable = double_variable;
```

The fact that the value 2.00 "comes out even" makes no difference. The value 2.00 is of type *double*, not of type *int*. As you will see shortly, you can replace 2.00 with 2 in the preceding assignment to the variable double_variable, but even that is not enough to make the assignment acceptable. The variables int_variable and double_variable are of different types, and that is the cause of the problem.

Even if the compiler will allow you to mix types in an assignment statement, in most cases you should not. Doing so makes your program less portable, and it can be confusing. For example, if your compiler lets you assign 2.99 to a variable of type *int*, the variable will receive the value 2, rather than 2.99, which can be confusing since the program seems to say the value will be 2.99.

There are some special cases where it is permitted to assign a value of one type to a variable of another type. It is acceptable to assign a value of type *int* to a variable of type *double*. For example, the following is both legal and acceptable style:

```
double double_variable;
double_variable = 2;
```

The above will set the value of the variable named double_variable equal to 2.0.

Although it is usually a bad idea to do so, you can store an *int* value such as 65 in a variable of type *char* and you can store a letter such as 'Z' in a variable of type *int*. For many purposes, the C language considers the characters to be small integers; and perhaps unfortunately, C++ inherited this from C. The reason for allowing this is that variables of type *char* consume less memory than variables of type *int* and so doing arithmetic with variables of type *char* can save some memory. However, it is clearer to use the type *int* when you are dealing with integers and to use the type *char* when you are dealing with characters.

The general rule is that you cannot place a value of one type in a variable of another type—though it may seem that there are more exceptions to the rule than there are cases that follow the rule. Even if the compiler does not enforce this rule very strictly, it is a good rule to follow. Placing data of one type in a variable of another type can cause problems, since the value must be changed to a value of the appropriate type and that value may not be what you would expect.

Values of type *bool* can be assigned to variables of an integer type (*short*, *int*, *long*) and integers can be assigned to variables of type *bool*. However, it is poor style to do this and you should not use these features. For completeness and to help you read other people's code, we do give the details: When assigned to a variable of type *bool*, any nonzero integer will be stored as the value *true*. Zero will be stored as the value *false*. When assigning a *bool* value to an integer variable, *true* will be stored as 1 and *false* will be stored as 0.

Arithmetic Operators and Expressions

In a C++ program, you can combine variables and/or numbers using the arithmetic operators + for addition, – for subtraction, * for multiplication, and / for division. For example, the following assignment statement, which appears in the program in Display 2.1, uses the * operator to multiply the numbers in two variables. (The result is then placed in the variable on the left-hand side of the equal sign.)

```
total_weight = one_weight * number_of_bars;
```

All of the arithmetic operators can be used with numbers of type *int*, numbers of type *double*, and even with one number of each type. However, the type of the value produced and the exact value of the result depends on the types of the numbers being combined. If both operands (that is, both numbers) are of type *int*, then the result of combining them with an arithmetic operator is of type *int*. If one, or both, of the operands is of type *double*, then the result is of type *double*. For example, if the variables base_amount and increase are of type *int*, then the number produced by the following expression is of type *int*:

```
base_amount + increase
```

However, if one or both of the two variables is of type *double*, then the result is of type *double*. This is also true if you replace the operator + with any of the operators −, *, or /.

The type of the result can be more significant than you might suspect. For example, 7.0/2 has one operand of type *double*, namely 7.0. Hence, the result is the type *double* number 3.5. However, 7/2 has two operands of type *int* and so it yields the type *int*, which is the result 3. Even if the result "comes out even," there is a difference. For example, 6.0/2 has one operand of type *double*, namely 6.0. Hence, the result is the type *double* number 3.0, which is only an approximate quantity. However, 6/2 has two operands of type *int*, so it yields the result 3, which is of type *int* and so is an exact quantity. The division operator is the operator that is affected most severely by the type of its arguments.

When used with one or both operands of type *double*, the division operator, /, behaves as you might expect. However, when used with two operands of type *int*, the division operator, /, yields the integer part resulting from division. In other words, integer division discards the part after the decimal point. So, 10/3 is 3 (not 3.3333), 5/2 is 2 (not 2.5), and 11/3 is 3 (not 3.6666). Notice that the number *is not rounded*; the part after the decimal point is discarded no matter how large it is.

The operator % can be used with operands of type *int* to recover the information lost when you use / to do division with numbers of type *int*. When used with values of type *int*, the two operators/ and % yield the two numbers produced when you perform the long division algorithm you learned in grade school. For example, 17 divided by 5 yields 3 with a remainder of 2. The / operation yields the number of times one number "goes into" another. The % operation gives the remainder. For example, the statements

```
cout << "17 divided by 5 is " << (17/5) << endl;
cout << "with a remainder of " << (17%5) << endl;
```

yield the following output:

```
17 divided by 5 is 3
with a remainder of 2
```

Display 2.5 illustrates how / and % work with values of type *int*.

DISPLAY 2.5   Integer Division

$$
\begin{array}{r}
4 \longleftarrow 12/3 \\
3 \overline{\smash{)}12} \\
\underline{12} \\
0 \longleftarrow 12\%3
\end{array}
\qquad
\begin{array}{r}
4 \longleftarrow 14/3 \\
3 \overline{\smash{)}14} \\
\underline{12} \\
2 \longleftarrow 14\%3
\end{array}
$$

When used with negative values of type *int*, the result of the operators / and % can be different for different implementations of C++. Thus, you should use / and % with *int* values only when you know that both values are nonnegative.

Any reasonable spacing will do in arithmetic expressions. You can insert spaces before and after operations and parentheses, or you can omit them. Do whatever produces a result that is easy to read.

You can specify the order of operations by inserting parentheses, as illustrated in the following two expressions:

(x + y) * z

x + (y * z)

VideoNote
Precedence and Arithmetic
Operators

To evaluate the first expression, the computer first adds x and y and then multiplies the result by z. To evaluate the second expression, it multiplies y and z and then adds the result to x. Although you may be used to using mathematical formulas that contain square brackets and various other forms of parentheses, that is not allowed in C++. C++ allows only one kind of parentheses in arithmetic expressions. The other varieties are reserved for other purposes.

If you omit parentheses, the computer will follow rules called **precedence rules** that determine the order in which the operators, such as + and *, are performed. These precedence rules are similar to rules used in algebra and other mathematics classes. For example,

x + y * z

is evaluated by first doing the multiplication and then the addition. Except in some standard cases, such as a string of additions or a simple multiplication embedded inside an addition, it is usually best to include the parentheses, even if the intended order of operations is the one dictated by the precedence rules. The parentheses make the expression easier to read and less prone to programmer error. A complete set of C++ precedence rules is given in Appendix 2.

Display 2.6 shows some examples of common kinds of arithmetic expressions and how they are expressed in C++.

DISPLAY 2.6   Arithmetic Expressions

Mathematical Formula	C++ Expression
$b^2 - 4ac$	b*b – 4*a*c
$x(y + z)$	x*(y + z)
$\dfrac{1}{x^2 + x + 3}$	1/(x*x + x + 3)
$\dfrac{a + b}{c - d}$	(a + b)/(c – d)

PITFALL   Whole Numbers in Division

When you use the division operator / on two whole numbers, the result is a whole number. This can be a problem if you expect a fraction. Moreover, the problem can easily go unnoticed, resulting in a program that looks fine but is producing incorrect output without your even being aware of the problem. For example, suppose you are a landscape architect who charges $5,000 per mile to landscape a highway, and suppose you know the length of the highway you are working on in feet. The price you charge can easily be calculated by the following C++ statement:

```
total_price = 5000 * (feet/5280.0);
```

This works because there are 5,280 feet in a mile. If the stretch of highway you are landscaping is 15,000 feet long, this formula will tell you that the total price is

```
5000 * (15000/5280.0)
```

Your C++ program obtains the final value as follows: 15000/5280.0 is computed as 2.84. Then the program multiplies 5000 by 2.84 to produce the value 14200.00. With the aid of your C++ program, you know that you should charge $14,200 for the project.

Now suppose the variable feet is of type *int*, and you forget to put in the decimal point and the zero, so that the assignment statement in your program reads:

```
total_price = 5000 * (feet/5280);
```

It still looks fine but will cause serious problems. If you use this second form of the assignment statement, you are dividing two values of type *int*, so the result of the division feet/5280 is 15000/5280, which is the *int* value 2 (instead of the value 2.84, which you think you are getting). So the value assigned to total_cost is 5000 * 2, or 10000.00. If you forget the decimal point, you will charge $10,000. However, as we have already seen, the correct value is $14,200. A missing decimal point has cost you $4,200. Note that this will be true whether the type of total_price is *int* or *double*; the damage is done before the value is assigned to total_price. ■

SELF-TEST EXERCISES

15. Convert each of the following mathematical formulas to a C++ expression:

$$3x \qquad 3x + y \qquad \frac{x + y}{7} \qquad \frac{3x + y}{z + 2}$$

16. What is the output of the following program lines when embedded in a correct program that declares all variables to be of type *char*?

```
a = 'b';
b = 'c';
c = a;
cout << a << b << c << 'c';
```

17. What is the output of the following program lines when embedded in a correct program that declares number to be of type *int*?

```
number = (1/3) * 3;
cout << "(1/3) * 3 is equal to " << number;
```

18. Write a complete C++ program that reads two whole numbers into two variables of type *int* and then outputs both the whole-number part and the remainder when the first number is divided by the second. This can be done using the operators / and %.

19. Given the following fragment that purports to convert from degrees Celsius to degrees Fahrenheit, answer the following questions:

```
double c = 20;
double f;
f = (9/5) * c + 32.0;
```

   a. What value is assigned to f?
   b. Explain what is actually happening, and what the programmer likely wanted.
   c. Rewrite the code as the programmer intended.

20. What is the output of the following program lines when embedded in a correct program that declares month, day, year, and date to be of type string?

```
month = "03";
day = "04";
year = "06";
date = month + day + year;
cout << date << endl;
```

More Assignment Statements

There is a shorthand notation that combines the assignment operator (=) and an arithmetic operator so that a given variable can have its value changed by adding, subtracting, multiplying by, or dividing by a specified value. The general form is

    Variable Op= Expression

which is equivalent to

    Variable = Variable Op (Expression)

Op is an operator such as +, *, or *. The *Expression* can be another variable, a constant, or a more complicated arithmetic expression. Following are examples:

Example	Equivalent to:
count += 2;	count = count + 2;
total −= discount;	total = total − discount;
bonus *= 2;	bonus = bonus * 2;
time /= rush_factor;	time = time / rush_factor;
change %= 100;	change = change % 100;
amount *= cnt1 + cnt2;	amount = amount * (cnt1 + cnt2);

2.4 SIMPLE FLOW OF CONTROL

"If you think we're wax-works," he said, "you ought to pay, you know. Wax-works weren't made to be looked at for nothing. Nohow!"

"Contrariwise," added the one marked "DEE," "if you think we're alive, you ought to speak."

LEWIS CARROLL, *Through the Looking-Glass*

The programs you have seen thus far each consist of a simple list of statements to be executed in the order given. However, to write more sophisticated programs, you will also need some way to vary the order in which statements are executed. The order in which statements are executed is often referred to as **flow of control**. In this section we will present two simple ways to add some flow of control to your programs. We will discuss a branching mechanism that lets your program choose between two alternative actions, choosing one or the other depending on the values of variables. We will also present a looping mechanism that lets your program repeat an action a number of times.

A Simple Branching Mechanism

Sometimes it is necessary to have a program choose one of two alternatives, depending on the input. For example, suppose you want to design a program to compute a week's salary for an hourly employee. Assume the firm pays an overtime rate of one-and-one-half times the regular rate for all hours after the first 40 hours worked. As long as the employee works 40 or more hours, the pay is then equal to

```
rate * 40 + 1.5 * rate * (hours - 40)
```

However, if there is a possibility that the employee will work less than 40 hours, this formula will unfairly pay a negative amount of overtime. (To see this, just substitute 10 for hours, 1 for rate, and do the arithmetic. The poor employee will get a negative paycheck.) The correct pay formula for an employee who works less than 40 hours is simply

```
rate * hours
```

If both more than 40 hours and less than 40 hours of work are possible, then the program will need to choose between the two formulas. In order to compute the employee's pay, the program action should be

Decide whether or not (hours > 40) is true.

If it is, do the following assignment statement:
```
gross_pay = rate * 40 + 1.5 * rate * (hours - 40);
```

If it is not, do the following:
```
gross_pay = rate * hours;
```

There is a C++ statement that does exactly this kind of branching action. The *if-else* **statement** chooses between two alternative actions. For example, the wage calculation we have been discussing can be accomplished with the following C++ statement:

```
if (hours > 40)
    gross_pay = rate * 40 + 1.5 * rate * (hours - 40);
else
    gross_pay = rate * hours;
```

A complete program that uses this statement is given in Display 2.7.

Two forms of an *if-else* statement are described in Display 2.8. The first is the simple form of an *if-else* statement; the second form will be discussed in the subsection entitled "Compound Statements." In the first form shown, the two statements may be any executable statements. The *Boolean_Expression* is a test that can be checked to see if it is true or false, that is, to see if it is satisfied or not. For example, the *Boolean_Expression* in the earlier *if-else* statement is

```
hours > 40
```

When the program reaches the *if-else* statement, exactly one of the two embedded statements is executed. If the *Boolean_Expression* is true (that is, if it is satisfied), then the *Yes_Statement* is executed; if the *Boolean_Expression* is false (that is, if it is not satisfied), then the *No_Statement* is executed. Notice that the *Boolean_Expression* must be enclosed in parentheses. (This is required by the syntax rules for if-else statements in C++.) Also notice that an *if-else* statement has two smaller statements embedded in it.

DISPLAY 2.7   An if-else Statement *(part 1 of 2)*

```
1     #include <iostream>
2     using namespace std;
3     int main( )
4     {
5         int hours;
6         double gross_pay, rate;
7         cout << "Enter the hourly rate of pay: $";
8         cin >> rate;
9         cout << "Enter the number of hours worked,\n"
10             << "rounded to a whole number of hours: ";
11        cin >> hours;
12        if (hours > 40)
13            gross_pay = rate * 40 + 1.5 * rate * (hours - 40);
14        else
15            gross_pay = rate * hours;

16        cout.setf(ios::fixed);
17        cout.setf(ios::showpoint);
18        cout.precision(2);
19        cout << "Hours = " << hours << endl;
20        cout << "Hourly pay rate = $" << rate << endl;
21        cout << "Gross pay = $" << gross_pay << endl;
22        return 0;
23    }
```

Sample Dialogue 1

```
Enter the hourly rate of pay: $20.00
Enter the number of hours worked,
rounded to a whole number of hours: 30
Hours = 30
Hourly pay rate = $20.00
Gross pay = $600.00
```

(continued)

DISPLAY 2.7   An `if-else` **Statement** *(part 2 of 2)*

Sample Dialogue 2

```
Enter the hourly rate of pay: $10.00
Enter the number of hours worked,
rounded to a whole number of hours: 41
Hours = 41
Hourly pay rate = $10.00
Gross pay = $415.00
```

DISPLAY 2.8   Syntax for an `if-else` **Statement**

A Single Statement for Each Alternative:

```
1      if (Boolean_Expression)
2            Yes_Statement
3      else
4            No_Statement
```

A Sequence of Statements for Each Alternative:

```
5      if (Boolean_Expression)
6      {
7           Yes_Statement_1
8           Yes_Statement_2
9              . . .
10          Yes_Statement_Last
10      }
12      else
13      {
14          No_Statement_1
15          No_Statement_2
16             . . .
17          No_Statement_Last
18      }
```

A **Boolean expression** is any expression that is either true or false. An *if-else* statement always contains a *Boolean_Expression*. The simplest form for a *Boolean_Expression* consists of two expressions, such as numbers or variables, that are compared with one of the comparison operators shown in Display 2.9. Notice that some of the operators are spelled with two symbols: for example, ==, !=, <=, >=. Be sure to notice that you use a double equal == for

DISPLAY 2.9   Comparison Operators

Math Symbol	English	C++ Notation	C++ Sample	Math Equivalent
=	equal to	==	x + 7 == 2 * y	x + 7 = 2y
≠	not equal to	!=	ans != 'n'	ans ≠ 'n'
<	less than	<	count < m + 3	count < m + 3
≤	less than or equal to	<=	time <= limit	time ≤ limit
>	greater than	>	time > limit	time > limit
≥	greater than or equal to	>=	age >= 21	age ≥ 21

the equal sign, and you use the two symbols != for not equal. Such operators should not have any space between the two symbols. The part of the compiler that separates the characters into C++ names and symbols will see the !=, for example, and tell the rest of the compiler that the programmer meant to test for INEQUALITY. When an *if-else* statement is executed, the two expressions being compared are evaluated and compared using the operator. If the comparison turns out to be true, then the first statement is performed. If the comparison fails, then the second statement is executed.

You can combine two comparisons using the "and" operator, which is spelled && in C++. For example, the following Boolean expression is true (that is, is satisfied) provided x is greater than 2 *and* x is less than 7:

    (2 < x) && (x < 7)

When two comparisons are connected using a &&, the entire expression is true, provided both of the comparisons are true (that is, provided both are satisfied); otherwise, the entire expression is false.

You can also combine two comparisons using the "or" operator, which is spelled || in C++. For example, the following is true provided y is less than 0 *or* y is greater than 12:

    (y < 0) || (y > 12)

When two comparisons are connected using a ||, the entire expression is true provided that one or both of the comparisons are true (that is, satisfied); otherwise, the entire expression is false.

Remember that when you use a Boolean expression in an *if-else* statement, the Boolean expression must be enclosed in parentheses. Therefore, an *if-else* statement that uses the && operator and two comparisons is parenthesized as follows:

    if ((temperature >= 95) && (humidity >= 90))
        . . .

The inner parentheses around the comparisons are not required, but they do make the meaning clearer, and we will normally include them.

You can negate any Boolean expression using the ! operator. If you want to negate a Boolean expression, place the expression in parentheses and place the ! operator in front of it. For example, !(x < y) means "x is *not* less than y."

The "and" Operator &&

You can form a more elaborate Boolean expression by combining two simple tests using the "and" operator &&.

SYNTAX (FOR A BOOLEAN EXPRESSION USING &&)

(*Comparison_1*) && (*Comparison_2*)

EXAMPLE (WITHIN AN *if-else* STATEMENT)

```
if ( (score > 0) && (score < 10) )
    cout << "score is between 0 and 10\n";
else
    cout << "score is not between 0 and 10.\n";
```

If the value of score is greater than 0 and the value of score is also less than 10, then the first cout statement will be executed; otherwise, the second cout statement will be executed.

Since the Boolean expression in an *if-else* statement must be enclosed in parentheses, you should place a second pair of parentheses around the negated expression when it is used in an *if-else* statement. For example, an *if-else* statement might begin as follows:

```
if (!(x < y))
    ...
```

The ! operator can usually be avoided. For example, our hypothetical *if-else* statement can instead begin with the following, which is equivalent and easier to read:

```
if (x >= y)
    ...
```

We will not have much call to use the ! operator until later in this book, so we will postpone any detailed discussion of it until then.

Sometimes you want one of the two alternatives in an *if-else* statement to do nothing at all. In C++ this can be accomplished by omitting the *else* part. These sorts of statements are referred to as *if* **statements** to distinguish them from *if-else* statements. For example, the first of the following two statements is an *if* statement:

```
if (sales >= minimum)
    salary = salary + bonus;
cout << "salary = $" << salary;
```

If the value of sales is greater than or equal to the value of minimum, the assignment statement is executed and then the following cout statement is executed. On the other hand, if the value of sales is less than minimum, then the embedded assignment statement is not executed, so the *if* statement causes no change (that is, no bonus is added to the base salary), and the program proceeds directly to the cout statement.

The "or" Operator ||

You can form a more elaborate Boolean expression by combining two simple tests using the "or" operator ||.

SYNTAX (FOR A BOOLEAN EXPRESSION USING ||)

(*Comparison_1*) || (*Comparison_2*)

EXAMPLE (WITHIN AN *if-else* STATEMENT)

```
if ( (x == 1) || (x == y) )
    cout << "x is 1 or x equals y.\n";
else
    cout << "x is neither 1 nor equal to y.\n";
```

If the value of x is equal to 1 or the value of x is equal to the value of y (or both), then the first cout statement will be executed; otherwise, the second cout statement will be executed.

PITFALL   Strings of Inequalities

Do not use a string of inequalities such as the following in your program:

```
if (x < z < y)          ←——————————  Do not do this!
    cout << "z is between x and y.";
```

If you do use this type of expression, your program will probably compile and run, but it will undoubtedly give incorrect output. We will explain why this happens after we learn more details about the C++ language. The same problem will occur with a string of comparisons using any of the comparison operators; the problem is not limited to < comparisons. The correct way to express a string of inequalities is to use the "and" operator && as follows:

```
if ( (x < z) && (z < y) )  ←————— correct form
    cout << "z is between x and y.";
```

■

VideoNote
Common Bugs with
= and ==

PITFALL   Using = in place of ==

Unfortunately, you can write many things in C++ that you would think are incorrectly formed C++ statements but turn out to have some obscure meaning. This means that if you mistakenly write something that you would expect to produce an error message, you may find out that the program compiles and runs with no error messages, but gives incorrect output. Since you may not realize you wrote something incorrectly, this can cause serious problems. By the time you realize something is wrong, the mistake may be very hard to find. One common mistake is to use the symbol = when you mean ==. For example, consider an *if-else* statement that begins as follows:

```
if (x = 12)
    Do_Something
else
    Do_Something_Else
```

Suppose you wanted to test to see if the value of x is equal to 12 so that you really meant to use == rather than =. You might think the compiler will catch your mistake. The expression

```
x = 12
```

is not something that is satisfied or not. It is an assignment statement, so surely the compiler will give an error message. Unfortunately, that is not the case. In C++ the expression x = 12 is an expression that returns (or has) a value, just like x + 12 or 2 + 3. An assignment expression's value is the value transferred to the variable on the left. For example, the value of x = 12 is 12. We saw in our discussion of Boolean value compatibility that *int* values may be converted to *true* or *false*. Since 12 is not zero, it is converted to *true*. If you use x = 12 as the Boolean expression in an *if* statement, the Boolean expression is always *true*, so the first branch (*Do_Something*) is always executed.

This error is very hard to find because it *looks correct*! The compiler can find the error without any special instructions if you put the 12 on the left side of the comparison, as in

```
if (12 == x)
    Do_Something;
else
    Do_Something_Else;
```

Then, the compiler will give an error message if you mistakenly use = instead of ==.

Remember that dropping one of the = in an == is a common error that is not caught by many compilers, is very hard to see, and is almost certainly not what you wanted. In C++, many executable statements can also be used as almost any kind of expression, including as a Boolean expression for an if-else statement. If you put an assignment statement where a Boolean expression is expected, the assignment statement will be interpreted as a Boolean expression. Of course the result of the "test" will undoubtedly not be what you intended as the Boolean expression. The if-else statement above looks fine at a quick glance and it will compile and run. But, in all likelihood, it will produce puzzling results when it is run. ∎

Compound Statements

You will often want the branches of an if-else statement to execute more than one statement each. To accomplish this, enclose the statements for each branch between a pair of braces, { and }, as indicated in the second syntax template in Display 2.8 and illustrated in Display 2.10. A list of statements enclosed in a pair of braces is called a **compound statement.** A compound statement is treated as a single statement by C++ and may be used anywhere that a single statement may be used. (Thus, the second syntax template in Display 2.8 is really just a special case of the first one.) Display 2.10 contains two compound statements, embedded in an if-else statement.

Syntax rules for if-else demand that the Yes statement and No statement be exactly one statement. If more statements are desired for a branch, the statements must be enclosed in braces to convert them to one compound statement. If two or more statements not enclosed by braces are placed between the if and the else, then the compiler will give an error message.

DISPLAY 2.10 Compound Statements Used With if-else

```
1    if (my_score > your_score)
2    {
3        cout << "I win!\n";
4        wager = wager + 100;
5    }
6    else
7    {
8        cout << "I wish these were golf scores.\n";
9        wager = 0;
10   }
```

SELF-TEST EXERCISES

21. Write an *if-else* statement that outputs the word High if the value of the variable score is greater than 100 and Low if the value of score is at most 100. The variable score is of type *int*.

22. Suppose savings and expenses are variables of type *double* that have been given values. Write an *if-else* statement that outputs the word Solvent, decreases the value of savings by the value of expenses, and sets the value of expenses to 0, provided that savings is at least as large as expenses. If, however, savings is less than expenses, the *if-else* statement simply outputs the word Bankrupt and does not change the value of any variables.

23. Write an *if-else* statement that outputs the word Passed provided the value of the variable exam is greater than or equal to 60 and the value of the variable programs_done is greater than or equal to 10. Otherwise, the *if-else* statement outputs the word Failed. The variables exam and programs_done are both of type *int*.

24. Write an *if-else* statement that outputs the word Warning provided that either the value of the variable temperature is greater than or equal to 100, or the value of the variable pressure is greater than or equal to 200, or both. Otherwise, the *if-else* statement outputs the word OK. The variables temperature and pressure are both of type *int*.

25. Consider a quadratic expression, say

    $x^2 - x - 2$

    Describing where this quadratic is positive (that is, greater than 0), involves describing a set of numbers that are either less than the smaller root (which is -1) or greater than the larger root (which is +2). Write a C++ Boolean expression that is true when this formula has positive values.

26. Consider the quadratic expression

    $x^2 - 4x + 3$

    Describing where this quadratic is negative involves describing a set of numbers that are simultaneously greater than the smaller root (+1) and less than the larger root (+3). Write a C++ Boolean expression that is true when the value of this quadratic is negative.

27. What is the output of the following cout statements embedded in these *if-else* statements? You are to assume that these are embedded in a complete correct program. Explain your answer.

a. `if (0)`
   ```
       cout << "0 is true";
   else
       cout << "0 is false";
   cout << endl;
   ```
b. `if (1)`
   ```
       cout << "1 is true";
   else
       cout << "1 is false";
   cout << endl;
   ```
c. `if (-1)`
   ```
       cout << "-1 is true";
   else
       cout << "-1 is false";
   cout << endl;
   ```

Note: This is an exercise only. This is *not* intended to illustrate programming style you should follow.

Simple Loop Mechanisms

Most programs include some action that is repeated a number of times. For example, the program in Display 2.7 computes the gross pay for one worker. If the company employs 100 workers, then a more complete payroll program would repeat this calculation 100 times. A portion of a program that repeats a statement or group of statements is called a **loop.** The C++ language has a number of ways to create loops. One of these constructions is called a *while* **statement** or *while* **loop.** We will first illustrate its use with a short toy example and then do a more realistic example.

The program in Display 2.11 contains a simple *while* statement shown in color. The portion between the braces, { and }, is called the **body** of the *while* loop; it is the action that is repeated. The statements inside the braces are executed in order, then they are executed again, then again, and so forth until the *while* loop ends. In the first sample dialogue, the body is executed three times before the loop ends, so the program outputs `Hello` three times. Each repetition of the loop body is called an **iteration** of the loop, and so the first sample dialogue shows three iterations of the loop.

The meaning of a *while* statement is suggested by the English word *while.* The loop is repeated *while the Boolean expression in the parentheses is satisfied.* In Display 2.11 this means that the loop body is repeated as long as the value of the variable `count_down` is greater than 0. Let's consider the first sample dialogue and see how the *while* loop performs. The user types in 3 so the `cin` statement sets the value of `count_down` to 3. Thus, in this case, when the program reaches the *while* statement, it is certainly true that `count_down` is greater than 0, so the statements in the loop body are executed. Every time the loop body is repeated, the following two statements are executed:

DISPLAY 2.11   A *while* **Loop**

```
 1    #include <iostream>
 2    using namespace std;
 3    int main( )
 4    {
 5        int count_down;
 6        cout << "How many greetings do you want? ";
 7        cin >> count_down;

 8        while (count_down > 0)
 9        {
10            cout << "Hello ";
11            count_down = count_down - 1;
12        }
13        cout << endl;
14        cout << "That's all!\n";
15        return 0;
16    }
17
```

Sample Dialogue 1

```
How many greetings do you want? 3
Hello Hello Hello
That's all!
```

Sample Dialogue 2

```
How many greetings do you want? 1
Hello
That's all!
```

Sample Dialogue 3

```
How many greetings do you want? 0

That's all!
```

The loop body is executed zero times.

```
cout << "Hello ";
count_down = count_down - 1;
```

Therefore, every time the loop body is repeated, "Hello " is output and the value of the variable count_down is decreased by one. After the computer repeats the loop body three times, the value of count_down is decreased to 0

DISPLAY 2.12 Syntax of the *while* Statement

A Loop Body with Several Statements:

```
1    while (Boolean_Expression )
2    {
3        Statement_1
4        Statement_2
5        ...
6        Statement_Last
7    }
```

Do NOT put a semicolon here.

body

A Loop Body with a Single Statement:

```
8    while (Boolean_Expression )
9        Statement
```

body

and the program in Display 2.11 and the Boolean expression in parentheses are no longer satisfied. So, this *while* statement ends after repeating the loop body three times.

The syntax for a *while* statement is given in Display 2.12. The *Boolean_ Expressions* allowed are exactly the same as the Boolean expressions allowed in an *if-else* statement. Just as in *if-else* statements, the Boolean expression in a *while* statement must be enclosed in parentheses. In Display 2.12 we have given the syntax templates for two cases: the case when there is more than one statement in the loop body and the case when there is just a single statement in the loop body. Note that when there is only a single statement in the loop body, you need not include the braces { and }.

Let's go over the actions performed by a *while* statement in greater detail. When the *while* statement is executed, the first thing that happens is that the Boolean expression following the word *while* is checked. It is either true or false. For example, the comparison

```
count_down > 0
```

is true if the value of count_down is positive. If it is false, then no action is taken and the program proceeds to the next statement after the *while* statement. If the comparison is true, then the entire body of the loop is executed. At least one of the expressions being compared typically contains something that might be changed by the loop body, such as the value of count_down in the *while* statement in Display 2.11. After the body of the loop is executed, the comparison is again checked. This process is repeated again and again as long as the comparison continues to be true. After each iteration of the loop body, the comparison is again checked and if it is true, then the entire loop body is executed again. When the comparison is no longer true, the *while* statement ends.

The first thing that happens when a *while* statement is executed is that the Boolean expression is checked. If the Boolean expression is not true when the *while* statement begins, then the loop body is never executed. That is exactly what happens in Sample Dialogue 3 of Display 2.11. In many programming situations you want the possibility of executing the loop body zero times. For example, if your *while* loop is reading a list consisting of all the failing scores on an exam and nobody failed the exam, then you want the loop body to be executed zero times.

As we just noted, a *while* loop might execute its loop body zero times, which is often what you want. If, on the other hand, you know that *under all circumstances* your loop body should be executed at least one time, then you can use a *do-while* statement. A *do-while* statement is similar to a *while* statement except that the loop body is always executed at least once. The syntax for a *do-while* statement is given in Display 2.13. A program with a sample *do-while* loop is given in Display 2.14. In that *do-while* loop, as in any *do-while* loop, the first thing that happens is that the statements in the loop body are executed. After that first iteration of the loop body, the *do-while* statement behaves the same as a *while* loop. The Boolean expression is checked. If the Boolean expression is true, the loop body is executed again; the Boolean expression is checked again, and so forth.

Increment and Decrement Operators

We discussed binary operators in the section entitled "Arithmetic Operators and Expressions." Binary operators have two operands. Unary operators have only one operand. You already know of two unary operators, + and –, as used in the expressions +7 and –7. The C++ language has two other very common unary operators, ++ and ––. The ++ operator is called the **increment operator**

DISPLAY 2.13 Syntax of the *do-while* Statement

A Loop Body with Several Statements:

```
1    do
2    {
3          Statement_1
4          Statement_2
5          . . .
6          Statement_Last
7    } while (Boolean_Expression);
```
body

Do not forget the
final semicolon.

A Loop Body with a Single Statement:

```
8    do
9          Statement
10   while (Boolean_Expression);
```
body

DISPLAY 2.14   A *do-while* **Loop**

```
1    #include <iostream>
2    using namespace std;
3    int main( )
4    {
5        char ans;

6        do
7        {
8            cout << "Hello\n";
9            cout << "Do you want another greeting?\n"
10                 << "Press y for yes, n for no,\n"
11                 << "and then press return: ";
12           cin >> ans;
13       } while (ans == 'y' || ans == 'Y');
14       cout << "Good-Bye\n";
15       return 0;
16   }
```

Sample Dialogue

```
Hello
Do you want another greeting?
Press y for yes, n for no, and then press return: y
Hello
Do you want another greeting?
Press y for yes, n for no, and then press return: Y
Hello
Do you want another greeting?
Press y for yes, n for no, and then press return: n
Good-Bye
```

and the `--` operator is called the **decrement operator.** They are usually used with variables of type *int*. If n is a variable of type *int*, then n++ increases the value of n by one and n-- decreases the value of n by one. So n++ and n-- (when followed by a semicolon) are executable statements. For example, the statements

```
int n = 1, m = 7;
n++;
cout << "The value of n is changed to " << n << endl;
m--;
cout << "The value of m is changed to " << m << endl;
```

yield the following output:

```
The value of n is changed to 2
The value of m is changed to 6
```

And now you know where the "++" came from in the name "C++."

Increment and decrement statements are often used in loops. For example, we used the following statement in the *while* loop in Display 2.11:

```
count_down = count_down - 1;
```

However, most experienced C++ programmers would use the decrement operator rather than the assignment statement, so the entire *while* loop would read as follows:

```
while (count_down > 0)
{
    cout << "Hello ";
    count_down-;
}
```

PROGRAMMING EXAMPLE   Charge Card Balance

Suppose you have a bank charge card with a balance owed of $50 and suppose the bank charges you 2% per month interest. How many months can you let pass without making any payments before your balance owed will exceed $100? One way to solve this problem is to simply read each monthly statement and count the number of months that go by until your balance reaches $100 or more. Better still, you can calculate the monthly balances with a program rather than waiting for the statements to arrive. In this way you will obtain an answer without having to wait so long (and without endangering your credit rating).

After one month the balance would be $50 plus 2% of $50, which is $51. After two months the balance would be $51 plus 2% of $51, which is $52.02. After three months the balance would be $52.02 plus 2% of $52.02, and so on. In general, each month increases the balance by 2%. The program could keep track of the balance by storing it in a variable called balance. The change in the value of balance for one month can be calculated as follows:

```
balance = balance + 0.02 * balance ;
```

If we repeat this action until the value of balance reaches (or exceeds) 100.00 and we count the number of repetitions, then we will know the number of months it will take for the balance to reach 100.00. To do this, we need another variable to count the number of times the balance is changed. Let us call this new variable count. The final body of our *while* loop will thus contain the following statements:

```
balance = balance + 0.02 * balance;
count++;
```

In order to make this loop perform correctly, we must give appropriate values to the variables balance and count before the loop is executed. In this case, we can initialize the variables when they are declared. The complete program is shown in Display 2.15 ▌

PITFALL   Infinite Loops

A *while* loop or a *do-while* loop does not terminate as long as the Boolean expression after the word *while* is true. This Boolean expression normally contains a variable that will be changed by the loop body, and usually the value of this variable eventually is changed in a way that makes the Boolean expression false and therefore terminates the loop. However, if you make a mistake and write your program so that the Boolean expression is always true, then the loop will run forever. A loop that runs forever is called an **infinite loop.**

First let's describe a loop that does terminate. The following C++ code will write out the positive even numbers less than 12. That is, it will output the numbers 2, 4, 6, 8, and 10, one per line, and then the loop will end.

```
x = 2;
while (x != 12)
{
    cout << x << endl;
    x = x + 2;
}
```

The value of x is increased by 2 on each loop iteration until it reaches 12. At that point, the Boolean expression after the word *while* is no longer true, so the loop ends.

Now suppose you want to write out the odd numbers less than 12, rather than the even numbers. You might mistakenly think that all you need do is change the initializing statement to

```
x = 1;
```

but this mistake will create an infinite loop. Because the value of x goes from 11 to 13, the value of x is never equal to 12, so the loop will never terminate.

This sort of problem is common when loops are terminated by checking a numeric quantity using == or !=. When dealing with numbers, it is always safer to test for passing a value. For example, the following will work fine as the first line of our *while* loop:

```
while (x < 12)
```

With this change, x can be initialized to any number and the loop will still terminate.

A program that is in an infinite loop will run forever unless some external force stops it. Since you can now write programs that contain an infinite loop, it is a good idea to learn how to force a program to terminate. The method for forcing a program to stop varies from system to system. The keystrokes Control-C will terminate a program on many systems. (To type a Control-C, hold down the Control key while pressing the C key.) ■

DISPLAY 2.15 Charge Card Program

```cpp
1     #include <iostream>
2     using namespace std;
3     int main( )
4     {
5         double balance = 50.00;
6         int count = 0;
7         cout << "This program tells you how long it takes\n"
8              << "to accumulate a debt of $100, starting with\n"
9              << "an initial balance of $50 owed.\n"
10             << "The interest rate is 2% per month.\n";

11        while (balance < 100.00)
12        {
13            balance = balance + 0.02 * balance;
14            count++;
15        }

16        cout << "After " << count << " months,\n";
17        cout.setf(ios::fixed);
18        cout.setf(ios::showpoint);
19        cout.precision(2);
20        cout << "your balance due will be $" << balance << endl;
21        return 0;
22    }
23
```

Sample Dialogue

```
This program tells you how long it takes
to accumulate a debt of $100, starting with
an initial balance of $50 owed.
The interest rate is 2% per month.
After 36 months,
your balance due will be $101.99
```

SELF-TEST EXERCISES

28. What is the output produced by the following (when embedded in a correct program with x declared to be of type *int*)?

```
x = 10;
while (x > 0)
{
    cout << x << endl;
    x = x - 3;
}
```

29. What output would be produced in the previous exercise if the > sign were replaced with < ?

30. What is the output produced by the following (when embedded in a correct program with x declared to be of type *int*)?

```
x = 10;
do
{
    cout << x << endl;
    x = x - 3;
} while (x > 0);
```

31. What is the output produced by the following (when embedded in a correct program with x declared to be of type *int*)?

```
x = -42;
do
{
    cout << x << endl;
    x = x - 3;
} while (x > 0);
```

32. What is the most important difference between a while statement and a do-while statement?

33. What is the output produced by the following (when embedded in a correct program with x declared to be of type *int*)?

```
x = 10;
while (x > 0)
{
    cout << x << endl;
    x = x + 3;
}
```

34. Write a complete C++ program that outputs the numbers 1 to 20, one per line. The program does nothing else.

2.5 PROGRAM STYLE

In matters of grave importance, style, not sincerity, is the vital thing.

OSCAR WILDE, *The Importance of Being Earnest*

All the variable names in our sample programs were chosen to suggest their use. Our sample programs were laid out in a particular format. For example, the declarations and statements were all indented the same amount. These and other matters of style are of more than aesthetic interest. A program that is written with careful attention to style is easier to read, easier to correct, and easier to change.

Indenting

A program should be laid out so that elements that are naturally considered a group are made to look like a group. One way to do this is to skip a line between parts that are logically considered separate. Indenting can also help to make the structure of the program clearer. A statement within a statement should be indented. In particular, *if-else* statements, *while* loops, and *do-while* loops should be indented either as in our sample programs or in some similar manner.

The braces {} determine a large part of the structure of a program. Placing each brace on a line by itself, as we have been doing, makes it easy to find the matching pairs. Notice that we have indented some pairs of braces. When one pair of braces is embedded in another pair, the embedded braces are indented more than the outer braces. Look back at the program in Display 2.15. The braces for the body of the *while* loop are indented more than the braces for the main part of the program.

There are at least two schools of thought on where you should place braces. The first, which we use in this book, is to reserve a separate line for each brace. This form is easiest to read. The second school of thought holds that the opening brace for a pair need not be on a line by itself. If used with care, this second method can be effective, and it does save space. The important point is to use a style that shows the structure of the program. The exact layout is not precisely dictated, but you should be consistent within any one program.

Comments

In order to make a program understandable, you should include some explanatory notes at key places in the program. Such notes are called **comments.** C++ and most other programming languages have provisions for including such comments within the text of a program. In C++ the symbols // are used to indicate the start of a comment. All of the text between the // and the end of the line is a comment. The compiler simply ignores anything that follows // on a line. If you want a comment that covers more than one line, place a // on each line of the comment. The symbols // are two slashes (without a space between them).

In this book, comments will always be written in italic so that they stand out from the program text. Some text editors indicate comments by showing them in a different color from the rest of the program text.

There is another way to insert comments in a C++ program. Anything between the symbol pair /* and the symbol pair */ is considered a comment and is ignored by the compiler. Unlike the // comments, which require an additional // on each line, the /* to */ comments can span several lines, like so:

```
/*This is a comment that spans
three lines. Note that there is no comment
symbol of any kind on the second line.*/
```

Comments of the /* */ type may be inserted anywhere in a program that a space or line break is allowed. However, they should not be inserted anywhere except where they are easy to read and do not distract from the layout of the program. Usually, comments are only placed at the ends of lines or on separate lines by themselves.

There are differing opinions on which kind of comment is best to use. Either variety (the // kind or the /* */ kind) can be effective if used with care. We will use the // kind in this book.

It is difficult to say just how many comments a program should contain. The only correct answer is "just enough," which of course conveys little to the novice programmer. It will take some experience to get a feel for when it is best to include a comment. Whenever something is important and not obvious, it merits a comment. However, too many comments are as bad as too few. A program that has a comment on each line will be so buried in comments that the structure of the program is hidden in a sea of obvious observations. Comments like the following contribute nothing to understanding and should not appear in a program:

```
distance = speed * time; //Computes the distance traveled
```

Notice the comment given at the start of the program in Display 2.16. All programs should begin with a comment similar to the one shown there. It gives all the essential information about the program: what file the program is in, who wrote the program, how to contact the person who wrote the program, what the program does, the date that the program was last modified, and any other particulars that are appropriate, such as the assignment number, if the program is a class assignment. Exactly what you include in this comment will depend on your particular situation. We will not include such long comments in the programs in the rest of this book, but you should always begin your programs with a similar comment.

DISPLAY 2.16   Comments and Named Constants

```
1    //File Name: health.cpp (Your system may require some suffix other than cpp.)
2    //Author: Your Name Goes Here.
3    //Email Address: you@yourmachine.bla.bla
4    //Assignment Number: 2
5    //Description: Program to determine if the user is ill.
6    //Last Changed: September 23, 2006
7
8    #include <iostream>
9    using namespace std;
10   int main( )
11   {
12       const double NORMAL = 98.6; //degrees Fahrenheit
13       double temperature;
14
15       cout << "Enter your temperature: ";
16       cin >> temperature;
17
18       if (temperature > NORMAL)
19       {
20           cout << "You have a fever.\n";
21           cout << "Drink lots of liquids and get to bed.\n";
22       }
23       else
24       {
25           cout << "You don't have a fever.\n";
26           cout << "Go study.\n";
27       }
28
29       return 0;
30   }
```

*Your programs should always begin
with a comment similar to this one.*

Sample Dialogue

```
Enter your temperature: 98.6
You don't have a fever.
Go study.
```

Naming Constants

There are two problems with numbers in a computer program. The first is that they carry no mnemonic value. For example, when the number 10 is encountered in a program, it gives no hint of its significance. If the program is a banking program, it might be the number of branch offices or the number of teller windows at the main office. In order to understand the program, you need to know the significance of each constant. The second problem is that when a program needs to have some numbers changed, the changing tends to introduce errors. Suppose that 10 occurs twelve times in a banking program, that four of the times it represents the number of branch offices, and that eight of the times it represents the number of teller windows at the main office. When the bank opens a new branch and the program needs to be updated, there is a good chance that some of the 10s that should be changed to 11 will not be, or some that should not be changed will be. The way to avoid these problems is to name each number and use the name instead of the number within your program. For example, a banking program might have two constants with the names BRANCH_COUNT and WINDOW_COUNT. Both these numbers might have a value of 10, but when the bank opens a new branch, all you need do in order to update the program is to change the definition of BRANCH_COUNT.

How do you name a number in a C++ program? One way is to initialize a variable to that number value, as in the following example:

```
int BRANCH_COUNT = 10;
int WINDOW_COUNT = 10;
```

There is, however, one problem with this method of naming number constants: You might inadvertently change the value of one of these variables. C++ provides a way of marking an initialized variable so that it cannot be changed. If your program tries to change one of these variables, it produces an error condition. To mark a variable declaration so that the value of the variable cannot be changed, precede the declaration with the word *const* (which is an abbreviation of *constant*). For example:

```
const int BRANCH_COUNT = 10;
const int WINDOW_COUNT = 10;
```

If the variables are of the same type, it is possible to combine the previous lines into one declaration, as follows:

```
const int BRANCH_COUNT = 10, WINDOW_COUNT = 10;
```

However, most programmers find that placing each name definition on a separate line is clearer. The word *const* is often called a **modifier,** because it modifies (restricts) the variables being declared.

A variable declared using the *const* modifier is often called a **declared constant.** Writing declared constants in all uppercase letters is not required by the C++ language, but it is standard practice among C++ programmers.

Once a number has been named in this way, the name can then be used anywhere the number is allowed, and it will have exactly the same meaning as the number it names. To change a named constant, you need change only the initializing value in the *const* variable declaration. The meaning of all occurrences of BRANCH_COUNT, for instance, can be changed from 10 to 11 simply by changing the initializing value of 10 in the declaration of BRANCH_COUNT.

Although unnamed numeric constants are allowed in a program, you should seldom use them. It often makes sense to use unnamed number constants for well-known, easily recognizable, and unchangeable quantities, such as 100 for the number of centimeters in a meter. However, all other numeric constants should be given names in the fashion we just described. This will make your programs easier to read and easier to change.

Display 2.16 contains a simple program that illustrates the use of the declaration modifier *const*.

Naming Constants with the *const* Modifier

When you initialize a variable inside a declaration, you can mark the variable so that the program is not allowed to change its value. To do this, place the word *const* in front of the declaration, as described below:

SYNTAX

```
const Type_Name Variable_Name = Constant;
```

EXAMPLES

```
const int MAX_TRIES = 3;
const double PI = 3.14159;
```

SELF-TEST EXERCISES

35. The following *if-else* statement will compile and run without any problems. However, it is not laid out in a way that is consistent with the other *if-else* statements we have used in our programs. Rewrite it so that the layout (indenting and line breaks) matches the style we used in this chapter.

    ```
    if (x < 0) {x = 7; cout << "x is now positive.";}
    else {x = - 7; cout << "x is now negative.";}
    ```

36. What output would be produced by the following two lines (when embedded in a complete and correct program)?

    ```
    //cout << "Hello from";
    cout << "Self-Test Exercise";
    ```

37. Write a complete C++ program that asks the user for a number of gallons and then outputs the equivalent number of liters. There are 3.78533 liters in a gallon. Use a declared constant. Since this is just an exercise, you need not have any comments in your program.

CHAPTER SUMMARY

- Use meaningful names for variables.

- Be sure to check that variables are declared to be of the correct data type.

- Be sure that variables are initialized before the program attempts to use their value. This can be done when the variable is declared or with an assignment statement before the variable is first used.

- Use enough parentheses in arithmetic expressions to make the order of operations clear.

- Always include a prompt line in a program whenever the user is expected to enter data from the keyboard, and always echo the user's input.

- An *if-else* statement allows your program to choose one of two alternative actions. An *if* statement allows your program to decide whether to perform some one particular action.

- A *do-while* loop always executes its loop body at least once. In some situations, a *while* loop might not execute the body of the loop at all.

- Almost all number constants in a program should be given meaningful names that can be used in place of the numbers. This can be done by using the modifier *const* in a variable declaration.

- Use an indenting, spacing, and line-break pattern similar to the sample programs.

- Insert comments to explain major subsections or any unclear part of a program.

Answers to Self-Test Exercises

1. *int* feet = 0, inches = 0;
   int feet(0), inches(0);

2. *int* count = 0;
   double distance = 1.5;

   Alternatively, you could use

   int count(0);
   double distance(1.5);

3. sum = n1 + n2;

4. length = length + 8.3;

5. product = product * n;

6. The actual output from a program such as this is dependent on the system and the history of the use of the system.

```cpp
#include <iostream>
using namespace std;
int main()
{
    int first, second, third, fourth, fifth;
    cout << first << " " << second << " " << third
         << " " << fourth << " " << fifth << endl;
    return 0;
}
```

7. There is no unique right answer for this one. Below are possible answers:

   a. speed
   b. pay_rate
   c. highest or max_score

8.
```cpp
cout << "The answer to the question of\n"
     << "Life, the Universe, and Everything is 42.\n";
```

9.
```cpp
cout << "Enter a whole number and press return: ";
cin >> the_number;
```

10.
```cpp
cout.setf(ios::fixed);
cout.setf(ios::showpoint);
cout.precision(3);
```

11.
```cpp
#include <iostream>
using namespace std;
int main()
{
    cout << "Hello world\n";
    return 0;
}
```

12.
```cpp
#include <iostream>
using namespace std;

int main()
{
    int n1, n2, sum;
    cout << "Enter two whole numbers\n";
    cin >> n1 >> n2;
    sum = n1 + n2;
    cout << "The sum of " << n1 << " and "
         << n2 << " is " << sum << endl;
    return 0;
}
```

13. cout << endl << "\t";

14. #include <iostream>
    using namespace std;

    int main( )
    {
        double one(1.0), two(1.414), three(1.732),
                four(2.0),five(2.236);
        cout << "\tN\tSquare Root\n";
        cout << "\t1\t" << one << endl
            << "\t2\t" << two << endl
            << "\t3\t" << three << endl
            << "\t4\t" << four << endl
            << "\t5\t" << five << endl;
        return 0;
    }

15. 3 * x
    3 * x + y
    (x + y) / 7 Note that x + y / 7 is not correct.
    (3 * x + y) / (z + 2)

16. bcbc

17. (1/3) * 3 is equal to 0

    Since 1 and 3 are of type *int*, the / operator performs integer
    division, which discards the remainder, so the value of 1/3 is 0, not
    0.3333. This makes the value of the entire expression 0 * 3, which
    of course is 0.

18. #include <iostream>
    using namespace std;

    int main()
    {
        int number1, number2;

        cout << "Enter two whole numbers: ";
        cin >> number1 >> number2;
        cout << number1 << " divided by " << number2
            << " equals " << (number1/number2) << endl
            << "with a remainder of " << (number1%number2)
            << endl;
        return 0;
    }

19. a. 52.0

b. 9/5 has *int* value 1; since numerator and denominator are both *int*, integer division is done; the fractional part is discarded.

```
f = (9.0 / 5) * c + 32.0;
```

or this

```
f = 1.8 * c + 32.0;
```

20. 030406

The strings are concatenated with the + operator.

21. ```
if (score > 100)
        cout << "High";
else
        cout << "Low";
```

You may want to add \n to the end of these quoted strings depending on the other details of the program.

22. ```
if (savings >= expenses)
    {
        savings = savings - expenses;
        expenses = 0;
        cout << "Solvent";
    }
else
    {
        cout << "Bankrupt";
    }
```

You may want to add \n to the end of these quoted strings depending on the other details of the program.

23. ```
if ((exam >= 60) && (programs_done >= 10))
        cout << "Passed";
else
        cout << "Failed";
```

You may want to add \n to the end of these quoted strings depending on the other details of the program.

24. ```
if ( (temperature >= 100) || (pressure >= 200) )
        cout << "Warning";
else
        cout << "OK";
```

You may want to add \n to the end of these quoted strings depending on the other details of the program.

25. ```
(x < -1) || (x > 2)
```
```

26. (1 < x) && (x < 3)

27. a. 0 is *false*. In the section on type compatibility, it is noted that the *int* value 0 converts to *false*.

    b. 1 is *true*. In the section on type compatibility, it is noted that a nonzero *int* value converts to *true*.

    c. -1 is *true*. In the section on type compatibility, it is noted that a non-zero *int* value converts to *true*.

28. 10
    7
    4
    1

29. There would be no output, since the Boolean expression (x < 0) is not satisfied and so the *while* statement ends without executing the loop body.

30. The output is exactly the same as it was for Self-Test Exercise 27.

31. The body of the loop is executed before the Boolean expression is checked, the Boolean expression is false, and so the output is

    -42

32. With a *do-while* statement the loop body is always executed at least once. With a *while* statement there can be conditions under which the loop body is not executed at all.

33. This is an infinite loop. The output would begin with the following and conceptually go on forever:

    10
    13
    16
    19

    (Once the value of x becomes larger than the largest integer allowed on your computer, the program may stop or exhibit other strange behavior, but the loop is conceptually an infinite loop.)

34. ```
#include <iostream>
using namespace std;

int main()
{
    int n = 1;
    while (n <= 20)
    {
```
```

```
            cout << n << endl;
            n++;
        }
        return 0;
    }
```

35.
```
if (x < 0)
{
    x = 7;
    cout << "x is now positive.";
}
else
{
    x = -7;
    cout << "x is now negative.";
}
```

36. The first line is a comment and is not executed. So the entire output is just the following line:

```
Self-Test Exercise
```

37.
```
#include <iostream>
using namespace std;

int main()
{
    const double LITERS_PER_GALLON = 3.78533;
    double gallons, liters;

    cout << "Enter the number of gallons:\n";
    cin >> gallons;

    liters = gallons*LITERS_PER_GALLON;
    cout << "There are " << liters << " in "
         << gallons << " gallons.\n";

    return 0;
}
```

PROGRAMMING PROJECTS

myprogramminglab

Visit www.myprogramminglab.com to complete many of these Programming Projects online and get instant feedback.

1. A kilogram is 1,000 grams. Write a program that will read the weight of a package of butter in grams and output the weight in kilograms, as well as the number of packages of butter needed to yield 1 kilogram of butter. Your program should allow the user to repeat this calculation as often as the user wishes.

2. A government research lab has concluded that an artificial sweetener commonly used in diet soda pop will cause death in laboratory mice. A friend of yours is desperate to lose weight but cannot give up soda pop. Your friend wants to know how much diet soda pop it is possible to drink without dying as a result. Write a program to supply the answer. The input to the program is the amount of artificial sweetener needed to kill a mouse, the weight of the mouse, and the weight of the dieter. To ensure the safety of your friend, be sure the program requests the weight at which the dieter will stop dieting, rather than the dieter's current weight. Assume that diet soda contains 1/10th of 1% artificial sweetener. Use a variable declaration with the modifier *const* to give a name to this fraction. You may want to express the percent as the *double* value 0.001. Your program should allow the calculation to be repeated as often as the user wishes.

3. Workers at a particular company have won an 8.2% pay increase retroactive for 9 months. Write a program that takes an employee's previous annual salary as input, and outputs the amount of retroactive pay due to the employee, the new annual salary, and the new monthly salary. Use a variable declaration with the modifier *const* to express the pay increase. Your program should allow the calculation to be repeated as often as the user wishes.

4. What is an escape sequence? Write a C++ program to display "Welcome to Chapter 2". The program should display the double quotes in the output.

5. Negotiating a consumer loan is not always straightforward. One form of loan is the discount installment loan, which works as follows. Suppose a loan has a face value of $1,000, the interest rate is 15%, and the duration is 18 months. The interest is computed by multiplying the face value of $1,000 by 0.15, to yield $150. That figure is then multiplied by the loan period of 1.5 years to yield $225 as the total interest owed. That amount is immediately deducted from the face value, leaving the consumer with only $775. Repayment is made in equal monthly installments based on the face value. So the monthly loan payment will be $1,000 divided by 18, which is $55.56. This method of calculation may not be too bad if the consumer needs $775 dollars, but the calculation is a bit more complicated if the consumer needs $1,000. Write a program that will take three inputs: the amount the consumer needs to receive, the interest rate, and the duration of the loan in months. The program should then calculate the face value required in order for the consumer to receive the amount needed. It should also calculate the monthly payment. Your program should allow the calculations to be repeated as often as the user wishes.

6. Write a program that determines whether a meeting room is in violation of fire law regulations regarding the maximum room capacity. The program will read in the maximum room capacity and the number of people

attending the meeting. If the number of people is less than or equal to the maximum room capacity, the program announces that it is legal to hold the meeting and tells how many additional people may legally attend. If the number of people exceeds the maximum room capacity, the program announces that the meeting cannot be held as planned due to fire regulations and tells how many people must be excluded in order to meet the fire regulations. For a harder version, write your program so that it allows the calculation to be repeated as often as the user wishes. If this is a class exercise, ask your instructor whether you should do this harder version.

7. An employee is paid at a rate of $16.78 per hour for the first 40 hours worked in a week. Any hours over that are paid at the overtime rate of one-and-one-half times that. From the worker's gross pay, 6% is withheld for Social Security tax, 14% is withheld for federal income tax, 5% is withheld for state income tax, and $10 per week is withheld for union dues. If the worker has three or more dependents, then an additional $35 is withheld to cover the extra cost of health insurance beyond what the employer pays. Write a program that will read in the number of hours worked in a week and the number of dependents as input and will then output the worker's gross pay, each withholding amount, and the net take-home pay for the week. For a harder version, write your program so that it allows the calculation to be repeated as often as the user wishes. If this is a class exercise, ask your instructor whether you should do this harder version.

8. It is difficult to make a budget that spans several years, because prices are not stable. If your company needs 200 pencils per year, you cannot simply use this year's price as the cost of pencils 2 years from now. Because of inflation the cost is likely to be higher than it is today. Write a program to gauge the expected cost of an item in a specified number of years. The program asks for the cost of the item, the number of years from now that the item will be purchased, and the rate of inflation. The program then outputs the estimated cost of the item after the specified period. Have the user enter the inflation rate as a percentage, like 5.6 (percent). Your program should then convert the percent to a fraction, like 0.056, and should use a loop to estimate the price adjusted for inflation. (*Hint:* This is similar to computing interest on a charge card account, which was discussed in this chapter.)

9. You have just purchased a stereo system that cost $1,000 on the following credit plan: no down payment, an interest rate of 18% per year (and hence 1.5% per month), and monthly payments of $50. The monthly payment of $50 is used to pay the interest and whatever is left is used to pay part of the remaining debt. Hence, the first month you pay 1.5% of $1,000 in interest. That is $15 in interest. So, the remaining $35 is deducted from your debt, which leaves you with a debt of $965.00. The next month you pay interest of 1.5% of $965.00, which is $14.48. Hence, you can

deduct $35.52 (which is $50 – $14.48) from the amount you owe. Write a program that will tell you how many months it will take you to pay off the loan, as well as the total amount of interest paid over the life of the loan. Use a loop to calculate the amount of interest and the size of the debt after each month. (Your final program need not output the monthly amount of interest paid and remaining debt, but you may want to write a preliminary version of the program that does output these values.) Use a variable to count the number of loop iterations and hence the number of months until the debt is zero. You may want to use other variables as well. The last payment may be less than $50. Do not forget the interest on the last payment. If you owe $50, then your monthly payment of $50 will not pay off your debt, although it will come close. One month's interest on $50 is only 75 cents.

10. Write a program that reads ten integer numbers and outputs the sum of all the positive numbers among them. The program should ignore all numbers which are less than or equal to 0. The user enters the ten numbers just once each, and can enter them in any order. Your program should not ask the user to enter the positive numbers and the negative numbers separately. The program should also display count of positive numbers and count of negative numbers or zero.

11. Write a program that reads ten integer numbers and outputs the number of inputs which are greater than 50, less than 50 and equal to 50. The program should also display the average of all numbers greater than 50 and the average of all numbers less than 50.

12. The Babylonian algorithm to compute the square root of a number n is as follows:

    1. Make a *guess* at the answer (you can pick $n/2$ as your initial guess).

    2. Compute $r = n\ /\ guess$

    3. Set *guess* = (*guess* + *r*) / 2

    4. Go back to step 2 for as many iterations as necessary. The more that steps 2 and 3 are repeated, the closer *guess* will become to the square root of *n.*

    Write a program that inputs an integer for *n,* iterates through the Babylonian algorithm until *guess* is within 1% of the previous guess, and outputs the answer as a *double.*

13. Many treadmills output the speed of the treadmill in miles per hour (mph) on the console, but most runners think of speed in terms of a pace. A common pace is the number of minutes and seconds per mile instead of mph.

VideoNote
Solution to Programming
Project 2.13

Write a program that starts with a quantity in mph and converts the quantity into minutes and seconds per mile. As an example, the proper output for an input of 6.5 mph should be 9 minutes and 13.8 seconds per mile. If you need to convert a *double* to an *int*, which will discard any value after the decimal point, then you may use

```
intValue = static_cast<int>(dblVal);
```

14. Write a program that plays the game of Mad Lib. Your program should prompt the user to enter the following strings:

   ■ The first or last name of your instructor

   ■ Your name

   ■ A food

   ■ A number between 100 and 120

   ■ An adjective

   ■ A color

   ■ An animal

   After the strings are input, they should be substituted into the story below and output to the console.

   Dear Instructor **[Instructor Name]**,

   I am sorry that I am unable to turn in my homework at this time. First, I ate a rotten **[Food]**, which made me turn **[Color]** and extremely ill. I came down with a fever of **[Number 100-120]**. Next, my **[Adjective]** pet **[Animal]** must have smelled the remains of the **[Food]** on my homework, because he ate it. I am currently rewriting my homework and hope you will accept it late.

   Sincerely,
   [Your Name]

15. Sound travels through air as a result of collisions between the molecules in the air. The temperature of the air affects the speed of the molecules, which in turn affects the speed of sound. The velocity of sound in dry air can be approximated by the formula:

   ```
   velocity ≈ 331.3 + 0.61 × Tc
   ```

   where T_c is the temperature of the air in degrees Celsius and the velocity is in meters/second.

Write a program that allows the user to input a starting and an ending temperature. Within this temperature range, the program should output the temperature and the corresponding velocity in 1° increments. For example, if the user entered 0 as the start temperature and 2 as the end temperature, then the program should output

```
At 0 degrees Celsius the velocity of sound is 331.3 m/s
At 1 degrees Celsius the velocity of sound is 331.9 m/s
At 2 degrees Celsius the velocity of sound is 332.5 m/s
```

16. The following is a short program that computes the volume of a sphere given the radius. It will compile and run, but it does not adhere to the program style recommended in Section 2.5. Rewrite the program using the style described in the chapter for indentation, adding comments, and appropriately named constants.

```cpp
#include <iostream>
using namespace std;
int main()
{
    double radius, vm;
    cout << "Enter radius of a sphere." << endl; cin >> radius;
    vm = (4.0 / 3.0) * 3.1415 * radius * radius * radius;
    cout << " The volume is " << vm << endl;
    return 0;
}
```

17. Many private water wells produce only 1 or 2 gallons of water per minute. One way to avoid running out of water with these low-yield wells is to use a holding tank. A family of four will use about 250 gallons of water per day. However, there is a "natural" water holding tank in the casing (that is, the hole) of the well itself. A deeper well stores more water that can be pumped out for household use. But how much water will be available?

VideoNote
Solution to Programming
Project 2.17

Write a program that allows the user to input the radius of the well casing in inches (a typical well will have a 3-inch radius) and the depth of the well in feet (assume water will fill this entire depth, although in practice that will not be true since the static water level will generally be 50 feet or more below the ground surface). The program should output the number of gallons stored in the well casing. For your reference, the volume of a cylinder is r^2h, where r is the radius and h is the height, and 1 cubic foot = 7.48 gallons of water.

For example, a 300-foot-well full of water with a radius of 3 inches for the casing holds about 441 gallons of water—plenty for a family of four and no need to install a separate holding tank.

18. The Harris–Benedict equation estimates the number of calories your body needs to maintain your weight if you do no exercise. This is called your basal metabolic rate, or BMR.

The formula for the calories needed for a woman to maintain her weight is

> BMR = 655 + (4.3 × weight in pounds) + (4.7 × height in inches) – (4.7 × age in years)

The formula for the calories needed for a man to maintain his weight is

> BMR = 66 + (6.3 × weight in pounds) + (12.9 × height in inches) – (6.8 × age in years)

A typical chocolate bar will contain around 230 calories. Write a program that allows the user to input his or her weight in pounds, height in inches, age in years, and the character M for male and F for female. The program should then output the number of chocolate bars that should be consumed to maintain one's weight for the appropriate sex of the specified weight, height, and age.

19. Write a program that calculates the total grade for N classroom exercises as a percentage. The user should input the value for N followed by each of the N scores and totals. Calculate the overall percentage (sum of the total points earned divided by the total points possible) and output it as a percentage. Sample input and output is shown below.

```
How many exercises to input? 3

Score received for exercise 1: 10
Total points possible for exercise 1: 10

Score received for exercise 2: 7
Total points possible for exercise 2: 12

Score received for exercise 3: 5
Total points possible for exercise 3: 8

Your total is 22 out of 30, or 73.33%.
```

More Flow of Control 3

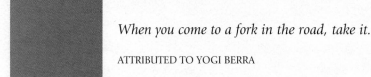

When you come to a fork in the road, take it.

ATTRIBUTED TO YOGI BERRA

INTRODUCTION

The order in which the statements in your program are performed is called **flow of control.** The *if-else* statement, the *while* statement, and the *do-while* statement are three ways to specify flow of control. This chapter explores some new ways to use these statements and introduces two new statements called the *switch* statement and the *for* statement, which are also used for flow of control. The actions of an *if-else* statement, a *while* statement, or a *do-while* statement are controlled by Boolean expressions. We begin by discussing Boolean expressions in more detail.

PREREQUISITES

This chapter uses material from Chapter 2.

3.1 USING BOOLEAN EXPRESSIONS

"Contrariwise," continued Tweedledee. "If it was so, it might be; and if it were so, it would be; but as it isn't, it ain't. That's logic."

LEWIS CARROLL, *Through the Looking-Glass*

Evaluating Boolean Expressions

A **Boolean expression** is an expression that can be thought of as being *true* or *false* (that is, *true* if satisfied or *false* if not satisfied). Thus far you have used Boolean expressions as the test condition in *if-else* statements and as the controlling expression in loops, such as a *while* loop. However, a Boolean expression has an independent identity apart from any *if-else* statement or loop statement you might use it in. The C++ type *bool* provides you the ability to declare variables that can carry the values *true* and *false*.

A Boolean expression can be evaluated in the same way that an arithmetic expression is evaluated. The only difference is that an arithmetic expression uses operations such as +, *, and / and produces a number as the final result, whereas a Boolean expression uses relational operations such as == and < and Boolean operations such as &&, ||, and ! to produce one of the two values *true* and *false* as the final result. Note that ==, !=, <, <=, and so forth operate on pairs of any built-in type to produce a Boolean value *true* or *false*.

If you understand the way Boolean expressions are evaluated, you will be able to write and understand complex Boolean expressions and be able to use Boolean expressions for the value returned by a function.

First let's review evaluating an arithmetic expression; the same technique will work to evaluate Boolean expressions. Consider the following arithmetic expression:

    (x + 1) * (x + 3)

Assume that the variable x has the value 2. To evaluate this arithmetic expression, you evaluate the two sums to obtain the numbers 3 and 5, then you combine these two numbers 3 and 5 using the * operator to obtain 15 as the final value. Notice that in performing this evaluation, you do not multiply the expressions (x + 1) and (x + 3). Instead, you multiply the values of these expressions. You use 3; you do not use (x + 1). You use 5; you do not use (x + 3).

The computer evaluates Boolean expressions the same way. Subexpressions are evaluated to obtain values, each of which is either *true* or *false*. These individual values of *true* or *false* are then combined according to the rules in the tables shown in Display 3.1. For example, consider the Boolean expression

    !((y < 3) || (y > 7))

which might be the controlling expression for an *if-else* statement or a *while* statement. Suppose the value of y is 8. In this case, (y < 3) evaluates to *false* and (y > 7) evaluates to *true*, so the Boolean expression above is equivalent to

    !(*false* || *true*)

Consulting the tables for || (which is labeled **OR** in Display 3.1), the computer sees that the expression inside the parentheses evaluates to *true*. Thus, the computer sees that the entire expression is equivalent to

    !(*true*)

Consulting the tables again, the computer sees that !(*true*) evaluates to *false*, and so it concludes that *false* is the value of the original Boolean expression.

Almost all the examples we have constructed thus far have been fully parenthesized to show exactly how each &&, ||, and ! is used to construct an expression. Parentheses are not always required. If you omit parentheses, the default precedence is as follows: perform ! first, then evaluate relational operators such as <, then evaluate &&, and then evaluate ||. However, it is a good practice to include most parentheses in order to make the expression easier to understand. One place where parentheses can safely be omitted is a simple string of &&'s or ||'s (but not a mixture of the two). The following expression is acceptable in terms of both the C++ compiler and readability:

    (temperature > 90) && (humidity > 0.90) && (pool_gate == OPEN)

DISPLAY 3.1   Truth Tables

AND

Exp_1	Exp_2	Exp_1 && Exp_2
true	true	true
true	false	false
false	true	false
false	false	false

NOT

Exp	!(Exp)
true	false
false	true

OR

Exp_1	Exp_2	Exp_1 || Exp_2
true	true	true
true	false	true
false	true	true
false	false	false

Since the relational operations > and == are evaluated before the && operation, you could omit the parentheses in the expression above and it would have the same meaning, but including some parentheses makes the expression easier to read.

When parentheses are omitted from an expression, the computer groups items according to rules known as **precedence rules.** Some of the precedence rules for C++ are given in Display 3.2. If one operation is evaluated before another, the operation that is evaluated first is said to have **higher precedence.** Binary operations of equal precedence are evaluated in left-to-right order. Unary operations of equal precedence are evaluated in right-to-left order. A complete set of precedence rules is given in Appendix 2.

Notice that the precedence rules include both arithmetic operators such as + and * as well as Boolean operators such as && and ||. This is because many expressions combine arithmetic and Boolean operations, as in the following simple example:

```
(x + 1) > 2 || (x + 1) < -3
```

If you check the precedence rules given in Display 3.2, you will see that this expression is equivalent to

```
((x + 1) > 2) || ((x + 1) < -3)
```

DISPLAY 3.2   Precedence Rules

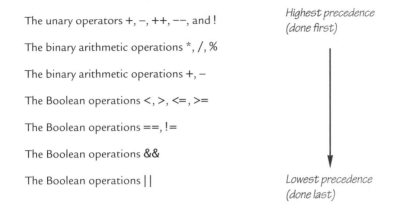

The unary operators +, −, ++, −−, and !   *Highest precedence*
                                                                  (done first)

The binary arithmetic operations *, /, %

The binary arithmetic operations +, −

The Boolean operations <, >, <=, >=

The Boolean operations ==, !=

The Boolean operations &&

The Boolean operations || *Lowest precedence*
                                                                  (done last)

because > and < have higher precedence than ||. In fact, you could omit all the parentheses in the expression above and it would have the same meaning, although it would be harder to read. Although we do not advocate omitting all the parentheses, it might be instructive to see how such an expression is interpreted using the precedence rules. Here is the expression without any parentheses:

```
x + 1 > 2 || x + 1 < -3
```

The precedence rules say first apply the unary −, then apply the + signs, then do the > and the <, and finally do the ||, which is exactly what the fully parenthesized version says to do.

The preceding description of how a Boolean expression is evaluated is basically correct, but in C++, the computer actually takes an occasional shortcut when evaluating a Boolean expression. Notice that in many cases you need to evaluate only the first of two subexpressions in a Boolean expression. For example, consider the following:

```
(x >= 0) && (y > 1)
```

If x is negative, then (x >= 0) is *false*, and as you can see in the tables in Display 3.1, when one subexpression in an && expression is *false*, then the whole expression is *false*, no matter whether the other expression is *true* or *false*. Thus, if we know that the first expression is *false*, there is no need to evaluate the second expression. A similar thing happens with || expressions. If the first of two expressions joined with the || operator is *true*, then you know the entire expression is *true*, no matter whether the second expression is *true* or *false*. The C++ language uses this fact to sometimes save itself the trouble of evaluating the second subexpression in a logical expression connected with an && or an ||. C++ first evaluates the leftmost of the two expressions joined by an && or an ||. If that gives it enough information to determine the final value of the expression (independent of the value of the second expression), then C++ does not bother to evaluate the second expression. This method of evaluation is called **short-circuit evaluation.**

Some languages, other than C++, use **complete evaluation.** In complete evaluation, when two expressions are joined by an **&&** or an **||**, both subexpressions are always evaluated and then the truth tables are used to obtain the value of the final expression.

Both short-circuit evaluation and complete evaluation give the same answer, so why should you care that C++ uses short-circuit evaluation? Most of the time you need not care. As long as both subexpressions joined by the **&&** or the **||** have a value, the two methods yield the same result. However, if the second subexpression is undefined, you might be happy to know that C++ uses short-circuit evaluation.

Let's look at an example that illustrates this point. Consider the following statement:

```
if ( (kids != 0) && ((pieces/kids) >= 2) )
    cout << "Each child may have two pieces!";
```

If the value of kids is not zero, this statement involves no subtleties. However, suppose the value of kids is zero and consider how short-circuit evaluation handles this case. The expression (kids!= 0) evaluates to *false*, so there would be no need to evaluate the second expression. Using short-circuit evaluation, C++ says that the entire expression is *false*, *without bothering to evaluate the second expression.* This prevents a run-time error, since evaluating the second expression would involve dividing by zero.

C++ sometimes uses integers as if they were Boolean values. In particular, C++ converts the integer 1 to *true* and converts the integer 0 to *false*. The situation is even a bit more complicated than simply using 1 for *true* and 0 for *false*. The compiler will treat any nonzero number as if it were the value *true* and will treat 0 as if it were the value *false*. As long as you make no mistakes in writing Boolean expressions, this conversion causes no problems and you usually need not even be aware of it. However, when you are debugging, it might help to know that the compiler is happy to combine integers using the Boolean operators **&&**, **||**, and **!**.

Boolean (*bool*) **values are** *true* **and** *false*

In C++, a Boolean expression evaluates to the *bool* value *true* when it is satisfied and to the *bool* value *false* when it is not satisfied.

PITFALL   **Boolean Expressions Convert to** *int* **Values**

Suppose you want to use a Boolean expression in an *if-else* statement, and you want it to be *true* provided that time has not yet run out (in some game or process). To phrase it a bit more precisely, suppose you want to use a Boolean expression in an *if-else* statement and you want it to be *true* provided the value of a variable time of type *int* is not greater than the value of a variable called limit. You might write the following (where *Something* and *Something_Else* are some C++ statements):

```
if (!time > limit)          ◄——————————— Wrong for what we want
     Something
else
     Something_Else
```

This sounds right if you read it out loud: "not time greater than limit." The Boolean expression is wrong, however, and unfortunately, the compiler will not give you an error message. We have been bitten by the precedence rules of C++. The compiler will instead apply the precedence rules from Display 3.2 and interpret your Boolean expression as the following:

```
(!time) > limit
```

This looks like nonsense, and intuitively it is nonsense. If the value of time is, for example, 36, what could possibly be the meaning of (!time)? After all, that is equivalent to "not 36." But in C++, any nonzero integer converts to *true* and 0 is converted to *false*. Thus, !36 is interpreted as "not *true*" and so it evaluates to *false*, which is in turn converted back to 0 because we are comparing to an *int*.

What we want as the value of this Boolean expression and what C++ gives us are not the same. If time has a value of 36 and limit has a value of 60, you want the displayed Boolean expression above to evaluate to *true* (because it is *not true* that time > limit). Unfortunately, the Boolean expression instead evaluates as follows: (!time) evaluates to *false*, which is converted to 0, so the entire Boolean expression is equivalent to

```
0 > limit
```

That in turn is equivalent to 0 > 60, because 60 is the value of limit. This evaluates to *false*. Thus, the above logical expression evaluates to *false*, when you want it to evaluate to *true*.

There are two ways to correct this problem. One way is to use the ! operator correctly. When using the operator !, be sure to include parentheses around the argument. The correct way to write the preceding Boolean expression is as follows:

```
if (!(time > limit))
     Something
else
     Something_Else
```

Another way to correct this problem is to completely avoid using the ! operator. For example, the following is also correct and easier to read:

```
if (time <= limit)
    Something
else
    Something_Else
```

Avoid using "not"   You can almost always avoid using the ! operator, and some programmers advocate avoiding it as much as possible. They say that just as *not* in English can make things not undifficult to read, so too can the "not" operator ! make C++ programs difficult to read. There is no need to be obsessive in avoiding the ! operator, but before using it, you should see if you can express the same thing more clearly without using the ! operator.   ■

The Type *bool* **Is New**

Older versions of C++ have no type *bool*, but instead use the integers 1 and 0 for *true* and *false*. If you have an older version of C++ that does not have the type *bool*, you should obtain a new compiler.

 SELF-TEST EXERCISES

1. Determine the value, *true* or *false*, of each of the following Boolean expressions, assuming that the value of the variable count is 0 and the value of the variable limit is 10. Give your answer as one of the values *true* or *false*.

   a.   (count == 0) && (limit < 20)
   b.   count == 0 && limit < 20
   c.   (limit > 20) || (count < 5)
   d.   !(count == 12)
   e.   (count == 1) && (x < y)
   f.   (count < 10) || (x < y)
   g.   !(((count < 10) || (x < y)) && (count >= 0))
   h.   ((limit/count) > 7) || (limit < 20)
   i.   (limit < 20) || ((limit/count) > 7)
   j.   ((limit/count) > 7) && (limit < 0)
   k.   (limit < 0) && ((limit/count) > 7)
   l.   (5 && 7) + (!6)

2. Name two kinds of statements in C++ that alter the order in which actions are performed. Give some examples.

3. In college algebra we see numeric intervals given as

   2 < x < 3

   In C++ this interval does not have the meaning you may expect. Explain and give the correct C++ Boolean expression that specifies that x lies between 2 and 3.

4. Does the following sequence produce division by zero?

   ```
   j = -1;
   if ((j > 0) && (1/(j + 1) > 10))
       cout << i << endl;
   ```

Enumeration Types (*Optional*)

An **enumeration type** is a type whose values are defined by a list of constants of type *int*. An enumeration type is very much like a list of declared constants.

When defining an enumeration type, you can use any *int* values and can have any number of constants defined in an enumeration type. For example, the following enumeration type defines a constant for the length of each month:

```
enum MonthLength { JAN_LENGTH = 31, FEB_LENGTH = 28,
MAR_LENGTH = 31, APR_LENGTH = 30, MAY_LENGTH = 31,
JUN_LENGTH = 30, JUL_LENGTH = 31, AUG_LENGTH = 31,
SEP_LENGTH = 30, OCT_LENGTH = 31, NOV_LENGTH = 30,
DEC_LENGTH = 31 };
```

As this example shows, two or more named constants in an enumeration type can receive the same *int* value.

If you do not specify any numeric values, the identifiers in an enumeration-type definition are assigned consecutive values beginning with 0. For example, the type definition

```
enum Direction { NORTH = 0, SOUTH = 1, EAST = 2, WEST = 3 };
```

is equivalent to

```
enum Direction { NORTH, SOUTH, EAST, WEST };
```

The form that does not explicitly list the *int* values is normally used when you just want a list of names and do not care about what values they have.

If you initialize only some enumeration constant to some values, say

```
enum MyEnum { ONE = 17, TWO, THREE, FOUR = -3, FIVE };
```

then ONE takes the value 17, TWO takes the next *int* value 18, THREE takes the next value 19, FOUR takes -3, and FIVE takes the next value, -2.

In short, the default for the first enumeration constant is 0. The rest increase by 1 unless you set one or more of the enumeration constants.

3.2 MULTIWAY BRANCHES

"Would you tell me, please, which way I ought to go from here?"

"That depends a good deal on where you want to get to," said the Cat.

LEWIS CARROLL, *Alice in Wonderland*

Any programming construct that chooses one from a number of alternative actions is called a **branching mechanism.** The *if-else* statement chooses between two alternatives. In this section we will discuss methods for choosing from among more than two alternatives.

Nested Statements

As you have seen, *if-else* statements and *if* statements contain smaller statements within them. Thus far we have used compound statements and simple statements such as assignment statements as these smaller substatements, but there are other possibilities. In fact, any statement at all can be used as a subpart of an *if-else* statement, of an *if* statement, of a *while* statement, or of a *do-while* statement. This is illustrated in Display 3.3. The statement in that display has three levels of nesting, as indicated by the boxes. Two cout statements are nested within an *if-else* statement, and that *if-else* statement is nested within an *if* statement.

When nesting statements, you normally indent each level of nested substatements. In Display 3.3 there are three levels of nesting, so there are three levels of indenting. Both cout statements are indented the same amount because they are both at the same level of nesting. Later in this chapter, you will see some specific cases where it makes sense to use other indenting patterns, but unless there is some rule to the contrary, you should indent each level of nesting as illustrated in Display 3.3.

DISPLAY 3.3   An *if-else* Statement Within an *if* Statement

```
1   if (count > 0)
2       if (score > 5)
3           cout << "count > 0 and score > 5\n";
4       else
5           cout << "count > 0 and score <= 5\n";
```

■ PROGRAMMING TIP   Use Braces in Nested Statements

Suppose we want to write an *if-else* statement to use in an onboard computer monitoring system for a racing car. This part of the program warns the driver when fuel is low but tells the driver to bypass pit stops if the fuel tank is close to full. In all other situations the program gives no output so as not to distract the driver. We design the following pseudocode:

> If the fuel gauge is below 3/4 full, then:
> Check whether the fuel gauge is below 1/4 full and issue a low fuel warning if it is.
> Otherwise (that is, if fuel gauge is over 3/4 full):
> Output a statement telling the driver not to stop.

If we are not being too careful, we might implement the pseudocode as follows:

Read text to see what is wrong with this.

```
if (fuel_gauge_reading < 0.75)
    if (fuel_gauge_reading < 0.25)
        cout << "Fuel very low. Caution!\n";
else
    cout << "Fuel over 3/4. Don't stop now!\n";
```

This implementation looks fine, and it is indeed a correctly formed C++ statement that the compiler will accept and that will run with no error messages. However, it does not implement the pseudocode. Notice that this statement has two occurrences of *if* and only one *else*. The compiler must decide which *if* gets paired with the one *else*. We have nicely indented this nested statement to show that the *else* should be paired with the first *if*, but the compiler does not care about indenting. To the compiler, the preceding nested statement is the same as the following version, which differs only in how it is indented:

```
if (fuel_gauge_reading < 0.75)
    if (fuel_gauge_reading < 0.25)
        cout << "Fuel very low. Caution!\n";
    else
        cout << "Fuel over 3/4. Don't stop now!\n";
```

Unfortunately for us, the compiler will use the second interpretation and will pair the one *else* with the second *if* rather than the first *if*. This is sometimes called the **dangling *else* problem**; it is illustrated by the program in Display 3.4.

The compiler always pairs an *else* with the nearest previous *if* that is not already paired with some *else*. But, do not try to work within this rule. Ignore the rule! Change the rules! You are the boss! Always tell the compiler what you want it to do and the compiler will then do what you want. How do you tell the compiler what you want? You use braces. Braces in nested statements are like parentheses in arithmetic expressions. The braces tell the compiler

rule for pairing *else*'s with *if*'s

DISPLAY 3.4   The Importance of Braces

```
1    //Illustrates the importance of using braces in if-else statements.
2    #include <iostream>
3    using namespace std;
4    int main( )
5    {
6        double fuel_gauge_reading;
7
8        cout << "Enter fuel gauge reading: ";
9        cin >> fuel_gauge_reading;
10
11       cout << "First with braces:\n";
12       if (fuel_gauge_reading < 0.75)
13       {
14           if (fuel_gauge_reading < 0.25)
15               cout << "Fuel very low. Caution!\n";
16       }
17       else
18       {
19           cout << "Fuel over 3/4. Don't stop now!\n";
20       }
21
22       cout << "Now without braces:\n";
23       if (fuel_gauge_reading < 0.75)
24           if (fuel_gauge_reading < 0.25)
25               cout << "Fuel very low. Caution!\n";
26       else
27           cout << "Fuel over 3/4. Don't stop now!\n";
28
29       return 0;
30   }
```

This indenting is nice, but is not what the computer follows.

Sample Dialogue 1

```
Enter fuel gauge reading: 0.1
First with braces:
Fuel very low. Caution!
Now without braces:
Fuel very low. Caution!
```

Braces make no difference in this case, but see Dialogue 2.

Sample Dialogue 2

```
Enter fuel gauge reading: 0.5
First with braces:
Now without braces:
Fuel over 3/4. Don't stop now!
```

There should be no output here, and thanks to braces, there is none.

Incorrect output from the version without braces.

how to group things, rather than leaving them to be grouped according to default conventions, which may or may not be what you want. To avoid problems and to make your programs easier to read, place braces, { and }, around substatements in *if-else* statements, as we have done in the first *if-else* statement in Display 3.4.

For very simple substatements, such as a single assignment statement or a single `cout` statement, you can safely omit the braces. In Display 3.4, the braces around the following substatement (within the first *if-else* statement) are not needed:

```
cout << "Fuel over 3/4. Don't stop now!\n";
```

However, even in these simple cases, the braces can sometimes aid readability. Some programmers advocate using braces around even the simplest substatements when they occur within *if-else* statements, which is what we have done in the first *if-else* statement in Display 3.4. ■

Multiway *if-else* Statements

An *if-else* statement is a two-way branch. It allows a program to choose one of two possible actions. Often you will want to have a three- or four-way branch so that your program can choose between more than two alternative actions. You can implement such multiway branches by nesting *if-else* statements. By way of example, suppose you are designing a game-playing program in which the user must guess the value of some number. The number can be in a variable named `number`, and the guess can be in a variable named `guess`. If you wish to give a hint after each guess, you might design the following pseudocode:

```
Output "Too high." when guess > number.
Output "Too low." when guess < number.
Output "Correct!" when guess == number.
```

Any time a branching action is described as a list of mutually exclusive conditions and corresponding actions, as in this example, it can be implemented by using a nested *if-else* statement. For example, this pseudocode translates to the following code:

```
if (guess > number)
    cout << "Too high.";
else if (guess < number)
    cout << "Too low.";
else if (guess == number)
    cout << "Correct!";
```

The indenting pattern used here is slightly different from what we have advocated previously. If we followed our indenting rules, we would produce something like the following:

```
if (guess > number)
    cout << "Too high.";
else
    if (guess < number)
        cout << "Too low.";
    else
        if (guess == number)
            cout << "Correct!";
```

Use the previous indenting pattern rather than this one.

This is one of those rare cases in which you should not follow our general guidelines for indenting nested statements. The reason is that by lining up all the *else*'s, you also line up all the condition/action pairs and so make the layout of the program reflect your reasoning. Another reason is that even for not-too-deeply nested *if-else* statements, you can quickly run out of space on your page!

Since the conditions are mutually exclusive, the last *if* in the nested *if-else* statement above is superfluous and can be omitted, but it is sometimes best to include it in a comment as follows:

```
if (guess > number)
    cout << "Too high.";
else if (guess < number)
    cout << "Too low.";
else //(guess == number)
    cout << "Correct!";
```

You can use this form of multiple-branch *if-else* statement even if the conditions are not mutually exclusive. Whether the conditions are mutually exclusive or not, the computer will evaluate the conditions in the order in which they appear until it finds the first condition that is *true* and then it will execute the action corresponding to this condition. If no condition is *true*, no action is taken. If the statement ends with a plain *else* without any *if*, then the last statement is executed when all the conditions are *false*.

Multiway *if-else* Statement

SYNTAX

```
if (Boolean_Expression_1)
    Statement_1
else if (Boolean_Expression_2)
    Statement_2
        .
        .
        .
else if (Boolean_Expression_n)
    Statement_n
else
    Statement_For_All_Other_Possibilities
```

(continued)

EXAMPLE>

```
if ((temperature <-10) && (day == SUNDAY))
    cout << "Stay home.";
else if (temperature <-10) //and day != SUNDAY
    cout << "Stay home, but call work.";
else if (temperature <= 0) //and temperature >= -10
    cout << "Dress warm.";
else //temperature > 0
    cout << "Work hard and play hard.";
```

The Boolean expressions are checked in order until the first *true* Boolean expression is encountered, and then the corresponding statement is executed. If none of the Boolean expressions is *true*, then the *Statement_For_All_Other_Possibilities* is executed.

PROGRAMMING EXAMPLE   State Income Tax

Display 3.5 contains a program that uses a multiway *if-else* statement. The program takes the taxpayer's net income rounded to a whole number of dollars and computes the state income tax due on this net income. This state computes tax according to the following rate schedule:

1. No tax is paid on the first $15,000 of net income.

2. A tax of 5 percent is assessed on each dollar of net income from $15,001 to $25,000.

3. A tax of 10 percent is assessed on each dollar of net income over $25,000.

The program defined in Display 3.5 uses a multiway *if-else* statement with one action for each of these three cases. The condition for the second case is actually more complicated than it needs to be. The computer will not get to the second condition unless it has already tried the first condition and found it to be *false*. Thus, you know that whenever the computer tries the second condition, it will know that net_income is greater than 15000. Hence, you can replace the line

```
else if ((net_income > 15000) && (net_income <= 25000))
```

with the following, and the program will perform exactly the same:

```
else if (net_income <= 25000)
```

DISPLAY 3.5   Multiway *if-else* Statement

```
1     //Program to compute state income tax.
2     #include <iostream>
3     using namespace std;
4
5     //This program outputs the amount of state income tax due computed
6     //as follows: no tax on income up to $15,000; 5% on income between
7     //$15,001 and $25,000; 10% on income over $25,000.
8
9     int main( )
10    {
11        int net_income;
12        double tax_bill;
13        double five_percent_tax, ten_percent_tax;
14
15
16        cout << "Enter net income (rounded to whole dollars) $";
17        cin >> net_income;
18
19        if (net_income <= 15000)
20            tax_bill = 0;
21        else if ((net_income > 15000) && (net_income <= 25000))
22            //5% of amount over $15,000
23            tax_bill = (0.05 * (net_income - 15000));
24        else //net_income > $25,000
25        {
26            //five_percent_tax = 5% of income from $15,000 to $25,000.
27            five_percent_tax = 0.05 * 10000;
28            //ten_percent_tax = 10% of income over $25,000.
29            ten_percent_tax = 0.10 * (net_income - 25000);
30            tax_bill = (five_percent_tax + ten_percent_tax);
31        }
32
33        cout.setf(ios::fixed);
34        cout.setf(ios::showpoint);
35        cout.precision(2);
36        cout << "Net income = $" << net_income << endl
37             << "Tax bill = $" << tax_bill << endl;
38
39        return 0;
40    }
```

Sample Dialogue

```
Enter net income (rounded to whole dollars) $25100
Net income = $25100.00
Tax bill = $510.00
```

SELF-TEST EXERCISES

5. What output will be produced by the following code, when embedded in a complete program?

```
int x = 2;
cout << "Start\n";
if (x <= 3)
    if (x != 0)
        cout << "Hello from the second if.\n";
    else
        cout << "Hello from the else.\n";
cout << "End\n";

cout << "Start again\n";
if (x > 3)
    if (x != 0)
        cout << "Hello from the second if.\n";
    else
        cout << "Hello from the else.\n";
cout << "End again\n";
```

6. What output will be produced by the following code, when embedded in a complete program?

```
int extra = 2;
if (extra < 0)
    cout << "small";
else if (extra = = 0)
    cout << "medium";
else
    cout << "large";
```

7. What would be the output in Self-Test Exercise 6 if the assignment were changed to the following?

```
int extra = -37;
```

8. What would be the output in Self-Test Exercise 6 if the assignment were changed to the following?

```
int extra = 0;
```

9. What output will be produced by the following code, when embedded in a complete program?

```
int x = 200;
cout << "Start\n";
if (x < 100)
    cout << "First Output.\n";
```

```
else if (x > 10)
    cout << "Second Output.\n";
else
    cout << "Third Output.\n";
cout << "End\n";
```

10. What would be the output in Self-Test Exercise 9 if the Boolean expression (x > 10) were changed to (x > 100)?

11. What output will be produced by the following code, when embedded in a complete program?

```
int x = SOME_CONSTANT;
cout << "Start\n";
if (x < 100)
    cout << "First Output.\n";
else if (x > 100)
    cout << "Second Output.\n";
else
    cout << x << endl;
cout << "End\n";
```

SOME_CONSTANT is a constant of type *int*. Assume that neither "First Output" nor "Second Output" is output. So, you know the value of x is output.

12. Write a multiway *if-else* statement that classifies the value of an *int* variable n into one of the following categories and writes out an appropriate message:

n < 0 or 0 ≤ n ≤ 100 or n > 100

13. Given the following declaration and output statement, assume that this has been embedded in a correct program and is run. What is the output?

```
enum Direction { N, S, E, W };
//...
cout << W << " " << E << " " << S << " " << N << endl;
```

14. Given the following declaration and output statement, assume that this has been embedded in a correct program and is run. What is the output?

```
enum Direction { N = 5, S = 7, E = 1, W };
// ...
cout << W << " " << E << " " << S << " " N << endl;
```

The *switch* Statement

You have seen *if-else* statements used to construct multiway branches. The **switch statement** is another kind of C++ statement that also implements multiway branches. A sample *switch* statement is shown in Display 3.6. This particular *switch* statement has four regular branches and a fifth branch for illegal input. The variable grade determines which branch is executed. There is one branch for each of the grades 'A', 'B', and 'C'. The grades 'D' and 'F' cause the same branch to be taken, rather than having a separate action for each of 'D' and 'F'. If the value of grade is any character other than 'A', 'B', 'C', 'D', or 'F', then the cout statement after the identifier *default* is executed.

DISPLAY 3.6   **A** *switch* **Statement** *(part 1 of 2)*

```
1    //Program to illustrate the switch statement.
2    #include <iostream>
3    using namespace std;
4    int main( )
5    {
6        char grade;
7        cout << "Enter your midterm grade and press Return: ";
8        cin >> grade;
9        switch (grade)
10       {
11           case 'A':
12               cout << "Excellent. "
13                    << "You need not take the final.\n";
14               break;
15           case 'B':
16               cout << "Very good. ";
17               grade = 'A';
18               cout << "Your midterm grade is now "
19                    << grade << endl;
20               break;
21           case 'C':
22               cout << "Passing.\n";
23               break;
24           case 'D':
25           case 'F':
26               cout << "Not good. "
27                    << "Go study.\n";
28               break;
29           default:
30               cout << "That is not a possible grade.\n";
31       }
32       cout << "End of program.\n";
33       return 0;
34   }
```

(continued)

DISPLAY 3.6   A *switch* **Statement** *(part 2 of 2)*

Sample Dialogue 1

```
Enter your midterm grade and press Return: A
Excellent. You need not take the final.
End of program.
```

Sample Dialogue 2

```
Enter your midterm grade and press Return: B
Very good. Your midterm grade is now A.
End of program.
```

Sample Dialogue 3

```
Enter your midterm grade and press Return: D
Not good. Go study.
End of program.
```

Sample Dialogue 4

```
Enter your midterm grade and press Return: E
That is not a possible grade.
End of program.
```

VideoNote
switch Statement Example

The syntax and preferred indenting pattern for the *switch* statement are shown in the sample *switch* statement in Display 3.6 and in the box entitled "*switch* Statement."

When a *switch* statement is executed, one of a number of different branches is executed. The choice of which branch to execute is determined by a **controlling expression** given in parentheses after the keyword *switch*. The controlling expression in the sample *switch* statement shown in Display 3.6 is of type *char*. The controlling expression for a *switch* statement must always return either a *bool* value, an *enum* constant, one of the integer types, or a character. When the *switch* statement is executed, this controlling expression is evaluated and the computer looks at the constant values given after the various occurrences of the *case* identifiers. If it finds a constant that equals the value of the controlling expression, it executes the code for that *case*. For example, if the expression evaluates to 'B', then it looks for the following and executes the statements that follow this line:

```
case 'B':
```

Notice that the constant is followed by a colon. Also note that you cannot have two occurrences of *case* with the same constant value after them, since that would be an ambiguous instruction.

A **break** statement consists of the keyword *break* followed by a semicolon. When the computer executes the statements after a *case* label, it continues until it reaches a *break* statement. When the computer encounters a *break* statement, the *switch* statement ends. If you omit the *break* statements, then after executing the code for one *case*, the computer will go on to execute the code for the next *case*.

Note that you can have two *case* labels for the same section of code. In the *switch* statement in Display 3.6, the same action is taken for the values 'D' and 'F'. This technique can also be used to allow for both upper- and lowercase letters. For example, to allow both lowercase 'a' and uppercase 'A' in the program in Display 3.6, you can replace

```
case 'A':
    cout << "Excellent. "
        << "You need not take the final.\n";
    break;
```

with the following:

```
case 'A':
case 'a':
    cout << "Excellent. "
        << "You need not take the final.\n";
    break;
```

Of course, the same can be done for all the other letters.

If no *case* label has a constant that matches the value of the controlling expression, then the statements following the *default* label are executed. You need not have a *default* section. If there is no *default* section and no match is found for the value of the controlling expression, then nothing happens when the *switch* statement is executed. However, it is safest to always have a *default* section. If you think your *case* labels list all possible outcomes, then you can put an error message in the *default* section. This is what we did in Display 3.6.

---

switch Statement

SYNTAX

```
switch (Controlling_Expression)
{
    case Constant_1:
        Statement_Sequence_1
        break;
```

(continued)

```
        case Constant_2:
            Statement_Sequence_2
            break;
        .
        .
        .
        case Constant_n:
            Statement_Sequence_n
            break;
        default:
            Default_Statement_Sequence
    }
```

EXAMPLE

```
    int vehicle_class;
    cout << "Enter vehicle class: ";
    cin >> vehicle_class;

    switch (vehicle_class)
    {
        case 1:
            cout << "Passenger car.";
            toll = 0.50;                    If you forget this break,
            break;    ←——————————    then passenger cars will
        case 2:                             pay $1.50.
            cout << "Bus.";
            toll = 1.50;
            break;
        case 3:
            cout << "Truck.";
            toll = 2.00;
            break;
        default:
            cout << "Unknown vehicle class!";
    }
```

PITFALL   Forgetting a *break* in a *switch* Statement

If you forget a *break* in a *switch* statement, the compiler will not issue an error message. You will have written a syntactically correct *switch* statement, but it will not do what you intended it to do. Consider the *switch* statement in the box entitled "*switch* Statement." If a *break* statement were omitted, as indicated by the arrow, then when the variable vehicle_class has the value 1, the *case* labeled

```
    case 1:
```

would be executed as desired, but then the computer would go on to also execute the next *case*. This would produce a puzzling output that says the vehicle is a passenger car and then later says it is a bus; moreover, the final value of to11 would be 1.50, not 0.50 as it should be. When the computer starts to execute a *case*, it does not stop until it encounters either a *break* or the end of the *switch* statement. ■

Using *switch* Statements for Menus

The multiway *if-else* statement is more versatile than the *switch* statement, and you can use a multiway *if-else* statement anywhere you can use a *switch* statement. However, sometimes the *switch* statement is clearer. For example, the *switch* statement is perfect for implementing *menus*.

DISPLAY 3.7 A Menu (*part 1 of 2*)

```
1    //Program to give out homework assignment information.
2    #include <iostream>
3    using namespace std;
4
5
6    int main( )
7    {
8        int choice;
9
10       do
11       {
12           cout << endl
13               << "Choose 1 to see the next homework assignment.\n"
14               << "Choose 2 for your grade on the last assignment.\n"
15               << "Choose 3 for assignment hints.\n"
16               << "Choose 4 to exit this program.\n"
17               << "Enter your choice and press Return: ";
18           cin >> choice;
19
20           switch(choice)
21           {
22               case 1:
23                   //code to display the next assignment on screen would go here.
24                   break;
25               case 2:
26                   //code to ask for a student number and give the corresponding
27                   //grade would go here.
28                   break;
29               case 3:
30                   //code to display a hint for the current assignment would go
```

(*continued*)

DISPLAY 3.7 **A Menu** (*part 2 of 2*)

```
31                      //here.
32                      break;
33                  case 4:
34                      cout << "End of Program.\n";
35                      break;
36                  default:
37                      cout << "Not a valid choice.\n"
38                           << "Choose again.\n";
39              }
40          } while (choice != 4);
41
42          return 0;
43      }
```

Sample Dialogue

```
Choose 1 to see the next homework assignment.
Choose 2 for your grade on the last assignment.
Choose 3 for assignment hints.
Choose 4 to exit this program.
Enter your choice and press Return: 3

Assignment hints:
Analyze the problem.                              The exact
Write an algorithm in pseudocode.                 output will
Translate the pseudocode into a C++ program.      depend on the
                                                  code inserted
                                                  into the switch
Choose 1 to see the next homework assignment.     statement.
Choose 2 for your grade on the last assignment.
Choose 3 for assignment hints.
Choose 4 to exit this program.
Enter your choice and press Return: 4
End of Program.
```

A *menu* in a restaurant presents a list of alternatives for a customer to choose from. A **menu** in a computer program does the same thing: It presents a list of alternatives on the screen for the user to choose from. Display 3.7 shows the outline of a program designed to give students information on homework assignments. The program uses a menu to let the student choose which information she or he wants. A more readable way to implement the menu actions is through functions. Functions are discussed in Chapter 4.

Blocks

Each branch of a *switch* statement or of an *if-else* statement is a separate subtask. As indicated in the previous Programming Tip, it is often best to make the action of each branch a function call. That way the subtask for each branch can be designed, written, and tested separately. On the other hand, sometimes the action of one branch is so simple that you can just make it a compound statement. Occasionally, you may want to give this compound statement its own local variables. For example, consider the program in Display 3.8. It calculates the final bill for a specified number of items at a given price. If the sale is a wholesale transaction, then no sales tax is charged (presumably because the tax will be paid when the items are resold to retail buyers). If, however, the sale is a retail transaction, then sales tax must be added. An *if-else* statement is used to produce different calculations for wholesale and retail purchases. For the retail purchase, the calculation uses a temporary variable called subtotal, and so that variable is declared within the compound statement for that branch of the *if-else* statement.

As shown in Display 3.8, the variable subtotal is declared within a compound statement. If we wanted to, we could have used the variable name subtotal for something else outside of the compound statement in which it is declared. A variable that is declared inside a compound statement is *local* to the compound statement. Local variables are created when the compound statement is executed and are destroyed when the compound statement is completed. In other words, **local variables** exist only within the compound statement in which they are declared. Within a compound statement, you can use all the variables declared outside of the compound statement, as well as the local variables declared inside the compound statement.

DISPLAY 3.8   Block with a Local Variable *(part 1 of 2)*

```
1    //Program to compute bill for either a wholesale or a retail purchase.
2    #include <iostream>
3    using namespace std;
4
5
6    int main( )
7    {
8        const double TAX_RATE = 0.05; //5% sales tax
9        char sale_type;
10       int number;
11       double price, total;
12
13       cout << "Enter price $";
14       cin >> price;
```

(continued)

DISPLAY 3.8 Block with a Local Variable *(part 2 of 2)*

```
15          cout << "Enter number purchased: ";
16          cin >> number;
17          cout << "Type W if this is a wholesale purchase.\n"
18                 << "Type R if this is a retail purchase.\n"
19                 << "Then press Return.\n";
20          cin >> sale_type;
21
22          if ((sale_type == 'W') || (sale_type == 'w'))
23          {
24              total = price * number;
25          }
26          else if ((sale_type == 'R') || (sale_type == 'r'))
27          {
28              double subtotal;                              Local to the block
29              subtotal = price * number;
30              total = subtotal + subtotal * TAX_RATE;
31          }
32          else
33          {
34              cout << "Error in input.\n";
35          }
36          cout.setf(ios::fixed);
37          cout.setf(ios::showpoint);
38          cout.precision(2);
39          cout << number << " items at $" << price << endl;
40          cout << "Total Bill = $" << total;
41          if ((sale_type == 'R') || (sale_type == 'r'))
42              cout << " including sales tax.\n";
43
44          return 0;
45      }
```

Sample Dialogue

```
Enter price: $10.00
Enter number purchased: 2
Type W if this is a wholesale purchase.
Type R if this is a retail purchase.
Then press Return.
R
2 items at $10.00
Total Bill = $21.00 including sales tax.
```

A compound statement with declarations is more than a simple compound statement, so it has a special name. A compound statement that contains variable declarations is usually called a **block**, and the variables declared within the block are said to be **local to the block** or to **have the block as their scope.** (A plain old compound statement that does not contain any variable declarations is also called a block. Any code enclosed in braces is called a block.)

In Chapter 4 we will show how to define functions. The body of a function definition is also a block. There is no standard name for a block that is not the body of a function. However, we want to talk about these kinds of blocks, so let us create a name for them. Let's call a block a **statement block** when it is not the body of a function (and not the body of the main part of a program).

Statement blocks can be nested within other statement blocks, and basically the same rules about local variable names apply to these nested statement blocks as those we have already discussed, but applying the rules can be tricky when statement blocks are nested. A better rule is to not nest statement blocks. Nested statement blocks make a program hard to read. If you feel the need to nest statement blocks, instead make some of the statement blocks into function definitions and use function calls rather than nested statement blocks. In fact, statement blocks of any kind should be used sparingly. In most situations, a function call is preferable to a statement block. For completeness, we include the scope rule for nested blocks in the accompanying summary box.

Blocks

A **block** is some C++ code enclosed in braces. The variables declared in a block are local to the block and so the variable names can be used outside of the block for something else (such as being reused as the name for a different variable).

Scope Rule for Nested Blocks

If an identifier is declared as a variable in each of two blocks, one within the other, then these are two different variables with the same name. One variable exists only within the inner block and cannot be accessed outside of the inner block. The other variable exists only in the outer block and cannot be accessed in the inner block. The two variables are distinct, so changes made to one of these variables will have no effect on the other of these two variables.

PITFALL   Inadvertent Local Variables

When you declare a variable within a pair of braces, { }, that variable becomes a local variable for the block enclosed in the pair. This is true whether you wanted the variable to be local or not. If you want a variable to be available outside of the braces, then you must declare it outside of the braces. ■

SELF-TEST EXERCISES

15. What output will be produced by the following code, when embedded in a complete program?

```cpp
int first_choice = 1;
switch (first_choice + 1)
{
    case 1:
        cout << "Roast beef\n";
        break;
    case 2:
        cout << "Roast worms\n";
        break;
    case 3:
        cout << "Chocolate ice cream\n";
    case 4:
        cout << "Onion ice cream\n";
        break;
    default:
        cout << "Bon appetit!\n";
}
```

16. What would be the output in Self-Test Exercise 15 if the first line were changed to the following?

```cpp
int first_choice = 3;
```

17. What would be the output in Self-Test Exercise 15 if the first line were changed to the following?

```cpp
int first_choice = 2;
```

18. What would be the output in Self-Test Exercise 15 if the first line were changed to the following?

```cpp
int first_choice = 4;
```

19. What output is produced by the following code, when embedded in a complete program?

```
int number = 22;
{
    int number = 42;
    cout << number << " ";
}
cout << number;
```

20. Though we urge you not to program using this style, we are providing an exercise that uses nested blocks to help you understand the scope rules. Give the output that this code fragment would produce if embedded in an otherwise complete, correct program.

```
{
    int x = 1;
    cout << x << endl;
    {
        cout << x << endl;
        int x = 2;
        cout << x << endl;
        {
            cout << x << endl;
            int x = 3;
            cout << x << endl;
        }
        cout << x << endl;
    }
    cout << x << endl;
}
```

3.3 MORE ABOUT C++ LOOP STATEMENTS

It is not true that life is one damn thing after another—

It's one damn thing over and over.

EDNA ST. VINCENT MILLAY, *Letter to Arthur Darison Ficke, October 24, 1930*

A **loop** is any program construction that repeats a statement or sequence of statements a number of times. The simple *while* loops and *do-while* loops that we have already seen are examples of loops. The statement (or group of statements) to be repeated in a loop is called the **body** of the loop, and each repetition of the loop body is called an **iteration** of the loop. The two main design questions when constructing loops are: What should the loop body be? How many times should the loop body be iterated?

The *while* Statements Reviewed

The syntax for the *while* statement and its variant, the *do-while* statement, is reviewed in Display 3.9. The important difference between the two types of loops involves *when* the controlling Boolean expression is checked. When a *while* statement is executed, the Boolean expression is checked *before* the loop body is executed. If the Boolean expression evaluates to *false*, then the body is not executed at all. With a *do-while* statement, the body of the loop is executed first and the Boolean expression is checked *after* the loop body is executed. Thus, the *do-while* statement always executes the loop body at least once. After this start-up, the *while* loop and the *do-while* loop behave very much the same. After each iteration of the loop body, the Boolean expression is again checked; if it is *true*, then the loop is iterated again. If it has changed from *true* to *false*, then the loop statement ends.

DISPLAY 3.9 Syntax of the *while* Statement and *do-while* Statement

A *while* Statement with a Single Statement Body

```
while (Boolean_Expression)
    Statement  ◄──────────  Body
```

A *while* Statement with a Multistatement Body

```
while (Boolean_Expression)
{
    Statement_1
    Statement_2
        .
        .           ⟩  Body
        .
    Statement_Last
}
```

A *do-while* Statement with a Single Statement Body

```
do
    Statement  ◄──────────  Body
while (Boolean_Expression);
```

A *do-while* Statement with a Multistatement Body

```
do
{
    Statement_1
    Statement_2
        .
        .           ⟩  Body
        .
    Statement_Last
} while (Boolean_Expression);
```

The first thing that happens when a *while* loop is executed is that the controlling Boolean expression is evaluated. If the Boolean expression evaluates to *false* at that point, then the body of the loop is never executed. It may seem pointless to execute the body of a loop zero times, but that is sometimes the desired action. For example, a *while* loop is often used to sum a list of numbers, but the list could be empty. To be more specific, a checkbook balancing program might use a *while* loop to sum the values of all the checks you have written in a month—but you might take a month's vacation and write no checks at all. In that case, there are zero numbers to sum and so the loop is iterated zero times.

executing the
body zero times

Increment and Decrement Operators Revisited

You have used the increment operator as a statement that increments the value of a variable by 1. For example, the following will output 42 to the screen:

```
int number = 41;
number++;
cout << number;
```

Thus far we have always used the increment operator as a statement. But the increment operator is also an operator, just like the + and ? operators. An expression like number++ also returns a value, so number++ can be used in an arithmetic expression such as

increment
operator in
expressions

```
2 * (number++)
```

The expression number++ first returns the value of the variable number, and *then* the value of number is increased by 1. For example, consider the following code:

```
int number = 2;
int value_produced = 2 * (number++);
cout << value_produced << endl;
cout << number << endl;
```

This code will produce the following output:

```
4
3
```

Notice the expression 2 * (number++). When C++ evaluates this expression, it uses the value that number has *before* it is incremented, not the value that it has after it is incremented. Thus, the value produced by the expression number++ is 2, even though the increment operator changes the value of number to 3. This may seem strange, but sometimes it is just what you want. And, as you are about to see, if you want an expression that behaves differently, you can have it.

The expression v++ evaluates to the value of the variable v, and *then* the value of the variable v is incremented by 1. If you reverse the order and place the ++ in front of the variable, the order of these two actions is reversed. The expression ++v first increments the value of the variable v and then returns this increased value of v. For example, consider the following code:

```
int number = 2;
int value_produced = 2 * (++number);
cout << value_produced << endl;
cout << number << endl;
```

This code is the same as the previous piece of code except that the ++ is before the variable, so this code produces the following output:

```
6
3
```

Notice that the two increment operators number++ and ++number have the same effect on a variable number: They both increase the value of number by 1. But the two expressions evaluate to different values. Remember, if the ++ is *before* the variable, then the incrementing is done *before* the value is returned; if the ++ is *after* the variable, then the incrementing is done *after* the value is returned.

The program in Display 3.10 uses the increment operator in a *while* loop to count the number of times the loop body is repeated. One of the main uses of the increment operator is to control the iteration of loops in ways similar to what is done in Display 3.10.

DISPLAY 3.10   The Increment Operator as an Expression
(part 1 of 2)

```
1     //Calorie-counting program.
2     #include <iostream>
3     using namespace std;
4
5     int main( )
6     {
7         int number_of_items, count,
8             calories_for_item, total_calories;
9
10        cout << "How many items did you eat today? ";
11        cin >> number_of_items;
12
13        total_calories = 0;
14        count = 1;
15        cout << "Enter the number of calories in each of the\n"
16             << number_of_items << " items eaten:\n";
17
18        while (count++ <= number_of_items)
```

(continued)

DISPLAY 3.10   The Increment Operator as an Expression
(part 2 of 2)

```
19          {
20              cin >> calories_for_item;
21              total_calories = total_calories
22                              + calories_for_item;
23          }
24
25          cout << "Total calories eaten today = "
26              << total_calories << endl;
27          return 0;
28      }
29
```

Sample Dialogue

```
How many items did you eat today?
7
Enter the number of calories in each of the
7 items eaten:
300 60 1200 600 150 1 120
Total calories eaten today = 2431
```

Everything we said about the increment operator applies to the decrement
operator as well, except that the value of the variable is decreased by 1 rather
than increased by 1. For example, consider the following code:

decrement
operator

```
int number = 8;
int value_produced = number--;
cout << value_produced << endl;
cout << number << endl;
```

This produces the output

```
8
7
```

On the other hand, the code

```
int number = 8;
int value_produced = --number;
    cout << value_produced << endl;
    cout << number << endl;
```

produces the output

```
7
7
```

number-- returns the value of number and then decrements number; on the other hand, --number first decrements number and then returns the value of number.

++ and -- can only be used with variables

You cannot apply the increment and decrement operators to anything other than a single variable. Expressions such as (x + y)++, --(x + y), 5++, and so forth are all illegal in C++.

SELF-TEST EXERCISES

21. What is the output of the following (when embedded in a complete program)?

```
int count = 3;
while (count-- > 0)
    cout << count << " ";
```

22. What is the output of the following (when embedded in a complete program)?

```
int count = 3;
while (--count > 0)
    cout << count << " ";
```

23. What is the output of the following (when embedded in a complete program)?

```
int n = 1;
do
    cout << n << " ";
while (n++ <= 3);
```

24. What is the output of the following (when embedded in a complete program)?

```
int n = 1;
do
    cout << n << " ";
while (++n <= 3);
```

The *for* Statement

The *while* statement and the *do-while* statement are all the loop mechanisms you absolutely need. In fact, the *while* statement alone is enough. However, there is one sort of loop that is so common that C++ includes a special statement for this. In performing numeric calculations, it is common to do a calculation with the number 1, then with the number 2, then with 3, and so forth, until some last value is reached. For example, to add 1 through 10, you want the computer to perform the following statement ten times, with the value of n equal to 1 the first time and with n increased by 1 each subsequent time:

```
sum = sum + n;
```

The following is one way to accomplish this with a *while* statement:

```
sum = 0;
n = 1;
while (n <= 10)
{
    sum = sum + n;
    n++;
}
```

Although a *while* loop will do here, this sort of situation is just what the **for statement** (also called the **for** loop) was designed for. The following *for* statement will neatly accomplish the same task:

```
sum = 0;
for (n = 1; n <= 10; n++)
    sum = sum + n;
```

Let's look at this *for* statement piece by piece.

First, notice that the *while* loop version and the *for* loop version are made by putting together the same pieces: They both start with an assignment statement that sets the variable sum equal to 0. In both cases, this assignment statement for sum is placed before the loop statement itself begins. The loop statements themselves are both made from the pieces.

```
n = 1; n <= 10; n++ and sum = sum + n;
```

These pieces serve the same function in the *for* statement as they do in the *while* statement. The *for* statement is simply a more compact way of saying the same thing. Although other things are possible, we will only use *for* statements to perform loops controlled by one variable. In our example, that would be the variable n. With the equivalence of the previous two loops to guide us, let's go over the rules for writing a *for* statement.

A *for* statement begins with the keyword *for* followed by three things in parentheses that tell the computer what to do with the controlling variable. The beginning of a *for* statement looks like the following:

```
for (Initialization_Action; Boolean_Expression; Update_Action)
```

The first expression tells how the variable is initialized, the second gives a Boolean expression that is used to check for when the loop should end, and the last expression tells how the loop control variable is updated after each iteration of the loop body. For example, the above *for* loop begins

```
for (n = 1; n <= 10; n++)
```

The n = 1 says that n is initialized to 1. The n <= 10 says the loop will continue to iterate the body as long as n is less than or equal to 10. The last expression, n++, says that n is incremented by 1 after each time the loop body is executed.

The three expressions at the start of a *for* statement are separated by two, and only two, semicolons. Do not succumb to the temptation to place a semicolon after the third expression. (The technical explanation is that these three things are expressions, not statements, and so do not require a semicolon at the end.)

Display 3.11 shows the syntax of a *for* statement and also describes the action of the *for* statement by showing how it translates into an equivalent *while* statement. Notice that in a *for* statement, as in the corresponding *while* statement, the stopping condition is tested before the first loop iteration. Thus, it is possible to have a *for* loop whose body is executed zero times.

DISPLAY 3.11 The *for* Statement *(part 1 of 2)*

for **Statement**

SYNTAX

```
1   for (Initialization_Action; Boolean_Expression; Update_Action)
2       Body_Statement
```

EXAMPLE

```
1   for (number = 100; number >= 0; number--)
2       cout << number
3           << " bottles of beer on the shelf.\n";
```

Equivalent *while* **Loop**

EQUIVALENT SYNTAX

```
1   Initialization_Action;
2   while (Boolean_Expression)
3   {
4       Body_Statement
5       Update_Action;
6   }
```

EQUIVALENT EXAMPLE

```
1   number = 100;
2   while (number >= 0)
```

(continued)

DISPLAY 3.11   The *for* Statement *(part 2 of 2)*

```
3    {
4        cout << number
5            << " bottles of beer on the shelf.\n";
6        number--;
7    }
```

Output

```
100 bottles of beer on the shelf.
99 bottles of beer on the shelf.
                .
                .
                .
0 bottles of beer on the shelf.
```

Display 3.12 shows a sample *for* statement embedded in a complete (although very simple) program. The *for* statement in Display 3.12 is similar to the one discussed above, but it has one new feature. The variable n is declared when it is initialized to 1. So, the declaration of n is inside the *for* statement. The initializing action in a *for* statement can include a variable declaration. When a variable is used only within the *for* statement, this can be the best place to declare the variable. However, if the variable is also used outside of the *for* statement, then it is best to declare the variable outside of the *for* statement.

> declaring variables within a *for* statement

The ANSI C++ standard requires that a C++ compiler claiming compliance with the standard treat any declaration in a *for* loop initializer as if it were local to the body of the loop. Earlier C++ compilers did not do this. You should determine how your compiler treats variables declared in a *for* loop initializer. In the interests of portability, you should not write code that depends on this behavior. The ANSI C++ standard requires that variables declared in the initialization expression of a *for* loop be local to the block of the *for* loop. The next generation of C++ compilers will likely comply with this rule, but compilers presently available may or may not comply.

Our description of a *for* statement was a bit less general than what is allowed. The three expressions at the start of a *for* statement may be any C++ expressions and therefore they may involve more (or even fewer!) than one variable. However, our *for* statements will always use only a single variable in these expressions.

In the *for* statement in Display 3.12, the body was the simple assignment statement

```
sum = sum + n;
```

DISPLAY 3.12 A *for* Statement

```
1    //Illustrates a for loop.
2    #include <iostream>
3    using namespace std;
4
5    int main( )
6    {
7        int sum = 0;
8
9        for (int n = 1; n <= 10; n++) //Note that the variable n is a local
10           sum = sum + n;            //variable of the body of the for loop!
11
12       cout << "The sum of the numbers 1 to 10 is "
13            << sum << endl;
14       return 0;
15   }
```

Initializing action

Repeat the loop as long as this is true.

Done after each loop body iteration

Output

```
The sum of the numbers 1 to 10 is 55
```

DISPLAY 3.13   *for* Loop with a Multistatement Body

SYNTAX

```
for (Initialization_Action; Boolean_Expression; Update_Action)
{
    Statement_1
    Statement_2
         .
         .
         .
    Statement_Last
}
```

Body

EXAMPLE

```
for (int number = 100; number >= 0; number--)
{
    cout << number
         << " bottles of beer on the shelf.\n";
    if (number > 0)
        cout << "Take one down and pass it around.\n";
}
```

The body may be any statement at all. In particular, the body may be a compound statement. This allows us to place several statements in the body of a *for* loop, as shown in Display 3.13.

Thus far, you have seen *for* loops that increase the loop control variable by 1 after each loop iteration, and you have seen *for* loops that decrease the loop control variable by 1 after each loop iteration. There are many more possible kinds of variable updates. The variable can be incremented or decremented by 2 or 3 or any number. If the variable is of type *double*, it can be incremented or decremented by a fractional amount. All of the following are legitimate *for* loops:

more possible update actions

```
int n;
for (n = 1; n <= 10; n = n + 2)
    cout << "n is now equal to " << n << endl;

for (n = 0; n > -100; n = n - 7)
    cout << "n is now equal to " << n << endl;

for (double size = 0.75; size <= 5; size = size + 0.05)
    cout << "size is now equal to " << size << endl;
```

The update need not even be an addition or subtraction. Moreover, the initialization need not simply set a variable equal to a constant. You can initialize and change a loop control variable in just about any way you wish. For example, the following demonstrates one more way to start a *for* loop:

```
for (double x = pow(y, 3.0); x > 2.0; x = sqrt(x))
    cout << "x is now equal to " << x << endl;
```

PITFALL   Extra Semicolon in a *for* Statement

Do not place a semicolon after the closing parentheses at the beginning of a *for* loop. To see what can happen, consider the following *for* loop:

```
for (int count = 1; count <= 10; count++);        Problem
    cout << "Hello\n";                             semicolon
```

If you did not notice the extra semicolon, you might expect this *for* loop to write Hello to the screen ten times. If you do notice the semicolon, you might expect the compiler to issue an error message. Neither of those things happens. If you embed this *for* loop in a complete program, the compiler will not complain. If you run the program, only one Hello will be output instead of ten Hellos. What is happening? To answer that question, we need a little background.

One way to create a statement in C++ is to put a semicolon after something. If you put a semicolon after x++, you change the expression

```
x++
```

into the statement

```
x++;
```

If you place a semicolon after nothing, you still create a statement. Thus, the semicolon by itself is a statement, which is called the **empty statement** or the **null statement.** The empty statement performs no action, but it is still a statement. Therefore, the following is a complete and legitimate *for* loop, whose body is the empty statement:

```
for (int count = 1; count <= 10; count++);
```

This *for* loop is indeed iterated ten times, but since the body is the empty statement, nothing happens when the body is iterated. This loop does nothing, and it does nothing ten times!

Now let's go back and consider the *for* loop code labeled *Problem semicolon.* Because of the extra semicolon, that code begins with a *for* loop that has an empty body, and as we just discussed, that *for* loop accomplishes nothing. After the *for* loop is completed, the following cout statement is executed and writes Hello to the screen one time:

```
cout << "Hello\n";
```

You will eventually see some uses for *for* loops with empty bodies, but at this stage, such a *for* loop is likely to be just a careless mistake. ■

What Kind of Loop to Use

When designing a loop, the choice of which C++ loop statement to use is best postponed to the end of the design process. First design the loop using pseudocode, then translate the pseudocode into C++ code. At that point it will be easy to decide what type of C++ loop statement to use.

If the loop involves a numeric calculation using a variable that is changed by equal amounts each time through the loop, use a *for* loop. In fact, whenever you have a loop for a numeric calculation, you should consider using a *for* loop. It will not always be suitable, but it is often the clearest and easiest loop to use for numeric calculations.

In most other cases, you should use a *while* loop or a *do-while* loop; it is fairly easy to decide which of these two to use. If you want to insist that the loop body will be executed at least once, you may use a *do-while* loop. If there are circumstances for which the loop body should not be executed at all, then you must use a *while* loop. A common situation that demands a *while* loop is reading input when there is a possibility of no data at all. For example, if the program reads in a list of exam scores, there may be cases of students who have taken no exams, and hence the input loop may be faced with an empty list. This calls for a *while* loop.

SELF-TEST EXERCISES

25. What is the output of the following (when embedded in a complete program)?

```
for (int count = 1; count < 5; count++)
    cout << (2 * count) << " ";
```

26. What is the output of the following (when embedded in a complete program)?

```
for (int n = 10; n > 0; n = n - 2)
{
    cout << "Hello ";
    cout << n << endl;
}
```

27. What is the output of the following (when embedded in a complete program)?

```
for (double sample = 2; sample > 0; sample = sample - 0.5)
    cout << sample << " ";
```

28. For each of the following situations, tell which type of loop (*while*, *do-while*, or *for*) would work best:

    a. Summing a series, such as $1/2 + 1/3 + 1/4 + 1/5 + \ldots + 1/10$.

    b. Reading in the list of exam scores for one student.

    c. Reading in the number of days of sick leave taken by employees in a department.

    d. Testing a function to see how it performs for different values of its arguments.

29. Rewrite the following loops as *for* loops.

    a.
```
int i = 1;
    while (i <= 10)
    {
        if (i < 5 && i != 2)
            cout << 'X';
        i++;
    }
```

    b.
```
int i = 1;
    while (i <= 10)
```

```
       {
           cout << 'X';
           i = i + 3;
       }
c.  long m = 100;
       do
       {
           cout << 'X';
           m = m + 100;
       } while (m < 1000);
```

30. What is the output of this loop? Identify the connection between the value of n and the value of the variable log.

```
int n = 1024;
int log = 0;
for (int i = 1; i < n; i = i * 2)
    log++;
cout << n << " " << log << endl;
```

31. What is the output of this loop? Comment on the code.

```
int n = 1024;
int log = 0;
for (int i = 1; i < n; i = i * 2);
    log++;
cout << n << " " << log << endl;
```

32. What is the output of this loop? Comment on the code.

```
int n = 1024;
int log = 0;
for (int i = 0; i < n; i = i * 2)
    log++;
cout << n << " " << log << endl;
```

PITFALL   Uninitialized Variables and Infinite Loops

When we first introduced simple *while* and *do-while* loops in Chapter 2, we warned you of two pitfalls associated with loops. We said that you should be sure all variables that need to have a value in the loop are initialized (that is, given a value) before the loop is executed. This seems obvious when stated in the abstract, but in practice it is easy to become so concerned with designing a loop that you forget to initialize variables before the loop. We also said that you should be careful to avoid infinite loops. Both of these cautions apply equally well to *for* loops. ∎

The *break* Statement

You have already used the *break* statement as a way of ending a *switch* statement. This same *break* statement can be used to exit a loop. Sometimes you want to exit a loop before it ends in the normal way. For example, the loop might contain a check for improper input and if some improper input is encountered, then you may want to simply end the loop. The code in Display 3.14 reads a list of negative numbers and computes their sum as the value of the variable sum. The loop ends normally provided the user types in ten negative numbers. If the user forgets a minus sign, the computation is ruined and the loop ends immediately when the *break* statement is executed.

DISPLAY 3.14   A *break* Statement in a Loop *(part 1 of 2)*

```
1    //Sums a list of ten negative numbers.
2    #include <iostream>
3    using namespace std;
4
5    int main( )
6    {
7        int number, sum = 0, count = 0;
8        cout << "Enter 10 negative numbers:\n";
9
10       while (++count <= 10)
11       {
12           cin >> number;
13
14           if (number >= 0)
15           {
16               cout << "ERROR: positive number"
17                       << " or zero was entered as the\n"
18                       << count << "th number! Input ends "
19                       << "with the " << count << "th number.\n"
20                       << count << "th number was not added in.\n";
21               break;
22           }
23
24           sum = sum + number;
25       }
26
27       cout << sum << " is the sum of the first "
28               << (count - 1) << " numbers.\n";
29
30       return 0;
31   }
```

(continued)

DISPLAY 3.14   A _break_ Statement in a Loop _(part 2 of 2)_

Sample Dialogue

```
Enter 10 negative numbers:
-1 -2 -3 4 -5 -6 -7 -8 -9 -10
ERROR: positive number or zero was entered as the
4th number! Input ends with the 4th number.
4th number was not added in.
-6 is the sum of the first 3 numbers.
```

The _break_ Statement

The _break_ statement can be used to exit a loop statement. When the _break_ statement is executed, the loop statement ends immediately and execution continues with the statement following the loop statement. The _break_ statement may be used in any form of loop— in a _while_ loop, in a _do-while_ loop, or in a _for_ loop. This is the same _break_ statement that we have already used in _switch_ statements.

PITFALL   The _break_ Statement in Nested Loops

A _break_ statement ends only the innermost loop that contains it. If you have a loop within a loop and a _break_ statement in the inner loop, then the _break_ statement will end only the inner loop. ∎

SELF-TEST EXERCISES

33. What is the output of the following (when embedded in a complete program)?

```cpp
int n = 5;
while (--n > 0)
{
    if (n == 2)
        break;
    cout << n << " ";
}
cout << "End of Loop.";
```

34. What is the output of the following (when embedded in a complete program)?

```
int n = 5;
while (--n > 0)
{
    if (n == 2)
        exit(0);
    cout << n << " ";
}
cout << "End of Loop.";
```

35. What does a *break* statement do? Where is it legal to put a *break* statement?

3.4 DESIGNING LOOPS

Round and round she goes, and where she stops nobody knows.

TRADITIONAL CARNIVAL BARKER'S CALL

When designing a loop, you need to design three things:

1. The body of the loop

2. The initializing statements

3. The conditions for ending the loop

We begin with a section on two common loop tasks and show how to design these three elements for each of the two tasks.

Loops for Sums and Products

Many common tasks involve reading in a list of numbers and computing their sum. If you know how many numbers there will be, such a task can easily be accomplished by the following pseudocode. The value of the variable this_many is the number of numbers to be added. The sum is accumulated in the variable sum.

```
sum = 0;
repeat the following this_many times:
    cin >> next;
    sum = sum + next;
end of loop.
```

This pseudocode is easily implemented as the following *for* loop:

```
int sum = 0;
    for (int count = 1; count <= this_many; count++)
```

```
    {
        cin >> next;
        sum = sum + next;
    }
```

Notice that the variable sum is expected to have a value when the following loop body statement is executed:

```
sum = sum + next;
```

Since sum must have a value the very first time this statement is executed, sum must be initialized to some value before the loop is executed. In order to determine the correct initializing value for sum, think about what you want to happen after one loop iteration. After adding in the first number, the value of sum should be that number. That is, the first time through the loop the value of sum + next should equal next. To make this true, the value of sum must be initialized to 0.

Repeat "This Many Times"

A *for* statement can be used to produce a loop that repeats the loop body a predetermined number of times.

PSEUDOCODE

```
Repeat the following this_many times:
    Loop_Body
```

EQUIVALENT *for* STATEMENT

```
for (int count = 1; count <= this_many; count++)
    Loop_Body
```

EXAMPLE

```
for (int count = 1; count <= 3; count++)
    cout << "Hip, Hip, Hurray\n";
```

You can form the **product** of a list of numbers in a way that is similar to how we formed the sum of a list of numbers. The technique is illustrated by the following code:

```
int product = 1;
for (int count = 1; count <= this_many; count++)
{
    cin >> next;
    product = product * next;
}
```

The variable `product` must be given an initial value. Do not assume that all variables should be initialized to zero. If `product` were initialized to 0, then it would still be zero after the loop above has finished. As indicated in the C++ code shown earlier, the correct initializing value for `product` is 1. To see that 1 is the correct initial value, notice that the first time through the loop this will leave `product` equal to the first number read in, which is what you want.

Ending a Loop

There are four commonly used methods for terminating an **input loop**. We will discuss them in order.

1. List headed by size

2. Ask before iterating

3. List ended with a sentinel value

4. Running out of input

If your program can determine the size of an input list beforehand, either by asking the user or by some other method, you can use a "repeat *n* times" loop to read input exactly *n* times, where *n* is the size of the list. This method is called **list headed by size.**

The second method for ending an input loop is simply to ask the user, after each loop iteration, whether or not the loop should be iterated again. For example:

```
sum = 0;
cout << "Are there any numbers in the list? (Type\n"
     << "Y and Return for Yes, N and Return for No): ";
char ans;
cin >> ans;
while ((ans = = 'Y') || (ans = = 'y'))
{
    cout << "Enter number: ";
    cin >> number;
    sum = sum + number;
    cout << "Are there any more numbers? (Type\n"
         << "Y for Yes, N for No. End with Return.): ";
    cin >> ans;
}
```

However, for reading in a long list, this is very tiresome to the user. Imagine typing in a list of 100 numbers this way. The user is likely to progress from happy to sarcastic and then to angry and frustrated. When reading in a long list, it is preferable to include only one stopping signal, which is the method we discuss next.

Perhaps the nicest way to terminate a loop that reads a list of values from the keyboard is with a *sentinel value*. A **sentinel value** is one that is somehow distinct from all the possible values on the list being read in and so can be used to signal the end of the list. For example, if the loop reads in a list of positive numbers, then a negative number can be used as a sentinel value to indicate the end of the list. A loop such as the following can be used to add a list of nonnegative numbers:

```
cout << "Enter a list of nonnegative integers.\n"
    << "Place a negative integer after the list.\n";
sum = 0;
cin >> number;
while (number >= 0)
{
    sum = sum + number;
    cin >> number;
}
```

Notice that the last number in the list is read but is not added into sum. To add the numbers 1, 2, and 3, the user appends a negative number to the end of the list like so:

```
1 2 3 -1
```

The final -1 is read in but not added into the sum.

To use a sentinel value this way, you must be certain there is at least one value of the data type in question that definitely will not appear on the list of input values and thus can be used as the sentinel value. If the list consists of integers that might be any value whatsoever, then there is no value left to serve as the sentinel value. In this situation, you must use some other method to terminate the loop.

When reading input from a file, you can use a sentinel value, but a more common method is to simply check to see if all the input in the file has been read and to end the loop when there is no more input left to be read. This method of ending an input loop is discussed in Chapter 6 in the Programming Tip section entitled "Checking for the End of a File" and in the section entitled "The eof Member Function."

The techniques we gave for ending an input loop are all special cases of more general techniques that can be used to end loops of any kind. The more general techniques are as follows:

- Count-controlled loops
- Ask before iterating
- Exit on a flag condition

A **count-controlled loop** is any loop that determines the number of iterations before the loop begins and then iterates the loop body that many times. The list-headed-by-size technique that we discussed for input loops is an example of a count-controlled loop. All of our "repeat this many times" loops are count-controlled loops.

We already discussed the **ask-before-iterating** technique. You can use it for loops other than input loops, but the most common use for this technique is for processing input.

Earlier in this section we discussed input loops that end when a sentinel value is read. In our example, the program read nonnegative integers into a variable called number. When number received a negative value, that indicated the end of the input; the negative value was the sentinel value. This is an example of a more general technique known as **exit on a flag condition.** A variable that changes value to indicate that some event has taken place is often called a **flag.** In our example input loop, the flag was the variable number; when it becomes negative, that indicates that the input list has ended.

Ending a file input loop by running out of input is another example of the exit-on-a-flag technique. In this case the flag condition is determined by the system. The system keeps track of whether or not input reading has reached the end of a file.

A flag can also be used to terminate loops other than input loops. For example, the following sample loop can be used to find a tutor for a student. Students in the class are numbered starting with 1. The loop checks each student number to see if that student received a high grade and stops the loop as soon as a student with a high grade is found. For this example, a grade of 90 or more is considered high. The code compute_grade(n) is a call to a user-defined function. In this case, the function will execute some code that will compute a numeric value from 0 to 100 that corresponds to student n's grade. The numeric value then is copied into the variable grade. Chapter 4 discusses functions in more detail.

```
int n = 1;
grade = compute_grade(n);
while (grade < 90)
{
    n++;
    grade = compute_grade(n);
}
cout << "Student number " << n << " may be a tutor.\n"
     << "This student has a score of " << grade << endl;
```

In this example, the variable grade serves as the flag.

The previous loop indicates a problem that can arise when designing loops. What happens if no student has a score of 90 or better? The answer depends on the definition for the function compute_grade. If grade is defined for all positive integers, it could be an infinite loop. Even worse, if grade is defined to be, say, 100 for all arguments n that are not students, then it may try to make a tutor out of a nonexistent student. In any event, something will go wrong. If there is a danger of a loop turning into an infinite loop or even a danger of it iterating more times than is sensible, then you should include a check to see that the loop is not iterated too many times. For example, a better condition for our example loop is the following, where the variable number_of_students has been set equal to the number of students in the class:

```
int n = 1;
grade = compute_grade(n);
while ((grade < 90) && (n < number_of_students))
{
    n++;
    grade = compute_grade(n);
}
if (grade >= 90)
    cout << "Student number " << n << " may be a tutor.\n"
            << "This student has a score of " << grade << endl;
else
    cout << "No student has a high score.";
```

Nested Loops

VideoNote
Nested Loop Example

The program in Display 3.15 was designed to help track the reproduction rate of the green-necked vulture, an endangered species. In the district where this vulture survives, conservationists annually perform a count of the number of eggs in green-necked vulture nests. The program in Display 3.15 takes the reports of each of the conservationists in the district and calculates the total number of eggs contained in all the nests they observed.

Each conservationist's report consists of a list of numbers. Each number is the count of the number of eggs observed in one green-necked vulture nest. The *void* function named get_one_total reads in the report of one conservationist and calculates the total number of eggs found by this conservationist. The list of numbers for each conservationist has a negative number added to the end of the list. This serves as a sentinel value. The function call to get_one_total is included in a *for* loop so that this function is called once for each conservationist report.

The body of a loop may contain any kind of statement, so it is possible to have loops nested within loops (as well as eggs nested within nests). The program in Display 3.15 contains a loop within a loop. The nested loop in Display 3.15 is executed once for each value of count from 1 to number_of_ reports. For each such iteration of the outer *for* loop there is one complete execution of the inner *while* loop. In Chapter 4 we'll use subroutines to make the program in Display 3.15 more readable.

DISPLAY 3.15   Explicitly Nested Loops *(part 1 of 2)*

```
1    //Determines the total number of green-necked vulture eggs
2    //counted by all conservationists in the conservation district.
3    #include <iostream>
4    using namespace std;
5
6    int main()
7    {
8        cout   << "This program tallies conservationist reports\n"
9               << "on the green-necked vulture.\n"
```

(continued)

DISPLAY 3.15   Explicitly Nested Loops *(part 2 of 2)*

```
10          << "Each conservationist's report consists of\n"
11          << "a list of numbers. Each number is the count of\n"
12          << "the eggs observed in one"
13          << "green-necked vulture nest.\n"
14          << "This program then tallies "
15          << "the total number of eggs.\n";
16
17       int number_of_reports;
18       cout << "How many conservationist reports are there? ";
19       cin >> number_of_reports;
20
21       int grand_total = 0, subtotal, count;
22       for (count = 1; count <= number_of_reports; count++)
23       {
24           cout << endl << "Enter the report of "
25                << "conservationist number " << count << endl;
26           cout << "Enter the number of eggs in each nest.\n"
27                << "Place a negative integer at the end of your list.\n";"
28           subtotal = 0;
29           int next;
30           cin >> next;
31           while (next >= 0)
32           {
33               subtotal = subtotal + next;
34               cin >> next;
35           }
36           cout << "Total egg count for conservationist "
37                << " number " << count << " is "
38                << subtotal << endl;
39           grand_total = grand_total + subtotal;
40       }
41
42       cout << endl << "Total egg count for all reports = "
43            << grand_total << endl;
44
45       return 0;
46   }
```

SELF-TEST EXERCISES   myprogramminglab

36. Write a loop that will write the word Hello to the screen ten times (when embedded in a complete program).

37. Write a loop that will read in a list of even numbers (such as 2, 24, 8, 6) and compute the total of the numbers on the list. The list is ended with a sentinel value. Among other things, you must decide what would be a good sentinel value to use.

38. Predict the output of the following nested loops:

```cpp
int n, m;
for (n = 1; n <= 10; n++)
    for (m = 10; m >= 1; m-)
        cout << n << " times " << m
             << " = " << n * m << endl;
```

Debugging Loops

No matter how carefully a program is designed, mistakes will still sometimes occur. In the case of loops, there is a pattern to the kinds of mistakes programmers most often make. Most loop errors involve the first or last iteration of the loop. If you find that your loop does not perform as expected, check to see if the loop is iterated one too many or one too few times. Loops that iterate one too many or one too few times are said to have an **off-by-one error;** these errors are among the most common loop bugs. Be sure you are not confusing less-than with less-than-or-equal-to. Be sure you have initialized the loop correctly. Remember that a loop may sometimes need to be iterated zero times and check that your loop handles that possibility correctly.

Infinite loops usually result from a mistake in the Boolean expression that controls the stopping of the loop. Check to see that you have not reversed an inequality, confusing less-than with greater-than. Another common source of infinite loops is terminating a loop with a test for equality, rather than something involving greater-than or less-than. With values of type *double*, testing for equality does not give meaningful answers, since the quantities being compared are only approximate values. Even for values of type *int*, equality can be a dangerous test to use for ending a loop, since there is only one way that it can be satisfied.

First, localize the problem

If you check and recheck your loop and can find no error, but your program still misbehaves, then you will need to do some more sophisticated testing. First, make sure that the mistake is indeed in the loop. Just because the program is performing incorrectly does not mean the bug is where you think it is. If your program is divided into functions, it should be easy to determine the approximate location of the bug or bugs.

Once you have decided that the bug is in a particular loop, you should watch the loop change the value of variables while the program is running. This way you can see what the loop is doing and thus see what it is doing wrong. Watching the value of a variable change while the program is running is called **tracing** the variable. Many systems have debugging utilities that allow you to easily trace variables without making any changes to your program. If your system has such a debugging utility, it would be well worth your effort to learn how to use it. If your system does not have a debugging utility, you can trace a variable by placing a temporary cout statement in the loop body; that way the value of the variable will be written to the screen on each loop iteration.

For example, consider the following piece of program code, which needs to be debugged:

```
int next = 2, product = 1;
while (next < 5)
{
    next++;
    product = product * next;
}
//The variable product contains
//the product of the numbers 2 through 5.
```

The comment at the end of the loop tells what the loop is supposed to do, but we have tested it and know that it gives the variable product an incorrect value. We need to find out what is wrong. To help us debug this loop, we trace the variables next and product. If you have a debugging utility, you could use it. If you do not have a debugging facility, you can trace the variables by inserting a cout statement as follows:

```
int next = 2, product = 1;
while (next < 5)
{
    next++;
    product = product * next;
    cout << "next = " << next
         << " product = " << product << endl;
}
```

When we trace the variables product and next, we find that after the first loop iteration, the values of product and next are both 3. It is then clear to us that we have multiplied only the numbers 3 through 5 and have missed multiplying by 2.

There are at least two good ways to fix this bug. The easiest fix is to initialize the variable next to 1, rather than 2. That way, when next is incremented the first time through the loop, it will receive the value 2 rather than 3. Another way to fix the loop is to place the increment after the multiplication, as follows:

```
int next = 2, product = 1;
while (next < 5)
{
    product = product * next;
    next++;
}
```

Let's assume we fix the bug by moving the statement next++ as indicated above. After we add this fix, we are not yet done. We must test this revised code. When we test it, we will see that it still gives an incorrect result. If we again trace variables, we will discover that the loop stops after multiplying by 4, and never multiplies by 5. This tells us that the Boolean expression should now use a less-than-or-equal sign, rather than a less-than sign. Thus, the correct code is

```
int next = 2, product = 1;
while (next <= 5)
{
    product = product * next;
    next++;
}
```

Every change
requires retesting

Every time you change a program, you should retest the program. Never assume that your change will make the program correct. Just because you found one thing to correct does not mean you have found all the things that need to be corrected. Also, as illustrated by this example, when you change one part of your program to make it correct, that change may require you to change some other part of the program as well.

Testing a Loop

Every loop should be tested with inputs that cause each of the following loop behaviors (or as many as are possible): zero iterations of the loop body, one iteration of the loop body, the maximum number of iterations of the loop body, and one less than the maximum number of iterations of the loop body. (This is only a minimal set of test situations. You should also conduct other tests that are particular to the loop you are testing.)

The techniques we have developed will help you find the few bugs that may find their way into a well-designed program. However, no amount of debugging can convert a poorly designed program into a reliable and readable one. If a program or algorithm is very difficult to understand or performs very poorly, do not try to fix it. Instead, throw it away and start over. This will result in a program that is easier to read and that is less likely to contain hidden errors. What may not be so obvious is that by throwing out the poorly designed code and starting over, you will produce a working program faster than if you try to repair the old code. It may seem like wasted effort to throw out all the code that you worked so hard on, but that is the most efficient way to proceed. The work that went into the discarded code is not wasted. The lessons you learned by writing it will help you to design a better program faster than if you started with no experience. The bad code itself is unlikely to help at all.

Debugging a Very Bad Program

If your program is very bad, do not try to debug it. Instead, throw it out and start over.

SELF-TEST EXERCISES

myprogramminglab

39. What does it mean to trace a variable? How do you trace a variable?

40. What is an off-by-one loop error?

41. You have a fence that is to be 100 meters long. Your fence posts are to be placed every 10 feet. How many fence posts do you need? Why is the presence of this problem in a programming book not as silly as it might seem? What problem that programmers have does this question address?

CHAPTER SUMMARY

- Boolean expressions are evaluated similarly to the way arithmetic expressions are evaluated.

- Most modern compilers have a *bool* type having the values *true* and *false*.

- You can write a function so that it returns a value of *true* or *false*. A call to such a function can be used as a Boolean expression in an *if-else* statement or anywhere else that a Boolean expression is permitted.

- One approach to solving a task or subtask is to write down conditions and corresponding actions that need to be taken under each condition. This can be implemented in C++ as a multiway *if-else* statement.

- A *switch* statement is a good way to implement a menu for the user of your program.

- A **block** is a compound statement that contains variable declarations. The variables declared in a block are local to the block. Among other uses, blocks can be used for the action in one branch of a multiway branch statement, such as a multiway *if-else* statement.

- A *for* loop can be used to obtain the equivalent of the instruction "repeat the loop body *n* times."

- There are four commonly used methods for terminating an input loop: list headed by size, ask before iterating, list ended with a sentinel value, and running out of input.

- It is usually best to design loops in pseudocode that does not specify a choice of C++ looping mechanism. Once the algorithm has been designed, the choice of which C++ loop statement to use is usually clear.

- One way to simplify your reasoning about nested loops is to make the loop body a function call.

- Always check loops to be sure that the variables used by the loop are properly initialized before the loop begins.

- Always check loops to be certain they are not iterated one too many or one too few times.

- When debugging loops, it helps to trace key variables in the loop body.

- If a program or algorithm is very difficult to understand or performs very poorly, do not try to fix it. Instead, throw it away and start over.

Answers to Self-Test Exercises

1. a. *true*.

   b. *true*. Note that expressions (a) and (b) mean exactly the same thing. Because the operators == and < have higher precedence than &&, you do not need to include the parentheses. The parentheses do, however, make it easier to read. Most people find the expression in (a) easier to read than the expression in (b), even though they mean the same thing.

   c. *true*.

   d. *true*.

   e. *false*. Since the value of the first subexpression (count == 1) is *false*, you know that the entire expression is *false* without bothering to evaluate the second subexpression. Thus, it does not matter what the values of x and y are. This is called *short-circuit evaluation*, which is what C++ does.

   f. *true*. Since the value of the first subexpression (count < 10) is *true*, you know that the entire expression is *true* without bothering to evaluate the second subexpression. Thus, it does not matter what the values of x and y are. This is called *short-circuit evaluation*, which is what C++ does.

   g. *false*. Notice that the expression in (g) includes the expression in (f) as a subexpression. This subexpression is evaluated using short-circuit evaluation as we described for (f). The entire expression in (g) is equivalent to

   ```
   !( (true || (x < y)) && true )
   ```

   which in turn is equivalent to !(*true* && *true*), and that is equivalent to !(*true*), which is equivalent to the final value of *false*.

   h. This expression produces an error when it is evaluated because the first subexpression ((limit/count) > 7) involves a division by zero.

i. *true*. Since the value of the first subexpression (`limit < 20`) is *true*, you know that the entire expression is *true* without bothering to evaluate the second subexpression. Thus, the second subexpression

    `((limit/count) > 7)`

is never evaluated and so the fact that it involves a division by zero is never noticed by the computer. This is short-circuit evaluation, which is what C++ does.

j. This expression produces an error when it is evaluated because the first subexpression (`(limit/count) > 7`) involves a division by zero.

k. *false*. Since the value of the first subexpression (`limit < 0`) is *false*, you know that the entire expression is *false* without bothering to evaluate the second subexpression. Thus, the second subexpression

    `((limit/count) > 7)`

is never evaluated and so the fact that it involves a division by zero is never noticed by the computer. This is short-circuit evaluation, which is what C++ does.

l. If you think this expression is nonsense, you are correct. The expression has no intuitive meaning, but C++ converts the *int* values to *bool* values and then evaluates the && and ! operations. Thus, C++ will evaluate this mess. Recall that in C++, any nonzero integer converts to *true*, and 0 converts to *false*. C++ will evaluate

    `(5 && 7) + (!6)`

as follows: In the expression (`5 && 7`), the 5 and 7 convert to *true*. *true* && *true* evaluates to *true*, which C++ converts to 1. In (`!6`), the 6 is converted to *true*, so `!(true)` evaluates to *false*, which C++ converts to 0. The entire expression thus evaluates to 1 + 0, which is 1. The final value is thus 1. C++ will convert the number 1 to *true*, but the answer has little intuitive meaning as *true*; it is perhaps better to just say the answer is 1.

   There is no need to become proficient at evaluating these nonsense expressions, but doing a few will help you to understand why the compiler does not give you an error message when you make the mistake of incorrectly mixing numeric and Boolean operators in a single expression.

2. To this point we have studied branching statements, iteration statements, and function call statements. Examples of branching statements we have studied are *if* and *if-else* statements. Examples of iteration statements are *while* and *do-while* statements.

3. The expression 2 < x < 3 is legal. It does not mean (2 < x)&&(x < 3) as many would wish. It means (2 < x) < 3. Since (2 < x) is a Boolean expression, its value is either *true* or *false*, which converts to 1 or 0, so that 2 < x < 3 is always *true*. The output is "true" regardless of the value of x.

4. No. The Boolean expression j > 0 is *false* (j was just assigned –1). The && uses short-circuit evaluation, which does not evaluate the second expression if the truth value can be determined from the first expression. The first expression is *false*, so the entire expression evaluates to *false* without evaluating the second expression. So, there is no division by zero.

5.
```
Start
Hello from the second if.
End
Start again
End again
```

6.
```
large
```

7.
```
small
```

8.
```
medium
```

9.
```
Start
Second Output
End
```

10. The statements are the same whether the second Boolean expression is (x > 10) or (x > 100). So, the output is the same as in Self-Test Exercise 9.

11.
```
Start
100
End
```

12. Both of the following are correct:

```
if (n < 0)
    cout << n << " is less than zero.\n";
else if ((0 <= n) && (n <= 100))
    cout << n << " is between 0 and 100 (inclusive).\n";
else if (n >100)
    cout << n << " is larger than 100.\n";
```

and

```
if (n < 0)
    cout << n << " is less than zero.\n";
```

```
else if (n <= 100)
    cout << n << " is between 0 and 100 (inclusive).\n";
else
    cout << n << " is larger than 100.\n";
```

13. *enum* constants are given default values starting at 0, unless otherwise assigned. The constants increment by 1. The output is 3 2 1 0.

14. *enum* constants are given values as assigned. Unassigned constants increment the previous value by 1. The output is 2 1 7 5.

15.   Roast worms

16.   Onion ice cream

17.   Chocolate ice cream
       Onion ice cream

   (This is because there is no *break* statement in *case* 3.)

18.   Bon appetit!

19.   42 22

20. It helps to slightly change the code fragment to understand to which declaration each usage resolves.

```
{
    int x1 = 1;    // output in this column
    cout << x1 << endl; // 1<cr>
    {
        cout << x1 << endl; // 1<cr>
        int x2 = 2;
        cout << x2 << endl; // 2<cr>
        {
            cout << x2 << endl; // 2<cr>
            int x3 = 3;
            cout << x3 << endl; // 3<cr>
        }
        cout << x2 << endl; // 2<cr>
    }
    cout << x1 << endl; // 1<cr>
}
```

   Here *<cr>* indicates that the output starts a new line.

21.   2 1 0

22.   2 1

23. 1 2 3 4

24. 1 2 3

25. 2 4 6 8

26.
```
Hello 10
Hello 8
Hello 6
Hello 4
Hello 2
```

27. 2.000000 1.500000 1.000000 0.500000

28. a. A *for* loop

b. and c. Both require a *while* loop since the input list might be empty.

c. A *do-while* loop can be used since at least one test will be performed.

29. a. *for* (*int* i = 1; i <= 10; i++)
    if (i < 5 && i != 2)
        cout << 'X';

b. *for* (i = 1; i <= 10; i = i + 3)
    cout << 'X';

c. cout << 'X'; *//necessary to keep output the same. Note*
    //also the change in initialization of m
    for (long m = 200; m < 1000; m = m + 100)
        cout << 'X';

30. The output is 1024 10. The second number is the base 2 log of the first number.

31. The output is: 1024 1. The ';' after the *for* is probably a pitfall error.

32. This is an infinite loop. Consider the update expression i = i * 2. It cannot change i because its initial value is 0, so it leaves i at its initial value, 0.

33. 4 3 End of Loop

34. 4 3

Notice that since the exit statement ends the program, the phrase End of Loop is not output.

35. A *break* statement is used to exit a loop (a *while*, *do-while*, or *for* statement) or to terminate a case in a *switch* statement. A *break* is not legal anywhere else in a C++ program. Note that if the loops are nested, a *break* statement only terminates one level of the loop.

36. ```
for (int count = 1; count <= 10; count++)
    cout << "Hello\n";
```

37. You can use any odd number as a sentinel value.

```
int sum = 0, next;
cout << "Enter a list of even numbers. Place an\n"
    << "odd number at the end of the list.\n";
cin >> next;
while ((next % 2) = = 0)
{
    sum = sum + next;
    cin >> next;
}
```

38. The output is too long to reproduce here. The pattern is as follows:

```
1 times 10 = 10
1 times 9 = 9
        .
        .
        .
1 times 1 = 1
2 times 10 = 20
2 times 9 = 18
        .
        .
        .
2 times 1 = 2
3 times 10 = 30
        .
        .
        .
```

39. *Tracing a variable* means watching a program variable change value while the program is running. This can be done with special debugging facilities or by inserting temporary output statements in the program.

40. Loops that iterate the loop body one too many or one too few times are said to have an off-by-one error.

41. Off-by-one errors abound in problem solving, not just writing loops. Typical reasoning from those who do not think carefully is

10 posts = 100 feet of fence / 10 feet between posts

This, of course, will leave the last 10 feet of fence without a post. You need 11 posts to provide 10 between-the-post 10-foot intervals to get 100 feet of fence.
```

PROGRAMMING PROJECTS

Visit www.myprogramminglab.com to complete many of these Programming Projects online and get instant feedback.

1. Using a nested *for* loop, create the following triangle structure:

   ```
   1
   2    3
   4    5    6
   7    8    9    10
   11   12   13   14   15
   ```

2. Write a program to compute the interest due, total amount due, and the minimum payment for a revolving credit account. The program accepts the account balance as input, and then adds on the interest to get the total amount due. The rate schedules are the following: the interest is 2.0 percent on the first $2,000 and 1.5 percent on any amount over that. The minimum payment is the total amount due, if that is $50 or less; otherwise, it is $50 or 20 percent of the total amount owed, whichever is larger. Your program should include a loop that lets the user repeat this calculation until the user says she or he is done.

3. Write an astrology program. The user types in a birthday, and the program responds with the sign and horoscope for that birthday. The month may be entered as a number from 1 to 12. Then enhance your program so that if the birthday is only one or two days away from an adjacent sign, the program announces that the birthday is on a "cusp" and also outputs the horoscope for that nearest adjacent sign. This program will have a long multiway branch. Make up a horoscope for each sign. Your program should include a loop that lets the user repeat this calculation until the user says she or he is done.

   The horoscope signs and dates are:

Aries	March 21–April 19
Taurus	April 20–May 20
Gemini	May 21–June 21
Cancer	June 22–July 22
Leo	July 23–August 22
Virgo	August 23–September 22
Libra	September 23–October 22
Scorpio	October 23–November 21
Sagittarius	November 22–December 21
Capricorn	December 22–January 19
Aquarius	January 20–February 18
Pisces	February 19–March 20

4. Write a program which will print the following triangle

```
                        1
               1                 1
          1              2              1
        1         3           3          1
      1       4         6           4        1
   1       5        10          10        5        1
```

You can use a nested *for* loop or *while* loop to write this program.

5. Write a program that computes the cost of a long-distance call. The cost of the call is determined according to the following rate schedule:

   a. Any call started between 8:00 am and 6:00 pm, Monday through Friday, is billed at a rate of $0.40 per minute.

   b. Any call starting before 8:00 am or after 6:00 pm, Monday through Friday, is charged at a rate of $0.25 per minute.

   c. Any call started on a Saturday or Sunday is charged at a rate of $0.15 per minute.

   The input will consist of the day of the week, the time the call started, and the length of the call in minutes. The output will be the cost of the call. The time is to be input in 24-hour notation, so the time 1:30 pm is input as

   13:30

   The day of the week will be read as one of the following pairs of character values, which are stored in two variables of type *char*:

   Mo Tu We Th Fr Sa Su

   Be sure to allow the user to use either uppercase or lowercase letters or a combination of the two. The number of minutes will be input as a value of type *int*. (You can assume that the user rounds the input to a whole number of minutes.) Your program should include a loop that lets the user repeat this calculation until the user says she or he is done.

6. (This Project requires that you know some basic facts about complex numbers, so it is only appropriate if you have studied complex numbers in some mathematics class.)

   Write a C++ program that solves a quadratic equation to find its roots. The roots of a quadratic equation

   ax² + bx + c = 0

   (where a is not zero) are given by the formula

   (–b ± sqrt(b² – 4ac)) / 2a

The value of the discriminant ($b^2 - 4ac$) determines the nature of roots. If the value of the discriminant is zero, then the equation has a single real root. If the value of the discriminant is positive then the equation has two real roots. If the value of the discriminant is negative, then the equation has two complex roots.

The program takes values of a, b, and c as input and outputs the roots. Be creative in how you output complex roots. Include a loop that allows the user to repeat this calculation for new input values until the user says she or he wants to end the program.

7. Using a nested *while* loop, create the following pyramid-like triangle structure:

```
                           1
                     2     3     4
               5     6     7     8     9
         10    11    12    13    14    15    16
      17 18    19    20    21    22    23    24    25
26    27 28    29    30    31    32    33    34    35    36
```

You can then modify your program using a *for* loop instead of a *while* loop.

8. Write a program that scores a blackjack hand. In blackjack, a player receives from two to five cards. The cards 2 through 10 are scored as 2 through 10 points each. The face cards—jack, queen, and king—are scored as 10 points. The goal is to come as close to a score of 21 as possible without going over 21. Hence, any score over 21 is called "busted." The ace can count as either 1 or 11, whichever is better for the user. For example, an ace and a 10 can be scored as either 11 or 21. Since 21 is a better score, this hand is scored as 21. An ace and two 8s can be scored as either 17 or 27. Since 27 is a "busted" score, this hand is scored as 17.

The user is asked how many cards she or he has, and the user responds with one of the integers 2, 3, 4, or 5. The user is then asked for the card values. Card values are 2 through 10, jack, queen, king, and ace. A good way to handle input is to use the type *char* so that the card input 2, for example, is read as the character '2', rather than as the number 2. Input the values 2 through 9 as the characters '2' through '9'. Input the values 10, jack, queen, king, and ace as the characters 't', 'j', 'q', 'k', and 'a'. (Of course, the user does not type in the single quotes.) Be sure to allow upper- as well as lowercase letters as input.

After reading in the values, the program should convert them from character values to numeric card scores, taking special care for aces. The output is either a number between 2 and 21 (inclusive) or the word Busted. You are likely to have one or more long multiway branches that use a *switch* statement or nested *if-else* statement. Your program should include a loop that lets the user repeat this calculation until the user says she or he is done.

9. Interest on a loan is paid on a declining balance, and hence a loan with an interest rate of, say, 12 percent can cost significantly less than 12 percent of the balance. Write a program that takes a loan amount and interest rate as input, and then outputs the monthly payments and balance of the loan until the loan is paid off. Assume that the monthly payments are one-tenth of the original loan amount, and that any amount in excess of the interest is credited toward decreasing the balance due. Thus, on a loan of $30,000, the payments would be $3,000 a month. If the interest rate is 15 percent, then each month the interest is one-twelfth of 15 percent of the remaining balance. The first month, (15 percent of $30,000)/12, or $375, would be paid in interest, and the remaining $2,625 would decrease the balance to $27,375. The following month the interest would be (15 percent of $27,375)/12, and so forth. Also have the program output the total interest paid over the life of the loan.

Finally, determine what simple annualized percentage of the original loan balance was paid in interest. Your program should allow the user to repeat this calculation as often as desired.

10. The Fibonacci numbers F_n are defined as follows. F_0 is 1, F_1 is 1, and

$$F_{i+2} = F_i + F_{i+1}$$

$i = 0, 1, 2, \ldots$. In other words, each number is the sum of the previous two numbers. The first few Fibonacci numbers are 1, 1, 2, 3, 5, and 8. One place that these numbers occur is as certain population growth rates. If a population has no deaths, then the series shows the size of the population after each time period. It takes an organism two time periods to mature to reproducing age, and then the organism reproduces once every time period. The formula applies most straightforwardly to asexual reproduction at a rate of one offspring per time period.

Assume that the green crud population grows at this rate and has a time period of 5 days. Hence, if a green crud population starts out as 10 pounds of crud, then in 5 days there is still 10 pounds of crud; in 10 days there is 20 pounds of crud, in 15 days 30 pounds, in 20 days 50 pounds, and so forth. Write a program that takes both the initial size of a green crud population (in pounds) and a number of days as input, and that outputs the number of pounds of green crud after that many days. Assume that the population size is the same for 4 days and then increases every fifth day. Your program should allow the user to repeat this calculation as often as desired.

11. The value e^x can be approximated by the sum

$$1 + x + x^2/2! + x^3/3! + \ldots + x^n/n!$$

Write a program that takes a value x as input and outputs this sum for n taken to be each of the values 1 to 100. The program should also output e^x calculated using the predefined function exp. The function exp is a predefined function such that exp(x) returns an approximation to the value e^x. The function exp is in the library with the header file cmath. Your program should repeat the calculation for new values of x until the user says she or he is through.

Use variables of type double to store the factorials or you are likely to produce integer overflow (or arrange your calculation to avoid any direct calculation of factorials). 100 lines of output might not fit comfortably on your screen. Output the 100 output values in a format that will fit all 100 values on the screen. For example, you might output 10 lines with 10 values on each line.

12. An approximated value of f(n) can be calculated using the series given below:

$$f(n) = 3 \; [- 1/2 + 1/4 - 1/6 + 1/8 - 1/10 \; ... \; - ((-1)^{n-1})/(2n + 2) \;]$$

Write a C++ program to calculate the approximated value of f(n) using this series. The program takes an input n that determines the number of terms in the approximation of the value of f(n) and outputs the approximation. Include a loop that allows the user to repeat this calculation for new values n until the user says she or he wants to end the program.

VideoNote
**Solution to Programming
Project 3.13**

13. The following problem is sometimes called "The Monty Hall Game Show Problem." You are a contestant on a game show and have won a shot at the grand prize. Before you are three closed doors. Behind one door is a brand new car. Behind the other two doors are consolation prizes. The location of the prizes is randomly selected. The game show host asks you to select a door, and you pick one. However, before revealing the contents behind your door, the game show host reveals one of the other doors with a consolation prize. At this point, the game show host asks if you would like to stick with your original choice or switch your choice to the other closed door. What choice should you make to optimize your chances of winning the car? Does it matter whether you stick with your original choice or switch doors?

Write a simulation program to solve the game show problem. Your program should make 10,000 simulated runs through the problem, randomly selecting locations for the prize, and then counting the number of times the car was won when sticking with the original choice, and counting the number of times the car was won when switching doors. Output the estimated probability of winning for both strategies. Be sure that your program exactly simulates the process of selecting the door, revealing one, and then switching. Do not make assumptions about the actual solution (for example, simply assuming that there is a 1/3 or 1/2 chance of getting the prize).

Appendix 4 gives library functions for generating random numbers. A more detailed description is provided in Chapter 4.

14. Write a program that finds and prints all of the prime numbers between 10 and 200. A prime number is a number such that 1 and itself are the only numbers that evenly divide it (for example, 11, 13, 17…).

> One way to solve this problem is to use a doubly nested loop. The outer loop can iterate from 10 to 200 while the inner loop checks to see if the counter value for the outer loop is prime. One way to see if number n is prime is to loop from 2 to $n - 1$ and if any of these numbers evenly divides n, then n cannot be prime. If none of the values from 2 to $n - 1$ evenly divides n, then n must be prime. (Note that there are several easy ways to make this algorithm more efficient.)

15. Buoyancy is the ability of an object to float. Archimedes' principle states that the buoyant force is equal to the weight of the fluid that is displaced by the submerged object. The buoyant force can be computed by

$$F_b = V \times y$$

where F_b is the buoyant force, V is the volume of the submerged object, and y is the specific weight of the fluid. If F_b is greater than or equal to the weight of the object, then it will float, otherwise it will sink.

Write a program that inputs the weight (in pounds) and radius (in feet) of a sphere and outputs whether the sphere will sink or float in water. Use $y = 62.4 \text{ lb/ft}^3$ as the specific weight of water. The volume of a sphere is computed by $(4/3)\pi r^3$.

16. Write a program that finds the temperature on the Kelvin scale and the corresponding Fahrenheit scale temperature value. The formula to convert from Kelvin to Fahrenheit is

Fahrenheit = ((Kelvin − 273) * 1.8) + 32

Your program should create two integer variables for the temperature in Kelvin and Fahrenheit and then initialize the Kelvin temperature to 0 degrees Kelvin. In a loop, increment the Kelvin value and compute the corresponding temperature in Fahrenheit until the Kelvin temperature becomes 273.

> Since you are working with integer values, the formula may not give an exact result for every possible Kelvin temperature. This will not affect your solution to this particular problem.

17. Repeat Programming Project 18 from Chapter 2 but in addition ask the user if he or she is:

a. Sedentary

b. Somewhat active (exercise occasionally)

c. Active (exercise 3–4 days per week)

d. Highly active (exercise every day)

If the user answers "Sedentary," then increase the calculated BMR by 20 percent. If the user answers "Somewhat active," then increase the calculated BMR by 30 percent. If the user answers "Active," then increase the calculated BMR by 40 percent. Finally, if the user answers "Highly active," then increase the calculated BMR by 50 percent. Output the number of chocolate bars based on the new BMR value.

VideoNote
Solution to Programming
Project 3.18

18. The keypad on your oven is used to enter the desired baking temperature and is arranged like the digits on a phone:

1	2	3
4	5	6
7	8	9
	0	

Unfortunately the circuitry is damaged and the digits in the leftmost column no longer function. In other words, the digits 1, 4, and 7 do not work. If a recipe calls for a temperature that can't be entered, then you would like to substitute a temperature that can be entered. Write a program that inputs a desired temperature. The temperature must be between 0 and 999 degrees. If the desired temperature does not contain 1, 4, or 7, then output the desired temperature. Otherwise, compute the next largest and the next smallest temperature that does not contain 1, 4, or 7 and output both.

For example, if the desired temperature is 450, then the program should output 399 and 500. Similarly, if the desired temperature is 375, then the program should output 380 and 369.

19. The game of "23" is a two-player game that begins with a pile of 23 tooth-picks. Players take turns, withdrawing either 1, 2, or 3 toothpicks at a time. The player to withdraw the last toothpick loses the game. Write a human vs. computer program that plays "23". The human should always move first. When it is the computer's turn, it should play according to the following rules:

- If there are more than 4 toothpicks left, then the computer should withdraw $4 - X$ toothpicks, where X is the number of toothpicks the human withdrew on the previous turn.
- If there are 2 to 4 toothpicks left, then the computer should withdraw enough toothpicks to leave 1.
- If there is 1 toothpick left, then the computer has to take it and loses.

When the human player enters the number of toothpicks to withdraw, the program should perform input validation. Make sure that the entered number is between 1 and 3 and that the player is not trying to withdraw more toothpicks than exist in the pile.

Procedural Abstraction and Functions That Return a Value

4

There was a most ingenious Architect who had contrived a new method for building Houses, by beginning at the Roof, and working downward to the Foundation.

JONATHAN SWIFT, *Gulliver's Travels*

INTRODUCTION

A program can be thought of as consisting of subparts, such as obtaining the input data, calculating the output data, and displaying the output data. C++, like most programming languages, has facilities to name and code each of these subparts separately. In C++ these subparts are called *functions*. In this chapter we present the basic syntax for one of the two main kinds of C++ functions—namely those designed to compute a single value. We also discuss how these functions can aid in program design. We begin with a discussion of a fundamental design principle.

Prerequisites

You should read Chapter 2 and at least look through Chapter 1 before reading this chapter.

4.1 TOP-DOWN DESIGN

Remember that the way to write a program is to first design the method that the program will use and to write out this method in English, as if the instructions were to be followed by a human clerk. As we noted in Chapter 1, this set of instructions is called an *algorithm*. A good plan of attack for designing the algorithm is to break down the task to be accomplished into a few subtasks, decompose each of these subtasks into smaller subtasks, and so forth. Eventually, the subtasks become so small that they are trivial to implement in C++. This method is called **top-down design.** (The method is also sometimes called **stepwise refinement,** or more graphically, **divide and conquer.**)

Using the top-down method, you design a program by breaking the program's task into subtasks and solving these subtasks by subalgorithms. Preserving this top-down structure in your C++ program makes the program easier to understand, easier to change if need be, and, as will become apparent, easier to write, test, and debug. C++, like most programming languages, has facilities to include separate subparts inside of a program. In other programming languages these subparts are called *subprograms*, *procedures*, or *methods*. In C++ these subparts are called **functions.**

One of the advantages of using functions to divide a programming task into subtasks is that the program becomes easier to understand, test, debug, and maintain. Additionally, dividing the task allows different people to work on the different subtasks. When producing a very large program, such as a compiler or office-management system, this sort of teamwork is needed if the program is to be produced in a reasonable amount of time. We will begin our discussion of functions by showing you how to use functions that were written by somebody else.

4.2 PREDEFINED FUNCTIONS

C++ comes with libraries of predefined functions that you can use in your programs. Before we show you how to define functions, we will first show you how to use some functions that are already defined for you.

Using Predefined Functions

We will use the `sqrt` function to illustrate how you use predefined functions. The `sqrt` function calculates the square root of a number. (The square root of a number is the number that, when multiplied by itself, will produce the number you started out with. For example, the square root of 9 is 3 because 3^2 is equal to 9.) The function `sqrt` starts with a number, such as 9.0, and computes its square root, in this case 3.0. The value the function starts out with is called its **argument.** The value it computes is called the **value returned.** Some functions may have more than one argument, but no function has more than one value returned. If you think of the function as being similar to a small program, then the arguments are analogous to the input and the value returned is analogous to the output.

The syntax for using functions in your program is simple. To set a variable named `the_root` equal to the square root of 9.0, you can use the following assignment statement:

```
the_root = sqrt(9.0);
```

The expression `sqrt(9.0)` is called a **function call** (or if you want to be fancy you can also call it a **function invocation**). An argument in a function call can be a constant, such as 9.0, or a variable, or a more complicated expression. A function call is an expression that can be used like any other expression. You can use a function call wherever it is legal to use an expression of the type specified for the value returned by the function. For example, the value returned by `sqrt` is of type *double*. Thus, the following is legal (although perhaps stingy):

```
bonus = sqrt(sales)/10;
```

`sales` and `bonus` are variables that would normally be of type *double*. The function call `sqrt(sales)` is a single item, just as if it were enclosed in parentheses. Thus, this assignment statement is equivalent to

```
bonus = (sqrt(sales))/10;
```

You can also use a function call directly in a cout statement, as in the following:

```
cout << "The side of a square with area " << area
    << " is " << sqrt(area);
```

Display 4.1 contains a complete program that uses the predefined function sqrt. The program computes the size of the largest square dog house that can be built for the amount of money the user is willing to spend. The program asks the user for an amount of money and then determines how many square feet of floor space can be purchased for that amount of money. That calculation yields an area in square feet for the floor area of the dog house. The function sqrt yields the length of one side of the dog house floor.

Notice that there is another new element in the program in Display 4.1:

```
#include <cmath>
```

Function Call

A function call is an expression consisting of the function name followed by arguments enclosed in parentheses. If there is more than one argument, the arguments are separated by commas. A function call is an expression that can be used like any other expression of the type specified for the value returned by the function.

SYNTAX

```
Function_Name(Argument_List)
```

where the *Argument_List* is a comma-separated list of arguments:

```
Argument_1, Argument_2, . . . , Argument_Last
```

EXAMPLES

```
side = sqrt(area);
cout << "2.5 to the power 3.0 is "
    << pow(2.5, 3.0);
```

That line looks very much like the line

```
#include <iostream>
```

and, in fact, these two lines are the same sort of thing. As we noted in Chapter 2, such lines are called include **directives.** The name inside the angular brackets <> is the name of a file known as a **header file.** A header file for a library provides

DISPLAY 4.1   A Function Call

```
1    //Computes the size of a dog house that can be purchased
2    //given the user's budget.
3    #include <iostream>
4    #include <cmath>
5    using namespace std;
6
7    int main( )
8    {
9        const double COST_PER_SQ_FT = 10.50;
10       double budget, area, length_side;
11
12       cout << "Enter the amount budgeted for your dog house $";
13       cin >> budget;
14
15       area = budget / COST_PER_SQ_FT;
16       length_side = sqrt(area);
17
18       cout.setf(ios::fixed);
19       cout.setf(ios::showpoint);
20       cout.precision(2);
21       cout << "For a price of $" << budget << endl
22            << "I can build you a luxurious square dog house\n"
23            << "that is " << length_side
24            << " feet on each side.\n";
25
26       return 0;
27   }
```

Sample Dialogue

```
Enter the amount budgeted for your dog house: $25.00
For a price of $25.00
I can build you a luxurious square dog house
that is 1.54 feet on each side.
```

the compiler with certain basic information about the library, and an include directive delivers this information to the compiler. This enables the linker to find object code for the functions in the library so that it can correctly link the library to your program. For example, the library iostream contains the definitions of cin and cout, and the header file for the iostream library is called iostream. The math library contains the definition of the function sqrt and a number of other mathematical functions, and the header file for this library is cmath. If your program uses a predefined function from some library, then it must contain a directive that names the header file for that library, such as the following:

```
#include <cmath>
```

Be sure to follow the syntax illustrated in our examples. Do not forget the symbols < and >; they are the same symbols as the less-than and greater-than symbols. There should be no space between the < and the filename, nor between the filename and the >. Also, some compilers require that directives have no spaces around the #, so it is always safest to place the # at the very start of the line and not to put any space between the # and the word `include`. These `#include` directives are normally placed at the beginning of the file containing your program.

As we noted before, the directive

```
#include <iostream>
```

requires that you also use the following *using* directive:

```
using namespace std;
```

This is because the definitions of names like `cin` and `cout`, which are given in `iostream`, define those names to be part of the `std` namespace. This is true of most standard libraries. If you have an `include` directive for a standard library such as

```
#include <cmath>
```

then you probably need the *using* directive:

```
using namespace std;
```

There is no need to use multiple copies of this *using* directive when you have multiple `include` directives.

**#include may
not be enough**

Usually, all you need to do to use a library is to place an `include` directive and a *using* directive for that library in the file with your program. If things work with just the `include` directive and the *using* directive, you need not worry about doing anything else. However, for some libraries on some systems, you may need to give additional instructions to the compiler or to explicitly run a linker program to link in the library. Early C and C++ compilers did not automatically search all libraries for linking. The details vary from one system to another, so you will have to check your manual or a local expert to see exactly what is necessary.

Some people will tell you that `include` directives are not processed by the compiler, but are processed by a **preprocessor.** They're right, but the difference is more of a word game than anything that need concern you. On almost all compilers the preprocessor is called automatically when you compile your program.

A few predefined functions are described in Display 4.2; more predefined functions are described in Appendix 4. Notice that the absolute value functions `abs` and `labs` are in the library with header file `cstdlib`, so any program that uses either of these functions must contain the following directive:

```
#include <cstdlib>
```

All the other functions listed are in the library with header file cmath, just like sqrt.

Also notice that there are three absolute value functions. If you want to produce the absolute value of a number of type *int*, you use abs; if you want to produce the absolute value of a number of type *long*, you use labs; and if you want to produce the absolute value of a number of type *double*, you use fabs. To complicate things even more, abs and labs are in the library with header file cstdlib, while fabs is in the library with header file cmath. fabs is an abbreviation for *floating-point absolute value*. Recall that numbers with a fraction after the decimal point, such as numbers of type *double*, are often called *floating-point numbers*.

Another example of a predefined function is pow, which is in the library with header file cmath. The function pow can be used to do exponentiation in C++. For example, if you want to set a variable result equal to x^y, you can use the following:

```
result = pow(x, y);
```

DISPLAY 4.2 Some Predefined Functions

Name	Description	Type of Arguments	Type of Value Returned	Example	Value	Library Header
sqrt	square root	*double*	*double*	sqrt(4.0)	2.0	cmath
pow	powers	*double*	*double*	pow(2.0,3.0)	8.0	cmath
abs	absolute value for *int*	*int*	*int*	abs(-7) abs(7)	7 7	cstdlib
labs	absolute value for *long*	*long*	*long*	labs(-70000) labs(70000)	70000 70000	cstdlib
fabs	absolute value for *double*	*double*	*double*	fabs(-7.5) fabs(7.5)	7.5 7.5	cmath
ceil	ceiling (round up)	*double*	*double*	ceil(3.2) ceil(3.9)	4.0 4.0	cmath
floor	floor (round down)	*double*	*double*	floor(3.2) floor(3.9)	3.0 3.0	cmath
srand	Seed random number generator	*none*	*none*	srand()	none	cstdlib
rand	Random number	*none*	*int*	rand()	0–RAND _MAX	cstdlib

Hence, the following three lines of program code will output the number 9.0 to the screen, because $(3.0)^{2.0}$ is 9.0:

```
double result, x = 3.0, y = 2.0;
result = pow(x, y);
cout << result;
```

Arguments have a type

Notice that the above call to pow returns 9.0, not 9. The function pow always returns a value of type *double*, not of type *int*. Also notice that the function pow requires two arguments. A function can have any number of arguments. Moreover, every argument position has a specified type and the argument used in a function call should be of that type. In many cases, if you use an argument of the wrong type, then some automatic type conversion will be done for you by C++. However, the results may not be what you intended. When you call a function, you should use arguments of the type specified for that function. One exception to this caution is the automatic conversion of arguments from type *int* to type *double*. In many situations, including calls to the function pow, you can safely use an argument of type *int* when an argument of type *double* is specified.

Restrictions on pow

Many implementations of pow have a restriction on what arguments can be used. In these implementations, if the first argument to pow is negative, then the second argument must be a whole number. Since you probably have enough other things to worry about when learning to program, it might be easiest and safest to use pow only when the first argument is nonnegative.

Random Number Generation

Random and pseudorandom numbers

Games and simulation programs often require the generation of random numbers. C++ has a predefined function to generate *pseudorandom numbers*. A pseudorandom number is one that appears to be random but is really determined by a predictable formula. For example, here is the formula for a very simple pseudorandom number generator that specifies the ith random number R_i based on the previously generated random number R_{i-1}:

$$R_i = (R_{i-1} \times 7) \% 11$$

Let's set the initial "seed," $R_0 = 1$. The first time we fetch a "random" number we compute R_1 with the formula:

$$R_1 = (R_0 \times 7) \% 11 = (1 \times 7) \% 11 = 7 \% 11 \quad = 7$$

The second time we fetch a "random" number we compute R_2 with:

$$R_2 = (R_1 \times 7) \% 11 = (7 \times 7) \% 11 = 49 \% 11 = 5$$

The third time we fetch a "random" number we compute R_3 with:

$$R_3 = (R_2 \times 7) \% 11 = (5 \times 7) \% 11 = 35 \% 11 = 2$$

and so on.

As you can see, each successive value seems random unless we know the formula. This is why they are called pseudorandom. This particular function would not be a very good pseudorandom number generator because it would repeat numbers rather quickly. The random number generator in C++ varies depending upon the library implementation but uses the same basic idea as our simple generator with some enhancements to achieve a random uniform distribution.

We can get a different sequence of random numbers if we start with a different seed value. In the example, the seed always started at 1. However, if the seed is initialized with a number that changes, such as the time on the computer's clock, then we will likely get a different sequence of random numbers every time we run the program.

To seed C++'s random number generator use the predefined method srand. It returns no value and takes as input an unsigned integer that is the initial seed value. To always seed the random number generator with the value 35, we would use:

```
srand(35);
```

To vary the random number sequence every time the program is executed, we can seed the random number generator with the time of day. Invoking the predefined function time(0) returns the number of seconds that have elapsed since January 1, 1970[1] on most systems. The time function requires you to include the ctime library.

```
#include <cstdlib>
#include <ctime>
...
srand(time(0));
```

We can get a random number by calling the function rand, which will return an integer in the range 0 to RAND_MAX. RAND_MAX is a constant defined in cstdlib and is guaranteed to be 32767 or higher. Usually, a number between 0 and RAND_MAX is not what is desired, in which case the random number can be scaled by modulus and addition. For example, to simulate rolling a six-sided die we could use the following:

```
int die = (rand() % 6) + 1;
```

The random number modulo 6 gives us a number between 0 and 5. Adding 1 results in a random integer that is in the range from 1 to 6.

It is important to seed the random number generator only once. A common error is to invoke srand every time a random number is generated. If both srand and rand are placed in a loop, then the likely result is a sequence of identical numbers, because the computer runs quickly enough that the time value will probably not change for repeated calls to srand.

---

[1]The number of seconds elapsed since January 1, 1970 is known as Unix time.

Type Casting

Division may
require the
type double

Recall that 9/2 is integer division and evaluates to 4, not 4.5. If you want division to produce an answer of type *double* (that is, including the fractional part after the decimal point), then at least one of the two numbers in the division must be of type *double*. For example, 9/2.0 evaluates to 4.5. If one of the two numbers is given as a constant, you can simply add a decimal point and a zero to one (or both) numbers, and the division will then produce a value that includes the digits after the decimal point.

But what if both of the operands in a division are variables, as in the following?

```
int total_candy, number_of_people;
double candy_per_person;
<The program somehow sets the value of total_candy to 9
        and the value of number_of_people to 2.
        It does not matter how the program does this.>
candy_per_person = total_candy/number_of_people;
```

Unless you convert the value in one of the variables total_candy or number_of_people to a value of type *double*, then the result of the division will be 4, not 4.5 as it should be. The fact that the variable candy_per_person is of type *double* does not help. The value of 4 obtained by division will be converted to a value of type *double* before it is stored in the variable candy_per_person, but that will be too late. The 4 will be converted to 4.0 and the final value of candy_per_person will be 4.0, not 4.5. If one of the quantities in the division were a constant, you could add a decimal point and a zero to convert the constant to type *double*, but in this case both quantities are variables. Fortunately, there is a way to convert from type *int* to type *double* that you can use with either a constant or a variable.

In C++ you can tell the computer to convert a value of type *int* to a value of type *double*. The way that you write "Convert the value 9 to a value of type *double*" is

```
static_cast<double>(9)
```

The notation *static_cast<double>* is a kind of predefined function that converts a value of some other type, such as 9, to a value of type *double*, in this case 9.0. An expression such as *static_cast<double>*(9) is called a **type cast**. You can use a variable or other expression in place of the 9. You can use other type names besides *double* to obtain a type cast to some type other than *double*, but we will postpone that topic until later.

For example, in the following we use a type cast to change the type of 9 from *int* to *double* and so the value of answer is set to 4.5:

```
double answer;
    answer = static_cast<double>(9)/2;
```

Type casting applied to a constant, such as 9, can make your code easier to read, since it makes your intended meaning clearer. But type casting applied to constants of type *int* does not give you any additional power. You can use 9.0 instead of *static_cast<double>*(9) when you want to convert 9 to a value of type *double*. However, if the division involves only variables, then type casting may be your only sensible alternative. Using type casting, we can rewrite our earlier example so that the variable candy_per_person receives the correct value of 4.5, instead of 4.0; in order to do this, the only change we need is the replacement of total_candy with *static_cast<double>*(total_candy), as shown in what follows:

```
int total_candy, number_of_people;
double candy_per_person;
<The program somehow sets the value of total_candy to 9
    and the value of number_of_people to 2.
    It does not matter how the program does this.>
candy_per_person =
    static_cast<double>(total_candy)/number_of_people;
```

Notice the placement of parentheses in the type casting used in the code. You want to do the type casting before the division so that the division operator is working on a value of type *double*. If you wait until after the division is completed, then the digits after the decimal point are already lost. If you mistakenly use the following for the last line of the previous code, then the value of candy_per_person will be 4.0, not 4.5.

Warning!

```
candy_per_person =
    static_cast<double>(total_candy/number_of_people); //WRONG!
```

A Function to Convert from *int* to *double*

The notation *static_cast<double>* can be used as a predefined function and will convert a value of some other type to a value of type *double*. For example, *static_cast<double>*(2) returns 2.0. This is called **type casting**. (Type casting can be done with types other than *double*, but until later in this book, we will do type casting only with the type *double*.)

SYNTAX

```
static_cast<double>(Expression_of_Type_int)
```

EXAMPLE

```
int total_pot, number_of_winners;
double your_winnings;
    . . .
your_winnings =
    static_cast<double>(total_pot)/number_of_winners;
```

Older Form of Type Casting

double used
as a function

The use of *static_cast<double>*, as we discussed in the previous section, is the preferred way to perform a type cast. However, older versions of C++ used a different notation for type casting. This older notation simply uses the type name as if it were a function name, so *double*(9) returns 9.0. Thus, if candy_per_person is a variable of type *double*, and if both total_candy and number_of_people are variables of type *int*, then the following two assignment statements are equivalent:

```
candy_per_person =
    static_cast<double>(total_candy)/number_of_people;
```

and

```
candy_per_person =
    double(total_candy)/number_of_people;
```

Although *static_cast<double>*(total_candy) and *double*(total_candy) are more or less equivalent, you should use the *static_cast<double>* form, since the form *double*(total_candy) may be discontinued in later versions of C++.

PITFALL Integer Division Drops the Fractional Part

In integer division, such as computing 11/2, it is easy to forget that 11/2 gives 5, not 5.5. The result is the next-lower integer. For example,

```
double d;
d = 11/2;
```

Here, the division is done using integer divide; the result of the division is 5, which is converted to *double*, then assigned to d. The fractional part is not generated. Observe that the fact that d is of type *double* does not change the division result. The variable d receives the value 5.0, not 5.5. ■

SELF-TEST EXERCISES

1. Determine the value of each of the following arithmetic expressions:

sqrt(16.0)	sqrt(16)	pow(2.0, 3.0)
pow(2, 3)	pow(2.0, 3)	pow(1.1, 2)
abs(3)	abs(-3)	abs(0)
fabs(-3.0)	fabs(-3.5)	fabs(3.5)
ceil(5.1)	ceil(5.8)	floor(5.1)
floor(5.8)	pow(3.0, 2)/2.0	pow(3.0, 2)/2
7/abs(-2)	(7 + sqrt(4.0))/3.0	sqrt(pow(3, 2))

2. Convert each of the following mathematical expressions to a C++ arithmetic expression:

$$\sqrt{x+y} \qquad\qquad x^{y+7} \qquad\qquad \sqrt{area+fudge}$$

$$\frac{\sqrt{time+tide}}{nobody} \qquad \frac{-b+\sqrt{b^2-4ac}}{2a} \qquad |x-y|$$

3. Write a complete C++ program to compute and output the square root of PI; PI is approximately 3.14159. The *const double* PI is predefined in cmath. You are encouraged to use this predefined constant.

4. Write and compile short programs to test the following issues:

   a. Determine whether your compiler will allow the #include <iostream> anywhere on the line, or if the # needs to be flush with the left margin.

   b. Determine whether your compiler will allow space between the # and the include.

4.3 PROGRAMMER-DEFINED FUNCTIONS

A custom-tailored suit always fits better than one off the rack.

MY UNCLE, *The Tailor*

In the previous section we told you how to use predefined functions. In this section we tell you how to define your own functions.

Function Definitions

You can define your own functions, either in the same file as the main part of your program or in a separate file so that the functions can be used by several different programs. The definition is the same in either case, but for now, we will assume that the function definition will be in the same file as the main part of your program.

Display 4.3 contains a sample function definition in a complete program that demonstrates a call to the function. The function is called total_cost. The function takes two arguments—the price for one item and number of items for a purchase. The function returns the total cost, including sales tax, for that many items at the specified price. The function is called in the same way a predefined function is called. The description of the function, which the programmer must write, is a bit more complicated.

The description of the function is given in two parts that are called the *function declaration* and the *function definition*. The **function declaration** (also known as the **function prototype**) describes how the function is called. C++ requires that either the complete function definition

DISPLAY 4.3   A Function Definition

```
1     #include <iostream>                                    function declaration
2     using namespace std;
3
4     double total_cost(int number_par, double price_par);
5     //Computes the total cost, including 5% sales tax,
6     //on number_par items at a cost of price_par each.
7
8     int main( )
9     {
10        double price, bill;
11        int number;
12
13        cout << "Enter the number of items purchased: ";
14        cin >> number;
15        cout << "Enter the price per item $";
16        cin >> price;
                                           function call
17
18        bill = total_cost(number, price);
19
20        cout.setf(ios::fixed);
21        cout.setf(ios::showpoint);
22        cout.precision(2);
23        cout << number << " items at "
24            << "$" << price << " each.\n"
25            << "Final bill, including tax, is $" << bill
26            << endl;
27
28        return 0;                                  function heading
29    }
30
31    double total_cost(int number_par, double price_par)
32    {
33        const double TAX_RATE = 0.05; //5% sales tax
34        double subtotal;                            function       function
35                                                    body           definition
36        subtotal = price_par * number_par;
37        return (subtotal + subtotal * TAX_RATE);
38    }
```

Sample Dialogue

```
Enter the number of items purchased: 2
Enter the price per item: $10.10
2 items at $10.10 each.
Final bill, including tax, is $21.21
```

or the function declaration appears in the code before the function is called. The function declaration for the function `total_cost` is in color at the top of Display 4.3 and is reproduced here:

```
double total_cost(int number_par, double price_par);
```

The function declaration tells you everything you need to know in order to write a call to the function. It tells you the name of the function, in this case `total_cost`. It tells you how many arguments the function needs and what type the arguments should be; in this case, the function `total_cost` takes two arguments, the first one of type *int* and the second one of type *double*. The identifiers `number_par` and `price_par` are called *formal parameters*. A **formal parameter** is used as a kind of blank, or place holder, to stand in for the argument. When you write a function declaration, you do not know what the arguments will be, so you use the formal parameters in place of the arguments. The names of the formal parameters can be any valid identifiers, but for a while we will end our formal parameter names with _par so that it will be easier for us to distinguish them from other items in a program. Notice that a function declaration ends with a semicolon.

The first word in a function declaration specifies the **type of the value returned** by the function. Thus, for the function `total_cost`, the type of the value returned is *double*.

As you can see, the function call in Display 4.3 satisfies all the requirements given by its function declaration. Let's take a look. The function call is in the following line:

```
bill = total_cost(number, price);
```

The function call is the expression on the right-hand side of the equal sign. The function name is `total_cost`, and there are two arguments: The first argument is of type *int*, the second argument is of type *double*, and since the variable `bill` is of type *double*, it looks like the function returns a value of type *double* (which it does). All that detail is determined by the function declaration.

The compiler does not care whether there's a comment along with the function declaration, but you should always include a comment that explains what value is returned by the function.

Function Declaration

A **function declaration** tells you all you need to know to write a call to the function. A function declaration is required to appear in your code prior to a call to a function whose definition has not yet appeared. Function declarations are normally placed before the `main` part of your program.

(continued)

SYNTAX

```
Type_Returned Function_Name(Parameter_List);
Function_Declaration_Comment
```
Do not forget this semicolon.

where the *Parameter_List* is a comma-separated list of parameters:

```
Type_1 Formal_Parameter_1, Type_2 Formal_Parameter_2,...
                   ..., Type_LastFormal_Parameter_Last
```

EXAMPLE

```
double total_weight(int number, double weight_of_one);
//Returns the total weight of number items that
//each weigh weight_of_one.
```

In Display 4.3 the function definition is in color at the bottom of the display. A **function definition** describes how the function computes the value it returns. If you think of a function as a small program within your program, then the function definition is like the code for this small program. In fact, the syntax for the definition of a function is very much like the syntax for the main part of a program. A function definition consists of a *function header* followed by a *function body*. The **function header** is written the same way as the function declaration, except that the header does *not* have a semicolon at the end. This makes the header a bit repetitious, but that's OK.

Although the function declaration tells you all you need to know to write a function call, it does not tell you what value will be returned. The value returned is determined by the statements in the *function body*. The **function body** follows the function header and completes the function definition. The function body consists of declarations and executable statements enclosed within a pair of braces. Thus, the function body is just like the body of the main part of a program. When the function is called, the argument values are plugged in for the formal parameters and then the statements in the body are executed. The value returned by the function is determined when the function executes a *return* statement. (The details of this "plugging in" will be discussed in a later section.)

A ***return* statement** consists of the keyword *return* followed by an expression. The function definition in Display 4.3 contains the following *return* statement:

```
return (subtotal + subtotal * TAX_RATE);
```

When this *return* statement is executed, the value of the following expression is returned as the value of the function call:

```
(subtotal + subtotal * TAX_RATE)
```

The parentheses are not needed. The program will run exactly the same if the *return* statement is written as follows:

```
return subtotal + subtotal * TAX_RATE;
```

However, on larger expressions, the parentheses make the *return* statement easier to read. For consistency, some programmers advocate using these parentheses even on simple expressions. In the function definition in Display 4.3, there are no statements after the *return* statement, but if there were, they would not be executed. When a *return* statement is executed, the function call ends.

A Function Is Like a Small Program

To understand functions, keep the following three points in mind:

- A function definition is like a small program and calling the function is the same thing as running this "small program."

- A function uses formal parameters, rather than `cin`, for input. The arguments to the function are the input and they are plugged in for the formal parameters.

- A function (of the kind discussed in this chapter) does not normally send any output to the screen, but it does send a kind of "output" back to the program. The function returns a value, which is like the "output" for the function. The function uses a *return* statement instead of a `cout` statement for this "output."

Let's see exactly what happens when the following function call is executed in the program shown in Display 4.3:

Anatomy of a function call

```
bill = total_cost(number, price);
```

First, the values of the arguments `number` and `price` are plugged in for the formal parameters; that is, the values of the arguments `number` and `price` are substituted in for `number_par` and `price_par`. In the Sample Dialogue, `number` receives the value 2 and `price` receives the value 10.10. So 2 and 10.10 are substituted for `number_par` and `price_par`, respectively. This substitution process is known as the **call-by-value mechanism,** and the formal parameters are often referred to as **call-by-value formal parameters,** or simply as **call-by-value parameters.** There are three things that you should note about this substitution process:

1. It is the values of the arguments that are plugged in for the formal parameters. If the arguments are variables, the values of the variables, not the variables themselves, are plugged in.

2. The first argument is plugged in for the first formal parameter in the parameter list, the second argument is plugged in for the second formal parameter in the list, and so forth.

3. When an argument is plugged in for a formal parameter (for instance, when 2 is plugged in for number_par), the argument is plugged in for *all* instances of the formal parameter that occur in the function body (for instance, 2 is plugged in for number_par each time it appears in the function body).

The entire process involved in the function call shown in Display 4.3 is described in detail in Display 4.4.

DISPLAY 4.4   Details of a Function Call

```
int main()
{
    double price, bill;
    int number;

    cout << "Enter the number of items purchased: ";
    cin >> number;
    cout << "Enter the price per item $";
    cin >> price;

    bill = total_cost (number, price);
                        2          10.10
    cout.setf (ios::fixed);
    cout.setf (ios::showpoint);
    cout.precision(2);
    cout << number << " items at "
         << "$" << price << " each.\n"
21.21    << "Final bill, including tax, is $" << bill
         << endl;
    return 0;
}

                            2              10.10
double total_cost (int number_par, double price_par)
{
    const double TAX_RATE = 0.05; //5% sales tax
    double subtotal;

    subtotal = price_par * number_par;
    return (subtotal + subtotal * TAX_RATE);
}

                    21.21
```

*1. Before the function is called, values of the variables **number** and **price** are set to 2 and 10.10, by cin statements (as you can see the Sample Dialogue in Display 4.3)*

*2. The function call executes and the value of **number** (which is 2) plugged in for **number_par** and value of **price** (which is 10.10) plugged in for **price_par**.*

*3. The body of the function executes with **number_par** set to 2 and **price_par** set to 10.10, producing the value 20.20 in subtotal.*

*4. When the return statement is executed, the value of the expression after return is evaluated and returned by the function. In this case, (**subtotal + subtotal * TAX_RATE**) is (20.20 + 20.20*0.05) or 21.21.*

*5. The value 21.21 is returned to where the function was invoked. The result is that **total_cost (number, price)** is replaced by the return value of 21.21. The value of **bill** (on the left-hand side of the equal sign) is set equal to 21.21 when the statement **bill = total_cost (number, price);** finally ends.*

Functions That Return a Boolean Value

A function may return a *bool* value. Such a function can be used in a Boolean expression to control an *if-else* statement or to control a loop statement, or it can be used anywhere else that a Boolean expression is allowed. The returned type for such a function should be the type *bool*.

A call to a function that returns a Boolean value of *true* or *false* can be used anywhere that a Boolean expression is allowed. This can often make a program easier to read. By means of a function declaration, you can associate a complex Boolean expression with a meaningful name and use the name as a Boolean expression in an *if-else* statement or anywhere else that a Boolean expression is allowed. For example, the statement

```
if (((rate >= 10) && (rate < 20)) || (rate == 0))
{
    ...
}
```

can be made to read

```
if (appropriate(rate))
{
    ...
}
```

provided that the following function has been defined:

```
bool appropriate(int rate)
{
    return (((rate >= 10) && (rate < 20)) || (rate == 0));
}
```

Alternate Form for Function Declarations

You are not required to list formal parameter names in a function declaration. The following two function declarations are equivalent:

```
double total_cost(int number_par, double price_par);
```

and

```
double total_cost(int, double);
```

We will always use the first form so that we can refer to the formal parameters in the comment that accompanies the function declaration. However, you will often see the second form in manuals that describe functions.[2]

---

[2] All C++ needs to link to your program to the library for your function is the function name and sequence of types of the formal parameters. The formal parameter names are important only to the function definition. However, programs should communicate to programmers as well as to compilers. It is frequently very helpful in understanding a function to use the name that the programmer attaches to the function's data.

This alternate form applies only to function declarations. *Function headers must always list the formal parameter names.*

PITFALL   Arguments in the Wrong Order

When a function is called, the computer substitutes the first argument for the first formal parameter, the second argument for the second formal parameter, and so forth. It does not check for reasonableness. If you confuse the order of the arguments in a function call, the program will not do what you want it to do. In order to see what can go wrong, consider the program in Display 4.5. The programmer who wrote that program carelessly reversed the order of the arguments in the call to the function grade. The function call should have been

```
letter_grade = grade(score, need_to_pass);
```

This is the only mistake in the program. Yet, some poor student has been mistakenly failed in a course because of this careless mistake. The function grade is so simple that you might expect this mistake to be discovered by the programmer when the program is tested. However, if grade were a more complicated function, the mistake might easily go unnoticed.

If the type of an argument does not match the formal parameter, then the compiler may give you a warning message. Unfortunately, not all compilers will give such warning messages. Moreover, in a situation like the one in

DISPLAY 4.5   Incorrectly Ordered Arguments *(part 1 of 2)*

```
1    //Determines user's grade. Grades are Pass or Fail.
2    #include <iostream>
3    using namespace std;
4
5    char grade(int received_par, int min_score_par);
6    //Returns 'P' for passing, if received_par is
7    //min_score_par or higher. Otherwise returns 'F' for failing.
8
9    int main( )
10   {
11       int score, need_to_pass;
12       char letter_grade;
13
14       cout << "Enter your score"
15            << " and the minimum needed to pass:\n";
16       cin >> score >> need_to_pass;
17
18       letter_grade = grade(need_to_pass, score);
19
```

(continued)

DISPLAY 4.5   Incorrectly Ordered Arguments *(part 2 of 2)*

```
20          cout << "You received a score of " << score << endl
21               << "Minimum to pass is " << need_to_pass << endl;
22
23          if (letter_grade == 'P')
24              cout << "You Passed. Congratulations!\n";
25          else
26              cout << "Sorry. You failed.\n";
27
28          cout << letter_grade
29               << " will be entered in your record.\n";
30
31          return 0;
32      }
33
34      char grade(int received_par, int min_score_par)
35      {
36          if (received_par >= min_score_par)
37              return 'P';
38          else
39              return 'F';
40      }
```

Sample Dialogue

```
Enter your score and the minimum needed to pass:
98 60
You received a score of 98
Minimum to pass is 60
Sorry. You failed.
F will be entered in your record.
```

Display 4.5, no compiler will complain about the ordering of the arguments, because the function argument types will match the formal parameter types no matter what order the arguments are in. ■

Function Definition–Syntax Summary

Function declarations are normally placed before the main part of your program and function definitions are normally placed after the main part of your program (or, as we will see later in this book, in a separate file). Display 4.6 gives a summary of the syntax for a function declaration and definition. There is actually a bit more freedom than that display indicates. The declarations and executable statements in the function definition can be intermixed, as

VideoNote
Programmer-Defined
Function Example

long as each variable is declared before it is used. The rules about intermixing declarations and executable statements in a function definition are the same as they are for the main part of a program. However, unless you have reason to do otherwise, it is best to place the declarations first, as indicated in Display 4.6.

Since a function does not return a value until it executes a *return* statement, a function must contain one or more *return* statements in the body of the function. A function definition may contain more than one *return* statement. For example, the body of the code might contain an *if-else* statement, and each branch of the *if-else* statement might contain a different *return* statement, as illustrated in Display 4.5.

Spacing and line breaks

Any reasonable pattern of spaces and line breaks in a function definition will be accepted by the compiler. However, you should use the same rules for indenting and laying out a function definition as you use for the main part of a program. In particular, notice the placement of braces {} in our function definitions and in Display 4.6. The opening and closing braces that mark the ends of the function body are each placed on a line by themselves. This sets off the function body.

More About Placement of Function Definitions

We have discussed where function definitions and function declarations are normally placed. Under normal circumstances these are the best locations for the function declarations and function definitions. However, the compiler will accept programs with the function definitions and function declarations in certain other locations. A more precise statement of the rules is as follows:

DISPLAY 4.6   Syntax for a Function That Returns a Value

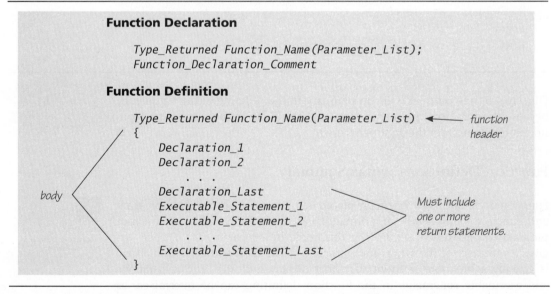

Function Declaration

```
Type_Returned Function_Name(Parameter_List);
Function_Declaration_Comment
```

Function Definition

```
Type_Returned Function_Name(Parameter_List)          function
{                                                    header
    Declaration_1
    Declaration_2
        . . .
    Declaration_Last
    Executable_Statement_1              Must include
    Executable_Statement_2             one or more
        . . .                          return statements.
    Executable_Statement_Last
}
```

body

Each function call must be preceded by either a function declaration for that function or the definition of the function. For example, if you place all of your function definitions before the main part of the program, then you need not include any function declarations. Knowing this more general rule will help you to understand C++ programs you see in some other books, but you should follow the example of the programs in this book. The style we are using sets the stage for learning how to build your own libraries of functions, which is the style that most C++ programmers use.

■ **PROGRAMMING TIP** Use Function Calls in Branching Statements

The *switch* statement and the multiway *if-else* statement allow you to place several different statements in each branch. However, doing so can make the *switch* statement or *if-else* statement difficult to read. Look at the *switch* statement in Display 3.7. Each of the branches for choices 1, 2, and 3 could be a single function call. This makes the layout of the *switch* statement and the overall structure of the program clear. If we had instead placed all the code for each branch in the *switch* statement, instead of in the function definitions, then the *switch* statement would be an incomprehensible sea of C++ statements. In fact, the *switch* statement would not even fit on one screen. ■

SELF-TEST EXERCISES

5. What is the output produced by the following program?

```cpp
#include <iostream>
using namespace std;
char mystery(int first_par, int second_par);
int main()
{
    cout << mystery(10, 9) << "ow\n";
    return 0;
}

char mystery(int first_par, int second_par)
{
    if (first_par >= second_par)
        return 'W';
    else
        return 'H';

}
```

6. Write a function declaration and a function definition for a function that takes three arguments, all of type *int*, and that returns the sum of its three arguments.

7. Write a function declaration and a function definition for a function that takes one argument of type *int* and one argument of type *double*, and that returns a value of type *double* that is the average of the two arguments.

8. Write a function declaration and a function definition for a function that takes one argument of type *double*. The function returns the character value 'P' if its argument is positive and returns 'N' if its argument is zero or negative.

9. Carefully describe the call-by-value parameter mechanism.

10. List the similarities and differences between use of a predefined (that is, library) function and a user-defined function.

11. Write a function definition for a function called in_order that takes three arguments of type *int*. The function returns *true* if the three arguments are in ascending order; otherwise, it returns *false*. For example, in_order(1, 2, 3) and in_order(1, 2, 2) both return *true*, while in_order(1, 3, 2) returns *false*.

12. Write a function definition for a function called even that takes one argument of type *int* and returns a *bool* value. The function returns *true* if its one argument is an even number; otherwise, it returns *false*.

13. Write a function definition for a function is_digit that takes one argument of type *char* and returns a *bool* value. The function returns *true* if the argument is a decimal digit; otherwise, it returns *false*.

14. Write a function definition for a function is_root_of that takes two arguments of type *int* and returns a *bool* value. The function returns *true* if the first argument is the square root of the second; otherwise, it returns *false*.

4.4 PROCEDURAL ABSTRACTION

The cause is hidden, but the result is well known.

OVID, *Metamorphoses IV*

The Black-Box Analogy

A person who uses a program should not need to know the details of how the program is coded. Imagine how miserable your life would be if you had to know and remember the code for the compiler you use. A program has a job to do, such as compile your program or check the spelling of words in your paper. You need to know *what* the program's job is so that you can use the program, but you do not (or at least should not) need to know *how* the program does its job. A function is like a small program and should be used in a similar way. A programmer who uses a function in a program needs to know *what* the function does (such as calculate a square root or convert a temperature from degrees Fahrenheit to degrees Celsius) but should not need to know *how* the function accomplishes its task. This is often referred to as treating the function like a *black box*.

Calling something a **black box** is a figure of speech intended to convey the image of a physical device that you know how to use but whose method of operation is a mystery, because it is enclosed in a black box and you cannot see inside the box (and cannot pry it open!). If a function is well designed, the programmer can use the function as if it were a black box. All the programmer needs to know is that if he or she puts appropriate arguments into the black box, then an appropriate returned value will come out of the black box. Designing a function so that it can be used as a black box is sometimes called **information hiding** to emphasize that the programmer acts as if the body of the function were hidden from view.

Display 4.7 contains the function declaration and two different definitions for a function named new_balance. As the function declaration comment explains, the function new_balance calculates the new balance in a bank account when simple interest is added. For instance, if an account starts with $100, and 4.5 percent interest is posted to the account, then the new balance is $104.50. Hence, the following code will change the value of vacation_fund from 100.00 to 104.50:

```
vacation_fund = 100.00;
vacation_fund = new_balance(vacation_fund, 4.5);
```

It does not matter which of the implementations of new_balance shown in Display 4.7 that a programmer uses. The two definitions produce functions that return exactly the same values. We may as well place a black box over the body of the function definition so that the programmer does not know which implementation is being used. In order to use the function new_balance, all the programmer needs to read is the function declaration and the accompanying comment.

Writing and using functions as if they were black boxes is also called **procedural abstraction.** When programming in C++ it might make more sense to call it *functional abstraction.* However, *procedure* is a more general term than *function.* Computer scientists use the term *procedure* for all "function-like" sets of instructions, and so they use the term *procedural abstraction.* The term *abstraction* is intended to convey the idea that when you use a function as a black box, you are abstracting away the details of the code contained in the function body. You can call this technique *the black-box principle* or *the principle*

DISPLAY 4.7 Definitions That Are Black-Box Equivalent

Function Declaration

```
1    double new_balance(double balance_par, double rate_par);
2    //Returns the balance in a bank account after
3    //posting simple interest. The formal parameter balance_par is
4    //the old balance. The formal parameter rate_par is the interest rate.
5    //For example, if rate_par is 5.0, then the interest rate is 5 percent
6    //and so new_balance(100, 5.0) returns 105.00.
```

Definition 1

```
double new_balance(double balance_par, double rate_par)
{
    double interest_fraction, interest;

    interest_fraction = rate_par/100;
    interest = interest_fraction * balance_par;
    return (balance_par + interest);
}
```

Definition 2

```
double new_balance(double balance_par, double rate_par)
{
    double interest_fraction, updated_balance;

    interest_fraction = rate_par/100;
    updated_balance = balance_par * (1 + interest_fraction);
    return updated_balance;
}
```

of *procedural abstraction* or *information hiding*. The three terms mean the same thing. Whatever you call this principle, the important point is that you should use it when designing and writing your function definitions.

Procedural Abstraction

When applied to a function definition, the principle of **procedural abstraction** means that your function should be written so that it can be used like a **black box**. This means that the programmer who uses the function should not need to look at the body of the function definition

(continued)

to see how the function works. The function declaration and the accompanying comment should be all the programmer needs to know in order to use the function. To ensure that your function definitions have this important property, you should strictly adhere to the following rules:

HOW TO WRITE A BLACK-BOX FUNCTION DEFINITION (THAT RETURNS A VALUE)

- The function declaration comment should tell the programmer any and all conditions that are required of the arguments to the function and should describe the value that is returned by the function when called with these arguments.

- All variables used in the function body should be declared in the function body. (The formal parameters do not need to be declared, because they are listed in the function declaration.)

■ PROGRAMMING TIP   Choosing Formal Parameter Names

The principle of procedural abstraction says that functions should be self-contained modules that are designed separately from the rest of the program. On large programming projects, a different programmer may be assigned to write each function. The programmer should choose the most meaningful names he or she can find for formal parameters. The arguments that will be substituted for the formal parameters may well be variables in the main part of the program. These variables should also be given meaningful names, often chosen by someone other than the programmer who writes the function definition. This makes it likely that some or all arguments will have the same names as some of the formal parameters. This is perfectly acceptable. No matter what names are chosen for the variables that will be used as arguments, these names will not produce any confusion with the names used for formal parameters. After all, the functions will use only the values of the arguments. When you use a variable as a function argument, the function takes only the value of the variable and disregards the variable name.

Now that you know you have complete freedom in choosing formal parameter names, we will stop placing a "_par" at the end of each formal parameter name. For example, in Display 4.8 we have rewritten the definition for the function total_cost from Display 4.3 so that the formal parameters are named number and price rather than number_par and price_par. If you replace the function declaration and definition of the function total_cost that appear in Display 4.3 with the versions in Display 4.8, then the program will perform in exactly the same way, even though there will be formal parameters named number and price and there will be variables in the main part of the program that are also named number and price.

DISPLAY 4.8   Simpler Formal Parameter Names

Function Declaration

```
1    double total_cost(int number, double price);
2    //Computes the total cost, including 5 percent sales tax,
3    //on number items at a cost of price each.
```

Function Definition

```
1    double total_cost(int number, double price)
2    {
3        const double TAX_RATE = 0.05; //5 percent sales tax
4        double subtotal;
5        subtotal = price * number;
6        return (subtotal + subtotal * TAX_RATE);
7    }
```

■

■ PROGRAMMING TIP   Nested Loops

When you see nested loops in your code, then you should consider whether or not to apply the principle of procedural abstraction. Consider the explicitly nested loops in Display 3.15 that computed the total number of green-necked vulture eggs counted by all conservationists. We can make this code more readable by moving the loops into procedure calls, as shown in Display 4.9.

The two versions of our program for totaling green-necked vulture eggs are equivalent. Both programs produce the same dialogue with the user. However, most people find the version in Display 4.9 easier to understand because the loop body is a function call. When considering the outer loop, you should think of computing the subtotal for one conservationist's report as a single operation and not think of it as a loop. ■

Make a Loop Body a Function Call

Whenever you have a loop nested within a loop, or any other complex computation included in a loop body, make the loop body a function call. This way you can separate the design of the loop body from the design of the rest of the program. This divides your programming task into two smaller subtasks.

DISPLAY 4.9 Nicely Nested Loops *(part 1 of 3)*

```
1    //Determines the total number of green-necked vulture eggs
2    //counted by all conservationists in the conservation district.
3    #include <iostream>
4    using namespace std;
5
6
7    int get_one_total();
8    //Precondition: User will enter a list of egg counts
9    //followed by a negative number.
10   //Postcondition: returns a number equal to the sum of all the egg counts.
11
12   int main( )
13   {
14       cout << "This program tallies conservationist reports\n"
15            << "on the green-necked vulture.\n"
16            << "Each conservationist's report consists of\n"
17            << "a list of numbers. Each number is the count of\n"
18            << "the eggs observed in one"
19            << " green-necked vulture nest.\n"
20            << "This program then tallies"
21            << " the total number of eggs.\n";
22
23       int number_of_reports;
24       cout << "How many conservationist reports are there? ";
25       cin >> number_of_reports;
26
27       int grand_total = 0, subtotal, count;
28       for (count = 1; count <= number_of_reports; count++)
29       {
30           cout << endl << "Enter the report of "
31                << "conservationist number " << count << endl;
32           subtotal = get_one_total();
33           cout << "Total egg count for conservationist "
34                << " number " << count << " is "
35                << subtotal << endl;
36           grand_total = grand_total + subtotal;
37       }
38
39       cout << endl << "Total egg count for all reports = "
40            << grand_total << endl;
41
42       return 0;
43   }
44
45
```

(continued)

DISPLAY 4.9   Nicely Nested Loops (*part 2 of 3*)

```
46    //Uses iostream:
47    int get_one_total()
48    {
49        int total;
50        cout << "Enter the number of eggs in each nest.\n"
51              << "Place a negative integer"
52              << " at the end of your list.\n";
53
54        total = 0;
55        int next;
56        cin >> next;
57        while (next >= 0)
58        {
59            total = total + next;
60            cin >> next;
61        }
62        return total;
63    }
```

Sample Dialogue

```
This program tallies conservationist reports
on the green-necked vulture.
Each conservationist's report consists of
a list of numbers. Each number is the count of
the eggs observed in one green-necked vulture nest.
This program then tallies the total number of eggs.
How many conservationist reports are there? 3

Enter the report of conservationist number 1
Enter the number of eggs in each nest.
Place a negative integer at the end of your list.
1 0 0 2 -1
Total egg count for conservationist number 1 is 3

Enter the report of conservationist number 2
Enter the number of eggs in each nest.
Place a negative integer at the end of your list.
0 3 1 -1
Total egg count for conservationist number 2 is 4

Enter the report of conservationist number 3
Enter the number of eggs in each nest.
```

(continued)

DISPLAY 4.9   Nicely Nested Loops *(part 3 of 3)*

```
Place a negative integer at the end of your list.
-1
Total egg count for conservationist number 3 is 0

Total egg count for all reports = 7
```

CASE STUDY   Buying Pizza

The large "economy" size of an item is not always a better buy than the smaller size. This is particularly true when buying pizzas. Pizza sizes are given as the diameter of the pizza in inches. However, the quantity of pizza is determined by the area of the pizza, and the area is not proportional to the diameter. Most people cannot easily estimate the difference in area between a 10-inch pizza and a 12-inch pizza and so cannot easily determine which size is the best buy—that is, which size has the lowest price per square inch. In this case study we will design a program that compares two sizes of pizza to determine which is the better buy.

Problem Definition

The precise specification of the program input and output are as follows:

Input

The input will consist of the diameter in inches and the price for each of two sizes of pizza.

Output

The output will give the cost per square inch for each of the two sizes of pizza and will tell which is the better buy, that is, which has the lowest cost per square inch. (If they are the same cost per square inch, we will consider the smaller one to be the better buy.)

Analysis of the Problem

We will use top-down design to divide the task to be solved by our program into the following subtasks:

> **Subtask 1:** Get the input data for both the small and large pizzas.
>
> **Subtask 2:** Compute the price per square inch for the small pizza.
>
> **Subtask 3:** Compute the price per square inch for the large pizza.
>
> **Subtask 4:** Determine which is the better buy.
>
> **Subtask 5:** Output the results.

Notice subtasks 2 and 3. They have two important properties:

Subtasks 2 and 3

1. They are exactly the same task. The only difference is that they use different data to do the computation. The only things that change between subtask 2 and subtask 3 are the size of the pizza and its price.

2. The result of subtask 2 and the result of subtask 3 are each a single value: the price per square inch of the pizza.

When to define a function

Whenever a subtask takes some values, such as some numbers, and returns a single value, it is natural to implement the subtask as a function. Whenever two or more such subtasks perform the same computation, they can be implemented as the same function called with different arguments each time it is used. We therefore decide to use a function called `unitprice` to compute the price per square inch of a pizza. The function declaration and explanatory comment for this function will be as follows:

```
double unitprice(int diameter, double price);
//Returns the price per square inch of a pizza. The formal
//parameter named diameter is the diameter of the pizza in
//inches. The formal parameter named price is the price of
//the pizza.
```

Algorithm Design

Subtask 1

Subtask 1 is straightforward. The program will simply ask for the input values and store them in four variables, which we will call `diameter_small`, `diameter_large`, `price_small`, and `price_large`.

Subtasks 4 and 5

Subtask 4 is routine. To determine which pizza is the best buy, we just compare the cost per square inch of the two pizzas using the less-than operator. Subtask 5 is a routine output of the results.

Subtasks 2 and 3

Subtasks 2 and 3 are implemented as calls to the function `unitprice`. Next, we design the algorithm for this function. The hard part of the algorithm is determining the area of the pizza. Once we know the area, we can easily determine the price per square inch using division, as follows:

```
price/area
```

where `area` is a variable that holds the area of the pizza. This expression will be the value returned by the function `unitprice`. But we still need to formulate a method for computing the area of the pizza.

A pizza is basically a circle (made up of bread, cheese, sauce, and so forth). The area of a circle (and hence of a pizza) is πr^2, where r is the radius of the circle and π is the number called "pi," which is approximately equal to 3.14159. The radius is one half of the diameter.

The algorithm for the function `unitprice` can be outlined as follows:

Algorithm Outline for the Function `unitprice`

1. Compute the radius of the pizza.

2. Compute the area of the pizza using the formula πr^2.

3. Return the value of the expression (`price/area`).

We will give this outline a bit more detail before translating it into C++ code. We will express this more detailed version of our algorithm in *pseudocode*. **Pseudocode** is a mixture of C++ and ordinary English. Pseudocode allows us to make our algorithm precise without worrying about the details of C++ syntax. We can then easily translate our pseudocode into C++ code. In our pseudocode, radius and area will be variables for holding the values indicated by their names.

Pseudocode for the Function unitprice

```
radius = one half of diameter;
area = π * radius * radius;
return (price/area);
```

That completes our algorithm for unitprice. We are now ready to convert our solutions to subtasks 1 through 5 into a complete C++ program.

Coding

Coding subtask 1 is routine, so we next consider subtasks 2 and 3. Our program can implement subtasks 2 and 3 by the following two calls to the function unitprice:

```
unitprice_small = unitprice(diameter_small, price_small);
unitprice_large = unitprice(diameter_large, price_large);
```

where unitprice_small and unitprice_large are two variables of type *double*. One of the benefits of a function definition is that you can have multiple calls to the function in your program. This saves you the trouble of repeating the same (or almost the same) code. But we still must write the code for the function unitprice.

When we translate our pseudocode into C++ code, we obtain the following for the body of the function unitprice:

```
{//First draft of the function body for unitprice
    const double PI = 3.14159;
    double radius, area;

    radius = diameter/2;
    area = PI * radius * radius;
    return (price/area);
}
```

Notice that we made PI a named constant using the modifier *const*. Also, notice the following line from the code:

```
radius = diameter/2;
```

This is just a simple division by 2, and you might think that nothing could be more routine. Yet, as written, this line contains a serious mistake. We want the division to produce the radius of the pizza including any fraction.

For example, if we are considering buying the "bad luck special," which is a 13-inch pizza, then the radius is 6.5 inches. But the variable `diameter` is of type *int*. The constant 2 is also of type *int*. Thus, as we saw in Chapter 2, this line would perform integer division and would compute the radius 13/2 to be 6 instead of the correct value of 6.5, and we would have disregarded a half inch of pizza radius. In all likelihood, this would go unnoticed, but the result could be that millions of subscribers to the Pizza Consumers Union could be wasting their money by buying the wrong size pizza. This is not likely to produce a major worldwide recession, but the program would be failing to accomplish its goal of helping consumers find the best buy. In a more important program, the result of such a simple mistake could be disastrous.

How do we fix this mistake? We want the division by 2 to be regular division that includes any fractional part in the answer. That form of division requires that at least one of the arguments to the division operator / must be of type *double*. We can use type casting to convert the constant 2 to a value of type *double*. Recall that *static_cast<double>(2)*, which is called a *type casting*, converts the *int* value 2 to a value of type *double*. Thus, if we replace 2 by *static_cast<double>(2)*, that will change the second argument in the division from type *int* to type *double*, and the division will then produce the result we want. The rewritten assignment statement is

```
radius = diameter/static_cast<double>(2);
```

The complete corrected code for the function definition of `unitprice`, along with the rest of the program, is shown in Display 4.10.

The type cast *static_cast<double>(2)* returns the value 2.0, so we could have used the constant 2.0 in place of *static_cast<double>(2)*. Either way, the function `unitprice` will return the same value. However, by using *static_cast<double>(2)*, we make it conspicuously obvious that we want to do the version of division that includes the fractional part in its answer. If we instead used 2.0, then when revising or copying the code, we can easily make the mistake of changing 2.0 to 2, and that would produce a subtle problem.

We need to make one more remark about the coding of our program. As you can see in Display 4.10, when we coded tasks 4 and 5, we combined these two tasks into a single section of code consisting of a sequence of `cout` statements followed by an *if-else* statement. When two tasks are very simple and are closely related, it sometimes makes sense to combine them into a single task.

Program Testing

Just because a program compiles and produces answers that look right does not mean the program is correct. In order to increase your confidence in your program, you should test it on some input values for which you know the correct answer by some other means, such as working out the answer with paper and pencil or by using a handheld calculator. For example, it does not make sense to buy a 2-inch pizza, but it can still be used as

DISPLAY 4.10   Buying Pizza *(part 1 of 2)*

```
1    //Determines which of two pizza sizes is the best buy.
2    #include <iostream>
3    using namespace std;
4
5    double unitprice (int diameter, double price);
6    //Returns the price per square inch of a pizza. The formal
7    //parameter named diameter is the diameter of the pizza in inches.
8    //The formal parameter named price is the price of the pizza.
9
10   int main( )
11   {
12       int diameter_small, diameter_large;
13       double price_small, unitprice_small,
14           price_large, unitprice_large;
15
16       cout << "Welcome to the Pizza Consumers Union.\n";
17       cout << "Enter diameter of a small pizza (in inches): ";
18       cin >> diameter_small;
19       cout << "Enter the price of a small pizza: $";
20       cin >> price_small;
21       cout << "Enter diameter of a large pizza (in inches): ";
22       cin >> diameter_large;
23       cout << "Enter the price of a large pizza: $";
24       cin >> price_large;
25
26       unitprice_small = unitprice(diameter_small, price_small);
27       unitprice_large = unitprice(diameter_large, price_large);
28
29       cout.setf(ios::fixed);
30       cout.setf(ios::showpoint);
31       cout.precision(2);
32       cout << "Small pizza:\n"
33           << "Diameter = " << diameter_small << " inches\n"
34           << "Price = $" << price_small
35           << " Per square inch = $" << unitprice_small << endl
36           << "Large pizza:\n"
37           << "Diameter = " << diameter_large << " inches\n"
38           << "Price = $" << price_large
39           << " Per square inch = $" << unitprice_large << endl;
40       if (unitprice_large < unitprice_small)
41           cout << "The large one is the better buy.\n";
42       else
43           cout << "The small one is the better buy.\n";
44
45       cout << "Buon Appetito!\n";
46       return 0;
```

(continued)

DISPLAY 4.10   Buying Pizza *(part 2 of 2)*

```
47      }
48
49      double unitprice(int diameter, double price)
50      {
51          const double PI = 3.14159;
52          double radius, area;
53
54          radius = diameter/static_cast<double>(2);
55          area = PI * radius * radius;
56          return (price/area);
57      }
58
```

Sample Dialogue

```
Welcome to the Pizza Consumers Union.
Enter diameter of a small pizza (in inches): 10
Enter the price of a small pizza: $7.50
Enter diameter of a large pizza (in inches): 13
Enter the price of a large pizza: $14.75
Small pizza:
Diameter = 10 inches
Price = $7.50 Per square inch = $0.10
Large pizza:
Diameter = 13 inches
Price = $14.75 Per square inch = $0.11
The small one is the better buy.
Buon Appetito!
```

an easy test case for this program. It is an easy test case because it is easy to compute the answer by hand. Let's calculate the cost per square inch of a 2-inch pizza that sells for $3.14. Since the diameter is 2 inches, the radius is 1 inch. The area of a pizza with radius 1 is $3.14159 * 1^2$, which is 3.14159. If we divide this into the price of $3.14, we find that the price per square inch is $3.14/3.14159$, which is approximately $1.00. Of course, this is an absurd size for a pizza and an absurd price for such a small pizza, but it is easy to determine the value that the function unitprice should return for these arguments.

Having checked your program on this one case, you can have more confidence in it, but you still cannot be certain your program is correct. An incorrect program can sometimes give the correct answer, even though it will give incorrect answers on some other inputs. You may have tested an incorrect program on one of the cases for which the program happens to give the correct output. For example, suppose we had not caught the mistake we discovered when coding the function `unitprice`. Suppose we mistakenly used 2 instead of *static_cast<double>*(2) in the following line:

```
radius = diameter/static_cast<double>(2);
```

So that line reads as follows:

```
radius = diameter/2;
```

As long as the pizza diameter is an even number, like 2, 8, 10, or 12, the program gives the same answer whether we divide by 2 or by *static_cast<double>*(2). It is unlikely that it would occur to you to be sure to check both even- and odd-size pizzas. However, if you test your program on several different pizza sizes, then there is a better chance that your test cases will contain samples of the relevant kinds of data.

■ PROGRAMMING TIP   Use Pseudocode

Algorithms are typically expressed in *pseudocode*. **Pseudocode** is a mixture of C++ (or whatever programming language you are using) and ordinary English (or whatever human language you are using). Pseudocode allows you to state your algorithm precisely without having to worrying about all the details of C++ syntax. When the C++ code for a step in your algorithm is obvious, there is little point in stating it in English. When a step is difficult to express in C++, the algorithm will be clearer if the step is expressed in English. You can see an example of pseudocode in the previous case study, where we expressed our algorithm for the function `unitprice` in pseudocode.   ■

SELF-TEST EXERCISES

myprogramminglab

15. What is the purpose of the comment that accompanies a function declaration?

16. What is the principle of procedural abstraction as applied to function definitions?

17. What does it mean when we say the programmer who uses a function should be able to treat the function like a black box? (*Hint:* This question is very closely related to the previous question.)

18. Carefully describe the process of program testing.

19. Consider two possible definitions for the function `unitprice`. One is the definition given in Display 4.10. The other definition is the same except that the type cast *static_cast<double>*(2) is replaced with the constant 2.0; in other words, the line

    ```
    radius = diameter/static_cast<double>(2);
    ```

    is replaced with the line

    ```
    radius = diameter/2.0;
    ```

    Are these two possible function definitions black-box equivalent?

4.5 SCOPE AND LOCAL VARIABLES

He was a local boy, not known outside his home town.

COMMON SAYING

In the last section we advocated using functions as if they were black boxes. In order to define a function so that it can be used as a black box, you often need to give the function variables of its own that do not interfere with the rest of your program. The variables that "belong to" a function are called *local variables*. As we will see, these variables simply conform to the scope rule for nested blocks described in Chapter 3. In this section we take another look at scoping with an emphasis on local variables and how to use them.

The Small Program Analogy

Look back at the program in Display 4.1. It includes a call to the predefined function `sqrt`. We did not need to know anything about the details of the function definition for `sqrt` in order to use this function. In particular, we did not need to know what variables were declared in the definition of `sqrt`. A function that you define is no different. Variable declarations in function definitions that you write are as separate as those in the function definitions for the predefined functions. Variable declarations within a function definition are the same as if they were variable declarations in another program. If you declare a variable in a function definition and then declare another variable of the same name in the `main` part of your program (or in the body of some other function definition), then these two variables are two different variables, even though they have the same name. Let's look at a program that does have a variable in a function definition with the same name as another variable in the program.

The program in Display 4.11 has two variables named `average_pea`; one is declared and used in the function definition for the function `est_total`, and the other is declared and used in the `main` part of the program. The variable

DISPLAY 4.11 Local Variables *(part 1 of 2)*

```
1    //Computes the average yield on an experimental pea growing patch.
2    #include <iostream>
3    using namespace std;
4
5    double est_total(int min_peas, int max_peas, int pod_count);
6    //Returns an estimate of the total number of peas harvested.
7    //The formal parameter pod_count is the number of pods.
8    //The formal parameters min_peas and max_peas are the minimum
9    //and maximum number of peas in a pod.
10                                                This variable named average_pea is
11   int main( )                                  local to the main part of the program.
12   {
13       int max_count, min_count, pod_count;
14       double average_pea, yield;
15
16       cout << "Enter minimum and maximum number of peas in a pod: ";
17       cin >> min_count >> max_count;
18       cout << "Enter the number of pods: ";
19       cin >> pod_count;
20       cout << "Enter the weight of an average pea (in ounces): ";
21       cin >> average_pea;
22
23       yield =
24           est_total(min_count, max_count, pod_count) * average_pea;
25
26       cout.setf(ios::fixed);
27       cout.setf(ios::showpoint);
28       cout.precision(3);
29       cout << "Min number of peas per pod = " << min_count << endl
30            << "Max number of peas per pod = " << max_count << endl
31            << "Pod count = " << pod_count << endl
32            << "Average pea weight = "
33            << average_pea << " ounces" << endl
34            << "Estimated average yield = " << yield << " ounces"
35            << endl;
36
37       return 0;
38   }
39
40   double est_total(int min_peas, int max_peas, int pod_count)
41   {
42       double average_pea;                      This variable named average_pea
43                                                is local to the function est_total.
44       average_pea = (max_peas + min_peas)/2.0;
45       return (pod_count * average_pea);
46   }
```

(continued)

DISPLAY 4.11   Local Variables *(part 2 of 2)*

Sample Dialogue

```
Enter minimum and maximum number of peas in a pod: 4 6
Enter the number of pods: 10
Enter the weight of an average pea (in ounces): 0.5
Min number of peas per pod = 4
Max number of peas per pod = 6
Pod count = 10
Average pea weight = 0.500 ounces
Estimated average yield = 25.000 ounces
```

average_pea in the function definition for est_total and the variable average_pea in the main part of the program are two different variables. It is the same as if the function est_total were a predefined function. The two variables named average_pea will not interfere with each other any more than two variables in two completely different programs would. When the variable average_pea is given a value in the function call to est_total, this does not change the value of the variable in the main part of the program that is also named average_pea. (The details of the program in Display 4.11, other than this coincidence of names, are explained in the Programming Example section that follows this section.)

Variables that are declared within the body of a function definition are said to be **local to that function** or to have that function as their **scope.** Variables that are defined within the main body of the program are said to be **local to the main part of the program** or to have the main part of the program as their scope. There are other kinds of variables that are not local to any function or to the main part of the program, but we will have no use for such variables. Every variable we will use is either local to a function definition or local to the main part of the program. When we say that a variable is a **local variable** without any mention of a function and without any mention of the main part of the program, we mean that the variable is local to some function definition.

Local Variables

Variables that are declared within the body of a function definition are said to be **local to that function** or to have that function as their **scope.** Variables that are declared within the main part of the program are said to be **local to the main part of the program** or to have the main part of the program as their **scope.** When we say that a variable is a **local variable** without any mention of a function and without any mention of the main part of the

(continued)

program, we mean that the variable is local to some function definition. If a variable is local to a function, then you can have another variable with the same name that is declared in the main part of the program or in another function definition, and these will be two different variables, even though they have the same name.

PROGRAMMING EXAMPLE   Experimental Pea Patch

The program in Display 4.11 gives an estimate for the total yield on a small garden plot used to raise an experimental variety of peas. The function est_total returns an estimate of the total number of peas harvested. The function est_total takes three arguments. One argument is the number of pea pods that were harvested. The other two arguments are used to estimate the average number of peas in a pod. Different pea pods contain differing numbers of peas, so the other two arguments to the function are the smallest and the largest number of peas that were found in any one pod. The function est_total averages these two numbers and uses this average as an estimate for the average number of peas in a pod.

Global Constants and Global Variables

As we noted in Chapter 2, you can and should name constant values using the *const* modifier. For example, in Display 4.10 we used the following declaration to give the name PI to the constant 3.14159:

```
const double PI = 3.14159;
```

In Display 4.3, we used the *const* modifier to give a name to the rate of sales tax with the following declaration:

```
const double TAX_RATE = 0.05; //5 percent sales tax
```

As with our variable declarations, we placed these declarations for naming constants inside the body of the functions that used them. This worked out fine because each named constant was used by only one function. However, it can easily happen that more than one function uses a named constant. In that case you can place the declaration for naming a constant at the beginning of your program, outside of the body of all the functions and outside the body of the main part of your program. The named constant is then said to be a **global named constant** and the named constant can be used in any function definition that follows the constant declaration.

Display 4.12 shows a program with an example of a global named constant. The program asks for a radius and then computes both the area of

DISPLAY 4.12 A Global Named Constant *(part 1 of 2)*

```
1    //Computes the area of a circle and the volume of a sphere.
2    //Uses the same radius for both calculations.
3    #include <iostream>
4    #include <cmath>
5    using namespace std;
6
7    const double PI = 3.14159;
8
9    double area (double radius);
10   //Returns the area of a circle with the specified radius.
11
12   double volume(double radius);
13   //Returns the volume of a sphere with the specified radius.
14
15   int main( )
16   {
17       double radius_of_both, area_of_circle, volume_of_sphere;
18
19       cout << "Enter a radius to use for both a circle\n"
20            << "and a sphere (in inches): ";
21       cin >> radius_of_both;
22
23       area_of_circle = area(radius_of_both);
24       volume_of_sphere = volume(radius_of_both);
25
26       cout << "Radius = " << radius_of_both << " inches\n"
27            << "Area of circle = " << area_of_circle
28            << " square inches\n"
29            << "Volume of sphere = " << volume_of_sphere
30            << " cubic inches\n";
31
32       return 0;
33   }
34
35   double area(double radius)
36   {
37       return (PI * pow(radius, 2));
38   }
39
40   double volume(double radius)
41   {
42       return ((4.0/3.0) * PI * pow(radius, 3));
43   }
```

(continued)

DISPLAY 4.12   A Global Named Constant *(part 2 of 2)*

Sample Dialogue

```
Enter a radius to use for both a circle
and a sphere (in inches): 2
Radius = 2 inches
Area of circle = 12.5664 square inches
Volume of sphere = 33.5103 cubic inches
```

---

a circle and the volume of a sphere with that radius. The programmer who wrote that program looked up the formulas for computing those quantities and found the following:

area = $\pi \times$ (radius)^2
volume = $(4/3) \times \pi \times$ (radius)^3

Both formulas include the constant π, which is approximately equal to 3.14159. The symbol π is the Greek letter called "pi." In previous programs we have used the following declaration to produce a named constant called PI to use when we convert such formulas to C++ code:

const double PI = 3.14159;

In the program in Display 4.12 we use the same declaration but place it near the beginning of the file so that it defines a global named constant that can be used in all the function bodies.

VideoNote
Walkthrough of Functions and Local Variables

The compiler allows you wide latitude with regard to where you place the declarations for your global named constants, but to aid readability you should place all your include directives together, all your global named constant declarations together in another group, and all your function declarations together. We will follow standard practice and place all our global named constant declarations after our include directives and before our function declarations.

Placing all named constant declarations at the start of your program can aid readability even if the named constant is used by only one function. If the named constant might need to be changed in a future version of your program, it will be easier to find if it is at the beginning of the program. For example, placing the constant declaration for the sales tax rate at the beginning of an accounting program will make it easy to revise the program should the tax rate increase.

It is possible to declare ordinary variables, without the *const* modifier, as **global variables**, which are accessible to all function definitions in the file. This is done the same way that it is done for global named constants, except that the modifier *const* is not used in the variable declaration. However, there is seldom any need to use such global variables. Moreover, global variables can make a program harder to understand and maintain, so we will not use any global variables. Once you have had more experience designing programs, you may choose to occasionally use global variables.

Call-by-Value Formal Parameters Are Local Variables

Formal parameters are more than just blanks that are filled in with the argument values for the function. Formal parameters are actually variables that are local to the function definition, so they can be used just like a local variable that is declared in the function definition. Earlier in this chapter we described the call-by-value mechanism that handles the arguments in a function call. We can now define this mechanism for "plugging in arguments" in more detail. When a function is called, the formal parameters for the function (which are local variables) are initialized to the values of the arguments. This is the precise meaning of the phrase "plugged in for the formal parameters" that we have been using. Typically, a formal parameter is used only as a kind of blank, or place holder, that is filled in by the value of its corresponding argument; occasionally, however, a formal parameter is used as a variable whose value is changed. In this section we will give one example of a formal parameter used as a local variable.

The program in Display 4.13 is the billing program for the law offices of Dewey, Cheatham, and Howe. Notice that, unlike other law firms, the firm of Dewey, Cheatham, and Howe does not charge for any time less than a quarter of an hour. That is why it's called "the law office with a heart." If they work for 1 hour and 14 minutes, they only charge for 4 quarter hours, not 5 quarter hours as other firms do; so you would pay only $600 for the consultation.

DISPLAY 4.13 Formal Parameter Used as a Local Variable *(part 1 of 2)*

```
1   //Law office billing program.
 2   #include <iostream>
 3   using namespace std;
 4
 5   const double RATE = 150.00; //Dollars per quarter hour.
 6
 7   double fee(int hours_worked, int minutes_worked);
 8   //Returns the charges for hours_worked hours and
 9   //minutes_worked minutes of legal services.
10
11   int main( )
12   {
13       int hours, minutes;
14       double bill;
15
```
(continued)

DISPLAY 4.13   Formal Parameter Used as a Local Variable (*part 2 of 2*)

```
16        cout << "Welcome to the offices of\n"
17              << "Dewey, Cheatham, and Howe.\n"
18              << "The law office with a heart.\n"
19              << "Enter the hours and minutes"
20              << " of your consultation:\n";
21        cin >> hours >> minutes;
22
23        bill = fee(hours, minutes);
24
25        cout.setf(ios::fixed);
26        cout.setf(ios::showpoint);
27        cout.precision(2);
28        cout << "For " << hours << " hours and " << minutes
29              << " minutes, your bill is $" << bill << endl;
30
31        return 0;
32    }
33
34    double fee(int hours_worked, int minutes_worked)
35    {
36        int quarter_hours;
37
38        minutes_worked = hours_worked * 60 + minutes_worked;
39        quarter_hours = minutes_worked/15;
40        return (quarter_hours * RATE);
41    }
```

The value of minutes is not changed by the call to fee.

minutes_worked is a local variable initialized to the value of minutes.

Sample Dialogue

```
Welcome to the offices of
Dewey, Cheatham, and Howe.
The law office with a heart.
Enter the hours and minutes of your consultation:
2 45
For 2 hours and 45 minutes, your bill is $1650.00
```

Notice the formal parameter minutes_worked in the definition of the function fee. It is used as a variable and has its value changed by the following line, which occurs within the function definition:

```
minutes_worked = hours_worked * 60 + minutes_worked;
```

Formal parameters are local variables just like the variables you declare within the body of a function. However, you should not add a variable

Do not add a declaration for a formal parameter

declaration for the formal parameters. Listing the formal parameter `minutes_` `worked` in the function declaration also serves as the variable declaration. The following is the *wrong way* to start the function definition for `fee` as it declares `minutes_worked` twice:

```
double fee(int hours_worked, int minutes_worked)
{
    int quarter_hours;                          — Do NOT do this!
    int minutes_worked;  ◄
        . . .
```

Block Scope

The scope of a local variable refers to the part of a program that can directly access that variable and is sometimes referred to as *local scope*. Similarly, global identifiers declared at the beginning of your program, outside of the body of all the functions, are sometimes referred to as having *global scope*. Despite their differences, local and global identifiers are really examples of *block scope* described in Chapter 3. A block is some C++ code enclosed in braces, with the exception of the "global block," which is an implied outermost block that encompasses all code. The scope rule states that identifiers declared within their block are local to that block and accessible only from the point they are defined to the end of their block. Blocks are commonly nested. For example, the braces of the `main` function defines a block and a `for` loop inside `main` defines a nested block.

The program outlined in Display 4.14 doesn't compute anything interesting but illustrates the scope of identifiers declared in different blocks. In this example, the constant `GLOBAL_CONST` has global scope, along with the functions `function1` and `main`, because they are declared outside the body of all functions. This allows us to access `GLOBAL_CONST` from both `main` and `function1`.

The `main` function declares the variables `x` and `d` that are local to `main`. Their scope extends to the end of `main`'s block. Similarly, the function `function1` has a parameter `param` and a local variable `y` that have scope extending to the end of `function1`. Neither of these variables is directly accessible from outside their scope. The scope of local variables and parameters really uses the same rule of block scope, but in this case the block refers to the function in which the variables or parameters are declared.

The *for* loop in Display 4.14 illustrates the scope of a nested block. The variable `i` is declared inside the *for* loop and thus only has scope to the end of the loop block. Attempts to reference `i` anywhere outside its scope, even if we are still inside `main` (for example, on line 17) would result in a compiler error.

You can think of variables as being created when their scope begins and destroyed when their scope ends. For example, the local variable `y` in Display 4.14 is created and initialized to `GLOBAL_CONST` every time `function1` is called. If code on line 23 changed the value stored in `y`, then these changes would be

DISPLAY 4.14 Local, Global, and Block Scope

Block Scope Revisited

```
1     #include <iostream>
2     using namespace std;
3
4     const double GLOBAL_CONST = 1.0;
5
6     int function1(int param);
7
8     int main()
9     {
10        int x;
11        double d = GLOBAL_CONST;
12
13        for (int i = 0; i < 10; i++)
14        {
15            x = function1(i);
16        }
17        return 0;
18    }
19
20    int function1(int param)
21    {
22        double y = GLOBAL_CONST;
23        ...
24        return 0;
25    }
```

Local and Global scope are examples of Block scope. A variable can be directly accessed only within its scope.

Block scope: Variable i has scope from lines 13-16

Local scope to main: Variable x has scope from lines 10-18 and variable d has scope from lines 11-18

Global scope: The constant GLOBAL_CONST has scope from lines 4-25 and the function function1 has scope from lines 6-25

Local scope to function1: Variable param has scope from lines 20-25 and variable y has scope from lines 22-25

lost when the function exits and y goes out of scope because the variable y is destroyed. A repeat call to function1 will not recall the previous value of y, but rather a new y will be created.

In addition to block scope there is also namespace scope and class scope. Class scope is discussed in Chapter 10 and namespace scope in Chapter 12. C++ also defines function prototype scope, which refers to the line of scope for parameters defined in a function prototype. Finally, C++ supports function scope, which is used for labels. Labels are a remnant from the C language and are used with goto statements. Their use is generally shunned because they can result in logic that is difficult to follow, whereas the same task can be performed by loops in an understandable fashion.

Namespaces Revisited

Thus far, we have started all of our programs with the following two lines:

```
#include <iostream>
using namespace std;
```

However, the start of the file is not always the best location for the line

using namespace std;

We will eventually be using more namespaces than just std. In fact, we may be using different namespaces in different function definitions. If you place the directive

using namespace std;

inside the brace { that starts the body of a function definition, then the *using* directive applies to only that function definition. This will allow you to use two different namespaces in two different function definitions, even if the two function definitions are in the same file and even if the two namespaces have some name(s) with different meanings in the two different namespaces.

Placing a *using* directive inside a function definition is analogous to placing a variable declaration inside a function definition. If you place a variable definition inside a function definition, the variable is local to the function; that is, the meaning of the variable declaration is confined to the function definition. If you place a *using* directive inside a function definition, the *using* directive is local to the function definition; in other words, the meaning of the *using* directive is confined to the function definition.

It will be some time before we use any namespace other than std in a *using* directive, but it will be good practice to start placing these *using* directives where they should go. In Display 4.15 we have rewritten the program in Display 4.12 with the *using* directives where they should be placed. The program in Display 4.15 will behave exactly the same as the one in Display 4.12. In this particular case, the difference is only one of style, but when you start to use more namespaces, the difference will affect how your programs perform.

DISPLAY 4.15 Using Namespaces *(part 1 of 2)*

```
1    //Computes the area of a circle and the volume of a sphere.
2    //Uses the same radius for both calculations.
3    #include <iostream>
4    #include <cmath>
5
6    const double PI = 3.14159;
7
8    double area(double radius);
9    //Returns the area of a circle with the specified radius.
10
11   double volume(double radius);
12   //Returns the volume of a sphere with the specified radius.
```

(continued)

DISPLAY 4.15   Using Namespaces *(part 2 of 2)*

```
13
14    int main( )
15    {
16        using namespace std;
17
18        double radius_of_both, area_of_circle, volume_of_sphere;
19
20        cout << "Enter a radius to use for both a circle\n"
21             << "and a sphere (in inches): ";
22        cin >> radius_of_both;
23
24        area_of_circle = area(radius_of_both);
25        volume_of_sphere = volume(radius_of_both);
26
27        cout << "Radius = " << radius_of_both << " inches\n"
28             << "Area of circle = " << area_of_circle
29             << " square inches\n"
30             << "Volume of sphere = " << volume_of_sphere
31             << " cubic inches\n";
32
33        return 0;
34    }
35
36
37    double area(double radius)
38    {
39        using namespace std;
40
41        return (PI * pow(radius, 2));
42    }
43
44    double volume(double radius)
45    {
46        using namespace std;
47
48        return ((4.0/3.0) * PI * pow(radius, 3));
49    }
```

> The sample dialogue for this program would be the same as the one for the program in Display 4.12.

SELF-TEST EXERCISES

myprogramminglab

20. If you use a variable in a function definition, where should you declare the variable? In the function definition? In the main part of the program? Any place that is convenient?

21. Suppose a function named Function1 has a variable named sam declared within the definition of Function1, and a function named Function2 also has a variable named sam declared within the definition of Function2. Will the program compile (assuming everything else is correct)? If the program will compile, will it run (assuming that everything else is correct)? If it runs, will it generate an error message when run (assuming everything else is correct)? If it runs and does not produce an error message when run, will it give the correct output (assuming everything else is correct)?

22. The following function is supposed to take as arguments a length expressed in feet and inches and return the total number of inches in that many feet and inches. For example, total_inches(1,2) is supposed to return 14, because 1 foot and 2 inches is the same as 14 inches. Will the following function perform correctly? If not, why not?

```
double total_inches(int feet, int inches)
{
    inches = 12 * feet + inches;
    return inches;
}
```

23. Write a function declaration and function definition for a function called read_filter that has no parameters and that returns a value of type double. The function read_filter prompts the user for a value of type double and reads the value into a local variable. The function returns the value read provided this value is greater than or equal to zero and returns zero if the value read is negative.

PROGRAMMING EXAMPLE   The Factorial Function

Display 4.16 contains the function declaration and definition for a commonly used mathematical function known as the *factorial* function. In mathematics texts, the factorial function is usually written $n!$ and is defined to be the product of all the integers from 1 to n. In traditional mathematical notation, you can define $n!$ as follows:

$$n! = 1 \times 2 \times 3 \times \ldots \times n$$

In the function definition we perform the multiplication with a *while* loop. Note that the multiplication is performed in the reverse order to what you might expect. The program multiplies by n, then n – 1, then n – 2, and so forth.

DISPLAY 4.16   Factorial Function

Function Declaration

```
1    int factorial(int n);
2    //Returns factorial of n.
3    //The argument n should be nonnegative.
```

Function Definition

```
1    int factorial(int n)
2    {
3        int product = 1;
4        while (n > 0)
5        {
6            product = n * product;
7            n--;  ←──────────────── formal parameter n
8        }                            used as a local variable
9
10       return product;
11   }
```

The function definition for `factorial` uses two local variables: `product`, which is declared at the start of the function body, and the formal parameter n. Since a formal parameter is a local variable, we can change its value. In this case we change the value of the formal parameter n with the decrement operator n--. (The decrement operator was discussed in Chapter 2.)

Formal parameter used as a local variable

Each time the body of the loop is executed, the value of the variable `product` is multiplied by the value of n, and then the value of n is decreased by one using n--. If the function `factorial` is called with 3 as its argument, then the first time the loop body is executed the value of `product` is 3, the next time the loop body is executed the value of `product` is 3 * 2, the next time the value of `product` is 3 * 2 * 1, and then the *while* loop ends. Thus, the following will set the variable x equal to 6 which is 3 * 2 * 1:

```
x = factorial(3);
```

Notice that the local variable `product` is initialized to the value 1 when the variable is declared. (This way of initializing a variable when it is declared was introduced in Chapter 2.) It is easy to see that 1 is the correct initial value for the variable `product`. To see that this is the correct initial value for `product`, note that after executing the body of the *while* loop the first time, we want the value of `product` to be equal to the (original) value of the formal parameter n; if `product` is initialized to 1, then this will be what happens. ▮

4.6 OVERLOADING FUNCTION NAMES

"...—and that shows that there are three hundred and sixty-four days when you might get un-birthday presents—"

"Certainly," said Alice.

"And only one for birthday presents, you know. There's glory for you!"

"I don't know what you mean by 'glory,'" Alice said.

Humpty Dumpty smiled contemptuously, "Of course you don't—till I tell you. I mean 'there's a nice knock-down argument for you!'"

"But 'glory' doesn't mean 'a nice knock-down argument,'" Alice objected.

"When I use a word," Humpty Dumpty said, in rather a scornful tone, "it means just what I choose it to mean—neither more nor less."

"The question is," said Alice, "whether you can make words mean so many different things."

"The question is," said Humpty Dumpty, "which is to be master—that's all."

LEWIS CARROLL, *Through the Looking-Glass*

C++ allows you to give two or more different definitions to the same function name, which means you can reuse names that have strong intuitive appeal across a variety of situations. For example, you could have three functions called max: one that computes the largest of two numbers, another that computes the largest of three numbers, and yet another that computes the largest of four numbers. When you give two (or more) function definitions for the same function name, that is called **overloading** the function name. Overloading does require some extra care in defining your functions and should not be used unless it will add greatly to your program's readability. But when it is appropriate, overloading can be very effective.

Introduction to Overloading

Suppose you are writing a program that requires you to compute the average of two numbers. You might use the following function definition:

```
double ave(double n1, double n2)
{
    return ((n1 + n2)/2.0);
}
```

Now suppose your program also requires a function to compute the average of three numbers. You might define a new function called ave3 as follows:

```
double ave3(double n1, double n2, double n3)
{
    return ((n1 + n2 + n3)/3.0);
}
```

This will work, and in many programming languages you have no choice but to do something like this. Fortunately, C++ allows for a more elegant solution. In C++ you can simply use the same function name ave for both functions; you can use the following function definition in place of the function definition ave3:

```
double ave(double n1, double n2, double n3)
{
    return ((n1 + n2 + n3)/3.0);
}
```

DISPLAY 4.17 Overloading a Function Name

```
1    //Illustrates overloading the function name ave.
2    #include <iostream>
3
4    double ave(double n1, double n2);
5    //Returns the average of the two numbers n1 and n2.
6
7    double ave(double n1, double n2, double n3);
8    //Returns the average of the three numbers n1, n2, and n3.
9
10   int main( )
11   {
12       using namespace std;
13       cout << "The average of 2.0, 2.5, and 3.0 is "
14            << ave(2.0, 2.5, 3.0) << endl;
15
16       cout << "The average of 4.5 and 5.5 is "
17            << ave(4.5, 5.5) << endl;
18
19       return 0;                              two arguments
20   }
21
22   double ave(double n1, double n2)
23   {
24       return ((n1 + n2)/2.0);
25   }                                          three arguments
26
27   double ave(double n1, double n2, double n3)
28   {
29       return ((n1 + n2 + n3)/3.0);
30   }
31
32
```

Output

```
The average of 2.0, 2.5, and 3.0 is 2.50000
The average of 4.5 and 5.5 is 5.00000
```

so that the function name ave then has two definitions. This is an example of overloading. In this case we have overloaded the function name ave. In Display 4.17 we have embedded these two function definitions for ave into a complete sample program. Be sure to notice that each function definition has its own function declaration.

Overloading is a great idea. It makes a program easier to read, and it saves you from going crazy trying to think up a new name for a function just because you already used the most natural name in some other function definition. But how does the compiler know which function definition to use when it encounters a call to a function name that has two or more definitions? The compiler cannot read a programmer's mind. In order to tell which function definition to use, the compiler checks the number of arguments and the types of the arguments in the function call. In the program in Display 4.17, one of the functions called ave has two arguments and the other has three arguments. To tell which definition to use, the compiler simply counts the number of arguments in the function call. If there are two arguments, it uses the first definition. If there are three arguments, it uses the second definition.

Determining which definition applies

Whenever you give two or more definitions to the same function name, the various function definitions must have different specifications for their arguments; that is, any two function definitions that have the same function name must use different numbers of formal parameters or use formal parameters of different types (or both). Notice that when you overload a function name, the function declarations for the two different definitions must differ in their formal parameters. *You cannot overload a function name by giving two definitions that differ only in the type of the value returned.*

Overloading a Function Name

If you have two or more function definitions for the same function name, that is called **overloading**. When you overload a function name, the function definitions must have different numbers of formal parameters or some formal parameters of different types. When there is a function call, the compiler uses the function definition whose number of formal parameters and types of formal parameters match the arguments in the function call.

Overloading is not really new to you. You saw a kind of overloading in Chapter 2 with the division operator /. If both operands are of type *int*, as in 13/2, then the value returned is the result of integer division, in this case 6. On the other hand, if one or both operands are of type *double*, then the value returned is the result of regular division; for example, 13/2.0 returned the value 6.5. There are two definitions for the division operator /, and the two definitions are distinguished not by having different numbers of operands, but rather by requiring operands of different types. The difference between overloading of / and overloading function names is that the compiler has already done the overloading of / but you program the overloading of the function name. We will see in a later chapter how to overload operators such as +, –, and so on.

| **PROGRAMMING EXAMPLE**   Revised Pizza-Buying Program |

The Pizza Consumers Union has been very successful with the program that we wrote for it in Display 4.10. In fact, now everybody always buys the pizza that is the best buy. One disreputable pizza parlor used to make money by fooling consumers into buying the more expensive pizza, but our program has put an end to their evil practices. However, the owners wish to continue their despicable behavior and have come up with a new way to fool consumers. They now offer both round pizzas and rectangular pizzas. They know that the program we wrote cannot deal with rectangularly shaped pizzas, so they hope they can again confuse consumers. We need to update our program so that we can foil their nefarious scheme. We want to change the program so that it can compare a round pizza and a rectangular pizza.

The changes we need to make to our pizza evaluation program are clear: We need to change the input and output a bit so that it deals with two different shapes of pizzas. We also need to add a new function that can compute the cost per square inch of a rectangular pizza. We could use the following function definition in our program so that we can compute the unit price for a rectangular pizza:

```
double unitprice_rectangular
    (int length, int width, double price)
{
    double area = length * width;
    return (price/area);
}
```

However, this is a rather long name for a function; in fact, it's so long that we needed to put the function heading on two lines. That is legal, but it would be nicer to use the same name, unitprice, for both the function that computes the unit price for a round pizza and for the function that computes the unit price for a rectangular pizza. Since C++ allows overloading of function names, we can do this. Having two definitions for the function unitprice will pose no problems to the compiler because the two functions will have different numbers of arguments. Display 4.18 shows the program we obtained when we modified our pizza evaluation program to allow us to compare round pizzas with rectangular pizzas.

DISPLAY 4.18   **Overloading a Function Name** *(part 1 of 2)*

```
1    //Determines whether a round pizza or a rectangular pizza is the best buy.
2    #include <iostream>
3
4    double unitprice(int diameter, double price);
5    //Returns the price per square inch of a round pizza.
6    //The formal parameter named diameter is the diameter of the pizza
7    //in inches. The formal parameter named price is the price of the pizza.
8
9    double unitprice(int length, int width, double price);
10   //Returns the price per square inch of a rectangular pizza
11   //with dimensions length by width inches.
12   //The formal parameter price is the price of the pizza.
13
14   int main( )
15   {
16       using namespace std;
17       int diameter, length, width;
18       double price_round, unit_price_round,
19       price_rectangular, unitprice_rectangular;
20
21       cout << "Welcome to the Pizza Consumers Union.\n";
22       cout << "Enter the diameter in inches"
23           << " of a round pizza: ";
24       cin >> diameter;
25       cout << "Enter the price of a round pizza: $";
26       cin >> price_round;
27       cout << "Enter length and width in inches\n"
28           << "of a rectangular pizza: ";
29       cin >> length >> width;
30       cout << "Enter the price of a rectangular pizza: $";
31       cin >> price_rectangular;
32
33       unitprice_rectangular =
34                   unitprice(length, width, price_rectangular);
35       unit_price_round = unitprice(diameter, price_round);
36
37       cout.setf(ios::fixed);
38       cout.setf(ios::showpoint);
39       cout.precision(2);
40       cout << endl
41           << "Round pizza: Diameter = "
42           << diameter << " inches\n"
43           << "Price = $" << price_round
44           << " Per square inch = $" << unit_price_round
45           << endl
46           << "Rectangular pizza: Length = "
47           << length << " inches\n"
```

(continued)

DISPLAY 4.18   Overloading a Function Name *(part 2 of 2)*

```
48              << "Rectangular pizza: Width = "
49              << width << " inches\n"
50              << "Price = $" << price_rectangular
51              << " Per square inch = $" << unitprice_rectangular
52              << endl;
53
54      if (unit_price_round < unitprice_rectangular)
55          cout << "The round one is the better buy.\n";
56      else
57          cout << "The rectangular one is the better buy.\n";
58
59      cout << "Buon Appetito!\n";
60      return 0;
61  }
62
63  double unitprice(int diameter, double price)
64  {
65      const double PI = 3.14159;
66      double radius, area;
67
68      radius = diameter/static_cast<double>(2);
69      area = PI * radius * radius;
70      return (price/area);
71  }
72
73  double unitprice(int length, int width, double price)
74  {
75      double area = length * width;
76      return (price/area);
77  }
```

Sample Dialogue

```
Welcome to the Pizza Consumers Union.
Enter the diameter in inches of a round pizza: 10
Enter the price of a round pizza: $8.50
Enter length and width in inches of a rectangular pizza: 6 4
Enter the price of a rectangular pizza: $7.55

Round pizza: Diameter = 10 inches
Price = $8.50 Per square inch = $0.11
Rectangular pizza: Length = 6 inches
Rectangular pizza: Width = 4 inches
Price = $7.55 Per square inch = $0.31
The round one is the better buy.
Buon Appetito!
```

Automatic Type Conversion

Suppose that the following function definition occurs in your program and that you have *not* overloaded the function name mpg (so this is the only definition of a function called mpg).

```
double mpg(double miles, double gallons)
//Returns miles per gallon.
{
    return (miles/gallons);
}
```

If you call the function mpg with arguments of type *int*, then C++ will automatically convert any argument of type *int* to a value of type *double*. Hence, the following will output 22.5 miles per gallon to the screen:

```
cout << mpg(45, 2) << " miles per gallon";
```

C++ converts the 45 to 45.0 and the 2 to 2.0, then performs the division 45.0/2.0 to obtain the value returned, which is 22.5.

Interaction of overloading and type conversion

If a function requires an argument of type *double* and you give it an argument of type *int*, C++ will automatically convert the *int* argument to a value of type *double*. This is so useful and natural that we hardly give it a thought. However, overloading can interfere with this automatic type conversion. Let's look at an example.

Now, suppose you had (foolishly) overloaded the function name mpg so that your program also contained the following definition of mpg (as well as the previous one):

```
int mpg(int goals, int misses)
//Returns the Measure of Perfect Goals
//which is computed as (goals - misses).
{
    return (goals - misses);
}
```

In a program that contains both of these definitions for the function name mpg, the following will (unfortunately) output 43 miles per gallon (since 43 is 45 – 2):

```
cout << mpg(45, 2) << " miles per gallon";
```

When C++ sees the function call mpg(45, 2), which has two arguments of type *int*, C++ *first* looks for a function definition of mpg that has two formal parameters of type *int*. If it finds such a function definition, C++ uses that function definition. C++ does not convert an *int* argument to a value of type *double* unless that is the only way it can find a matching function definition.

The mpg example illustrates one more point about overloading. You should not use the same function name for two unrelated functions. Such careless use of function names is certain to eventually produce confusion.

SELF-TEST EXERCISES

myprogramminglab

24. Suppose you have two function definitions with the following function declarations:

    ```
    double score(double time, double distance);
    int score(double points);
    ```

    Which function definition would be used in the following function call and why would it be the one used? (x is of type *double*.)

    ```
    final_score = score(x);
    ```

25. Suppose you have two function definitions with the following function declarations:

    ```
    double the_answer(double data1, double data2);
    double the_answer(double time, int count);
    ```

    Which function definition would be used in the following function call and why would it be the one used? (x and y are of type *double*.)

    ```
    x = the_answer(y, 6.0);
    ```

26. Suppose you have two function definitions with the function declarations given in Self-Test Exercise 25. Which function definition would be used in the following function call and why would it be the one used?

    ```
    x = the_answer(5, 6);
    ```

27. Suppose you have two function definitions with the function declarations given in Self-Test Exercise 25. Which function definition would be used in the following function call and why would it be the one used?

    ```
    x = the_answer(5, 6.0);
    ```

28. This question has to do with the Programming Example "Revised Pizza-Buying Program." Suppose the evil pizza parlor that is always trying to fool customers introduces a square pizza. Can you overload the function unitprice so that it can compute the price per square inch of a square pizza as well as the price per square inch of a round pizza? Why or why not?

29. Look at the program in Display 4.18. The main function contains the *using* directive:

    ```
    using namespace std;
    ```

    Why doesn't the method unitprice contain this *using* directive?

CHAPTER SUMMARY

- A good plan of attack for designing the algorithm for a program is to break down the task to be accomplished into a few subtasks, then decompose each subtask into smaller subtasks, and so forth until the subtasks are simple enough that they can easily be implemented as C++ code. This approach is called **top-down design.**

- A function that returns a value is like a small program. The arguments to the function serve as the input to this "small program" and the value returned is like the output of the "small program."

- When a subtask for a program takes some values as input and produces a single value as its only result, then that subtask can be implemented as a function.

- A function should be defined so that it can be used as a black box. The programmer who uses the function should not need to know any details about how the function is coded. All the programmer should need to know is the function declaration and the accompanying comment that describes the value returned. This rule is sometimes called the **principle of procedural abstraction.**

- A variable that is declared in a function definition is said to be **local to the function.**

- Global named constants are declared using the *const* modifier. Declarations for global named constants are normally placed at the start of a program after the *include* directives and before the function declarations.

- Call-by-value formal parameters (which are the only kind of formal parameter discussed in this chapter) are variables that are local to the function. Occasionally, it is useful to use a formal parameter as a local variable.

- When you have two or more function definitions for the same function name, that is called **overloading** the function name. When you overload a function name, the function definitions must have different numbers of formal parameters or some formal parameters of different types.

Answers to Self-Test Exercises

1.
4.0	4.0	8.0
8.0	8.0	1.21
3	3	0
3.0	3.5	3.5
6.0	6.0	5.0
5.0	4.5	4.5
3	3.0	3.0

2. sqrt(x + y)
   pow(x, y + 7)
   sqrt(area + fudge)
   sqrt(time + tide)/nobody
   (-b + sqrt(b * b - 4 * a * c))/(2 * a)
   abs(x - y) or labs(x - y) or fabs(x - y)

3. *//Computes the square root of 3.14159.*
   #include <iostream>
   #include <cmath>*//provides sqrt and PI.*
   using namespace std;
   int main()
   {
        cout << "The square root of " >> PI
             << sqrt(PI) << endl;
        return 0;
   }

4. a. *//To determine whether the compiler will tolerate*
      //spaces before the # in the #include:
      #include <iostream>
      using namespace std;
      int main( )
      {
           cout << "hello world" << endl;
           return 0;
      }

   b. *//To determine if the compiler will allow spaces*
      //between the # and include in the #include:
      # include<iostream>
      using namespace std;
      //The rest of the program can be identical to the above.

5.   Wow

6. The function declaration is:

   int sum(*int* n1, *int* n2, *int* n3);
   //Returns the sum of n1, n2, and n3.

   The function definition is:

   int sum(*int* n1, *int* n2, *int* n3)
   {
        return (n1 + n2 + n3);
   }

7. The function declaration is:

```
double ave(int n1, double n2);
//Returns the average of n1 and n2.
```

The function definition is:

```
double ave(int n1, double n2)
{
    return ((n1 + n2)/2.0);
}
```

8. The function declaration is:

```
char positive_test(double number);
//Returns 'P' if number is positive.
//Returns 'N' if number is negative or zero.
```

The function definition is:

```
char positive_test(double number)
{
    if (number > 0)
        return 'P';
    else
        return 'N';
}
```

9. Suppose the function is defined with arguments, say param1 and param2. The function is then called with corresponding arguments arg1 and arg2. The values of the arguments are "plugged in" for the corresponding formal parameters, arg1 into param1, arg2 into param2. The formal parameters are then used in the function.

10. Predefined (library) functions usually require that you #include a header file. For a programmer-defined function, the programmer puts the code for the function either into the file with the main part of the program or in another file to be compiled and linked to the main program.

11. ```
bool in_order(int n1, int n2, int n3)
{
    return ((n1 <= n2) && (n2 <= n3));
}
```

12. ```
bool even(int n)
{
    return ((n % 2) == 0);
}
```

13. *bool* is digit(*char* ch)
    {
        return ('0' <= ch) && (ch <= '9');
    }

14. *bool* is_root_of(*int* root_candidate, *int* number)
    {
        return (number == root_candidate * root_candidate);
    }

15. The comment explains what value the function returns and gives any other information that you need to know in order to use the function.

16. The principle of procedural abstraction says that a function should be written so that it can be used like a black box. This means that the programmer who uses the function need not look at the body of the function definition to see how the function works. The function declaration and accompanying comment should be all the programmer needs to know in order to use the function.

17. When we say that the programmer who uses a function should be able to treat the function like a black box, we mean the programmer should not need to look at the body of the function definition to see how the function works. The function declaration and accompanying comment should be all the programmer needs to know in order to use the function.

18. In order to increase your confidence in your program, you should test it on input values for which you know the correct answers. Perhaps you can calculate the answers by some other means, such as pencil and paper or hand calculator.

19. Yes, the function would return the same value in either case, so the two definitions are black-box equivalent.

20. If you use a variable in a function definition, you should declare the variable in the body of the function definition.

21. Everything will be fine. The program will compile (assuming everything else is correct). The program will run (assuming that everything else is correct). The program will not generate an error message when run (assuming everything else is correct). The program will give the correct output (assuming everything else is correct).

22. The function will work fine. That is the entire answer, but here is some additional information: The formal parameter inches is a call-by-value parameter and, as discussed in the text, it is therefore a local variable. Thus, the value of the argument will not be changed.

23. The function declaration is:

```
double read_filter();
//Reads a number from the keyboard. Returns the number
//read provided it is >= 0; otherwise returns zero.
```

The function definition is:

```
//uses iostream
double read_filter()
{
    using namespace std;
    double value_read;
    cout << "Enter a number:\n";
    cin >> value_read;

    if (value_read >= 0)
        return value_read;
    else
        return 0.0;
}
```

24. The function call has only one argument, so it would use the function definition that has only one formal parameter.

25. The function call has two arguments of type *double*, so it would use the function corresponding to the function declaration with two arguments of type *double* (that is, the first function declaration).

26. The second argument is of type *int* and the first argument would be automatically converted to type *double* by C++ if needed, so it would use the function corresponding to the function declaration with the first argument of type *double* and the second argument of type *int* (that is, the second function declaration).

27. The second argument is of type *double* and the first argument would be automatically converted to type *double* by C++ if needed, so it would use the function corresponding to the function declaration with two arguments of type *double* (that is, the first function declaration).

28. This cannot be done (at least not in any nice way). The natural ways to represent a square and a round pizza are the same. Each is naturally represented as one number, which is the diameter for a round pizza and the length of a side for a square pizza. In either case the function unitprice would need to have one formal parameter of type *double* for the price and one formal parameter of type *int* for the size (either radius or side). Thus, the two function declarations would have the same number and

types of formal parameters. (Specifically, they would both have one formal parameter of type *double* and one formal parameter of type *int*.) Thus, the compiler would not be able to decide which definition to use. You can still defeat this evil pizza parlor's strategy by defining two functions, but they will need to have different names.

29. The definition of `unitprice` does not do any input or output and so does not use the library `iostream`. In `main` we needed the *using* directive because `cin` and `cout` are defined in `iostream` and those definitions place `cin` and `cout` in the `std` namespace.

PROGRAMMING PROJECTS

Visit www.myprogramminglab.com to complete many of these Programming Projects online and get instant feedback. `myprogramminglab`

1. Write a C++ program that will read a *double* number from the keyboard, store it in a variable `num`, and perform the following operations:

   a. `abs`
   b. `floor`
   c. `ceil`

   Test the program by storing positive and negative values in the variable `num`. Your program should allow the user to repeat this calculation as often as they wish.

2. Modify your program from Programming Project 1 so that the program reads two numbers from the keyboard and stores them in the variables `num1` and `num2` respectively. Perform the `pow` operation by raising `num1` to the power of `num2`.

3. The price of stocks is sometimes given to the nearest eighth of a dollar; for example, 297/8 or 891/2. Write a program that computes the value of the user's holding of one stock. The program asks for the number of shares of stock owned, the whole-dollar portion of the price, and the fraction portion. The fraction portion is to be input as two *int* values, one for the numerator and one for the denominator. The program then outputs the value of the user's holdings. Your program should allow the user to repeat this calculation as often as the user wishes and will include a function definition that has three *int* arguments consisting of the whole-dollar portion of the price and the two integers that make up the fraction part. The function returns the price of one share of stock as a single number of type *double*.

4. Write a program to determine the difference in the price of an item over the past year. The program asks for the price of an item (such as a pizza or 1 kilogram of gold) both one year ago and today. It then estimates the difference in price. Define a function to compute the difference in price. The

difference in price for the past year should be a value of type *double*, for example $10.3. Your program should allow the user to repeat this calculation as often as the user wishes.

5. Modify your program from Programming Project 4 so that the program defines a function to determine the rate of inflation for the past year. The inflation rate can be calculated as the difference in price divided by the year–ago price. Define a second function to determine and print the estimated cost of an item in one year. The function should receive the current price of the item and the inflation rate as arguments.

6. Write a function declaration for a function that computes interest on a credit card account balance. The function takes arguments for the initial balance, the monthly interest rate, and the number of months for which interest must be paid. The value returned is the interest due. Do not forget to compound the interest—that is, to charge interest on the interest due. The interest due is added into the balance due, and the interest for the next month is computed using this larger balance. Use a *while* loop that is similar to (but need not be identical to) the one shown in Display 2.14. Embed the function in a program that reads the values for the interest rate, initial account balance, and number of months, then outputs the interest due. Embed your function definition in a program that lets the user compute interest due on a credit account balance. The program should allow the user to repeat the calculation until the user says he or she wants to end the program.

VideoNote
Solution to Programming
Project 4.7

7. The gravitational attractive force between two bodies with masses m_1 and m_2 separated by a distance d is given by:

$$F = \frac{Gm_1m_2}{d^2}$$

where G is the universal gravitational constant:

$$G = 6.673 \times 10^{-8} \left(\frac{cm^3}{g \times sec^2} \right)$$

Write a function definition that takes arguments for the masses of two bodies and the distance between them and that returns the gravitational force. Since you will use the preceding formula, the gravitational force will be in dynes. One dyne equals

$$\left(\frac{g \times cm}{sec^2} \right)$$

You should use a globally defined constant for the universal gravitational constant. Embed your function definition in a complete program that computes the gravitational force between two objects given suitable inputs. Your program should allow the user to repeat this calculation as often as the user wishes.

8. A college maintains an interactive student database system that keeps track of its students. The database system must store each student's name, roll number, address, three subjects taken and their corresponding scores. Give the class specification. Your program should provide the necessary input and display methods. There should be a function to find the average of all the three scores for each student. Provide another function that displays whether the student has passed or failed, depending on the average scores calculated in the previous function (assume that a score that is greater or equal to 50 is a pass score). Your program should allow the user to repeat this calculation as often as the user wishes.

9. Write a program that asks for the user's height, weight, and age, and then computes clothing sizes according to the formulas:

   ■ Hat size = weight in pounds divided by height in inches and all that multiplied by 2.9.

   ■ Jacket size (chest in inches) = height times weight divided by 288 and then adjusted by adding 1/8 of an inch for each 10 years over age 30. (Note that the adjustment only takes place after a full 10 years. So, there is no adjustment for ages 30 through 39, but 1/8 of an inch is added for age 40.)

   ■ Waist in inches = weight divided by 5.7 and then adjusted by adding 1/10 of an inch for each 2 years over age 28. (Note that the adjustment only takes place after a full 2 years. So, there is no adjustment for age 29, but 1/10 of an inch is added for age 30.)

   Use functions for each calculation. Your program should allow the user to repeat this calculation as often as the user wishes.

10. Modify your program from Programming Project 8 so that it also calculates and displays the details of the student with the highest average score.

11. That we are "blessed" with several absolute value functions is an accident of history. C libraries were already available when C++ arrived; they could be easily used, so they were not rewritten using function overloading. You are to find all the absolute value functions you can and rewrite all of them overloading the abs function name. At a minimum, you should have the *int*, *long*, *float*, and *double* types represented.

12. Write an overloaded function min that takes either two or three parameters of type int and returns the smallest of them.

13. Write a program that outputs the lyrics for the song "Ninety-Nine Bottles of Beer on the Wall." Your program should print the number of bottles in English, not as a number. For example:

> Ninety-nine bottles of beer on the wall,
>
> Ninety-nine bottles of beer,
>
> Take one down, pass it around,
>
> Ninety-eight bottles of beer on the wall.
>
> …
>
> One bottle of beer on the wall,
>
> One bottle of beer,
>
> Take one down, pass it around,
>
> Zero bottles of beer on the wall.

Design your program with a function that takes as an argument an integer between 0 and 99 and returns a string that contains the integer value in English. Your function should not have 100 different *if-else* statements! Instead, use % and / to extract the tens and ones digits to construct the English string. You may need to test specifically for values such as 0, 10–19, etc.

14. To maintain one's body weight, an adult human needs to consume enough calories daily to (1) meet the basal metabolic rate (energy required to breathe, maintain body temperature, etc.), (2) account for physical activity such as exercise, and (3) account for the energy required to digest the food that is being eaten. For an adult that weighs P pounds, we can estimate these caloric requirements using the following formulas:

1. Basal metabolic rate: Calories required = $70 * (P / 2.2)^{0.756}$

2. Physical activity: Calories required = $0.0385 * Intensity * P * Minutes$

Here, *Minutes* is the number of minutes spent during the physical activity, and *Intensity* is a number that estimates the intensity of the activity. Here are some sample numbers for the range of values:

Activity	Intensity
Running 10 mph:	17
Running 6 mph:	10
Basketball:	8
Walking 1 mph:	1

3. Energy to digest food: calories required = $TotalCaloriesConsumed * 0.1$

In other words, 10 percent of the calories we consume goes towards digestion.

Write a function that computes the calories required for the basal metabolic rate, taking as input a parameter for the person's weight. Write another function that computes the calories required for physical activity, taking as input parameters for the intensity, weight, and minutes spent exercising.

Use these functions in a program that inputs a person's weight, an estimate for the intensity of physical activity, the number of minutes spent performing the physical activity, and the number of calories in one serving of your favorite food. The program should then calculate and output how many servings of that food should be eaten per day to maintain the person's current weight at the specified activity level. The computation should include the energy that is required to digest food.

> You can find estimates of the caloric content of many foods on the Web. For example, a double cheeseburger has approximately 1000 calories.

15. You have invented a vending machine capable of dispensing candies. Write a program to simulate the vending machine. It costs $1.50 to buy a packet of candies, and the machine only takes coins in denominations of a dollar, quarter, dime, or nickel. Write code to simulate a person putting money into the vending machine by repeatedly prompting the user for the next coin to be inserted. Output the total entered so far when each coin is inserted. When $1.50 or more is added, the program should output "Enjoy your candies. Please visit again." along with any change that should be returned. Use top-down design to determine appropriate functions for the program.

16. Your time machine is capable of going forward in time up to 24 hours. The machine is configured to jump ahead in minutes. To enter the proper number of minutes into your machine, you would like a program that can take a start time (in hours, minutes, and a Boolean indicating AM or PM) and a future time (in hours, minutes, and a Boolean indicating AM or PM) and calculate the difference in minutes between the start and future time.

A time is specified in your program with three variables:

```
int hours, minutes;
bool isAM;
```

For example, to represent 11:50 PM, you would store:

```
hours = 11
minutes = 50
isAM = false;
```

This means that you need six variables to store a start and future time.

Write a program that allows the user to enter a start time and a future time. Include a function named computeDifference that takes the six variables as parameters that represent the start time and future time. Your function should return, as an int, the time difference in minutes. For example, given a start time of 11:59 AM and a future time of 12:01 PM, your program should compute 2 minutes as the time difference. Given a start time of 11:59 AM and a future time of 11:58 AM, your program should compute 1439 minutes as the time difference (23 hours and 59 minutes).

You may need "AM" or "PM" from the user's input by reading in two character values. (Display 2.3 illustrates character input.) Characters can be compared just like numbers. For example, if the variable a_char is of type char, then (a_char == 'A') is a Boolean expression that evaluates to true if a_char contains the letter A.

VideoNote
Solution to Programming
Project 4.17

17. Do Programming Project 18 from Chapter 3 except write a function named containsDigit that determines if a number contains a particular digit. The header should look like:

```
bool containsDigit(int number, int digit);
```

If number contains digit, then the function should return true. Otherwise, the function should return false. Your program should use this function to find the closest numbers that can be entered on the keypad.

Functions for All Subtasks 5

Everything is possible.

COMMON MAXIM

INTRODUCTION

The top-down design strategy discussed in Chapter 4 is an effective way to design an algorithm for a program. You divide the program's task into subtasks and then implement the algorithms for these subtasks as functions. Thus far, we have seen how to define functions that start with the values of some arguments and return a single value as the result of the function call. A subtask that computes a single value is a very important kind of subtask, but it is not the only kind. In this chapter we will complete our description of C++ functions and present techniques for designing functions that perform other kinds of subtasks.

PREREQUISITES

You should read Chapters 2 through 4 before reading this chapter.

5.1 *void* FUNCTIONS

void functions return no value

Subtasks are implemented as functions in C++. The functions discussed in Chapter 4 always return a single value, but there are other forms of subtasks. A subtask might produce several values or it might produce no values at all. In C++, a function must either return a single value or return no values at all. As we will see later in this chapter, a subtask that produces several different values is usually (and perhaps paradoxically) implemented as a function that returns no value. For the moment, however, let us avoid that complication and focus on subtasks that intuitively produce no values at all, and let us see how these subtasks are implemented. A function that returns no value is called a *void* function. For example, one typical subtask for a program is to output the results of some calculation. This subtask produces output on the screen, but it produces no values for the rest of the program to use. This kind of subtask would be implemented as a *void* function.

Definitions of *void* Functions

In C++ a *void* function is defined in almost the same way as a function that returns a value. For example, the following is a *void* function that outputs the result of a calculation that converts a temperature expressed in Fahrenheit

278

degrees to a temperature expressed in Celsius degrees. The actual calculation would be done elsewhere in the program. This *void* function implements only the subtask for outputting the results of the calculation. For now, we do not need to worry about how the calculation will be performed.

```
void show_results(double f_degrees, double c_degrees)
{
    using namespace std;
    cout.setf(ios::fixed);
    cout.setf(ios::showpoint);
    cout.precision(1);
    cout << f_degrees
         << " degrees Fahrenheit is equivalent to\n"
         << c_degrees << " degrees Celsius.\n";
    return;
}
```

As this function definition illustrates, there are only two differences between a function definition for a *void* function and the function definitions we discussed in Chapter 4. One difference is that we use the keyword *void* where we would normally specify the type of the value to be returned. This tells the compiler that this function will not return any value. The name *void* is used as a way of saying "no value is returned by this function." The second difference is that the *return* statement does not contain an expression for a value to be returned, because, after all, there is no value returned. The syntax is summarized in Display 5.1.

Function definition

A *void* function call is an executable statement. For example, our function show_results might be called as follows:

Function call

```
show_results(32.5, 0.3);
```

If this statement were executed in a program, it would cause the following to appear on the screen:

```
32.5 degrees Fahrenheit is equivalent to
0.3 degrees Celsius.
```

Notice that the function call ends with a semicolon, which tells the compiler that the function call is an executable statement.

When a *void* function is called, the arguments are substituted for the formal parameters and the statements in the function body are executed. For example, a call to the *void* function show_results, which we gave earlier in this section, will cause some output to be written to the screen. One way to think of a call to a *void* function is to imagine that the body of the function definition is copied into the program in place of the function call. When the function is called, the arguments are substituted for the formal parameters, and then it is just as if the body of the function were lines in the program.

DISPLAY 5.1 Syntax for a *void* Function Definition

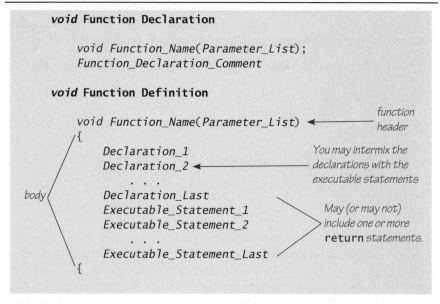

Functions with no arguments

It is perfectly legal, and sometimes useful, to have a function with no arguments. In that case, there simply are no formal parameters listed in the function declaration and no arguments are used when the function is called. For example, the *void* function `initialize_screen`, defined next, simply sends a new line command to the screen:

```
void initialize_screen()
{
    using namespace std;
    cout << endl;
    return;
}
```

If your program includes the following call to this function as its first executable statement, then the output from the previously run program will be separated from the output for your program:

```
initialize_screen();
```

Be sure to notice that even when there are no parameters to a function, you still must include the parentheses in the function declaration and in a call to the function. The next programming example shows these two sample *void* functions in a complete program.

PROGRAMMING EXAMPLE	Converting Temperatures

The program in Display 5.2 takes a Fahrenheit temperature as input and outputs the equivalent Celsius temperature. A Fahrenheit temperature F can be converted to an equivalent Celsius temperature C as follows:

$$C = (5/9)(F \times 32)$$

The function celsius shown in Display 5.2 uses this formula to do the temperature conversion.

return Statements in *void* Functions

Both *void* functions and functions that return a value can have *return* statements. In the case of a function that returns a value, the *return* statement specifies the value returned. In the case of a *void* function, the *return* statement simply ends the function call. As we saw in the previous chapter, every function that returns a value must end by executing a *return* statement. However, a *void* function need not contain a *return* statement. If it does not contain a *return* statement, it will end after executing the code in the function body. It is as if there were an implicit *return* statement just before the final closing brace } at the end of the function body. For example, the functions initialize_screen and show_results in Display 5.2 would perform exactly the same if we omitted the *return* statements from their function definitions.

> *void* functions and *return* statements

The fact that there is an implicit *return* statement before the final closing brace in a function body does not mean that you never need a *return* statement in a *void* function. For example, the function definition in Display 5.3 might be used as part of a restaurant management program. That function outputs instructions for dividing a given amount of ice cream among the people at a table. If there are no people at the table (that is, if number equals 0), then the *return* statement within the *if* statement terminates the function call and avoids a division by zero. If number is not 0, then the function call ends when the last cout statement is executed at the end of the function body.

By now you may have guessed that the main part of a program is actually the definition of a function called main. When the program is run, the function main is automatically called and it, in turn, may call other functions. Although it may seem that the *return* statement in the main part of a program should be optional, officially it is not. Technically, the main part of a program is a function that returns a value of type *int*, so it requires a *return* statement. However, the function main is used as if it were a *void* function. Treating the main part of your program as a function that returns an integer may sound

> The main part of a program is a function

DISPLAY 5.2 *void* **Functions** *(part 1 of 2)*

```
1    //Program to convert a Fahrenheit temperature to a Celsius temperature.
2    #include <iostream>
3
4    void initialize_screen( );
5    //Separates current output from
6    //the output of the previously run program.
7
8    double celsius(double fahrenheit);
9    //Converts a Fahrenheit temperature
10   //to a Celsius temperature.
11
12   void show_results(double f_degrees, double c_degrees);
13   //Displays output. Assumes that c_degrees
14   //Celsius is equivalent to f_degrees Fahrenheit.
15
16   int main( )
17   {
18       using namespace std;
19       double f_temperature, c_temperature;
20
21       initialize_screen( );
22       cout << "I will convert a Fahrenheit temperature"
23            << " to Celsius.\n"
24            << "Enter a temperature in Fahrenheit: ";
25       cin >> f_temperature;
26
27       c_temperature = celsius(f_temperature);
28
29       show_results(f_temperature, c_temperature);
30       return 0;
31   }
32
33   //Definition uses iostream:
34   void initialize_screen( )
35   {
36       using namespace std;
37       cout << endl;
38       return;            ◄───────── This return is optional.
39   }
40   double celsius(double fahrenheit)
41   {
42       return ((5.0/9.0)*(fahrenheit - 32));
43   }
44   //Definition uses iostream:
45   void show_results(double f_degrees, double c_degrees)
46   {
```

(continued)

DISPLAY 5.2 *void* **Functions** *(part 2 of 2)*

```
47      using namespace std;
48      cout.setf(ios::fixed);
49      cout.setf(ios::showpoint);
50      cout.precision(1);
51      cout << f_degrees
52           << " degrees Fahrenheit is equivalent to\n"
53           << c_degrees << " degrees Celsius.\n";
54      return; ◄─────────────────── This return is optional.
55   }
```

Sample Dialogue

```
I will convert a Fahrenheit temperature to Celsius.
Enter a temperature in Fahrenheit: 32.5
32.5 degrees Fahrenheit is equivalent to
0.3 degrees Celsius.
```

DISPLAY 5.3 **Use of** *return* **in a** *void* **Function**

Function Declaration

```
1    void ice_cream_division(int number, double total_weight);
2    //Outputs instructions for dividing total_weight ounces of
3    //ice cream among number customers.
4    //If number is 0, nothing is done.
```

Function Definition

```
1    //Definition uses iostream:
2    void ice_cream_division(int number, double total_weight)
3    {
4        using namespace std;
5        double portion;
6                                          If number is 0, then the
7        if (number == 0)                  function execution ends here.
8            return; ◄─────
9        portion = total_weight/number;
10       cout.setf(ios::fixed);
11       cout.setf(ios::showpoint);
12       cout.precision(2);
13       cout << "Each one receives "
14            << portion << " ounces of ice cream." << endl;
15   }
```

crazy, but that's the tradition. It might be best to continue to think of the main part of the program as just "the main part of the program" and not worry about this minor detail.[1]

SELF-TEST EXERCISES

1. What is the output of the following program?

```
#include <iostream>
void friendly();
void shy(int audience_count);
int main()
{
    using namespace std;
    friendly();
    shy(6);
    cout << "One more time:\n";
    shy(2);
    friendly();
    cout << "End of program.\n";
    return 0;
}

void friendly()
{
    using namespace std;
    cout << "Hello\n";
}

void shy(int audience_count)
{
    using namespace std;
    if (audience_count < 5)
        return;
    cout << "Goodbye\n";
}
```

2. Are you required to have a *return* statement in a *void* function definition?

3. Suppose you omitted the *return* statement in the function definition for initialize_screen in Display 5.2. What effect would it have on the program? Would the program compile? Would it run? Would the program behave any differently? What about the *return* statement in the function

---

[1] The C++ Standard says that you can omit the *return* 0 in the main part, but many compilers still require it.

definition for show_results in that same program? What effect would it have on the program if you omitted the *return* statement in the definition of show_results? What about the *return* statement in the function definition for celsius in that same program? What effect would it have on the program if you omitted the *return* statement in the definition of celsius?

4. Write a definition for a *void* function that has three arguments of type *int* and that outputs to the screen the product of these three arguments. Put the definition in a complete program that reads in three numbers and then calls this function.

5. Does your compiler allow *void* main() and *int* main()? What warnings are issued if you have *int* main() and do not supply a *return* 0; statement? To find out, write several small test programs and perhaps ask your instructor or a local guru.

6. Is a call to a *void* function used as a statement or is it used as an expression?

5.2 CALL-BY-REFERENCE PARAMETERS

When a function is called, its arguments are substituted for the formal parameters in the function definition, or to state it less formally, the arguments are "plugged in" for the formal parameters. There are different mechanisms used for this substitution process. The mechanism we used in Chapter 4, and thus far in this chapter, is known as the *call-by-value* mechanism. The second main mechanism for substituting arguments is known as the *call-by-reference* mechanism.

A First View of Call-by-Reference

The call-by-value mechanism that we used until now is not sufficient for certain subtasks. For example, one common subtask is to obtain one or more input values from the user. Look back at the program in Display 5.2. Its tasks are divided into four subtasks: initialize the screen, obtain the Fahrenheit temperature, compute the corresponding Celsius temperature, and output the results. Three of these four subtasks are implemented as the functions initialize_screen, celsius, and show_results. However, the subtask of obtaining the input is implemented as the following four lines of code (rather than as a function call):

```
cout << "I will convert a Fahrenheit temperature"
     << " to Celsius.\n"
     << "Enter a temperature in Fahrenheit: ";
cin >> f_temperature;
```

The subtask of obtaining the input should be accomplished by a function call. To do this with a function call, we will use a call-by-reference parameter.

A function for obtaining input should set the values of one or more variables to values typed in at the keyboard, so the function call should have one or more variables as arguments and should change the values of these argument variables. With the call-by-value formal parameters that we have used until now, an argument in a function call can be a variable, but the function takes only the value of the variable and does not change the variable in any way. With a call-by-value formal parameter only the value of the argument is substituted for the formal parameter. For an input function, we want the variable (not the value of the variable) to be substituted for the formal parameter. The call-by-reference mechanism works in just this way. With a **call-by-reference** formal parameter (also called simply a **reference** parameter), the corresponding argument in a function call must be a variable and this argument variable is substituted for the formal parameter. It is as if the argument variable were literally copied into the body of the function definition in place of the formal parameter. After the argument is substituted in, the code in the function body is executed and this code can change the value of the argument variable.

A call-by-reference parameter must be marked in some way so that the compiler will know it from a call-by-value parameter. The way that you indicate a call-by-reference parameter is to attach the ampersand sign, **&**, to the end of the type name in the formal parameter list in both the function declaration and the header of the function definition. For example, the following function definition has one formal parameter, f_variable, and that formal parameter is a call-by-reference parameter:

```
void get_input (double& f_variable)
{
    using namespace std;
    cout << "I will convert a Fahrenheit temperature"
         << " to Celsius.\n"
         << "Enter a temperature in Fahrenheit: ";
    cin >> f_variable;
}
```

In a program that contains this function definition, the following function call sets the variable f_temperature equal to a value read from the keyboard:

```
get_input(f_temperature);
```

Using this function definition, we could easily rewrite the program shown in Display 5.2 so that the subtask of reading the input is accomplished by this function call. However, rather than rewrite an old program, let's look at a completely new program.

Display 5.4 demonstrates call-by-reference parameters. The program doesn't do very much. It just reads in two numbers and writes the same numbers out, but in the reverse order. The parameters in the functions get_numbers and swap_values are call-by-reference parameters. The input is performed by the function call

```
get_numbers(first_num, second_num);
```

DISPLAY 5.4   Call-by-Reference Parameters

```
1    //Program to demonstrate call-by-reference parameters.
2    #include <iostream>

3    void get_numbers(int& input1, int& input2);
4    //Reads two integers from the keyboard.

5    void swap_values(int& variable1, int& variable2);
6    //Interchanges the values of variable1 and variable2.

7    void show_results(int output1, int output2);
8    //Shows the values of variable1 and variable2, in that order.
9    int main( )
10   {
11       int first_num = 0, second_num = 0;
12
13       get_numbers(first_num, second_num);
14       swap_values(first_num, second_num);
15       show_results(first_num, second_num);
16       return 0;
17   }
18   //Uses iostream:
19   void get_numbers (int& input1, int& input2)
20   {
21       using namespace std;
22       cout << "Enter two integers: ";
23       cin >> input1
24           >> input2;
25   }
26   void swap_values(int& variable1, int& variable2)
27   {
28       int temp;
29       temp = variable1;
30       variable1 = variable2;
31       variable2 = temp;
32   }
33   //Uses iostream:
34   void show_results(int output1, int output2)
35   {
36       using namespace std;
37       cout << "In reverse order the numbers are: "
38           << output1 << " " << output2 << endl;
39   }
```

Sample Dialogue

```
Enter two integers: 5 10
In reverse order the numbers are: 10 5
```

The values of the variables `first_num` and `second_num` are set by this function call. After that, the following function call reverses the values in the two variables `first_num` and `second_num`:

```
swap_values(first_num, second_num);
```

In the next few subsections we describe the call-by-reference mechanism in more detail and also explain the particular functions used in Display 5.4.

Call-by-Reference in Detail

In most situations, the call-by-reference mechanism works as if the name of the variable given as the function argument were literally substituted for the call-by-reference formal parameter. However, the process is a bit more subtle than that. In some situations, this subtlety is important, so we need to examine more details of this call-by-reference substitution process.

Recall that program variables are implemented as memory locations. The compiler assigns one memory location to each variable. For example, when the program in Display 5.4 is compiled, the variable `first_num` might be assigned location 1010, and the variable `second_num` might be assigned 1012. For purposes of this example, consider these variables to be stored at these memory locations. In other words, after executing the line

```
int first_num = 0, second_num = 0;
```

the value 0 will be stored at memory locations 1010 and 1012. The arrows in the diagram below point to the memory locations referenced by the variables.

Memory Location	Value
...	
1008	
1010	0	◀— first_num
1012	0	◀— second_num
1014	
...	

Next, consider the following function declaration from Display 5.4:

```
void get_numbers(int& input1, int& input2);
```

The call-by-reference formal parameters `input1` and `input2` are place holders for the actual arguments used in a function call.

Call-by-Reference

To make a formal parameter a **call-by-reference** parameter, append the **ampersand sign &** to its type name. The corresponding argument in a call to the function should then be a variable, not a constant or other expression. When the function is called, the corresponding variable argument (not its value) will be substituted for the formal parameter. Any change made to the formal parameter in the function body will be made to the argument variable when the function is called. The exact details of the substitution mechanisms are given in the text of this chapter.

EXAMPLE (OF CALL-BY-REFERENCE PARAMETERS IN A FUNCTION DECLARATION):

```
void get_data(int& first_in, double& second_in);
```

Now consider a function call like the following from the same display:

```
get_numbers(first_num, second_num);
```

When the function call is executed, the function is not given values stored in `first_num` and `second_num`. Instead, it is given the memory locations associated with each name. In this example, the locations are

```
1010
1012
```

which are the locations assigned to the argument variables `first_num` and `second_num`, in that order. It is these memory locations that are associated with the formal parameters. The first memory location is associated with the first formal parameter, the second memory location is associated with the second formal parameter, and so forth. In our example `input1` is the first parameter, so it gets the same memory location as `first_num`. The second parameter is `input2` and it gets the same memory location as `second_num`. Diagrammatically, the correspondence is

Memory Location	Value
...	
1008	
1010	0
1012	0
1014	
...	

input1 → 1010 0 ← *first_num*
input2 → 1012 0 ← *second_num*

When the function statements are executed, whatever the function body says to do to a formal parameter is actually done to the variable in the memory location associated with that formal parameter. In this case, the instructions in the body of the function get_numbers say that a value should be stored in the formal parameter input1 using a cin statement, and so that value is stored in the variable in memory location 1010 (which happens to be where the variable first_num is stored). Similarly, the instructions in the body of the function get_numbers say that a value should then be stored in the formal parameter input2 using a cin statement, and so that value is stored in the variable in memory location 1012 (which happens to be where the variable second_num is stored). Thus, whatever the function instructs the computer to do to input1 and input2 is actually done to the variables first_num and second_num. For example, if the user enters 5 and 10 as in Display 5.4, then the result is

Memory Location	Value
...	
1008	
1010	5
1012	10
1014	
...	

input1 → (points to 1010) first_num ← (points to 1010, value 5)
input2 → (points to 1012) second_num ← (points to 1012, value 10)

When the function get_numbers exits, the variables input1 and input2 go out of scope and are lost. This means we can no longer retrieve the data values at 1010 and 1012 through the variables input1 and input2. However, the data still exists in memory location 1010 and 1012 and is accessible through the variables first_num and second_num within the scope of the main function. These details of how the call-by-reference mechanism works in this function call to get_numbers are described in Display 5.5.

It may seem that there is an extra level of detail, or at least an extra level of verbiage. If first_num is the variable with memory location 1010, why do we insist on saying "the variable at memory location 1010" instead of simply saying "first_num"? This extra level of detail is needed if the arguments and formal parameters contain some confusing coincidence of names. For example, the function get_numbers has formal parameters named input1 and input2. Suppose you want to change the program in Display 5.4 so that it uses the function get_numbers with arguments that are also named input1 and input2, and suppose that you want to do something less than obvious. Suppose you want the first number typed in to be stored in a variable named input2, and the second

DISPLAY 5.5   Behavior of Call-by-Reference Arguments *(part 1 of 2)*

**Anatomy of a Function Call from Display 5.4
Using Call-by-Reference Arguments**

0   Assume the variables `first_num` and `second_num` have been assigned the following memory address by the compiler:

```
first_num  ────►  1010
second_num ────►  1012
```

(We do not know what addresses are assigned and the results will not depend on the actual addresses, but this will make the process very concrete and thus perhaps easier to follow.)

1   In the program in Display 5.4, the following function call begins executing:

```
get_numbers(first_num, second_num);
```

2   The function is told to use the memory location of the variable `first_num` in place of the formal parameter `input1` and the memory location of the `second_num` in place of the formal parameter `input2`. The effect is the same as if the function definition were rewritten to the following (which is not legal C++ code, but does have a clear meaning to us):

```
void get_numbers(int& <the variable at memory location 1010>,
                 int& <the variable at memory location 1012>)
{
    using namespace std;
    cout << "Enter two integers: ";
    cin >> <the variable at memory location 1010>
        >> <the variable at memory location 1012>;
}
```

Anatomy of the Function Call in Display 5.4 (*concluded*)

Since the variables in locations 1010 and 1012 are `first_num` and `second_num`, the effect is thus the same as if the function definition were rewritten to the following:

```
void get_numbers(int& first_num, int& second_num)
{
    using namespace std;
    cout << "Enter two integers: ";
    cin >> first_num
        >> second_num;
}
```

3   The body of the function is executed. The effect is the same as if the following were executed:

(continued)

DISPLAY 5.5 **Behavior of Call-by-Reference Arguments** *(part 2 of 2)*

```
        {
            using namespace std;
            cout << "Enter two integers: ";
            cin >> first_num
                >> second_num;
        }
```

4   When the `cin` statement is executed, the values of the variables `first_num` and `second_num` are set to the values typed in at the keyboard. (If the dialogue is as shown in Display 5.4, then the value of `first_num` is set to 5 and the value of `second_num` is set to 10.)

5   When the function call ends, the variables `first_num` and `second_num` retain the values that they were given by the `cin` statement in the function body. (If the dialogue is as shown in Display 5.4, then the value of `first_num` is 5 and the value of `second_num` is 10 at the end of the function call.)

---

number typed in to be stored in the variable named `input1`—perhaps because the second number will be processed first, or because it is the more important number. Now, let's suppose that the variables `input1` and `input2`, which are declared in the `main` part of your program, have been assigned memory locations 1014 and 1016. The function call could be as follows:

```
int input1, input 2;
get_numbers(input2, input1);
```
Notice the order of the arguments

In this case if you say "input1," we do not know whether you mean the variable named `input1` that is declared in the `main` part of your program or the formal parameter `input1`. However, if the variable `input1` declared in the `main` part of your program is assigned memory location 1014, the phrase "the variable at memory location 1014" is unambiguous. Let's go over the details of the substitution mechanisms in this case.

In this call the argument corresponding to the formal parameter `input1` is the variable `input2`, and the argument corresponding to the formal parameter `input2` is the variable `input1`. This can be confusing to us, but it produces no problem at all for the computer, since the computer never does actually "substitute input2 for input1" or "substitute input1 for input2." The computer simply deals with memory locations. The computer substitutes "the variable at memory location 1016" for the formal parameter `input1`, and "the variable at memory location 1014" for the formal parameter `input2`.

PROGRAMMING EXAMPLE   The swap_values Function

The function swap_values defined in Display 5.4 interchanges the values stored in two variables. The description of the function is given by the following function declaration and accompanying comment:

```
void swap_values(int& variable1, int& variable2);
//Interchanges the values of variable1 and variable2.
```

To see how the function is supposed to work, assume that the variable first_num has the value 5 and the variable second_num has the value 10 and consider the function call:

```
swap_values(first_num, second_num);
```

After this function call, the value of first_num will be **10** and the value of second_num will be 5.

As shown in Display 5.4, the definition of the function swap_values uses a local variable called temp. This local variable is needed. You might be tempted to think the function definition could be simplified to the following:

```
void swap_values(int& variable1, int& variable2)
{
    variable1 = variable2;                    This does not work!
    variable2 = variable1;
}
```

To see that this alternative definition cannot work, consider what would happen with this definition and the function call

```
swap_values(first_num, second_num);
```

The variables first_num and second_num are substituted for the formal parameters variable1 and variable2 so that, with this incorrect function definition, the function call is equivalent to the following:

```
first_num = second_num;
second_num = first_num;
```

This code does not produce the desired result. The value of first_num is set equal to the value of second_num, just as it should be. But then, the value of second_num is set equal to the changed value of first_num, which is now the original value of second_num. Thus the value of second_num is not changed at all. (If this is unclear, go through the steps with specific values for the variables first_num and second_num.) What the function needs to do is to save the original value of first_num so that value is not lost. This is what the local variable temp in the correct function definition is used for. That correct definition is the one in Display 5.4. When that correct version is used and the function is called with the arguments `first_num` and `second_num`, the function call is equivalent to the following code, which works correctly:

```
temp = first_num;
first_num = second_num;
second_num = temp;
```

Parameters and Arguments

All the different terms that have to do with parameters and arguments can be confusing. However, if you keep a few simple points in mind, you will be able to easily handle these terms.

1. The **formal parameters** for a function are listed in the function declaration and are used in the body of the function definition. A formal parameter (of any sort) is a kind of blank or place holder that is filled in with something when the function is called.

2. An **argument** is something that is used to fill in a formal parameter. When you write down a function call, the arguments are listed in parentheses after the function name. When the function call is executed, the arguments are "plugged in" for the formal parameters.

3. The terms *call-by-value* and *call-by-reference* refer to the mechanism that is used in the "plugging in" process. In the **call-by-value** method, only the value of the argument is used. In this call-by-value mechanism, the formal parameter is a local variable that is initialized to the value of the corresponding argument. In the **call-by-reference** mechanism, the argument is a variable and the entire variable is used. In the call-by-reference mechanism, the argument variable is substituted for the formal parameter so that any change that is made to the formal parameter is actually made to the argument variable.

Mixed Parameter Lists

Whether a formal parameter is a call-by-value parameter or a call-by-reference parameter is determined by whether there is an ampersand attached to its type specification. If the ampersand is present, then the formal parameter is a call-by-reference parameter. If there is no ampersand associated with the formal parameter, then it is a call-by-value parameter.

Mixing call-by-reference and call-by-value

It is perfectly legitimate to mix call-by-value and call-by-reference formal parameters in the same function. For example, the first and last of the formal parameters in the following function declaration are call-by-reference formal parameters and the middle one is a call-by-value parameter:

```
void good_stuff(int& par1, int par2, double& par3);
```

Call-by-reference parameters are not restricted to *void* functions. You can also use them in functions that return a value. Thus, a function with a call-by-reference parameter could both change the value of a variable given as an argument and return a value.

■ PROGRAMMING TIP   What Kind of Parameter to Use

VideoNote
Call by Reference and Call
by Value

Display 5.6 illustrates the differences between how the compiler treats call-by-value and call-by-reference formal parameters. The parameters par1_value and par2_ref are both assigned a value inside the body of the function definition. But since they are different kinds of parameters, the effect is different in the two cases.

par1_value is a call-by-value parameter, so it is a local variable. When the function is called as follows

```
do_stuff(n1, n2);
```

the local variable par1_value is initialized to the value of n1. That is, the local variable par1_value is initialized to 1 and the variable n1 is then ignored by the function. As you can see from the sample dialogue, the formal parameter par1_value (which is a local variable) is set to 111 in the function body and this value is output to the screen. However, the value of the argument n1 is not changed. As shown in the sample dialogue, n1 has retained its value of 1.

DISPLAY 5.6   **Comparing Argument Mechanisms** *(part 1 of 2)*

```
1    //Illustrates the difference between a call-by-value
2    //parameter and a call-by-reference parameter.
3    #include <iostream>
4    void do_stuff(int par1_value, int& par2_ref);
5    //par1_value is a call-by-value formal parameter and
6    //par2_ref is a call-by-reference formal parameter.
7    int main( )
8    {
9        using namespace std;
10       int n1, n2;
11
12       n1 = 1;
13       n2 = 2;
14       do_stuff(n1, n2);
15       cout << "n1 after function call = " << n1 << endl;
16       cout << "n2 after function call = " << n2 << endl;
17       return 0;
18   }
19   void do_stuff(int par1_value, int& par2_ref)
20   {
21       using namespace std;
```

(continued)

DISPLAY 5.6 Comparing Argument Mechanisms *(part 2 of 2)*

```
22        par1_value = 111;
23        cout << "par1_value in function call = "
24             << par1_value << endl;
25        par2_ref = 222;
26        cout << "par2_ref in function call = "
27             << par2_ref << endl;
28    }
```

Sample Dialogue

```
par1_value in function call = 111
par2_ref in function call = 222
n1 after function call = 1
n2 after function call = 222
```

On the other hand, par2_ref is a call-by-reference parameter. When the function is called, the variable argument n2 (not just its value) is substituted for the formal parameter par2_ref. So that when the following code is executed:

```
par2_ref = 222;
```

it is the same as if the following were executed:

```
n2 = 222;
```

Thus, the value of the variable n2 is changed when the function body is executed, so as the dialogue shows, the value of n2 is changed from 2 to 222 by the function call.

If you keep in mind the lesson of Display 5.6, it is easy to decide which parameter mechanism to use. If you want a function to change the value of a variable, then the corresponding formal parameter must be a call-by-reference formal parameter and must be marked with the ampersand sign, &. In all other cases, you can use a call-by-value formal parameter. ∎

PITFALL   Inadvertent Local Variables

If you want a function to change the value of a variable, the corresponding formal parameter must be a call-by-reference parameter and must have the ampersand, &, attached to its type. If you carelessly omit the ampersand, the function will have a call-by-value parameter where you meant to have a call-by-reference parameter, and when the program is run, you will discover that the function call does not change the value of the corresponding argument. This is because a formal call-by-value parameter is a local variable, so if it has its value changed in the function, then as with any local variable, that change has no effect outside of the function body. This is a logic error that can be very difficult to see because it looks right.

For example, the program in Display 5.7 is identical to the program in Display 5.4, except that the ampersands were mistakenly omitted from the function swap_values. As a result, the formal parameters variable1 and variable2 are local variables. The argument variables first_num and second_num are never substituted in for variable1 and variable2; variable1 and variable2 are instead initialized to the values of first_num and second_num. Then, the values of variable1 and variable2 are interchanged, but the values of first_num and second_num are left unchanged. The omission of two ampersands has made the program completely wrong, yet it looks almost identical to the correct program and will compile and run without any error messages.

DISPLAY 5.7   Inadvertent Local Variable

```
1    //Program to demonstrate call-by-reference parameters.
2    #include <iostream>

3    void get_numbers(int& input1, int& input2);
4    //Reads two integers from the keyboard.              ── forgot the & here

5    void swap_values(int variable1, int variable2);
6    //Interchanges the values of variable1 and variable2.

7    void show_results(int output1, int output2);
8    //Shows the values of variable1 and variable2, in that order.

9    int main( )
10   {
11       int first_num, second_num;

12       get_numbers(first_num, second_num);
13       swap_values(first_num, second_num);
14       show_results(first_num, second_num);        forgot the & here
15       return 0;
16   }

17   void swap_values(int variable1, int variable2)
18   {
19       int temp;                          inadvertent
                                            local variables
20       temp = variable1;
21       variable1 = variable2;
22       variable2 = temp;
23   }
24            <The definitions of get_numbers and
25                show_results are the same as in Display 5.4.>
```

Sample Dialogue

```
Enter two integers: 5 10
In reverse order the numbers are: 5 10
```

SELF-TEST EXERCISES

7. What is the output of the following program?

```cpp
#include <iostream>
void figure_me_out(int& x, int y, int& z);
int main()
{
    using namespace std;
    int a, b, c;
    a = 10;
    b = 20;
    c = 30;
    figure_me_out(a, b, c);
    cout << a << " " << b << " " << c;
    return 0;
}

void figure_me_out(int& x, int y, int& z)
{
    using namespace std;
    cout << x << " " << y << " " << z << endl;
    x = 1;
    y = 2;
    z = 3;
    cout << x << " " << y << " " << z << endl;
}
```

8. What would be the output of the program in Display 5.4 if you omit the ampersands, &, from the first parameter in the function declaration and function heading of swap_values? The ampersand is not removed from the second parameter.

9. What would be the output of the program in Display 5.6 if you change the function declaration for the function do_stuff to the following and you change the function header to match, so that the formal parameter par2_ref is changed to a call-by-value parameter:

```cpp
void do_stuff(int par1_value, int par2_ref);
```

10. Write a *void* function definition for a function called zero_both that has two reference parameters, both of which are variables of type *int*, and sets the values of both variables to 0.

11. Write a *void* function definition for a function called add_tax. The function add_tax has two formal parameters: tax_rate, which is the amount of sales tax expressed as a percentage, and cost, which is the cost of an item before tax. The function changes the value of cost so that it includes sales tax.

12. Can a function that returns a value have a call-by-reference parameter? May a function have both call-by-value and call-by-reference parameters?

5.3 USING PROCEDURAL ABSTRACTION

My memory is so bad, that many times I forget my own name!

MIGUEL DE CERVANTES SAAVEDRA, *Don Quixote*

Recall that the principle of procedural abstraction says that functions should be designed so that they can be used as black boxes. For a programmer to use a function effectively, all the programmer should need to know is the function declaration and the accompanying comment that says what the function accomplishes. The programmer should not need to know any of the details contained in the function body. In this section we discuss a number of topics that deal with this principle in more detail.

Functions Calling Functions

A function body may contain a call to another function. The situation for these sorts of function calls is exactly the same as it would be if the function call had occurred in the `main` function of the program; the only restriction is that the function declaration should appear before the function is used. If you set up your programs as we have been doing, this will happen automatically, since all function declarations come before the `main` function and all function definitions come after the `main` function. Although you may include a function call within the definition of another function, you cannot place the definition of one function within the body of another function definition.

Display 5.8 shows an enhanced version of the program shown in Display 5.4. The program in Display 5.4 always reversed the values of the variables `first_num` and `second_num`. The program in Display 5.8 reverses these variables only some of the time. The program in Display 5.8 uses the function `order` to reorder the values in these variables so as to ensure that

    first_num <= second_num

If this condition is already true, then nothing is done to the variables `first_num` and `second_num`. If, however, `first_num` is greater than `second_num`, then the function `swap_values` is called to interchange the values of these two variables. This testing for order and exchanging of variable values all takes place within the body of the function `order`. Thus, the function `swap_values` is called within the body of the function `order`. This presents no special problems. Using the principle of procedural abstraction, we think of the function `swap_values` as performing an action (namely, interchanging the values of two variables); this action is the same no matter where it occurs.

DISPLAY 5.8 Function Calling Another Function *(part 1 of 2)*

```
1    //Program to demonstrate a function calling another function.
2    #include <iostream>
3
4    void get_input(int& input1, int& input2);
5    //Reads two integers from the keyboard.
6
7    void swap_values(int& variable1, int& variable2);
8    //Interchanges the values of variable1 and variable2.
9
10   void order(int& n1, int& n2);
11   //Orders the numbers in the variables n1 and n2
12   //so that after the function call n1 <= n2.
13
14   void give_results(int output1, int output2);
15   //Outputs the values in output1 and output2.
16   //Assumes that output1 <= output2
17
18   int main( )
19   {
20       int first_num, second_num;
21
22       get_input(first_num, second_num);
23       order(first_num, second_num);
24       give_results(first_num, second_num);
25       return 0;
26   }
27
28   //Uses iostream:
29   void get_input(int& input1, int& input2)
30   {
31       using namespace std;
32       cout << "Enter two integers: ";
33       cin >> input1 >> input2;
34   }
35
36   void swap_values(int& variable1, int& variable2)
37   {
38       int temp;
39
40       temp = variable1;
41       variable1 = variable2;
42       variable2 = temp;
43   }
44
```

(continued)

DISPLAY 5.8 Function Calling Another Function *(part 2 of 2)*

```
45    void order(int& n1, int& n2)
46    {
47        if (n1 > n2)
48            swap_values(n1, n2);
49    }
```
These function definitions can be in any order.

```
50
51    //Uses iostream:
52    void give_results(int output1, int output2)
53    {
54        using namespace std;
55        cout << "In increasing order the numbers are: "
56             << output1 << " " << output2 << endl;
57    }
```

Sample Dialogue

```
Enter two integers: 10 5
In increasing order the numbers are: 5 10
```

Preconditions and Postconditions

One good way to write a function declaration comment is to break it down into two kinds of information, called a precondition and a postcondition. The **precondition** states what is assumed to be true when the function is called. The function should not be used and cannot be expected to perform correctly unless the precondition holds. The **postcondition** describes the effect of the function call; that is, the postcondition tells what will be true after the function is executed in a situation in which the precondition holds. For a function that returns a value, the postcondition will describe the value returned by the function. For a function that changes the value of some argument variables, the postcondition will describe all the changes made to the values of the arguments.

For example, the function declaration comment for the function swap_values shown in Display 5.8 can be put into this format as follows:

```
void swap_values(int& variable1, int& variable2);
//Precondition: variable1 and variable2 have been given
//values.
//Postcondition: The values of variable1 and variable2
//have been interchanged.
```

The comment for the function celsius from Display 5.2 can be put into this format as follows:

```
double celsius(double fahrenheit);
//Precondition: fahrenheit is a temperature expressed
```

```
//in degrees Fahrenheit.
//Postcondition: Returns the equivalent temperature
//expressed in degrees Celsius.
```

When the only postcondition is a description of the value returned, programmers often omit the word postcondition. A common and acceptable alternative form for the previous function declaration comments is the following:

```
//Precondition: fahrenheit is a temperature expressed
//in degrees Fahrenheit.
//Returns the equivalent temperature expressed in
//degrees Celsius.
```

Another example of preconditions and postconditions is given by the following function declaration:

```
void post_interest(double& balance, double rate);
//Precondition: balance is a nonnegative savings
//account balance.rate is the interest rate
//expressed as a percent, such as 5 for 5%.
//Postcondition: The value of balance has been
//increased by rate percent.
```

You do not need to know the definition of the function post_interest in order to use this function, so we have given only the function declaration and accompanying comment.

Preconditions and postconditions are more than a way to summarize a function's actions. They should be the first step in designing and writing a function. When you design a program, you should specify what each function does before you start designing how the function will do it. In particular, the function declaration comments and the function declaration should be designed and written down before starting to design the function body. If you later discover that your specification cannot be realized in a reasonable way, you may need to back up and rethink what the function should do, but by clearly specifying what you think the function should do, you will minimize both design errors and wasted time writing code that does not fit the task at hand.

Some programmers prefer not to use the words precondition and postcondition in their function comments. However, whether you use the words or not, your function comment should always contain the precondition and postcondition information.

CASE STUDY Supermarket Pricing

This case study solves a very simple programming task. It may seem that it contains more detail than is needed for such a simple task. However, if you see the design elements in the context of a simple task, you can concentrate on learning them without the distraction of any side issues. Once you learn the techniques that are illustrated in this simple case study, you can apply these same techniques to much more complicated programming tasks.

Problem Definition

We have been commissioned by the Quick-Shop supermarket chain to write a program that will determine the retail price of an item given suitable input. Their pricing policy is that any item that is expected to sell in one week or less is marked up 5 percent, and any item that is expected to stay on the shelf for more than one week is marked up 10 percent over the wholesale price. Be sure to notice that the low markup of 5 percent is used for up to 7 days and that at 8 days the markup changes to 10 percent. It is important to be precise about exactly when a program should change from one form of calculation to a different one.

As always, we should be sure we have a clear statement of the input required and the output produced by the program.

Input

The input will consist of the wholesale price of an item and the expected number of days until the item is sold.

Output

The output will give the retail price of the item.

Analysis of the Problem

Like many simple programming tasks, this one breaks down into three main subtasks:

1. Input the data.

2. Compute the retail price of the item.

3. Output the results.

These three subtasks will be implemented by three functions. The three functions are described by their function declarations and accompanying comments, which are given below. Note that only those items that are changed by the functions are call-by-reference parameters. The remaining formal parameters are call-by-value parameters.

```
void get_input(double& cost, int& turnover);
//Precondition: User is ready to enter values correctly.
//Postcondition: The value of cost has been set to the
//wholesale cost of one item. The value of turnover has been
//set to the expected number of days until the item is sold.

double price(double cost, int turnover);
//Precondition: cost is the wholesale cost of one item.
//turnover is the expected number of days
//until sale of the item.
//Returns the retail price of the item.
```

```
void give_output(double cost, int turnover, double price);
//Precondition: cost is the wholesale cost of one item;
//turnover is the expected time until sale of the item;
//price is the retail price of the item.
//Postcondition: The values of cost, turnover, and price have
//been written to the screen.
```

Now that we have the function headings, it is trivial to write the main part of our program:

```
int main()
{
    double wholesale_cost, retail_price;
    int shelf_time;

    get_input(wholesale_cost, shelf_time);
    retail_price = price(wholesale_cost, shelf_time);
    give_output(wholesale_cost, shelf_time, retail_price);
    return 0;
}
```

Even though we have not yet written the function bodies and have no idea of how the functions work, we can write the above code that uses the functions. That is what is meant by the principle of procedural abstraction. The functions are treated like black boxes.

Algorithm Design

The implementations of the functions `get_input` and `give_output` are straightforward. They simply consist of a few `cin` and `cout` statements. The algorithm for the function `price` is given by the following pseudocode:

```
if turnover ≤ 7 days then
    return (cost +5% of cost);
else
    return (cost +10% of cost);
```

Coding

There are three constants used in this program: a low markup figure of 5 percent, a high markup figure of 10 percent, and an expected shelf stay of 7 days as the threshold above which the high markup is used. Since these constants might need to be changed to update the program should the company decide to change its pricing policy, we declare global named constants at the start of our program for each of these three numbers. The declarations with the *const* modifier are the following:

```
const double LOW_MARKUP = 0.05; //5%
const double HIGH_MARKUP = 0.10; //10%
const int THRESHOLD = 7; //Use HIGH_MARKUP if do not
                         //expect to sell in 7 days or less
```

The body of the function `price` is a straightforward translation of our algorithm from pseudocode to C++ code:

```
{
    if (turnover <= THRESHOLD)
        return ( cost + (LOW_MARKUP * cost) );
    else
        return ( cost + (HIGH_MARKUP * cost) );
}
```

The complete program is shown in Display 5.9.

DISPLAY 5.9 Supermarket Pricing *(part 1 of 2)*

```
 1    //Determines the retail price of an item according to
 2    //the pricing policies of the Quick-Shop supermarket chain.
 3    #include <iostream>
 4    const double LOW_MARKUP = 0.05; //5%
 5    const double HIGH_MARKUP = 0.10; //10%
 6    const int THRESHOLD = 7;//Use HIGH_MARKUP if not expected
 7                            //to sell in 7 days or less.
 8    void introduction();
 9    //Postcondition: Description of program is written on the screen.
10    void get_input(double& cost, int& turnover);
11    //Precondition: User is ready to enter values correctly.
12    //Postcondition: The value of cost has been set to the
13    //wholesale cost of one item. The value of turnover has been
14    //set to the expected number of days until the item is sold.
15    double price(double cost, int turnover);
16    //Precondition: cost is the wholesale cost of one item.
17    //turnover is the expected number of days until sale of the item.
18    //Returns the retail price of the item.
19    void give_output(double cost, int turnover, double price);
20    //Precondition: cost is the wholesale cost of one item; turnover is the
21    //expected time until sale of the item; price is the retail price of the item.
22    //Postcondition: The values of cost, turnover, and price have been
23    //written to the screen.
24    int main( )
25    {
26        double wholesale_cost, retail_price;
27        int shelf_time;
28        introduction( );
29        get_input(wholesale_cost, shelf_time);
30        retail_price = price(wholesale_cost, shelf_time);
31        give_output(wholesale_cost, shelf_time, retail_price);
32        return 0;
33    }
34    //Uses iostream:
35    void introduction( )
```

(continued)

DISPLAY 5.9   **Supermarket Pricing** *(part 2 of 2)*

```
36    {
37        using namespace std;
38        cout<< "This program determines the retail price for\n"
39            << "an item at a Quick-Shop supermarket store.\n";
40    }
41    //Uses iostream:
42    void get_input(double& cost, int& turnover)
43    {
44        using namespace std;
45        cout << "Enter the wholesale cost of item: $";
46        cin >> cost;
47        cout << "Enter the expected number of days until sold: ";
48        cin >> turnover;
49    }
50    //Uses iostream:
51    void give_output(double cost, int turnover, double price)
52    {
53        using namespace std;
54        cout.setf(ios::fixed);
55        cout.setf(ios::showpoint);
56        cout.precision(2);
57        cout << "Wholesale cost = $" << cost << endl
58            << "Expected time until sold = "
59            << turnover << " days" << endl
60            << "Retail price = $" << price << endl;
61    }
62    //Uses defined constants LOW_MARKUP, HIGH_MARKUP, and THRESHOLD:
63    double price(double cost, int turnover)
64    {
65        if (turnover <= THRESHOLD)
66            return ( cost + (LOW_MARKUP * cost) );
67        else
68            return ( cost + (HIGH_MARKUP * cost) );
69
70    }
```

Sample Dialogue

```
This program determines the retail price for an item at a Quick-Shop
supermarket store. Enter the wholesale cost of item: $1.21
Enter the expected number of days until sold: 5
Wholesale cost = $1.21
Expected time until sold = 5 days
Retail price = $1.27
```

Program Testing

An important technique in testing a program is to test all kinds of input. There is no precise definition of what we mean by a "kind" of input, but in practice, it is often easy to decide what kinds of input data a program deals with. In the case of our supermarket program, there are two main kinds of input: input that uses the low markup of 5 percent and input that uses the high markup of 10 percent. Thus, we should test at least one case in which the item is expected to remain on the shelf for less than 7 days and at least one case in which the item is expected to remain on the shelf for more than 7 days.

Test all kinds of input

Another testing strategy is to test boundary values. Unfortunately, boundary value is another vague concept. An input (test) value is a boundary value if it is a value at which the program changes behavior. For example, in our supermarket program, the program's behavior changes at an expected shelf stay of 7 days. Thus, 7 is a boundary value; the program behaves differently for a number of days that is less than or equal to 7 than it does for a number of days that is greater than 7. Hence, we should test the program on at least one case in which the item is expected to remain on the shelf for exactly 7 days. Normally, you should also test input that is one step away from the boundary value as well, since you can easily be off by one in deciding where the boundary is. Hence, we should test our program on input for an item that is expected to remain on the shelf for 6 days, an item that is expected to remain on the shelf for 7 days, and an item that is expected to remain on the shelf for 8 days. (This is in addition to the test inputs described in the previous paragraph, which should be well below and well above 7 days.)

Test boundary values

 SELF-TEST EXERCISES

13. Can a function definition appear inside the body of another function definition?

14. Can a function definition contain a call to another function?

15. Rewrite the function declaration comment for the function order shown in Display 5.8 so that it is expressed in terms of preconditions and postconditions.

16. Give a precondition and a postcondition for the predefined function sqrt, which returns the square root of its argument.

5.4 TESTING AND DEBUGGING FUNCTIONS

"I beheld the wretch—the miserable monster whom I had created."

MARY WOLLSTONECRAFT SHELLEY, *Frankenstein*

Stubs and Drivers

Each function should be designed, coded, and tested as a separate unit from the rest of the program. This is the essence of the top-down design strategy. When you treat each function as a separate unit, you transform one big task into a series of smaller, more manageable tasks. But how do you test a function outside of the program for which it is intended? You write a special program to do the testing. For example, Display 5.10 shows a program to test the function get_input, which was used in the program in Display 5.9.

DISPLAY 5.10   Driver Program *(part 1 of 2)*

```
1     //Driver program for the function get_input.
2     #include <iostream>
3
4     void get_input(double& cost, int& turnover);
5     //Precondition: User is ready to enter values correctly.
6     //Postcondition: The value of cost has been set to the
7     //wholesale cost of one item. The value of turnover has been
8     //set to the expected number of days until the item is sold.
9
10    int main( )
11    {
12        using namespace std;
13        double wholesale_cost;
14        int shelf_time;
15        char ans;
16
17        cout.setf(ios::fixed);
18        cout.setf(ios::showpoint);
19        cout.precision(2);
20        do
21        {
22            get_input(wholesale_cost, shelf_time);
23
24            cout << "Wholesale cost is now $"
25                 << wholesale_cost << endl;
26            cout << "Days until sold is now "
27                 << shelf_time << endl;
28
29            cout << "Test again?"
30                 << " (Type y for yes or n for no): ";
31            cin >> ans;
32            cout << endl;
33        } while (ans == 'y' || ans == 'Y');
34
35        return 0;
36    }
```

(continued)

DISPLAY 5.10 Driver Program *(part 2 of 2)*

```
37    //Uses iostream:
38    void get_input(double& cost, int& turnover)
39    {
40        using namespace std;
41        cout << "Enter the wholesale cost of item: $";
42        cin >> cost;
43        cout << "Enter the expected number of days until sold: ";
44        cin >> turnover;
45    }
```

Sample Dialogue

```
Enter the wholesale cost of item: $123.45
Enter the expected number of days until sold: 67
Wholesale cost is now $123.45
Days until sold is now 67
Test again? (Type y for yes or n for no): y

Enter the wholesale cost of item: $9.05
Enter the expected number of days until sold: 3
Wholesale cost is now $9.05
Days until sold is now 3
Test again? (Type y for yes or n for no): n
```

Programs like this one are called **driver** programs. These driver programs are temporary tools and can be quite minimal. They need not have fancy input routines. They need not perform all the calculations the final program will perform. All they need do is obtain reasonable values for the function arguments in as simple a way as possible—typically from the user—then execute the function and show the result. A loop, as in the program shown in Display 5.10, will allow you to retest the function on different arguments without having to rerun the program.

If you test each function separately, you will find most of the mistakes in your program. Moreover, you will find out which functions contain the mistakes. If you were to test only the entire program, you would probably find out if there were a mistake but may have no idea where the mistake is. Even worse, you may think you know where the mistake is but be wrong.

Once you have fully tested a function, you can use it in the driver program for some other function. Each function should be tested in a program in which it is the only untested function. However, it's fine to use a fully tested function when testing some other function. If a bug is found, you know the bug is in the untested function. For example, after fully testing the function get_input with the driver program in Display 5.10, you can use get_input as the input routine in driver programs to test the remaining functions.

It is sometimes impossible or inconvenient to test a function without using some other function that has not yet been written or has not yet been tested. In this case, you can use a simplified version of the missing or untested function. These simplified functions are called **stubs**. These stubs will not necessarily perform the correct calculation, but they will deliver values that suffice for testing, and they are simple enough that you can have confidence in their performance. For example, the program in Display 5.11 is designed to test the function give_output from Display 5.9 as well as the basic layout of the program. This program uses the function get_input, which we already

DISPLAY 5.11   **Program with a Stub** *(part 1 of 2)*

```
1    //Determines the retail price of an item according to
2    //the pricing policies of the Quick-Shop supermarket chain.
3    #include <iostream>

4    void introduction( );
5    //Postcondition: Description of program is written on the screen.

6    void get_input(double& cost, int& turnover);
7    //Precondition: User is ready to enter values correctly.
8    //Postcondition: The value of cost has been set to the
9    //wholesale cost of one item. The value of turnover has been
10   //set to the expected number of days until the item is sold.

11   double price(double cost, int turnover);
12   //Precondition: cost is the wholesale cost of one item.
13   //turnover is the expected number of days until sale of the item.
14   //Returns the retail price of the item.

15   void give_output(double cost, int turnover, double price);
16   //Precondition: cost is the wholesale cost of one item; turnover is the
17   //expected time until sale of the item; price is the retail price of the item.
18   //Postcondition: The values of cost, turnover, and price have been
19   //written to the screen.

20   int main( )
21   {
22       double wholesale_cost, retail_price;
23       int shelf_time;

24       introduction( );
25           get_input(wholesale_cost, shelf_time);
26       retail_price = price(wholesale_cost, shelf_time);
27       give_output(wholesale_cost, shelf_time, retail_price);
28       return 0;
29   }
```

(continued)

DISPLAY 5.11   Program with a Stub *(part 2 of 2)*

```
30    //Uses iostream:
31    void introduction( )          fully tested
32    {                             function
33        using namespace std;
34        cout << "This program determines the retail price for\n"
35                << "an item at a Quick-Shop supermarket store.\n";
36    }
37    //Uses iostream:               fully tested
38    void get_input(double& cost, int& turnover)   function
39    {
40        using namespace std;
41        cout << "Enter the wholesale cost of item: $";
42        cin >> cost;
43        cout << "Enter the expected number of days until sold: ";
44        cin >> turnover;
45    }
                                      function
                                      being tested
46    //Uses iostream:
47    void give_output(double cost, int turnover, double price)
48    {
49        using namespace std;
50        cout.setf(ios::fixed);
51        cout.setf(ios::showpoint);
52        cout.precision(2);
53        cout << "Wholesale cost = $" << cost << endl
54                << "Expected time until sold = "
55                << turnover << " days" << endl
56                << "Retail price= $" << price << endl;
57    }
                                                      stub
58    //This is only a stub:
59    double price(double cost, int turnover)
60    {
61        return 9.99; //Not correct, but good enough for some testing.
62    }
```

Sample Dialogue

```
This program determines the retail price for
an item at a Quick-Shop supermarket store.
Enter the wholesale cost of item: $1.21
Enter the expected number of days until sold: 5
Wholesale cost = $1.21
Expected time until sold = 5 days
Retail price = $9.99
```

fully tested using the driver program shown in Display 5.10. This program also includes the function `initialize_screen`, which we assume has been tested in a driver program of its own, even though we have not bothered to show that simple driver program. Since we have not yet tested the function `price`, we have used a stub to stand in for it. Notice that we could use this program before we have even written the function `price`. This way we can test the basic program layout before we fill in the details of all the function definitions.

Using a program outline with stubs allows you to test and then "flesh out" the basic program outline, rather than write a completely new program to test each function. For this reason, a program outline with stubs is usually the most efficient method of testing. A common approach is to use driver programs to test some basic functions, like the input and output functions, and then use a program with stubs to test the remaining functions. The stubs are replaced by functions one at a time: One stub is replaced by a complete function and tested; once that function is fully tested, another stub is replaced by a full function definition, and so forth until the final program is produced.

The Fundamental Rule for Testing Functions

Every function should be tested in a program in which every other function in that program has already been fully tested and debugged.

SELF-TEST EXERCISES

17. What is the fundamental rule for testing functions? Why is this a good way to test functions?

18. What is a driver program?

19. Write a driver program for the function introduction shown in Display 5.11.

20. Write a driver program for the function add_tax from Self-Test Exercise 11.

21. What is a stub?

22. Write a stub for the function whose function declaration is given next. Do not write a whole program, only the stub that would go in a program. (*Hint:* It will be very short.)

```
double rain_prob(double pressure, double humidity,
                 double temp);
//Precondition: pressure is the barometric
```

```
//pressure in inches of mercury,
//humidity is the relative humidity as a percent, and
//temp is the temperature in degrees Fahrenheit.
//Returns the probability of rain, which is a number
//between 0 and 1.
//0 means no chance of rain. 1 means rain is 100%
//certain.
```

5.5 GENERAL DEBUGGING TECHNIQUES

VideoNote
Debugging

Careful testing through the use of stubs and drivers can detect a large number of bugs that may exist in a program. However, examination of the code and the output of test cases may be insufficient to track down many logic errors. In this case, there are a number of general debugging techniques that you may employ.

Keep an Open Mind

Examine the system as a whole and don't assume that the bug occurs in one particular place. If the program is giving incorrect output values, then you should examine the source code, different test cases for the input and output values, and the logic behind the algorithm itself. For example, consider the code to determine price for the supermarket example in Display 5.9. If the wrong price is displayed, the error might simply be that the input values were different from those you were expecting in the test case, leading to an apparently incorrect program.

Some novice programmers will "randomly" change portions of the code hoping that it will fix the error. Avoid this technique at all costs! Sometimes this approach will work for the first few simple programs that you write. However, it will almost certainly fail for larger programs and will often introduce new errors to the program. Make sure that you understand what logical impact a change to the code will make before committing the modification.

Finally, if allowed by your instructor, you could show the program to someone else. A fresh set of eyes can sometimes quickly pinpoint an error that you have been missing. Taking a break and returning to the problem a few hours later or the next day can also sometimes help in discovering an error.

Check Common Errors

One of the first mistakes you should look for are common errors that are easy to make, as described throughout the textbook in the Pitfall and Programming Tip sections. Examples of sources for common errors include (1) uninitialized variables, (2) off-by-one errors, (3) exceeding a data boundary, (4) automatic type conversion, and (5) using = instead of ==.

Localize the Error

Determining the precise cause and location of a bug is one of the first steps to fixing the error. Examining the input and output behavior for different test cases is one way to localize the error. A related technique is to add cout statements to strategic locations in the program that print out the values for critical variables. The cout statements also serve to show what code the program is executing. This is the strategy of tracing variables that was described in Chapter 3 for loops, but it can be used even when there are no loops present in the code.

For example, consider the code in Display 5.12 that is intended to convert a temperature from Fahrenheit to Celsius using the formula

$$C = \frac{5(F - 32)}{9}$$

When this program is executed with an input of 100 degrees Fahrenheit, the output is "Temperature in Celsius is 0". This is obviously incorrect, as the correct answer is 37.8 degrees Celsius.

To track down the error we can print out the value of critical variables. In this case, something appears to be wrong with the conversion formula, so we try a two-step approach. In the first step we compute (Fahrenheit – 32) and in the second step we compute (5 / 9) and then output both values. This

DISPLAY 5.12   Temperature Conversion Program with a Bug

```
1    #include <iostream>
2    using namespace std;
3
4    int main()
5    {
6        double fahrenheit;
7        double celsius;
8
9        cout << "Enter temperature in Fahrenheit." << endl;
10       cin >> fahrenheit;
11       celsius = (5 / 9) * (fahrenheit - 32);
12       cout << "Temperature in Celsius is " << celsius << endl;
13
14       return 0;
15   }
```

Sample Dialogue

```
Enter temperature in Fahrenheit.
100
Temperature in Celsius is 0
```

is illustrated in Display 5.13. We have also commented out the original line of code by placing // at the beginning of the line. This tells the compiler to ignore the original line of code but still leave it in the program for our reference. If we ever wish to restore the code, we simply remove the // instead of having to type the line in again if it was deleted.

By examining the result of the cout statements we have now identified the precise location of the bug. In this case, the conversion factor is not computed correctly. Since we are setting the conversion factor to 5 / 9,

DISPLAY 5.13   **Debugging with cout Statements**

```
1    #include <iostream>
2    using namespace std;
3
4    int main()
5    {
6        double fahrenheit;
7        double celsius;
8
9        cout << "Enter temperature in Fahrenheit." << endl;
10       cin >> fahrenheit;
11
12       // Comment out original line of code but leave it          code that is
13       // in the program for our reference                        commented out
14       // celsius = (5 / 9) * (fahrenheit - 32);
15
16       // Add cout statements to verify (5 / 9) and (fahrenheit - 32)
17       // are computed correctly
18       double conversionFactor = 5 / 9;
19       double tempFahrenheit = (fahrenheit - 32);                 debugging
20                                                                  with cout
21       cout << "fahrenheit - 32 = " << tempFahrenheit << endl;    statements
22       cout << "conversionFactor = " << conversionFactor << endl;
23       celsius = conversionFactor * tempFahrenheit;
24       cout << "Temperature in Celsius is " << celsius << endl;
25
26       return 0;
27   }
```

Sample Dialogue

```
Enter temperature in Fahrenheit.
100
fahrenheit - 32 = 68
conversionFactor = 0
Temperature in Celsius is 0
```

this instructs the compiler to compute the division of two integers, which results in zero. The simple fix is to perform floating-point division instead of integer division by changing one of the operands to a floating-point type, for example:

```
double conversionFactor = 5.0 / 9;
```

Once the bug has been identified we can now remove or comment out the debug code and return to a corrected version of the original program by modifying the line that computes the formula to the following:

```
celsius = (5.0 / 9) * (fahrenheit - 32);
```

Adding debugging code and introducing cout statements is a simple technique that works in almost any programming environment. However, it can sometimes be tedious to add a large number of cout statements to a program. Moreover, the output of the cout statements may be long or difficult to interpret, and the introduction of debugging code might even introduce new errors. Many compilers and integrated developing environments include a separate program, a **debugger,** that allows the programmer to stop execution of the program at a specific line of code called a breakpoint and step through the execution of the code one line at a time. As the debugger steps through the code, the programmer can inspect the contents of variables and even manually change the values stored in those variables. No cout statements are necessary to view the values of critical variables. The interface, commands, and capabilities of debuggers vary among C++ compilers, so check your user manual or check with your instructor for help on how to use these features.

The assert Macro

In Section 5.3 we discussed the concept of preconditions and postconditions for subroutines. The assert macro is a tool to ensure that the expected conditions are true at the location of the assert statement. If the condition is not met, then the program will display an error message and abort. To use assert, first include the definition of assert in your program with the following include statement:

```
#include <cassert>
```

To use assert, add the following line of code at the location where you would like to enforce the assertion with a boolean expression that should evaluate to true:

```
assert(boolean_expression);
```

The assert statement is a macro, which is a construct similar to a function. As an example, consider a subroutine that uses Newton's method to calculate the square root of a number n:

$$sqrt_{i+1} = \frac{1}{2}\left(sqrt_i + \frac{n}{sqrt_i}\right)$$

Here $sqrt_0 = 1$ and $sqrt_i$ approaches the square root of n as i approaches infinity. A subroutine that implements this algorithm requires that n be a positive number and that the number of iterations we will repeat the calculation is also a positive number. We can guarantee this condition by adding assert to the subroutine as shown below:

```
// Approximates the square root of n using Newton's
// Iteration.
// Precondition: n is positive, num_iterations is positive
// Postcondition: returns the square root of n
double newton_sqroot(double n, int num_iterations)
{
    double answer = 1;
    int i = 0;

    assert((n > 0) && (num_iterations> 0));
    while (i <num_iterations)
    {
        answer = 0.5 * (answer + n / answer);
        i++;
    }
    return answer;
}
```

If we try to execute this subroutine with any negative parameters, then the program will abort and display the assertion that failed. The assert statement can be used in a similar manner for any assertion that you would like to enforce and is an excellent technique for defensive programming.

If you are going to distribute your program, you might not want the executable program to include the assert statements, since users could then get error messages that they might not understand. If you have added many assert statements to your code, it can be tedious to remove them all. Fortunately, you can disable all assert macros by adding the following line to the beginning of your program, before the include statement for <cassert> as follows:

```
#define NDEBUG
#include <cassert>
```

If you later change your program and need to debug it again, you can turn the assert statements back on by deleting the line #define NDEBUG (or commenting it out).

SELF-TEST EXERCISES

23. If computing the statement: x = (x * y / z); how can you use the assert macro to avoid division by zero?

24. What is a debugger?

25. What general techniques can you use to determine the source of an error?

CHAPTER SUMMARY

- All subtasks in a program can be implemented as functions, either as functions that return a value or as *void* functions.

- A **formal parameter** is a kind of place holder that is filled in with a function **argument** when the function is called. There are two methods of performing this substitution, call-by-value and call-by-reference.

- In the **call-by-value** substitution mechanism, the value of an argument is substituted for its corresponding formal parameter. In the **call-by-reference** substitution mechanism, the argument should be a variable and the entire variable is substituted for the corresponding argument.

- The way to indicate a call-by-reference parameter in a function definition is to attach the ampersand sign, &, to the type of the formal parameter.

- An argument corresponding to a call-by-value parameter cannot be changed by a function call. An argument corresponding to a call-by-reference parameter can be changed by a function call. If you want a function to change the value of a variable, then you must use a call-by-reference parameter.

- A good way to write a function declaration comment is to use a precondition and a postcondition. The **precondition** states what is assumed to be true when the function is called. The **postcondition** describes the effect of the function call; that is, the postcondition tells what will be true after the function is executed in a situation in which the precondition holds.

- Every function should be tested in a program in which every other function in that program has already been fully tested and debugged.

- A **driver program** is a program that does nothing but test a function.

- A simplified version of a function is called a **stub.** A stub is used in place of a function definition that has not yet been tested (or possibly not even written) so that the rest of the program can be tested.

- A debugger, strategic placement of cout statements, and the assert macro are tools that can help you debug a program.

Answers to Self-Test Exercises

1.
    ```
    Hello
    Goodbye
    One more time:
    Hello
    End of program.
    ```

2. No, a *void* function definition need not contain a *return* statement. A *void* function definition may contain a *return* statement, but one is not required.

3. Omitting the *return* statement in the function definition for initialize_screen in Display 5.2 would have absolutely no effect on how the program behaves. The program will compile, run, and behave exactly the same. Similarly, omitting the *return* statement in the function definition for show_results also will have no effect on how the program behaves. However, if you omit the *return* statement in the function definition for celsius, that will be a serious error that will keep the program from running. The difference is that the functions initialize_screen and show_results are *void* functions, but celsius is not a *void* function.

4.
    ```cpp
    #include <iostream>

    void product_out(int n1, int n2, int n3);
    int main()
    {
        using namespace std;
        int num1, num2, num3;
        cout << "Enter three integers: ";
        cin >> num1 >> num2 >> num3;
        product_out(num1, num2, num3);
        return 0;
    }

    void product_out(int n1, int n2, int n3)
    {
        using namespace std;
        cout << "The product of the three numbers "
             << n1 << ", " << n2 << ", and "
             << n3 << " is " << (n1 * n2 * n3) << endl;
    }
    ```

5. These answers are system dependent.

6. A call to a *void* function followed by a semicolon is a statement. A call to a function that returns a value is an expression.

7.
```
10 20 30
1 2 3
1 20 3
```

8.
```
Enter two integers: 5 10
In reverse order the numbers are: 5 5    ←———— different
```

9.
```
par1_value in function call = 111
par2_ref in function call = 222
n1 after function call = 1
n2 after function call = 2  ←———— different
```

10. *void* zero_both(*int*& n1, *int*& n2)
```
{
    n1 = 0;
    n2 = 0;
}
```

11. *void* add_tax(*double* tax_rate, *double*& cost)
```
{
    cost = cost + ( tax_rate/100.0 ) * cost;
}
```

The division by 100 is to convert a percent to a fraction. For example, 10% is 10/100.0 or 1/10th of the cost.

12. Yes, a function that returns a value can have a call-by-reference parameter. Yes, a function can have a combination of call-by-value and call-by-reference parameters.

13. No, a function definition cannot appear inside the body of another function definition.

14. Yes, a function definition can contain a call to another function.

15. *void* order(*int*& n1, *int*& n2);
```
//Precondition: The variables n1 and n2 have values.
//Postcondition: The values in n1 and n2 have been
//ordered so that n1 <= n2.
```

16. *double* sqrt(*double* n);
```
//Precondition: n >= 0.
//Returns the squareroot of n.
```

You can rewrite the second comment line to the following if you prefer, but the previous version is the usual form used for a function that returns a value:

```
//Postcondition: Returns the squareroot of n.
```

17. The fundamental rule for testing functions is that every function should be tested in a program in which every other function in that program has already been fully tested and debugged. This is a good way to test a function because if you follow this rule, then when you find a bug, you will know which function contains the bug.

18. A driver program is a program written for the sole purpose of testing a function.

19.
```cpp
#include <iostream>

void introduction();
//Postcondition: Description of program is written on
//the screen.
int main()
{
    using namespace std;
    introduction();
    cout << "End of test.\n";
    return 0;
}
//Uses iostream:
void introduction()
{
    using namespace std;
    cout << "This program determines the retail price for\n"
         << "an item at a Quick-Shop supermarket store.\n";
}
```

20.
```cpp
//Driver program for the function add_tax.
#include <iostream>

void add_tax(double tax_rate, double& cost);
//Precondition: tax_rate is the amount of sales tax as
//a percentage and cost is the cost of an item before
//tax.
//Postcondition: cost has been changed to the cost of
//the item after adding sales tax.

int main()
{
    using namespace std;
    double cost, tax_rate;
    char ans;
    cout.setf(ios::fixed);
    cout.setf(ios::showpoint);
    cout.precision(2);
    do
    {
        cout << "Enter cost and tax rate:\n";
```

```
        cin >> cost >> tax_rate;
        add_tax(tax_rate, cost);

        cout << "After call to add_tax\n"
             << "tax_rate is " << tax_rate << endl
             << "cost is " << cost << endl;

        cout << "Test again?"
             << " (Type y for yes or n for no): ";
        cin >> ans;
        cout << endl;
    } while (ans == 'y' || ans == 'Y');

    return 0;
}

void add_tax(double tax_rate, double& cost)
{
    cost = cost + ( tax_rate/100.0 )* cost;
}
```

21. A stub is a simplified version of a function that is used in place of the function so that other functions can be tested.

22. ```
    //THIS IS JUST A STUB.
    double rain_prob(double pressure, double humidity, double temp)
    {
        return 0.25; //Not correct, but good enough for some testing.
    }
    ```

23. `assert(z != 0).`

24. A debugger is a tool that allows the programmer to set breakpoints, step through the code line by line, and inspect or modify the value of variables.

25. Keeping an open mind, adding cout statements to narrow down the cause of the error, using a debugger, searching for common errors, and devising a variety of tests are a few techniques that you can use to debug a program.

PROGRAMMING PROJECTS

myprogramminglab *Visit www.myprogramminglab.com to complete many of these Programming Projects online and get instant feedback.*

1. Write a program that converts from 24-hour notation to 12-hour notation. For example, it should convert 14:25 to 2:25 PM. The input is given as two integers. There should be at least three functions, one for input, one to do the conversion, and one for output. Record the AM/PM information as a value of
    ```

type char, 'A' for AM and 'P' for PM. Thus, the function for doing the conversions will have a call-by-reference formal parameter of type char to record whether it is AM or PM. (The function will have other parameters as well.) Include a loop that lets the user repeat this computation for new input values again and again until the user says he or she wants to end the program.

2. Write a program that uses the fundamental idea of Euclid's algorithm, which is one of the oldest known algorithms, for calculating the greatest common divisor of two numbers using a function. If p and q are the numbers, the gcd() function will perform the calculation in the following manner:

```
gcd(p,0) = p
gcd(p,q) = gcd(q, p%q)
```

3. Write a program to find the factorial of a number using a function. For example, the factorial of 5 = 5 x 4 x 3 x 2 x 1 = 120.

4. Write a program that computes the "to the power" calculation of a given number, where the base and exponent are given by the user. Your program should take two integers, one for the exponent, and another for the base. You should use three functions: one for input, another for exponent calculation, and another for output. The calculation function must take two parameters: one for the exponent, and another for the base.

5. Write a program that tells what coins to give out for any amount of change from 1 cent to 99 cents. For example, if the amount is 86 cents, the output would be something like the following:

```
86 cents can be given as
3 quarter(s) 1 dime(s) and 1 penny(pennies)
```

Use coin denominations of 25 cents (quarters), 10 cents (dimes), and 1 cent (pennies). Do not use nickel and half-dollar coins. Your program will use the following function (among others):

```
void compute_coins(int coin_value, int& num, int& amount_left);
//Precondition: 0 < coin_value < 100; 0 <= amount_left < 100.
//Postcondition: num has been set equal to the maximum number
//of coins of denomination coin_value cents that can be obtained
//from amount_left. Additionally, amount_left has been decreased
//by the value of the coins, that is, decreased by
//num * coin_value.
```

For example, suppose the value of the variable amount_left is 86. Then, after the following call, the value of number will be 3 and the value of amount_left will be 11 (because if you take 3 quarters from 86 cents, that leaves 11 cents):

```
compute_coins(25, number, amount_left);
```

Include a loop that lets the user repeat this computation for new input values until the user says he or she wants to end the program. (*Hint:* Use integer division and the % operator to implement this function.)

6. Write a program that reads in a length in miles and yards and outputs the equivalent length in kilometers and meters. Use at least three functions: one for input, one or more for calculating, and one for output. Include a loop that lets the user repeat this computation for new input values until the user says he or she wants to end the program. There are 1,609.3 meters in a mile and 1,000 meters in a kilometer; 1 yard is 0.9144 meters and 0.000600 miles.

7. Write a program like that of the previous exercise that converts from kilometers and meters into miles and yards. Use functions for the subtasks.

8. (You should do the previous two programming projects before doing this one.) Write a program that combines the functions in the previous two programming projects. The program asks the user if he or she wants to convert from miles and yards to kilometers and meters or from kilometers and meters to miles and yards. The program then performs the desired conversion. Have the user respond by typing the integer 1 for one type of conversion and 2 for the other conversion. The program reads the user's answer and then executes an *if-else* statement. Each branch of the *if-else* statement will be a function call. The two functions called in the *if-else* statement will have function definitions that are very similar to the programs for the previous two programming projects. Thus, they will be fairly complicated function definitions that call other functions in their function bodies. Include a loop that lets the user repeat this computation for new input values until the user says he or she wants to end the program.

VideoNote
Solution to Programming
Project 5.9

9. Write a program that reads in a weight in pounds and ounces and outputs the equivalent weight in kilograms and grams. Use at least three functions: one for input, one or more for calculating, and one for output. Include a loop that lets the user repeat this computation for new input values until the user says he or she wants to end the program. There are 2.2046 pounds in a kilogram, 1000 grams in a kilogram, and 16 ounces in a pound.

10. Write a program like that of the previous exercise that converts from kilograms and grams into pounds and ounces. Use functions for the subtasks.

11. There are 35,273 ounces in a ton, 1,000 kilograms in a ton, and 437 grains in a ounce. The program asks the user if he or she wants to convert from ounces and grains to tons and kilograms or from tons and kilograms to ounces and grains. The program then performs the desired conversion. Have the user respond by typing the integer 1 for one type of conversion and 2 for the other. The program reads the user's answer and then executes

an *if-else* statement. Each branch of the *if-else* statement will be a function call. The two functions called in the *if-else* statement will have function definitions that are very conceptually similar to the programs for the previous two programming projects. Thus, they will be fairly complicated function definitions that call other functions in their function bodies. Include a loop that lets the user repeat this computation for new input values until the user says he or she wants to end the program.

12. (You need to do Programming Projects 8 and 11 before doing this programming project.) Write a program that combines the functions of Programming Projects 8 and 11. The program asks the user if he or she wants to convert lengths or weights. If the user chooses lengths, then the program asks the user if he or she wants to convert from miles and yards to kilometers and meters or from kilometers and meters to miles and yards. If the user chooses weights, a similar question about ounces, grains, tons and kilograms, is asked. The program then performs the desired conversion. Have the user respond by typing the integer 1 for one type of conversion and 2 for the other. The program reads the user's answer and then executes an *if-else* statement. Each branch of the *if-else* statement will be a function call. The two functions called in the *if-else* statement will have function definitions that are very similar to the programs for Programming Projects 8 and 11. Thus, these functions will be fairly complicated function definitions that call other functions in their function bodies; however, they will be very easy to write by adapting the programs you wrote for Programming Projects 8 and 11.

Notice that your program will have *if-else* statements embedded inside of *if-else* statements, but only in an indirect way. The outer *if-else* statement will include two function calls as its two branches. These two function calls will each in turn include an *if-else* statement, but you need not think about that. They are just function calls and the details are in a black box that you create when you define these functions. If you try to create a four-way branch, you are probably on the wrong track. You should only need to think about two-way branches (even though the entire program does ultimately branch into four cases). Include a loop that lets the user repeat this computation for new input values until the user says he or she wants to end the program.

13. The area of an arbitrary triangle can be computed using the formula

$$\text{area} = \sqrt{s(s-a)(s-b)(s-c)}$$

where a, b, and c are the lengths of the sides, and s is the semiperimeter.

$$s = (a + b + c)/2$$

Write a *void* function that computes the area and perimeter *(not the semi-perimeter)* of a triangle based on the length of the sides. The function should use five parameters—three value parameters that provide the lengths of the edges and two reference parameters that store the computed area and perimeter. Make your function robust. Note that not all combinations of *a*, *b*, and *c* produce a triangle. Your function should produce correct results for legal data and reasonable results for illegal combinations.

14. In cold weather, meteorologists report an index called the windchill factor, that takes into account the wind speed and the temperature. The index provides a measure of the chilling effect of wind at a given air temperature. Windchill may be approximated by the formula:

$$W = 13.12 + 0.6215 * t - 11.37 * v^{0.16} + 0.3965 * t * v^{0.016}$$

where
v = wind speed in m/sec
t = temperature in degrees Celsius: $t <= 10$
W = windchill index (in degrees Celsius)

Write a function that returns the windchill index. Your code should ensure that the restriction on the temperature is not violated. Look up some weather reports in back issues of a newspaper in your university library and compare the windchill index you calculate with the result reported in the newspaper.

VideoNote
Solution to Programming
Project 5.15

15. In the land of Puzzlevania, Aaron, Bob, and Charlie had an argument over which one of them was the greatest puzzler of all time. To end the argument once and for all, they agreed on a duel to the death. Aaron is a poor shooter and only hits his target with a probability of 1/3. Bob is a bit better and hits his target with a probability of 1/2. Charlie is an expert marksman and never misses. A hit means a kill and the person hit drops out of the duel.

To compensate for the inequities in their marksmanship skills, it is decided that the contestants would fire in turns starting with Aaron, followed by Bob, and then by Charlie. The cycle would repeat until there was one man standing. And that man would be remembered as the greatest puzzler of all time.

a. Write a function to simulate a single shot. It should use the following declaration:

```
void shoot(bool& targetAlive, double accuracy);
```

This would simulate someone shooting at `targetAlive` with the given accuracy by generating a random number between 0 and 1. If the random number is less than `accuracy`, then the target is hit and `targetAlive` should be set to false. Chapter 4 illustrates how to generate random numbers.

For example, if Bob is shooting at Charlie, this could be invoked as:

```
shoot(charlieAlive, 0.5);
```

Here, `charlieAlive` is a Boolean variable that indicates if Charlie is alive. Test your function using a driver program before moving on to step b.

b. An obvious strategy is for each man to shoot at the most accurate shooter still alive on the grounds that this shooter is the deadliest and has the best chance of hitting back. Write a second function named `startDuel` that uses the `shoot` function to simulate an entire duel using this strategy. It should loop until only one contestant is left, invoking the `shoot` function with the proper target and probability of hitting the target according to who is shooting. The function should return a variable that indicates who won the duel.

c. In your main function, invoke the `startDuel` function 1000 times in a loop, keeping track of how many times each contestant wins. Output the probability that each contestant will win when everyone uses the strategy of shooting at the most accurate shooter left alive.

d. A counterintuitive strategy is for Aaron to intentionally miss on his first shot. Thereafter, everyone uses the strategy of shooting at the most accurate shooter left alive. This strategy means that Aaron is guaranteed to live past the first round, since Bob and Charlie will fire at each other. Modify the program to accommodate this new strategy and output the probability of winning for each contestant.

16. Write a program that inputs a date (for example, July 4, 2008) and outputs the day of the week that corresponds to that date. The following algorithm is from http://en.wikipedia.org/wiki/Calculating_the_day_of_the_week. The implementation will require several functions.

```
bool isLeapYear(int year);
```

This function should return `true` if year is a leap year and `false` if it is not. Here is pseudocode to determine a leap year:

```
leap_year = (year divisible by 400) or (year divisible by 4 and
     year not divisible by 100))
int getCenturyValue(int year);
```

This function should take the first two digits of the year (that is, the century), divide by 4, and save the remainder. Subtract the remainder from 3 and return this value multiplied by 2. For example, the year 2008 becomes: (20/4) = 5 with a remainder of 0. 3 – 0 = 3. Return 3 * 2 = 6.

int getYearValue(*int* year);

This function computes a value based on the years since the beginning of the century. First, extract the last two digits of the year. For example, 08 is extracted for 2008. Next, factor in leap years. Divide the value from the previous step by 4 and discard the remainder. Add the two results together and return this value. For example, from 2008 we extract 08. Then (8/4) = 2 with a remainder of 0. Return 2 + 8 = 10.

int getMonthVa0lue(*int* month, *int* year);

This function should return a value based on the table below and will require invoking the isLeapYear function.

Month	Return Value
January	0 (6 if year is a leap year)
February	3 (2 if year is a leap year)
March	3
April	6
May	1
June	4
July	6
August	2
September	5
October	0
November	3
December	5

Finally, to compute the day of the week, compute the sum of the date's day plus the values returned by getMonthValue, getYearValue, and getCenturyValue. Divide the sum by 7 and compute the remainder. A remainder of 0 corresponds to Sunday, 1 corresponds to Monday, etc., up to 6, which corresponds to Saturday. For example, the date July 4, 2008 should be computed as (day of month) +(getMonthValue) + (getYearValue) + (getCenturyValue) = 4 + 6 + 10 + 6 = 26. 26/7 = 3 with a remainder of 5. The fifth day of the week corresponds to Friday.

Your program should allow the user to enter any date and output the corresponding day of the week in English.

This program should include a `void` function named `getInput` that prompts the user for the date and returns the month, day, and year using pass-by-reference parameters. You may choose to have the user enter the date's month as either a number (1–12) or a month name.

17. Complete the previous Programming Project and create a top-level function named dayOfWeek with the header:

    ```
    int dayOfWeek(int month, int day, int year);
    ```

    The function should encapsulate the necessary logic to return the day of the week of the specified date as an `int` (Sunday = 0, Monday = 1, etc.) You should add validation code to the function that tests if any of the inputs are invalid. If so, the function should return –1 as the day of the week. In your main function write a test driver that checks if dayOfWeek is returning the correct values. Your set of test cases should include at least two cases with invalid inputs.

I/O Streams as an Introduction to Objects and Classes 6

Fish say, they have their stream and pond; But is there anything beyond?

RUPERT BROOKE, *"Heaven"* (1913)

As a leaf is carried by a stream, whether the stream ends in a lake or in the sea, so too is the output of your program carried by a stream not knowing if the stream goes to the screen or to a file.

WASHROOM WALL OF A COMPUTER SCIENCE DEPARTMENT (1995)

INTRODUCTION

I/O refers to program input and output. Input can be taken from the keyboard or from a file. Similarly, output can be sent to the screen or to a file. This chapter explains how you can write your programs to take input from a file and send output to another file.

Input is delivered to your program via a C++ construct known as a *stream*, and output from your program is delivered to the output device via a stream. Streams are our first examples of *objects*. An object is a special kind of variable that has its own special-purpose functions that are, in a sense, attached to the variable. The ability to handle objects is one of the language features that sets C++ apart from earlier programming languages. In this chapter we tell you what streams are and explain how to use them for program I/O. In the process of explaining streams, we will introduce you to the basic ideas about what objects are and about how objects are used in a program.

PREREQUISITES

This chapter uses the material from Chapters 2 through 5.

6.1 STREAMS AND BASIC FILE I/O

Good Heavens! For more than forty years I have been speaking prose without knowing it.

MOLIÈRE, *Le Bourgeois Gentilhomme*

You are already using files to store your programs. You can also use files to store input for a program or to receive output from a program. The files used for program I/O are the same kind of files you use to store your programs. Streams, which we discuss next, allow you to write programs that handle file input and keyboard input in a unified way and that handle file output and screen output in a unified way.

A **stream** is a flow of characters (or other kind of data). If the flow is into your program, the stream is called an **input stream.** If the flow is out of your program, the stream is called an **output stream.** If the input stream flows from the keyboard, then your program will take input from the keyboard. If the input stream flows from a file, then your program will take its input from that file. Similarly, an output stream can go to the screen or to a file.

Although you may not realize it, you have already been using streams in your programs. The cin that you have already used is an input stream connected to the keyboard, and cout is an output stream connected to the screen. These two streams are automatically available to your program, as long as it has an include directive that names the header file iostream. You can define other streams that come from or go to files; once you have defined them, you can use them in your program in the same way you use the streams cin and cout.

cin and cout are streams

For example, suppose your program defines a stream called in_stream that comes from some file. (We'll tell you how to define it shortly.) You can then fill an *int* variable named the_number with a number from this file by using the following in your program:

```
int the_number;
in_stream >> the_number;
```

Similarly, if your program defines an output stream named out_stream that goes to another file, then you can output the value of this variable to this other file. The following will output the string "the_number is" followed by the contents of the variable the_number to the output file that is connected to the stream out_stream.

```
out_stream << "the_number is" << the_number << endl;
```

Once the streams are connected to the desired files, your program can do file I/O the same way it does I/O using the keyboard and screen.

Why Use Files for I/O?

The keyboard input and screen output we have used so far deal with temporary data. When the program ends, the data typed in at the keyboard and the data left on the screen go away. Files provide you with a way to store data permanently. The contents of a file remain until a person or program changes the file. If your program sends its output to a file, the output file will remain after the program has finished running. An input file can be used over and over again by many programs without the need to type in the data separately for each program.

Permanent storage

The input and output files used by your program are the same kind of files that you read and write with an editor, such as the editor you use to write your programs. This means you can create an input file for your program or read an output file produced by your program whenever it's convenient for you, as opposed to having to do all your reading and writing while the program is running.

Files also provide you with a convenient way to deal with large quantities of data. When your program takes its input from a large input file, the program receives a lot of data without making the user do a lot of typing.

File I/O

When your program takes input from a file, it is said to be **reading** from the file; when your program sends output to a file, it is said to be **writing** to the file. There are other ways of reading input from a file, but the method we will use reads the file from the beginning to the end (or as far as the program gets before ending). Using this method, your program is not allowed to back up and read anything in the file a second time. This is exactly what happens when the program takes input from the keyboard, so this should not seem new or strange. (As we will see, the program can reread a file starting from the beginning of the file, but this is "starting over," not "backing up.") Similarly, for the method we present here, your program writes output into a file starting at the beginning of the file and proceeding forward. It is not allowed to back up and change any output that it has previously written to the file. This is exactly what happens when your program sends output to the screen. You can send more output to the screen, but you cannot back up and change the screen output. The way that you get input from a file into your program or send output from your program into a file is to connect the program to the file by means of a stream.

A stream is a variable

In C++, a stream is a special kind of variable known as an *object*. We will discuss objects in the next section, but we will first describe how your program can use stream objects to do simple file I/O. If you want to use a stream to get input from a file (or give output to a file), you must declare the stream and you must connect the stream to the file.

You can think of the file that a stream is connected to as the value of the stream. You can disconnect a stream from one file and connect it to another file, so you can change the value of these stream variables. However, you must use special functions that apply only to streams in order to perform these changes. You *cannot* use a stream variable in an assignment statement the way that you can use a variable of type *int* or *char*. Although streams are variables, they are unusual sorts of variables.

Declaring streams ifstream and ofstream

The streams cin and cout are already declared for you, but if you want a stream to connect to a file, you must declare it just as you would declare any other variable. The type for input-file stream variables is named ifstream (for "input-file stream"). The type for output-file stream variables is named ofstream (for "output-file stream"). Thus, you can declare in_stream to be an input stream for a file and out_stream to be an output stream for another file as follows:

```
ifstream in_stream;
ofstream out_stream;
```

The types `ifstream` and `ofstream` are defined in the library with the header file `fstream`, and so any program that declares stream variables in this way must contain the following directive (normally near the beginning of the file):

```
#include <fstream>
```

When using the types `ifstream` and `ofstream`, your program must also contain the following, normally either at the start of the file or at the start of the function body that uses the types `ifstream` or `ofstream`:

```
using namespace std;
```

Stream variables, such as `in_stream` and `out_stream` declared earlier, must each be **connected to** a file. This is called **opening the file** and is done with a function named open. For example, suppose you want the input stream `in_stream` connected to the file named `infile.dat`. Your program must then contain the following before it reads any input from this file:

Connecting a stream to a file open

```
in_stream.open("infile.dat");
```

This may seem like rather strange syntax for a function call. We will have more to say about this peculiar syntax in the next section. For now, just notice a couple of details about how this call to open is written. First, the stream variable name and a dot (that is, a period) is placed before the function named open, and the file name is given as an argument to open. Also notice that the file name is given in quotes. The file name that is given as an argument is the same as the name you would use for the file if you wanted to write in it using the editor. If the input file is in the same directory as your program, you probably can simply give the name of the file in the manner just described. In some situations you might also need to specify the directory that contains the file. The details about specifying directories varies from one system to another. If you need to specify a directory, ask your instructor or some other local expert to explain the details.

Once you have declared an input stream variable and connected it to a file using the open function, your program can take input from the file using the extraction operator >>. For example, the following reads two input numbers from the file connected to `in_stream` and places them in the variables `one_number` and `another_number`:

```
int one_number, another_number;
in_stream >> one_number >> another_number;
```

An output stream is opened (that is, connected to a file) in the same way as just described for input streams. For example, the following declares the output stream `out_stream` and connects it to the file named `outfile.dat`:

```
ofstream out_stream;
out_stream.open("outfile.dat");
```

When used with a stream of type `ofstream`, the member function `open` will create the output file if it does not already exist. If the output file does already exist, the member function `open` will discard the contents of the file so that the output file is empty after the call to `open`.

After a file is connected to the stream `out_stream` with a call to `open`, the program can send output to that file using the insertion operator `<<`. For example, the following writes two strings and the contents of the variables `one_number` and `another_number` to the file that is connected to the stream `out_stream` (which in this example is the file named `outfile.dat`):

```
out_stream << "one_number = " << one_number
<< " another_number = " << another_number;
```

Notice that when your program is dealing with a file, it is as if the file had two names. One is the usual name for the file that is used by the operating system. This name is called the **external file name.** In our sample code the external file names were `infile.dat` and `outfile.dat`. The external file name is in some sense the "real name" for the file. It is the name used by the operating system. The conventions for spelling these external file names vary from one system to another; you will need to learn these conventions from your instructor or from some other local expert. The names `infile.dat` and `outfile.dat` that we used in our examples might or might not look like file names on your system. You should name your files following whatever conventions your system uses. Although the external file name is the real name for the file, it is typically used only once in a program. The external file name is given as an argument to the function `open`, but *after the file is opened, the file is always referred to by naming the stream that is connected to the file*. Thus, within your program, the stream name serves as a second name for the file.

The sample program in Display 6.1 reads three numbers from one file and writes their sum, as well as some text, to another file.

A File Has Two Names

Every input and every output file used by your program has two names. The **external file name** is the real name of the file, but it is used only in the call to the function open, which connects the file to a stream. After the call to open, you always use the stream name as the name of the file.

Every file should be closed when your program is finished getting input from the file or sending output to the file. Closing a file disconnects the stream from the file. A file is closed with a call to the function `close`. The following lines from the program in Display 6.1 illustrate how to use the function `close`:

```
in_stream.close( );
out_stream.close( );
```

DISPLAY 6.9   Some Predefined Character Functions in cctype

Function	Description	Example
toupper(*Char_Exp*)	Returns the uppercase version of *Char_Exp*.	*char* c = toupper('a'); cout << c; **Outputs:** A
tolower(*Char_Exp*)	Returns the lowercase version of *Char_Exp*.	*char* c = tolower('A'); cout << c; **Outputs:** a

isupper(*Char_Exp*)	Returns *true* provided *Char_Exp* is an uppercase letter; otherwise, returns *false*.	*if* (isupper(c))
		    cout << c <<
		        << " isuppercase.";
		else
		    cout << c
		        << " is not uppercase.";

islower(*Char_Exp*)	Returns *true* provided *Char_Exp* is a lowercase letter; otherwise, returns *false*.	*char* c = 'a'; *if* (islower(c)) cout << c <<<< " islowercase."; **Outputs:** a is lowercase.

isalpha(*Char_Exp*)	Returns *true* provided *Char_Exp* is a letter of the alphabet; otherwise, returns *false*.	*char* c = '$';
		if (isalpha(c))
		    cout << c << " is a letter.";
		else
		    cout << c
		        <<" is not a letter.";
		Outputs: $ is not a letter.

isdigit(*Char_Exp*)	Returns *true* provided *Char_Exp* is one of the digits '0' through '9'; otherwise, returns *false*.	*if* (isdigit('3'))
		    cout << "It's a digit.";
		else
		    cout << "It's not a digit.";
		Outputs: It's a digit.

isspace(*Char_Exp*)	Returns *true* provided *Char_Exp* is a whitespace character, such as the blank or new-line symbol; otherwise, returns *false*.	*//Skips over one "word" and*
		//sets c equal to the first
		//whitespace character after
		//the "word":
		do
		{
		    cin.get(c);
		
		} *while* (! isspace(c));

In order to get the computer to treat the value returned by `toupper` or `tolower` as a value of type *char* (as opposed to a value of type *int*), you need to indicate that you want a value of type *char*. One way to do this is to place the value returned in a variable of type *char*. The following will output the character `'A'`, which is usually what we want:

```
char c = toupper('a');        Places 'A' in the
    cout << c;                variable c
```

Another way to get the computer to treat the value returned by `toupper` or `tolower` as a value of type *char* is to use a type cast as follows:

```
cout << static_cast<char>(toupper('a'));
```

(Type casts were discussed in Chapter 4 in the section "Type Casting.") ■

myprogramminglab ■ **SELF-TEST EXERCISES**

36. Consider the following code (and assume that it is embedded in a complete and correct program and then run):

```
cout << "Enter a line of input:\n";
char next;
do
{
    cin.get(next);
    cout << next;
} while ( (! isdigit(next)) && (next != '\n') );
cout << "<END OF OUTPUT";
```

If the dialogue begins as follows, what will be the next line of output?

```
Enter a line of input:
I'll see you at 10:30 AM.
```

37. Write some C++ code that will read a line of text and echo the line with all uppercase letters deleted.

CHAPTER SUMMARY

■ A stream of type `ifstream` can be connected to a file with a call to the member function open. Your program can then take input from that file.

■ A stream of type `ofstream` can be connected to a file with a call to the member function open. Your program can then send output to that file.

■ You should use the member function `fail` to check whether a call to open was successful.

■ An **object** is a variable that has functions associated with it. These functions are called **member functions.** A **class** is a type whose variables are objects. A stream is an example of an object. The types `ifstream` and `ofstream` are examples of classes.

■ The following is the syntax you use when you write a call to a member function of an object:

```
Calling_Object.Member_Function_Name(Argument_List);
```

An example with the stream `cout` as the calling object and `precision` as the member function is the following:

```
cout.precision(2);
```

■ Stream member functions, such as `width`, `setf`, and `precision`, can be used to format output. These output functions work the same for the stream `cout`, which is connected to the screen, and for output streams connected to files.

■ Every input stream has a member function named `get` that can be used to read one character of input. The member function `get` does not skip over whitespace. Every output stream also has a member function named `put` that can be used to write one character to the output stream.

■ The member function `eof` can be used to test for when a program has reached the end of an input file. The member function `eof` works well for text processing. However, when processing numeric data, you might prefer to test for the end of a file by using the other method we discussed in this chapter.

■ A function may have formal parameters of a stream type, but they must be call-by-reference parameters; they cannot be call-by-value parameters. The type `ifstream` can be used for an input-file stream, and the type `ofstream` can be used for an output-file stream. (See the next summary point for other type possibilities.)

■ If you use `istream` (spelled without the f) as the type for an input-stream parameter, then the argument corresponding to that formal parameter can be either the stream `cin` or an input-file stream of type `ifstream` (spelled with the f). If you use `ostream` (spelled without the f) as the type for an output stream parameter, then the argument corresponding to that formal parameter can be either the stream `cout` or an output-file stream of type `ofstream` (spelled with the f).

Answers to Self-Test Exercises

1. The streams `fin` and `fout` are declared as follows:

```
ifstream fin;
ofstream fout;
```

The `include` directive that goes at the top of your file is

```
#include <fstream>
```

Your code also needs the following:

```
using namespace std;
```

2. `fin.open("stuff1.dat");`

```
if (fin.fail( ))
{
    cout << "Input file opening failed.\n";
    exit(1);
}

fout.open("stuff2.dat");
if (fout.fail( ))
{
    cout << "Output file opening failed.\n";
    exit(1);
}
```

3. `fin.close( );`
   `fout.close( );`

4. You need to replace the stream `out_stream` with the stream `cout`. Note that you do not need to declare `cout`, you do not need to call `open` with `cout`, and you do not need to close `cout`.

5. `#include <cstdlib>`

Your code also needs the following:

```
using namespace std;
```

6. The `exit(1)` function returns the argument to the operating system. By convention, the operating system uses a 1 as an indication of error status and 0 as an indication of success. What is actually done is system-dependent.

7. `bla.dobedo(7);`

8. Both files and program variables store values and can have values retrieved from them. Program variables exist only while the program runs, whereas files may exist before a program is run and may continue to exist after a program stops. In short, files may be permanent; variables are not. Files provide the ability to store large quantities of data, whereas program variables do not provide quite so large a store.

9. We have seen the `open`, `close`, and `fail` member functions at this point. The following illustrate their use.

```
int c;
ifstream in;
ofstream out;
in.open("in.dat");
if (in.fail( ))
{
    cout << "Input file opening failed.\n";
    exit(1);
}
in >> c;

out.open("out.dat");
if (out.fail( ))
{
    cout << "Output file opening failed.\n";
    exit(1);
}
out << c;

out.close( );
in.close( );
```

10. This is the "starting over" the text describes at the beginning of this chapter. The file must be closed and opened again. This action puts the read position at the start of the file, ready to be read again.

11. The two names are the *external file name* and the *stream name*. The external file name is the one used by the operating system. It is the real name of the file, but it is used only in the call to the function open, which connects the file to a stream. The stream name is a stream variable (typically of type ifstream or ofstream). After the call to open, your program always uses the stream name as the name of the file.

12.
```
*  123*123*
*  123*123*
```

Each of the spaces contains exactly two blank characters. Notice that a call to width or call to setw only lasts for one output item.

13.
```
*  123*123  *  123*
```

Each of the spaces consists of exactly two blank characters.

14.
```
*  123*123*
*  +123*+123*
*123  *123  *
```

There is just one space between the * and the + on the second line. Each of the other spaces contains exactly two blank characters.

15. The output to the file `stuff.dat` will be exactly the same as the output given in the answer to Exercise 14.

16.

    12345

    Notice that the entire integer is output even though this requires more space than was specified by `setw`.

17. a. `ios::fixed`. Setting this flag causes floating-point numbers not to be displayed in e-notation, that is, not in scientific notation. Setting this flag unsets `ios::scientific`.

    b. `ios::scientific`. Setting this flag causes floating-point numbers to be displayed in e-notation, that is, in scientific notation. Setting this flag unsets `ios::fixed`.

    c. `ios::showpoint`. Setting this flag causes the decimal point and trailing zeros to be always displayed.

    d. `ios::showpos`. Setting this flag causes a plus sign to be output before positive integer values.

    e. `ios::right`. Setting this flag causes subsequent output to be placed at the right end of any field that is set with the `width` member function. That is, any extra blanks are put before the output. Setting this flag unsets `ios::left`.

    f. `ios::left`. Setting this flag causes subsequent output to be placed at the left end of any field that is set with the `width` member function. That is, any extra blanks are put after the output. Setting this flag unsets `ios::right`.

18. You need to replace `outstream` with `cout` and delete the `open` and `close` calls for `outstream`. You do not need to declare `cout`, open `cout`, or close `cout`. The `#include <fstream>` directive has all the `iostream` members you need for screen I/O, though it does no harm, and may make the program clearer, to `#include <iostream>`.

19.

    1
    2
    3
    3

20. *void* to_screen(ifstream& file_stream)
    {
        int next;
        while (file_stream >> next)
            cout << next << endl;
    }

21. The maximum number of characters that can be typed in for a string variable is one less than the declared size. Here the value is 20.

22. The statement

    ```
    cin >> c;
    ```

    reads the next *nonwhite* character, whereas

    ```
    cin.get(c);
    ```

    reads the next character whether the character is nonwhite or not.

23. The two statements are equivalent. Both of the statements output the value of the variable c.

24. The character that is "put back" into the input stream with the member function putback need not be the last character read. If your program reads an 'a' from the input stream, it can use the putback function to put back a 'b'. (The text in the input file will not be changed by putback, although your program will behave as if the text in the input file had been changed.)

25. The complete dialogue is

    ```
    Enter a line of input:
    a b c d e f g
    a b END OF OUTPUT
    ```

26. The complete dialogue is

    ```
    Enter a line of input:
    abcdef gh
    ace h
    ```

    Note that the output is simply every other character of the input, and note that the blank is treated just like any other character.

27. The complete dialogue is

    ```
    Enter a line of input:
    0 1 2 3 4 5 6 7 8 9 10 11
    01234567891 1
    ```

    Be sure to note that only the '1' in the input string 10 is output. This is because cin.get is reading characters, not numbers, and so it reads the input 10 as the two characters, '1' and '0'. Since this code is written to echo only every other character, the '0' is not output. Since the '0' is not output, the next character, which is a blank, is output, and so there is one blank in the output. Similarly, only one of the two '1' characters in 11 is output. If this is unclear, write the input on a sheet of paper and use a small square for the blank character. Then, cross out every other character; the output shown above is what is left.

28. This code contains an infinite loop and will continue as long as the user continues to give it input. The Boolean expression (`next != '\n'`) is always *true* because `next` is filled via the statement

```
cin >> next;
```

and this statement always skips the new-line character `'\n'` (as well as any blanks). The code will run and if the user gives no additional input, the dialogue will be as follows:

```
Enter a line of input:
0 1 2 3 4 5 6 7 8 9 10 11
0246811
```

Notice that the code in Self-Test Exercise 27 used `cin.get`, so it reads every character, *whether the character is a blank or not*, and then it outputs every other character. So the code in Self-Test Exercise 27 outputs every other character even if the character is a blank. On the other hand, the code in this Self-Test Exercise uses `cin` and `>>`, so it *skips over all blanks* and considers only nonblank characters (which in this case are the digits `'0'` through `'9'`). Thus, this code outputs every other *nonblank* character. The two `'1'` characters in the output are the first character in the input 10 and the first character in the input 11.

29. *void* copy_char(istream& source_file)
```
{
    char next;
    source_file.get(next);
    cout << next;
}
```

30. *void* copy_line(istream& source_file)
```
{
    char next;
    do
    {
        source_file.get(next);
        cout << next;
    } while (next != '\n');
}
```

31. *void* send_line(ostream& target_stream)
```
{
    char next;
    do
    {
        cin.get(next);
        target_stream << next;
    } while (next != '\n');
}
```

32. a. 2.0 1.1 2.3
    b. 2.0 3.0 2.3
    c. 2.0 3.0 4.0

33. One set of functions follows:

```
void func(double x)
{
    double y = 1.1;
    double z = 2.3;
    cout << x << " " << y << " " << z << endl;
}
void func(double x, double y)
{
    double z = 2.3;
    cout << x << " " << y << " " << z << endl;
}
void func(double x, double y, double z)
{
    cout << x << " " << y << " " << z << endl;
}
```

34. It would evaluate to *false*. Your program must attempt to read one more character (beyond the last character) before it changes to *true*.

35.
```
void text_to_screen(ifstream& file_stream)
{
    char next;
    file_stream.get(next);
    while (! file_stream.eof( ))
    {
        cout << next;
        file_stream.get(next);
    }
}
```

If you prefer, you can use `cout.put(next);` instead of `cout << next;`.

36. The complete dialogue is as follows:

```
Enter a line of input:
I'll see you at 10:30 AM.
I'll see you at 1 <END OF OUTPUT
```

37.
```
cout << "Enter a line of input:\n";
char next;
do
{
    cin.get(next);
    if (!isupper(next))
        cout << next;
} while (next != '\n');
```

Note that you should use `!isupper(next)` and not use `islower(next)`. This is because `islower(next)` is *false* if next contains a character that is not a letter (such as the blank or comma symbol).

PROGRAMMING PROJECTS

myprogramminglab   *Visit www.myprogramminglab.com to complete many of these Programming Projects online and get instant feedback.*

1. Write a program that will search a file of numbers of type *int* and writes the numbers which cannot be divided by 2 (odd numbers) to the screen. The file contains nothing but numbers of type *int* separated by blanks or line breaks. If this is being done as a class assignment, obtain the file name from your instructor.

2. Write a program that takes its input from a file of numbers of type *double* and outputs the number of negative or positive numbers present in the file to the screen. The file contains nothing but numbers of type *double* separated by blanks and/or line breaks. If this is being done as a class assignment, obtain the file name from your instructor.

3. a. Compute the median of a data file. The median is the number that has the same number of data elements greater than the number as there are less than the number. For purposes of this problem, you are to assume that the data is *sorted* (that is, is in increasing order). The median is the middle element of the file if there are an odd number of elements, or the average of the two middle elements if the file has an even number of elements. You will need to open the file, count the members, close the file and calculate the location of the middle of the file, open the file again (recall the "start over" discussion in this chapter), count up to the file entries you need, and calculate the middle.

   If your instructor has assigned this problem, ask for a data file to test your program with. Otherwise, construct several files on your own, including one with an even number of data points, increasing, and one with an odd number, also increasing.

   b. For a sorted file, a quartile is one of three numbers: The first has one-fourth the data values less than or equal to it, one-fourth the data values between the first and second numbers, one-fourth the data points between the second and the third, and one-fourth above the third quartile. Find the three quartiles for the data file you used for part (a).

   (*Hint*: You should recognize that having done part (a) you have one-third of your job done—you have the second quartile already. You also should recognize that you have done almost all the work toward finding the other two quartiles as well.)

4. Write a program that takes its input from a file of numbers of type *double*. The program outputs to the screen the average and standard deviation of the numbers in the file. The file contains nothing but numbers of type *double* separated by blanks and/or line breaks. The standard deviation of a list of numbers n_1, n_2, n_3, and so forth is defined as the square root of the average of the following numbers:

$(n_1 - a)^2$, $(n_2 - a)^2$, $(n_3 - a)^2$, and so forth

The number a is the average of the numbers n_1, n_2, n_3, and so forth. If this is being done as a class assignment, obtain the file name from your instructor.

(*Hint*: Write your program so that it first reads the entire file and computes the average of all the numbers, and then closes the file, then reopens the file and computes the standard deviation.)

5. Write a program that gives and takes advice on program writing. The program starts by writing a piece of advice to the screen and asking the user to type in a different piece of advice. The program then ends. The next person to run the program receives the advice given by the person who last ran the program. The advice is kept in a file, and the contents of the file change after each run of the program. You can use your editor to enter the initial piece of advice in the file so that the first person who runs the program receives some advice. Allow the user to type in advice of any length so that it can be any number of lines long. The user is told to end his or her advice by pressing the Return key two times. Your program can then test to see that it has reached the end of the input by checking to see when it reads two consecutive occurrences of the character '\n'.

6. Write a program that reads text from one file and writes an edited version of the same text to another file. The edited version is identical to the unedited version except that there will be no single quote and double quote strings in the edited version. Thus, the text is edited to remove single quote and double quotes characters. Your program should define a function that is called with the input- and output-file streams as arguments. If this is being done as a class assignment, obtain the file names from your instructor.

7. Write a program that merges the numbers in two files and writes all the numbers into a third file. Your program takes input from two different files and writes its output to a third file. Each input file contains a list of numbers of type *int* in sorted order from the smallest to the largest. After the program is run, the output file will contain all the numbers in the two input files in one longer list in sorted order from smallest to largest. Your program should define a function that is called with the two input-file streams and the output-file stream as three arguments. If this is being done as a class assignment, obtain the file names from your instructor.

8. Write a program to generate personalized junk mail. The program takes input both from an input file and from the keyboard. The input file contains the text of a letter, except that the name of the recipient is indicated by the three characters #N#. The program asks the user for a name and then writes the letter to a second file but with the three letters #N# replaced by the name. The three-letter string #N# will occur exactly once in the letter.

   (*Hint*: Have your program read from the input file until it encounters the three characters #N#, and have it copy what it reads to the output file as it goes. When it encounters the three letters #N#, it then sends output to the screen asking for the name from the keyboard. You should be able to figure out the rest of the details. Your program should define a function that is called with the input- and output-file streams as arguments. If this is being done as a class assignment, obtain the file names from your instructor.)

   Harder version (using material in the optional section "File Names as Input"): Allow the string #N# to occur any number of times in the file. In this case, the name is stored in two string variables. For this version, assume that there is a first name and last name but no middle names or initials.

9. Write a program to compute numeric grades for a course. The course records are in a file that will serve as the input file. The input file is in exactly the following format: Each line contains a student's first name, then one space, then the student's last name, then one space, then five quiz scores all on one line. The quiz scores are whole numbers and are separated by one space. Your program will take its input from this file and send its output to a second file. The data in the output file will be the same as the data in the input file except that there will be one additional number (of type *double*) at the end of each line. This number will be the highest of the student's five quiz scores. If this is being done as a class assignment, obtain the file names from your instructor. Use at least one function that has file streams as all or some of its arguments.

10. Enhance the program you wrote for Programming Project 9 in all of the following ways.

   a. The list of quiz scores on each line will contain ten or fewer quiz scores. (If there are fewer than ten quiz scores, that means the student missed one or more quizzes.) The average score is still the sum of the quiz scores divided by 10. This amounts to giving the student a 0 for any missed quiz.

   b. The output file will contain a line (or lines) at the beginning of the file explaining the output. Use formatting instructions to make the layout neat and easy to read.

c. After placing the desired output in an output file, your program will close all files and then copy the contents of the "output" file to the "input" file so that the net effect is to change the contents of the input file.

Use at least two functions that have file streams as all or some of their arguments. If this is being done as a class assignment, obtain the file names from your instructor.

11. Write a program that will compute the average sentence length (average number of characters per sentence) for a file that contains some text. A sentence is defined to be any string of symbols that is preceded and followed by one of the following at each end: a period, a question mark, an exclamation mark, or the end of a file. Your program should define a function that is called with the input-file stream as an argument. This function should also work with the stream `cin` as the input stream, although the function will not be called with `cin` as an argument in this program. If this is being done as a class assignment, obtain the file names from your instructor.

12. Write a program that will correct a C++ program that has errors in which operator, << or >>, it uses with `cin` and `cout`. The program replaces each (incorrect) occurrence of

```
cin <<
```

with the corrected version

```
cin >>
```

and each (incorrect) occurrence of

```
cout >>
```

with the corrected version

```
cout <<
```

For an easier version, assume that there is always exactly one blank space between any occurrence of `cin` and a following <<, and similarly assume that there is always exactly one blank space between each occurrence of `cout` and a following >>.

For a harder version, allow for the possibility that there may be any number of blanks, even zero blanks, between `cin` and << and between `cout` and >>. In this harder case, the replacement corrected version has only one blank between the `cin` or `cout` and the following operator. The program to be corrected is in one file and the corrected version is output to a second file. Your program should define a function that is called with the input- and output-file streams as arguments.

If this is being done as a class assignment, obtain the file names from your instructor and ask your instructor whether you should do the easier version or the harder version.

(*Hint*: Even if you are doing the harder version, you will probably find it easier and quicker to first do the easier version and then modify your program so that it performs the harder task.)

13. Write a program that allows the user to type in any one-line question and then answers that question. The program will not really pay any attention to the question, but will simply read the question line and discard all that it reads. It always gives one of the following answers:

```
I'm not sure, but I think you will find the answer in Chapter #N.
That's a good question.
If I were you, I would not worry about such things.
That question has puzzled philosophers for centuries.
I don't know. I'm just a machine.
Think about it and the answer will come to you.
I used to know the answer to that question, but I've forgotten it.
The answer can be found in a secret place in the woods.
```

These answers are stored in a file (one answer per line), and your program simply reads the next answer from the file and writes it out as the answer to the question. After your program has read the entire file, it simply closes the file, reopens the file, and starts down the list of answers again.

Whenever your program outputs the first answer, it should replace the two symbols #N with a number between 1 and 18 (including the possibility of 1 and 18). In order to choose a number between 1 and 18, your program should initialize a variable to 18 and decrease the variable's value by 1 each time it outputs a number so that the chapter numbers count backward from 18 to 1. When the variable reaches the value 0, your program should change its value back to 18. Give the number 17 the name NUMBER_OF_CHAPTERS with a global named constant declaration using the *const* modifier.

(*Hint*: Use the function new_line defined in this chapter.)

14. This project is the same as Programming Project 13, except that in this project your program will use a more sophisticated method for choosing the answer to a question. When your program reads a question, it counts the number of characters in the question and stores the number in a variable named count. It then responds with answer number count % ANSWERS. The first answer in the file is answer number 0, the next is answer number 1, then 2, and so forth. ANSWERS is defined in a constant declaration, as shown next, so that it is equal to the number of answers in the answer file:

const int ANSWERS = 8;

This way you can change the answer file so that it contains more or fewer answers and you need change only the constant declaration to make your program work correctly for a different number of possible answers. Assume that the answer listed first in the file will always be the following, even if the answer file is changed:

```
I'm not sure, but I think you will find the answer in Chapter #N.
```

When replacing the two characters #N with a number, use the number (count % NUMBER_OF_CHAPTERS + 1), where count is the variable discussed above, and NUMBER_OF_CHAPTERS is a global named constant defined to be equal to the number of chapters in this book.

15. This program numbers the lines found in a text file. Write a program that reads text from a file and outputs each line to the screen and to another file preceded by a line number. Print the line number at the start of the line and right-adjusted in a field of three spaces. Follow the line number with a colon, then one space, then the text of the line. You should get a character at a time and write code to ignore leading blanks on each line. You may assume that the lines are short enough to fit within a line on the screen. Otherwise, allow default printer or screen output behavior if the line is too long (that is, wrap or truncate).

    A somewhat harder version determines the number of spaces needed in the field for the line numbers by counting lines before processing the lines of the file. This version of the program should insert a new line after the last complete word that will fit within a 72-character line.

16. Write a program that computes all of the following statistics for a file and outputs the statistics to both the screen and another file: the total number of occurrences of special characters in the file, the total number of lines in the file, and the total number of occurrences of 'T' or 't' letters in the file.

17. The text file babynames2004.txt, which is included in the source code for this book and is available online from the book's Web site, contains a list of the 1000 most popular boy and girl names in the United States for the year 2004 as compiled by the Social Security Administration.

    This is a space-delimited file of 1000 entries in which the rank is listed first, followed by the corresponding boy name and girl name. The most popular names are listed first and the least popular names are listed last. For example, the file begins with

```
1 Jacob Emily
2 Michael Emma
3 Joshua Madison
```

This indicates that Jacob is the most popular boy name and Emily is the most popular girl name. Michael is the second most popular boy name and Emma is the second most popular girl name.

Write a program that allows the user to input a name. The program should then read from the file and search for a matching name among the girls and boys. If a match is found, it should output the rank of the name. The program should also indicate if there is no match.

For example, if the user enters the name "Justice," then the program should output:

```
Justice is ranked 406 in popularity among boys.
Justice is ranked 497 in popularity among girls.
```

If the user enters the name "Walter," then the program should output:

```
Walter is ranked 366 in popularity among boys.
Walter is not ranked among the top 1000 girl names.
```

VideoNote
Solution to Programming
Project 6.18

18. To complete this problem you must have a computer that is capable of viewing Scalable Vector Graphics (SVG) files. Your Web browser may already be able to view these files. To test to see if your browser can display SVG files, type in the `rectline.svg` file below and see if you can open it in your Web browser. If your Web browser cannot view the file, then you can search on the Web and download a free SVG viewer.

The graphics screen to draw an image uses a coordinate system in which (0, 0) is located in the upper-left corner. The x coordinate increases to the right, and the y coordinate increases to the bottom. Consequently, coordinate (100, 0) would be located 100 pixels directly toward the right from the upper-left corner, and coordinate (0, 100) would be located 100 pixels directly toward the bottom from the upper-left corner. This is illustrated in the figure below.

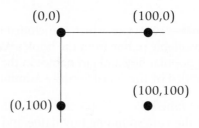

The SVG format defines a graphics image using XML. The specification for the image is stored in a text file and can be displayed by an SVG viewer. Here is a sample SVG file that draws two rectangles and a line. To view it, save it to a text file with the ".svg" extension, such as `rectline.svg`, and open it with your SVG viewer.

```
<?xml version="1.0" standalone="no"?>
<!DOCTYPE svg PUBLIC "-//W3C//DTD SVG 1.1//EN"
"http://www.w3.org/Graphics/SVG/1.1/DTD/svg11.dtd">
<svg width="500" height="500"
xmlns="http://www.w3.org/2000/svg">

<rect x="20" y="20" width="50" height="250"
style="fill:blue;"/>
<rect x="75" y="100" width="150" height="50"
style="fill:rgb(0,255,0);"/>
<line x1="0" y1="0" x2="300" y2="300"
style="stroke:purple;stroke-width:2"/>

</svg>
```

For purposes of this problem, you can ignore the first five lines and the last line and consider them "boilerplate" that must be inserted to properly create the image.

The lines that begins with `<rect x="20"`...draw a blue rectangle whose upper-left corner is at coordinate (20, 20) and whose width is 50 pixels and height is 250 pixels.

The lines that begin with `<rect x="75"`...draw a green rectangle (RGB color value of 0,255,0 is all green) whose upper-left corner is at coordinate (75, 100) and whose width is 150 pixels and height is 50 pixels.

Finally, the `<line>` tag draws a purple line from (0, 0) to (300, 300) with a width of 2.

Based on this example, write a program that inputs four nonnegative integer values and creates the SVG file that displays a simple bar chart that depicts the integer values. Your program should scale the values so they are always drawn with a maximum height of 400 pixels. For example, if your input values to graph were 20, 40, 60, and 120, you might generate a SVG file that would display as follows:

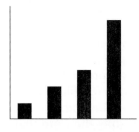

19. Refer to Programming Project 18 for information about the SVG format. Shown below is another example that illustrates how to draw circles, ellipses, and multiple lines:

```
<?xml version="1.0" standalone="no"?>
<!DOCTYPE svg PUBLIC "-//W3C//DTD SVG 1.1//EN"
"http://www.w3.org/Graphics/SVG/1.1/DTD/svg11.dtd">
<svg width="500" height="500"
xmlns="http://www.w3.org/2000/svg">

<circle cx="100" cy="50" r="30"
stroke="green" stroke-width="3" fill="gold"/>

<ellipse cx="100" cy="200" rx="50" ry="100"
style="fill:purple;stroke:black;stroke-width:2"/>

<polyline points="10,10 40,40 20,100 120,140"
style="fill-opacity:0;stroke:red;stroke-width:2"/>

</svg>
```

The <circle> tag draws a circle centered at (100, 50) with radius 30 and pen width of 3. It is filled in with gold and has a border in green.

The <ellipse> tag draws an ellipse centered at (100, 200) with *x* radius of 30 and *y* radius of 100. It is filled using purple with a black border.

The <polyline> tag draws a red line from (10, 10) to (40, 40) to (20, 100) to (120, 140). The fill-opacity is set to 0, making the fill of the polygon transparent.

Based on these examples and those presented in Project 18, write a program that creates an SVG image that draws a picture of your professor. It can be somewhat abstract and simple. If you wish to draw a fancier image, you can research the SVG picture format; there are additional tags that can draw using filters, gradients, and polygons.

20. Write a program that prompts the user to input the name of a text file and then outputs the number of sentences in the file. You can consider a "sentence" to be any text that ends with a delimiter (for example, a period, exclamation sign, question mark) or borders the beginning or end of the file.

21. The following is an old word puzzle: "Name a common word, besides tremendous, stupendous and horrendous, that ends in dous." If you think about this for a while, it will probably come to you. However, we can also solve this puzzle by reading a text file of English words and outputting the word if it contains "dous" at the end. The text file "words.txt" contains 87, 314 English words, including the word that completes the puzzle. This file is available online with the source code for the book. Write a program that reads each word from the text file and outputs only those containing "dous" at the end to solve the puzzle.

Arrays 7

It is a capital mistake to theorize before one has data.

SIR ARTHUR CONAN DOYLE, *Scandal in Bohemia* (Sherlock Holmes)

INTRODUCTION

An array is used to process a collection of data all of which is of the same type, such as a list of temperatures or a list of names. This chapter introduces the basics of defining and using arrays in C++ and presents many of the basic techniques used when designing algorithms and programs that use arrays.

PREREQUISITES

This chapter uses material from Chapters 2 through 6.

7.1 INTRODUCTION TO ARRAYS

Suppose we wish to write a program that reads in five test scores and performs some manipulations on these scores. For instance, the program might compute the highest test score and then output the amount by which each score falls short of the highest. The highest score is not known until all five scores are read in. Hence, all five scores must be retained in storage so that after the highest score is computed each score can be compared to it.

To retain the five scores, we will need something equivalent to five variables of type *int*. We could use five individual variables of type *int*, but five variables are hard to keep track of, and we may later want to change our program to handle 100 scores; certainly, 100 variables are impractical. An array is the perfect solution. An **array** behaves like a list of variables with a uniform naming mechanism that can be declared in a single line of simple code. For example, the names for the five individual variables we need might be score[0], score[1], score[2], score[3], and score[4]. The part that does not change—in this case, score—is the name of the array. The part that can change is the integer in the square brackets, [ ].

Declaring and Referencing Arrays

In C++, an array consisting of five variables of type *int* can be declared as follows:

```
int score[5];
```

This declaration is like declaring the following five variables to all be of type *int*:

```
score[0], score[1], score[2], score[3], score[4]
```

The individual variables that together make up the array are referred to in a variety of different ways. We will call them **indexed variables,** though they are also sometimes called **subscripted variables** or **elements** of the array. The number in square brackets is called an **index** or a **subscript.** In C++, indexes are numbered starting with 0, not with 1 or any other number except 0. The number of indexed variables in an array is called the **declared size** of the array, or sometimes simply the **size** of the array. When an array is declared, the size of the array is given in square brackets after the array name. The indexed variables are then numbered (also using square brackets), starting with 0 and ending with the integer that is one less than the size of the array.

In our example, the indexed variables were of type *int*, but an array can have indexed variables of any type. For example, to declare an array with indexed variables of type *double*, simply use the type name *double* instead of *int* in the declaration of the array. All the indexed variables for one array are, however, of the same type. This type is called the **base type** of the array. Thus, in our example of the array score, the base type is *int*.

You can declare arrays and regular variables together. For example, the following declares the two *int* variables next and max in addition to the array score:

```
int next, score[5], max;
```

An indexed variable like score[3] can be used anyplace that an ordinary variable of type *int* can be used.

Do not confuse the two ways to use the square brackets [ ] with an array name. When used in a declaration, such as

```
int score[5];
```

the number enclosed in the square brackets specifies how many indexed variables the array has. When used anywhere else, the number enclosed in the square brackets tells which indexed variable is meant. For example, score[0] through score[4] are indexed variables.

The index inside the square brackets need not be given as an integer constant. You can use any expression in the square brackets as long as the expression evaluates to one of the integers 0 through the integer that is one less than the size of the array. For example, the following will set the value of score[3] equal to 99:

```
int n = 2;
score[n + 1] = 99;
```

Although they may look different, score[n+1] and score[3] are the same indexed variable in the code above. That is because n + 1 evaluates to 3.

The identity of an indexed variable, such as score[i], is determined by the value of its index, which in this instance is i. Thus, you can write programs that say things such as "do such and such to the ith indexed variable," where the value of i is computed by the program. For example, the program in Display 7.1 reads in scores and processes them in the way we described at the start of this chapter.

■ **PROGRAMMING TIP**   Use *for* Loops with Arrays

The second *for* loop in Display 7.1 illustrates a common way to step through an array using a *for* loop:

```
for (i = 0; i < 5; i++)
    cout << score[i] << " off by "
         << (max - score[i]) << endl;
```

The *for* statement is ideally suited to array manipulations.   ■

PITFALL   Array Indexes Always Start with Zero

The indexes of an array always start with 0 and end with the integer that is one less than the size of the array.   ■

■ **PROGRAMMING TIP**   Use a Defined *Constant* for the Size of an Array

Look again at the program in Display 7.1. It only works for classes that have exactly five students. Most classes do not have exactly five students. One way to make a program more versatile is to use a defined constant for the size of each array. For example, the program in Display 7.1 could be rewritten to use the following defined constant:

```
const int NUMBER_OF_STUDENTS = 5;
```

The line with the array declaration would then be

```
int i, score[NUMBER_OF_STUDENTS], max;
```

Of course, all places that have a 5 for the size of the array should also be changed to have NUMBER_OF_STUDENTS instead of 5. If these changes are made to the program (or better still, if the program had been written this way in the first place), then the program can be rewritten to work for any number of students by simply changing the one line that defines the constant NUMBER_OF_STUDENTS. Note that on many compilers you cannot use a variable for the array size, such as the following:

```
cout << "Enter number of students:\n";
cin >> number;
int score[number]; //ILLEGAL ON MANY COMPILERS!
```

DISPLAY 7.1   Program Using an Array

```
1     //Reads in 5 scores and shows how much each
2     //score differs from the highest score.
3     #include <iostream>

4     int main( )
5     {
6         using namespace std;
7         int i, score[5], max;

8         cout << "Enter 5 scores:\n";
9         cin >> score[0];
10        max = score[0];
11        for (i = 1; i < 5; i++)
12        {
13            cin >> score[i];
14            if (score[i] > max)
15                max = score[i];
16            //max is the largest of the values score[0],..., score[i].
17        }

18        cout << "The highest score is " << max << endl
19             << "The scores and their\n"
20             << "differences from the highest are:\n";
21        for (i = 0; i < 5; i++)
22            cout << score[i] << " off by "
23                 << (max - score[i]) << endl;

24        return 0;
25    }
```

Sample Dialogue

```
Enter 5 scores:
5 9 2 10 6
The highest score is 10
The scores and their
differences from the highest are:
5 off by 5
9 off by 1
2 off by 8
10 off by 0
6 off by 4
```

Some but not all compilers will allow you to specify an array size with a variable in this way. However, for the sake of portability you should not do so, even if your compiler permits it. (In Chapter 9 we will discuss a different kind of array whose size can be determined when the program is run. ■

Arrays in Memory

Before discussing how arrays are represented in a computer's memory, let's first see how a simple variable, such as a variable of type *int* or *double*, is represented in the computer's memory. A computer's memory consists of a list of numbered locations called bytes.[1] The number of a byte is known as its address. A simple variable is implemented as a portion of memory consisting of some number of consecutive bytes. The number of bytes is determined by the type of the variable. Thus, a simple variable in memory is described by two pieces of information: an **address** in memory (giving the location of the first byte for that variable) and the type of the variable, which tells how many bytes of memory the variable requires. When we speak of the address of a variable, it is this address we are talking about. When your program stores a value in the variable, what really happens is that the value (coded as 0s and 1s) is placed in those bytes of memory that are assigned to that variable. Similarly, when a variable is given as a (call-by-reference) argument to a function, it is the address of the variable that is actually given to the calling function. Now let's move on to discuss how arrays are stored in memory.

Array indexed variables are represented in memory the same way as ordinary variables, but with arrays there is a little more to the story. The locations of the various array indexed variables are always placed next to one another in memory. For example, consider the following:

```
int a[6];
```

When you declare this array, the computer reserves enough memory to hold six variables of type *int*. Moreover, the computer always places these variables one after the other in memory. The computer then remembers the address of indexed variable a[0], but it does not remember the address of any other indexed variable. When your program needs the address of some other indexed variable, the computer calculates the address for this other indexed variable from the address of a[0]. For example, if you start at the address of a[0] and count past enough memory for three variables of type *int*, then you will be at the address of a[3]. To obtain the address of a[3], the computer starts with the address of a[0] (which is a number). The computer then adds the number of bytes needed to hold three variables of type *int* to the number for the address of a[0]. The result is the address of a[3]. This implementation is diagrammed in Display 7.2.

---

[1] A byte consists of 8 bits, but the exact size of a byte is not important to this discussion.

Array Declaration

SYNTAX

Type_Name Array_Name[*Declared_Size*];

EXAMPLES

int big_array[100];
double a[3];
double b[5];
char grade[10], one_grade;

An array declaration, of the form shown, will define *Declared_Size* indexed variables, namely, the indexed variables *Array_Name*[0] through *Array_Name*[*Declared_Size*-1]. Each indexed variable is a variable of type *Type_Name*.

The array a consists of the indexed variables a[0], a[1], and a[2], all of type *double*. The array b consists of the indexed variables b[0], b[1], b[2], b[3], and b[4], also all of type *double*. You can combine array declarations with the declaration of simple variables such as the variable one_grade shown above.

Many of the peculiarities of arrays in C++ can be understood only in terms of these details about memory. For example, in the next Pitfall section, we use these details to explain what happens when your program uses an illegal array index.

VideoNote
Array Walkthrough

PITFALL   Array Index Out of Range

The most common programming error made when using arrays is attempting to reference a nonexistent array index. For example, consider the following array declaration:

int a[6];

When using the array a, every index expression must evaluate to one of the integers 0 through 5. For example, if your program contains the indexed variable a[i], the i must evaluate to one of the six integers 0, 1, 2, 3, 4, or 5. If i evaluates to anything else, that is an error. When an index expression evaluates to some value other than those allowed by the array declaration, the index is said to be out of range or simply **illegal.** On most systems, the result of an illegal array index is that your program will do something wrong, possibly disastrously wrong, and will do so without giving you any warning.

DISPLAY 7.2   An Array in Memory

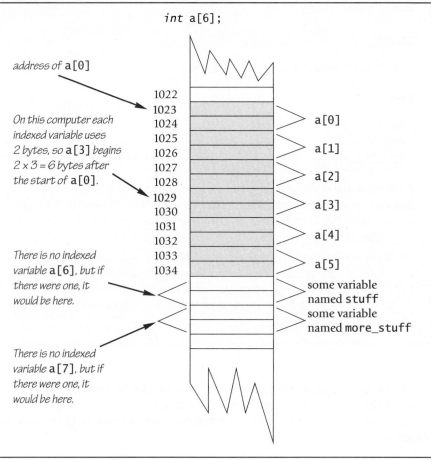

int a[6];

address of a[0]

On this computer each
indexed variable uses
2 bytes, so a[3] begins
2 x 3 = 6 bytes after
the start of a[0].

There is no indexed
variable a[6], but if
there were one, it
would be here.

There is no indexed
variable a[7], but if
there were one, it
would be here.

| 1022 |
| 1023 |
| 1024 | a[0] |
| 1025 |
| 1026 | a[1] |
| 1027 |
| 1028 | a[2] |
| 1029 |
| 1030 | a[3] |
| 1031 |
| 1032 | a[4] |
| 1033 |
| 1034 | a[5] |

some variable
named stuff
some variable
named more_stuff

For example, suppose your system is typical, the array a is declared as
shown, and your program contains the following:

    a[i] = 238;

Now, suppose the value of i, unfortunately, happens to be 7. The computer
proceeds as if a[7] were a legal indexed variable. The computer calculates
the address where a[7] would be (if only there were an a[7]), and places the
value 238 in that location in memory. However, there is no indexed variable
a[7], and the memory that receives this 238 probably belongs to some other
variable, maybe a variable named more_stuff. So the value of more_stuff
has been unintentionally changed. The situation is illustrated in Display 7.2.

Array indexes get out of range most commonly at the first or last
iteration of a loop that processes the array. So, it pays to carefully check
all array processing loops to be certain that they begin and end with legal
array indexes. ■

Initializing Arrays

An array can be initialized when it is declared. When initializing the array, the values for the various indexed variables are enclosed in braces and separated with commas. For example,

```
int children[3] = {2, 12, 1};
```

This declaration is equivalent to the following code:

```
int children[3];
children[0] = 2;
children[1] = 12;
children[2] = 1;
```

If you list fewer values than there are indexed variables, those values will be used to initialize the first few indexed variables, and the remaining indexed variables will be initialized to a 0 of the array base type. In this situation, indexed variables not provided with initializers are initialized to 0. However, arrays with no initializers and other variables declared within a function definition, including the main function of a program, are not initialized. Although array indexed variables (and other variables) may sometimes be automatically initialized to 0, you cannot and should not count on it.

If you initialize an array when it is declared, you can omit the size of the array, and the array will automatically be declared to have the minimum size needed for the initialization values. For example, the following declaration

```
int b[ ] = {5, 12, 11};
```

is equivalent to

```
int b[3] = {5, 12, 11};
```

SELF-TEST EXERCISES

myprogramming**lab**

1. Describe the difference in the meaning of *int* a[5] and the meaning of a[4]. What is the meaning of the [5] and [4] in each case?

2. In the array declaration

   double score[5];

   state the following:

   a. The array name
   b. The base type
   c. The declared size of the array
   d. The range of values that an index for this array can have
   e. One of the indexed variables (or elements) of this array

3. Identify any errors in the following array declarations.

   a. *int* x[4] = { 8, 7, 6, 4, 3 };

   b. *int* x[ ] = { 8, 7, 6, 4 };

   c. *const int* SIZE = 4;

   d. *int* x[SIZE];

4. What is the output of the following code?

   ```
   char symbol[3] = {'a', 'b', 'c'};

   for (int index = 0; index < 3; index++)
       cout << symbol[index];
   ```

5. What is the output of the following code?

   ```
   double a[3] = {1.1, 2.2, 3.3};
   cout << a[0] << " " << a[1] << " " << a[2] << endl;
   a[1] = a[2];
   cout << a[0] << " " << a[1] << " " << a[2] << endl;
   ```

6. What is the output of the following code?

   ```
   int i, temp[10];

   for (i = 0; i < 10; i++)
       temp[i] = 2 * i;

   for (i = 0; i < 10; i++)
       cout << temp[i] << " ";
   cout << endl;

   for (i = 0; i < 10; i = i + 2)
       cout << temp[i] << " ";
   ```

7. What is wrong with the following piece of code?

   ```
   int sample_array[10];

   for (int index = 1; index <= 10; index++)
       sample_array[index] = 3 * index;
   ```

8. Suppose we expect the elements of the array a to be ordered so that

   a[0] ≤ a[1] ≤ a[2] ≤ ...

   However, to be safe we want our program to test the array and issue a warning in case it turns out that some elements are out of order. The following code is supposed to output such a warning, but it contains a bug. What is it?

   ```
   double a[10];
   <Some code to fill the array a goes here.>
   ```

```
for (int index = 0; index < 10; index++)
    if (a[index] > a[index + 1])
        cout << "Array elements " << index << " and "
            << (index + 1) << " are out of order.";
```

9. Write some C++ code that will fill an array a with 20 values of type *int* read in from the keyboard. You need not write a full program, just the code to do this, but do give the declarations for the array and for all variables.

10. Suppose you have the following array declaration in your program:

    ```
    int your_array[7];
    ```

    Also, suppose that in your implementation of C++, variables of type *int* use 2 bytes of memory. When you run your program, how much memory will this array consume? Suppose that when you run your program, the system assigns the memory address 1000 to the indexed variable your_array[0]. What will be the address of the indexed variable your_array[3]?

7.2 ARRAYS IN FUNCTIONS

You can use both array indexed variables and entire arrays as arguments to functions. We first discuss array indexed variables as arguments to functions.

Indexed Variables as Function Arguments

An indexed variable can be an argument to a function in exactly the same way that any variable can be an argument. For example, suppose a program contains the following declarations:

```
int i, n, a[10];
```

If my_function takes one argument of type *int*, then the following is legal:

```
my_function(n);
```

Since an indexed variable of the array a is also a variable of type *int*, just like n, the following is equally legal:

```
my_function(a[3]);
```

There is one subtlety that does apply to indexed variables used as arguments. For example, consider the following function call:

```
my_function(a[i]);
```

If the value of i is 3, then the argument is a[3]. On the other hand, if the value of i is 0, then this call is equivalent to the following:

```
my_function(a[0]);
```

The indexed expression is evaluated in order to determine exactly which indexed variable is given as the argument.

Display 7.3 contains an example of indexed variables used as function arguments. The program shown gives five additional vacation days to each of three employees in a small business. The program is extremely simple, but it does illustrate how indexed variables are used as arguments to functions. Notice the function adjust_days. This function has a formal parameter called old_days that is of type *int*. In the main body of the program, this function is called with the argument vacation[number] for various values of number. Notice that there was nothing special about the formal parameter old_days. It is just an ordinary formal parameter of type *int*, which is the base type of the array vacation. In Display 7.3 the indexed variables are call-by-value arguments. The same remarks apply to call-by-reference arguments. An indexed variable can be a call-by-value argument or a call-by-reference argument.

DISPLAY 7.3   Indexed Variable as an Argument *(part 1 of 2)*

```
1    //Illustrates the use of an indexed variable as an argument.
2    //Adds 5 to each employee's allowed number of vacation days.
3    #include <iostream>
4    const int NUMBER_OF_EMPLOYEES = 3;

5    int adjust_days(int old_days);
6    //Returns old_days plus 5.

7    int main( )
8    {
9        using namespace std;
10       int vacation[NUMBER_OF_EMPLOYEES], number;
11       cout << "Enter allowed vacation days for employees 1"
12            << " through " << NUMBER_OF_EMPLOYEES << ":\n";
13       for (number = 1; number <= NUMBER_OF_EMPLOYEES; number++)
14           cin >> vacation[number - 1];
15       for (number = 0; number < NUMBER_OF_EMPLOYEES; number++)
16           vacation[number] = adjust_days(vacation[number]);
17       cout << "The revised number of vacation days are:\n";
18       for (number = 1; number <= NUMBER_OF_EMPLOYEES; number++)
19           cout << "Employee number " << number
20                << " vacation days = " << vacation[number-1] << endl;
21       return 0;
22   }

23   int adjust_days(int old_days)
24   {
25       return (old_days + 5);
26   }
```

(continued)

DISPLAY 7.3 Indexed Variable as an Argument *(part 2 of 2)*

Sample Dialogue

```
Enter allowed vacation days for employees 1 through 3:
10 20 5
The revised number of vacation days are:
Employee number 1 vacation days = 15
Employee number 2 vacation days = 25
Employee number 3 vacation days = 10
```

SELF-TEST EXERCISES

11. Consider the following function definition:

    ```
    void tripler(int& n)
    {
        n = 3*n;
    }
    ```

    Which of the following are acceptable function calls?

    ```
    int a[3] = {4, 5, 6}, number = 2;
    tripler(number);
    tripler(a[2]);
    tripler(a[3]);
    tripler(a[number]);
    tripler(a);
    ```

12. What (if anything) is wrong with the following code? The definition of
    `tripler` is given in Self-Test Exercise 11.

    ```
    int b[5] = {1, 2, 3, 4, 5};
    for (int i = 1; i <= 5; i++)
        tripler(b[i]);
    ```

Entire Arrays as Function Arguments

A function can have a formal parameter for an entire array so that when the
function is called, the argument that is plugged in for this formal parameter
is an entire array. However, a formal parameter for an entire array is neither a
call-by-value parameter nor a call-by-reference parameter; it is a new kind of
formal parameter referred to as an **array parameter.** Let's start with an example.

VideoNote
Passing Arrays to Functions

The function defined in Display 7.4 has one array parameter, a, which will be replaced by an entire array when the function is called. It also has one ordinary call-by-value parameter (size) that is assumed to be an integer value equal to the size of the array. This function fills its array argument (that is, fills all the array's indexed variables) with values typed in from the keyboard, and then the function outputs a message to the screen telling the index of the last array index used.

The formal parameter *int* a[ ] is an array parameter. The square brackets, with no index expression inside, are what C++ uses to indicate an array parameter. An array parameter is not quite a call-by-reference parameter, but for most practical purposes it behaves very much like a call-by-reference parameter. Let's go through this example in detail to see how an array argument works in this case. (An **array argument** is, of course, an array that is plugged in for an array parameter, such as a[ ].)

When the function fill_up is called it must have two arguments: The first gives an array of integers, and the second should give the declared size of the array. For example, the following is an acceptable function call:

```
int score[5], number_of_scores = 5;
fill_up(score, number_of_scores);
```

This call to fill_up will fill the array score with five *int*egers typed in at the keyboard. Notice that the formal parameter a[ ] (which is used in the function declaration and the heading of the function definition) is given with square brackets, but no index expression. (You may insert a number inside the square brackets for an array parameter, but the compiler will simply

DISPLAY 7.4 Function with an Array Parameter

Function Declaration

```
1    void fill_up(int a[], int size);
2    //Precondition: size is the declared size of the array a.
3    //The user will type in size integers.
4    //Postcondition: The array a is filled with size integers
5    //from the keyboard.
```

Function Definition

```
1    //Uses iostream:
2    void fill_up(int a[], int size)
3    {
4        using namespace std;
5        cout << "Enter " << size << " numbers:\n";
6        for (int i = 0; i < size; i++)
7            cin >> a[i];
8        size--;
9        cout << "The last array index used is " << size << endl;
10   }
```

ignore the number, so we do not use such numbers in this book.) On the other hand, the argument given in the function call (score in this example) is given without any square brackets or any index expression. What happens to the array argument score in this function call? Very loosely speaking, the argument score is plugged in for the formal array parameter a in the body of the function, and then the function body is executed. Thus, the function call

```
fill_up(score, number_of_scores);
```

is equivalent to the following code:

```
{
    using namespace std;          5  is the value of
    size = 5;  ◄————————           number_of_scores
    cout << "Enter " << size << " numbers:\n";
    for (int i = 0; i < size; i++)
        cin >> score[i];
    size--;
    cout << "The last array index used is " << size << endl;
}
```

The formal parameter a is a different kind of parameter from the ones we have seen before now. The formal parameter a is merely a placeholder for the argument score. When the function fill_up is called with score as the array argument, the computer behaves as if a were replaced with the corresponding argument score. *When an array is used as an argument in a function call, any action that is performed on the array parameter is performed on the array argument, so the values of the indexed variables of the array argument can be changed by the function.* If the formal parameter in the function body is changed (for example, with a cin statement), then the array argument will be changed.

So far it looks like an array parameter is simply a call-by-reference parameter for an array. That is close to being true, but an array parameter is slightly different from a call-by-reference parameter. To help explain the difference, let's review some details about arrays.

Recall that an array is stored as a contiguous chunk of memory. For example, consider the following declaration for the array score: Arrays in memory

```
int score[5];
```

When you declare this array, the computer reserves enough memory to hold five variables of type *int*, which are stored one after the other in the computer's memory. The computer does not remember the addresses of each of these five indexed variables; it remembers only the address of indexed variable score[0]. For example, when your program needs score[3], the computer calculates the address of score[3] from the address of score[0]. The computer knows that score[3] is located three *int* variables past score[0]. Thus, to obtain the address of score[3], the computer takes the address of score[0] and adds a number that represents the amount of memory used by three *int* variables; the result is the address of score[3].

Array argument

Viewed this way, an array has three parts: the address (location in memory) of the first indexed variable, the base type of the array (which determines how much memory each indexed variable uses), and the size of the array (that is, the number of indexed variables). When an array is used as an array argument to a function, only the first of these three parts is given to the function. When an array argument is plugged in for its corresponding formal parameter, all that is plugged in is the address of the array's first indexed variable. The base type of the array argument must match the base type of the formal parameter, so the function also knows the base type of the array. However, the array argument does not tell the function the size of the array. When the code in the function body is executed, the computer knows where the array starts in memory and how much memory each indexed variable uses, but(unless you make special provisions) it does not know how many indexed variables the array has. That is why it is critical that you always have another *int* argument telling the function the size of the array. That is also why an array parameter is not the same as a call-by-reference parameter. You can think of an array parameter as a weak form of call-by-reference parameter in which everything about the array is told to the function except for the size of the array.[2]

Different size array arguments can be plugged in for the same array parameter

These array parameters may seem a little strange, but they have at least one very nice property as a direct result of their seemingly strange definition. This advantage is best illustrated by again looking at our example of the function fill_up given in Display 7.4. *That same function can be used to fill an array of any size*, as long as the base type of the array is *int*. For example, suppose you have the following array declarations:

```
int score[5], time[10];
```

The first of the following calls to fill_up fills the array score with five values and the second fills the array time with ten values:

```
fill_up(score, 5);
fill_up(time, 10);
```

You can use the same function for array arguments of different sizes because the size is a separate argument.

The *const* Parameter Modifier

When you use an array argument in a function call, the function can change the values stored in the array. This is usually fine. However, in a complicated function definition, you might write code that inadvertently changes one or more of the values stored in an array, even though the array should not be changed at all. As a precaution, you can tell the compiler that you do not

---

[2] If you have heard of pointers, this will sound like pointers, and indeed an array argument is passed by passing a pointer to its first (zeroth) index variable. We will discuss this in Chapter 9. If you have not yet learned about pointers, you can safely ignore this footnote.

intend to change the array argument, and the computer will then check to make sure your code does not inadvertently change any of the values in the array. To tell the compiler that an array argument should not be changed by your function, you insert the modifier *const* before the array parameter for that argument position. An array parameter that is modified with a *const* is called a **constant array parameter.**

For example, the following function outputs the values in an array but does not change the values in the array:

```
void show_the_world(int a[ ], int size_of_a)
//Precondition: size_of_a is the declared size of the array a.
//All indexed variables of a have been given values.
//Postcondition: The values in a have been written
//to the screen.
{
    cout << "The array contains the following values:\n";
    for (int i = 0; i < size_of_a; i++)
        cout << a[i] << " ";
    cout << endl;
}
```

This function will work fine. However, as an added safety measure you can add the modifier *const* to the function heading as follows:

```
void show_the_world(const int a[ ], int size_of_a)
```

With the addition of this modifier *const*, the computer will issue an error message if your function definition contains a mistake that changes any of the

---

Array Formal Parameters and Arguments

An argument to a function may be an entire array, but an argument for an entire array is neither a call-by-value argument nor a call-by-reference argument. It is a new kind of argument known as an **array argument.** When an array argument is plugged in for an **array parameter,** all that is given to the function is the address in memory of the first indexed variable of the array argument (the one indexed by 0). The array argument does not tell the function the size of the array. Therefore, when you have an array parameter to a function, you normally must also have another formal parameter of type *int* that gives the size of the array (as in the example below).

An array argument is like a call-by-reference argument in the following way: If the function body changes the array parameter, then when the function is called, that change is actually made to the array argument. Thus, a function can change the values of an array argument (that is, can change the values of its indexed variables).

(continued)

The syntax for a function declaration with an array parameter is as follows:

SYNTAX

Type_Returned Function_Name(..., *Base_Type Array_Name*[],...);

EXAMPLE

void sum_array(*double*& sum, *double* a[ ], *int* size);

values in the array argument. For example, the following is a version of the function show_the_world that contains a mistake that inadvertently changes the value of the array argument. Fortunately, this version of the function definition includes the modifier *const*, so that an error message will tell us that the array a is changed. This error message will help to explain the mistake:

```
void show_the_world(const int a[ ], int size_of_a)
//Precondition: size_of_a is the declared size of the array a.
//All indexed variables of a have been given values.
//Postcondition: The values in a have been written
//to the screen.
{
    cout << "The array contains the following values:\n";
    for (int i = 0; i < size_of_a; a[i]++)
        cout << a[i] << " ";          Mistake, but the compiler
    cout << endl;                     will not catch it unless you
}                                     use the const modifier.
```

If we had not used the *const* modifier in this function definition and if we made the mistake shown, the function would compile and run with no error messages. However, the code would contain an infinite loop that continually increments a[0] and writes its new value to the screen.

The problem with this incorrect version of show_the_world is that the wrong item is incremented in the *for* loop. The indexed variable a[i] is incremented, but it should be the index i that is incremented. In this incorrect version, the index i starts with the value 0 and that value is never changed. But a[i], which is the same as a[0], is incremented. When the indexed variable a[i] is incremented, that changes a value in the array, and since we included the modifier *const*, the computer will issue a warning message. That error message should serve as a clue to what is wrong.

You normally have a function declaration in your program in addition to the function definition. When you use the *const* modifier in a function definition, you must also use it in the function declaration so that the function heading and the function declaration are consistent.

The modifier *const* can be used with any kind of parameter, but it is normally used only with array parameters and call-by-reference parameters for classes, which are discussed in Chapter 11.

PITFALL   Inconsistent Use of *const* Parameters

The *const* parameter modifier is an all-or-nothing proposition. If you use it for one array parameter of a particular type, then you should use it for every other array parameter that has that type and that is not changed by the function. The reason has to do with function calls within function calls. Consider the definition of the function show_difference, which is given below along with the declaration of a function used in the definition:

```
double compute_average(int a[ ], int number_used);
//Returns the average of the elements in the first number_used
//elements of the array a. The array a is unchanged.

void show_difference(const int a[ ], int number_used)
{
    double average = compute_average(a, number_used);
    cout << "Average of the " << number_used
         << " numbers = " << average << endl
         << "The numbers are:\n";
    for (int index = 0; index < number_used; index++)
        cout << a[index] << " differs from average by "
             << (a[index] - average) << endl;
}
```

This code will generate an error message or warning message with most compilers. The function compute_average does not change its parameter a. However, when the compiler processes the function definition for show_ difference, it will think that compute_average does (or at least might) change the value of its parameter a. This is because, when it is translating the function definition for show_difference, all the compiler knows about the function compute_average is the function declaration for compute_ average, and the function declaration does not contain a *const* to tell the compiler that the parameter a will not be changed. Thus, if you use *const* with the parameter a in the function show_difference, then you should also use the modifier *const* with the parameter a in the function compute_ average. The function declaration for compute_average should be as follows:

```
double compute_average(const int a[ ], int number_used);    ■
```

Functions That Return an Array

A function may not return an array in the same way that it returns a value of type *int* or *double*. There is a way to obtain something more or less equivalent to a function that returns an array. The thing to do is to return a pointer to the array. However, we have not yet covered pointers. We will discuss returning a pointer to an array when we discuss the interaction of arrays and pointers in Chapter 9. Until then, you have no way to write a function that returns an array.

CASE STUDY   Production Graph

In this case study we use arrays in the top-down design of a program. We use both indexed variables and entire arrays as arguments to the functions for subtasks.

Problem Definition

The Apex Plastic Spoon Manufacturing Company has commissioned us to write a program that will display a bar graph showing the productivity of each of its four manufacturing plants for any given week. Plants keep separate production figures for each department, such as the teaspoon department, soup spoon department, plain cocktail spoon department, colored cocktail spoon department, and so forth. Moreover, each plant has a different number of departments. For example, only one plant manufactures colored cocktail spoons. The input is entered plant-by-plant and consists of a list of numbers giving the production for each department in that plant. The output will consist of a bar graph in the following form:

```
Plant #1 **********
Plant #2 *************
Plant #3 ********************
Plant #4 *****
```

Each asterisk represents 1000 units of output.

We decide to read in the input separately for each department in a plant. Since departments cannot produce a negative number of spoons, we know that the production figure for each department will be nonnegative. Hence, we can use a negative number as a sentinel value to mark the end of the production numbers for each plant.

Since output is in units of 1000, it must be scaled by dividing it by 1000. This presents a problem since the computer must display a whole number of asterisks. It cannot display 1.6 asterisks for 1600 units. We will thus round to the nearest 1000th. Thus, 1600 will be the same as 2000 and will produce two asterisks. A precise statement of the program's input and output is as follows.

Input

There are four manufacturing plants numbered 1 through 4. The following input is given for each of the four plants: a list of numbers giving the production for each department in that plant. The list is terminated with a negative number that serves as a sentinel value.

Output

A bar graph showing the total production for each plant. Each asterisk in the bar graph equals 1000 units. The production of each plant is rounded to the nearest 1000 units.

Analysis of the Problem

We will use an array called `production`, which will hold the total production for each of the four plants. In C++, array indexes always start with 0. But since the plants are numbered 1 through 4, rather than 0 through 3, we will not use the plant number as the array index. Instead, we will place the total production for plant number n in the indexed variable `production[n-1]`. The total output for plant number 1 will be held in `production[0]`, the figures for plant 2 will be held in `production[1]`, and so forth.

Since the output is in thousands of units, the program will scale the values of the array elements. If the total output for plant number 3 is 4040 units, then the value of `production[2]` will initially be set to 4040. This value of 4040 will then be scaled to 4 so that the value of `production[2]` is changed to 4, and four asterisks will be output in the graph to represent the output for plant number 3.

The task for our program can be divided into the following subtasks: Subtasks

- `input_data`: Read the input data for each plant and set the value of the indexed variable `production[plant_number-1]` equal to the total production for that plant, where `plant_number` is the number of the plant.

- `scale`: For each `plant_number`, change the value of the indexed variable `production[plant_number - 1]` to the correct number of asterisks.

- `graph`: Output the bar graph.

The entire array `production` will be an argument for the functions that carry out these subtasks. As is usual with an array parameter, this means we must have an additional formal parameter for the size of the array, which in this case is the same as the number of plants. We will use a defined constant for the number of plants, and this constant will serve as the size of the array `production`. The `main` part of our program, together with the function declarations for the functions that perform the subtasks and the defined constant for the number of plants, is shown in Display 7.5. Notice that, since there is no reason to change the array parameter to the function `graph`, we have made that array parameter a constant parameter by adding the *const* parameter modifier. The material in Display 7.5 is the outline for our program, and if it is in a separate file, that file can be compiled so that we can check for any syntax errors in this outline before we go on to define the functions corresponding to the function declarations shown.

Having compiled the file shown in Display 7.5, we are ready to design the implementation of the functions for the three subtasks. For each of these three functions, we will design an algorithm, write the code for the function, and test the function before we go on to design the next function.

Algorithm Design for input_data

The function declaration and descriptive comment for the function input_data is shown in Display 7.5. As indicated in the body of the main part of our program (also shown in Display 7.5), when input_data is called, the formal array parameter a will be replaced with the array production, and since the last plant number is the same as the number of plants, the formal parameter last_plant_number will be replaced by NUMBER_OF_PLANTS. The algorithm for input_data is straightforward:

For plant_number equal to each of 1, 2, through last_plant_number do the following:

Read in all the data for plant whose number is plant_number.

Sum the numbers.

Set production[plant_number -1] equal to that total.

Coding for input_data

The algorithm for the function input_data translates to the following code:

```
//Uses iostream:
void input_data(int a[ ], int last_plant_number)
{
    using namespace std;
    for (int plant_number = 1;
        plant_number <= last_plant_number; plant_number++)
    {
        cout << endl
            << "Enter production data for plant number "
            << plant_number << endl;
        get_total(a[plant_number - 1]);
    }
}
```

The code is routine since all the work is done by the function get_total, which we still need to design. But before we move on to discuss the function get_total, let's observe a few things about the function input_data. Notice that we store the figures for plant number plant_number in the indexed variable with index plant_number-1; this is because arrays always start with index 0, while the plant numbers start with 1. Also, notice that we use an indexed variable for the argument to the function get_total. The function get_total really does all the work for the function input_data.

The function get_total does all the input work for one plant. It reads the production figures for that plant, sums the figures, and stores the total in the indexed variable for that plant. But get_total does not need to know that its argument is an indexed variable. To a function such as get_total, an indexed variable is just like any other variable of type *int*. Thus, get_total will have an ordinary call-by-reference parameter of type *int*. That means that

DISPLAY 7.5 Outline of the Graph Program

```
1    //Reads data and displays a bar graph showing productivity for each plant.
2    #include <iostream>
3    const int NUMBER_OF_PLANTS = 4;
4

5    void input_data(int a[], int last_plant_number);
6    //Precondition: last_plant_number is the declared size of the array a.
7    //Postcondition: For plant_number = 1 through last_plant_number:
8    //a[plant_number - 1] equals the total production for plant number plant_number.
9
10   void scale(int a[], int size);
11   //Precondition: a[0] through a[size - 1] each has a nonnegative value.
12   //Postcondition: a[i] has been changed to the number of 1000s (rounded to
13   //an integer) that were originally in a[i], for all i such that 0 <= i <= size - 1.
14
15   void graph(const int asterisk_count[], int last_plant_number);
16   //Precondition: asterisk_count[0] through asterisk_count[last_plant_number - 1]
17   //have nonnegative values.
18   //Postcondition: A bar graph has been displayed saying that plant
19   //number N has produced asterisk_count[N - 1] 1000s of units, for each N such that
20   //1 <= N <= last_plant_number
21
22   int main( )
23   {
24       using namespace std;
25       int production[NUMBER_OF_PLANTS];
26
27       cout << "This program displays a graph showing\n"
28           << "production for each plant in the company.\n";
29
30       input_data(production, NUMBER_OF_PLANTS);
31       scale(production, NUMBER_OF_PLANTS);
32       graph(production, NUMBER_OF_PLANTS);
33
34       return 0;
35   }
36
```

get_total is just an ordinary input function like others that we have seen before we discussed arrays. The function get_total reads in a list of numbers ended with a sentinel value, sums the numbers as it reads them in, and sets the value of its argument, which is a variable of type *int*, equal to this sum. There is nothing new to us in the function get_total. Display 7.6 shows the function definitions for both get_total and input_data. The functions are embedded in a simple test program.

Testing input_data

Every function should be tested in a program in which it is the only untested function. The function input_data includes a call to the function get_total. Therefore, we should test get_total in a driver program of its own. Once get_total has been completely tested, we can use it in a program, like the one in Display 7.6, to test the function input_data.

When testing the function input_data, we should include tests with all possible kinds of production figures for a plant. We should include a plant that has no production figures (as we did for plant 4 in Display 7.6); we should include a test for a plant with only one production figure (as we did for plant 3 in Display 7.6); and we should include a test for a plant with more than one production figure (as we did for plants 1 and 2 in Display 7.6). We should test for both nonzero and zero production figures, which is why we included a 0 in the input list for plant 2 in Display 7.6.

Algorithm Design for scale

The function scale changes the value of each indexed variable in the array production so that it shows the number of asterisks to print out. Since there should be one asterisk for every 1000 units of production, the value of each indexed variable must be divided by 1000.0. Then to get a whole number of asterisks, this number is rounded to the nearest integer. This method can be used to scale the values in any array a of any size, so the function declaration for scale, shown in Display 7.5 and repeated here, is stated in terms of an arbitrary array a of some arbitrary size:

```
void scale(int a[ ], int size);
//Precondition: a[0] through a[size - 1] each has a
//nonnegative value.
//Postcondition: a[i] has been changed to the number of 1000s
//(rounded to an integer) that were originally in a[i], for
//all i such that 0 <= i <= size - 1.
```

When the function scale is called, the array parameter a will be replaced by the array production, and the formal parameter size will be replaced by NUMBER_OF_PLANTS so that the function call looks like the following:

```
scale(production, NUMBER_OF_PLANTS);
```

The algorithm for the function scale is as follows:

```
for (int index = 0; index < size; index++)
```

Divide the value of a[index] by 1000 and round the result to the nearest whole number; the result is the new value of a[index].

Coding for scale

The algorithm for scale translates into the C++ code given next, where round is a function we still need to define. The function round takes one argument of type *double* and returns a type *int* value that is the integer nearest to its argument; that is, the function round will round its argument to the nearest whole number.

DISPLAY 7.6   Test of Function input_data *(part 1 of 3)*

```
1     //Tests the function input_data.
2     #include <iostream>
3     const int NUMBER_OF_PLANTS = 4;
4
5     void input_data(int a[], int last_plant_number);
6     //Precondition: last_plant_number is the declared size of the array a.
7     //Postcondition: For plant_number = 1 through last_plant_number:
8     //a[plant_number-1] equals the total production for plant number plant_number.
9
10    void get_total(int& sum);
11    //Reads nonnegative integers from the keyboard and
12    //places their total in sum.
13
14    int main( )
15    {
16        using namespace std;
17        int production[NUMBER_OF_PLANTS];
18        char ans;
19
20        do
21        {
22            input_data(production, NUMBER_OF_PLANTS);
23            cout << endl
24                << "Total production for each"
25                << " of plants 1 through 4:\n";
26            for (int number = 1; number <= NUMBER_OF_PLANTS; number++)
27                cout << production[number - 1] << " ";
28
29            cout << endl
30                << "Test Again?(Type y or n and Return): ";
31            cin >> ans;
32        } while ( (ans != 'N') && (ans != 'n') );
33
34        cout << endl;
35
36        return 0;
37    }
38    //Uses iostream:
39    void input_data(int a[], int last_plant_number)
40    {
41        using namespace std;
42        for (int plant_number = 1;
43            plant_number <= last_plant_number; plant_number++)
44        {
45            cout << endl
46                << "Enter production data for plant number "
```

(continued)

DISPLAY 7.6   Test of Function input_data *(part 2 of 3)*

```
47                        << plant_number << endl;
48                get_total(a[plant_number - 1]);
49          }
50      }
51
52
53      //Uses iostream:
54      void get_total(int& sum)
55      {
56          using namespace std;
57          cout << "Enter number of units produced by each department.\n"
58              << "Append a negative number to the end of the list.\n";
59
60          sum = 0;
61          int next;
62          cin >> next;
63          while (next >= 0)
64          {
65              sum = sum + next;
66              cin >> next;
67          }
68
69          cout << "Total = " << sum << endl;
70      }
```

Sample Dialogue

```
Enter production data for plant number 1.
Enter number of units produced by each department.
Append a negative number to the end of the list.
1 2 3 -1
Total = 6

Enter production data for plant number 2.
Enter number of units produced by each department.
Append a negative number to the end of the list.
0 2 3 -1
Total = 5

Enter production data for plant number 3.
Enter number of units produced by each department.
Append a negative number to the end of the list.
2 -1
Total = 2
```

(continued)

DISPLAY 7.6   Test of Function input_data *(part 3 of 3)*

```
Enter production data for plant number 4.
Enter number of units produced by each department.
Append a negative number to the end of the list.
-1
Total = 0

Total production for each of plants 1 through 4:
6 5 2 0
Test Again?(Type y or n and Return): n
```

```
void scale(int a[], int size)
{
    for (int index = 0; index < size; index++)
        a[index] = round(a[index]/1000.0 );
}
```

Notice that we divided by 1000.0, not by 1000 (without the decimal point). If we had divided by 1000, we would have performed integer division. For example, 2600/1000 would give the answer 2, but 2600/1000.0 gives the answer 2.6. It is true that we want an integer for the final answer after rounding, but we want 2600 divided by 1000 to produce 3, not 2, when it is rounded to a whole number.

We now turn to the definition of the function round, which rounds its argument to the nearest integer. For example, round(2.3) returns 2, and round(2.6) returns 3. The code for the function round, as well as that for scale, is given in Display 7.7. The code for round may require a bit of explanation.

The function round uses the predefined function floor from the library with the header file cmath. The function floor returns the whole number just below its argument. For example, floor(2.1) and floor(2.9) both return 2. To see that round works correctly, let's look at some examples. Consider round(2.4). The value returned is

floor(2.4 + 0.5)

which is floor(2.9), and that is 2.0. In fact, for any number that is greater than or equal to 2.0 and strictly less than 2.5, that number plus 0.5 will be less than 3.0, and so floor applied to that number plus 0.5 will return 2.0. Thus, round applied to any number that is greater than or equal to 2.0 and strictly less than 2.5 will return 2. (Since the function declaration for round specifies that the type for the value returned is *int*, the computed value of 2.0 is type cast to the integer value 2 without a decimal point using *static_cast<int>*.)

Now consider numbers greater than or equal to 2.5, for example, 2.6. The value returned by the call round(2.6) is

floor(2.6 + 0.5)

DISPLAY 7.7   The Function scale

```
1    //Demonstration program for the function scale.
2    #include <iostream>
3    #include <cmath>
4
5    void scale(int a[], int size);
6    //Precondition: a[0] through a[size - 1] each has a nonnegative value.
7    //Postcondition: a[i] has been changed to the number of 1000s (rounded to
8    //an integer) that were originally in a[i], for all i such that 0 <= i <= size - 1.
9
10   int round(double number);
11   //Precondition: number >= 0.
12   //Returns number rounded to the nearest integer.
13
14   int main( )
15   {
16       using namespace std;
17       int some_array[4], index;
18       cout << "Enter 4 numbers to scale: ";
19       for (index = 0; index < 4; index++)
20           cin >> some_array[index];
21       scale(some_array, 4);
22       cout << "Values scaled to the number of 1000s are: ";
23       for (index = 0; index < 4; index++)
24           cout << some_array[index] << " ";
25       cout << endl;
26       return 0;
27   }
28
29   void scale(int a[], int size)
30   {
31       for (int index = 0; index < size; index++)
32           a[index] = round(a[index]/1000.0);
33   }
34
35   //Uses cmath:
36   int round(double number)
37   {
38       using namespace std;
39       return static_cast<int>(floor(number + 0.5));
40   }
```

Sample Dialogue

```
Enter 4 numbers to scale: 2600 999 465 3501
Values scaled to the number of 1000s are: 3 1 0 4
```

which is floor(3.1) and that is 3.0. In fact, for any number that is greater than or equal to 2.5 and less than or equal to 3.0, that number plus 0.5 will be greater than 3.0. Thus, round called with any number that is greater than or equal to 2.5 and less than or equal to 3.0 will return 3.

Thus, round works correctly for all arguments between 2.0 and 3.0. Clearly, there is nothing special about arguments between 2.0 and 3.0. A similar argument applies to all nonnegative numbers. So, round works correctly for all nonnegative arguments.

Testing scale

Display 7.7 contains a demonstration program for the function scale, but the testing programs for the functions round and scale should be more elaborate than this simple program. In particular, they should allow you to retest the tested function several times rather than just once. We will not give the complete testing programs, but you should first test round (which is used by scale) in a driver program of its own, and then test scale in a driver program. The program to test round should test arguments that are 0, arguments that round up (like 2.6), and arguments that round down like 2.3. The program to test scale should test a similar variety of values for the elements of the array.

The Function graph

The complete program for producing the desired bar graph is shown in Display 7.8. We have not taken you step-by-step through the design of the function graph because it is quite straightforward.

DISPLAY 7.8 **Production Graph Program** *(part 1 of 3)*

```
1     //Reads data and displays a bar graph showing productivity for each plant.
2     #include <iostream>
3     #include <cmath>
4     const int NUMBER_OF_PLANTS = 4;

5     void input_data(int a[], int last_plant_number);
6     //Precondition: last_plant_number is the declared size of the array a.
7     //Postcondition: For plant_number = 1 through last_plant_number:
8     //a[plant_number - 1] equals the total production for plant number plant_number.

9     void scale(int a[], int size);
10    //Precondition: a[0] through a[size - 1] each has a nonnegative value.
11    //Postcondition: a[i] has been changed to the number of 1000s (rounded to
12    //an integer) that were originally in a[i], for all i such that 0 <= i <= size - 1.

13    void graph(const int asterisk_count[], int last_plant_number);
14    //Precondition: asterisk_count[0] through asterisk_count[last_plant_number - 1]
15    //have nonnegative values.
16    //Postcondition: A bar graph has been displayed saying that plant
17    //number N has produced asterisk_count[N - 1] 1000s of units, for each N such that
18    //1 <= N <= last_plant_number
```

(continued)

DISPLAY 7.8 **Production Graph Program** *(part 2 of 3)*

```
19    void get_total(int& sum);
20    //Reads nonnegative integers from the keyboard and
21    //places their total in sum.
22    int round(double number);
23    //Precondition: number >= 0.
24    //Returns number rounded to the nearest integer.

25    void print_asterisks(int n);
26    //Prints n asterisks to the screen.

27    int main( )
28    {
29        using namespace std;
30        int production[NUMBER_OF_PLANTS];

31        cout << "This program displays a graph showing\n"
32             << "production for each plant in the company.\n";
33        input_data(production, NUMBER_OF_PLANTS);
34        scale(production, NUMBER_OF_PLANTS);
35        graph(production, NUMBER_OF_PLANTS);
36        return 0;
37    }

38    //Uses iostream:
39    void input_data(int a[], int last_plant_number)

    <The rest of the definition of input_data is given in Display 7.6.>

40    //Uses iostream:
41    void get_total(int& sum)

    <The rest of the definition of get_total is given in Display 7.6.>

42    void scale(int a[], int size)

    <The rest of the definition of scale is given in Display 7.7.>

43    //Uses cmath:
44    int round(double number)

    <The rest of the definition of round is given in Display 7.7.>

45    //Uses iostream:
46    void graph(const int asterisk_count[], int last_plant_number)
47    {
48        using namespace std;
49        cout << "\nUnits produced in thousands of units:\n";
50        for (int plant_number = 1;
51             plant_number <= last_plant_number; plant_number++)
52        {
53            cout << "Plant #" << plant_number << " ";
54            print_asterisks(asterisk_count[plant_number - 1]);
55            cout << endl;
56        }
57    }
```

(continued)

DISPLAY 7.8   Production Graph Program *(part 3 of 3)*

```
58      //Uses iostream:
59      void print_asterisks(int n)
60      {
61          using namespace std;
62          for (int count = 1; count <= n; count++)
63              cout << "*";
64      }
```

Sample Dialogue

```
This program displays a graph showing
production for each plant in the company.
Enter production data for plant number 1.
Enter number of units produced by each department.
Append a negative number to the end of the list.
2000 3000 1000 -1
Total = 6000

Enter production data for plant number 2.
Enter number of units produced by each department.
Append a negative number to the end of the list.
2050 3002 1300 -1
Total = 6352

Enter production data for plant number 3.
Enter number of units produced by each department.
Append a negative number to the end of the list.
5000 4020 500 4348 -1
Total = 13868

Enter production data for plant number 4.
Enter number of units produced by each department.
Append a negative number to the end of the list.
2507 6050 1809 -1
Total = 10366

Units produced in thousands of units: Plant #1 ******
Plant #2 ******
Plant #3 **************
Plant #4 **********
```

myprogramminglab

SELF-TEST EXERCISES

13. Write a function definition for a function called one_more, which has a formal parameter for an array of integers and increases the value of each array element by one. Add any other formal parameters that are needed.

14. Consider the following function definition:

```
void too2(int a[ ], int how_many)
{
    for (int index = 0; index < how_many; index++)
        a[index] = 2;
}
```

Which of the following are acceptable function calls?

```
int my_array[29];
too2(my_array, 29);
too2(my_array, 10);
too2(my_array, 55);
"Hey too2. Please, come over here."
int your_array[100];
too2(your_array, 100);
too2(my_array[3], 29);
```

15. Insert *const* before any of the following array parameters that can be changed to constant array parameters:

```
void output(double a[], int size);
//Precondition: a[0] through a[size - 1] have values.
//Postcondition: a[0] through a[size - 1] have been
//written out.

void drop_odd(int a[ ], int size);
//Precondition: a[0] through a[size - 1] have values.
//Postcondition: All odd numbers in a[0] through
//a[size - 1] have been changed to 0.
```

16. Write a function named out_of_order that takes as parameters an array of *double*s and an *int* parameter named size and returns a value of type *int*. This function will test this array for being out of order, meaning that the array violates the following condition:

```
a[0] <= a[1] <= a[2] <= ...
```

The function returns –1 if the elements are not out of order; otherwise, it will return the index of the first element of the array that is out of order. For example, consider the declaration

```
double a[10] = {1.2, 2.1, 3.3, 2.5, 4.5,
                7.9, 5.4, 8.7, 9.9, 1.0};
```

In this array, a[2] and a[3] are the first pair out of order, and a[3] is the first element out of order, so the function returns 3. If the array were sorted, the function would return -1.

7.3 PROGRAMMING WITH ARRAYS

Never trust to general impressions, my boy, but concentrate yourself upon details.

SIR ARTHUR CONAN DOYLE, *A Case of Identity (Sherlock Holmes)*

In this section we discuss partially filled arrays and give a brief introduction to sorting and searching of arrays. This section includes no new material about the C++ language, but does include more practice with C++ array parameters.

Partially Filled Arrays

Often the exact size needed for an array is not known when a program is written, or the size may vary from one run of the program to another. One common and easy way to handle this situation is to declare the array to be of the largest size the program could possibly need. The program is then free to use as much or as little of the array as is needed.

Partially filled arrays require some care. The program must keep track of how much of the array is used and must not reference any indexed variable that has not been given a value. The program in Display 7.9 illustrates this point. The program reads in a list of golf scores and shows how much each score differs from the average. This program will work for lists as short as one score, as long as ten scores, and for any length in between. The scores are stored in the array score, which has ten indexed variables, but the program uses only as much of the array as it needs. The variable number_used keeps track of how many elements are stored in the array. The elements (that is, the scores) are stored in positions score[0] through score[number_used - 1].

The details are very similar to what they would be if number_used were the declared size of the array and the entire array were used. In particular, the variable number_used usually must be an argument to any function that manipulates the partially filled array. Since the argument number_used (when used properly) can often ensure that the function will not reference an illegal array index, this sometimes (but not always) eliminates the need for an argument that gives the declared size of the array. For example, the functions show_difference and compute_average use the argument number_used to ensure that only legal array indexes are used. However, the function fill_array needs to know the maximum declared size for the array so that it does not overfill the array.

DISPLAY 7.9 Partially Filled Array *(part 1 of 2)*

```
1    //Shows the difference between each of a list of golf scores and their average.
2    #include <iostream>
3    const int MAX_NUMBER_SCORES = 10;

4    void fill_array(int a[], int size, int& number_used);
5    //Precondition: size is the declared size of the array a.
6    //Postcondition: number_used is the number of values stored in a.
7    //a[0] through a[number_used - 1] have been filled with
8    //nonnegative integers read from the keyboard.

9    double compute_average(const int a[], int number_used);
10   //Precondition: a[0] through a[number_used - 1] have values; number_used> 0.
11   //Returns the average of numbers a[0] through a[number_used - 1].

12   void show_difference(const int a[],int number_used);
13   //Precondition: The first number_used indexed variables of a have values.
14   //Postcondition: Gives screen output showing how much each of the first
15   //number_used elements of a differs from their average.

16   int main( )
17   {
18       using namespace std;
19       int score[MAX_NUMBER_SCORES], number_used;

20       cout << "This program reads golf scores and shows\n"
21            << "how much each differs from the average.\n";
22
23       cout << "Enter golf scores:\n";
24       fill_array(score, MAX_NUMBER_SCORES, number_used);
25       show_difference(score, number_used);

26       return 0;
27   }
28   //Uses iostream:
29   void fill_array(int a[], int size, int& number_used)
30   {
31       using namespace std;
32       cout << "Enter up to " << size << " nonnegative whole numbers.\n"
33            << "Mark the end of the list with a negative number.\n";
34       int next, index = 0;
35       cin >> next;
36       while ((next >= 0) && (index < size))
37       {
38           a[index] = next;
39           index++;
40           cin >> next;
41       }

42       number_used = index;
43   }
```

(continued)

DISPLAY 7.9   **Partially Filled Array** *(part 2 of 2)*

```
44    double compute_average(const int a[], int number_used)
45    {
46        double total = 0;
47        for (int index = 0; index < number_used; index++)
48            total = total + a[index];
49        if (number_used> 0)
50        {
51            return (total/number_used);
52        }
53        else
54        {
55            using namespace std;
56            cout << "ERROR: number of elements is 0 in compute_average.\n"
57                 << "compute_average returns 0.\n";
58            return 0;
59        }
60    }
61    void show_difference(const int a[], int number_used)
62    {
63        using namespace std;
64        double average = compute_average(a, number_used);
65        cout << "Average of the " << number_used
66             << " scores = " << average << endl
67             << "The scores are:\n";
68        for (int index = 0; index < number_used; index++)
69        cout << a[index] << " differs from average by "
70             << (a[index] - average) << endl;
71    }
```

Sample Dialogue

```
This program reads golf scores and shows
how much each differs from the average.
Enter golf scores:
Enter up to 10 nonnegative whole numbers.
Mark the end of the list with a negative number.
69 74 68 -1

Average of the 3 scores = 70.3333
The scores are:
69 differs from average by -1.33333
74 differs from average by 3.66667
68 differs from average by -2.33333
```

■ PROGRAMMING TIP   Do Not Skimp on Formal Parameters

Notice the function `fill_array` in Display 7.9. When `fill_array` is called, the declared array size `MAX_NUMBER_SCORES` is given as one of the arguments, as shown in the following function call from Display 7.9:

```
fill_array(score, MAX_NUMBER_SCORES, number_used);
```

You might protest that `MAX_NUMBER_SCORES` is a globally defined constant and so could be used in the definition of `fill_array` without the need to make it an argument. You would be correct, and if we did not use `fill_array` in any program other than the one in Display 7.9, we could get by without making `MAX_NUMBER_SCORES` an argument to `fill_array`. However, `fill_array` is a generally useful function that you may want to use in several different programs. We do in fact also use the function `fill_array` in the program in Display 7.10, discussed in the next subsection. In the program in Display 7.10, the argument for the declared array size is a different named global constant. If we had written the global constant `MAX_NUMBER_SCORES` into the body of the function `fill_array`, we would not have been able to reuse the function in the program in Display 7.10.   ■

PROGRAMMING EXAMPLE   Searching an Array

A common programming task is to search an array for a given value. For example, the array may contain the student numbers for all students in a given course. To tell whether a particular student is enrolled, the array is searched to see if it contains the student's number. The program in Display 7.10 fills an array and then searches the array for values specified by the user. A real application program would be much more elaborate, but this shows all the essentials of the sequential search algorithm. The sequential search algorithm is the most straightforward searching algorithm you could imagine: The program looks at the array elements in the order first to last to see if the target number is equal to any of the array elements.

In Display 7.10, the function `search` is used to search the array. When searching an array, you often want to know more than simply whether or not the target value is in the array. If the target value is in the array, you often want to know the index of the indexed variable holding that target value, since the index may serve as a guide to some additional information about the target value. Therefore, we designed the function `search` to return an index giving the location of the target value in the array, provided the target value is, in fact, in the array. If the target value is not in the array, `search` returns -1. Let's look at the function `search` in a little more detail.

The function `search` uses a *while* loop to check the array elements one after the other to see whether any of them equals the target value. The variable

DISPLAY 7.10 Searching an Array *(part 1 of 2)*

```
1    //Searches a partially filled array of nonnegative integers.
2    #include <iostream>
3    const int DECLARED_SIZE = 20;

4    void fill_array(int a[], int size, int& number_used);
5    //Precondition: size is the declared size of the array a.
6    //Postcondition: number_used is the number of values stored in a.
7    //a[0] through a[number_used - 1] have been filled with
8    //nonnegative integers read from the keyboard.

9    int search(const int a[], int number_used, int target);
10   //Precondition: number_used is <= the declared size of a.
11   //Also, a[0] through a[number_used - 1] have values.
12   //Returns the first index such that a[index] == target,
13   //provided there is such an index; otherwise, returns -1.

14   int main( )
15   {
16       using namespace std;
17       int arr[DECLARED_SIZE], list_size, target;

18       fill_array(arr, DECLARED_SIZE, list_size);

19       char ans;
20       int result;
21       do
22       {
23           cout << "Enter a number to search for: ";
24           cin >> target;

25           result = search(arr, list_size, target);
26           if (result == -1)
27               cout << target << " is not on the list.\n";
28           else
29               cout << target << " is stored in array position "
30                    << result << endl
31                    << "(Remember: The first position is 0.)\n";

32           cout << "Search again?(y/n followed by Return): ";
33           cin >> ans;
34       } while ((ans != 'n') && (ans != 'N'));

35       cout << "End of program.\n";
36       return 0;
37   }
38   //Uses iostream:
39   void fill_array(int a[], int size, int& number_used)
```

    <The rest of the definition of fill_array is given in Display 7.9.>

```
40
```

(continued)

DISPLAY 7.10 Searching an Array *(part 2 of 2)*

```
41    int search(const int a[], int number_used, int target)
42    {
43
44        int index = 0;
45        bool found = false;
46        while ((!found) && (index < number_used))
47            if (target == a[index])
48                found = true;
49            else
50                index++;
51
52        if (found)
53            return index;
54        else
55            return -1;
56    }
```

Sample Dialogue

```
Enter up to 20 nonnegative whole numbers.
Mark the end of the list with a negative number.
10 20 30 40 50 60 70 80 -1
Enter a number to search for: 10
10 is stored in array position 0.
(Remember: The first position is 0.)
Search again?(y/n followed by Return): y
Enter a number to search for: 40
40 is stored in array position 3.
(Remember: The first position is 0.)
Search again?(y/n followed by Return): y
Enter a number to search for: 42
42 is not on the list.
Search again?(y/n followed by Return): n
End of program.
```

found is used as a flag to record whether or not the target element has been found. If the target element is found in the array, found is set to *true*, which in turn ends the *while* loop.

Even if we used fill_array in only one program, it can still be a good idea to make the declared array size an argument to fill_array. Displaying the declared size of the array as an argument reminds us that the function needs this information in a critically important way.

PROGRAMMING EXAMPLE   Sorting an Array

One of the most widely encountered programming tasks, and certainly the most thoroughly studied, is sorting a list of values, such as a list of sales figures that must be sorted from lowest to highest or from highest to lowest, or a list of words that must be sorted into alphabetical order. In this section we describe a function called sort that sorts a partially filled array of numbers so that they are ordered from smallest to largest.

The procedure sort has one array parameter a. The array a will be partially filled, so there is an additional formal parameter called number_used, which tells how many array positions are used. Thus, the declaration and precondition for the function sort is

```
void sort(int a[], int number_used);
//Precondition: number_used <= declared size of the array a.
//Array elements a[0] through a[number_used - 1] have values.
```

The function sort rearranges the elements in array a so that after the function call is completed the elements are sorted as follows:

```
a[0] ≤ a[1] ≤ a[2] ≤ ... ≤ a[number_used - 1]
```

The algorithm we use to do the sorting is called selection sort. It is one of the easiest of the sorting algorithms to understand.

One way to design an algorithm is to rely on the definition of the problem. In this case the problem is to sort an array a from smallest to largest. That means rearranging the values so that a[0] is the smallest, a[1] the next smallest, and so forth. That definition yields an outline for the selection sort algorithm:

```
for (int index = 0; index < number_used; index++)
    Place the indexth smallest element in a[index]
```

There are many ways to realize this general approach. The details could be developed using two arrays and copying the elements from one array to the other in sorted order, but one array should be both adequate and economical. Therefore, the function sort uses only the one array containing the values to be sorted. The function sort rearranges the values in the array a by interchanging pairs of values. Let us go through a concrete example so that you can see how the algorithm works.

VideoNote
Selection Sort Walkthrough

Consider the array shown in Display 7.11. The algorithm will place the smallest value in a[0]. The smallest value is the value in a[3]. So the algorithm interchanges the values of a[0] and a[3]. The algorithm then looks for the next smallest element. The value in a[0] is now the smallest element and so the next smallest element is the smallest of the remaining elements a[1], a[2], a[3], ..., a[9]. In the example in Display 7.11, the next smallest element is in a[5], so the algorithm interchanges the values of a[1] and a[5]. This positioning of the second smallest element is illustrated in the fourth and fifth array pictures in Display 7.11. The algorithm then positions the third smallest element, and so forth.

DISPLAY 7.11 Selection Sort

a[0]	a[1]	a[2]	a[3]	a[4]	a[5]	a[6]	a[7]	a[8]	a[9]
8	6	10	2	16	4	18	14	12	20

8	6	10	2	16	4	18	14	12	20

2	6	10	8	16	4	18	14	12	20

2	6	10	8	16	4	18	14	12	20

2	4	10	8	16	6	18	14	12	20

As the sorting proceeds, the beginning array elements are set equal to the correct sorted values. The sorted portion of the array grows by adding elements one after the other from the elements in the unsorted end of the array. Notice that the algorithm need not do anything with the value in the last indexed variable, a[9]. That is because once the other elements are positioned correctly, a[9] must also have the correct value. After all, the correct value for a[9] is the smallest value left to be moved, and the only value left to be moved is the value that is already in a[9].

The definition of the function sort, included in a demonstration program, is given in Display 7.12. sort uses the function index_of_smallest to find the index of the smallest element in the unsorted end of the array, and then it does an interchange to move this element down into the sorted part of the array.

The function swap_values, shown in Display 7.12, is used to interchange the values of indexed variables. For example, the following call will interchange the values of a[0] and a[3]:

```
swap_values(a[0], a[3]);
```

The function swap_values was explained in Chapter 5.

DISPLAY 7.12 Sorting an Array *(part 1 of 2)*

```
1    //Tests the procedure sort.
2    #include <iostream>

3    void fill_array(int a[], int size, int&number_used);
4    //Precondition: size is the declared size of the array a.
5    //Postcondition: number_used is the number of values stored in a.
6    //a[0] through a[number_used - 1] have been filled with
7    //nonnegative integers read from the keyboard.

8    void sort(int a[], int number_used);
9    //Precondition: number_used <= declared size of the array a.
10   //The array elements a[0] through a[number_used - 1] have values.
11   //Postcondition: The values of a[0] through a[number_used - 1] have
12   //been rearranged so that a[0] <= a[1] <= ... <= a[number_used - 1].

13   void swap_values(int &v1, int &v2);
14   //Interchanges the values of v1 and v2.

15   int index_of_smallest(const int a[], int start_index, int number_used);
16   //Precondition: 0 <= start_index < number_used. Referenced array elements have
17   //values.
18   //Returns the index i such that a[i] is the smallest of the values
19   //a[start_index], a[start_index + 1], ..., a[number_used - 1].

20   int main( )
21   {
22       using namespace std;
23       cout << "This program sorts numbers from lowest to highest.\n";

24       int sample_array[10], number_used;
25       fill_array(sample_array, 10, number_used);
26       sort(sample_array, number_used);

27       cout << "In sorted order the numbers are:\n";
28       for (int index = 0; index < number_used; index++)
29       cout << sample_array[index] << " ";
30       cout << endl;

31       return 0;
32   }

33   //Uses iostream:
34   void fill_array(int a[], int size, int&number_used)
```

<The rest of the definition of fill_array is given in Display 7.9.>

```
35   void sort(int a[], int number_used)
36   {
37       int index_of_next_smallest;
38       for (int index = 0; index < number_used - 1; index++)
```

(continued)

DISPLAY 7.12 Sorting an Array *(part 2 of 2)*

```
39          {//Place the correct value in a[index]:
40              index_of_next_smallest =
41                          index_of_smallest(a, index, number_used);
42              swap_values(a[index], a[index_of_next_smallest]);
43              //a[0] <= a[1] <=...<= a[index] are the smallest of the original array
44              //elements. The rest of the elements are in the remaining positions.
45          }
46      }
47

48      void swap_values(int& v1, int& v2)
49      {
50          int temp;
51          temp = v1;
52          v1 = v2;
53          v2 = temp;
54      }
55

56      int index_of_smallest(const int a[], int start_index, int number_used)
57      {
58          int min = a[start_index],
59              index_of_min = start_index;
60          for (int index = start_index + 1; index < number_used; index++)
61              if (a[index] < min)
62              {
63                  min = a[index];
64                  index_of_min = index;
65                  //min is the smallest of a[start_index] through a[index]
66              }
67
68          return index_of_min;
69      }
```

Sample Dialogue

```
This program sorts numbers from lowest to highest.
Enter up to 10 nonnegative whole numbers.
Mark the end of the list with a negative number.
80 30 50 70 60 90 20 30 40 -1
In sorted order the numbers are:
20 30 30 40 50 60 70 80 90
```

SELF-TEST EXERCISES

17. Write a program that will read up to ten nonnegative integers into an array called `number_array` and then write the integers back to the screen. For this exercise you need not use any functions. This is just a toy program and can be very minimal.

18. Write a program that will read up to ten letters into an array and write the letters back to the screen in the reverse order. For example, if the input is

    abcd.

    then the output should be

    dcba

    Use a period as a sentinel value to mark the end of the input. Call the array `letter_box`. For this exercise you need not use any functions. This is just a toy program and can be very minimal.

19. Following is the declaration for an alternative version of the function search defined in Display 7.12. In order to use this alternative version of the search function, we would need to rewrite the program slightly, but for this exercise all you need to do is to write the function definition for this alternative version of search.

    ```
    bool search(const int a[], int number_used,
    int target, int& where);
    //Precondition: number_used is <= the declared size of the
    //array a; a[0] through a[number_used - 1] have values.
    //Postcondition: If target is one of the elements a[0]
    //through a[number_used - 1], then this function returns
    //true and sets the value of where so that a[where] ==
    //target; otherwise this function returns false and the
    //value of where is unchanged.
    ```

7.4 MULTIDIMENSIONAL ARRAYS

Two indexes are better than one.

FOUND ON THE WALL OF A COMPUTER SCIENCE DEPARTMENT RESTROOM

C++ allows you to declare arrays with more than one index. In this section we describe these multidimensional arrays.

Multidimensional Array Basics

It is sometimes useful to have an array with more than one index, and this is allowed in C++. The following declares an array of characters called page. The array page has two indexes: The first index ranges from 0 to 29, and the second from 0 to 99.

```
char page[30][100];
```

The indexed variables for this array each have two indexes. For example, page[0][0], page[15][32], and page[29][99] are three of the indexed variables for this array. Note that each index must be enclosed in its own set of square brackets. As was true of the one-dimensional arrays we have already seen, each indexed variable for a multidimensional array is a variable of the base type.

An array may have any number of indexes, but perhaps the most common number of indexes is two. A two-dimensional array can be visualized as a two-dimensional display with the first index giving the row and the second index giving the column. For example, the array indexed variables of the two-dimensional array page can be visualized as follows:

```
page[0][0], page[0][1], ..., page[0][99]
page[1][0], page[1][1], ..., page[1][99]
page[2][0], page[2][1], ..., page[2][99]
                .
                .
                .
page[29][0], page[29][1], ..., page[29][99]
```

You might use the array page to store all the characters on a page of text that has 30 lines (numbered 0 through 29) and 100 characters on each line (numbered 0 through 99).

A multidimensional array is an array of arrays

In C++, a two-dimensional array, such as page, is actually an array of arrays. The example array page is actually a one-dimensional array of size 30, whose base type is a one-dimensional array of characters of size 100. Normally, this need not concern you, and you can usually act as if the array page is actually an array with two indexes (rather than an array of arrays, which is harder to keep track of). There is, however, at least one situation where a two-dimensional array looks very much like an array of arrays, namely, when you have a function with an array parameter for a two-dimensional array, which is discussed in the next subsection.

Multidimensional Array Parameters

The following declaration of a two-dimensional array is actually declaring a one-dimensional array of size 30, whose base type is a one-dimensional array of characters of size 100:

Multidimensional Array Declaration

SYNTAX

Type Array_Name[*Size_Dim_1*][*Size_Dim_2*]...[*Size_Dim_Last*];

EXAMPLES

char page[30][100];
int matrix[2][3];
double three_d_picture[10][20][30];

An array declaration, of the form shown, defines one indexed variable for each combination of array indexes. For example, the second of the sample declarations defines the following six indexed variables for the array matrix:

matrix[0][0], matrix[0][1], matrix[0][2],
matrix[1][0], matrix[1][1], matrix[1][2]

---

char page[30][100];

Viewing a two-dimensional array as an array of arrays will help you to understand how C++ handles parameters for multidimensional arrays. For example, the following function takes an array argument, like page, and prints it to the screen:

```
void display_page(const char p[][100], int size_dimension_1)
{
    for (int index1 = 0; index1 < size_dimension_1; index1++)
    {//Printing one line:
        for (int index2 = 0; index2 < 100; index2++)
            cout << p[index1][index2];
        cout << endl;
    }
}
```

Notice that with a two-dimensional array parameter, the size of the first dimension is not given, so we must include an *int* parameter to give the size of this first dimension. (As with ordinary arrays, the compiler will allow you to specify the first dimension by placing a number within the first pair of square brackets. However, such a number is only a comment; the compiler ignores any such number.) The size of the second dimension (and all other dimensions if there are more than two) is given after the array parameter, as shown for the parameter

const char p[ ][100]

> **Multidimensional Array Parameters**
>
> When a multidimensional array parameter is given in a function heading or function declaration, the size of the first dimension is not given, but the remaining dimension sizes must be given in square brackets. Since the first dimension size is not given, you usually need an additional parameter of type *int* that gives the size of this first dimension. Below is an example of a function declaration with a two-dimensional array parameter p:
>
> *void* get_page(*char* p[][100], *int* size_dimension_1);

If you realize that a multidimensional array is an array of arrays, then this rule begins to make sense. Since the two-dimensional array parameter

```
const char p[ ][100]
```

is a parameter for an array of arrays, the first dimension is really the index of the array and is treated just like an array index for an ordinary, one-dimensional array. The second dimension is part of the description of the base type, which is an array of characters of size 100.

PROGRAMMING EXAMPLE — Two-Dimensional Grading Program

Display 7.13 contains a program that uses a two-dimensional array, named grade, to store and then display the grade records for a small class. The class has four students and includes three quizzes. Display 7.14 illustrates how the array grade is used to store data. The first array index is used to designate a student, and the second array index is used to designate a quiz. Since the students and quizzes are numbered starting with 1 rather than 0, we must subtract 1 from the student number and subtract 1 from the quiz number to obtain the indexed variable that stores a particular quiz score. For example, the score that student number 4 received on quiz number 1 is recorded in grade[3][0].

Our program also uses two ordinary one-dimensional arrays. The array st_ave will be used to record the average quiz score for each of the students. For example, the program will set st_ave[0] equal to the average of the quiz scores received by student 1, st_ave[1] equal to the average of the quiz scores received by student 2, and so forth. The array quiz_ave will be used to record the average score for each quiz. For example, the program will set quiz_ave[0] equal to the average of all the student scores for quiz 1, quiz_ave[1] will record the average

DISPLAY 7.13 Two-Dimensional Array *(part 1 of 3)*

```
1    //Reads quiz scores for each student into the two-dimensional array grade (but
2    //the input code is not shown in this display). Computes the average score
3    //for each student and the average score for each quiz. Displays the quiz scores
4    //and the averages.
5    #include <iostream>
6    #include <iomanip>
7    const int NUMBER_STUDENTS = 4, NUMBER_QUIZZES = 3;
8
9    void compute_st_ave(const int grade[][NUMBER_QUIZZES], double st_ave[]);
10   //Precondition: Global constants NUMBER_STUDENTS and NUMBER_QUIZZES
11   //are the dimensions of the array grade. Each of the indexed variables
12   //grade[st_num - 1, quiz_num - 1] contains the score for student st_num on quiz
13   //quiz_num.
14   //Postcondition: Each st_ave[st_num - 1] contains the average for student
15   //number stu_num.
16
17   void compute_quiz_ave(const int grade[][NUMBER_QUIZZES], double quiz_ave[]);
18   //Precondition: Global constants NUMBER_STUDENTS and NUMBER_QUIZZES
19   //are the dimensions of the array grade. Each of the indexed variables
20   //grade[st_num - 1, quiz_num - 1] contains the score for student st_num on quiz
21   //quiz_num.
22   //Postcondition: Each quiz_ave[quiz_num - 1] contains the average for quiz number
23   //quiz_num.
24
25   void display(const int grade[][NUMBER_QUIZZES],
26   const double st_ave[], const double quiz_ave[]);
27   //Precondition: Global constants NUMBER_STUDENTS and NUMBER_QUIZZES are the
28   //dimensions of the array grade. Each of the indexed variables grade[st_num - 1,
29   //quiz_num - 1] contains the score for student st_num on quiz quiz_num. Each
30   //st_ave[st_num - 1] contains the average for student stu_num. Each
31   //quiz_ave[quiz_num - 1] contains the average for quiz number quiz_num.
32   //Postcondition: All the data in grade, st_ave, and quiz_ave has been output.
33
34   int main( )
35   {
36       using namespace std;
37       int grade[NUMBER_STUDENTS][NUMBER_QUIZZES];
38       double st_ave[NUMBER_STUDENTS];
39       double quiz_ave[NUMBER_QUIZZES];
40
     <The code for filling the array grade goes here, but is not shown.>
```

(continued)

DISPLAY 7.13 Two-Dimensional Array *(part 2 of 3)*

```
41          compute_st_ave(grade, st_ave);
42          compute_quiz_ave(grade, quiz_ave);
43          display(grade, st_ave, quiz_ave);
44          return 0;
45      }
46      void compute_st_ave(const int grade[][NUMBER_QUIZZES], double st_ave[])
47      {
48          for (int st_num = 1; st_num <= NUMBER_STUDENTS; st_num++)
49          {//Process one st_num:
50              double sum = 0;
51              for (int quiz_num = 1; quiz_num <= NUMBER_QUIZZES; quiz_num++)
52                  sum = sum + grade[st_num - 1][quiz_num - 1];
53              //sum contains the sum of the quiz scores for student number st_num.
54              st_ave[st_num - 1] = sum/NUMBER_QUIZZES;
55              //Average for student st_num is the value of st_ave[st_num-1]
56          }
57      }
58
59
60      void compute_quiz_ave(const int grade[][NUMBER_QUIZZES], double quiz_ave[])
61      {
62          for (int quiz_num = 1; quiz_num <= NUMBER_QUIZZES; quiz_num++)
63          {//Process one quiz (for all students):
64              double sum = 0;
65              for (int st_num = 1; st_num <= NUMBER_STUDENTS; st_num++)
66                  sum = sum + grade[st_num - 1][quiz_num - 1];
67              //sum contains the sum of all student scores on quiz number quiz_num.
68              quiz_ave[quiz_num - 1] = sum/NUMBER_STUDENTS;
69              //Average for quiz quiz_num is the value of quiz_ave[quiz_num - 1]
70          }
71      }
72
73
74      //Uses iostream and iomanip:
75      void display(const int grade[][NUMBER_QUIZZES],
76          const double st_ave[], const double quiz_ave[])
77      {
78          using namespace std;
79          cout.setf(ios::fixed);
80          cout.setf(ios::showpoint);
81          cout.precision(1);
82          cout << setw(10) << "Student"
83              << setw(5) << "Ave"
84              << setw(15) << "Quizzes\n";
85          for (int st_num = 1; st_num <= NUMBER_STUDENTS; st_num++)
86          {//Display for one st_num:
```

(continued)

DISPLAY 7.13 Two-Dimensional Array *(part 3 of 3)*

```
87              cout << setw(10) << st_num
88                   << setw(5) << st_ave[st_num - 1] << " ";
89              for (int quiz_num = 1; quiz_num <= NUMBER_QUIZZES; quiz_num++)
90                   cout << setw(5) << grade[st_num - 1][quiz_num - 1];
91              cout << endl;
92          }
93
94          cout << "Quiz averages = ";
95          for (int quiz_num = 1; quiz_num <= NUMBER_QUIZZES; quiz_num++)
95              cout << setw(5) << quiz_ave[quiz_num - 1];
96          cout << endl;
97      }
```

Sample Dialogue

<The dialogue for filling the array grade is not shown.>

Student	Ave		Quizzes	
1	10.0	10	10	10
2	1.0	2	0	1
3	7.7	8	6	9
4	7.3	8	4	10
Quiz averages =		7.0	5.0	7.5

DISPLAY 7.14 The Two-Dimensional Array grade

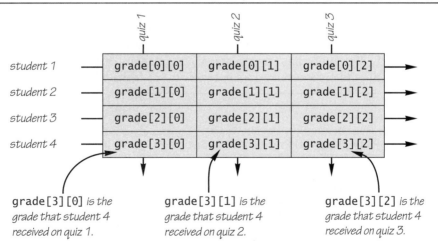

grade[3][0] *is the grade that student 4 received on quiz 1.*   grade[3][1] *is the grade that student 4 received on quiz 2.*   grade[3][2] *is the grade that student 4 received on quiz 3.*

DISPLAY 7.15   The Two-Dimensional Array grade (Another View)

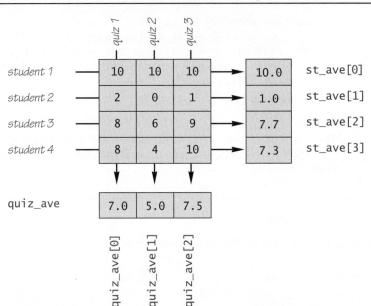

score for quiz 2, and so forth. Display 7.15 illustrates the relationship between the arrays grade, st_ave, and quiz_ave. In that display, we have shown some sample data for the array grade. This data, in turn, determines the values that the program stores in st_ave and in quiz_ave. Display 7.15 also shows these values, which the program computes for st_ave and quiz_ave.

The complete program for filling the array grade and then computing and displaying both the student averages and the quiz averages is shown in Display 7.13. In that program we have declared array dimensions as global named constants. Since the procedures are particular to this program and could not be reused elsewhere, we have used these globally defined constants in the procedure bodies, rather than having parameters for the size of the array dimensions. Since it is routine, the display does not show the code that fills the array.

PITFALL   Using Commas Between Array Indexes

Note that in Display 7.13 we wrote an indexed variable for the two-dimensional array grade as grade[st_num - 1][quiz_num - 1] with two pairs of square brackets. In some other programming languages it would be written with one pair of brackets and commas as follows: grade[st_num - 1, quiz_num - 1]; this is incorrect in C++. If you use grade[st_num - 1, quiz_num - 1] in C++ you are unlikely to get any error message, but it is incorrect usage and will cause your program to misbehave. ∎

SELF-TEST EXERCISES   myprogramminglab

20. What is the output produced by the following code?

```
int my_array[4][4], index1, index2;
for (index1 = 0; index1 < 4; index1++)
    for (index2 = 0; index2 < 4; index2++)
        my_array[index1][index2] = index2;
for (index1 = 0; index1 < 4; index1++)
{
    for (index2 = 0; index2 < 4; index2++)
        cout << my_array[index1][index2] << " ";
    cout << endl;
}
```

21. Write code that will fill the array a (declared below) with numbers typed in at the keyboard. The numbers will be input five per line, on four lines (although your solution need not depend on how the input numbers are divided into lines).

```
int a[4][5];
```

22. Write a function definition for a *void* function called echo such that the following function call will echo the input described in Self-Test Exercise 21 and will echo it in the same format as we specified for the input (that is, four lines of five numbers per line):

```
echo(a, 4);
```

CHAPTER SUMMARY

■ An array can be used to store and manipulate a collection of data that is all of the same type.

■ The indexed variables of an array can be used just like any other variables of the base type of the array.

■ A *for* loop is a good way to step through the elements of an array and perform some program action on each indexed variable.

■ The most common programming error made when using arrays is attempting to access a nonexistent array index. Always check the first and last iterations of a loop that manipulates an array to make sure it does not use an index that is illegally small or illegally large.

■ An array formal parameter is neither a call-by-value parameter nor a call-by-reference parameter, but a new kind of parameter. An array parameter is similar to a call-by-reference parameter in that any change that is made to the formal parameter in the body of the function will be made to the array argument when the function is called.

- The indexed variables for an array are stored next to each other in the computer's memory so that the array occupies a contiguous portion of memory. When the array is passed as an argument to a function, only the address of the first indexed variable (the one numbered 0) is given to the calling function. Therefore, a function with an array parameter usually needs another formal parameter of type *int* to give the size of the array.

- When using a partially filled array, your program needs an additional variable of type *int* to keep track of how much of the array is being used.

- To tell the compiler that an array argument should not be changed by your function, you can insert the modifier *const* before the array parameter for that argument position. An array parameter that is modified with a *const* is called a **constant array parameter.**

- If you need an array with more than one index, you can use a multidimensional array, which is actually an array of arrays.

Answers to Self-Test Exercises

1. The statement *int* a[5]; is a declaration, where 5 is the number of array elements. The expression a[4] is an access into the array defined by the previous statement. The access is to the element having index 4, which is the fifth (and last) array element.

2. a. score

    b. double

    c. 5

    d. 0 through 4

    e. Any of score[0], score[1], score[2], score[3], score[4]

3. a. One too many initializers

    b. Correct. The array size is 4.

    c. Correct. The array size is 4.

4. abc

5. 1.1 2.2 3.3
   1.1 3.3 3.3

   (Remember that the indexes start with 0, not 1.)

6. 2 4 6 8 10 12 14 16 18 0 4 8 12 16

7. The indexed variables of sample_array are sample_array[0] through sample_array[9], but this piece of code tries to fill sample_array[1] through sample_array[10]. The index 10 in sample_array[10] is out of range.

8. There is an index out of range. When index is equal to 9, index + 1 is equal to 10, so a[index + 1], which is the same as a[10], has an illegal index. The loop should stop with one less iteration. To correct the code, change the first line of the *for* loop to

   ```
   for (int index = 0; index < 9; index++)
   ```

9. ```
   int i, a[20];

   cout << "Enter 20 numbers:\n";

   for (i = 0; i < 20; i++)
       cin >> a[i];
   ```

10. The array will consume 14 bytes of memory. The address of the indexed variable your_array[3] is 1006.

11. The following function calls are acceptable:

    ```
    tripler(number);
    tripler(a[2]);
    tripler(a[number]);
    ```

    The following function calls are incorrect:

    ```
    tripler(a[3]);
    tripler(a);
    ```

    The first one has an illegal index. The second has no indexed expression at all. You cannot use an entire array as an argument to tripler, as in the second call. The section "Entire Arrays as Function Arguments" discusses a different situation in which you can use an entire array as an argument.

12. The loop steps through indexed variables b[1] through b[5], but 5 is an illegal index for the array b. The indexes are 0, 1, 2, 3, and 4. The correct version of the code is:

    ```
    int b[5] = {1, 2, 3, 4, 5};
        for (int i = 0; i < 5; i++)
            tripler(b[i]);
    ```

13. ```
    void one_more(int a[ ], int size)
    //Precondition: size is the declared size of the array a.
    //a[0] through a[size - 1] have been given values.
    //Postcondition: a[index] has been increased by 1.
    //for all indexed variables of a.
    {
    ```

```
        for (int index = 0; index < size; index++)
            a[index] = a[index] + 1;
}
```

14. The following function calls are all acceptable:

    ```
    too2(my_array, 29);
    too2(my_array, 10);
    too2(your_array, 100);
    ```

    The call

    ```
    too2(my_array, 10);
    ```

    is legal, but will fill only the first ten indexed variables of my_array. If that is what is desired, the call is acceptable.

    The following function calls are all incorrect:

    ```
    too2(my_array, 55);
    "Hey too2. Please, come over here."
    too2(my_array[3], 29);
    ```

    The first of these is incorrect because the second argument is too large. The second is incorrect because it is missing a final semicolon (and for other reasons). The third one is incorrect because it uses an indexed variable for an argument where it should use the entire array.

15. You can make the array parameter in output a constant parameter, since there is no need to change the values of any indexed variables of the array parameter. You cannot make the parameter in drop_odd a constant parameter because it may have the values of some of its indexed variables changed.

    ```
    void output(const double a[ ], int size);
    //Precondition: a[0] through a[size - 1] have values.
    //Postcondition: a[0] through a[size - 1] have been
    //written out.

    void drop_odd(int a[], int size);
    //Precondition: a[0] through a[size - 1] have values.
    //Postcondition: All odd numbers in a[0] through
    //a[size - 1] have been changed to 0.
    ```

16. ```
    int out_of_order(double array[], int size)
    {
        for (int i = 0; i < size - 1; i++)
            if (array[i] > array[i+1]) //fetch a[i+1] for each i.
            return i+1;
        return -1;
    }
    ```
    ```

17.
```cpp
#include <iostream>
using namespace std;
const int DECLARED_SIZE = 10;

int main( )
{
    cout << "Enter up to ten nonnegative integers.\n"
         << "Place a negative number at the end.\n";
    int number_array[DECLARED_SIZE], next, index = 0;
    cin >> next;
    while ( (next >= 0) && (index < DECLARED_SIZE) )
    {
        number_array[index] = next;
        index++;
        cin >> next;
    }

    int number_used = index;
    cout << "Here they are back at you:";
    for (index = 0; index < number_used; index++)
        cout << number_array[index] << " ";
    cout<< endl;
    return 0;
}
```

18.
```cpp
#include <iostream>
using namespace std;
const int DECLARED_SIZE = 10;

int main()
{
    cout << "Enter up to ten letters"
         << " followed by a period:\n";
    char letter_box[DECLARED_SIZE], next;
    int index = 0;
    cin >> next;
    while ( (next != '.') && (index < DECLARED_SIZE) )
    {
        letter_box[index] = next;
        index++;
        cin >> next;
    }
    int number_used = index;
    cout << "Here they are backwards:\n";
    for(index = number_used - 1; index >= 0; index--)
        cout << letter_box[index];
    cout << endl;
    return 0;
}
```

19. ```
    bool search(const int a[ ], int number_used,
                                 int target, int& where)
    {
        int index = 0;
        bool found = false;
        while ((!found) && (index < number_used))
            if (target == a[index])
                found = true;
            else
                index++;
        //If target was found, then
        //found == true and a[index] == target.
        if (found)
            where = index;
        return found;
    }
    ```

20. ```
    0 1 2 3
    0 1 2 3
    0 1 2 3
    0 1 2 3
    ```

21. ```
    int a[4][5];
    int index1, index2;
    for (index1 = 0; index1 < 4; index1++)
        for (index2 = 0; index2 < 5; index2++)
            cin >> a[index1][index2];
    ```

22. ```
    void echo(const int a[][5], int size_of_a)
    //Outputs the values in the array a on size_of_a lines
    //with 5 numbers per line.
    {
        for (int index1 = 0; index1 < size_of_a; index1++)
        {
            for (int index2 = 0; index2 < 5; index2++)
                cout << a[index1][index2] << " ";
            cout << endl;
        }
    }
    ```

PROGRAMMING PROJECTS

Visit www.myprogramminglab.com to complete many of these Programming Projects online and get instant feedback.

Projects 7 through 11 can be written more elegantly using structures or classes. Projects 12 through 15 are meant to be written using multidimensional arrays and do not require structures or classes. See Chapters 10 and 11 for information on defining classes and structures.

1. There are three versions of this project.

Version 1 (all interactive). Write a program that reads in the average monthly rainfall for a city for each month of the year and then reads in the actual monthly rainfall for each of the previous 12 months. The program then prints out a nicely formatted table showing the rainfall for each of the previous 12 months as well as how much above or below average the rainfall was for each month. The average monthly rainfall is given for the months January, February, and so forth, in order. To obtain the actual rainfall for the previous 12 months, the program first asks what the current month is and then asks for the rainfall figures for the previous 12 months. The output should correctly label the months.

> There are a variety of ways to deal with the month names. One straight-forward method is to code the months as integers and then do a conversion before doing the output. A large *switch* statement is acceptable in an output function. The month input can be handled in any manner you wish, as long as it is relatively easy and pleasant for the user.

After you have completed this program, produce an enhanced version that also outputs a graph showing the average rainfall and the actual rainfall for each of the previous 12 months. The graph should be similar to the one shown in Display 7.8, except that there should be two bar graphs for each month and they should be labeled as the average rainfall and the rainfall for the most recent month. Your program should ask the user whether she or he wants to see the table or the bar graph and then should display whichever format is requested. Include a loop that allows the user to see either format as often as the user wishes until the user requests that the program end.

Version 2 (combines interactive and file output). For a more elaborate version, also allow the user to request that the table and graph be output to a file. The file name is entered by the user. This program does everything that the Version 1 program does but has this added feature. To read a file name, you must use material presented in the optional section of Chapter 5 entitled "File Names as Input."

Version 3 (all I/O with files). This version is like Version 1 except that input is taken from a file and the output is sent to a file. Since there is no user to interact with, there is no loop to allow repeating the display; both the table and the graph are output to the same file. If this is a class assignment, ask your instructor for instructions on what file names to use.

2. Hexadecimal numerals are integers written in base 16. The 16 digits used are '0' through '9' plus 'a' for the "digit 10", 'b' for the "digit 11", 'c' for the "digit 12", 'd' for the "digit 13", 'e' for the "digit 14", and 'f' for the "digit 15". For example, the hexadecimal numeral d is the same as base

10 numeral 13 and the hexadecimal numeral 1d is the same as the base 10 numeral 29. Write a C++ program to perform addition of two hexadecimal numerals each with up to 10 digits. If the result of the addition is more than 10 digits long, then simply give the output message "Addition Overflow" and not the result of the addition. Use arrays to store hexadecimal numerals as arrays of characters. Include a loop to repeat this calculation for new numbers until the user says she or he wants to end the program.

VideoNote
Solution to Programming
Project 7.3

3. Write a function called delete_repeats that has a partially filled array of characters as a formal parameter and that deletes all repeated letters from the array. Since a partially filled array requires two arguments, the function will actually have two formal parameters: an array parameter and a formal parameter of type *int* that gives the number of array positions used. When a letter is deleted, the remaining letters are moved forward to fill in the gap. This will create empty positions at the end of the array so that less of the array is used. Since the formal parameter is a partially filled array, a second formal parameter of type *int* will tell how many array positions are filled. This second formal parameter will be a call-by-reference parameter and will be changed to show how much of the array is used after the repeated letters are deleted.

For example, consider the following code:

```
char a[10];
a[0] = 'a';
a[1] = 'b';
a[2] = 'a';
a[3] = 'c';
int size = 4;
delete_repeats(a, size);
```

After this code is executed, the value of a[0] is 'a', the value of a[1] is 'b', the value of a[2] is 'c', and the value of size is 3. (The value of a[3] is no longer of any concern, since the partially filled array no longer uses this indexed variable.)

You may assume that the partially filled array contains only lowercase letters. Embed your function in a suitable test program.

4. The standard deviation of a list of numbers is a measure of how much the numbers deviate from the average. If the standard deviation is small, the numbers are clustered close to the average. If the standard deviation is large, the numbers are scattered far from the average. The standard deviation, S, of a list of N numbers x is defined as follows:

$$S = \sqrt{\dfrac{\displaystyle\sum_{i=1}^{N} = (x_i - \bar{x})^2}{N}}$$

where x is the average of the N numbers $x1$, $x2$, ... Define a function that takes a partially filled array of numbers as its arguments and returns the standard deviation of the numbers in the partially filled array. Since a partially filled array requires two arguments, the function will actually have two formal parameters: an array parameter and a formal parameter of type *int* that gives the number of array positions used. The numbers in the array will be of type *double*. Embed your function in a suitable test program.

5. Write a program that reads in a list of integers into an array with base type *int*. Provide the facility to either read this array from the keyboard or from a file, at the user's option. If the user chooses file input, the program should request a file name. You may assume that there are fewer than 50 entries in the array. Your program determines how many entries there are. The output is to be a two-column list. The first column is a list of the distinct array elements; the second column is the count of the number of occurrences of each element. The list should be sorted on entries in the first column, largest to smallest.

For example, for the input

-12 3 -12 4 1 1 -12 1 -1 1 2 3 4 2 3 -12

the output should be

```
N    Count
4    2
3    3
2    2
1    4
-1   1
-12  4
```

6. The text discusses the selection sort. We propose a different "sort" routine, the insertion sort. This routine is in a sense the opposite of the selection sort in that it picks up successive elements from the array and *inserts* each of these into the correct position in an already sorted subarray (at one end of the array we are sorting).

The array to be sorted is divided into a sorted subarray and an unexamined subarray. Initially, the sorted subarray is empty. Each element of the unexamined subarray is picked and inserted into its correct position in the sorted subarray.

Write a function and a test program to implement the selection sort. Thoroughly test your program.

> *Example and hints:* The implementation involves an outside loop that selects successive elements in the unsorted subarray and a nested loop that inserts each element in its proper position in the sorted subarray.

Initially, the sorted subarray is empty, and the unsorted subarray is all of the array:

a[0]	a[1]	a[2]	a[3]	a[4]	a[5]	a[6]	a[7]	a[8]	a[9]
8	6	10	2	16	4	18	14	12	10

Pick the first element, a[0] (that is, 8), and place it in the first position. The inside loop has nothing to do in this first case. The array and subarrays look like this:

sorted	unsorted								
a[0]	a[1]	a[2]	a[3]	a[4]	a[5]	a[6]	a[7]	a[8]	a[9]
8	6	10	2	16	4	18	14	12	10

The first element from the unsorted subarray is a[1], which has value 6. Insert this into the sorted subarray in its proper position. These are out of order, so the inside loop must swap values in position 0 and position 1. The result is as follows:

sorted		unsorted							
a[0]	a[1]	a[2]	a[3]	a[4]	a[5]	a[6]	a[7]	a[8]	a[9]
6	8	10	2	16	4	18	14	10	12

Note that the sorted subarray has grown by one entry.

Repeat the process for the first unsorted subarray entry, a[2], finding a place where a[2] can be placed so that the subarray remains sorted. Since a[2] is already in place—that is, it is larger than the largest element in the sorted subarray—the inside loop has nothing to do. The result is as follows:

sorted			unsorted						
a[0]	a[1]	a[2]	a[3]	a[4]	a[5]	a[6]	a[7]	a[8]	a[9]
6	8	10	2	16	4	18	14	10	12

Again, pick the first unsorted array element, a[3]. This time the inside loop has to swap values until the value of a[3] is in its proper position. This involves some swapping:

sorted				unsorted					
a[0]	a[1]	a[2]	a[3]	a[4]	a[5]	a[6]	a[7]	a[8]	a[9]
6	8	10<-->2		16	4	18	14	10	12

sorted				unsorted					
a[0]	a[1]	a[2]	a[3]	a[4]	a[5]	a[6]	a[7]	a[8]	a[9]
6	8<--->2		10	16	4	18	14	10	12

sorted				unsorted					
a[0]	a[1]	a[2]	a[3]	a[4]	a[5]	a[6]	a[7]	a[8]	a[9]
6<--->2		8	10	16	4	18	14	10	12

The result of placing the 2 in the sorted subarray is

sorted				unsorted					
a[0]	a[1]	a[2]	a[3]	a[4]	a[5]	a[6]	a[7]	a[8]	a[9]
2	6	8	10	16	4	18	14	10	12

The algorithm continues in this fashion until the unsorted array is empty and the sorted array has all the original array's elements.

7. An array can be used to store large integers one digit at a time. For example, the integer 1234 could be stored in the array a by setting a[0] to 1, a[1] to 2, a[2] to 3, and a[3] to 4. However, for this exercise you might find it more useful to store the digits backward, that is, place 4 in a[0], 3 in a[1], 2 in a[2], and 1 in a[3].

In this exercise you will write a program that reads in two positive integers that are 20 or fewer digits in length and then outputs the sum of the two numbers. Your program will read the digits as values of type *char* so that the number 1234 is read as the four characters '1', '2', '3', and '4'. After they are read into the program, the characters are changed to values of type *int*. The digits will be read into a partially filled array, and you might find it useful to reverse the order of the elements in the array after the array is filled with data from the keyboard. (Whether or not you reverse the order of the elements in the array is up to you. It can be done either way, and each way has its advantages and disadvantages.)

Your program will perform the addition by implementing the usual paper-and-pencil addition algorithm. The result of the addition is stored in an array of size 20, and the result is then written to the screen. If the result of the addition is an integer with more than the maximum number of digits (that is, more than 20 digits), then your program should issue a message saying that it has encountered "integer overflow." You should be able to change the maximum length of the integers by changing only one globally defined constant. Include a loop that allows the user to continue to do more additions until the user says the program should end.

8. Write a program that will read a line of text and output a list of all the letters that occur in the text together with the number of times each letter occurs in the line. End the line with a period that serves as a sentinel value. The letters should be listed in the following order: the most frequently oc-curring letter, the next most frequently occurring letter, and so forth. Use two arrays, one to hold integers and one to hold letters. You may assume that the input uses all lowercase letters. For example, the input

do be do bo.

should produce output similar to the following:

Letter	Number of Occurrences
o	3
d	2
b	2
e	1

Your program will need to sort the arrays according to the values in the integer array. This will require that you modify the function sort given in Display 7.12. You cannot use sort to solve this problem without changing the function. If this is a class assignment, ask your instructor if input/output should be done with the keyboard and screen or if it should be done with files. If it is to be done with files, ask your instructor for instructions on file names.

9. Write a program to score five-card poker hands into one of the following categories: nothing, one pair, two pairs, three of a kind, straight (in order, with no gaps), flush (all the same suit, for example, all spades), full house (one pair and three of a kind), four of a kind, straight flush (both a straight and a flush). Use two arrays, one to hold the value of the card and one to hold the suit. Include a loop that allows the user to continue to score more hands until the user says the program should end.

10. Write a program that will allow two users to play tic-tac-toe. The program should ask for moves alternately from player X and player O. The program displays the game positions as follows:

```
1 2 3
4 5 6
7 8 9
```

The players enter their moves by entering the position number they wish to mark. After each move, the program displays the changed board. A sample board configuration is as follows:

```
X X 0
4 5 6
0 8 9
```

11. Write a program to assign passengers seats in an airplane. Assume a small airplane with seat numbering as follows:

```
1 A B C D
2 A B C D
3 A B C D
4 A B C D
5 A B C D
6 A B C D
7 A B C D
```

The program should display the seat pattern, with an X marking the seats already assigned. For example, after seats 1A, 2B, and 4C are taken, the display should look like this:

```
1 X B C D
2 A X C D
3 A B C D
4 A B X D
5 A B C D
6 A B C D
7 A B C D
```

After displaying the seats available, the program prompts for the seat desired, the user types in a seat, and then the display of available seats is updated. This continues until all seats are filled or until the user signals that the program should end. If the user types in a seat that is already assigned, the program should say that that seat is occupied and ask for another choice.

12. Matrix multiplication is an important function that is required to execute in different software systems. Write a program that accepts input data for two 3 X 3 (3 rows and 3 columns), 2D matrices and finds the multiplication of the two matrices. Your program must have well- formatted input and output sections.

13. The mathematician John Horton Conway invented the "Game of Life." Though not a "game" in any traditional sense, it provides interesting behavior that is specified with only a few rules. This project asks you to write a program that allows you to specify an initial configuration. The program follows the rules of LIFE to show the continuing behavior of the configuration.

    LIFE is an organism that lives in a discrete, two-dimensional world. While this world is actually unlimited, we don't have that luxury, so we restrict the array to 80 characters wide by 22 character positions high. If you have access to a larger screen, by all means use it.

    This world is an array with each cell capable of holding one LIFE cell. Generations mark the passing of time. Each generation brings births and deaths to the LIFE community. The births and deaths follow the following set of rules.

    ■ We define each cell to have eight *neighbor* cells. The neighbors of a cell are the cells directly above, below, to the right, to the left, diagonally above to the right and left, and diagonally below to the right and left.

    ■ If an occupied cell has zero or one neighbors, it dies of *loneliness*. If an occupied cell has more than three neighbors, it dies of *overcrowding*.

    ■ If an empty cell has exactly three occupied neighbor cells, there is a *birth* of a new cell to replace the empty cell.

    ■ Births and deaths are instantaneous and occur at the changes of generation. A cell dying for whatever reason may help cause birth, but a newborn cell cannot resurrect a cell that is dying, nor will a cell's death prevent the death of another, say, by reducing the local population.

      Notes: Some configurations grow from relatively small starting configurations. Others move across the region. It is recommended that for text output you use a rectangular array of *char* with 80 columns and 22 rows to store the LIFE world's successive generations. Use an asterisk * to indicate a living cell, and use a blank to indicate an empty (or dead) cell. If you have a screen with more rows than that, by all means make use of the whole screen.

    Examples:

    ***

    becomes

    *

    *

    *

    then becomes

    ***

    again, and so on.

Suggestions: Look for stable configurations. That is, look for communities that repeat patterns continually. The number of configurations in the repetition is called the *period*. There are configurations that are fixed, which continue without change. A possible project is to find such configurations.

Hints: Define a *void* function named *generation* that takes the array we call *world*, an 80-column by 22-row array of *char*, which contains the initial configuration. The function scans the array and modifies the cells, marking the cells with births and deaths in accord with the rules listed earlier. This involves examining each cell in turn, either killing the cell, letting it live, or, if the cell is empty, deciding whether a cell should be born. There should be a function *display* that accepts the array *world* and displays the array on the screen. Some sort of time delay is appropriate between calls to *generation* and *display*. To do this, your program should generate and display the next generation when you press Return. You are at liberty to automate this, but automation is not necessary for the program.

14. Redo (or do for the first time) Programming Project 17 from Chapter 6. Your program should first load all boy names and girl names from the file into separate arrays. Search for the target name from the arrays, not directly from the file.

15. Redo (or do for the first time) Programming Project 18 from Chapter 6. Your program should not be hard-coded to create a bar chart of exactly four integers, but should be able to graph an array of up to 100 integers. Scale the graph appropriately in the horizontal and vertical dimensions so the bar chart fits within a 400 by 400 pixel area. You can impose the constraint that all integers in the array are nonnegative. Use the sentinel value of −1 to indicate the end of the values to draw in the bar chart. For example, to create the bar chart with values 20, 40, 60, and 120, your program would operate on the array:

```
a[0]  =  20
a[1]  =  40
a[2]  =  60
a[3]  =  120
a[4]  =  -1
```

Test your program by creating several bar charts with different values and up to 100 entries and view the resulting SVG files to ensure that they are drawn correctly.

16. A common memory matching game played by young children is to start with a deck of cards that contains identical pairs. For example, given six cards in the deck, two might be labeled "1," two might be labeled "2," and two might be labeled "3." The cards are shuffled and placed face down on the table. The player then selects two cards that are face down, turns them face up, and if they match they are left face up. If the two cards do not match, they are returned to their original position face down. The game continues in this fashion until all cards are face up.

Write a program that plays the memory matching game. Use 16 cards that are laid out in a 4 X 4 square and are labeled with pairs of numbers from 1 to 8. Your program should allow the player to specify the cards that she would like to select through a coordinate system.

For example, suppose the cards are in the following layout:

```
        1   2   3   4
      ----------------------------
   1 | 8   *   *   *
   2 | *   *   *   *
   3 | *   8   *   *
   4 | *   *   *   *
```

All of the cards are face down except for the pair 8, which has been located at coordinates (1, 1) and (2, 3). To hide the cards that have been temporarily placed face up, output a large number of newlines to force the old board off the screen.

(*Hint:* Use a two-dimensional array for the arrangement of cards and another two-dimensional array that indicates if a card is face up or face down. Write a function that "shuffles" the cards in the array by repeatedly selecting two cards at random and swapping them. Random number generation is described in Chapter 4.)

17. Your swim school has two swimming instructors, Jeff and Anna. Their current schedules are shown below. An "X" denotes a 1-hour time slot that is occupied with a lesson.

Jeff	Monday	Tuesday	Wednesday	Thursday
11–12	X	X		
12–1		X	X	X
1–2		X	X	
2–3	X	X	X	

Anna	Monday	Tuesday	Wednesday	Thursday
11–12	X	X		X
12–1		X		X
1–2	X	X		
2–3	X		X	X

Write a program with array(s) capable of storing the schedules. Create a main menu that allows the user to mark a time slot as busy or free for either instructor. Also, add an option to output the schedules to the screen. Next, add an option to output all time slots available for individual lessons (slots when at least one instructor is free). Finally, add an option to output all time slots available for group lessons (when both instructors are free).

18. Modify Programming Project 17 by adding menu options to load and save the schedules from a file.

19. Traditional password entry schemes are susceptible to "shoulder surfing" in which an attacker watches an unsuspecting user enter their password or PIN number and uses it later to gain access to the account. One way to combat this problem is with a randomized challenge-response system. In these systems, the user enters different information every time based on a secret in response to a randomly generated challenge. Consider the following scheme in which the password consists of a five-digit PIN number (00000 to 99999). Each digit is assigned a random number that is 1, 2, or 3. The user enters the random numbers that correspond to their PIN instead of their actual PIN numbers.

For example, consider an actual PIN number of 12345. To authenticate the user would be presented with a screen such as:

```
PIN:    0 1 2 3 4 5 6 7 8 9
NUM:    3 2 3 1 1 3 2 2 1 3
```

The user would enter 23113 instead of 12345. This doesn't divulge the password even if an attacker intercepts the entry because 23113 could correspond to other PIN numbers, such as 69440 or 70439. The next time the user logs in, a different sequence of random numbers would be generated, such as:

```
PIN:    0 1 2 3 4 5 6 7 8 9
NUM:    1 1 2 3 1 2 2 3 3 3
```

Your program should simulate the authentication process. Store an actual PIN number in your program. The program should use an array to assign random numbers to the digits from 0 to 9. Output the random digits to the screen, input the response from the user, and output whether or not the user's response correctly matches the PIN number.

Strings and Vectors 8

Polonius: What do you read my lord?

Hamlet: Words, words, words.

WILLIAM SHAKESPEARE, *Hamlet*

INTRODUCTION

This chapter discusses two topics that use arrays or are related to arrays: strings and vectors. Although strings and vectors are very closely related, this relationship is not always obvious, and no one of these topics depends on the other. The topics of strings and vectors can be covered in either order.

Sections 8.1 and 8.2 present two types whose values represent strings of characters, such as "Hello". One type, discussed in Section 8.1, is just an array with base type *char* that stores strings of characters in the array and marks the end of the string with the null character '\0'. This is the older way of representing strings, which C++ inherited from the C programming language. These sorts of strings are called C strings. Although C strings are an older way of representing strings, it is difficult to do any sort of string processing in C++ without at least passing contact with C strings. For example, quoted strings, such as "Hello", are implemented as C strings in C++.

The ANSI/ISO C++ standard includes a more modern string-handling facility in the form of the class string. The class string is the second string type that we will discuss in this chapter and is covered in Section 8.2.

Vectors can be thought of as arrays that can grow (and shrink) in length while your program is running. In C++, once your program creates an array, it cannot change the length of the array. Vectors serve the same purpose as arrays except that they can change length while the program is running.

PREREQUISITES

Sections 8.1 and 8.2, which cover strings, and Section 8.3 which covers vectors, are independent of each other. If you wish to cover vectors before strings, that is fine.

Section 8.1 on C strings uses material from Chapters 2 through 6, and Sections 7.1, 7.2, and 7.3 of Chapter 7. Section 8.2 on the string class uses Section 8.1 and material from Chapters 2 through 6 and Sections 7.1, 7.2, and 7.3 of Chapter 7. Section 8.3 on vectors uses material from Chapters 2 through 6 and Sections 7.1, 7.2, and 7.3 of Chapter 7.

8.1 AN ARRAY TYPE FOR STRINGS

In everything one must consider the end.

JEAN DE LA FONTAINE, FABLES, BOOK III (1668)

In this section we describe one way to represent strings of characters, which C++ has inherited from the C language. In Section 8.2 we describe a string class that is a more modern way to represent strings. Although the string type described here may be a bit "old-fashioned," it is still widely used and is an integral part of the C++ language.

C-String Values and C-String Variables

One way to represent a string is as an array with base type *char*. If the string is "Hello", it is handy to represent it as an array of characters with six indexed variables: five for the five letters in "Hello" plus one for the character '\0', which serves as an end marker. The character '\0' is called the **null character** and is used as an end marker because it is distinct from all the "real" characters. The end marker allows your program to read the array one character at a time and know that it should stop reading when it reads the end marker '\0'. A string stored in this way (as an array of characters terminated with '\0') is called a **C string.**

We write '\0' with two symbols when we write it in a program, but just like the new-line character '\n', the character '\0' is really only a single character value. Like any other character value, '\0' can be stored in one variable of type *char* or one indexed variable of an array of characters.

The Null Character, '\0'

The null character, '\0', is used to mark the end of a C string that is stored in an array of characters. When an array of characters is used in this way, the array is often called a C-string variable. Although the null character '\0' is written using two symbols, it is a single character that fits in one variable of type *char* or one indexed variable of an array of characters.

You have already been using C strings. In C++, a literal string, such as "Hello", is stored as a C string, although you seldom need to be aware of this detail.

A **C-string variable** is just an array of characters. Thus, the following array declaration provides us with a C-string variable capable of storing a C-string value with nine or fewer characters:

```
char s[10];
```

The 10 is for the nine letters in the string plus the null character '\0' to mark the end of the string.

A C-string variable is a partially filled array of characters. Like any other partially filled array, a C-string variable uses positions starting at indexed variable 0 through as many as are needed. However, a C-string variable does not use an *int* variable to keep track of how much of the array is currently being used. *Instead, a string variable places the special symbol* '\0' *in the array immediately after the last character of the C string.* Thus, if s contains the string "Hi Mom"!, then the array elements are filled as shown here:

s[0]	s[1]	s[2]	s[3]	s[4]	s[5]	s[6]	s[7]	s[8]	s[9]
H	I		M	o	m	!	\0	?	?

The character '\0' is used as a sentinel value to mark the end of the C string. If you read the characters in the C string starting at indexed variable s[0], proceed to s[1], and then to s[2], and so forth, you know that when you encounter the symbol '\0', you have reached the end of the C string. Since the symbol '\0' always occupies one element of the array, the length of the longest string that the array can hold is 1 less than the size of the array.

C-string variables vs. arrays of characters

The thing that distinguishes a C-string variable from an ordinary array of characters is that a C-string variable must contain the null character '\0' at the end of the C-string value. This is a distinction in how the array is used rather than a distinction about what the array is. *A C-string variable is an array of characters, but it is used in a different way.*

C-String Variable Declaration

A **C-string variable** is the same thing as an array of characters, but it is used differently. A C-string variable is declared to be an array of characters in the usual way.

SYNTAX

```
char Array_Name[Maximum_C_string_Size + 1];
```

EXAMPLE

```
char my_c_string[11];
```

The + 1 allows for the null character '\0', which terminates any C string stored in the array. For example, the C-string variable my_c_string in the example can hold a C string that is ten or fewer characters long.

Initializing C-string variables

You can initialize a C-string variable when you declare it, as illustrated by the following example:

```
char my_message[20] = "Hi there.";
```

Notice that the C string assigned to the C-string variable need not fill the entire array.

When you initialize a C-string variable, you can omit the array size. C++ will automatically make the size of the C-string variable 1 more than the length of the quoted string. (The one extra indexed variable is for '\0'.) For example,

```
char short_string[] = "abc";
```

is equivalent to

```
char short_string[4] = "abc";
```

Be sure you do not confuse the following initializations:

```
char short_string[] = "abc";
```

and

```
char short_string[] = {'a', 'b', 'c'};
```

They are *not equivalent*. The first of these two possible initializations places the null character '\0' in the array after the characters 'a', 'b', and 'c'. The second one does not put a '\0' anywhere in the array.

Initializing a C-String Variable

A C-string variable can be initialized when it is declared, as illustrated by the following example:

```
char your_string[11] = "Do Be Do";
```

Initializing in this way automatically places the null character, '\0', in the array at the end of the C string specified.

If you omit the number inside the square brackets, [], then the C-string variable will be given a size one character longer than the length of the C string. For example, the following declares my_string to have nine indexed variables (eight for the characters of the C string "Do Be Do" and one for the null character '\0'):

```
char my_string[] = "Do Be Do";
```

A C-string variable is an array, so it has **indexed variables** that can be used just like those of any other array. For example, suppose your program contains the following C-string variable declaration:

```
char our_string[5] = "Hi";
```

With our_string declared as shown previously, your program has the following indexed variables: our_string[0], our_string[1], our_string[2], our_string[3], and our_string[4]. For example, the following will change the C-string value in `our_string` to a C string of the same length consisting of all `'X'` characters:

```
int index = 0;
while (our_string[index] != '\0')
{
    our_string[index] = 'X';
    index++;
}
```

Do not destroy the '\0'

When manipulating these indexed variables, you should be very careful not to replace the null character `'\0'` with some other value. If the array loses the value `'\0'`, it will no longer behave like a C-string variable. For example, the following will change the array `happy_string` so that it no longer contains a C string:

```
char happy_string[7] = "DoBeDo";
happy_string[6] = 'Z';
```

After this code is executed, the array `happy_string` will still contain the six letters in the C-string "DoBeDo", but `happy_string` will no longer contain the null character `'\0'` to mark the end of the C string. Many string-manipulating functions depend critically on the presence of `'\0'` to mark the end of the C-string value.

As another example, consider the previous *while* loop that changed characters in the C-string variable `our_string`. That *while* loop changes characters until it encounters a `'\0'`. If the loop never encounters a `'\0'`, then it could change a large chunk of memory to some unwanted values, which could make your program do strange things. As a safety feature, it would be wise to rewrite that *while* loop as follows, so that if the null character `'\0'` is lost, the loop will not inadvertently change memory locations beyond the end of the array:

```
int index = 0;
while ( (our_string[index] != '\0') && (index < SIZE) )
{
    our_string[index] = 'X';
    index++;
}
```

SIZE is a defined constant equal to the declared size of the array `our_string`.

PITFALL   Using = and == with C Strings

C-string values and C-string variables are not like values and variables of other data types, and many of the usual operations do not work for C strings. You cannot use a C-string variable in an assignment statement using =. If you use == to test C strings for equality, you will not get the result you expect. The reason for these problems is that C strings and C-string variables are arrays.

Assigning a value to a C-string variable is not as simple as it is for other kinds of variables. The following is illegal:

```
char a_string[10];                        Illegal!
a_string = "Hello";
```

Although you can use the equal sign to assign a value to a C-string variable when the variable is declared, you cannot do it anywhere else in your program. Technically, a use of the equal sign in a declaration, as in

```
char happy_string[7] = "DoBeDo";
```

is an initialization, not an assignment. If you want to assign a value to a C-string variable, you must do something else.

There are a number of different ways to assign a value to a C-string variable. The easiest way is to use the predefined function strcpy as shown:

```
strcpy(a_string, "Hello");
```

This will set the value of a_string equal to "Hello". Unfortunately, this version of the function strcpy does not check to make sure the copying does not exceed the size of the string variable that is the first argument.

Many, but not all, versions of C++ also have a safer version of strcpy. This safer version is spelled strncpy (with an n). The function strncpy takes a third argument that gives the maximum number of characters to copy. For example:

```
char another_string[10];
strncpy(another_string, a_string_variable, 9);
```

With this strncpy function, at most nine characters (leaving room for '\0') will be copied from the C-string variable a_string_variable, no matter how long the string in a_string_variable may be.

You also cannot use the operator == in an expression to test whether two C strings are the same. (Things are actually much worse than that. You can use == with C strings, but it does not test for the C strings being equal. So if you use == to test two C strings for equality, you are likely to get incorrect results, but no error message!) To test whether two C strings are the same, you can use the predefined function strcmp. For example:

```
if (strcmp(c_string1, c_string2))
    cout << "The strings are NOT the same.";
else
    cout << "The strings are the same.";
```

Note that the function strcmp works differently than you might guess. The comparison is true if the strings do not match. The function strcmp compares the characters in the C-string arguments a character at a time. If at any point the numeric encoding of the character from c_string1 is less than the numeric encoding of the corresponding character from c_string2, the testing stops, and a negative number is returned. If the character from c_string1 is greater than the character from c_string2, then a positive number is returned. (Some implementations of strcmp return the difference of the character encodings, but you should not depend on that.) If the C strings are the same, a 0 is returned. The ordering relationship used for comparing characters is called **lexicographic order.** The important point to note is that if both strings are all in uppercase or all in lowercase, then lexicographic order is just alphabetic order.

We see that strcmp returns a negative value, a positive value, or zero, depending on whether the C strings compare lexicographically as less, greater, or equal. If you use strcmp as a Boolean expression in an *if* or a looping statement to test C strings for equality, then the nonzero value will be converted to *true* if the strings are different, and the zero will be converted to *false.* Be sure that you remember this inverted logic in your testing for C-string equality. C++ compilers that are compliant with the standard have a safer version of strcmp that has a third argument that gives the maximum number of characters to compare.

The functions strcpy and strcmp are in the library with the header file <cstring>, so to use them you would insert the following near the top of the file:

```
#include <cstring>
```

The functions strcpy and strcmp do not require the following or anything similar (although other parts of your program are likely to require it):[1]

```
using namespace std;
```
■

The <cstring> Library

You do not need any include directive or *using* directive in order to declare and initialize C strings. However, when processing C strings, you inevitably will use some of the predefined string functions in the library <cstring>. So, when using C strings, you will normally give the following include directive near the beginning of the file with your code:

```
#include <cstring>
```

Other Functions in <cstring>

Display 8.1 contains a few of the most commonly used functions from the library with the header file <cstring>. To use them, you insert the following near the top of the file:

```
#include <cstring>
```

---

[1] As you will see in Chapter 12, the definitions of strcpy and strcmp, and all other string functions in <cstring>, are placed in the global namespace, not in the std namespace, and so no *using* directive is required.

DISPLAY 8.1   Some Predefined C-String Functions in `<cstring>`

Function	Description	Cautions
strcpy(*Target_String_Var*, *Src_String*)	Copies the C-string value *Src_String* into the C-string variable *Target_String_Var*.	Does not check to make sure *Target_String_Var* is large enough to hold the value *Src_String*.
strncpy(*Target_String_Var*, *Src_String*, *Limit*)	The same as the two-argument strcpy except that at most *Limit* characters are copied.	If *Limit* is chosen carefully, this is safer than the two-argument version of strcpy. Not implemented in all versions of C++.
strcat(*Target_String_Var*, *Src_String*)	Concatenates the C-string value *Src_String* onto the end of the C string in the C-string variable *Target_String_Var*.	Does not check to see that *Target_String_Var* is large enough to hold the result of the concatenation.
strncat(*Target_String_Var*, *Src_String*, *Limit*)	The same as the two-argument strcat except that at most *Limit* characters are appended.	If *Limit* is chosen carefully, this is safer than the two-argument version of strcat. Not implemented in all versions of C++.
strlen(*Src_String*)	Returns an integer equal to the length of *Src_String*. (The null character, '\0', is not counted in the length.)	
strcmp(*String_1*, *String_2*)	Returns 0 if *String_1* and *String_2* are the same. Returns a value < 0 if *String_1* is less than *String_2*. Returns a value > 0 if *String_1* is greater than *String_2* (that is, returns a nonzero value if *String_1* and *String_2* are different). The order is lexicographic.	If *String_1* equals *String_2*, this function returns 0, which converts to *false*. Note that this is the reverse of what you might expect it to return when the strings are equal.
strncmp(*String_1*, *String_2*, *Limit*)	The same as the two-argument strcat except that at most *Limit* characters are compared.	If *Limit* is chosen carefully, this is safer than the two-argument version of strcmp. Not implemented in all versions of C++.

Like the functions `strcpy` and `strcmp`, all the other functions in `<cstring>` also do not require the following or anything similar (although other parts of your program are likely to require it):[1]

```
using namespace std;
```

We have already discussed `strcpy` and `strcmp`. The function `strlen` is easy to understand and use. For example, `strlen("dobedo")` returns 6 because there are six characters in `"dobedo"`.

The function `strcat` is used to concatenate two C strings, that is, to form a longer string by placing the two shorter C strings end-to-end. The first argument must be a C-string variable. The second argument can be anything that evaluates to a C-string value, such as a quoted string. The result is placed in the C-string variable that is the first argument. For example, consider the following:

```
char string_var[20] = "The rain";
strcat(string_var, "in Spain");
```

This code will change the value of `string_var` to `"The rainin Spain"`. As this example illustrates, you need to be careful to account for blanks when concatenating C strings.

If you look at the table in Display 8.1, you will see that safer, three-argument versions of the functions `strcpy`, `strcat`, and `strcmp` are available in many, but not all, versions of C++. Also, note that these three-argument versions are spelled with an added letter n: `strncpy`, `strncat`, and `strncmp`.

C-String Arguments and Parameters

A C-string variable is an array, so a C-string parameter to a function is simply an array parameter.

As with any array parameter, whenever a function changes the value of a C-string parameter, it is safest to include an additional *int* parameter giving the declared size of the C-string variable.

On the other hand, if a function only uses the value in a C-string argument but does not change that value, then there is no need to include another parameter to give either the declared size of the C-string variable or the amount of the C-string variable array that is filled. The null character `'\0'` can be used to detect the end of the C-string value that is stored in the C-string variable.

$$S = \sqrt{\frac{\sum_{i=1}^{N} = (x_i - \bar{x})^2}{N}}$$

SELF-TEST EXERCISES

1. Which of the following declarations are equivalent?

   ```
   char string_var[10] = "Hello";
   char string_var[10] = {'H', 'e', 'l', 'l', 'o', '\0'};
   char string_var[10] = {'H', 'e', 'l', 'l', 'o'};
   char string_var[6] = "Hello";
   char string_var[] = "Hello";
   ```

2. What C string will be stored in `singing_string` after the following code is run?

   ```
   char singing_string[20] = "DoBeDo";
   strcat(singing_string, " to you");
   ```

   Assume that the code is embedded in a complete and correct program and that an `include` directive for `<cstring>` is in the program file.

3. What (if anything) is wrong with the following code?

   ```
   char string_var[] = "Hello";
   strcat(string_var, " and Good-bye.");
   cout << string_var;
   ```

   Assume that the code is embedded in a complete program and that an `include` directive for `<cstring>` is in the program file.

4. Suppose the function `strlen` (which returns the length of its string argument) was not already defined for you. Give a function definition for `strlen`. Note that `strlen` has only one argument, which is a C string. Do not add additional arguments; they are not needed.

5. What is the maximum length of a string that can be placed in the string variable declared by the following declaration? Explain.

   ```
   char s[6];
   ```

6. How many characters are in each of the following character and string constants?

   a.   `'\n'`
   b.   `'n'`
   c.   `"Mary"`
   d.   `"M"`
   e.   `"Mary\n"`

7. Since character strings are just arrays of *char*, why does the text caution you not to confuse the following declaration and initialization?

```
char short_string[] = "abc";
char short_string[] = {'a', 'b', 'c'};
```

8. Given the following declaration and initialization of the string variable, write a loop to assign 'X' to all positions of this string variable, keeping the length the same.

```
char our_string[15] = "Hi there!";
```

9. Given the declaration of a C-string variable, where SIZE is a defined constant:

```
char our_string[SIZE];
```

The C-string variable our_string has been assigned in code not shown here. For correct C-string variables, the following loop reassigns all positions of our_string the value 'X', leaving the length the same as before. Assume this code fragment is embedded in an otherwise complete and correct program. Answer the questions following this code fragment:

```
int index = 0;
while (our_string[index] != '\0')
{
    our_string[index] = 'X';
    index++;
}
```

  a. Explain how this code can destroy the contents of memory beyond the end of the array.
  b. Modify this loop to protect against inadvertently changing memory beyond the end of the array.

10. Write code using a library function to copy the string constant "Hello" into the string variable declared below. Be sure to include the necessary header file to get the declaration of the function you use.

```
char a_string[10];
```

11. What string will be output when this code is run? (Assume, as always, that this code is embedded in a complete, correct program.)

```
char song[10] = "I did it ";
char franks_song[20];
strcpy( franks_song, song );
strcat( franks_song, "my way!");
cout << franks_song << endl;
```

12. What is the problem (if any) with this code?

```
char a_string[20] = "How are you? ";
strcat(a_string, "Good, I hope.");
```

C-String Input and Output

C strings can be output using the insertion operator <<. In fact, we have already been doing so with quoted strings. You can use a C-string variable in the same way; for example,

```
cout << news << "Wow.\n";
```

where news is a C-string variable.

It is possible to fill a C-string variable using the input operator >>, but there is one thing to keep in mind. As for all other types of data, all whitespace (blanks, tabs, and line breaks) are skipped when C strings are read this way. Moreover, each reading of input stops at the next space or line break. For example, consider the following code:

```
char a[80], b[80];
cout << "Enter some input:\n";
cin >> a >> b;
cout << a << b << "END OF OUTPUT\n";
```

When embedded in a complete program, this code produces a dialogue like the following:

```
Enter some input:
Do bedo to you!
Dobe END OF OUTPUT
```

The C-string variables a and b each receive only one word of the input: a receives the C-string value "Do" because the input character following Do is a blank; b receives "be" because the input character following be is a blank.

If you want your program to read an entire line of input, you can use the extraction operator >> to read the line one word at a time. This can be tedious and it still will not read the blanks in the line. There is an easy way to read an entire line of input and place the resulting C string into a C-string variable: Just use the predefined member function getline, which is a member function of every input stream (such as cin or a file input stream). The function getline has two arguments. The first argument is a C-string variable to receive the input and the second is an integer that typically is the declared size of the C-string variable. The second argument tells the maximum number of array elements in the C-string variable that getline will be allowed to fill with characters. For example, consider the following code:

```
char a[80];
cout << "Enter some input:\n";
cin.getline(a, 80);
cout << a << "END OF OUTPUT\n";
```

When embedded in a complete program, this code produces a dialogue like the following:

```
Enter some input:
Do bedo to you!
Do be do to you!END OF OUTPUT
```

With the function `cin.getline`, the entire line is read. The reading ends when the line ends, even though the resulting C string may be shorter than the maximum number of characters specified by the second argument.

When `getline` is executed, the reading stops after the number of characters given by the second argument have been filled in the C-string array, even if the end of the line has not been reached. For example, consider the following code:

```
char short_string[5];
cout << "Enter some input:\n";
cin.getline(short_string, 5);
cout << short_string << "END OF OUTPUT\n";
```

When embedded in a complete program, this code produces a dialogue like the following:

```
Enter some input:
dobedowap
dobeEND OF OUTPUT
```

Notice that four, not five, characters are read into the C-string variable short_ string, even though the second argument is 5. This is because the null character '\0' fills one array position. Every C string is terminated with the null character when it is stored in a C-string variable, and this always consumes one array position.

The C-string input and output techniques we illustrated for cout and cin work the same way for input and output with files. The input stream cin can be replaced by an input stream that is connected to a file. The output stream cout can be replaced by an output stream that is connected to a file. (File I/O is discussed in Chapter 6.)

---

getline

The member function getline can be used to read a line of input and place the C string of characters on that line into a C-string variable.

SYNTAX

```
cin.getline(String_Var, Max_Characters + 1);
```

One line of input is read from the stream *Input_Stream*, and the resulting C string is placed in *String_Var*. If the line is more than *Max_Characters* long, then only the first *Max_Characters* on the line

(continued)

are read. (The +1 is needed because every C string has the null character '\0' added to the end of the C string and so the string stored in *String_Var* is 1 longer than the number of characters read in.)

EXAMPLE

```
char one_line[80];
cin.getline(one_line, 80);
```

(You can use an input stream connected to a text file in place of cin.)

SELF-TEST EXERCISES

13. Consider the following code (and assume it is embedded in a complete and correct program and then run):

```
char a[80], b[80];
cout << "Enter some input:\n";
cin >> a >> b;
cout << a << '-' << b << "END OF OUTPUT\n";
```

If the dialogue begins as follows, what will be the next line of output?

```
Enter some input:

The
    time is now.
```

14. Consider the following code (and assume it is embedded in a complete and correct program and then run):

```
char my_string[80];
cout << "Enter a line of input:\n";
cin.getline(my_string, 6);
cout << my_string << "<END OF OUTPUT";
```

If the dialogue begins as follows, what will be the next line of output?

```
Enter a line of input:
May the hair on your toes grow long and curly.
```

C-String-to-Number Conversions and Robust Input

The C string "1234" and the number 1234 are not the same things. The first is a sequence of characters; the second is a number. In everyday life, we write them the same way and blur this distinction, but in a C++ program this distinction cannot be ignored. If you want to do arithmetic, you need 1234, not "1234". If you want to add a comma to the numeral for one thousand two hundred thirty four, then you want to change the C string "1234" to the C string "1,234". When designing numeric input, it is often useful to read the input as a string of characters, edit the string, and then convert the string to a number. For example, if you want your program to read an amount of money, the input may or may not begin with a dollar sign. If your program is reading percentages, the input may or may not have a percent sign at the end. If your program reads the input as a string of characters, it can store the string in a C-string variable and remove any unwanted characters, leaving only a C string of digits. Your program then needs to convert this C string of digits to a number, which can easily be done with the predefined function atoi.

The function atoi takes one argument that is a C string and returns the *int* value that corresponds to that C string. For example, atoi ("1234") returns the integer 1234. If the argument does not correspond to an *int* value, then atoi returns 0. For example, atoi("#37") returns 0, because the character '#' is not a digit. You pronounce atoi as "A to I," which is an

---

C-String-to-Number Functions

The functions atoi, atol, and atof can be used to convert a C string of digits to the corresponding numeric value. The functions atoi and atoll convert C strings to integers. The only difference between atoi and atol is that atoi returns a value of type *int* whereas atol returns a value of type *long*. The function atof converts a C string to a value of type *double*. If the C-string argument (to either function) is such that the conversion cannot be made, then the function returns zero. For example

```
int x = atoi("657");
```

sets the value of x to 657, and

```
double y = atof("12.37");
```

sets the value of y to 12.37.

Any program that uses atoi or atof must contain the following directive:

```
#include <cstdlib>
```

abbreviation of "alphabetic to integer." The function `atoi` is in the library with header file `cstdlib`, so any program that uses it must contain the following directive:

```
#include <cstdlib>
```

If your numbers are too large to be values of type *int*, you can convert them from C strings to values of type *long*. The function `atol` performs the same conversion as the function `atoi` except that `atol` returns values of type *long* and thus can accommodate larger integer values (on systems where this is a concern).

Display 8.2 contains the definition of a function called `read_and_clean` that reads a line of input and discards all characters other than the digits `'0'` through `'9'`. The function then uses the function `atoi` to convert the "cleaned-up" C string of digits to an integer value. As the demonstration program indicates, you can use this function to read money amounts and it will not matter whether the user included a dollar sign or not. Similarly, you can read percentages and it will not matter whether the user types in a percent sign or not. Although the output makes it look as if the function `read_and_clean` simply removes some symbols, more than that is happening. The value produced is a true *int* value that can be used in a program as a number; it is not a C string of characters.

The function `read_and_clean` shown in Display 8.2 will delete any nondigits from the string typed in, but it cannot check that the remaining digits will yield the number the user has in mind. The user should be given a chance to look at the final value and see whether it is correct. If the value is not correct, the user should be given a chance to reenter the input. In Display 8.3 we have used the function `read_and_clean` in another function called `get_int`, which will accept anything the user types and will allow the user to reenter the input until she or he is satisfied with the number that is computed from the input string. It is a very robust input procedure. (The function `get_int` is an improved version of the function of the same name given in Display 6.7.)

The functions `read_and_clean` in Display 8.2 and `get_int` in Display 8.3 are samples of the various input functions you can design by reading numeric input as a string value. Programming Project 3 at the end of this chapter asks you to define a function similar to `get_int` that reads in a number of type *double*, as opposed to a number of type *int*. To write that function, it would be nice to have a predefined function that converts a string value to a number of type *double*. Fortunately, the predefined function `atof`, which is also in the library with header file `cstdlib`, does just that. For example, `atof ("9.99")` returns the value `9.99` of type *double*. If the argument does not correspond to a number of type *double*, then `atof` returns `0.0`. You pronounce `atof` as "A to F," which is an abbreviation of "alphabetic to floating point." Recall that numbers with a decimal point are often called *floating-point* numbers because of the way the computer handles the decimal point when storing these numbers in memory.

DISPLAY 8.2   C Strings to Integers *(part 1 of 2)*

```
1    //Demonstrates the function read_and_clean.
2    #include <iostream>
3    #include <cstdlib>
4    #include <cctype>
5
6    void read_and_clean(int& n);
7    //Reads a line of input. Discards all symbols except the digits. Converts
8    //the C string to an integer and sets n equal to the value of this integer.
9
10   void new_line( );
11   //Discards all the input remaining on the current input line.
12   //Also discards the '\n' at the end of the line.
13
14   int main( )
15   {
16       using namespace std;
17       int n;
18       char ans;
19       do
20       {
21           cout << "Enter an integer and press Return: ";
22           read_and_clean(n);
23           cout << "That string converts to the integer " << n <<endl;
24           cout << "Again? (yes/no): ";
25           cin >> ans;
26           new_line( );
27       } while ( (ans != 'n') && (ans != 'N') );
28       return 0;
29   }
30   //Uses iostream, cstdlib, and cctype:
31   void read_and_clean(int& n)
32   {
33       using namespace std;
34       const int ARRAY_SIZE = 6;
35       char digit_string[ARRAY_SIZE];
36
37       char next;
38       cin.get(next);
39       int index = 0;
40       while (next != '\n')
41       {
42           if ((isdigit(next)) && (index < ARRAY_SIZE - 1))
43           {
44               digit_string[index] = next;
45               index++;
46           }
```

(continued)

DISPLAY 8.2   C Strings to Integers *(part 2 of 2)*

```
47              cin.get(next);
48          }
49          digit_string[index] = '\0';
50          n = atoi(digit_string);
51      }
52      //Uses iostream:
53      void new_line( )
54      {
55          using namespace std;
            <The rest of the definition of new_line is given in Display 6.7.>
```

Sample Dialogue

```
Enter an integer and press Return: $ 100
That string converts to the integer 100
Again? (yes/no): yes
Enter an integer and press Return: 100
That string converts to the integer 100
Again? (yes/no): yes
Enter an integer and press Return: 99%
That string converts to the integer 99
Again? (yes/no): yes
Enter an integer and press Return: 23% &&5 *12
That string converts to the integer 23512
Again? (yes/no): no
```

DISPLAY 8.3   **Robust Input Function** *(part 1 of 2)*

```
1    //Demonstration program for improved version of get_int.
2    #include <iostream>
3    #include <cstdlib>
4    #include <cctype>

5    void read_and_clean(int& n);
6    //Reads a line of input. Discards all symbols except the digits. Converts
7    //the C string to an integer and sets n equal to the value of this integer.

8    void new_line( );
9    //Discards all the input remaining on the current input line.
10   //Also discards the '\n' at the end of the line.

11   void get_int(int& input_number);
12   //Gives input_number a value that the user approves of.
```

(continued)

DISPLAY 8.3 Robust Input Function *(part 2 of 2)*

```
13    int main( )
14    {
15        using namespace std;
16        int input_number;
17        get_int(input_number);
18        cout << "Final value read in = " <<input_number<<endl;
19        return 0;
20    }
```

```
21    //Uses iostream and read_and_clean:
22    void get_int(int& input_number)
23    {
24        using namespace std;
25        char ans;
26        do
27        {
28            cout << "Enter input number: ";
29            read_and_clean(input_number);
30            cout << "You entered " <<input_number
31                << " Is that correct? (yes/no): ";
32            cin >> ans;
33            new_line( );
34        } while ((ans != 'y') && (ans != 'Y'));
35    }
36    //Uses iostream, cstdlib, and cctype:
37    void read_and_clean(int& n)
```

<The rest of the definition of read_and_clean is given in Display 8.2.>

```
38    //Uses iostream:
39    void new_line( )
```

<The rest of the definition of new_line is given in Display 8.2.>

Sample Dialogue

```
Enter input number: $57
You entered 57 Is that correct? (yes/no): no
Enter input number: $77*5xa
You entered 775 Is that correct? (yes/no): no
Enter input number: 77
You entered 77 Is that correct? (yes/no): no
Enter input number: $75
You entered 75 Is that correct? (yes/no): yes
Final value read in = 75
```

8.2 THE STANDARD string CLASS

I try to catch every sentence, every word you and I say, and quickly lock all these sentences and words away in my literary storehouse because they might come in handy.

ANTON CHEKHOV, *The Seagull*

In Section 8.1, we introduced C strings. These C strings were simply arrays of characters terminated with the null character '\0'. In order to manipulate these C strings, you needed to worry about all the details of handling arrays. For example, when you want to add characters to a C string and there is not enough room in the array, you must create another array to hold this longer string of characters. In short, C strings require the programmer to keep track of all the low-level details of how the C strings are stored in memory. This is a lot of extra work and a source of programmer errors. The latest ANSI/ISO standard for C++ specified that C++ must now also have a class string that allows the programmer to treat strings as a basic data type without needing to worry about implementation details. In this section we introduce you to this string type.

Introduction to the Standard Class string

The class string is defined in the library whose name is also <string>, and the definitions are placed in the std namespace. So, in order to use the class string, your code must contain the following (or something more or less equivalent):

```
#include <string>
using namespace std;
```

The class string allows you to treat string values and string expressions very much like values of a simple type. You can use the = operator to assign a value to a string variable, and you can use the + sign to concatenate two strings. For example, suppose s1, s2, and s3 are objects of type string and both s1 and s2 have string values. Then s3 can be set equal to the concatenation of the string value in s1 followed by the string value in s2 as follows:

+ operator does
concatenation

```
s3 = s1 + s2;
```

There is no danger of s3 being too small for its new string value. If the sum of the lengths of s1 and s2 exceeds the capacity of s3, then more space is automatically allocated for s3.

As we noted earlier in this chapter, quoted strings are really C strings and so they are not literally of type string. However, C++ provides automatic type casting of quoted strings to values of type string. So, you can use quoted strings as if they were literal values of type string, and we (and most others) will often refer to quoted strings as if they were values of type string. For example,

```
s3 = "Hello Mom!";
```

sets the value of the string variable s3 to a string object with the same characters as in the C string "Hello Mom!".

The class `string` has a default constructor that initializes a `string` object to the empty string. The class `string` also has a second constructor that takes one argument that is a standard C string and so can be a quoted string. This second constructor initializes the `string` object to a value that represents the same string as its C-string argument. For example,

```
string phrase;
string noun("ants");
```

The first line declares the string variable phrase and initializes it to the empty string. The second line declares noun to be of type `string` and initializes it to a string value equivalent to the C string "ants". Most programmers when talking loosely would say that "noun is initialized to "ants"," but there really is a type conversion here. The quoted string "ants" is a C string, not a value of type `string`. The variable noun receives a string value that has the same characters as "ants" in the same order as "ants", but the string value is not terminated with the null character '\0'. In fact, in theory at least, you do not know or care whether the string value of noun is even stored in an array, as opposed to some other data structure.

There is an alternate notation for declaring a string variable and invoking a constructor. The following two lines are exactly equivalent:

```
string noun("ants");
string noun = "ants";
```

These basic details about the class `string` are illustrated in Display 8.4. Note that, as illustrated there, you can output `string` values using the operator `<<`.

Consider the following line from Display 8.4:

```
phrase = "I love " + adjective + " " + noun + "!";
```

Converting C-string constants to the type `string`

C++ must do a lot of work to allow you to concatenate strings in this simple and natural fashion. The string constant "I love" is not an object of type `string`. A string constant like "I love" is stored as a C string (in other words, as a null-terminated array of characters). When C++ sees "I love" as an argument to +, it finds the definition (or overloading) of + that applies to a value such as "I love". There are overloadings of the + operator that have a C string on the left and a string on the right, as well as the reverse of this positioning. There is even a version that has a C string on both sides of the + and produces a `string` object as the value returned. Of course, there is also the overloading you expect, with the type `string` for both operands.

C++ did not really need to provide all those overloading cases for +. If these overloadings were not provided, C++ would look for a constructor that could perform a type conversion to convert the C string "I love" to a value for which + did apply. In this case, the constructor with the one C-string parameter would perform just such a conversion. However, the extra overloadings are presumably more efficient.

The class `string` is often thought of as a modern replacement for C strings. However, in C++ you cannot easily avoid also using C strings when you program with the class `string`.

DISPLAY 8.4 Program Using the Class string

```
1    //Demonstrates the standard class string.
2    #include <iostream>
3    #include <string>
4    using namespace std;

5    int main( )
6    {
7        string phrase;
8        string adjective("fried"), noun("ants");
9        string wish = "Bon appetit!";

10       phrase = "I love " + adjective + " " + noun + "!";
11       cout << phrase << endl
12             << wish << endl;

13       return 0;
14   }
```

Initialized to the empty string

Two ways of initializing a string variable

Sample Dialogue

```
I love fried ants!
Bon appetit!
```

The Class string

The class string can be used to represent values that are strings of characters. The class string provides more versatile string representation than the C strings discussed in Section 8.1.

The class string is defined in the library that is also named <string>, and its definition is placed in the std namespace. So, programs that use the class string should contain the following (or something more or less equivalent):

```
#include <string>
using namespace std;
```

The class string has a default constructor that initializes the string object to the empty string and a constructor that takes a C string as an argument and initializes the string object to a value that represents the string given as the argument. For example:

```
string s1, s2("Hello");
```

I/O with the Class string

You can use the insertion operator << and cout to output string objects just as you do for data of other types. This is illustrated in Display 8.4. Input with the class string is a bit more subtle.

The extraction operator >> and cin work the same for string objects as for other data, but remember that the extraction operator ignores initial whitespace and stops reading when it encounters more whitespace. This is as true for strings as it is for other data. For example, consider the following code;

```
string s1, s2;
cin >> s1;
cin >> s2;
```

If the user types in

```
May the hair on your toes grow long and curly!
```

then s1 will receive the value "May" with any leading (or trailing) whitespace deleted. The variable s2 receives the string "the". Using the extraction operator >> and cin, you can only read in words; you cannot read in a line or other string that contains a blank. Sometimes this is exactly what you want, but sometimes it is not at all what you want.

If you want your program to read an entire line of input into a variable of type string, you can use the function getline. The syntax for using getline with string objects is a bit different from what we described for C strings in Section 8.1. You do not use cin.getline; instead, you make cin the first argument to getline.[2] (Thus, this version of getline is not a member function.)

```
string line;
cout << "Enter a line of input:\n";
getline(cin, line);
cout << line << "END OF OUTPUT\n";
```

When embedded in a complete program, this code produces a dialogue like the following:

```
Enter some input:
Do bedo to you!
Do bedo to you!END OF OUTPUT
```

If there were leading or trailing blanks on the line, then they too would be part of the string value read by getline. This version of getline is in the

---

[2] This is a bit ironic, since the class string was designed using more modern object-oriented techniques, and the notation it uses for getline is the old fashioned, less object-oriented notation. This is an accident of history. This getline function was defined after the iostream library was already in use, so the designers had little choice but to make this getline a stand-alone function.

library <string>. You can use a stream object connected to a text file in place of cin to do input from a file using getline.

You cannot use cin and >> to read in a blank character. If you want to read one character at a time, you can use cin.get, which we discussed in Chapter 6. The function cin.get reads values of type *char*, not of type string, but it can be helpful when handling string input. Display 8.5 contains a program that illustrates both getline and cin.get used for string input. The significance of the function new_line is explained in the Pitfall subsection entitled "??"

DISPLAY 8.5   Program Using the Class string *(part 1 of 2)*

```
1    //Demonstrates getline and cin.get.
2    #include <iostream>
3    #include <string>

4    void new_line( );

5    int main( )
6    {
7        using namespace std;

8
9        string first_name, last_name, record_name;
10       string motto = "Your records are our records.";

11       cout << "Enter your first and last name:\n";
12       cin >> first_name>>last_name;
13       new_line( );

14       record_name = last_name + ", " + first_name;
15       cout << "Your name in our records is: ";
16       cout << record_name<<endl;

17       cout << "Our motto is\n"
18           << motto <<endl;
19       cout << "Please suggest a better (one-line) motto:\n";
20       getline(cin, motto);
21       cout << "Our new motto will be:\n";
22       cout << motto <<endl;

23       return 0;
24   }
25
26   //Uses iostream:
27   void new_line( )
28   {
29       using namespace std;
30
```

(continued)

DISPLAY 8.5   Program Using the Class string *(part 2 of 2)*

```
31        char next_char;
32        do
33        {
34            cin.get(next_char);
35        } while (next_char != '\n');
36    }
```

Sample Dialogue

```
Enter your first and last name:
B'Elanna Torres
Your name in our records is: Torres, B'Elanna
Our motto is
Your records are our records.
Please suggest a better (one-line) motto:
Our records go where no records dared to go before.
Our new motto will be:
Our records go where no records dared to go before.
```

I/O with string **Objects**

You can use the insertion operator << with cout to output string objects. You can input a string with the extraction operator >> and cin. When using >> for input, the code reads in a string delimited with whitespace. You can use the function getline to input an entire line of text into a string object.

EXAMPLES

```
string greeting("Hello"), response, next_word;
cout << greeting << endl;
getline(cin, response);
cin >> next_word;
```

SELF-TEST EXERCISES

15. Consider the following code (and assume that it is embedded in a complete and correct program and then run):

```
string s1, s2;
```

```
cout << "Enter a line of input:\n";
cin >> s1 >> s2;
cout << s1 << "*" << s2 << "<END OF OUTPUT";
```

If the dialogue begins as follows, what will be the next line of output?

```
Enter a line of input:
A string is a joy forever!
```

16. Consider the following code (and assume that it is embedded in a complete and correct program and then run):

```
string s;
cout << "Enter a line of input:\n";
getline(cin, s);
cout << s << "<END OF OUTPUT";
```

If the dialogue begins as follows, what will be the next line of output?

```
Enter a line of input:
A string is a joy forever!
```

■ PROGRAMMING TIP   More Versions of getline

So far, we have described the following way of using getline:

```
string line;
cout << "Enter a line of input:\n";
getline(cin, line);
```

This version stops reading when it encounters the end-of-line marker '\n'. There is a version that allows you to specify a different character to use as a stopping signal. For example, the following will stop when the first question mark is encountered:

```
string line;
cout << "Enter some input:\n";
getline(cin, line, '?');
```

It makes sense to use getline as if it were a *void* function, but it actually returns a reference to its first argument, which is cin in the code above. Thus, the following will read a line of text into s1 and a string of nonwhitespace characters into s2:

```
string s1, s2;
getline(cin, s1) >> s2;
```

The invocation getline (cin,s1) returns a reference to cin, so that after the invocation of getline, the next thing to happen is equivalent to

```
cin >> s2;
```

This kind of use of getline seems to have been designed for use in a C++ quiz show rather than to meet any actual programming need, but it can come in handy sometimes. ∎

VideoNote
Example using cin and getline with the string class

PITFALL   Mixing cin >> variable; and getline

Take care in mixing input using cin >> variable; with input using getline. For example, consider the following code:

```
int n;
string line;
cin >> n;
getline(cin, line);
```

---

getline for Objects of the Class string

The getline function for string objects has two versions:

```
istream& getline(istream& ins, string& str_var,
                 char delimiter);
```

and

```
istream& getline(istream& ins, string& str_var);
```

The first version of this function reads characters from the istream object given as the first argument (always cin in this chapter), inserting the characters into the string variable str_var until an instance of the delimiter character is encountered. The delimiter character is removed from the input and discarded. The second version uses '\n' for the default value of delimiter; otherwise, it works the same.

These getline functions return their first argument (always cin in this chapter), but they are usually used as if they were *void* functions.

When this code reads the following input, you might expect the value of n to be set to 42 and the value of line to be set to a string value representing "Hello hitchhiker.":

```
42
Hello hitchhiker.
```

However, while n is indeed set to the value of 42, line is set equal to the empty string. What happened?

Using cin >> n skips leading whitespace on the input, but leaves the rest of the line, in this case just '\n', for the next input. A statement like

```
cin >> n;
```

always leaves something on the line for a following getline to read (even if it is just the '\n'). In this case, the getline sees the '\n' and stops reading, so getline reads an empty string. If you find your program appearing to mysteriously ignore input data, see if you have mixed these two kinds of input. You may need to use either the new_line function from Display 8.5 or the function ignore from the library iostream. For example,

```
cin.ignore(1000, '\n');
```

With these arguments, a call to the ignore member function will read and discard the entire rest of the line up to and including the '\n' (or until it discards 1000 characters if it does not find the end of the line after 1000 characters).

There can be other baffling problems with programs that use cin with both >> and getline. Moreover, these problems can come and go as you move from one C++ compiler to another. When all else fails, or if you want to be certain of portability, you can resort to character-by-character input using cin.get.

These problems can occur with any of the versions of getline that we discuss in this chapter. ∎

String Processing with the Class string

The class string allows you to perform the same operations that you can perform with the C strings we discussed in Section 8.1 and more. You can access the characters in a string object in the same way that you access array elements, so string objects have all the advantages of arrays of characters plus a number of advantages that arrays do not have, such as automatically increasing their capacity. If last_name is the name of a string object, then last_name[i] gives access to the ith character in the string represented by last_name. This use of array square brackets is illustrated in Display 8.6.

Display 8.6 also illustrates the member function length. Every string object has a member function named length that takes no arguments and returns the length of the string represented by the string object. Thus, not only can a string object be used like an array but the length member function makes it behave like a partially filled array that automatically keeps track of how many positions are occupied.

When used with an object of the class string, the array square brackets do not check for illegal indexes. If you use an illegal index (that is, an index that is greater than or equal to the length of the string in the object), then the results are unpredictable but are bound to be bad. You may just get strange behavior without any error message that tells you that the problem is an illegal index value.

There is a member function named at that does check for illegal index values. This member function behaves basically the same as the square brackets, except for two points: You use function notation with at, so instead

DISPLAY 8.6   A `string` **Object Can Behave Like an Array**

```
1    //Demonstrates using a string object as if it were an array.
2    #include <iostream>
3    #include <string>
4    using namespace std;
5    int main( )
6    {
7        string first_name, last_name;
8        cout << "Enter your first and last name:\n";
9        cin >> first_name>>last_name;
10       cout << "Your last name is spelled:\n";
11       int i;
12       for (i = 0; i <last_name.length( ); i++)
13       {
14           cout << last_name[i] << " ";
15           last_name[i] = '-';
16       }
17       cout << endl;
18       for (i = 0; i <last_name.length( ); i++)
19           cout << last_name[i] << " "; //Places a "-" under each letter.
20       cout << endl;
21       cout << "Good day " << first_name << endl;
22       return 0;
23    }
```

Sample Dialogue

```
Enter your first and last name:
John Crichton
Your last name is spelled:
C r i c h t o n
- - - - - - - -
Good day John
```

of a[i], you use a.at(i); and the at member function checks to see if i evaluates to an illegal index. If the value of i in a.at(i) is an illegal index, then you should get a run-time error message telling you what is wrong. In the following two example code fragments, the attempted access is out of range, yet the first of these probably will not produce an error message, although it will be accessing a nonexistent indexed variable:

```
string str("Mary");
cout << str[6] << endl;
```

The second example, however, will cause the program to terminate abnormally, so you at least know that something is wrong:

```
string str("Mary");
cout << str.at(6) << endl;
```

But be warned that some systems give very poor error messages when str.at(i) has an illegal index i.

You can change a single character in the string by assigning a *char* value to the indexed variable, such as str[i]. This may also be done with the member function at. For example, to change the third character in the string object str to 'X', you can use either of the following code fragments:

```
str.at(2) = 'X';
```

or

```
str[2] = 'X';
```

As in an ordinary array of characters, character positions for objects of type string are indexed starting with 0, so the third character in a string is in index position 2.

Display 8.7 gives a partial list of the member functions of the class string. In many ways, objects of the class string are better behaved than the C strings we introduced in Section 8.1. In particular, the == operator on objects of the string class returns a result that corresponds to our intuitive notion of strings being equal—namely, it returns *true* if the two strings contain the same characters in the same order, and returns *false* otherwise. Similarly, the comparison operators <, >, < =, > = compare string objects using lexicographic ordering. (Lexicographic ordering is alphabetic ordering using the order of symbols given in the ASCII character set in Appendix 3. If the strings consist of all letters and are both either all uppercase or all lowercase letters, then for this case lexicographic ordering is the same as everyday alphabetical ordering.)

DISPLAY 8.7   **Member Functions of the Standard Class** string *(part 1 of 2)*

Example	Remarks
Constructors	
string str;	Default constructor creates empty string object str.
string str("sample");	Creates a string object with data "sample".
string str (a_string);	Creates a string object str that is a copy of a_string; a_string is an object of the class string.

(continued)

DISPLAY 8.7 **Member Functions of the Standard Class** string *(part 2 of 2)*

Accessors	
str[i]	Returns read/write reference to character in str at index i. Does not check for illegal index.
str.at(i)	Returns read/write reference to character in str at index i. Same as str[i], but this version checks for illegal index.
str.substr(position, length)	Returns the substring of the calling object starting at position and having length characters.
str.length( )	Returns the length of str.

Assignment/Modifiers	
str1 = str2;	Initializes str1 to str2's data.
str1 += str2;	Character data of str2 is concatenated to the end of str1.
str.empty( )	Returns true if str is an empty string; false otherwise.
str1 + str2	Returns a string that has str2's data concatenated to the end of str1's data.
str.insert(pos, str2);	Inserts str2 into str beginning at position pos.
str.erase(pos, length);	Removes substring of size length, starting at position pos.

Comparison	
str1 == str2 str1 != str2	Compare for equality or inequality; returns a Boolean value.
str1 < str2 str1 > str2	Four comparisons. All are lexicographical comparisons.
str1 <= str2 str1 >= str2	

Finds	
str.find(str1)	Returns index of the first occurrence of str1 in str. If str1 is not found, then the special value string::npos is returned.
str.find(str1, pos)	Returns index of the first occurrence of string str1 in str; the search starts at position pos.
str.find_first_of(str1, pos)	Returns the index of the first instance in str of any character in str1, starting the search at position pos.
str.find_first_not_of (str1, pos)	Returns the index of the first instance in str of any character not in str1, starting the search at position pos.

PROGRAMMING EXAMPLE   Palindrome Testing

A palindrome is a string that reads the same front to back as it does back to front. The program in Display 8.8 tests an input string to see if it is a palindrome. Our palindrome test will disregard all spaces and punctuations and will consider upper- and lowercase versions of a letter to be the same when deciding if something is a palindrome. Some palindrome examples are as follows:

```
Able was I ere I saw Elba.
I Love Me, Vol. I.
Madam, I'm Adam.
A man, a plan, a canal, Panama.
Rats live on no evil star.
radar
deed
mom
racecar
```

The remove_punct function is of interest in that it uses the string member functions substr and find. The member function substr extracts a substring of the calling object, given the position and length of the desired substring.

DISPLAY 8.8   Palindrome Testing Program *(part 1 of 3)*

```
1    //Test for palindrome property.
2    #include <iostream>
3    #include <string>
4    #include <cctype>
5    using namespace std;

6    void swap (char& v1, char& v2);
7    //Interchanges the values of v1 and v2.

8    string reverse(const string& s);
9    //Returns a copy of s but with characters in reverse order.

10   string remove_punct(const string& s, const string& punct);
11   //Returns a copy of s with any occurrences of characters
12   //in the string punct removed.

13   string make_lower(const string& s);
14   //Returns a copy of s that has all uppercase
15   //characters changed to lowercase, other characters unchanged.

16   bool is_pal(const string& s);
17   //Returns true if s is a palindrome, false otherwise.

18   int main( )
19   {
20       string str;
```

(continued)

DISPLAY 8.8   **Palindrome Testing Program** *(part 2 of 3)*

```
21          cout << "Enter a candidate for palindrome test\n"
22               << "followed by pressing Return.\n";
23          getline(cin, str);

24          if (is_pal(str))
25              cout << "\"" <<str + "\" is a palindrome.";
26          else
27              cout << "\"" <<str + "\" is not a palindrome.";
28          cout << endl;

29          return 0;
30      }
31
32      void swap(char& v1, char& v2)
33      {
34          char temp = v1;
35          v1 = v2;
36          v2 = temp;
37      }
38
39      string reverse(const string& s)
40      {
41          int start = 0;
42          int end = s.length( );
43          string temp(s);
44
45          while (start < end)
46          {
47              end--;
48              swap(temp[start], temp[end]);
49              start++;
50          }
51          return temp;
52      }
53      //Uses <cctype> and <string>
54      string make_lower(const string& s)
55      {
56          string temp(s);
57          for (int i = 0; i < s.length( ); i++)
58              temp[i] = tolower(s[i]);

59          return temp;
60      }
61      string remove_punct(const string& s, const string& punct)
62      {
63          string no_punct; //initialized to empty string
64          int s_length = s.length( );
65          int punct_length = punct.length( );
```

(continued)

DISPLAY 8.8   Palindrome Testing Program *(part 3 of 3)*

```
66        for (int i = 0; i < s_length; i++)
67        {
68            string a_char = s.substr(i,1); //A one-character string
69            int location = punct.find(a_char, 0);
70            //Find location of successive characters
71            //of src in punct.
72        if (location < 0 || location >= punct_length)
73            no_punct = no_punct + a_char; //a_char not in punct, so keep it
74        }
75        return no_punct;
76    }
77
78    //uses functions make_lower, remove_punct
79    bool is_pal(const string& s)
80    {
81        stringpunct (",;:.?!'\" "); //includes a blank
82        string str(s);
83        str = make_lower(str);
84        string lower_str = remove_punct(str, punct);
85        return (lower_str == reverse(lower_str));
86    }
```

Sample Dialogue

```
Enter a candidate for palindrome test
followed by pressing Return.
Madam, I'm Adam.

"Madam, I'm Adam." is a palindrome.
```

Sample Dialogue

```
Enter a candidate for palindrome test
followed by pressing Return.
Radar

"Radar" is a palindrome.
```

Sample Dialogue

```
Enter a candidate for palindrome test
followed by pressing Return.
Am I a palindrome?
"Am I a palindrome?" is not a palindrome.
```

The first three lines of `remove_punct` declare variables for use in the function. The *for* loop runs through the characters of the parameters one at a time and tries to find them in the `punct string`. To do this, a string that is the substring of s, of length 1 at each character position, is extracted. The position of this substring in the `punct string` is determined using the `find` member function. If this one-character string is not in the `punct string`, then the one-character string is concatenated to the no_punct string that is to be returned.

= and == Are Different for strings and C Strings

The operators =, ==, !=, <, >, <=, >=, when used with the standard C++ type `string`, produce results that correspond to our intuitive notion of how strings compare. They do not misbehave as they do with the C strings, as we discussed in Section 8.1

SELF-TEST EXERCISES

17. Consider the following code:

```
string s1, s2("Hello");
cout << "Enter a line of input:\n";
cin >> s1;
if (s1 == s2)
    cout << "Equal\n";
else
    cout << "Not equal\n";
```

If the dialogue begins as follows, what will be the next line of output?

```
Enter a line of input:
Hello friend!
```

18. What is the output produced by the following code?

```
string s1, s2("Hello");
s1 = s2;
s2[0] = 'J';
cout << s1 << " " << s2;
```

Converting Between string Objects and C Strings

You have already seen that C++ will perform an automatic type conversion to allow you to store a C string in a variable of type `string`. For example, the following will work fine:

```
char a_c_string[] = "This is my C string.";
string string_variable;
string_variable = a_c_string;
```

However, the following will produce a compiler error message:

```
a_c_string = string_variable; //ILLEGAL
```

The following is also illegal:

```
strcpy(a_c_string, string_variable); //ILLEGAL
```

strcpy cannot take a string object as its second argument, and there is no automatic conversion of string objects to C strings, which is the problem we cannot seem to get away from.

To obtain the C string corresponding to a string object, you must perform an explicit conversion. This can be done with the string member function c_str( ). The correct version of the copying we have been trying to do is the following:

```
strcpy(a_c_string, string_variable.c_str( )); //Legal;
```

Note that you need to use the strcpy function to do the copying. The member function c_str( ) returns the C string corresponding to the string calling object. As we noted earlier in this chapter, the assignment operator does not work with C strings. So, just in case you thought the following might work, we should point out that it too is illegal.

```
a_c_string = string_variable.c_str( ); //ILLEGAL
```

8.3 VECTORS

"Well, I'll eat it," said Alice, "and if it makes me grow larger, I can reach the key; and if it makes me grow smaller, I can creep under the door; so either way I'll get into the garden...."

LEWIS CARROLL, *Alice's Adventures in Wonderland*

Vectors can be thought of as arrays that can grow (and shrink) in length while your program is running. In C++, once your program creates an array, it cannot change the length of the array. Vectors serve the same purpose as arrays except that they can change length while the program is running. Vectors are part of a standard C++ library known as the STL (Standard Template Library), which we cover in more detail in Chapter 18.

You need not read the previous sections of this chapter before covering this section.

Vector Basics

Like an array, a vector has a base type, and like an array, a vector stores a collection of values of its base type. However, the syntax for a vector type and a vector variable declaration are different from the syntax for arrays.

Declaring a vector variable

You declare a variable v for a vector with base type *int* as follows:

```
vector<int> v;
```

The notation vector *<Base_Type>* is a **template class,** which means you can plug in any type for *Base_Type* and that will produce a class for vectors with that base type. You can think of this as specifying the base type for a vector in the same sense as you specify a base type for an array. You can use any type, including class types, as the base type for a vector. The notation vector *<int>* is a class name, and so the previous declaration of v as a vector of type vector *<int>* includes a call to the default constructor for the class vector *<int>*, which creates a vector object that is empty (has no elements).

Vector elements are indexed starting with 0, the same as arrays. The array square brackets notation can be used to read or change these elements, just as with an array. For example, the following changes the value of the ith element of the vector v and then outputs that changed value. (i is an *int* variable.)

```
v[i] = 42;
cout << "The answer is " << v[i];
```

There is, however, a restriction on this use of the square brackets notation with vectors that is unlike the same notation used with arrays. You can use v[i] to change the value of the ith element. However, you cannot initialize the ith element using v[i]; you can only change an element that has already been given some value. To add an element to an index position of a vector for the first time, you would normally use the member function push_back.

You add elements to a vector in order of positions, first at position 0, then position 1, then 2, and so forth. The member function push_back adds an element in the next available position. For example, the following gives initial values to elements 0, 1, and 2 of the vector sample:

```
vector<double> sample;
sample.push_back(0.0);
sample.push_back(1.1);
sample.push_back(2.2);
```

The number of elements in a vector is called the **size** of the vector. The member function size can be used to determine how many elements are in a vector. For example, after the previously shown code is executed, sample.size( ) returns 3. You can write out all the elements currently in the vector sample as follows:

```
for (int i = 0; i < sample.size( ); i++)
    cout << sample[i] << endl;
```

The function size returns a value of type *unsigned int*, not a value of type *int*. (The type *unsigned int* allows only nonnegative integer values.) This returned value should be automatically converted to type *int* when it needs to be of type *int*, but some compilers may warn you that you are using an *unsigned int* where an *int* is required. If you want to be very safe, you can always apply a type cast to convert the returned *unsigned int* to an *int* or, in cases like this *for* loop, use a loop control variable of type *unsigned int* as follows:

```
for (unsigned int i = 0; i < sample.size( ); i++)
    cout << sample[i] << endl;
```

A simple demonstration illustrating some basic vector techniques is given in Display 8.9.

DISPLAY 8.9   Using a Vector

```
1    #include <iostream>
2    #include <vector>
3    using namespace std;

4    int main( )
5    {
6        vector<int> v;
7        cout << "Enter a list of positive numbers.\n"
8             << "Place a negative number at the end.\n";

9        int next;
10       cin >> next;
11       while (next > 0)
12       {
13           v.push_back(next);
14           cout << next << " added. ";
15           cout << "v.size( ) = " <<v.size( ) <<endl;
16           cin >> next;
17       }

18       cout << "You entered:\n";
19       for (unsigned int i = 0; i <v.size( ); i++)
20           cout << v[i] << " ";
21       cout << endl;

22       return 0;
23   }
```

Sample Dialogue

```
Enter a list of positive numbers.
Place a negative number at the end.
2 4 6 8 -1
2 added. v.size( ) = 1
4 added. v.size( ) = 2
6 added. v.size( ) = 3
8 added. v.size( ) = 4
You entered:
2 4 6 8
```

There is a vector constructor that takes one integer argument and will initialize the number of positions given as the argument. For example, if you declare v as follows:

```
vector<int> v(10);
```

then the first ten elements are initialized to 0, and v.size( ) would return 10. You can then set the value of the ith element using v[i] for values of i equal to 0 through 9. In particular, the following could immediately follow the declaration:

```
for (unsigned int i = 0; i < 10; i++)
    v[i] = i;
```

To set the ith element, for i greater than or equal to 10, you would use push_back.

When you use the constructor with an integer argument, vectors of numbers are initialized to the zero of the number type. If the vector base type is a class type, the default constructor is used for initialization.

The vector definition is given in the library vector, which places it in the std namespace. Thus, a file that uses vectors would include the following (or something similar):

```
#include <vector>
using namespace std;
```

PITFALL   Using Square Brackets Beyond the Vector Size

If v is a vector and i is greater than or equal to v.size( ), then the element v[i] does not yet exist and needs to be created by using push_back to add elements up to and including position i. If you try to set v[i] for i greater than or equal to v.size( ), as in

```
v[i] = n;
```

then you may or may not get an error message, but your program will undoubtedly misbehave at some point. ■

Vectors

Vectors are used very much like arrays are used, but a vector does not have a fixed size. If it needs more capacity to store another element, its capacity is automatically increased. Vectors are defined in the library <vector>, which places them in the std namespace. Thus, a file that uses vectors would include the following (or something similar):

(continued)

```
#include <vector>
using namespace std;
```

The vector class for a given *Base_Type* is written vector <*Base_Type*>.
Two sample vector declarations are

```
vector<int> v; //default constructor
               //producing an empty vector.
vector<AClass> record(20); //vector constructor
                           //for AClass to initialize 20
                               elements.
```

Elements are added to a vector using the member function push_back, as
illustrated below:

```
v.push_back(42);
```

Once an element position has received its first element, either with
push_back or with a constructor initialization, that element position can
then be accessed using square bracket notation, just like an array element.

■ **PROGRAMMING TIP**   Vector Assignment Is Well Behaved

The assignment operator with vectors does an element-by-element assignment
to the vector on the left-hand side of the assignment operator (increasing
capacity if needed and resetting the size of the vector on the left-hand side of
the assignment operator). Thus, provided the assignment operator on the base
type makes an independent copy of the element of the base type, then the
assignment operator on the vector will make an independent copy.

Note that for the assignment operator to produce a totally independent
copy of the vector on the right-hand side of the assignment operator requires
that the assignment operator on the base type make completely independent
copies. The assignment operator on a vector is only as good (or bad)
as the assignment operator on its base type. (Details on overloading the
assignment operator for classes that need it are given in Chapter 11.)   ■

Efficiency Issues

At any point in time a vector has a **capacity,** which is the number of elements for
which it currently has memory allocated. The member function capacity( )
can be used to find out the capacity of a vector. Do not confuse the capacity
of a vector with the size of a vector. The *size* is the number of elements
in a vector, while the *capacity* is the number of elements for which there
is memory allocated. Typically, the capacity is larger than the size, and the
capacity is always greater than or equal to the size.

Whenever a vector runs out of capacity and needs room for an additional member, the capacity is automatically increased. The exact amount of the increase is implementation-dependent but always allows for more capacity than is immediately needed. A commonly used implementation scheme is for the capacity to double whenever it needs to increase. Since increasing capacity is a complex task, this approach of reallocating capacity in large chunks is more efficient than allocating numerous small chunks.

Size and Capacity

The **size** of a vector is the number of elements in the vector. The **capacity** of a vector is the number of elements for which it currently has memory allocated. For a vector v, the size and capacity can be recovered with the member functions v.size( ) and v.capacity( ).

You can completely ignore the capacity of a vector and that will have no effect on what your program does. However, if efficiency is an issue, you might want to manage capacity yourself and not simply accept the default behavior of doubling capacity whenever more is needed. You can use the member function reserve to explicitly increase the capacity of a vector. For example,

```
v.reserve(32);
```

sets the capacity to at least 32 elements, and

```
v.reserve(v.size( ) + 10);
```

sets the capacity to at least 10 more than the number of elements currently in the vector. Note that you can rely on v.reserve to increase the capacity of a vector, but it does not necessarily decrease the capacity of a vector if the argument is smaller than the current capacity.

You can change the size of a vector using the member function resize. For example, the following resizes a vector to 24 elements:

```
v.resize(24);
```

If the previous size was less than 24, then the new elements are initialized as we described for the constructor with an integer argument. If the previous size was greater than 24, then all but the first 24 elements are lost. The capacity is automatically increased if need be. Using resize and reserve, you can shrink the size and capacity of a vector when there is no longer any need for some elements or some capacity.

SELF-TEST EXERCISES

19. Is the following program legal? If so, what is the output?

```cpp
#include <iostream>
#include <vector>
using namespace std;

int main( )
{
    vector<int> v(10);
    int i;

    for (i = 0; i < v.size( ); i++)
        v[i] = i;

    vector<int> copy;
    copy = v;
    v[0] = 42;

    for (i = 0; i < copy.size( ); i++)
        cout << copy[i] << " ";
    cout << endl;

    return 0;
}
```

20. What is the difference between the size and the capacity of a vector?

CHAPTER SUMMARY

- A C-string variable is the same thing as an array of characters, but it is used in a slightly different way. A string variable uses the null character '\0' to mark the end of the string stored in the array.

- C-string variables usually must be treated like arrays, rather than simple variables of the kind we used for numbers and single characters. In particular, you cannot assign a C-string value to a C-string variable using the equal sign, =, and you cannot compare the values in two C-string variables using the == operator. Instead, you must use special C-string functions to perform these tasks.

- The ANSI/ISO standard <string> library provides a fully featured class called string that can be used to represent strings of characters.

- Objects of the class string are better behaved than C strings. In particular, the assignment and equal operators, = and ==, have their intuitive meaning when used with objects of the class string.

- Vectors can be thought of as arrays that can grow (and shrink) in length while your program is running.

Answers to Self-Test Exercises

1. The following two are equivalent to each other (but not equivalent to any others):

```
char string_var[10] = "Hello";
char string_var[10] = {'H', 'e', 'l', 'l', 'o', '\0'};
```

The following two are equivalent to each other (but not equivalent to any others):

```
char string_var[6] = "Hello";
char string_var[] = "Hello";
```

The following is not equivalent to any of the others:

```
char string_var[10] = {'H', 'e', 'l', 'l', 'o'};
```

2. "DoBeDo to you"

3. The declaration means that `string_var` has room for only six characters (including the null character `'\0'`). The function `strcat` does not check that there is room to add more characters to `string_var`, so `strcat` will write all the characters in the string "and Good-bye." into memory, even though that requires more memory than has been assigned to `string_var`. This means memory that should not be changed will be changed. The net effect is unpredictable, but bad.

4. If `strlen` were not already defined for you, you could use the following definition:

```
int strlen(const char str[])
//Precondition: str contains a string value terminated
//with '\0'.
//Returns the number of characters in the string str (not
//counting '\0').
{
    int index = 0;
    while (str[index] != '\0')
        index++;
    return index;
}
```

5. The maximum number of characters is five because the sixth position is needed for the null terminator (`'\0'`).

6. a. 1
   b. 1
   c. 5 (including the `'\0'`)
   d. 2 (including the `'\0'`)
   e. 6 (including the `'\0'`)

7. These are *not equivalent*. The first of these places the null character '\0' in the array after the characters 'a', 'b', and 'c'. The second only assigns the successive positions 'a', 'b', and 'c' but *does not put a* '\0' *anywhere*.

8.
```
int index = 0;
while ( our_string[index] != '\0' )
{
    our_string[index] = 'X';
    index++;
}
```

9. a. If the C-string variable does not have a null terminator, '\0', the loop can run beyond memory allocated for the C string, destroying the contents of memory there. To protect memory beyond the end of the array, change the *while* condition as shown in (b).

   b. `while ( our_string[index] != '\0' && index < SIZE )`

10.
```
#include <cstring>
//needed to get the declaration of strcpy
...
strcpy(a_string, "Hello");
```

11. `I did it my way!`

12. The string "good, I hope." is too long for a_string. A chunk of memory that doesn't belong to the array a_string will be overwritten.

13.
```
Enter some input:
The
    time is now.
The-timeEND OF OUTPUT
```

14. The complete dialogue is as follows:

```
Enter a line of input:
May the hair on your toes grow long and curly.
May t<END OF OUTPUT
```

15. `A*string<END OF OUTPUT`

16. `A string is a joy forever!<END OF OUTPUT`

17. The complete dialogue is

```
Enter a line of input:
Hello friend!
Equal
```

Remember, cin stops reading when it reaches a whitespace character such as a blank.

18. `Hello Jello`

19. The program is legal. The output is

    `0 1 2 3 4 5 6 7 8 9`

    Note that changing v does not change copy. A true independent copy is made with the assignment

    `copy = v;`

20. The size is the number of elements in a vector, whereas the capacity is the number of elements for which there is memory allocated. Typically, the capacity is larger than the size.

PROGRAMMING PROJECTS

VideoNote
Solution to Programming Project 8.1

Visit www.myprogramminglab.com to complete many of these Programming Projects online and get instant feedback.

1. Write a program that reads in a sentence of up to 100 characters and outputs the sentence with spacing corrected and with letters corrected for capitalization. In other words, in the output sentence, all strings of two or more blanks should be compressed to a single blank. The sentence should start with an uppercase letter but should contain no other uppercase letters. Do not worry about proper names; if their first letters are changed to lowercase, that is acceptable. Treat a line break as if it were a blank, in the sense that a line break and any number of blanks are compressed to a single blank. Assume that the sentence ends with a period and contains no other periods. For example, the input

   ```
   the    Answer to life, the Universe, and  everything
   IS 42.
   ```

   should produce the following output:

   ```
   The  answer to life, the universe, and   everything is 42.
   ```

2. Write a program that will read in a line of text and output the number of words in the line and the number of occurrences of each letter. Define a word to be any string of letters that is delimited at each end by either whitespace, a period, a comma, or the beginning or end of the line. You can assume that the input consists entirely of letters, whitespace, commas, and periods. When outputting the number of letters that occur in a line, be sure to count upper- and lowercase versions of a letter as the same letter. Output the letters in alphabetical order and list only those letters that do occur in the input line. For example, the input line

   ```
   I say Hi.
   ```

should produce output similar to the following:

```
3 words
1 a
1 h
2 i
1 s
1 y
```

3. Give the function definition for the function with the following function declaration. Embed your definition in a suitable test program.

```
void get_double(double& input_number);
//Postcondition: input_number is given a value
//that the user approves of.
```

You can assume that the user types in the input in normal everyday notation, such as 23.789, and does not use e-notation to type in the number. Model your definition after the definition of the function get_int given in Display 8.3 so that your function reads the input as characters, edits the string of characters, and converts the resulting string to a number of type *double*. You will need to define a function like read_and_clean that is more sophisticated than the one in Display 8.2, since it must cope with the decimal point. This is a fairly easy project. For a more difficult project, allow the user to enter the number in either the normal everyday notation, as discussed above, or in e-notation. Your function should decide whether or not the input is in e-notation by reading the input, *not* by asking the user whether she or he will use e-notation.

4. Write a program that reads a person's name in the following format: first name, then middle name or initial, and then last name. The program then outputs the name in the following format:

```
Last_Name, First_Name Middle_Initial.
```

For example, the input

```
Mary Average User
```

should produce the output:

```
User, Mary A.
```

The input

```
Mary A. User
```

should also produce the output:

```
User, Mary A.
```

Your program should work the same and place a period after the middle initial even if the input did not contain a period. Your program should allow for users who give no middle name or middle initial. In that case, the output, of course, contains no middle name or initial. For example, the input

```
Mary User
```

should produce the output

```
User, Mary
```

If you are using C strings, assume that each name is at most 20 characters long. Alternatively, use the class string.

> (*Hint:* You may want to use three string variables rather than one large string variable for the input. You may find it easier to *not* use getline.)

5. Write a program that reads in a line of text and replaces all four-letter words with the word "love". For example, the input string

```
I hate you, you dodo!
```

should produce the output

```
I love you, you love!
```

Of course, the output will not always make sense. For example, the input string

```
John will run home.
```

should produce the output

```
Love love run love.
```

If the four-letter word starts with a capital letter, it should be replaced by "Love", not by "love". You need not check capitalization, except for the first letter of a word. A word is any string consisting of the letters of the alphabet and delimited at each end by a blank, the end of the line, or any other character that is not a letter. Your program should repeat this action until the user says to quit.

6. Write a program that reads in a line of text and outputs the line with all the digits in all integer numbers replaced with 'x'. For example,

Input:

```
My userID is john17 and my 4 digit pin is 1234 which is secret.
```

Output:

```
My userID is john17 and my x digit pin is xxxx which is secret.
```

Note that if a digit is part of a word, then the digit is not changed to an 'x'. For example, note that john17 is NOT changed to johnxx. Include a loop that allows the user to repeat this calculation again until the user says she or he wants to end the program.

7. Write a program that can be used to train the user to use less sexist language by suggesting alternative versions of sentences given by the user. The program will ask for a sentence, read the sentence into a string variable, and replace all occurrences of masculine pronouns with gender-neutral pronouns. For example, it will replace "he" with "she or he". Thus, the input sentence

See an adviser, talk to him, and listen to him.

should produce the following suggested changed version of the sentence:

See an adviser, talk to her or him, and listen to her or him.

Be sure to preserve uppercase letters for the first word of the sentence. The pronoun "his" can be replaced by "her (s)"; your program need not decide between "her" and "hers". Allow the user to repeat this for more sentences until the user says she or he is done.

This will be a long program that requires a good deal of patience. Your program should not replace the string "he" when it occurs inside another word, such as "here". A word is any string consisting of the letters of the alphabet and delimited at each end by a blank, the end of the line, or any other character that is not a letter. Allow your sentences to be up to 100 characters long.

8. Write a sorting function that is similar to Display 7.12 in Chapter 7 except that it has an argument for a vector of *ints* rather than an array. This function will not need a parameter like number_used as in Display 7.12, since a vector can determine the number used with the member function size(). This sort function will have only this one parameter, which will be of a vector type. Use the selection sort algorithm (which was used in Display 7.12).

9. Redo Programming Project 6 from Chapter 7, but this time use vectors instead of arrays. (It may help to do the previous Programming Project first.)

10. Redo Programming Project 5 from Chapter 7, but this time use vectors instead of arrays. You should do either Programming Project 8 or 9 before doing this one. However, you will need to write your own (similar) sorting code for this project rather than using the sorting function from Programming Project 7 or 8 with no changes.

11. Write a program that inputs two string variables, first and last, each of which the user should enter with his or her name. First, convert both

strings to all lowercase. Your program should then create a new string that contains the full name in pig latin with the first letter capitalized for the first and last name. The rules to convert a word into pig latin are as follows:

If the first letter is a consonant, move it to the end and add "ay" to the end.

If the first letter is a vowel, add "way" to the end.

For example, if the user inputs "Erin" for the first name and "Jones" for the last name, then the program should create a new string with the text "Erinway Onesjay" and print it.

12. Your country is at war and your enemies are using a secret code to communicate with each other. You have managed to intercept a message that reads as follows:

```
:mmZ\dxZmx]Zpgy
```

The message is obviously encrypted using the enemy's secret code. You have just learned that their encryption method is based upon the ASCII code. Appendix 3 shows the ASCII character set. Individual characters in a string are encoded using this system. For example, the letter "A" is encoded using the number 65 and "B" is encoded using the number 66.

Your enemy's secret code takes each letter of the message and encrypts it as follows:

```
If (OriginalChar + Key > 126) then
    EncryptedChar = 32 + ((OriginalChar + Key) - 127)
Else
    EncryptedChar = (OriginalChar + Key)
```

For example, if the enemy uses Key = 10 then the message "Hey" would be encrypted as:

Character	ASCII code
H	72
e	101
y	121

```
Encrypted H = (72 + 10) = 82 = R in ASCII
Encrypted e = (101 + 10) = 111 = o in ASCII
Encrypted y = 32 + ((121 + 10) - 127) = 36 = $ in ASCII
```

Consequently, "Hey" would be transmitted as "Ro$."

Write a program that decrypts the intercepted message. You only know that the key used is a number between 1 and 100. Your program should try to decode the message using all possible keys between 1 and 100. When you try the valid key, the message will make sense. For all other keys, the message will appear as gibberish.

13. Write a program that inputs a time from the console. The time should be in the format "HH:MM AM" or "HH:MM PM". Hours may be one or two digits, for example, "1:10 AM" or "11:30 PM". Your program should include a function that takes a string parameter containing the time. This function should convert the time into a four-digit military time based on a 24-hour clock. For example, "1:10 AM" would output "0110 hours", "11:30 PM" would output "2330 hours", and "12:15 AM" would output "0015 hours". The function may either write the time to the console or return a string to be written to the console by the main function.

14. The XML (eXtensible Markup Language) is a common format used to structure and store data on the Web. The following is a small sample XML file that could be used to store names in an address book. Type it in using a text editor and save it to a file named address.xml (or find it on the accompanying CD).

```
<?xml version="1.0"?>
<address_book>
    <contact>
        <name>George Clooney</name>
        <street>1042 El Camino Real</street>
        <city>Beverly Hills</city>
        <state>CA</state>
        <zip>90214</zip>
    </contact>
    <contact>
        <name>Cathy Pearl</name>
        <street>405 A St.</street>
        <city>Palmdale</city>
        <state>CA</state>
        <zip>93352</zip>
    </contact>
    <contact>
        <name>Paris Hilton</name>
        <street>200 S. Elm St.</street>
        <city>Beverly Hills</city>
        <state>CA</state>
        <zip>90212</zip>
    </contact>
    <contact>
        <name>Wendy Jones</name>
        <street>982 Boundary Ave.</street>
```

```
                    <city>Palmdale</city>
                    <state>CA</state>
                    <zip>93354</zip>
            </contact>
    </address_book>
```

The sample file contains four contacts. The <> tag denotes the start of a field and the </> tag denotes the end of the field.

a. You are hosting a party in Palmdale, CA. Write a program that reads in the address.xml file and outputs the names and addresses of everyone in Palmdale. Your program shouldn't output any of the tag information, just the address content.

b. You would like to send an advertising flyer to everyone in zip codes 90210 through 90214. Write a program that reads in the address. xml file and outputs the names and addresses of everyone whose zip code falls within the specified range.

You may assume that each contact in the address file has the same structure and the same fields. However, your solution should be able to handle an input file with any number of contacts and should not assume that the fields within each contact are in the same order.

VideoNote
Solution to Programming
Project 8.15

15. Given the following header:

```
vector<string> split(string target, string delimiter);
```

implement the function split so that it returns a vector of the strings in target that are separated by the string delimiter. For example:

```
split("10,20,30", ",")
```

should return a vector with the strings "10", "20", and "30". Similarly,

```
split("do re mi fa so la ti do", " ")
```

should return a vector with the strings "do", "re", "mi", "fa", "so", "la", "ti", and "do".

16. Write a function that determines if two strings are anagrams. The function should not be case sensitive and should disregard any punctuation or spaces. Two strings are anagrams if the letters can be rearranged to form each other. For example, "Eleven plus two" is an anagram of "Twelve plus one." Each string contains one "v", three "e's", two "l's", etc. Test your function with several strings that are anagrams and non-anagrams. You may use either the string class or a C-style string.

Pointers and Dynamic Arrays 9

Memory is necessary for all the operations of reason.

BLAISE PASCAL, *Pensées*

INTRODUCTION

A *pointer* is a construct that gives you more control of the computer's memory. This chapter shows how pointers are used with arrays and introduces a new form of array called a *dynamic array*. Dynamic arrays are arrays whose size is determined while the program is running, rather than being fixed when the program is written.

PREREQUISITES

Section 9.1, which covers the basics of pointers, uses material from Chapters 2 through 6. It does not require any of the material from Chapters 7 or 8. Section 9.2, which covers dynamic arrays, uses material from Section 9.1, and Chapters 2 through 7. It does not require any of the material from Chapter 8.

9.1 POINTERS

Do not mistake the pointing finger for the moon.

ZEN SAYING

A **pointer** is the memory address of a variable. Recall that the computer's memory is divided into numbered memory locations (called bytes) and that variables are implemented as a sequence of adjacent memory locations. Recall also that sometimes the C++ system uses these memory addresses as names for the variables. If a variable is implemented as, say, three memory locations, then the address of the first of these memory locations is sometimes used as a name for that variable. For example, when the variable is used as a call-by-reference argument, it is this address, not the identifier name of the variable, that is passed to the calling function.

An address that is used to name a variable in this way (by giving the address in memory where the variable starts) is called a *pointer* because the address can be thought of as "pointing" to the variable. The address "points" to the variable because it identifies the variable by telling *where* the variable is, rather than telling what the variable's name is. A variable that is, say, at location number 1007 can be pointed out by saying "it's the variable over there at location 1007."

You have already been using pointers in a number of situations. As we noted in the previous paragraph, when a variable is a call-by-reference argument in a function call, the function is given this argument variable in the form of a pointer to the variable. This is an important and powerful use for pointers, but it is done automatically for you by the C++ system. In this chapter, we show you how to write programs that manipulate pointers in any way you want, rather than relying on the system to manipulate the pointers for you.

Pointer Variables

A pointer can be stored in a variable. However, even though a pointer is a memory address and a memory address is a number, you cannot store a pointer in a variable of type *int* or *double* without type casting. A variable to hold a pointer must be declared to have a pointer type. For example, the following declares p to be a pointer variable that can hold one pointer that points to a variable of type *double*:

Declaring pointer variables

```
double *p;
```

The variable p can hold pointers to variables of type *double*, but it cannot normally contain a pointer to a variable of some other type, such as *int* or *char*. Each variable type requires a different pointer type.

In general, to declare a variable that can hold pointers to other variables of a specific type, you declare the pointer variable just as you would declare an ordinary variable of that type, but you place an asterisk in front of the variable name. For example, the following declares the variables p1 and p2 so that they can hold pointers to variables of type *int*; it also declares two ordinary variables, v1 and v2, of type *int*:

```
int *p1, *p2, v1, v2;
```

There must be an asterisk before *each* of the pointer variables. If you omit the second asterisk in the previous declaration, then p2 will not be a pointer variable; it will instead be an ordinary variable of type *int*. The asterisk is the same symbol you have been using for multiplication, but in this context it has a totally different meaning.

When discussing pointers and pointer variables, we usually speak of *pointing* rather than of *addresses*. When a pointer variable, such as p1, contains the address of a variable, such as v1, the pointer variable is said to *point to the variable* v1 or to be *a pointer to the variable* v1.

Pointer variables, like p1 and p2 declared earlier, can contain pointers to variables like v1 and v2. You can use the operator & to determine the address of a variable, and you can then assign that address to a pointer variable. For example, the following will set the variable p1 equal to a pointer that points to the variable v1:

```
p1 = &v1;
```

Pointer Variable Declarations

A variable that can hold pointers to other variables of type *Type_Name* is declared similarly to the way you declare a variable of type *Type_Name*, except that you place an asterisk at the beginning of the variable name.

SYNTAX

```
Type_Name *Variable_Name1, *Variable_Name2, . . .;
```

EXAMPLE

```
double *pointer1, *pointer2;
```

Addresses and Numbers

A pointer is an address, and an address is an integer, but a pointer is not an integer. That is not crazy. That is abstraction! C++ insists that you use a pointer as an address and that you not use it as a number. A pointer is not a value of type *int* or of any other numeric type. You normally cannot store a pointer in a variable of type *int*. If you try, most C++ compilers will give you an error message or a warning message. Also, you cannot perform the normal arithmetic operations on pointers. (You can perform a kind of addition and a kind of subtraction on pointers, but they are not the usual integer addition and subtraction.)

You now have two ways to refer to v1: You can call it v1 or you can call it "the variable pointed to by p1." In C++, the way that you say "the variable pointed to by p1" is *p1. This is the same asterisk that we used when we declared p1, but now it has yet another meaning. When the asterisk is used in this way, it is often called the **dereferencing operator,** and the pointer variable is said to be **dereferenced.**

Putting these pieces together can produce some surprising results. Consider the following code:

```
v1 = 0;
p1 = &v1;
*p1 = 42;
cout << v1 << endl;
cout << *p1 << endl;
```

This code outputs the following to the screen:

```
42
42
```

As long as p1 contains a pointer that points to v1, then v1 and *p1 refer to the same variable. So when you set *p1 equal to 42, you are also setting v1 equal to 42.

The symbol & that is used to obtain the address of a variable is the same symbol that you use in function declarations to specify a call-by-reference parameter. This use is not a coincidence. Recall that a call-by-reference argument is implemented by giving the address of the argument to the calling function. So, these two uses of the symbol & are very much the same. However, the usages are slightly different and we will consider them to be two different (although very closely related) usages of the symbol &.

The * and & Operators

The *operator in front of a pointer variable produces the variable it points to. When used this way, the *operator is called the **dereferencing operator.**

The operator & in front of an ordinary variable produces the address of that variable; that is, produces a pointer that points to the variable. The & operator is called the address-of operator.

For example, consider the declarations

```
double *p, v;
```

The following sets the value of p so that p points to the variable v:

```
p = &v;
```

*p produces the variable pointed to by p, so after the assignment above, *p and v refer to the same variable. For example, the following sets the value of v to 9.99, even though the name v is never explicitly used:

```
*p = 9.99;
```

You can assign the value of one pointer variable to another pointer variable. This copies an address from one pointer variable to another pointer variable. For example, if p1 is still pointing to v1, then the following will set p2 so that it also points to v1:

Pointers in assignment statements

```
p2 = p1;
```

Provided we have not changed v1's value, the following also outputs a 42 to the screen:

```
cout << *p2;
```

Be sure that you do not confuse

```
p1 = p2;
```

and

```
*p1 = *p2;
```

When you add the asterisk, you are not dealing with the pointers p1 and p2, but with the variables that the pointers are pointing to. This is illustrated in Display 9.1.

Since a pointer can be used to refer to a variable, your program can manipulate variables even if the variables have no identifiers to name them. The operator *new* can be used to create variables that have no identifiers to serve as their names. These nameless variables are referred to via pointers. For example, the following creates a new variable of type *int* and sets the pointer variable p1 equal to the address of this new variable (that is, p1 points to this new, nameless variable):

```
p1 = new int;
```

This new, nameless variable can be referred to as *p1 (that is, as the variable pointed to by p1). You can do anything with this nameless variable that you can do with any other variable of type *int*. For example, the following reads a value of type *int* from the keyboard into this nameless variable, adds 7 to the value, then outputs this new value:

```
cin >> *p1;
*p1 = *p1 + 7;
cout << *p1;
```

DISPLAY 9.1   Uses of the Assignment Operator

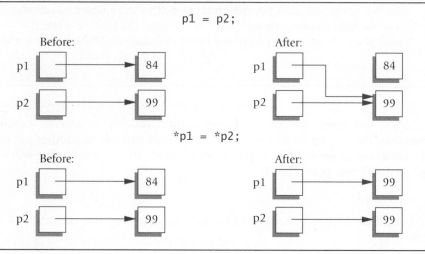

The *new* operator produces a new, nameless variable and returns a pointer that points to this new variable. You specify the type for this new variable by writing the type name after the *new* operator. Variables that are created using the *new* operator are called **dynamic variables** because they are created and destroyed while the program is running. The program in Display 9.2 demonstrates some simple operations on pointers and dynamic variables. Display 9.3 illustrates the working of the program in Display 9.2. In Display 9.3, variables are represented as boxes and the value of the variable is written inside the box. We have not shown the actual numeric addresses in the pointer variables. The actual numbers are not important. What is important is that the number is the address of some particular variable. So, rather than use the actual number of the address, we have merely indicated the address with an arrow that points to the variable with that address. For example, in illustration (b) in Display 9.3, p1 contains the address of a variable that has a question mark written in it.

DISPLAY 9.2   Basic Pointer Manipulations *(part 1 of 2)*

```
1     //Program to demonstrate pointers and dynamic variables.
2     #include <iostream>
3     using namespace std;
4
5     int main( )
6     {
7         int *p1, *p2;
8
9         p1 = new int;
10        *p1 = 42;
11        p2 = p1;
12        cout<< "*p1 == " << *p1 << endl;
13        cout<< "*p2 == " << *p2 << endl;
14
15        *p2 = 53;
16        cout<< "*p1 == " << *p1 << endl;
17        cout<< "*p2 == " << *p2 << endl;
18
19        p1 = new int;
20        *p1 = 88;
21        cout<< "*p1 == " << *p1 << endl;
22        cout<< "*p2 == " << *p2 << endl;
23        cout<< "Hope you got the point of this example!\n";
24        return 0;
25    }
```

(continued)

DISPLAY 9.2   Basic Pointer Manipulations *(part 2 of 2)*

Sample Dialogue

```
*p1 == 42
*p2 == 42
*p1 == 53
*p2 == 53
*p1 == 88
*p2 == 53
Hope you got the point of this example!
```

Pointer Variables Used with =

If p1 and p2 are pointer variables, then the statement

```
p1 = p2;
```

changes p1 so that it points to the same thing that p2 is currently pointing to.

The *new* Operator

The *new* operator creates a new dynamic variable of a specified type and returns a pointer that points to this new variable. For example, the following creates a new dynamic variable of type MyType and leaves the pointer variable p pointing to this new variable:

```
MyType *p;
p = new MyType;
```

The C++ standard specifies that if there is not sufficient memory available to create the new variable, then the *new* operator, by default, terminates the program.[1]

---

[1] Technically, the *new* operator throws an exception, which, if not caught, terminates the program. It is possible to "catch" the exception or install a new handler, but these topics are not covered until Chapter 16.

DISPLAY 9.3 Explanation of Display 9.2

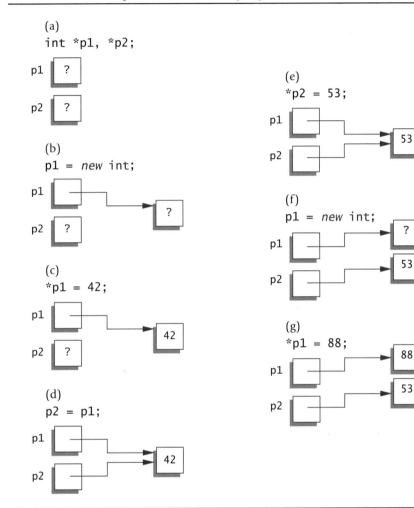

(a)
int *p1, *p2;

p1 [?]

p2 [?]

(b)
p1 = *new* int;

(c)
*p1 = 42;

(d)
p2 = p1;

(e)
*p2 = 53;

(f)
p1 = *new* int;

(g)
*p1 = 88;

▮ SELF-TEST EXERCISES

1. Explain the concept of a pointer in C++.

2. What unfortunate misinterpretation can occur with the following declaration?

   *int** int_ptr1, int_ptr2;

3. Give at least two uses of the * operator. State what the * is doing, and name the use of the * that you present.

4. What is the output produced by the following code?

```
int *p1, *p2;
p1 = new int;
p2 = new int;
*p1 = 10;
*p2 = 20;
cout << *p1 << " " << *p2 << endl;
p1 = p2;
cout << *p1 << " " << *p2 << endl;
*p1 = 30;
cout << *p1 << " " << *p2 << endl;
```

How would the output change if you were to replace

```
*p1 = 30;
```

with the following?

```
*p2 = 30;
```

5. What is the output produced by the following code?

```
int *p1, *p2;
p1 = new int;
p2 = new int;
*p1 = 10;
*p2 = 20;
cout << *p1 << " " << *p2 << endl;
*p1 = *p2; //This is different from Exercise 4
cout << *p1 << " " << *p2 << endl;
*p1 = 30;
cout << *p1 << " " << *p2 << endl;
```

Basic Memory Management

A special area of memory, called the **freestore,** is reserved for dynamic variables. Any new dynamic variable created by a program consumes some of the memory in the freestore.[2] If your program creates too many dynamic variables, it will consume all of the memory in the freestore. If this happens, any additional calls to *new* will fail.

The size of the freestore varies by computer and implementation of C++. It is typically large, and a modest program is not likely to use all the memory in the freestore. However, even on modest programs it is a good practice to recycle any freestore memory that is no longer needed. If your program no

---

[2] The freestore is also sometimes called the *heap.*

longer needs a dynamic variable, the memory used by that dynamic variable can be recycled. The *delete* operator eliminates a dynamic variable and returns the memory that the dynamic variable occupied to the freestore so that the memory can be reused. Suppose that p is a pointer variable that is pointing to a dynamic variable. The following will destroy the dynamic variable pointed to by p and return the memory used by the dynamic variable to the freestore:

> *delete* p;

After this call to *delete*, the value of p is undefined and p should be treated like an uninitialized variable.

The *delete* Operator

The *delete* operator eliminates a dynamic variable and returns the memory that the dynamic variable occupied to the freestore. The memory can then be reused to create new dynamic variables. For example, the following eliminates the dynamic variable pointed to by the pointer variable p:

> *delete* p;

After a call to *delete*, the value of the pointer variable, like p above, is undefined. (A slightly different version of *delete*, discussed later in this chapter, is used when the dynamic variable is an array.)

PITFALL   Dangling Pointers

When you apply *delete* to a pointer variable, the dynamic variable it is pointing to is destroyed. At that point, the value of the pointer variable is undefined, which means that you do not know where it is pointing, nor what the value is where it is pointing. Moreover, if some other pointer variable was pointing to the dynamic variable that was destroyed, then this other pointer variable is also undefined. These undefined pointer variables are called **dangling pointers.** If p is a dangling pointer and your program applies the dereferencing operator * to p (to produce the expression *p), the result is unpredictable and usually disastrous. Before you apply the dereferencing operator *to a pointer variable, you should be certain that the pointer variable points to some variable. ■

Static Variables and Automatic Variables

Variables created with the *new* operator are called **dynamic variables,** because they are created and destroyed while the program is running. When compared with these dynamic variables, ordinary variables seem static, but the terminology used by C++ programmers is a bit more involved than that, and ordinary variables are not called *static variables.*

The ordinary variables we have been using in previous chapters are not really static. If a variable is local to a function, then the variable is created by the C++ system when the function is called and is destroyed when the function call is completed. Since the main part of a program is really just a function called `main`, this is even true of the variables declared in the main part of your program. (Since the call to `main` does not end until the program ends, the variables declared in `main` are not destroyed until the program ends, but the mechanism for handling local variables is the same for `main` as it is for any other function.) The ordinary variables that we have been using (that is, the variables declared within `main` or within some other function definition) are called **automatic variables,** because their dynamic properties are controlled automatically for you; they are automatically created when the function in which they are declared is called and automatically destroyed when the function call ends. We will usually call these variables **ordinary variables,** but other books call them *automatic variables.*

There is one other category of variables, namely, **global variables.** Global variables are variables that are declared outside of any function definition (including being outside of `main`). We discussed global variables briefly in Chapter 4. As it turns out, we have no need for global variables and have not used them.

■ **PROGRAMMING TIP**   Define Pointer Types

You can define a pointer type name so that pointer variables can be declared like other variables without the need to place an asterisk in front of each pointer variable. For example, the following defines a type called `IntPtr`, which is the type for pointer variables that contain pointers to *int* variables:

```
typedef int* IntPtr;
```

Thus, the following two pointer variable declarations are equivalent:

```
IntPtr p;
```

and

```
int *p;
```

You can use *typedef* to define an alias for any type name or definition. For example, the following defines the type name `Kilometers` to mean the same thing as the type name *double*:

```
typedef double Kilometers;
```

Once you have given this type definition, you can define a variable of type *double* as follows:

```
Kilometers distance;
```

Renaming existing types this way can occasionally be useful. However, our main use of *typedef* will be to define types for pointer variables.

There are two advantages to using defined pointer type names, such as `IntPtr` defined earlier. First, it avoids the mistake of omitting an asterisk. Remember, if you intend p1 and p2 to be pointers, then the following is a mistake:

```
int *p1, p2;
```

Since the * was omitted from the p2, the variable p2 is just an ordinary *int* variable, not a pointer variable. If you get confused and place the * on the *int*, the problem is the same but is more difficult to notice. C++ allows you to place the * on the type name, such as *int*, so that the following is legal:

```
int* p1, p2;
```

Although this line is legal, it is misleading. It looks like both p1 and p2 are pointer variables, but in fact only p1 is a pointer variable; p2 is an ordinary *int* variable. As far as the C++ compiler is concerned, the *that is attached to the identifier *int* may as well be attached to the identifier p1. One correct way to declare both p1 and p2 to be pointer variables is

```
int *p1, *p2;
```

An easier and less error-prone way to declare both p1 and p2 to be pointer variables is to use the defined type name `IntPtr` as follows:

```
IntPtr p1, p2;
```

The second advantage of using a defined pointer type, such as `IntPtr`, is seen when you define a function with a call-by-reference parameter for a pointer variable. Without the defined pointer type name, you would need to include both an * and an & in the function declaration for the function, and the details can get confusing. If you use a type name for the pointer type, then a call-by-reference parameter for a pointer type involves no complications. You define a call-by-reference parameter for a defined pointer type just like you define any other call-by-reference parameter. Here's a sample:

```
void sample_function(IntPtr& pointer_variable);
```

Type Definitions

You can assign a name to a type definition and then use the type name to declare variables. This is done with the keyword *typedef*. These type definitions are normally placed outside of the body of the main part of your program (and outside the body of other functions) . We will use type definitions to define names for pointer types, as shown in the example below.

SYNTAX

```
typedef Known_Type_Definition New_Type_Name;
```

EXAMPLE

```
typedef int* IntPtr;
```

The type name IntPtr can then be used to declare pointers to dynamic variables of type *int*, as in the following:

```
IntPtr pointer1, pointer2;
```

myprogramminglab

SELF-TEST EXERCISES

6. Suppose a dynamic variable were created as follows:

   ```
   char *p;
   p = new char;
   ```

   Assuming that the value of the pointer variable p has not changed (so it still points to the same dynamic variable), how can you destroy this new dynamic variable and return the memory it uses to the freestore so that the memory can be reused to create new dynamic variables?

7. Write a definition for a type called NumberPtr that will be the type for pointer variables that hold pointers to dynamic variables of type *int*. Also, write a declaration for a pointer variable called my_point that is of type NumberPtr.

8. Describe the action of the *new* operator. What does the operator *new* return?

9.2 DYNAMIC ARRAYS

In this section you will see that array variables are actually pointer variables. You will also find out how to write programs with dynamic arrays. A **dynamic array** is an array whose size is not specified when you write the program, but is determined while the program is running.

Array Variables and Pointer Variables

In Chapter 7 we described how arrays are kept in memory. At that point we had not learned about pointers, so we discussed arrays in terms of memory addresses. But, a memory address is a pointer. So, in C++ an array variable is actually a pointer variable that points to the first indexed variable of the array. Given the following two variable declarations, p and a are the same kind of variable:

```
int a[10];
typedef int* IntPtr;
IntPtr p;
```

The fact that a and p are the same kind of variable is illustrated in Display 9.4. Since a is a pointer that points to a variable of type *int* (namely the variable a[0]), the value of a can be assigned to the pointer variable p as follows:

```
p = a;
```

After this assignment, p points to the same memory location that a points to. So, p[0], p[1], ... p[9] refer to the indexed variables a[0], a[1], ... a[9]. The square bracket notation you have been using for arrays applies to pointer variables as long as the pointer variable points to an array in memory. After this assignment, you can treat the identifier p as if it were an array identifier. You can also treat the identifier a as if it were a pointer variable, but there is one important reservation. *You cannot change the pointer value in an array variable, such as* a. You might be tempted to think the following is legal, but it is not:

```
IntPtr p2;
...//p2 is given some pointer value.
a = p2;//ILLEGAL. You cannot assign a different address to a.
```

Display 9.5 illustrates the working of the program in Display 9.4. As in Display 9.3, variables are represented as boxes and the value of the variable is written inside the box. An arrow indicates a pointer or reference to another memory location, in this case, the first element of the array.

DISPLAY 9.4 Arrays and Pointer Variables

```
1    //Program to demonstrate that an array variable is a kind of pointer variable.
2    #include <iostream>
3    using namespace std;
4
5    typedef int* IntPtr;
6
7    int main( )
8    {
9        IntPtr p;
10       int a[10];
11       int index;
12
13       for (index = 0; index < 10; index++)
14           a[index] = index;
15
16       p = a;
17
18       for (index = 0; index < 10; index++)
19           cout << p[index] << " ";
20       cout << endl;
21
22       for (index = 0; index < 10; index++)          Note that changes to the array p
23           p[index] = p[index] + 1;                   are also changes to the array a.
24
25       for (index = 0; index < 10; index++)
26           cout << a[index] << " ";
27       cout << endl;
28
29       return 0;
30   }
```

Output

```
0 1 2 3 4 5 6 7 8 9
1 2 3 4 5 6 7 8 9 10
```

Creating and Using Dynamic Arrays

One problem with the kinds of arrays you have used thus far is that you must specify the size of the array when you write the program—but you may not know what size array you need until the program is run. For example, an array might hold a list of student identification numbers, but the size of the class may be different each time the program is run. With the kinds of arrays you have used thus far, you must estimate the largest possible size you may need

DISPLAY 9.5   Explanation of Display 9.4

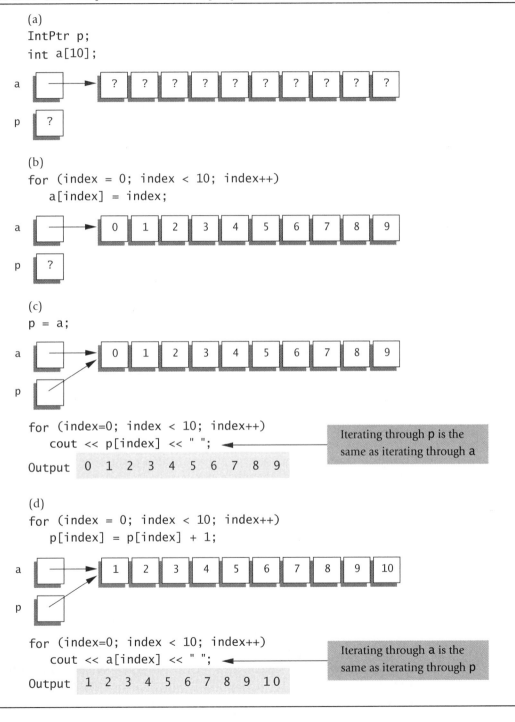

for the array and hope that size is large enough. There are two problems with this. First, you may estimate too low, and then your program will not work in all situations. Second, since the array might have many unused positions, this can waste computer memory. Dynamic arrays avoid these problems. If your program uses a dynamic array for student identification numbers, then the size of the class can be entered as input to the program and the dynamic array can be created to be exactly that size.

Creating a dynamic array

Dynamic arrays are created using the *new* operator. The creation and use of dynamic arrays is surprisingly simple. Since array variables are pointer variables, you can use the *new* operator to create dynamic variables that are arrays and treat these dynamic array variables as if they were ordinary arrays. For example, the following creates a dynamic array variable with ten array elements of type *double*:

```
typedef double* DoublePtr;
DoublePtr p;
p = new double [10];
```

To obtain a dynamic array of elements of any other type, simply replace *double* with the desired type. To obtain a dynamic array variable of any other size, simply replace 10 with the desired size.

There are also a number of less obvious things to notice about this example. First, the pointer type that you use for a pointer to a dynamic array is the same as the pointer type you would use for a single element of the array. For instance, the pointer type for an array of elements of type *double* is the same as the pointer type you would use for a simple variable of type *double*. The pointer to the array is actually a pointer to the first indexed variable of the array. In the previous example, an entire array with ten indexed variables is created and the pointer p is left pointing to the first of these ten indexed variables.

Also notice that when you call *new*, the size of the dynamic array is given in square brackets after the type, which in this example is the type *double*. This tells the computer how much storage to reserve for the dynamic array. If you omit the square brackets and the 10, the computer will allocate enough storage for only one variable of type *double*, rather than for an array of ten indexed variables of type *double*. As illustrated in Display 9.6, you can use an *int* variable in place of the constant 10 so that the size of the dynamic array can be read into the program.

The program in Display 9.6 sorts a list of numbers. This program works for lists of any size because it uses a dynamic array to hold the numbers. The size of the array is determined when the program is run. The user is asked how many numbers there will be, and then the *new* operator creates a dynamic array of that size. The size of the dynamic array is given by the variable array_ size.

Notice the *delete* statement, which destroys the dynamic array variable a in Display 9.6. Since the program is about to end anyway, we did not really need this *delete* statement; however, if the program went on to do other

DISPLAY 9.6   A Dynamic Array *(part 1 of 2)*

```
1    //Sorts a list of numbers entered at the keyboard.
2    #include <iostream>
3    #include <cstdlib>
4    #include <cstddef>
5
6    typedef int* IntArrayPtr;
7
8    void fill_array(int a[], int size);                          Ordinary array
9    //Precondition: size is the size of the array a.             parameters
10   //Postcondition: a[0] through a[size- 1] have been
11   //filled with values read from the keyboard.
12
13   void sort(int a[], int size);
14   //Precondition: size is the size of the array a.
15   //The array elements a[0] through a[size-1] have values.
16   //Postcondition: The values of a[0] through a[size-1] have been rearranged
17   //so that a[0] <= a[1] <= ... <= a[size-1].
18
19   int main( )
20   {
21       using namespace std;
22       cout << "This program sorts numbers from lowest to highest.\n";
23
24       int array_size;
25       cout << "How many numbers will be sorted? ";
26       cin >> array_size;
27
28       IntArrayPtr a;
29       a = new int[array_size];
30
31       fill_array(a, array_size);
32       sort(a, array_size);
33
34       cout << "In sorted order the numbers are:\n";
35       for (int index = 0; index < array_size; index++)
36           cout << a[index] << " ";                    The dynamic array a is
37       cout << endl;                                   used like an ordinary array.
38
39       delete [] a;
40
41       return 0;
42   }
43
44   //Uses the library iostream:
45   void fill_array(int a[], int size)
46   {
```

(continued)

DISPLAY 9.6 A Dynamic Array *(part 2 of 2)*

```
47          using namespace std;
48          cout << "Enter " << size << " integers.\n";
49          for (int index = 0; index < size; index++)
50              cin >> a[index];
51      }
52
53      void sort(int a[], int size)
```

<Any implementation of sort may be used. This may or may not require some additional function definitions. The implementation need not even know that sort will be called with a dynamic array. For example, you can use the implementation in Display 7.12 (with suitable adjustments to parameter names).>

things with dynamic variables, you would want such a *delete* statement so that the memory used by this dynamic array is returned to the freestore. The *delete* statement for a dynamic array is similar to the *delete* statement you saw earlier, except that with a dynamic array you must include an empty pair of square brackets, like so:

```
delete [] a;
```

The square brackets tell C++ that a dynamic array variable is being eliminated, so the system checks the size of the array and removes that many indexed variables. If you omit the square brackets, you would be telling the computer to eliminate only one variable of type *int*. For example,

```
delete a;
```

is not legal, but the error is not detected by most compilers. The ANSI C++ standard says that what happens when you do this is "undefined." That means the author of the compiler can have this do anything that is convenient— convenient for the compiler writer, not for you. Even if it does something useful, you have no guarantee that either the next version of that compiler or any other compiler you compile this code with will do the same thing. The moral is simple: Always use the

```
delete [] array_ptr;
```

syntax when you are deleting memory that was allocated with something like

```
array_ptr = new MyType[37];
```

You create a dynamic array with a call to *new* using a pointer, such as the pointer a in Display 9.6. After the call to *new*, you should not assign any other pointer value to this pointer variable, because that can confuse the system when the memory for the dynamic array is returned to the freestore with a call to *delete*.

How to Use a Dynamic Array

- *Define a pointer type:* Define a type for pointers to variables of the same type as the elements of the array. For example, if the dynamic array is an array of *double*, you might use the following:

    ```
    typedef double* DoubleArrayPtr;
    ```

- *Declare a pointer variable:* Declare a pointer variable of this defined type. The pointer variable will point to the dynamic array in memory and will serve as the name of the dynamic array.

    ```
    DoubleArrayPtr a;
    ```

- *Call new:* Create a dynamic array using the *new* operator:

    ```
    a = new double[array_size];
    ```

    The size of the dynamic array is given in square brackets as in the example above. The size can be given using an *int* variable or other *int* expression. In the example above, `array_size` can be a variable of type *int* whose value is determined while the program is running.

- *Use like an ordinary array:* The pointer variable, such as a, is used just like an ordinary array. For example, the indexed variables are written in the usual way: `a[0]`, `a[1]`, and so forth. The pointer variable should not have any other pointer value assigned to it, but should be used like an array variable.

- *Call delete[ ]:* When your program is finished with the dynamic variable, use *delete* and empty square brackets along with the pointer variable to eliminate the dynamic array and return the storage that it occupies to the freestore for reuse. For example:

    ```
    delete [] a;
    ```

Dynamic arrays are created using *new* and a pointer variable. When your program is finished using a dynamic array, you should return the array memory to the freestore with a call to *delete*. Other than that, a dynamic array can be used just like any other array.

SELF-TEST EXERCISES

myprogramminglab

9. Write a type definition for pointer variables that will be used to point to dynamic arrays. The array elements are to be of type *char*. Call the type CharArray.

10. Suppose your program contains code to create a dynamic array as follows:

```
int *entry;
entry = new int[10];
```

so that the pointer variable entry is pointing to this dynamic array. Write code to fill this array with ten numbers typed in at the keyboard.

11. Suppose your program contains code to create a dynamic array as in Self-Test Exercise 10, and suppose the pointer variable entry has not had its (pointer) value changed. Write code to destroy this new dynamic array and return the memory it uses to the freestore.

12. What is the output of the following code fragment? The code is assumed to be embedded in a correct and complete program.

```
int a[10];
int *p = a;
int i;
for (i = 0; i < 10; i++)
    a[i] = i;

for (i = 0; i < 10; i++)
    cout << p[i] << " ";
cout << endl;
```

13. What is the output of the following code fragment? The code is assumed to be embedded in a correct and complete program.

```
int array_size = 10;
int *a;
a = new int [array_size];
int *p = a;
int i;
for (i = 0; i < array_size; i++)
    a[i] = i;
p[0] = 10;

for (i = 0; i < array_size; i++)
    cout << a[i] << " ";
cout << endl;
```

Pointer Arithmetic (*Optional*)

There is a kind of arithmetic you can perform on pointers, but it is an arithmetic of addresses, not an arithmetic of numbers. For example, suppose your program contains the following code:

```
typedef double* DoublePtr;
DoublePtr d;
d = new double[10];
```

After these statements, d contains the address of the indexed variable d[0]. The expression d + 1 evaluates to the address of d[1], d + 2 is the address of d[2], and so forth. Notice that although the value of d is an address and an address is a number, d+1 does not simply add 1 to the number in d. If a variable of type *double* requires 8bytes (eight memory locations) and d contains the address 2001, then d+1 evaluates to the memory address 2009. Of course, the type *double* can be replaced by any other type and then pointer addition moves in units of variables for that type.

This pointer arithmetic gives you an alternative way to manipulate arrays. For example, if array_size is the size of the dynamic array pointed to by d, then the following will output the contents of the dynamic array:

```
for (int i = 0; i < array_size; i++)
    cout << *(d + i)<< " ";
```

This code is equivalent to the following:

```
for(int i = 0; i < array_size; i++)
    cout << d[i] << " ";
```

You may not perform multiplication or division of pointers. All you can do is add an integer to a pointer, subtract an integer from a pointer, or subtract two pointers of the same type. When you subtract two pointers, the result is the number of indexed variables between the two addresses. Remember, for subtraction of two pointer values, these values must point into the same array! It makes little sense to subtract a pointer that points into one array from another pointer that points into a different array. You can use the increment and decrement operators ++ and −−. For example, d++ will advance the value of d so that it contains the address of the next indexed variable, and d−− will change d so that it contains the address of the previous indexed variable.

VideoNote
Dynamic Arrays and Pointer
Arithmetic

SELF-TEST EXERCISES

myprogramming**lab**

These exercises apply to the optional section on pointer arithmetic.

14. What is the output of the following code fragment? The code is assumed to be embedded in a correct and complete program.

```
int array_size = 10;
int *a;
a = new int[array_size];
int i;
for (i = 0; i < array_size; i++)
    *(a + i) = i;

for (i = 0; i < array_size; i++)
    cout << a[i] << " ";
cout << endl;
```

15. What is the output of the following code fragment? The code is assumed to be embedded in a correct and complete program.

```
int array_size = 10;
int *a;
a = new int[array_size];
int i;
for (i = 0; i < array_size; i++)
    a[i] = i;
while (*a < 9)
{
    a++;
    cout << *a << " ";
}
cout << endl;
```

Multidimensional Dynamic Arrays (*Optional*)

You can have multidimensional dynamic arrays. You just need to remember that multidimensional arrays are arrays of arrays, or arrays of arrays of arrays, or so forth. For example, to create a two-dimensional dynamic array, you must remember that it is an array of arrays. To create a two-dimensional array of integers, you first create a one-dimensional dynamic array of pointers of type *int**, which is the type for a one-dimensional array of *int*s. Then you create a dynamic array of *int*s for each indexed variable of the array of pointers.

A type definition may help to keep things straight. The following is the variable type for an ordinary one-dimensional dynamic array of *int*s:

```
typedef int* IntArrayPtr;
```

To obtain a 3-by-4 array of *int*s, you want an array whose base type is IntArrayPtr. For example:

```
IntArrayPtr *m = new IntArrayPtr[3];
```

This is an array of three pointers, each of which can name a dynamic array of *int*s, as follows:

```
for (int i = 0; i < 3; i++)
    m[i] = new int[4];
```

The resulting array m is a 3-by-4 dynamic array. A simple program to illustrate this is given in Display 9.7.

Be sure to notice the use of *delete* in Display 9.7. Since the dynamic array m is an array of arrays, each of the arrays created with *new* in the *for* loop must be returned to the freestore manager with a call to *delete*[];

then, the array m itself must be returned to the freestore with another call to *delete*[]. There must be one call to *delete*[] for each call to *new* that created an array. (Since the program ends right after the calls to *delete*[], we could safely omit these calls, but we wanted to illustrate their usage.)

DISPLAY 9.7   A Two-Dimensional Dynamic Array *(part 1 of 2)*

```
1    #include <iostream>
2     using namespace std;
3
4     typedef int* IntArrayPtr;
5
6     int main( )
7     {
8         int d1, d2;
9         cout << "Enter the row and column dimensions of the array:\n";
10        cin >> d1 >> d2;
11
12        IntArrayPtr *m = new IntArrayPtr[d1];
13        int i, j;
14        for (i = 0; i < d1; i++)
15            m[i] = new int[d2];
16        //m is now a d1 by d2 array.
17
18        cout << "Enter " << d1 << " rows of "
19            << d2 << " integers each:\n";
20        for (i = 0; i < d1; i++)
21            for (j = 0; j < d2; j++)
22                cin >> m[i][j];
23
24        cout << "Echoing the two-dimensional array:\n";
25        for (i = 0; i < d1; i++)
26        {
27            for (j = 0; j < d2; j++)
28                cout << m[i][j] << " ";
29            cout << endl;
30        }
31        for (i = 0; i < d1; i++)
32            delete[] m[i];
33        delete[] m;
34
35        return 0;
36    }
```

Note that there must be one call to delete[ ] for each call to new that created an array. (These calls to delete[ ] are not really needed, since the program is ending, but in another context it could be important to include them.)

(continued)

DISPLAY 9.7 A Two-Dimensional Dynamic Array *(part2 of 2)*

Sample Dialogue

```
Enter the row and column dimensions of the array:
3 4
Enter 3 rows of 4 integers each:
1 2 3 4
5 6 7 8
9 0 1 2
Echoing the two-dimensional array:
1 2 3 4
5 6 7 8
9 0 1 2
```

CHAPTER SUMMARY

- A **pointer** is a memory address, so a pointer provides a way to indirectly name a variable by naming the address of the variable in the computer's memory.

- **Dynamic variables** are variables that are created (and destroyed) while a program is running.

- Memory for dynamic variables is in a special portion of the computer's memory called the **freestore**. When a program is finished with a dynamic variable, the memory used by the dynamic variable can be returned to the freestore for reuse; this is done with a *delete* statement.

- A **dynamic array** is an array whose size is determined when the program is running. A dynamic array is implemented as a dynamic variable of an array type.

Answers to Self-Test Exercises

1. A pointer is the memory address of a variable.

2. To the unwary, or to the neophyte, this looks like two objects of type pointer to *int*, that is, *int**. Unfortunately, the * binds to the *identifier*, not to the type (that is, not to the *int*). The result is that this declaration declares *int_ptr1* to be an *int* pointer, while *int_ptr2* is just an ordinary *int* variable.

3. *int* *p;   //*This declares a pointer variable that can*
          //*hold a pointer to an int variable.*
   *p = 17;   //*Here,* * *is the dereference operator.*
   //*This assigns 17 to the memory location pointed to by p.*

4.
   ```
   10 20
   20 20
   30 30
   ```

   If you replace *p1 = 30; with *p2 = 30;, the output would be the same.

5.
   ```
   10 20
   20 20
   30 20
   ```

6. *delete* p;

7. *typedef int** NumberPtr;
   NumberPtr my_point;

8. The *new* operator takes a type for its argument. *new* allocates space on the freestore of an appropriate size for a variable of the type of the argument. It returns a pointer to that memory (that is, a pointer to that new dynamic variable), provided there is enough available memory in the freestore. If there is not enough memory available in the freestore, your program ends.

9. *typedef char** CharArray;

10. cout << "Enter 10 integers:\n";
    for (*int* i = 0; i < 10; i++)
        cin >> entry[i];

11. *delete* [] entry;

12. 0 1 2 3 4 5 6 7 8 9

13. 10 1 2 3 4 5 6 7 8 9

14. 0 1 2 3 4 5 6 7 8 9

15. 1 2 3 4 5 6 7 8 9

PROGRAMMING PROJECTS

Visit www.myprogramminglab.com to complete many of these Programming Projects online and get instant feedback.   (myprogramminglab)

1. Do Programming Project 7 in Chapter 7 using a dynamic array. In this version of the problem, use dynamic arrays to store the digits in each large integer. Allow an arbitrary number of digits instead of capping the number of digits at 20.

2. Do Programming Project 3 in Chapter 7. In this version of the problem, return a new dynamic array where all repeated letters are deleted instead of modifying the partially filled array. Don't forget to free the memory allocated for these returned dynamic arrays when the data is no longer needed.

3. Do Programming Project 11 in Chapter 7 using a dynamic array (or arrays). In this version, your program will ask the user how many rows the plane has and will handle that many rows (and so not always assume the plane has 7 rows as it did in Programming Project 11 of Chapter 7).

4. Write a function that takes a C string as an input parameter and reverses the string. The function should use two pointers, *front* and *rear*. The *front* pointer should initially reference the first character in the string, and the *rear* pointer should initially reference the last character in the string. Reverse the string by swapping the characters referenced by *front* and *rear*, then increment *front* to point to the next character and decrement *rear* to point to the preceding character, and so on, until the entire string is reversed. Write a main program to test your function on various strings of both even and odd length.

5. You run four computer labs. Each lab contains computer stations that are numbered as shown in the table below:

Lab Number	Computer Station Numbers
1	1–5
2	1–6
3	1–4
4	1–3

Each user has a unique five-digit ID number. Whenever a user logs on, the user's ID, lab number, and the computer station number are transmitted to your system. For example, if user 49193 logs onto station 2 in lab 3, then your system receives (49193, 2, 3) as input data. Similarly, when a user logs off a station, then your system receives the lab number and computer station number.

Write a computer program that could be used to track, by lab, which user is logged onto which computer. For example, if user 49193 is logged into station 2 in lab 3 and user 99577 is logged into station 1 of lab 4, then your system might display the following:

```
Lab Number Computer Stations
1          1: empty 2: empty 3: empty 4: empty 5: empty
2          1: empty 2: empty 3: empty 4: empty 5: empty 6: empty
3          1: empty 2: 49193 3: empty 4: empty
4          1: 99577 2: empty 3: empty
```

Create a menu that allows the administrator to simulate the transmission of information by manually typing in the login or logoff data. Whenever someone logs in or out, the display should be updated. Also write a search option so that the administrator can type in a user ID and the system will output what lab and station number that user is logged into, or "None" if the user ID is not logged into any computer station.

You should use a fixed array of length 4 for the labs. Each array entry points to a dynamic array that stores the user login information for each respective computer station.

The structure is shown in the figure below. This structure is sometimes called a ragged array since the columns are of unequal length.

Lab Array   Dynamic Arrays for Computer Stations

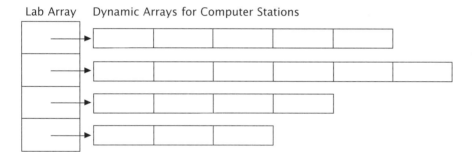

6. One problem with dynamic arrays is that once the array is created using the new operator, the size cannot be changed. For example, you might want to add or delete entries from the array as you can with a vector. This project asks you to create functions that use dynamic arrays to emulate the behavior of a vector.

VideoNote
Solution to Programming
Project 9.6

First, write a program that creates a dynamic array of five strings. Store five names of your choice into the dynamic array. Next, complete the following two functions:

```
string* addEntry(string *dynamicArray, int &size, string
             newEntry);
```

This function should create a new dynamic array one element larger than dynamicArray, copy all elements from dynamicArray into the new array, add the new entry onto the end of the new array, increment size, delete dynamicArray, and return the new dynamic array.

```
string* deleteEntry(string *dynamicArray, int &size, string
              entryToDelete);
```

This function should search dynamicArray for entryToDelete. If not found, the request should be ignored and the unmodified dynamicArray returned. If found, create a new dynamic array one element smaller than dynamicArray. Copy all elements except entryToDelete into the new array, delete dynamicArray, decrement size, and return the new dynamic array.

Test your functions by adding and deleting several names to the array while outputting the contents of the array. You will have to assign the array returned by addEntry or deleteEntry back to the dynamic array variable in your main function.

7. What if C++ had no built-in facility for two-dimensional arrays? It is possible to emulate them yourself with wrapper functions around a one-dimensional array. The basic idea is shown below. Consider the following two-dimensional array:

```
int matrix[2][3];
```

It can be visualized as a table:

matrix[0][0]	matrix[0][1]	matrix[0][2]
matrix[1][0]	matrix[1][1]	matrix[1][2]

The two-dimensional array can be mapped to storage in a one-dimensional array where each row is stored in consecutive memory locations (your compiler actually does something very similar to map two-dimensional arrays to memory).

```
int matrix1D[6];
```

matrix[0][0]	matrix1D[0][1]	matrix1D[0][2]	matrix1D[1][0]	matrix1D[1][1]	matrix1D[1][2]

Here, the mapping is as follows:

```
matrix[0][0] would be stored in matrix1D[0]
matrix[0][1] would be stored in matrix1D[1]
matrix[0][2] would be stored in matrix1D[2]
matrix[1][0] would be stored in matrix1D[3]
matrix[1][1] would be stored in matrix1D[4]
matrix[1][2] would be stored in matrix1D[5]
```

Based on this idea, complete the definitions for the following functions:

```
int* create2DArray(int rows, int columns);
```

This creates a one-dimensional dynamic array to emulate a two-dimensional array and returns a pointer to the one-dimensional dynamic array.

rows is the number of rows desired in the two-dimensional array.

columns is the number of columns desired in the two-dimensional array.

Return value: a pointer to a one-dimensional dynamic array large enough to hold a two-dimensional array of size rows * columns.

Note that `int ptr = create2DArray(2,3);` would create an array analogous to that created by `int ptr[2][3];`

```
void set(int *arr, int rows, int columns,
        int desired_row, int desired_column, int val);
```

This stores `val` into the emulated two-dimensional array at position `desired_row, desired_column`. The function should print an error message and exit if the desired indices are invalid.

arr is the one-dimensional array used to emulate a two-dimensional array.

rows is the total number of rows in the two-dimensional array.

columns is the total number of columns in the two-dimensional array.

desired_row is the zero-based index of the row the caller would like to access.

desired_column is the zero-based index of the column the caller would like to access.

val is the value to store at desired_row and desired_column.

```
int get(int *arr, int rows, int columns,
        int desired_row, int desired_column);
```

This returns the value in the emulated two-dimensional array at position `desired_row, desired_column`. The function should print an error message and exit if the desired indices are invalid.

arr is the one-dimensional array used to emulate a two-dimensional array.

rows is the total number of rows in the two-dimensional array.

columns is the total number of columns in the two-dimensional array.

desired_row is the zero-based index of the row the caller would like to access.

desired_column is the zero-based index of the column the caller would like to access.

Create a suitable test program that invokes all three functions.

8. Write a program that outputs a histogram of student grades for an assignment. The program should input each student's grade as an integer and store the grade in a vector (covered in Chapter 8). Grades should be

entered until the user enters -1 for a grade. The program should then scan through the vector and compute the histogram. In computing the histogram, the minimum value of a grade is 0 but your program should determine the maximum value entered by the user. Use a dynamic array to store the histogram. Output the histogram to the console. For example, if the input is:

```
20
30
4
20
30
30
-1
```

Then the output should be:

```
Number of 4's:    1
Number of 20's:   2
Number of 30's:   3
```

Defining Classes 10

"The time has come," the Walrus said,
"To talk of many things:
Of shoes—and ships—and sealing wax—
Of cabbages—and kings—"

LEWIS CARROLL, *Through the Looking-Glass*

INTRODUCTION

In Chapter 6 you learned how to use classes and objects, but not how to define classes. In this chapter we will show you how to define your own classes. A class is a data type. You can use the classes you define in the same way you use the predefined data types, such as *int*, *char*, and ifstream. However, unless you define your classes the right way, they will not be as well behaved as the predefined data types. Thus, we spend a good deal of time explaining what makes for a good class definition and give you some techniques to help you define your classes in a way that is consistent with modern programming practices.

Before we introduce classes, we will first present *structures* (also known as *structs*). When used in the way we present them here, a structure is a kind of simplified class and structures will prove to be a stepping-stone to understanding classes.

PREREQUISITES

This chapter uses material from Chapters 2 through 6.

10.1 STRUCTURES

As we said in Chapter 6, an object is a variable that has member functions, and a class is a data type whose variables are objects. Thus, the definition of a class should be a data type definition that describes two things: (1) what kinds of values the variables can hold and (2) what the member functions are. We will approach class definitions in two steps. We will first tell you how to give a type definition for a *structure*. A structure (of the kind discussed here) can be thought of as an object without any member functions. After you learn about structures, it will be a natural extension to define classes.

Structures for Diverse Data

Sometimes it is useful to have a collection of values of different types and to treat the collection as a single item. For example, consider a bank certificate of deposit, which is often called a CD. A CD is a bank account that does not allow withdrawals for a specified number of months. A CD naturally has three pieces of data associated with it: the account balance, the interest rate for the account, and the term, which is the number of months until maturity. The first two items can be represented as values of type *double*, and the number of months can be represented as a value of type *int*. Display 10.1 shows the definition of a structure called CDAccount that can be used for this kind of account. The definition is embedded in a complete program that demonstrates this structure type definition. As you can see from the sample dialogue, this particular bank specializes in short-term CDs, so the term will always be 12 or fewer months. Let's look at how this sample structure is defined and used.

The structure definition is as follows:

```
struct CDAccount
{
    double balance;
    double interest_rate;
    int term; //months until maturity
};
```

The keyword *struct* announces that this is a structure type definition. The identifier CDAccount is the name of the structure type. The name of a structure type is called the **structure tag.** The tag can be any legal identifier (but not a keyword). Although this convention is not required by the C++ language, structure tags are usually spelled with a mix of uppercase and lowercase letters, beginning with an uppercase letter. The identifiers declared inside the braces, {}, are called **member names.** As illustrated in this example, a structure type definition ends with both a brace, }, and a semicolon.

A structure definition is usually placed outside of any function definition (in the same way that globally defined constant declarations are placed outside of all function definitions). The structure type is then available to all the code that follows the structure definition.

Where to place a structure definition

Once a structure type definition has been given, the structure type can be used just like the predefined types *int*, *char*, and so forth. For example, the following will declare two variables, named my_account and your_account, both of type CDAccount:

```
CDAccount my_account, your_account;
```

A structure variable can hold values just like any other variable can hold values. A **structure value** is a collection of smaller values called **member values.** There is one member value for each member name declared in the structure definition. For example, a value of the type CDAccount is a collection of three member values: two of type *double* and one of type *int*. The member values that together make up the structure value are stored in *member variables*, which we discuss next.

Each structure type specifies a list of member names. In Display 10.1 the structure CDAccount has the three member names balance, interest_rate,

DISPLAY 10.1   A Structure Definition *(part 1 of 2)*

```
1    //Program to demonstrate the CDAccount structure type.
2    #include <iostream>
3    using namespace std;
4    //Structure for a bank certificate of deposit:
5    struct CDAccount
6    {
7        double balance;
8        double interest_rate;
9        int term; //months until maturity
10   };
11
12
13   void get_data(CDAccount& the_account);
14   //Postcondition: the_account.balance and the_account.interest_rate
15   //have been given values that the user entered at the keyboard.
16
17
18   int main( )
19   {
20       CDAccount account;
21       get_data(account);
22
23       double rate_fraction, interest;
24       rate_fraction = account.interest_rate / 100.0;
25       interest = account.balance * rate_fraction * (account.term / 12.0);
26       account.balance = account.balance + interest;
27
28       cout.setf(ios::fixed);
29       cout.setf(ios::showpoint);
30       cout.precision(2);
31       cout << "When your CD matures in "
32            << account.term << " months,\n"
33            << "it will have a balance of $"
34            << account.balance << endl;
35       return 0;
36   }
37
38   //Uses iostream:
39   void get_data(CDAccount& the_account)
40   {
41       cout << "Enter account balance: $";
42       cin >> the_account.balance;
43       cout << "Enter account interest rate: ";
44       cin >> the_account.interest_rate;
45       cout << "Enter the number of months until maturity\n"
46            << "(must be 12 or fewer months): ";
47       cin >> the_account.term;
48   }
```

(continued)

DISPLAY 10.1   A Structure Definition *(part 2 of 2)*

Sample Dialogue

```
Enter account balance: $100.00
Enter account interest rate: 10.0
Enter the number of months until maturity
(must be 12 or fewer months): 6
When your CD matures in 6 months,
it will have a balance of $105.00
```

and `term`. Each of these member names can be used to pick out one smaller variable that is a part of the larger structure variable. These smaller variables are called **member variables.** Member variables are specified by giving the name of the structure variable followed by a dot (that is, followed by a period) and then the member name. For example, if account is a structure variable of type CDAccount (as declared in Display 10.1), then the structure variable account has the following three member variables:

```
account.balance
account.interest_rate
account.term
```

The first two member variables are of type *double*, and the last is of type *int*. These member variables can be used just like any other variables of those types. For example, the member variables above can be given values with the following three assignment statements:

```
account.balance = 1000.00;
account.interest_rate = 4.7;
account.term = 11;
```

The result of these three statements is diagrammed in Display 10.2. Member variables can be used in all the ways that ordinary variables can be used. For example, the following line from the program in Display 10.1 will add the value contained in the member variable account.balance and the value contained in the ordinary variable interest and will then place the result in the member variable account.balance:

```
account.balance = account.balance + interest;
```

Notice that you specify a member variable for a structure variable by using the dot operator in the same way you used it in Chapter 6, where the dot operator was used to specify a member function of a class. The only difference is that in the case of structures, the members are variables rather than functions.

DISPLAY 10.2   Member Values

```
1     struct CDAccount
2     {
3         double balance;
4         double interest_rate;
5         int term; //months until maturity
6     };
7     int main( )
8     {
9         CDAccount account;
10            ...
11
12

13        account.balance = 1000.00;
14
15

16        account.interest_rate = 4.7;
17
18

19        account.term = 11;
20
21
22
```

balance	?	
interest_rate	?	} account
term	?	

balance	1000.00	
interest_rate	?	} account
term	?	

balance	1000.00	
interest_rate	4.7	} account
term	?	

balance	1000.00	
interest_rate	4.7	} account
term	11	

Reusing member names

Two or more structure types may use the same member names. For example, it is perfectly legal to have the following two type definitions in the same program:

```
struct FertilizerStock
{
    double quantity;
    double nitrogen_content;
};
```

and

```
struct CropYield
{
    int quantity;
    double size;
};
```

This coincidence of names will produce no problems. For example, if you declare the following two structure variables:

```
FertilizerStock super_grow;
CropYield apples;
```

then the quantity of `super_grow` fertilizer is stored in the member variable `super_grow.quantity` and the quantity of apples produced is stored in the member variable `apples.quantity`. The dot operator and the structure variable specify which `quantity` is meant in each instance.

A structure value can be viewed as a collection of member values. Viewed this way, a structure value is many different values. A structure value can also be viewed as a single (complex) value (which just happens to be made up of member values). Since a structure value can be viewed as a single value, structure values and structure variables can be used in the same ways that you use simple values and simple variables of the predefined types such as *int*. In particular, you can assign structure values using the equal sign. For example, if `apples` and `oranges` are structure variables of the type `CropYield` defined earlier, then the following is perfectly legal:

Structure variables in assignment statements

```
apples = oranges;
```

This assignment statement is equivalent to:

```
apples.quantity = oranges.quantity;
apples.size = oranges.size;
```

PITFALL   Forgetting a Semicolon in a Structure Definition

When you add the final brace, }, to a structure definition, it feels like the structure definition is finished, but it is not. You must also place a semicolon after that final brace. There is a reason for this, even though the reason is a feature that we will have no occasion to use. A structure definition is more than a definition. It can also be used to declare structure variables. You are allowed to list structure variable names between that final brace and that final semicolon. For example, the following defines a structure called `WeatherData` and declares two structure variables, `data_point1` and `data_point2`, both of type `WeatherData`:

```
struct WeatherData
{
    double temperature;
    double wind_velocity;
} data_point1, data_point2;
```

However, as we said, we will always separate a structure definition and the declaration of variables of that structure type, so our structure definitions will always have a semicolon immediately after the final brace.   ■

The Dot Operator

The **dot operator** is used to specify a member variable of a structure variable.

SYNTAX

— Dot operator

Structure_Variable_Name.Member_Variable_Name

```
struct StudentRecord
{
    int student_number;
    char grade;
};

int main()
{
    StudentRecord your_record;
    your_record.student_number = 2001;
    your_record.grade = 'A';
```

Some writers call the dot operator the *structure member access operator* although we will not use that term.

Structures as Function Arguments

A function can have call-by-value parameters of a structure type and/or call-by-reference parameters of a structure type. The program in Display 10.1, for example, includes a function named get_data that has a call-by-reference parameter with the structure type CDAccount.

Functions can return structures

A structure type can also be the type for the value returned by a function. For example, the following defines a function that takes three appropriate arguments and returns a value of type CDAccount:

```
CDAccount shrink_wrap(double the_balance,
                      double the_rate, int the_term)
{
    CDAccount temp;
    temp.balance = the_balance;
    temp.interest_rate = the_rate;
    temp.term = the_term;
    return temp;
}
```

Notice the local variable temp of type CDAccount; temp is used to build up a complete structure value, which is then returned by the function. Once you have defined the function shrink_wrap, you can give a value to a variable of type CDAccount as illustrated by the following:

```
CDAccount new_account;
new_account = shrink_wrap(10000.00, 5.1, 11);
```

■ PROGRAMMING TIP   Use Hierarchical Structures

Sometimes it makes sense to have structures whose members are themselves smaller structures. For example, a structure type called PersonInfo, which can be used to store a person's height, weight, and birth date, can be defined as follows:

Structures within structures

```
struct Date
{
    int month;
    int day;
    int year;
};

struct PersonInfo
{
    double height; //in inches
    int weight; //in pounds
    Date birthday;
};
```

A structure variable of type PersonInfo is declared in the usual way:

```
PersonInfo person1;
```

If the structure variable person1 has had its value set to record a person's birth date, then the year the person was born can be output to the screen as follows:

```
cout << person1.birthday.year;
```

The way to read such expressions is left to right, and very carefully. Starting at the left end, person1 is a structure variable of type PersonInfo. To obtain the member variable with the name birthday, use the dot operator as follows:

```
person1.birthday
```

This member variable is itself a structure variable of type Date. Thus, this member variable has member variables itself. A member variable of the structure variable person1.birthday is obtained by adding a dot and the member variable name, such as year, which produces the expression person1.birthday.year shown previously.   ■

Simple Structure Types

You define a **structure type** as shown below. The *Structure_Tag* is the name of the structure type.

SYNTAX

```
struct Structure_Tag
{
    Type_1 Member_Variable_Name_1;
    Type_2 Member_Variable_Name_2;
        .
        .
        .
    Type_Last Member_Variable_Name_Last;
};  ←————————— Do not forget this semicolon.
```

EXAMPLE

```
struct Automobile
{
    int year;
    int doors;
    double horse_power;
    char model;
};
```

Although we will not use this feature, you can combine member names of the same type into a single list separated by commas. For example, the following is equivalent to the previous structure definition:

```
struct Automobile
{
    int year, doors;
    double horse_power;
    char model;
};
```

Variables of a structure type can be declared in the same way as variables of other types. For example:

```
Automobile my_car, your_car;
```

The member variables are specified using the **dot operator.** For example,

```
my_car.year, my_car.doors, my_car.horse_power, and
my_car.model.
```

Initializing Structures

You can initialize a structure at the time that it is declared. To give a structure variable a value, you follow it by an equal sign and a list of the member values enclosed in braces. For example, the following definition of a structure type for a date was given in the previous subsection:

```
struct Date
{
    int month;
    int day;
    int year;
};
```

Once the type Date is defined, you can declare and initialize a structure variable called due_date as follows:

```
Date due_date = {12, 31, 2004};
```

Be sure to notice that the initializing values must be given in the order that corresponds to the order of member variables in the structure type definition. In this example, due_date.month receives the first initializing value of 12, due_date.day receives the second value of 31, and due_date.year receives the third value of 2004.

It is an error if there are more initializers than *struct* members. If there are fewer initializer values than *struct* members, the provided values are used to initialize data members, in order. Each data member without an initializer is initialized to a zero value of an appropriate type for the variable.

SELF-TEST EXERCISES

myprogramminglab

1. Given the following structure and structure variable declaration:

```
struct TermAccount
{
    double balance;
    double interest_rate;
    int term;
    char initial1;
    char initial2;
};
TermAccount account;
```

what is the type of each of the following? Mark any that are not correct.

a. `account.balance`

b. `account.interest_rate`

    c.   `TermAccount.term`

    d.   `savings_account.initial1`

    e.   `account.initial2`

    f.   `account`

2. Consider the following type definition:

```
struct ShoeType
{
    char style;
    double price;
};
```

Given this structure type definition, what will be the output produced by the following code?

```
ShoeType shoe1, shoe2;
shoe1.style ='A';
shoe1.price = 9.99;
cout << shoe1.style << " $" << shoe1.price << endl;
shoe2 = shoe1;

shoe2.price = shoe2.price/9;
cout << shoe2.style << " $" << shoe2.price << endl;
```

3. What is the error in the following structure definition? What is the message your compiler gives for this error? State what the error is, in your own words.

```
struct Stuff
{
    int b;
    int c;
}
int  main( )
{
    Stuff x;
    //other code
}
```

4. Given the following *struct* definition:

```
struct A
{
    int member_b;
    int member_c;
};
```

declare x to have this structure type. Initialize the members of x, member_b and member_c, to the values 1 and 2, respectively.

(*Note:* This requests an initialization, not an assignment of the members. This distinction is important and will be made in a later chapter.)

5. Here is an initialization of a structure type. Tell what happens with each initialization. Note any problems with these initializations.

```
struct Date
{
    int month;
    int day;
    int year;
};
```

a. Date due_date = {12, 21};

b. Date due_date = {12, 21, 20, 22};

c. Date due_date = {12, 21, 20, 22};

d. Date due_date = {12, 21, 22};

6. Write a definition for a structure type for records consisting of a person's wage rate, accrued vacation (which is some whole number of days), and status (which is either hourly or salaried). Represent the status as one of the two *char* values 'H' and 'S'. Call the type EmployeeRecord.

7. Give a function definition corresponding to the following function declaration. (The type ShoeType is given in Self-Test Exercise 2.)

```
void read_shoe_record(ShoeType& new_shoe);
//Fills new_shoe with values read from the keyboard.
```

8. Give a function definition corresponding to the following function declaration. (The type ShoeType is given in Self-Test Exercise 2.)

```
ShoeType discount(ShoeType old_record);
//Returns a structure that is the same as its argument,
//but with the price reduced by 10%.
```

9. Give the structure definition for a type named StockRecord that has two member variables, one named shoe_info of the type ShoeType given in Self-Test Exercise 2 and one named arrival_date of type Date given in Self-Test Exercise 5.

10. Declare a variable of type StockRecord (given in the previous exercise) and write a statement that will set the year of the arrival date to 2006.

10.2 CLASSES

I don't care to belong to any club that will accept me as a member.

GROUCHO MARX, *The Groucho Letters*

Defining Classes and Member Functions

A **class** is a data type whose variables are objects. In Chapter 6 we described an **object** as a variable that has member functions as well as the ability to hold data values.[1] Thus, within a C++ program, the definition of a class should be a data type definition that describes what kinds of values the variables can hold and also what the member functions are. A structure definition describes some of these things. A structure is a defined type that allows you to define values of the structure type by defining member variables. To obtain a class from a structure, all you need to do is add some member functions.

A sample class definition is given in the program shown in Display 10.3. The type DayOfYear defined there is a class definition for objects whose values are dates, such as January 1 or July 4. These values can be used to record holidays, birthdays, and other special dates. In this definition of DayOfYear, the month is recorded as an *int* value, with 1 standing for January, 2 standing for February, and so forth. The day of the month is recorded in a second *int* member variable. The class DayOfYear has one member function called output, which has no arguments and outputs the month and day values to the screen. Let's look at the definition for the class DayOfYear in detail.

A member function

The definition of the class DayOfYear is shown near the top of Display 10.3. For the moment, ignore the line that contains the keyword *public*. This line simply says that the member variables and functions have no restriction on them. We will explain this line later in this chapter. The rest of the definition of the class DayOfYear is very much like a structure definition, except that it uses the keyword *class* instead of *struct* and it lists the member function output (as well as the member variables month and day). Notice that the member function output is listed by giving only its function declaration. The definitions for the member functions are given elsewhere. (In a C++ class definition, you can intermix the ordering of the member variables and member functions in any way you wish, but the style we will follow has a tendency to list the member functions before the member variables.) Objects (that is, variables) of a class type are declared in the same way as variables of the predefined types and in the same way as structure variables.

---

[1] The object is actually the value of the variable rather than the variable itself, but since we use the variable to name the value it holds, we can simplify our discussion by ignoring this nicety and talking as if the variable and its value were the same thing.

DISPLAY 10.3 Class with a Member Function *(part 1 of 2)*

```
1    //Program to demonstrate a very simple example of a class.
2    //A better version of the class DayOfYear will be given in
     Display 10.4.
3    #include <iostream>
4    using namespace std;

5    class DayOfYear
6    {
7    public:
8        void output( );          ←——— Member function declaration
9        int month;
10       int day;
11   };

12   int main( )
13   {
14       DayOfYear today, birthday;

15       cout << "Enter today's date:\n";
16       cout << "Enter month as a number: ";
17       cin >> today.month;
18       cout << "Enter the day of the month: ";
19       cin >> today.day;
20       cout << "Enter your birthday:\n";
21       cout << "Enter month as a number: ";
22       cin >> birthday.month;
23       cout << "Enter the day of the month: ";
24       cin >> birthday.day;

25       cout << "Today's date is ";
26       today.output( );          ←
27       cout << "Your birthday is ";        Calls to the member
28       birthday.output( );       ←         function output

29       if (today.month == birthday.month
30           && today.day == birthday.day)
31           cout << "Happy Birthday!\n";
32       else
33           cout << "Happy Unbirthday!\n";

34       return 0;
35   }

36   //Uses iostream:
37   void DayOfYear::output( )
38   {
39       cout << "month = " << month                Member function
40           << ", day = " << day << endl;          definition
41   }
```

(continued)

DISPLAY 10.3   Class with a Member Function *(part 2 of 2)*

Sample Dialogue

```
Enter today's date:
Enter month as a number: 10
Enter the day of the month: 15
Enter your birthday:
Enter month as a number: 2
Enter the day of the month: 21
Today's date is month = 10, day = 15
Your birthday is month = 2, day = 21
Happy Unbirthday!
```

Calling member
functions

Member functions for classes that you define are called in the same way as we described in Chapter 6 for predefined classes. For example, the program in Display 10.3 declares two objects of type DayOfYear in the following way:

```
DayOfYear today, birthday;
```

The member function output is called with the object today as follows:

```
today.output();
```

and the member function output is called with the object birthday as follows:

```
birthday.output();
```

Encapsulation

Combining a number of items, such as variables and functions, into a single package, such as an object of some class, is called **encapsulation**.

Defining member
functions

When a member function is defined, the definition must include the class name because there may be two or more classes that have member functions with the same name. In Display 10.3 there is only one class definition, but in other situations you may have many class definitions, and each class may have a member function called output. The definition for the member function output of the class DayOfYear is shown in Display 10.3. The definition is similar to an ordinary function definition, but there are some differences.

The heading of the function definition for the member function output is as follows:

```
void DayOfYear::output()
```

The operator :: is called the **scope resolution operator,** and it serves a purpose similar to that of the dot operator. Both the dot operator and the scope resolution operator are used to tell what a member function is a member of. However, the scope resolution operator :: is used with a class name, whereas the dot operator is used with objects (that is, with class variables). The scope resolution operator consists of two colons with no space between them. The class name that precedes the scope resolution operator is often called a **type qualifier,** because it specializes ("qualifies") the function name to one particular type.

Look at the definition of the member function DayOfYear::output given in Display 10.3. Notice that in the function definition of DayOfYear::output, we used the member names month and day by themselves without first giving the object and dot operator. That is not as strange as it may at first appear. At this point we are simply defining the member function output. This definition of output will apply to all objects of type DayOfYear, but at this point we do not know the names of the objects of type DayOfYear that we will use, so we cannot give their names. When the member function is called, as in

Member variables in function definitions

```
today.output();
```

all the member names in the function definition are specialized to the name of the calling object. So the function call above is equivalent to the following:

```
{
    cout << "month = " << today.month
         << ", day = " << today.day << endl;
}
```

In the function definition for a member function, you can use the names of all members of that class (both the data members and the function members) without using the dot operator.

Member Function Definition

A member function is defined the same way as any other function except that the *Class_Name* and the scope resolution operator :: are given in the function heading.

SYNTAX

```
Returned_Type Class_Name::Function_Name(Parameter_List)
{
    Function_Body_Statements
}
```

(continued)

EXAMPLE

```
//Uses iostream:
void DayOfYear::output()
{
    cout << "month = " << month
         << ", day = " << day << endl;
}
```

The class definition for the example class DayOfYear above is given in Display 10.3, where month and day are defined as the names of member variables for the class DayOfYear. Note that month and day are not preceded by an object name and dot.

The Dot Operator and the Scope Resolution Operator

Both the dot operator and the scope resolution operator are used with member names to specify what thing they are members of. For example, suppose you have declared a class called DayOfYear and you declare an object called today as follows:

```
DayOfYear today;
```

You use the **dot operator** to specify a member of the object today. For example, output is a member function for the class DayOfYear (defined in Display 10.3), and the following function call will output the data values stored in the object today:

```
today.output();
```

You use the **scope resolution operator** :: to specify the class name when giving the function definition for a member function. For example, the heading of the function definition for the member function output would be as follows:

```
void DayOfYear::output()
```

Remember, the scope resolution operator :: is used with a class name, whereas the dot operator is used with an object of that class.

SELF-TEST EXERCISES

11. Below we have redefined the class DayOfYear from Display 10.3 so that it now has one additional member function called input. Write an appropriate definition for the member function input.

```
class DayOfYear
{
public:
    void input();
    void output();
    int month;
    int day;
};
```

12. Given the following class definition, write an appropriate definition for the member function set:

```
class Temperature
{
public:
    void set(double new_degrees, char new_scale);
    //Sets the member variables to the values given as
    //arguments.

    double degrees;
    char scale; //'F' for Fahrenheit or 'C' for Celsius.
};
```

13. Carefully distinguish between the meaning and use of the dot operator and the scope resolution operator ::.

Public and Private Members

The predefined types such as *double* are not implemented as C++ classes, but the people who wrote your C++ compiler did design some way to represent values of type *double* in your computer. It is possible to implement the type *double* in many different ways. In fact, different versions of C++ do implement the type *double* in slightly different ways, but if you move your C++ program from one computer to another with a different implementation of the type *double*, your program should still work correctly.[2] Classes are types that you define, and the types that you define should behave as well as the predefined types. You can build a library of your own class type definitions and use your types as if they were predefined types. For example, you could place each class definition in a separate file and copy it into any program that uses the type.

---

[2] Sometimes this ideal is not quite realized, but in the ideal world it should be realized, and at least for simple programs, it is realized even in the imperfect world that we live in.

Your class definitions should separate the rules for using the class and the details of the class implementation in as strong a way as was done for the predefined types. If you change the implementation of a class (for example, by changing some details in the definition of a member function in order to make function calls run faster), then you should not need to change any of the other parts of your programs. In order to realize this ideal, we need to describe one more feature of class definitions.

Look back at the definition of the type DayOfYear given in Display 10.3. The type DayOfYear is designed to hold values that represent dates such as birthdays and holidays. We chose to represent these dates as two integers, one for the month and one for the day of the month. We might later decide to change the representation of the month from one variable of type *int* to three variables of type *char*. In this changed version, the three characters would be an abbreviation of the month's name. For example, the three *char* values 'J', 'a', and 'n' would represent the month January. However, whether you use a single member variable of type *int* to record the month or three member variables of type *char* is an implementation detail that need not concern a programmer who uses the type DayOfYear. Of course, if you change the way the class DayOfYear represents the month, then you must change the implementation of the member function output—but that is all you should need to change. You should not need to change any other part of a program that uses your class definition for DayOfYear. Unfortunately, the program in Display 10.3 does not meet this ideal. For example, if you replace the one member variable named month with three member variables of type *char*, then there will be no member variable named month, so you must change those parts of the program that perform input and also change the *if-else* statement.

With an ideal class definition, you should be able to change the details of how the class is implemented and the only things you should need to change in any program that uses the class are the definitions of the member functions. In order to realize this ideal, you must have enough member functions so that you never need to access the member variables directly, but access them only through the member functions. Then, if you change the member variables, you need change only the definitions of the member functions to match your changes to the member variables, and nothing else in your programs need change. In Display 10.4 we have redefined the class DayOfYear so that it has enough member functions to do everything we want our programs to do, and so the program does not need to directly reference any member variables. If you look carefully at the program in Display 10.4, you will see that the only place the member variable names month and day are used is in the definitions of the member functions. There is no reference to today.month, today.day, bach_birthday.month, nor bach_birthday.day anywhere outside of the definitions of member functions.

The program in Display 10.4 has one new feature that is designed to ensure that no programmer who uses the class DayOfYear will ever

DISPLAY 10.4   Class with Private Members *(part 1 of 2)*

```
1     //Program to demonstrate the class DayOfYear.
2     #include <iostream>                    This is an improved version
3     using namespace std;                   of the class DayOfYear that
                                             we gave in Display 10.3.
4     class DayOfYear
5     {
6     public:
7         void input( );
8         void output( );

9         void set(int new_month, int new_day);
10        //Precondition: new_month and new_day form a possible date.
11        //Postcondition: The date is reset according to the arguments.

12        int get_month( );
13        //Returns the month, 1 for January, 2 for February, etc.

14        int get_day( );
15        //Returns the day of the month.
16    private:
17        void check_date( );  ←──────────────── Private member function
18        int month;  ←
19        int day;  ←─────────────── Private member variables
20    };

21    int main( )
22    {
23        DayOfYear today, bach_birthday;
24        cout << "Enter today's date:\n";
25        today.input( );
26        cout << "Today's date is ";
27        today.output( );

28        bach_birthday.set(3, 21);
29        cout << "J. S. Bach's birthday is ";
30        bach_birthday.output( );

31        if (today.get_month( ) == bach_birthday.get_month( ) &&
32            today.get_day( ) == bach_birthday.get_day( ) )
33            cout << "Happy Birthday Johann Sebastian!\n";
34        else
35            cout << "Happy Unbirthday Johann Sebastian!\n";
36        return 0;
37    }
38    //Uses iostream:
39    void DayOfYear::input( )
40    {
41        cout << "Enter the month as a number: ";
```

(continued)

DISPLAY 10.4   Class with Private Members *(part 2 of 2)*

```
42          cin >> month;
43          cout << "Enter the day of the month: ";
44          cin >> day;
45          check_date( );
46      }
47
48      void DayOfYear::output( )
         <The rest of the definition of DayOfYear::output is
          given in Display 10.3.>
49
50      void DayOfYear::set(int new_month, int new_day)
51      {
52          month = new_month;
53          day = new_day;
54          check_date();
55      }
56
57      void DayOfYear::check_date( )
58      {
59          if ((month < 1) || (month > 12) || (day < 1) || (day > 31))
60          {
61              cout << "Illegal date. Aborting program.\n";
62              exit(1);
63          }
64      }
65
66      int DayOfYear::get_month( )
67      {
68          return month;
69      }
70
71      int DayOfYear::get_day( )
72      {
73          return day;
74      }
```

Private members may be used in member function definitions (but not elsewhere).

A better definition of the member function input *would ask the user to reenter the date if the user enters an incorrect date.*

The member function check_date *does not check for all illegal dates, but it would be easy to make the check complete by making it longer. See Self-Test Exercise 14.*

The function exit *is discussed in Chapter 6. It ends the program.*

Sample Dialogue

```
Enter today's date:
Enter the month as a number: 3
Enter the day of the month: 21
Today's date is month = 3, day = 21
J. S. Bach's birthday is month = 3, day = 21
Happy Birthday Johann Sebastian!
```

directly reference any of its member variables. Notice the line in the definition of the class DayOfYear that contains the keyword *private*. All the member variable names that are listed after this line are **private members,** which means that they cannot be directly accessed in the program except within the definition of a member function. If you try to access one of these member variables in the main part of your program or in the definition of some function that is not a member function of this particular class, the compiler will give you an error message. If you insert the keyword *private* and a colon in the list of member variables and member functions, all the members that follow the label *private:* will be private members. The variables that follow the label *private:* will be **private member variables,** and the functions that follow it will be **private member functions.**

All the member variables for the class DayOfYear defined in Display 10.4 are private members. A private member variable may be used in the definition of any of the member functions, but nowhere else. For example, with this changed definition of the class DayOfYear, the following two assignments are no longer permitted in the main part of the program:

```
DayOfYear today; //This line is OK.
today.month = 12; //ILLEGAL
today.day = 25; //ILLEGAL
```

Any reference to these private variables is illegal (except in the definition of member functions). Since this new definition makes month and day private member variables, the following are also illegal in the main part of any program that declares today to be of type DayOfYear:

```
cout << today.month; //ILLEGAL
cout << today.day; //ILLEGAL
if (today.month == 1) //ILLEGAL
    cout << "January";
```

Once you make a member variable a private member variable, there is then no way to change its value (or to reference the member variable in any other way) except by using one of the member functions. This is a severe restriction, but it is usually a wise restriction to impose. Programmers find that it usually makes their code easier to understand and easier to update if they make all member variables private.

It may seem that the program in Display 10.4 does not really disallow direct access to the private member variables, since they can be changed using the member function DayOfYear::set, and their values can be discovered using the member functions DayOfYear::get_month and DayOfYear::get_day. While that is almost true for the program in Display 10.4, it might not be so true if we changed the implementation of how we represented the month and/or day in our dates. For example, suppose we change the type definition of DayOfYear to the following:

```
class DayOfYear
{
public:
    void input();
    void output();

    void set(int new_month, int new_day);
    //Precondition: new_month and new_day form a possible date.
    //Postcondition: The date is reset according to the
    //arguments.

    int get_month();
    //Returns the month, 1 for January, 2 for February, etc.

    int get_day();
    //Returns the day of the month.
private:
    void DayOfYear::check_date( );
    char first_letter; //of month
    char second_letter; //of month
    char third_letter; //of month
    int day;
};
```

It would then be slightly more difficult to define the member functions, but they could be redefined so that they would behave *exactly* as they did before. For example, the definition of the function get_month might start as follows:

```
int DayOfYear::get_month()
{
    if (first_letter == 'J' && second_letter == 'a'
            && third_letter == 'n')
        return 1;
    if (first_letter == 'F' && second_letter == 'e'
            && third_letter == 'b')
        return 2;
        . . .
```

This approach would be rather tedious, but not difficult.

Also notice that the member functions DayOfYear::set and DayOfYear::input check to make sure the member variables month and day are set to legal values. This is done with a call to the member function DayOfYear::check_date. If the member variables month and day were public instead of private, then these member variables could be set to any values, including illegal values. By making the member variables private and manipulating them only via member functions, we can ensure that the member variables are never set to illegal or meaningless values. (In Self-Test Exercise 14 you are asked to redefine the member function DayOfYear::check_date so that it does a complete check for illegal dates.)

It is also possible to make a member function private. Like a private member variable, a private member function can be used in the definition of any other member function, but nowhere else, such as in the `main` part of a program that uses the class type. For example, the member function `DayOfYear::check_date` in Display 10.4 is a private member function. The normal practice is to make a member function private if you only expect to use that member function as a helping function in the definitions of the member functions.

The keyword *public* is used to indicate **public members** the same way that the keyword *private* is used to indicate private members. For example, for the class `DayOfYear` defined in Display 10.4, all the member functions except `DayOfYear::check_date` are public members (and all the member variables are private members). A public member can be used in the `main` body of your program or in the definition of any function, even a nonmember function.

VideoNote
Class Scope, Public and
Private Members

You can have any number of occurrences of *public* and *private* in a class definition. Every time you insert the label

>   *public*:

the list of members changes from private to public. Every time you insert the label

>   *private*:

the list of members changes back to being private members. For example, the member function `do_something_else` and the member variable `more_stuff` in the following structure definition are private members, while the other four members are all public:

```
class SampleClass
{
public:
    void do_something();
    int stuff;
private:
    void do_something_else();
    char more_stuff;
public:
    double do_yet_another_thing();
    double even_more_stuff;
};
```

If you list members at the start of your class definition and do not insert either *public*: or *private*: before these first members, then they will be private members. However, it is a good idea to always explicitly label each group of members as either *public* or *private*.

Classes and Objects

A **class** is a type whose variables are **objects**. These objects can have both member variables and member functions. The syntax for a class definition is as follows.

SYNTAX

```
class Class_Name
{
public:
    Member_Specification_1
    Member_Specification_2
              .
              .
              .
    Member_Specification_n
private:
    Member_Specification_n+1
    Member_Specification_n+2
       .
       .
       .
};
```

Each *Member_Specification_i* is either a member variable declaration or a member function declaration. (Additional *public* and *private* sections are permitted.)

EXAMPLE

```
class Bicycle
{
public:
    char get_color();
    int number_of_speeds();
    void set(int the_speeds, char the_color);
private:
    int speeds;
    char color;
};
```

Once a class is defined, an object (which is just a variable of the class type) can be declared in the same way as variables of any other type. For example, the following declares two objects of type Bicycle:

```
Bicycle my_bike, your_bike;
```

■ PROGRAMMING TIP   Make All Member Variables Private

When defining a class, the normal practice is to make all member variables private. This means that the member variables can only be accessed or changed using the member functions. Much of this chapter is dedicated to explaining how and why you should define classes in this way.   ■

■ PROGRAMMING TIP   Define Accessor and Mutator Functions

The operator == can be used to test two values of a simple type to see if they are equal. Unfortunately, the predefined operator == does not automatically apply to objects. In Chapter 11 we will show you how you can make the operator == apply to the objects of the classes you define. Until then, you will not be able to use the equality operator == with objects (nor can you use it with structures). This can produce some complications. When defining a class, the preferred style is to make all member variables private. Thus, in order to test two objects to see if they represent the same value, you need some way to access the values of the member variables (or something equivalent to the values of the member variables). This allows you to test for equality by testing the values of each pair of corresponding member variables. To do this in Display 10.4, we used the member functions get_month and get_day in the *if-else* statement.

Member functions, such as get_month and get_day, that allow you to find out the values of the private member variables are called **accessor functions.** Given the techniques you have learned to date, it is important to always include a complete set of accessor functions with each class definition so that you can test objects for equality. The accessor functions need not literally return the values of each member variable, but they must return something equivalent to those values. In Chapter 11 we will develop a more elegant method to test two objects for equality, but even after you learn that technique, it will still be handy to have accessor functions.

Member functions, such as set in Display 10.4, that allow you to change the values of the private member variables are called **mutator functions.** It is important to always include mutator functions with each class definition so that you can change the data stored in an object.

Accessor and Mutator Functions

Member functions that allow you to find out the values of the private member variables of a class are called **accessor functions.** The accessor functions need not literally return the values of each member variable, but they must return something equivalent to those values. Although this is not required by the C++ language, the names of accessor functions normally include the word get.

(continued)

> Member functions that allow you to change the values of the private member variables of a class are called **mutator functions.** Although this is not required by the C++ language, the names of mutator functions normally include the word set.
>
> It is important to always include accessor and mutator functions with each class definition so that you can change the data stored in an object.

SELF-TEST EXERCISES

14. The private member function DayOfYear::check_date in Display 10.4 allows some illegal dates to get through, such as February 30. Redefine the member function DayOfYear::check_date so that it ends the program whenever it finds any illegal date. Allow February to contain 29 days, so you account for leap years. (*Hint:* This is a bit tedious and the function definition is a bit long, but it is not very difficult.)

15. Suppose your program contains the following class definition:

```
class Automobile
{
public:
    void set_price(double new_price);
    void set_profit(double new_profit);
    double get_price();
private:
    double price;
    double profit;
    double get_profit();
};
```

and suppose the main part of your program contains the following declaration and that the program somehow sets the values of all the member variables to some values:

```
Automobile hyundai, jaguar;
```

Which of the following statements are then allowed in the main part of your program?

```
hyundai.price = 4999.99;
jaguar.set_price(30000.97);
double a_price, a_profit;
a_price = jaguar.get_price();
a_profit = jaguar.get_profit();
a_profit = hyundai.get_profit();
```

```
if (hyundai == jaguar)
    cout << "Want to swap cars?";
hyundai = jaguar;
```

16. Suppose you change Self-Test Exercise 15 so that the definition of the class Automobile omits the line that contains the keyword *private*. How would this change your answer to the question in Self-Test Exercise 15?

17. Explain what *public*: and *private*: do in a class definition. In particular, explain why we do not just make everything *public*: and save difficulty in access.

18. a. How many *public*: sections are required in a class for the class to be useful?

    b. How many *private*: sections are required in a class?

    c. What kind of section do you have between the opening { and the first *public:* or *private:* section label of a class?

    d. What kind of section do you have between the opening { and the first *public:* or *private:* section label of a structure?

■ PROGRAMMING TIP   Use the Assignment Operator with Objects

It is perfectly legal to use the assignment operator = with objects or with structures. For example, suppose the class DayOfYear is defined as shown in Display 10.4 so that it has two private member variables named month and day, and suppose that the objects due_date and tomorrow are declared as follows:

```
DayOfYear due_date, tomorrow;
```

The following is then perfectly legal (provided the member variables of the object tomorrow have already been given values):

```
due_date = tomorrow;
```

The previous assignment is equivalent to the following:

```
due_date.month = tomorrow.month;
due_date.day = tomorrow.day;
```

Moreover, this is true even though the member variables named month and day are private members of the class DayOfYear.[3]   ■

---

[3] In Chapter 11 we see situations in which the assignment operator = should be redefined (overloaded) for a class.

PROGRAMMING EXAMPLE	BankAccount Class—Version 1

Display 10.5 contains a class definition for a bank account that illustrates all of the points about class definitions you have seen thus far. This type of bank account allows you to withdraw your money at any time, so it has no term as did the type CDAccount that you saw earlier. A more important difference is that the class BankAccount has member functions for all the operations you would expect to use in a program. Objects of the class BankAccount have two private member variables: one to record the account balance and one to record the interest rate. Let's discuss some of features of the class BankAccount.

First, notice that the class BankAccount has a private member function called fraction. Since fraction is a private member function, it cannot be called in the body of main or in the body of any function that is not a member function of the class BankAccount. The function fraction can only be called in the definitions of other member functions of the class BankAccount. The only reason we have this (or any) private member function is to aid us in defining other member functions for the same class. In our definition of the class BankAccount, we included the member function fraction so that we could use it in the definition of the function update. The function fraction takes one argument that is a percentage figure, like 10.0 for 10.0%, and converts it to a fraction, like 0.10. That allows us to compute the amount of interest on the account at the given percentage. If the account contains $100.00 and the interest rate is 10%, then the interest is equal to $100 times 0.10, which is $10.00.

When you call a public member function, such as update, in the main body of your program, you must include an object name and a dot, as in the following line from Display 10.5:

```
account1.update();
```

One member function calling another

However, when you call a private member function (or any other member function) within the definition of another member function, you use only the member function name without any calling object or dot operator. For example, the following definition of the member function BankAccount::update includes a call to BankAccount::fraction (as shown in Display 10.5):

```
void BankAccount::update()
{
    balance = balance + fraction(interest_rate) * balance;
}
```

The calling object for the member function fraction and for the member variables balance and interest_rate are determined when the function update is called. For example, the meaning of

```
account1.update();
```

is the following:

DISPLAY 10.5   The BankAccount Class *(part 1 of 3)*

```
1    //Program to demonstrate the class BankAccount.
2    #include <iostream>
3    using namespace std;

4    //Class for a bank account:
5    class BankAccount
6    {                                                        The member function
7    public:                                                  set is overloaded.
8        void set(int dollars, int cents, double rate);
9        //Postcondition: The account balance has been set to $dollars.cents;
10       //The interest rate has been set to rate percent.

11       void set(int dollars, double rate);
12       //Postcondition: The account balance has been set to $dollars.00.
13       //The interest rate has been set to rate percent.

14       void update( );
15       //Postcondition: One year of simple interest has been
16       //added to the account balance.

17       double get_balance( );
18       //Returns the current account balance.

19       double get_rate( );
20       //Returns the current account interest rate as a percentage.

21       void output(ostream& outs);
22       //Precondition: If outs is a file output stream, then
23       //outs has already been connected to a file.
24       //Postcondition: Account balance and interest rate have
25       //been written to the stream outs.
26   private:
27       double balance;
28       double interest_rate;
29
30       double fraction(double percent);
31       //Converts a percentage to a fraction. For example, fraction(50.3)
32       //returns 0.503.
33   };

34   int main( )
35   {
36       BankAccount account1, account2;
37       cout << "Start of Test:\n";
38       account1.set(123, 99, 3.0);                          Calls to the overloaded
39       cout << "account1 initial statement:\n";            member function set
40       account1.output(cout);
41       account1.set(100, 5.0);
```

(continued)

DISPLAY 10.5   The BankAccount **Class** *(part 2 of 3)*

```
42          cout << "account1 with new setup:\n";
43          account1.output(cout);

44          account1.update( );
45          cout << "account1 after update:\n";
46          account1.output(cout);

47          account2 = account1;
48          cout << "account2:\n";
49          account2.output(cout);
50          return 0;
51      }
52
53      void BankAccount::set(int dollars, int cents, double rate)
54      {
55          if ((dollars < 0) || (cents < 0) || (rate < 0))
56          {
57              cout << "Illegal values for money or interest rate.\n";
58              exit(1);
59          }

60          balance = dollars + 0.01*cents;
61          interest_rate = rate;
62      }
63
64      void BankAccount::set(int dollars, double rate)
65      {
66          if ((dollars < 0) || (rate < 0))
67          {
68              cout << "Illegal values for money or interest rate.\n";
69              exit(1);
70          }

71          balance = dollars;
72          interest_rate = rate;
73      }
74
75      void BankAccount::update( )
76      {
77          balance = balance + fraction(interest_rate)*balance;
78      }
79
80      double BankAccount::fraction(double percent_value)
81      {
82          return (percent_value / 100.0);
83      }
84
```

Definitions of overloaded member function set

In the definition of a member function, you call another member function like this.

(continued)

DISPLAY 10.5   The BankAccount Class *(part 3 of 3)*

```
85    double BankAccount::get_balance( )
86    {
87        return balance;
88    }
89
90    double BankAccount::get_rate( )
91    {
92        return interest_rate;
93    }
94
95    //Uses iostream:
96    void BankAccount::output(ostream& outs)
97    {
98        outs.setf(ios::fixed);
99        outs.setf(ios::showpoint);
100       outs.precision(2);
101       outs << "Account balance $" << balance << endl;
102       outs << "Interest rate " << interest_rate << "%" << endl;
103   }
```

Stream parameter that can be replaced either with cout or with a file output stream

Sample Dialogue

```
Start of Test:
account1 initial statement:
Account balance $123.99
Interest rate 3.00%
account1 with new setup:
Account balance $100.00
Interest rate 5.00%
account1 after update:
Account balance $105.00
Interest rate 5.00%
account2:
Account balance $105.00
Interest rate 5.00%
```

```
    {
        account1.balance = account1.balance +
        account1.fraction(account1.interest_rate) * account1.balance;
    }
```

Notice that the call to the member function fraction is handled in the same way in this regard as the references to the member variables.

Input/output
stream arguments

Like the classes we discussed earlier, the class BankAccount has a member function that outputs the data information stored in the object. In this program we are sending output to the screen. However, we want to write this class definition so that it can be copied into other programs and used unchanged in those other programs. Since some other program may want to send output to a file, we have given the member function output a formal parameter of type ostream so that the function output can be called with an argument that is either the stream cout or a file output stream. In the sample program we want the output to go to the screen, so the first function call to the member function output has the form

```
account1.output(cout);
```

Other calls to output also use cout as the argument, so all output is sent to the screen. If you want the output to go to a file instead, then you must first connect the file to an output stream, as we discussed in Chapter 6. If the file output stream is called fout and is connected to a file, then the following would write the data information for the object account1 to this file rather than to the screen:

```
account1.output(fout);
```

Overloading
member functions

The value of an object of type BankAccount represents a bank account that has some balance and pays some interest rate. The balance and interest rate can be set with the member function set. Notice that we have overloaded the member function named set so that there are two versions of set. One version has three formal parameters, and the other has only two formal parameters. Both versions have a formal parameter of type *double* for the interest rate, but the two versions of set use different formal parameters to set the account balance. One version has two formal parameters to set the balance, one for the dollars and one for the cents in the account balance. The other version has only a single formal parameter, which gives the number of dollars in the account and assumes that the number of cents is zero. This second version of set is handy, since most people open an account with some "even" amount of money, such as $1,000 and no cents. Notice that this overloading is nothing new. A member function is overloaded in the same way as an ordinary function is overloaded.

Summary of Some Properties of Classes

Classes have all of the properties that we described for structures plus all the properties associated with member functions. The following is a list of some points to keep in mind when using classes.

- Classes have both member variables and member functions.
- A member (either a member variable or a member function) may be either public or private.

- Normally, all the member variables of a class are labeled as private members.
- A private member of a class cannot be used except within the definition of another member function of the same class.
- The name of a member function for a class may be overloaded just like the name of an ordinary function.
- A class may use another class as the type for a member variable.
- A function may have formal parameters whose types are classes. (See Self-Test Exercises 19 and 20.)
- A function may return an object; that is, a class may be the type for the value returned by a function. (See Self-Test Exercise 21.)

Structures Versus Classes

Structures are normally used with all member variables being public and having no member functions. However, in C++ a structure can have private member variables and both public and private member functions. Aside from some notational differences, a C++ structure can do anything a class can do. Having said this and satisfied the "truth in advertising" requirement, we advocate that you forget this technical detail about structures. If you take this technical detail seriously and use structures in the same way that you use classes, then you have two names (with different syntax rules) for the same concept. On the other hand, if you use structures as we described them, then you will have a meaningful difference between structures (as you use them) and classes, and your usage will be the same as that of most other programmers.

SELF-TEST EXERCISES

myprogramminglab

19. Give a definition for the function with the following function declaration. The class BankAccount is defined in Display 10.5.

    ```
    double difference(BankAccount account1, BankAccount account2);
    //Precondition: account1 and account2 have been given values
    //(that is, their member variables have been given values).
    //Returns the balance in account1 minus the balance in
    account2.
    ```

20. Give a definition for the function with the following function declaration. The class BankAccount is defined in Display 10.5. (*Hint:* It's easy if you use a member function.)

```
void double_update(BankAccount& the_account);
//Precondition: the_account has previously been given a value
//(that is, its member variables have been given values).
//Postcondition: The account balance has been changed so that
//two years' interest has been posted to the account.
```

21. Give a definition for the function with the following function declaration. The class BankAccount is defined in Display 10.5.

```
BankAccount new_account(BankAccount old_account);
//Precondition: old_account has previously been given a value
//(that is, its member variables have been given values).
//Returns the value for a new account that has a balance of zero
//and the same interest rate as the old_account.
```

For example, after this function is defined, a program could contain the following:

```
BankAccount account3, account4;
account3.set(999, 99, 5.5);
account4 = new_account(account3);
account4.output(cout);
```

This would produce the following output:

```
Account balance $0.00
Interest rate 5.50%
```

Constructors for Initialization

You often want to initialize some or all the member variables for an object when you declare the object. As we will see later in this book, there are other initializing actions you might also want to take, but initializing member variables is the most common sort of initialization. C++ includes special provisions for such initializations. When you define a class, you can define a special kind of member function known as a **constructor.** A constructor is a member function that is automatically called when an object of that class is declared. A constructor is used to initialize the values of member variables and to do any other sort of initialization that may be needed. You can define a constructor the same way that you define any other member function, except for two points:

1. A constructor must have the same name as the class. For example, if the class is named BankAccount, then any constructor for this class must be named BankAccount.

2. A constructor definition cannot return a value. Moreover, no return type, not even *void*, can be given at the start of the function declaration or in the function header.

For example, suppose we wanted to add a constructor for initializing the balance and interest rate for objects of type BankAccount shown in Display 10.5. The class definition could be as follows. (We have omitted some of the comments to save space, but they should be included.)

```
class BankAccount
{
public:
    BankAccount(int dollars, int cents, double rate);
    //Initializes the account balance to $dollars.cents and
    //initializes the interest rate to rate percent.

    void set(int dollars, int cents, double rate);
    void set(int dollars, double rate);
    void update();

    double get_balance();
    double get_rate();
    void output(ostream& outs);
private:
    double balance;
    double interest_rate;
    double fraction(double percent);
};
```

Notice that the constructor is named BankAccount, which is the name of the class. Also notice that the function declaration for the constructor BankAccount does not start with *void* or with any other type name. Finally, notice that the constructor is placed in the public section of the class definition. Normally, you should make your constructors public member functions. If you were to make all your constructors private members, then you would not be able to declare any objects of that class type, which would make the class completely useless.

With the redefined class BankAccount, two objects of type BankAccount can be declared and initialized as follows:

```
BankAccount account1(10, 50, 2.0), account2(500, 0, 4.5);
```

Assuming that the definition of the constructor performs the initializing action that we promised, the previous declaration will declare the object account1, set the value of account1.balance to 10.50, and set the value of account1.interest_rate to 2.0. Thus, the object account1 is initialized so that it represents a bank account with a balance of $10.50 and an interest rate of 2.0%. Similarly, account2 is initialized so that it represents a bank account with a balance of $500.00 and an interest rate of 4.5%. What happens is that the object account1 is declared and then the constructor BankAccount is called with the three arguments 10, 50, and 2.0. Similarly, account2 is declared and then the constructor BankAccount is called with the arguments 500, 0, and 4.5. The result is conceptually equivalent to the following (although you cannot write it this way in C++):

```
BankAccount account1, account2; //PROBLEMS--BUT FIXABLE
account1.BankAccount(10, 50, 2.0); //VERY ILLEGAL
account2.BankAccount(500, 0, 4.5); //VERY ILLEGAL
```

As the comments indicate, you cannot place those three lines in your program. The first line can be made to be acceptable, but the two calls to the constructor BankAccount are illegal. A constructor cannot be called in the same way as an ordinary member function is called. Still, it is clear what we want to happen when we write those three lines, and that happens automatically when you declare the objects account1 and account2 as follows:

```
BankAccount account1(10, 50, 2.0), account2(500, 0, 4.5);
```

The definition of a constructor is given in the same way as any other member function. For example, if you revise the definition of the class BankAccount by adding the constructor just described, you need to also add the following definition of the constructor:

```
BankAccount::BankAccount(int dollars, int cents, double rate)
{
    if ((dollars < 0) || (cents < 0) || (rate < 0))
    {
        cout << "Illegal values for money or interest rate.\n";
        exit(1);
    }
    balance = dollars + 0.01*cents;
    interest_rate = rate;
}
```

Since the class and the constructor function have the same name, the name BankAccount occurs twice in the function heading: The BankAccount before the scope resolution operator :: is the name of the class, and the BankAccount after the scope resolution operator is the name of the constructor function. Also notice that no return type is specified in the heading of the constructor definition, not even the type *void*. Aside from these points, a constructor can be defined in the same way as an ordinary member function.

You can overload a constructor name like BankAccount::BankAccount, just as you can overload any other member function name, such as we did with BankAccount::set in Display 10.5. In fact, constructors usually are overloaded so that objects can be initialized in more than one way. For example, in Display 10.6 we have redefined the class BankAccount so that it has three versions of its constructor. This redefinition overloads the constructor name BankAccount so that it may have three arguments (as we just discussed), two arguments, or no arguments.

For example, suppose you give only two arguments when you declare an object of type BankAccount, as in the following example:

```
BankAccount account1(100, 2.3);
```

Then the object account1 is initialized so that it represents an account with a balance of $100.00 and an interest rate of 2.3%.

On the other hand, if no arguments are given, as in the following example,

```
BankAccount account2;
```

then the object is initialized to represent an account with a balance of $0.00 and an interest rate of 0.0%. Notice that when the constructor has no arguments, you do not include any parentheses in the object declaration. The following is incorrect:

```
BankAccount account2(); //WRONG! DO NOT DO THIS!
```

In some cases, you can omit mutator member functions such as set once you have a good set of constructor definitions. You can use the overloaded constructor BankAccount in Display 10.6 to create a new BankAccount object with the values of your choice. However, invoking the constructor will create a new object, so if you want to change the existing member variables in the object, then you should use a mutator function.

DISPLAY 10.6 Class with Constructors *(part 1 of 3)*

```
1    //Program to demonstrate the class BankAccount.
2    #include <iostream>
3    using namespace std;

4    //Class for a bank account:
5    class BankAccount
6    {
7    public:
8        BankAccount(int dollars, int cents, double rate);
9        //Initializes the account balance to $dollars.cents and
10       //initializes the interest rate to rate percent.

11       BankAccount(int dollars, double rate);
12       //Initializes the account balance to $dollars.00 and
13       //initializes the interest rate to rate percent.

14       BankAccount( );
15       //Initializes the account balance to $0.00
16       //and the interest rate to 0.0%.

17       void set(int dollars, int cents, double rate);
18       //Postcondition: The account balance has been set to $dollars.cents;
19       //The interest rate has been set to rate percent.

20       void set(int dollars, double rate);
21       //Postcondition: The account balance has been set to $dollars.00.
22       //The interest rate has been set to rate percent.

23       void update( );
```

This definition of **BankAccount** is an improved version of the class **BankAccount** given in Display 10.5.

(continued)

DISPLAY 10.6   Class with Constructors *(part 2 of 3)*

```
24        //Postcondition: One year of simple interest has been added
25        //to the account balance.

26        double get_balance( );
27        //Returns the current account balance.

28        double get_rate( );
29        //Returns the current account interest rate as a percentage.

30        void output(ostream& outs);
31        //Precondition: If outs is a file output stream, then
32        //outs has already been connected to a file.
33        //Postcondition: Account balance and interest rate
34        //have been written to the stream outs.
35    private:
36        double balance;
37        double interest_rate;

38        double fraction(double percent);
39        //Converts a percentage to a fraction. For example, fraction(50.3)
40        //returns 0.503.
41    };

42    int main( )
43    {
44        BankAccount account1(100, 2.3), account2;

45        cout << "account1 initialized as follows:\n";
46        account1.output(cout);
47        cout << "account2 initialized as follows:\n";
48        account2.output(cout);

49        account1 = BankAccount(999, 99, 5.5);
50        cout << "account1 reset to the following:\n";
51        account1.output(cout);
52        return 0;
53    }

54    BankAccount::BankAccount(int dollars, int cents, double rate)
55    {
56        if ((dollars < 0) || (cents < 0) || (rate < 0))
57        {
58            cout << "Illegal values for money or interest rate.\n";
59            exit(1);
60        }
61        balance = dollars + 0.01 * cents;
62        interest_rate = rate;
63    }

64    BankAccount::BankAccount(int dollars, double rate)
65    {
```

This declaration causes a call to the default constructor. Notice that there are no parentheses.

An explicit call to the constructor
BankAccount::BankAccount

(continued)

DISPLAY 10.6   Class with Constructors *(part 3 of 3)*

```
66        if ((dollars < 0) || (rate < 0))
67        {
68            cout << "Illegal values for money or interest rate.\n";
69            exit(1);
70        }
71        balance = dollars;
72        interest_rate = rate;
73    }

74    BankAccount::BankAccount( ) : balance(0), interest_rate(0.0)
75    {
76        //Body intentionally empty
77    }
```

<Definitions of the other member functions are the same as in Display 10.5.

Screen Output

```
account1 initialized as follows:
Account balance $100.00
Interest rate 2.30%
account2 initialized as follows:
Account balance $0.00
Interest rate 0.00%
account1 reset to the following:
Account balance $999.99
Interest rate 5.50%
```

Constructor

A **constructor** is a member function of a class that has the same name as the class. A constructor is called automatically when an object of the class is declared. Constructors are used to initialize objects. A constructor must have the same name as the class of which it is a member.

The constructor with no parameters in Display 10.6 deserves some extra discussion since it contains something we have not seen before. For reference, we reproduce the defining of the constructor with no parameters:

```
BankAccount::BankAccount() : balance(0), interest_rate(0.0)
{
    //Body intentionally empty
}
```

The new element, which is shown on the first line, is the part that starts with a single colon. This part of the constructor definition is called the **initialization section.** As this example shows, the initialization section goes after the parentheses that ends the parameter list and before the opening brace of the function body. The initialization section consists of a colon followed by a list of some or all the member variables separated by commas. Each member variable is followed by its initializing value in parentheses. This constructor definition is completely equivalent to the following way of writing the definition:

```
BankAccount::BankAccount( )
{
    balance = 0;
    interest_rate = 0.0;
}
```

The function body in a constructor definition with an initialization section need not be empty. For example, the following definition of the two-parameter constructor is equivalent to the one given in Display 10.6:

```
BankAccount::BankAccount(int dollars, double rate)
        : balance(dollars), interest_rate(rate)
{
    if ((dollars < 0) || (rate < 0))
    {
        cout << "Illegal values for money or interest rate.\n";
        exit(1);
    }
}
```

Notice that the initializing values can be given in terms of the constructor parameters.

Constructor Initialization Section

Some or all of the member variables in a class can (optionally) be initialized in the **constructor initialization section** of a constructor definition. The constructor initialization section goes after the parentheses that end the parameter list and before the opening brace of the function body. The initialization section consists of a colon followed by a list of some or all the member variables separated by commas. Each member variable is followed by its initializing value in parentheses. The example given below uses a constructor initialization section and is equivalent to the three-parameter constructor given in Display 10.6.

(continued)

EXAMPLE

```
BankAccount::BankAccount(int dollars, int cents,
                          double rate)
    : balance(dollars + 0.01*cents), interest_rate(rate)
{
    if ((dollars < 0) || (cents < 0) || (rate < 0))
    {
        cout <<
            "Illegal values for money or interest rate.\n";
        exit(1);
    }
}
```

Notice that the initializing values can be given in terms of the constructor parameters.

Calling a Constructor

A constructor is called automatically when an object is declared, but you must give the arguments for the constructor when you declare the object. A constructor can also be called explicitly in order to create a new object for a class variable.

SYNTAX (for an object declaration when you have constructors)

```
Class_Name Object_Name(Arguments_for_Constructor);
```

EXAMPLE

```
BankAccount account1(100, 2.3);
```

SYNTAX (for an explicit constructor call)

```
Object = Constructor_Name(Arguments_For_Constructor);
```

EXAMPLE

```
account1 = BankAccount(200, 3.5);
```

A constructor must have the same name as the class of which it is a member. Thus, in the syntax descriptions above, *Class_Name* and *Constructor_Name* are the same identifier.

Initializers can also be specified if the object is created as a dynamic variable.

```
BankAccount *myAcct; myAcct = new BankAccount (300, 4.2);
```

A constructor is called automatically whenever you declare an object of the class type, but it can also be called again after the object has been declared. This allows you to conveniently set all the members of an object. The technical details are as follows. Calling the constructor creates an anonymous object with new values. An anonymous object is an object that is not named (as yet) by any variable. The anonymous object can be assigned to the named object (that is, to the class variable). For example, the following line of code is a call to the constructor BankAccount that creates an anonymous object with a balance of $999.99 and interest rate of 5.5%. This anonymous object is assigned to object account1 so that it too represents an account with a balance of $999.99 and an interest rate of 5.5%:

```
account1 = BankAccount(999, 99, 5.5);
```

As you might guess from the notation, a constructor behaves like a function that returns an object of its class type. However, since a call to a constructor always creates a new object and a call to a set member function merely changes the values of existing member variables, a call to set may be a more efficient way to change the values of member variables than a call to a constructor. Thus, for efficiency reasons or if you need to change the values of member variables without creating a new object, you may wish to have both the set member functions and the constructors in your class definition.

■ PROGRAMMING TIP   Always Include a Default Constructor

C++ does not always generate a default constructor for the classes you define. If you give no constructor, the compiler will generate a default constructor that does nothing. This constructor will be called if class objects are declared. On the other hand, if you give at least one constructor definition for a class, then the C++ compiler will generate no other constructors. Every time you declare an object of that type, C++ will look for an appropriate constructor definition to use. If you declare an object without using arguments for the constructor, C++ will look for a default constructor, and if you have not defined a default constructor, none will be there for it to find.

For example, suppose you define a class as follows:

```
class SampleClass
{                              Constructor that requires two arguments
public:
    SampleClass(int parameter1, double parameter2);
    void do_stuff();
private:
    int data1;
    double data2;
};
```

You should recognize the following as a legal way to declare an object of type `SampleClass` and call the constructor for that class:

```
SampleClass my_object(7, 7.77);
```

However, you may be surprised to learn that the following is illegal:

```
SampleClass your_object;
```

The compiler interprets this declaration as including a call to a constructor with no arguments, but there is no definition for a constructor with zero arguments. You must either add two arguments to the declaration of `your_object` or add a constructor definition for a constructor with no arguments.

A constructor that can be called with no arguments is called a **default constructor**, since it applies in the default case where you declare an object without specifying any arguments. Since it is likely that you will sometimes want to declare an object without giving any constructor arguments, you should always include a default constructor. The following redefined version of `SampleClass` includes a default constructor:

```
class SampleClass
{
public:
    SampleClass(int parameter1, double parameter2);
    SampleClass();            Default constructor
    void do_stuff();
private:          ◄───────
    int data1;
    double data2;
};
```

If you redefine the class `SampleClass` in this manner, then the previous declaration of `your_object` would be legal.

If you do not want the default constructor to initialize any member variables, you can simply give it an empty body when you implement it. The following constructor definition is perfectly legal. It does nothing when called except make the compiler happy:

```
SampleClass::SampleClass()
{
    //Do nothing.
}
```

Note that if a class is created as a dynamic variable using the new operator then the default constructor is invoked.   ■

PITFALL   Constructors with No Arguments

If a constructor for a class called `BankAccount` has two formal parameters, you declare an object and give the arguments to the constructor as follows:

```
BankAccount account1(100, 2.3);
```

To call the constructor with no arguments, you would naturally think that you would declare the object as follows:

```
BankAccount account2(); //THIS WILL CAUSE PROBLEMS.
```

After all, when you call a function that has no arguments, you include a pair of empty parentheses. However, this is wrong for a constructor. Moreover, it may not produce an error message, since it does have an unintended meaning. The compiler will think that this code is the function declaration for a function called account2 that takes no arguments and returns a value of type BankAccount.

Do not include parentheses when you declare an object and want C++ to use the constructor with no arguments. The correct way to declare account2 using the constructor with no arguments is as follows:

```
BankAccount account2;
```

However, if you explicitly call a constructor in an assignment statement, you do use the parentheses. If the definitions and declarations are as in Display 10.6, then the following will set the account balance for account1 to $0.00 and set the interest rate to 0.0%:

```
account1 = BankAccount();
```

Constructors with No Arguments

When you declare an object and want the constructor with zero arguments to be called, you do not include any parentheses. For example, to declare an object and pass two arguments to the constructor, you might do the following:

```
BankAccount account1(100, 2.3);
```

However, if you want the constructor with zero arguments to be used, declare the object as follows:

```
BankAccount account1;
```

You do *not* declare the object as follows:

```
BankAccount account1(); //INCORRECT DECLARATION
```

(The problem is that this syntax declares a function named account1 that returns a BankAccount object and has no parameters.)

SELF-TEST EXERCISES

22. Suppose your program contains the following class definition (along with definitions of the member functions):

```
class YourClass
{
public:
    YourClass(int new_info, char more_new_info);
    YourClass();
    void do_stuff();
private:
    int information;
    char more_information;
};
```

Which of the following are legal?

```
YourClass an_object(42, 'A');
YourClass another_object;
YourClass yet_another_object();
an_object = YourClass(99, 'B');
an_object = YourClass();
an_object = YourClass;
```

23. How would you change the definition of the class DayOfYear in Display 10.4 so that it has two versions of an (overloaded) constructor? One version should have two *int* formal parameters (one for the month and one for the day) and should set the private member variables to represent that month and day. The other should have no formal parameters and should set the date represented to January 1. Do this without using a constructor initialization section in either constructor.

24. Redo the previous exercise, but this time use a constructor initialization section to initialize all member functions in each constructor.

10.3 ABSTRACT DATA TYPES

We all know — the Times knows — but we pretend we don't.

VIRGINIA WOOLF, *Monday or Tuesday*

A data type, such as the type *int*, has certain specified values, such as 0, 1, −1, 2, and so forth. You tend to think of the data type as being these values, but the operations on these values are just as important as the values. Without the operations, you could do nothing of interest with the values. The operations for the type *int* consist of +, −, *, /, %, and a few other operators and predefined library functions. You should not think of a data type as being simply a collection of values. A **data type** consists of a collection of values together with a set of basic operations defined on those values.

A data type is called an **abstract data type** (abbreviated ADT) if the programmers who use the type do not have access to the details of how the values and operations are implemented. The predefined types, such as *int*, are abstract data types (ADTs). You do not know how the operations, such as + and *, are implemented for the type *int*. Even if you did know, you would not use this information in any C++ program.

Programmer-defined types, such as the structure types and class types, are not automatically ADTs. Unless they are defined and used with care, programmer-defined types can be used in unintuitive ways that make a program difficult to understand and difficult to modify. The best way to avoid these problems is to make sure all the data types that you define are ADTs. The way that you do this in C++ is to use classes, but not every class is an ADT. To make it an ADT you must define the class in a certain way, and that is the topic of the next subsection.

Classes to Produce Abstract Data Types

A class is a type that you define, as opposed to the types, such as *int* and *char*, that are already defined for you. A value for a class type is the set of values of the member variables. For example, a value for the type BankAccount in Display 10.6 consists of two numbers of type *double*. For easy reference, we repeat the class definition (omitting only the comments):

```
class BankAccount
{
public:
    BankAccount(int dollars, int cents, double rate);
    BankAccount(int dollars, double rate);
    BankAccount();
    void set(int dollars, int cents, double rate);
    void set(int dollars, double rate);
    void update();
    double get_balance();
    double get_rate();
    void output(ostream& outs);
private:
    double balance;
    double interest_rate;
    double fraction(double percent);
};
```

The programmer who uses the type BankAccount need not know how you implemented the definition of BankAccount::update or any of the

other member functions. The function definition for the member function
BankAccount::update that we used is as follows:

```
void BankAccount::update()
{
    balance = balance + fraction(interest_rate) * balance;
}
```

However, we could have dispensed with the private function fraction and
implemented the member function update with the following slightly more
complicated formula:

```
void BankAccount::update()
{
    balance = balance + (interest_rate / 100.0) * balance;
}
```

The programmer who uses the class BankAccount need not be concerned with
which implementation of update we used, since both implementations have
the same effect.

Similarly, the programmer who uses the class BankAccount need not be
concerned about how the values of the class are implemented. We chose to
implement the values as two values of type *double*. If vacation_savings
is an object of type BankAccount, the value of vacation_savings consists
of the two values of type *double* stored in the following two member
variables:

```
vacation_savings.balance
vacation_savings.interest_rate
```

However, you do not want to think of the value of the object vacation_
savings as two numbers of type *double*, such as 1.3546e + 2 and 4.5. You
want to think of the value of vacation_savings as the single entry

Account balance $135.46
Interest rate 4.50%

That is why our implementation of BankAccount::output writes the class
value in this format.

The fact that we chose to implement this BankAccount value as the two
double values 1.3546e + 2 and 4.5 is an implementation detail. We could
instead have implemented this BankAccount value as the two *int* values 135
and 46 (for the dollars and cents part of the balance) and the single value
0.045 of type *double*. The value 0.045 is simply 4.5% converted to a fraction,
which might be a more useful way to implement a percentage figure. After
all, in order to compute interest on the account we convert a percentage
to just such a fraction. With this alternative implementation of the class
BankAccount, the public members would remain unchanged but the private
members would change to the following:

```
class BankAccount
{
public:
    <This part is exactly the same as before>
private:
    int dollars_part;
    int cents_part;
    double interest_rate;
    double fraction(double percent);
};
```

We would need to change the member function definitions to match this change, but that is easy to do. For example, the function definitions for get_balance and one version of the constructor could be changed to the following:

```
double BankAccount::get_balance()
{
    return (dollars_part + 0.01 * cents_part);
}

BankAccount::BankAccount(int dollars, int cents, double rate)
{
    if ((dollars < 0) || (cents < 0) || (rate < 0))
    {
        cout << "Illegal values for money or interest rate.\n";
        exit(1);
    }
    dollars_part = dollars;
    cents_part = cents;
    interest_rate = rate;
}
```

Similarly, each of the other member functions could be redefined to accommodate this new way of storing the account balance and the interest rate.

Notice that even though the user may think of the account balance as a single number, that does not mean the implementation has to be a single number of type *double*. You have just seen that it could, for example, be two numbers of type *int*. The programmer who uses the type BankAccount need not know any of this detail about how the values of the type BankAccount are implemented.

How to write an ADT

These comments about the type BankAccount illustrate the basic technique for defining a class so that it will be an abstract data type. In order to define a class so that it is an abstract data type, you need to separate the specification of how the type is used by a programmer from the details of how the type is implemented. The separation should be so complete that you can change the implementation of the class without needing to make any changes in any program that uses the class ADT. One way to ensure this separation is to follow these rules:

1. Make all the member variables private members of the class.

2. Make each of the basic operations that the programmer needs a public member function of the class, and fully specify how to use each such public member function.

3. Make any helping functions private member functions.

In Chapters 11 and 12 you will learn some alternative approaches to defining ADTs, but these three rules are one common way to ensure that a class is an abstract data type.

The **interface** of an ADT tells you how to use the ADT in your program. When you define an ADT as a C++ class, the interface consists of the public member functions of the class along with the comments that tell you how to use these public member functions. The interface of the ADT should be all you need to know in order to use the ADT in your program.

The **implementation** of the ADT tells how this interface is realized as C++ code. The implementation of the ADT consists of the private members of the class and the definitions of both the public and private member functions. Although you need the implementation in order to run a program that uses the ADT, you should not need to know anything about the implementation in order to write the rest of a program that uses the ADT; that is, you should not need to know anything about the implementation in order to write the main part of the program and to write any nonmember functions used by the main part of the program. The situation is similar to what we advocated for ordinary function definitions in Chapters 4 and 5. The implementation of an ADT, like the implementation of an ordinary function, should be thought of as being in a black box that you cannot see inside.

In Chapter 12 you will learn how to place the interface and implementation of an ADT in files separate from each other and separate from the programs that use the ADT. That way a programmer who uses the ADT literally does not see the implementation. Until then, we will place all of the details about our ADT classes in the same file as the main part of our program, but we still think of the interface (given in the public section of the class definitions) and the implementation (the private section of the class definition and the member function definitions) as separate parts of the ADT. We will strive to write our ADTs so that the user of the ADT need only know about the interface of the ADT and need not know anything about the implementation. To be sure you are defining your ADTs this way, simply make sure that if you change the implementation of your ADT, your program will still work without your needing to change any other part of the program. This is illustrated in the next Programming Example.

The most obvious benefit you derive from making your classes ADTs is that you can change the implementation without needing to change the other parts of your program. But ADTs provide more benefits than that. If you make your classes ADTs, you can divide work among different programmers,

Separate interface and implementation

VideoNote
Separate Interface and Implementation

with one programmer designing and writing the ADT and other programmers using the ADT. Even if you are the only programmer working on a project, you have divided one larger task into two smaller tasks, which makes your program easier to design and easier to debug.

| **PROGRAMMING EXAMPLE** | Alternative Implementation of a Class |

Display 10.7 contains the alternative implementation of the ADT class BankAccount discussed in the previous subsection. In this version, the data for a bank account is implemented as three member values: one for the dollars part of the account balance, one for the cents part of the account balance, and one for the interest rate.

Notice that, although both the implementation in Display 10.6 and the implementation in Display 10.7 each have a member variable called interest_ rate, the value stored is slightly different in the two implementations. If the account pays interest at a rate of 4.7%, then in the implementation in Display 10.6 (which is basically the same as the one in Display 10.5), the value of interest_rate is 4.7. However, in the implementation in Display 10.7, the value of interest_rate would be 0.047. This alternative implementation, shown in Display 10.7, stores the interest rate as a fraction rather than as a percentage figure. The basic difference in this new implementation is that when an interest rate is set, the function fraction is used to immediately convert the interest rate to a fraction. Hence, in this new implementation the private member function fraction is used in the definitions of constructors, but it is not needed in the definition of the member function update because the value in the member variable interest_rate has already been converted to a fraction. In the old implementation (shown in Display 10.5 and Display 10.6), the situation was just the reverse. In the old implementation, the private member function fraction was not used in the definition of constructors, but was used in the definition of update.

The public interface is not changed

Although we have changed the private members of the class BankAccount, we have not changed anything in the public section of the class definition. The public member functions have the same function declarations and they behave exactly as they did in the old version of the ADT class given in Display 10.6. For example, although this new implementation stores a percentage such as 4.7% as the fraction 0.047, the member function get_rate still returns the value 4.7, just as it would for the old implementation in Display 10.5. Similarly, the member function get_balance returns a single value of type *double*, which gives the balance as a number with a decimal point, just as it did in the old implementation in Display 10.5. This is true even though the balance is now stored in two member variables of type *int*, rather than in a single member variable of type *double* (as in the old versions).

DISPLAY 10.7 **Alternative** BankAccount **Class Implementation** *(part 1 of 4)*

```
1    //Demonstrates an alternative implementation of the class BankAccount.
2    #include <iostream>
3    #include <cmath>
4    using namespace std;
5    //Class for a bank account:
6    class BankAccount
7    {
8    public:
9        BankAccount(int dollars, int cents, double rate);
10       //Initializes the account balance to $dollars.cents and
11       //initializes the interest rate to rate percent.

12       BankAccount(int dollars, double rate);
13       //Initializes the account balance to $dollars.00 and
14       //initializes the interest rate to rate percent.

15       BankAccount( );
16       //Initializes the account balance to $0.00 and the
17       //interest rate to 0.0%.

18       void set(int dollars, int cents, double rate);
19       //Postcondition: The account balance has been set to $dollars.cents;
20       //The interest rate has been set to rate percent.

21       void set(int dollars, double rate);
22       //Postcondition: The account balance has been set to $dollars.00.
23       //The interest rate has been set to rate percent.

24       void update( );
25       //Postcondition: One year of simple interest has been
26       //added to the account balance.

27       double get_balance( );
28       //Returns the current account balance.

29       double get_rate( );
30       //Returns the current account interest rate as a percentage.

31       void output(ostream& outs);
32       //Precondition: If outs is a file output stream, then
33       //outs has already been connected to a file.
34       //Postcondition: Account balance and interest rate
35       //have been written to the stream outs.
36   private:
37       int dollars_part;
38       int cents_part;
39       double interest_rate;
40       //Expressed as a fraction, for example, 0.057 for 5.7%
```

> Notice that the public members of
> **BankAccount** look and behave
> exactly the same as in Display 10.6

(continued)

DISPLAY 10.7   Alternative BankAccount **Class Implementation** *(part 2 of 4)*

```
41        double fraction(double percent);
42        //Converts a percentage to a fraction. For example, fraction(50.3)
43        //returns 0.503.

44        double percent(double fraction_value);        ←——  New
45        //Converts a fraction to a percentage. For example, percent(0.503)
46        //returns 50.3.
47    };
48    int main( )
49    {
50        BankAccount account1(100, 2.3), account2;
51
52        cout << "account1 initialized as follows:\n";
53        account1.output(cout);
54        cout << "account2 initialized as follows:\n";
55        account2.output(cout);
56
57        account1 = BankAccount(999, 99, 5.5);
58        cout << "account1 reset to the following:\n";
59        account1.output(cout);
60        return 0;
61    }
62    BankAccount::BankAccount(int dollars, int cents, double rate)
63    {
64        if ((dollars < 0) || (cents < 0) || (rate < 0))
65        {
66            cout << "Illegal values for money or interest rate.\n";
67            exit(1);
68        }
69        dollars_part = dollars;
70        cents_part = cents;
71        interest_rate = fraction(rate);
72    }
73    BankAccount::BankAccount(int dollars, double rate)
74    {
75        if ((dollars < 0) || (rate < 0))
76        {
77            cout << "Illegal values for money or interest rate.\n";
78            exit(1);
79        }
80        dollars_part = dollars;
81        cents_part = 0;
82        interest_rate = fraction(rate);
83    }
84    BankAccount::BankAccount( ) : dollars_part(0), cents_part(0), interest_rate(0.0)
85
```

Since the body of **main** is identical to that in Display 10.6, the screen output is also identical to that in Display 10.6

In the old implementation of this ADT, the private member function **fraction** was used in the definition of **update**. In this implementation, **fraction** is instead used in the definition of constructors and in the set function.

(continued)

DISPLAY 10.7   Alternative BankAccount **Class Implementation** *(part 3 of 4)*

```
86      {
87          //Body intentionally empty.
88      }
89      double BankAccount::fraction(double percent_value)
90      {
91          return (percent_value/100.0);
92      }
93      //Uses cmath:
94      void BankAccount::update( )
95      {
96          double balance = get_balance( );
97          balance = balance + interest_rate * balance;
98          dollars_part = static_cast<int>(floor(balance));
99          cents_part = static_cast<int>(floor((balance - dollars_part)*100));
100     }
101     double BankAccount::get_balance( )
102     {
103         return (dollars_part + 0.01 * cents_part);
104     }
105     double BankAccount::percent(double fraction_value)
106     {
107         return (fraction_value * 100);
108     }
109     double BankAccount::get_rate( )
110     {
111         return percent(interest_rate);
112     }
113     //Uses iostream:
114     void BankAccount::output(ostream& outs)
115     {
116         outs.setf(ios::fixed);
117         outs.setf(ios::showpoint);
118         outs.precision(2);
119         outs << "Account balance $" << get_balance( ) << endl;
120         outs << "Interest rate "<< get_rate( ) << "%" << endl;
121     }
122     void BankAccount::set(int dollars, int cents, double rate)
123     {
124         if ((dollars < 0) || (cents < 0) || (rate < 0))
125         {
126             cout << "Illegal values for money or interest rate.\n";
127             exit(1);
128         }
```

The new definitions of get_balance and get_rate *ensure that the output will still be in the correct units.*

(continued)

DISPLAY 10.7 Alternative BankAccount **Class Implementation** *(part 4 of 4)*

```
129        dollars_part = dollars;
130        cents_part = cents;
131        interest_rate = fraction(rate);
132    }

133    void BankAccount::set(int dollars, double rate)
134    {
135        if ((dollars < 0) || (rate < 0))
136        {
137            cout << "Illegal values for money or interest rate.\n";
138            exit(1);
139        }
140        dollars_part = dollars;
141        interest_rate = fraction(rate);
142    }
```

Changing private
member functions

Notice that there is an important difference between how you treat the public member functions and how you treat the private member functions. If you want to preserve the interface of an ADT class so that any programs that use it need not change (other than changing the definitions of the class and its member functions), then you must leave the public member function declarations unchanged. However, you are free to add, delete, or change any of the private member functions. In this example, we have added one additional private function called percent, which is the inverse of the function fraction. The function fraction converts a percentage to a fraction, and the function percent converts a fraction back to a percentage. For example, fraction(4.7) returns 0.047, and percent(0.047) returns 4.7.

Information Hiding

We discussed information hiding when we introduced functions in Chapter 3. We said that **information hiding,** as applied to functions, means that you should write your functions so that they could be used as black boxes, that is, so that the programmer who uses the function need not know any details about how the function is implemented. This principle means that all the programmer who uses a function needs to know is the function declaration and the accompanying comment that explains how to use the function. The use of private member variables and private member functions in the definition of an abstract data type is another way to implement information hiding, but now we apply the principle to data values as well as to functions.

SELF-TEST EXERCISES

25. When you define an ADT as a C++ class, should you make the member variables public or private? Should you make the member functions public or private?

26. When you define an ADT as a C++ class, what items are considered part of the interface for the ADT? What items are considered part of the implementation for the ADT?

27. Suppose your friend defines an ADT as a C++ class in the way we described in Section 10.3. You are given the task of writing a program that uses this ADT. That is, you must write the main part of the program as well as any nonmember functions that are used in the main part of the program. The ADT is very long and you do not have a lot of time to write this program. What parts of the ADT do you need to read and what parts can you safely ignore?

28. Redo the three- and two-parameter constructors in Display 10.7 so that all member variables are set using a constructor initialization section.

10.4 INTRODUCTION TO INHERITANCE

One of the most powerful features of C++ is the use of *derived classes*. The word *inheritance* is just another name for the topic of derived classes. When we say that one class was derived from another class, we mean that the derived class was obtained from the other class by adding features. For example, suppose we define a class for vehicles that has member variables to record the vehicle's number of wheels and maximum number of occupants. The class also has accessor and mutator functions. Imagine that we then define a class for automobiles that has member variables and functions just like the ones in the class of vehicles. In addition, our automobile class would have added member variables for such things as the amount of fuel in the fuel tank and the license plate number and would also have some added member functions. Instead of repeating the definitions of the member variables and functions of the class of vehicles within the class of automobiles, we could use C++'s inheritance mechanism and let the automobile class inherit all the member variables and functions of the class for vehicles.

Inheritance allows you to define a general class and then later define more specialized classes that add some new details to the existing general class. This saves work because the more specialized, or derived, class inherits all the properties of the general class and you, the programmer, need only program the new features. This section will first introduce the notion of inheritance and a derived class and then we briefly describe how to create your own derived classes. Details of inheritance are left to Chapter 15. It may take a while before you are completely comfortable with the idea of a derived class, but you easily can learn enough about derived classes to start using them in some simple, and very useful, ways.

Derived Classes

Consider the BankAccount class defined in Display 10.7. This class keeps track of an amount and interest rate for a bank account—fairly generic features that apply to any interest-bearing account. If we would like to implement more specific types of bank accounts, then there is a natural hierarchy for grouping the account types. Display 10.8 depicts a part of this hierarchical arrangement for bank accounts, checking accounts, money market accounts, savings accounts, and Certificate of Deposit (CD) accounts. In the hierarchy, BankAccount is the most general type of account; more specific types of accounts are shown underneath. An arrow points from a specific account type to a more general account type. In addition to representing different types of bank accounts, each box also corresponds to a class that we can implement in C++.

For example, a checking account does everything a bank account can do (store an amount and interest rate) but in addition allows customers to make deposits and write checks. Similarly, a savings account does everything a bank account can do but in addition allows customers to make deposits and withdrawals. Unlike a checking account, a savings account may not allow customers to write checks. Since both checking accounts and savings accounts are types of bank accounts they are shown in Display 10.8 directly underneath the BankAccount class. When we say that some class A is a **derived class** of some other class B, it means that class A has all the features of class B but it also has *added features*. The convention for indicating this relationship in a diagram is to draw an an unfilled arrow from the specific to the more general class. For example, in Display 10.8 the CheckingAccount and SavingsAccount classes are derived classes of the BankAccount class.

DISPLAY 10.8   A Class Hierarchy

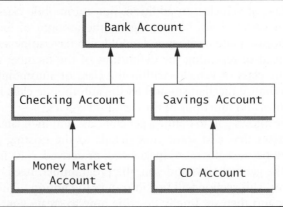

In C++, some class **A** can be a derived class of some other class **B**, which in turn can be a derived class of some other class **C**, and so on. For example, a CD account is similar to a savings account except the funds and any accrued interest must not be withdrawn until after a "maturity" date. If the funds are withdrawn prior to the maturity date, then there is a penalty. Due to these restrictions, a CD account normally accrues interest at a higher rate than a savings account. In the hierarchy, this is shown by deriving CDAccount from SavingsAccount. Similarly, a money market account is a special type of checking account in which the customer normally has a limit on the number of checks that can be written, along with higher minimum balances, but pays a higher interest rate. In the hierarchy, this is shown by deriving MoneyMarketAccount from CheckingAccount.

Derived classes are often discussed using the metaphor of inheritance and family relationships. If class B is a derived class of class A, then class B is called a **child** of class A and class A is called a **parent** of class B. The parent class is also referred to as the **base** class. The derived class is said to **inherit** the member functions of its parent class. For example, every convertible inherits the fact that it has four wheels from the class of all automobiles. This is why the topic of derived classes is often called *inheritance*.

Defining Derived Classes

If we want to create a class to represent a savings account, we could start by making a copy of the BankAccount class and renaming it to SavingsAccount. We would need to add new public member functions to deposit and withdraw funds. While this approach would work, it would be very inefficient, because the SavingsAccount class would duplicate most of the functionality in the BankAccount class. Not only does this waste memory space, it also becomes more difficult to make modifications. For example, if we later decide to change the update( ) function to accrue interest daily instead of annually, then we would have two places to make the change: in the SavingsAccount class and also in the BankAccount class. These problems can be solved by defining the SavingsAccount class as a derived class of the BankAccount class. The SavingsAccount class then can share member variables and functions defined in the BankAccount class. We specify this relationship when defining the derived class by adding a colon followed by the keyword public and the name of the parent or base class:

```
class SavingsAccount : public BankAccount
{
public:
    SavingsAccount(int dollars, int cents, double rate);
    <Other constructors would normally go here>
    void deposit(int dollars, int cents);
    void withdraw(int dollars, int cents);
private:
};
```

The colon separates the derived class, Savings Account, *from the parent class,* BankAccount

Notice that we only defined functions and data that specifically relate to savings accounts, in this case, functions to deposit and withdraw money. We don't need to redefine all of the variables and functions relating to bank accounts—such as storing the interest rate, dollars, cents, or defining the update( ) function—because those members will be inherited from the BankAccount class and are automatically created when we construct a SavingsAccount object. For example, if we create a SavingsAccount object, we could invoke the following functions:

```
SavingsAccount account(100, 50, 5.5);
account.deposit(10,25);
account.output(cout);
```

Invoking a function in the derived class,

Invoking a function in the parent class, BankAccount

In this example, inheritance allowed us to reuse code defined in the parent class from the context of the derived class. Moreover, if we later change one of BankAccount's functions—such as update( )—then the new code automatically will be used from the context of its derived classes when the program is recompiled and linked. An implementation of the SavingsAccount class along with a main function to test the deposit and withdraw functions is given in Display 10.9. For simplicity, we have left verification out of the deposit and withdraw functions, for example, checking for negative amounts, but you should be able to add them easily with some *if* statements.

Once the SavingsAccount class is defined we can go one step further and derive more specialized classes from the SavingsAccount. For example, to define the CD account class we need a new private member variable to store the days until maturity and define functions to access this variable:

```
class CDAccount : public SavingsAccount
{
public:
    CDAccount(int dollars, int cents, double rate,
              int days_to_maturity);
    <Other constructors would normally go here>
    int get_days_to_maturity( );
    //Returns the number of days until the CD matures
    void decrement_days_to_maturity( );
    //Subtracts one from the days_to_maturity variable
private:
    int days_to_maturity; //Days until the CD matures
};
```

Once again, we only defined functions and data that specifically relate to CD accounts, in this case, storing and manipulating the number of days to maturity. We don't need to redefine all of the variables and functions relating to bank accounts or savings accounts because those members will be inherited from the parent classes. For example, once the functions in the CDAccount class are implemented, we could invoke the following functions from the CDAccount, SavingsAccount, or BankAccount classes given a CDAccount object:

DISPLAY 10.9   A SavingsAccount **Derived Class** (part 1 of 2)

<Everything from Display 10.6 should be inserted here except for the **main** *function.>*

```
1    class SavingsAccount : public BankAccount
2    {
3    public:
4        SavingsAccount(int dollars, int cents, double rate);
5        //Other constructors would go here
6        void deposit(int dollars, int cents);
7        //Adds $dollars.cents to the account balance
8        void withdraw(int dollars, int cents);
9        //Subtracts $dollars.cents from the account balance
10   private:
11   };
12   int main( )
13   {
14       SavingsAccount account(100, 50, 5.5);
15       account.output(cout);
16       cout << endl;
17       cout << "Depositing $10.25." << endl;
18       account.deposit(10,25);
19       account.output(cout);
20       cout << endl;
21       cout << "Withdrawing $11.80." << endl;
22       account.withdraw(11,80);
23       account.output(cout);
24       cout << endl;
25       return 0;
26   }
27   SavingsAccount::SavingsAccount(int dollars, int cents, double rate):
28       BankAccount(dollars, cents, rate)
29   {
30       //deliberately empty
31   }
32   void SavingsAccount::deposit(int dollars, int cents)
33   {
34       double balance = get_balance();
35       balance += dollars;
36       balance += (static_cast<double>(cents) / 100);
37       int new_dollars = static_cast<int>(balance);
38       int new_cents = static_cast<int>((balance - new_dollars) * 100);
```

The colon indicates that the class **SavingsAccount** is derived from the class **BankAccount**

Only new member functions or variables need to be defined

The **SavingsAccount** constructor invokes the **BankAccount** constructor. Note the preceding colon.

The **deposit** function adds the new amount to the balance and changes the member variables via the **set** function

(continued)

DISPLAY 10.9 A SavingsAccount Derived Class *(part 2 of 2)*

```
39          set(new_dollars, new_cents, get_rate());
40      }

41      void SavingsAccount::withdraw(int dollars, int cents)
42      {
43          double balance = get_balance();
44          balance -= dollars;
45          balance -= (static_cast<double>(cents) / 100);
46          int new_dollars = static_cast<int>(balance);
47          int new_cents = static_cast<int>((balance - new_dollars) * 100);
48          set(new_dollars, new_cents, get_rate());
49      }
```

The **withdraw** *function subtracts the amount from the balance and changes the member variables via the* **set** *function*

Screen Output

```
Account balance $100.50
Interest rate 5.50%
Depositing $10.25.
Account balance $110.75
Interest rate 5.50%
Withdrawing $11.80.
Account balance $98.95
Interest rate 5.50%
```

```
//Create a new CD with $1000, 6% interest, 180 days to maturity
CDAccountnewCD(1000, 0, 6.0, 180);

newCD.deposit(100,50);
days_to_maturity = newCD.get_days_to_maturity( );
//Returns 180
balance = newCD.get_balance( );
//Returns 1100.50
```

Invoking a function in SavingsAccount

Invoking a function in CDAccount

Invoking a function in BankAccount

This short example has only scratched the surface of what is possible using inheritance. Additional details are described in Chapter 15. While it does take some effort to learn how to effectively design classes using inheritance, the effort will pay off in the long run. You will end up writing less code that is easier to understand and maintain than code that does not use inheritance.

SELF-TEST EXERCISES

29. How does inheritance support code reuse and make code easier to maintain?

30. Can a derived class directly access by name a private member variable of the parent class?

31. Suppose the class SportsCar is a derived class of a class Automobile. Suppose also that the class Automobile has public member functions named accelerate and addGas. Will an object of the class SportsCar have member functions named accelerate and addGas?

CHAPTER SUMMARY

- A structure can be used to combine data of different types into a single (compound) data value.

- A class can be used to combine data and functions into a single (compound) object.

- A member variable or a member function for a class may be either public or private. If it is public, it can be used outside of the class. If it is private, it can be used only in the definition of another member function in the class.

- A function may have formal parameters of a class or structure type. A function may return values of a class or structure type.

- A member function for a class can be overloaded in the same way as ordinary functions are overloaded.

- A **constructor** is a member function of a class that is called automatically when an object of the class is declared. A constructor must have the same name as the class of which it is a member.

- A data type consists of a collection of values together with a set of basic operations defined on these values.

- A data type is called an **abstract data type** (abbreviated **ADT**) if a programmer who uses the type does not need to know any of the details about how the values and operations for that type are implemented.

- One way to implement an abstract data type in C++ is to define a class with all member variables being private and with the operations implemented as public member functions.

- Inheritance refers to a parent/child relationship between classes. The child or derived class inherits members from the parent class.

Answers to Self-Test Exercises

1. a. *double*

    b. *double*

    c. illegal—cannot use struct tag instead of a structure variable

    d. illegal—savings_account undeclared

    e. *char*

    f. *TermAccount*

2. ```
   A $9.99
   A $1.11
   ```

3. Many compilers give poor error messages. Surprisingly, the error message from g++ is quite informative.

    ```
    g++ -fsyntax-only c10testq3.cc
    c10testq3.cc:8: semicolon missing after declaration of
    'Stuff'
    c10testq3.cc:8: extraneous 'int' ignored
    c10testq3.cc:8: semicolon missing after declaration of
    'struct Stuff'
    ```

4. A x = {1,2};

5. a. Too few initializers, not a syntax error. After initialization, due_date. month == 12, due_date.day == 21, due_date.year == 0. Member variables not provided an initializer are initialized to a zero of appropriate type.

    b. Correct after initialization: 12 == due_date.month, 21 == due_date. day, 2022 == due_date.year.

    c. Error: too many initializers.

    d. May be a design error, that is, an error in intent. The author of the code provides only two digits for the date initializer. There should be four digits used for the year because a program using two-digit dates could fail in ways that vary from amusing to disastrous at the turn of the century.

6. *struct* EmployeeRecord

    ```
    {
        double wage_rate;
        int vacation;
        char status;
    };
    ```

7. *void* read_shoe_record(ShoeType& new_shoe)

    ```
    {
    ```
    ```

```
        cout << "Enter shoe style (one letter): ";
        cin >> new_shoe.style;
        cout << "Enter shoe price $";
        cin >> new_shoe.price;
    }
```

8. `ShoeType discount(ShoeType old_record)`

```
    {
        ShoeType temp;
        temp.style = old_record.style;
        temp.price = 0.90 * old_record.price;
        return temp;
    }
```

9. `struct StockRecord`

```
    {
        ShoeType shoe_info;
        Date arrival_date;
    };
```

10. `StockRecord aRecord;`

```
    aRecord.arrival_date.year = 2006;
```

11. `void DayOfYear::input()`

```
    {
        cout << "Enter month as a number: ";
        cin >> month;
        cout << "Enter the day of the month: ";
        cin >> day;
    }
```

12. `void Temperature::set(double new_degrees, char new_scale)`

```
    {
        degrees = new_degrees;
        scale = new_scale;
    }
```

13. Both the dot operator and the scope resolution operator are used with
    member names to specify the class or struct of which the member name
    is a member. If class DayOfYear is as defined in Display 10.3 and today
    is an object of the class DayOfYear, then the member month may be ac-
    cessed with the dot operator: today.month. When we give the definition
    of a member function, the scope resolution operator is used to tell the
    compiler that this function is the one declared in the class whose name is
    given before the scope resolution operator.

14. ```
    void DayOfYear::check_date( )
    {
        if ((month < 1) || (month > 12)
            || (day < 1) || (day > 31))
        {
            cout << "Illegal date. Aborting program.\n";
            exit(1);
        }
        if (((month == 4) || (month == 6) || (month == 9)
                                          || (month == 11))
                                          && (day == 31))
        {
            cout << "Illegal date. Aborting program.\n";
            exit(1);
        }
        if ((month == 2) && (day > 29))
        {
            cout << "Illegal date. Aborting program.\n";
            exit(1);
        }
    }
    ```

15. ```
    hyundai.price = 4999.99; //ILLEGAL. price is private.

    jaguar.set_price(30000.97); //LEGAL
    double a_price, a_profit; //LEGAL
    a_price = jaguar.get_price(); //LEGAL
    a_profit = jaguar.get_profit(); //ILLEGAL. get_profit is private.
    a_profit = hyundai.get_profit(); //ILLEGAL. get_profit is private.
    if (hyundai == jaguar) //ILLEGAL. Cannot use == with classes.
        cout << "Want to swap cars?";
    hyundai = jaguar; //LEGAL
    ```

16. After the change, they would all be legal except for the following, which is still illegal:

    ```
    if (hyundai == jaguar) //ILLEGAL. Cannot use == with classes.
        cout << "Want to swap cars?";
    ```

17. *private* restricts access to function definitions to member functions of the same class. This restricts any change of *private* variables to functions provided by the class author. The class author is then in control of these changes to the *private* data, preventing inadvertent corruption of the class data.

18. a. Only one. The compiler warns if you have no *public*: members in a class (or *struct* for that matter).

    b. None; we normally expect to find at least one *private*: section in a class.

c. In a class, such a section is by default a `private:` section.

d. In a *struct*, such a section is by default a *public:* section.

19. A possible correct answer is as follows:

```
double difference(BankAccount account1, BankAccount account2)
{
    return (account1.get_balance() - account2.get_balance());
}
```

Note that the following is not correct, because `balance` is a private member.

```
double difference(BankAccount account1, BankAccount account2)
{
    return (account1.balance - account2.balance); //ILLEGAL
}
```

20. `void double_update(BankAccount& the_account)`

```
{
    the_account.update();
    the_account.update();
}
```

Note that since this is not a member function, you must give the object name and dot operator when you call `update`.

21. `BankAccount new_account(BankAccount old_account)`

```
{
    BankAccount temp;
    temp.set(0, old_account.get_rate( ));
    return temp;
}
```

22.
```
YourClass an_object(42, 'A'); //LEGAL
YourClass another_object; //LEGAL
YourClass yet_another_object(); //PROBLEM
an_object = YourClass(99, 'B'); //LEGAL
an_object = YourClass(); //LEGAL
an_object = YourClass; //ILLEGAL
```

The statement marked *//PROBLEM* is not, strictly speaking, illegal, but it does not mean what you might think it means. If you mean this to be a declaration of an object called `yet_another_object`, then it is wrong. It is a correct function declaration for a function called `yet_another_object` that takes zero arguments and that returns a value of type `YourClass`, but that is not the intended meaning. As a practical matter, you can probably consider it illegal. The correct way to declare an object called yet_another_object so that it will be initialized with the default constructor is as follows:

```
YourClass yet_another_object;
```

23. The modified class definition is as follows:

```
class DayOfYear
{
public:
    DayOfYear(int the_month, int the_day);
    //Precondition: the_month and the_day form a
    //possible date. Initializes the date according to
    //the arguments.
    DayOfYear();
    //Initializes the date to January first.
    void input();
    void output();
    int get_month();
    //Returns the month, 1 for January, 2 for February, etc.
    int get_day();
    //Returns the day of the month.
private:
    void check_date( );
    int month;
    int day;
};
```

Notice that we have omitted the member function set, since the constructors make set unnecessary. You must also add the following function definitions (and delete the function definition for DayOfYear::set):

```
DayOfYear::DayOfYear(int the_month, int the_day)
{
    month = the_month;
    day = the_day;
    check_date();
}
DayOfYear::DayOfYear()
{
    month = 1;
    day = 1;
}
```

24. The class definition is the same as in the previous exercise. The constructor definitions would change to the following:

```
DayOfYear::DayOfYear(int the_month, int the_day)
    : month(the_month), day(the_day)
```

```
{
    check_date();
}
DayOfYear::DayOfYear() : month(1), day(1)
{
    //Body intentionally empty.
}
```

25. The member variables should all be private. The member functions that are part of the interface for the ADT (that is, the member functions that are operations for the ADT) should be public. You may also have auxiliary helping functions that are used only in the definitions of other member functions. These auxiliary functions should be private.

26. All the declarations of private member variables are part of the implementation. (There should be no public member variables.) All the function declarations for public member functions of the class (which are listed in the class definitions) as well as the explanatory comments for these function declarations are part of the interface. All the function declarations for private member functions are part of the implementation. All member function definitions (whether the function is public or private) are part of the implementation.

27. You need to read only the interface parts. That is, you need to read only the function declarations for public members of the class (which are listed in the class definitions) as well as the explanatory comments for these function declarations. You need not read any of the function declarations of the private member functions, the declarations of the private member variables, the definitions of the public member functions, or the definitions of the private member functions.

28.
```
BankAccount::BankAccount(int dollars, int cents,
                         double rate) : dollars_part(dollars),
                         cents_part(cents), interest_
                         rate(fraction(rate))
{
    if ((dollars < 0) || (cents < 0) || (rate < 0))
    {
        cout << "Illegal values for money or interest rate.\n";
        exit(1);
    }
}

BankAccount::BankAccount(int dollars, double rate)
    : dollars_part(dollars), cents_part(0),
                    interest_rate(fraction(rate))
{
    if ((dollars < 0) || (rate < 0))
```

```
        {
            cout << "Illegal values for money or interest rate.\n";
            exit(1);
        }
```

29. Functions and data defined for the parent class can be made available in the derived class, eliminating the need to redefine the functions and data again in the derived class. This enhances maintainability because there is now no duplication of code among multiple classes and hence only a single location in the code that may be subject to change. Additionally, inheritance provides a clean way to isolate code that is only applicable to a derived class. Since such code only appears in the definition of the derived class, it is usually easier to read.

30. No, but a derived class can indirectly access a private member variable of the parent class through a public function.

31. Yes, the derived class will have access to the same functions. In Chapter 15 we will discuss how we can make the functions do different things for an object of class SportsCar versus an object of class Automobile.

PROGRAMMING PROJECTS

myprogramminglab   *Visit www.myprogramminglab.com to complete many of these Programming Projects online and get instant feedback.*

1. Write a grading program for a class with the following grading policies:

   a. There are two quizzes, each graded on the basis of 10 points.

   b. There is one midterm exam and one final exam, each graded on the basis of 100 points.

   c. The final exam counts for 50 percent of the grade, the midterm counts for 25 percent, and the two quizzes together count for a total of 25 percent. (Do not forget to normalize the quiz scores. They should be converted to a percent before they are averaged in.)

   Any grade of 90 or more is an A, any grade of 80 or more (but less than 90) is a B, any grade of 70 or more (but less than 80) is a C, any grade of 60 or more (but less than 70) is a D, and any grade below 60 is an F.

   The program will read in the student's scores and output the student's record, which consists of two quiz and two exam scores as well as the student's average numeric score for the entire course and the final letter grade. Define and use a structure for the student record. If this is a class assignment, ask your instructor if input/output should be done with the keyboard and screen or if it should be done with files. If it is to be done with files, ask your instructor for instructions on file names.

2. Redo Programming Project 1 (or do it for the first time), but this time make the student record type a class type rather than a structure type. The student record class should have member variables for all the input data described in Programing Project 1 and a member variable for the student's weighted average numeric score for the entire course as well as a member variable for the student's final letter grade. Make all member variables private. Include member functions for each of the following: member functions to set each of the member variables to values given as an argument(s) to the function, member functions to retrieve the data from each of the member variables, a *void* function that calculates the student's weighted average numeric score for the entire course and sets the corresponding member variable, and a *void* function that calculates the student's final letter grade and sets the corresponding member variable.

3. Redefine CDAccount from Display 10.1 so that it is a class rather than a structure. Use the same member variables as in Display 10.1 but make them private. Include member functions for each of the following: one to return the initial balance, one to return the balance at maturity, one to return the interest rate, and one to return the term. Include a constructor that sets all of the member variables to any specified values, as well as a default constructor. Embed your class definition in a test program.

VideoNote
Solution to Programming
Project 10.3

4. Redo your definition of the class CDAccount from Programming Project 3 so that it has the same interface but a different implementation. The new implementation is in many ways similar to the second implementation for the class BankAccount given in Display 10.7. Your new implementation for the class CDAccount will record the balance as two values of type *int*: one for the dollars and one for the cents. The member variable for the interest rate will store the interest rate as a fraction rather than as a percentage. For example, an interest rate of 4.3% will be stored as the value 0.043 of type *double*. Store the term in the same way as in Display 10.1.

5. Define a class for a type called ComplexType. An object of this type is used to represent complex numbers, so it records the real and imaginary parts of a complex number. Include a default constructor that sets real and imaginary parts to zero and a constructor with one argument that sets the real and imaginary parts to the value specified by its argument. Add another constructor which will pass a *float* value in real and imaginary parts of the complex number. Include member functions to display the complex number in real and imaginary parts. Also, include a member function that will add two complex numbers and return the complex number object. The member function for output will have to pass a character pointer. Embed your class definition in a test program. Create two objects, then add those objects and display them.

6. Define a class called Month that is an abstract data type for a month. Your class will have one member variable of type *int* to represent a month

(1 for January, 2 for February, and so forth). Include all the following member functions: a constructor to set the month using the first three letters in the name of the month as three arguments, a constructor to set the month using an integer as an argument (1 for January, 2 for February, and so forth), a default constructor, an input function that reads the month as an integer, an input function that reads the month as the first three letters in the name of the month, an output function that outputs the month as an integer, an output function that outputs the month as the first three letters in the name of the month, and a member function that returns the next month as a value of type Month. The input and output functions will each have one formal parameter for the stream. Embed your class definition in a test program.

7. Redefine the implementation of the class Month described in Programming Project 6 (or do the definition for the first time, but do the implementation as described here). This time the month is implemented as three member variables of type *char* that store the first three letters of the name of the month. Embed your definition in a test program.

8. (In order to do this project you must have first done either Project 6 or Project 7.) Rewrite the program in Display 10.4, but use the class Month that you defined in Project 6 or Project 7 as the type for the member variable to record the month. (You may define the class Month either as described in Project 6 or as described in Project 7.) Redefine the member function output so that it has one formal parameter of type ostream for the output stream. Modify the program so that everything that is output to the screen is *also* output to a file. This means that all output statements will occur twice: once with the argument cout and once with an output-stream argument. If you are in a class, obtain the file name from your instructor. The input will still come from the keyboard. Only the output will be sent to a file.

9. My mother always took a little red counter to the grocery store. The counter was used to keep a tally of the amount of money she would have spent so far on that visit to the store, if she bought all the items in her basket. There was a four-digit display, increment buttons for each digit, and a reset button. There was an overflow indicator that came up red if more money was entered than the $99.99 it would register. (This was a long time ago.)

Write and implement the member functions of a class Counter that simulates and slightly generalizes the behavior of this grocery store counter. The constructor should create a Counter object that can count up to the constructor's argument. That is, Counter(9999) should provide a counter that can count up to 9999. A newly constructed counter displays a reading of 0. The member function *void* reset(); sets the counter's number to 0. The member functions *void* incr1(); increments the units digit by 1, *void* incr10(); increments the tens digit by 1, and *void* incr100(); and *void* incr1000( ); increment the next two digits, respectively. Accounting for any carry when you increment should require no further action than adding an appropriate number to the private data member. A member function *bool* overflow(); detects overflow. (Overflow is the result of incrementing the counter's private data member beyond the maximum entered at counter construction.)

Use this class to provide a simulation of my mother's little red clicker. Even though the display is an integer, in the simulation, the rightmost (lower-order) two digits are always thought of as cents and tens of cents, the next digit is dollars, and the fourth digit is tens of dollars.

Provide keys for cents, dimes, dollars, and tens of dollars. Unfortunately, no choice of keys seems particularly mnemonic. One choice is to use the keys asdfo: a for cents, followed by a digit 1 to 9; s for dimes, followed by digits 1 to 9; d for dollars, followed by a digit 1 to 9; and f for tens of dollars, again followed by a digit 1 to 9. Each entry (one of asdf followed by 1 to 9) is followed by pressing the Return key. Any overflow is reported after each operation. Overflow can be requested by pressing the o key.

10. Write a rational number class. This problem will be revisited in Chapter 11, where operator overloading will make the problem much easier. For now we will use member functions add, sub, mul, div, and less that each carry out the operations +, -, *, /, and <. For example, a + b will be written a.add(b), and a < b will be written a.less(b).

Define a class for rational numbers. A rational number is a "ratio-nal" number, composed of two integers with division indicated. The division is not carried out, it is only indicated, as in 1/2, 2/3, 15/32, 65/4, 16/5. You should represent rational numbers by two *int* values, numerator and denominator.

A principle of abstract data type construction is that constructors must be present to create objects with any legal values. You should provide constructors to make objects out of pairs of *int* values; this is a constructor with two *int* parameters. Since every *int* is also a rational number, as in 2/1 or 17/1, you should provide a constructor with a single *int* parameter.

Provide member functions input and output that take an istream and ostream argument, respectively, and fetch or write rational numbers in the form 2/3 or 37/51 to or from the keyboard (and to or from a file).

Provide member functions add, sub, mul, and div that return a rational value. Provide a function less that returns a *bool* value. These functions should do the operation suggested by the name. Provide a member function neg that has no parameters and returns the negative of the calling object.

Provide a `main` function that thoroughly tests your class implementation. The following formulas will be useful in defining functions.

```
a/b + c/d = (a * d + b * c) / (b * d)
a/b - c/d = (a * d - b * c) / (b * d)
(a/b) * (c/d) = (a * c) / (b * d)
(a/b) / (c/d) = (a * d) / (c * b)
-(a/b) = (-a/b)
(a/b) < (c/d) means (a * d) < (c * b)
(a/b) == (c/d) means (a * d) == (c * b)
```

Let any sign be carried by the numerator; keep the denominator positive.

11. Define a class called `Odometer` that will be used to track fuel and mileage for an automotive vehicle. Include private member variables to track the miles driven and the fuel efficiency of the vehicle in miles per gallon. The class should have a constructor that initializes these values to zero. Include a member function to reset the odometer to zero miles, a member function to set the fuel efficiency, a member function that accepts miles driven for a trip and adds it to the odometer's total, and a member function that returns the number of gallons of gasoline that the vehicle has consumed since the odometer was last reset.

    Use your class with a test program that creates several trips with different fuel efficiencies.

12. Redo Programming Project 16 from Chapter 5 (or do it for the first time), but this time use a class to encapsulate the date. Use private member variables to store the day, month, and year along with an appropriate constructor and member functions to get and set the data. Create a public function that returns the day of the week. All helper functions should be declared private. Embed your class definition in a suitable test program.

13. The U.S. Postal Service printed a bar code on every envelope that represented a five- (or more) digit zip code using a format called POSTNET (this format was deprecated in favor of a new system, OneCode, in 2009). The bar code consists of long and short bars as shown:

For this program, we will represent the bar code as a string of digits. The digit 1 represents a long bar, and the digit 0 represents a short bar. Therefore, the bar code would be represented in our program as

11010010100010101011000010011

The first and last digits of the bar code are always 1. Removing these leaves 25 digits. If these 25 digits are split into groups of 5 digits each, we have

10100   10100   01010   11000   01001

Next, consider each group of 5 digits. There will always be exactly two 1s in each group of digits. Each digit stands for a number. From left to right, the digits encode the values 7, 4, 2, 1, and 0. Multiply the corresponding value with the digit and compute the sum to get the final encoded digit for the zip code. The table below shows the encoding for 10100.

Bar Code Digits	1	0	1	0	0
Value	7	4	2	1	0
Product of Digit * Value	7	0	2	0	0

```
Zip Code Digit = 7 + 0 + 2 + 0 + 0 = 9
```

Repeat this for each group of 5 digits and concatenate to get the complete zip code. There is one special value. If the sum of a group of 5 digits is 11, then this represents the digit 0 (this is necessary because with two digits per group it is not possible to represent zero). The zip code for the sample bar code decodes to 99504. Although the POSTNET scheme may seem unnecessarily complex, its design allows machines to detect if errors have been made in scanning the zip code.

Write a zip code class that encodes and decodes 5-digit bar codes used by the U.S. Postal Service on envelopes. The class should have two constructors. The first constructor should input the zip code as an integer, and the second constructor should input the zip code as a bar code string consisting of 0s and 1s, as described above. Although you have two ways to input the zip code, internally, the class should store the zip code using only one format (you may choose to store it as a bar code string or as a zip code number). The class should also have at least two public member functions, one to return the zip code as an integer, and the other to return the zip code in bar code format as a string. All helper functions should be declared private. Embed your class definition in a suitable test program. Your program should print an error message if an invalid bar code is passed to the constructor.

14. Consider a class Movie that contains information about a movie. The class has the following attributes:

- The movie name
- The MPAA rating (for example, G, PG, PG-13, R)
- The number of people that have rated this movie as a 1 (Terrible)
- The number of people that have rated this movie as a 2 (Bad)
- The number of people that have rated this movie as a 3 (OK)
- The number of people that have rated this movie as a 4 (Good)
- The number of people that have rated this movie as a 5 (Great)

Implement the class with accessor and mutator functions for the movie name and MPAA rating. Write a function addRating that takes an integer as an input parameter. The function should verify that the parameter is a number between 1 and 5, and if so, increment the number of people rating the movie that match the input parameter. For example, if 3 is the input parameter, then the number of people that rated the movie as a 3 should be incremented by 1. Write another function, getAverage, that returns the average value for all of the movie ratings. Finally, add a constructor that allows the programmer to create the object with a specified name and MPAA rating. The number of people rating the movie should be set to 0 in the constructor.

Test the class by writing a main function that creates at least two movie objects, adds at least five ratings for each movie, and outputs the movie name, MPAA rating, and average rating for each movie object.

Friends, Overloaded Operators, and Arrays in Classes

Give us the tools, and we'll finish the job.

WINSTON CHURCHILL, *Radio Broadcast, February 9, 1941*

INTRODUCTION

This chapter teaches you more techniques for defining functions and operators for classes, including overloading common operators such as +, *, and / so that they can be used with the classes you define in the same way that they are used with the predefined types such as *int* and *double*.

PREREQUISITES

This chapter uses material from Chapters 2 through 10.

11.1 FRIEND FUNCTIONS

Trust your friends.

COMMON ADVICE

Until now we have implemented class operations, such as input, output, accessor functions, and so forth, as member functions of the class, but for some operations, it is more natural to implement the operations as ordinary (nonmember) functions. In this section, we discuss techniques for defining operations on objects as nonmember functions. We begin with a simple example.

PROGRAMMING EXAMPLE   An Equality Function

In Chapter 10, we developed a class called DayOfYear that records a date, such as January 1 or July 4, that might be a holiday or birthday or some other annual event. We gave progressively better versions of the class. The final version was produced in Self-Test Exercise 23 of Chapter 10. In Display 11.1, we repeat this final version of the class DayOfYear and have enhanced the class one more time by adding a function called equal that can test two objects of type DayOfYear to see if their values represent the same date.

DISPLAY 11.1 Equality Function *(part 1 of 3)*

```
1    //Program to demonstrate the function equal. The class DayOfYear
2    //is the same as in Self-Test Exercises 23-24 in Chapter 10.
3    #include <iostream>
4    using namespace std;

5    class DayOfYear
6    {
7    public:
8        DayOfYear(int the_month, int the_day);
9        //Precondition: the_month and the_day form a
10       //possible date. Initializes the date according
11       //to the arguments.

12       DayOfYear( );
13       //Initializes the date to January first.

14       void input( );

15       void output( );

16       int get_month( );
17       //Returns the month, 1 for January, 2 for February, etc.

18       int get_day( );
19       //Returns the day of the month.
20   private:
21       void check_date( );
22       int month;
23       int day;
24   };
25
26   bool equal(DayOfYear date1, DayOfYear date2);
27   //Precondition: date1 and date2 have values.
28   //Returns true if date1 and date2 represent the same date;
29   //otherwise, returns false.
30
31   int main( )
32   {
33       DayOfYear today, bach_birthday(3, 21);
34
35       cout << "Enter today's date:\n";
36       today.input( );
37       cout << "Today's date is ";
38       today.output( );
39
40       cout << "J. S. Bach's birthday is ";
```

(continued)

DISPLAY 11.1 Equality Function *(part 2 of 3)*

```
41          bach_birthday.output( );
42
43          if (equal(today, bach_birthday))
44              cout << "Happy Birthday Johann Sebastian!\n";
45          else
46              cout << "Happy Unbirthday Johann Sebastian!\n";
47          return 0;
48      }
49
50      bool equal(DayOfYear date1, DayOfYear date2)
51      {
52          return ( date1.get_month( ) == date2.get_month( ) &&
53              date1.get_day( ) == date2.get_day( ));
54      }
55
56      DayOfYear::DayOfYear(int the_month, int the_day)
57              : month(the_month), day(the_day)
58      {
59          check_date();
60      }
61
62      int DayOfYear::get_month( )
63      {
64          return month;
65      }
66
67      int DayOfYear::get_day( )
68      {
69          return day;
70      }
71
72      //Uses iostream:
73      void DayOfYear::input( )
74      {
75          cout << "Enter the month as a number: ";
76          cin >> month;
77          cout << "Enter the day of the month: ";
78          cin >> day;
79      }
80
81      //Uses iostream:
82      void DayOfYear::output( )
83      {
84          cout << "month = " << month
85              << ", day = " << day << endl;
86      }
```

> *Omitted function and constructor definitions are as in Chapter 10, Self-Test Exercises 14 and 24, but those details are not needed for what we are doing here.*

(continued)

DISPLAY 11.1   Equality Function *(part 3 of 3)*

Sample Dialogue

```
Enter today's date:
Enter the month as a number: 3
Enter the day of the month: 21
Today's date is month = 3, day = 21
J. S. Bach's birthday is month = 3, day = 21
Happy Birthday Johann Sebastian!
```

Suppose today and bach_birthday are two objects of type DayOfYear that have been given values representing some dates. You can test to see if they represent the same date with the following Boolean expression:

```
equal(today, bach_birthday)
```

This call to the function equal returns *true* if today and bach_birthday represent the same date. In Display 11.1 this Boolean expression is used to control an *if-else* statement.

The definition of the function equal is straight forward. Two dates are equal if they represent the same month and the same day of the month. The definition of equal uses accessor functions get_month and get_day to compare the months and the days represented by the two objects.

Notice that we did not make the function equal a member function. It would be possible to make equal a member function of the class DayOfYear, but equal compares *two* objects of type DayOfYear. If you make equal a member function, you must decide whether the calling object should be the first date or the second date. Rather than arbitrarily choosing one of the two dates as the calling object, we instead treated the two dates in the same way. We made equal an ordinary (nonmember) function that takes two dates as its arguments. ∎

SELF-TEST EXERCISE

myprogramminglab

1. Write a function definition for a function called before that takes two arguments of the type DayOfYear, which is defined in Display 11.1. The function returns a *bool* value and returns *true* if the first argument represents a date that comes before the date represented by the second argument; otherwise, the function returns *false*; for example, January 5 comes before February 2.

Friend Functions

If your class has a full set of accessor functions, you can use the accessor functions to define a function to test for equality or to do any other kind of computing that depends on the private member variables. However, although this may give you access to the private member variables, it may not give you efficient access to them. Look again at the definition of the function `equal` given in Display 11.1. To read the month, it must make a call to the accessor function `get_month`. To read the day, it must make a call to the accessor function `get_day`. This works, but the code would be simpler and more efficient if we could just access the member variables.

A simpler and more efficient definition of the function `equal` given in Display 11.1 would be as follows:

```
bool equal(DayOfYear date1, DayOfYear date2)
{
    return (date1.month == date2.month &&
            date1.day == date2.day);
}
```

There is just one problem with this definition: It's illegal! It's illegal because the member variables `month` and `day` are private members of the class `DayOfYear`. Private member variables (and private member functions) cannot normally be referenced in the body of a function unless the function is a member function, and `equal` is not a member function of the class `DayOfYear`. But there is a way to give a nonmember function the same access privileges as a member function. If we make the function `equal` a *friend* of the class `DayOfYear`, then the previous definition of `equal` will be legal.

Friends can access private members

A **friend function** of a class is not a member function of the class, but a friend function has access to the private members of that class just as a member function does. A friend function can directly read the value of a member variable and can even directly change the value of a member variable, for example, with an assignment statement that has a private member variable on one side of the assignment operator. To make a function a friend function, you must name it as a friend in the class definition. For example, in Display 11.2 we have rewritten the definition of the class `DayOfYear` so that the function `equal` is a friend of the class. You make a function a friend of a class by listing the function declaration in the definition of the class and placing the keyword `friend` in front of the function declaration.

A friend is not a member

A friend function is added to a class definition by listing its function declaration, just as you would list the declaration of a member function, except that you precede the function declaration by the keyword `friend`. However, a friend is not a member function; rather, it really is an ordinary function with extraordinary access to the data members of the class. The friend is defined and called exactly like the ordinary function it is. In particular, the function definition for `equal` shown in Display 11.2 does

DISPLAY 11.2   Equality Function as a Friend

```
1     //Demonstrates the function equal.
2     //In this version equal is a friend of the class DayOfYear.
3     #include <iostream>
4     using namespace std;
5
6     class DayOfYear
7     {
8     public:
9         friend bool equal(DayOfYear date1, DayOfYear date2);
10        //Precondition: date1 and date2 have values.
11        //Returns true if date1 and date2 represent the same date;
12        //otherwise, returns false.
13
14        DayOfYear(int the_month, int the_day);
15        //Precondition: the_month and the_day form a
16        //possible date. Initializes the date according
17        //to the arguments.
18
19        DayOfYear( );
20        //Initializes the date to January first.
21
22        void input( );
23
24        void output( );
25
26        int get_month( );
27        //Returns the month, 1 for January, 2 for February, etc.
28
29        int get_day( );
30        //Returns the day of the month.
31    private:
32        void check_date( );
33        int month;
34        int day;
35    };
36
37    int main( )
38    {
```

<The main part of the program is the same as in Display 11.1.>

```
33    }
34
35    bool equal(DayOfYear date1, DayOfYear date2)
36    {
37        return (date1.month == date2.month &&
38                date1.day == date2.day);
39    }
40
```

Note that the private member variables month *and* day *can be accessed by name.*

<The rest of this display, including the Sample Dialogue, is the same as in Display 11.1.>

not include the qualifier DayOfYear:: in the function heading. Also, the equal function is not called by using the dot operator. The function equal takes objects of type DayOfYear as arguments the same way that any other nonmember function would take arguments of any other type. However, a friend function definition can access the private member variables and private member functions of the class by name, so it has the same access privileges as a member function.

■ PROGRAMMING TIP   Define Both Accessor Functions and Friend Functions

It may seem that if you make all your basic functions friends of a class, then there is no need to include accessor and mutator functions in the class. After all, friend functions have access to the private member variables and so do not need accessor or mutator functions. This is not entirely wrong. It is true that if you made all the functions in the world friends of a class, you would not need accessor or mutator functions. However, making all functions friends is not practical.

In order to see why you still need accessor functions, consider the example of the class DayOfYear given in Display 11.2. You might use this class in another program, and that other program might very well want to do something with the month part of a DayOfYear object. For example, the program might want to calculate how many months there are remaining in the year. Specifically, the main part of the program might contain the following:

```
DayOfYear today;
cout << "enter today's date: \n";
today.input();
cout << "There are " << (12 - today.get_month())
     << " months left in this year.\n";
```

You cannot replace today.get_month() with today.month because month is a private member of the class. You need the accessor function get_month.

You have just seen that you definitely need to include accessor functions in your class. Other cases require mutator functions. You may think that, because you usually need accessor and mutator functions, you do not need friends. In a sense, that is true. Notice that you could define the function equal either as a friend without using accessor functions (Display 11.2) or not as a friend and use accessor functions (as in Display 11.1). In most situations, the only reason to make a function a friend is to make the definition of the function simpler and more efficient; but sometimes, that is reason enough.

Friend Functions

A **friend function** of a class is an ordinary function except that it has access to the private members of objects of that class. To make a function a friend of a class, you must list the function declaration for the friend function in the class definition. The function declaration is preceded by the keyword *friend*. The function declaration may be placed in either the private section or the public section, but it will be a public function in either case, so it is clearer to list it in the public section.

SYNTAX (of a class definition with friend functions)

```
class Class_Name
{
public:
    friend Declaration_for_Friend_Function_1
    friend Declaration_for_Friend_Function_2
                    .
                    .
                    .
    Member_Function_Declarations
private:
    Private_Member_Declarations
};
```

You need not list the friend functions first. You can inter mix the order of these function declarations.

EXAMPLE

```
class FuelTank
{
public:
    friend double need_to_fill(FuelTank tank);
    //Precondition: Member variables of tank have values.
    //Returns the number of liters needed to fill tank.
    FuelTank(double the_capacity, double the_level);
    FuelTank();
    void input();
    void output();
private:
    double capacity;//in liters
    double level;
};
```

A friend function is *not* a member function. A friend function is defined and called the same way as an ordinary function. You do not use the dot operator in a call to a friend function and you do not use a type qualifier in the definition of a friend function.

■

■ PROGRAMMING TIP   Use Both Member and Nonmember Functions

Member functions and friend functions serve a very similar role. In fact, sometimes it is not clear whether you should make a particular function a friend of your class or a member function of the class. In most cases, you can make a function either a member function or a friend and have it perform the same task in the same way. There are, however, places where it is better to use a member function and places where it is better to use a friend function (or even a plain old function that isn't a friend, like the version of equal in Display 11.1). A simple rule to help you decide between member functions and nonmember functions is the following:

■ Use a member function if the task being performed by the function involves only one object.

■ Use a nonmember function if the task being performed involves more than one object. For example, the function equal in Display 11.1 (and Display 11.2) involves two objects, so we made it a nonmember (friend) function.

Whether you make a nonmember function a friend function or use accessor and mutator functions is a matter of efficiency and personal taste. As long as you have enough accessor and mutator functions, either approach will work.

The choice of whether to use a member or nonmember function is not always as simple as the above two rules. With more experience, you will discover situations in which it pays to violate those rules. A more accurate but harder to understand rule is to use member functions if the task is intimately related to a single object; use a nonmember function when the task involves more than one object and the objects are used symmetrically. However, this more accurate rule is not clear-cut, and the two simple rules given above will serve as a reliable guide until you become more sophisticated in handling objects.   ■

PROGRAMMING EXAMPLE   Money Class (Version 1)

Display 11.3 contains the definition of a class called Money, which represents amounts of U.S. currency. The value is implemented as a single integer value that represents the amount of money as if it were converted to all pennies. For example, $9.95 would be stored as the value 995. Since we use an integer to represent the amount of money, the amount is represented as an exact quantity. We did not use a value of type *double* because values of type *double* are stored as approximate values and we want our money amounts to be exact quantities.

This integer for the amount of money (expressed as all cents) is stored in a member variable named all_cents. We could use *int* for the type of the member variable all_cents, but with some compilers that would severely limit the amounts of money we could represent. In some implementations of C++, only 2 bytes are used to store the *int* type.[1] The result of the 2-byte implementation is that the largest value of type *int* is only slightly larger than 32000, but 32000 cents represents only $320, which is a fairly small amount of money. Since we may want to deal with amounts of money much larger than $320, we have used *long* for the type of the member variable all_cents. C++ compilers that implement the *int* type in 2 bytes usually implement the type *long* in 4 bytes. Values of type *long* are integers just like the values of the type *int*, except that the 4-byte *long* implementation enables the largest allowable value of type *long* to be much larger than the largest allowable value of type *int*. On most systems the largest allowable value of type *long* is 2 billion or larger. (The type *long* is also called *long int*. The two names *long* and *long int* refer to the same type.)

The class Money has two operations that are friend functions: equal and add (which are defined in Display 11.3). The function add returns a Money object whose value is the sum of the values of its two arguments. A function call of the form equal(amount1, amount2) returns *true* if the two objects amount1 and amount2 have values that represent equal amounts of money.

Notice that the class Money reads and writes amounts of money as we normally write amounts of money, such as $9.95 or –$9.95. First, consider the member function input (also defined in Display 11.3). That function first reads a single character, which should be either the dollar sign ('$') or the minus sign ('-'). If this first character is the minus sign, then the function remembers that the amount is negative by setting the value of the variable negative to *true*. It then reads an additional character, which should be the dollar sign. On the other hand, if the first symbol is not '-', then negative is set equal to *false*. At this point the negative sign (if any) and the dollar sign have been read. The function input then reads the number of dollars as a value of type *long* and places the number of dollars in the local variable named dollars. After reading the dollars part of the input, the function input reads the remainder of the input as values of type *char*; it reads in three characters, which should be a decimal point and two digits.

(You might be tempted to define the member function input so that it reads the decimal point as a value of type *char* and then reads the number of cents as a value of type *int*. This is not done because of the way that some C++ compilers treat leading zeros. As explained in the Pitfall section entitled "Leading Zeros in Number Constants," many compilers still in use do not read numbers with leading zeros as you would like them to, so an amount like $7.09 may be read incorrectly if your C++ code were to read the 09 as a value of type *int*.)

---

[1] See Chapter 2 for details. Display 2.2 has a description of data types as most recent compilers implement them.

DISPLAY 11.3   Money Class—Version 1 *(part 1 of 4)*

```
1    //Program to demonstrate the class Money.
2    #include <iostream>
3    #include <cstdlib>
4    #include <cctype>
5    using namespace std;

6    //Class for amounts of money in U.S. currency.
7    class Money
8    {
9    public:
10       friend Money add(Money amount1, Money amount2);
11       //Precondition: amount1 and amount2 have been given values.
12       //Returns the sum of the values of amount1 and amount2.

13       friend bool equal(Money amount1, Money amount2);
14       //Precondition: amount1 and amount2 have been given values.
15       //Returns true if the amount1 and amount2 have the same value;
16       //otherwise, returns false.

17       Money(long dollars, int cents);
18       //Initializes the object so its value represents an amount with the
19       //dollars and cents given by the arguments. If the amount is negative,
20       //then both dollars and cents must be negative.

21       Money(long dollars);
22       //Initializes the object so its value represents $dollars.00.

23       Money( );
24       //Initializes the object so its value represents $0.00.

25       double get_value( );
26       //Precondition: The calling object has been given a value.
27       //Returns the amount of money recorded in the data of the calling object.

28       void input(istream& ins);
29       //Precondition: If ins is a file input stream, then ins has already been
30       //connected to a file. An amount of money, including a dollar sign, has been
31       //entered in the input stream ins. Notation for negative amounts is -$100.00.
32       //Postcondition: The value of the calling object has been set to
33       //the amount of money read from the input stream ins.

34       void output(ostream& outs);
35       //Precondition: If outs is a file output stream, then outs has already been
36       //connected to a file.
37       //Postcondition: A dollar sign and the amount of money recorded
38       //in the calling object have been sent to the output stream outs.
39    private:
40       long all_cents;
41    };
```

(continued)

DISPLAY 11.3 Money Class—Version 1 *(part 2 of 4)*

```
42    int digit_to_int(char c);
43    //Function declaration for function used in the definition of Money::input:
44    //Precondition: c is one of the digits '0' through '9'.
45    //Returns the integer for the digit; for example, digit_to_int ('3') returns 3.

46    int main( )
47    {
48        Money your_amount, my_amount(10, 9), our_amount;
49        cout << "Enter an amount of money: ";
50        your_amount.input(cin);
51        cout << "Your amount is ";
52        your_amount.output(cout);
53        cout << endl;
54        cout << "My amount is ";
55        my_amount.output(cout);
56        cout << endl;

57        if (equal(your_amount, my_amount))
58            cout << "We have the same amounts.\n";
59        else
60            cout << "One of us is richer.\n";
61        our_amount = add(your_amount, my_amount);
62        your_amount.output(cout);
63        cout << " + ";
64        my_amount.output(cout);
65        cout << " equals ";
66        our_amount.output(cout);
67        cout << endl;
68        return 0;
69    }
70    Money add(Money amount1, Money amount2)
71    {
72        Money temp;
73
74        temp.all_cents = amount1.all_cents + amount2.all_cents;
75        return temp;
76    }
77
78    bool equal(Money amount1, Money amount2)
79    {
80        return (amount1.all_cents == amount2.all_cents);
81    }
82
83    Money::Money(long dollars, int cents)
84    {
85        if (dollars * cents < 0) //If one is negative and one is positive
```

(continued)

DISPLAY 11.3   Money Class—Version 1 *(part 3 of 4)*

```
86          {
87              cout << "Illegal values for dollars and cents.\n";
88              exit(1);
89          }
90          all_cents = dollars * 100 + cents;
91      }
92
93      Money::Money(long dollars) : all_cents(dollars * 100)
94      {
95          //Body intentionally blank.
96      }
97
98      Money::Money( ) : all_cents(0)
99      {
100         //Body intentionally blank.
101     }
102
103     double Money::get_value( )
104     {
105         return (all_cents * 0.01);
106     }
107     //Uses iostream, cctype, cstdlib:
108     void Money::input(istream& ins)
109     {
110         char one_char, decimal_point, digit1, digit2;
111         //digits for the amount of cents
112         long dollars;
113         int cents;
114         bool negative;//set to true if input is negative.
115
116         ins >> one_char;
117         if (one_char == ' ')
118         {
119             negative = true;
120             ins >> one_char; //read '$'
121         }
122         else
123             negative = false;
124         //if input is legal, then one_char == '$'
125
126         ins >> dollars >> decimal_point >> digit1 >> digit2;
127
128         if (one_char != '$' || decimal_point != '.'
129             || !isdigit(digit1) || !isdigit(digit2))
```

(continued)

DISPLAY 11.3   Money Class—Version 1 *(part 4 of 4)*

```
130          {
131               cout << "Error illegal form for money input\n";
132               exit(1);
133          }
134          cents = digit_to_int(digit1) * 10 + digit_to_int(digit2);
135
136          all_cents = dollars * 100 + cents;
137          if (negative)
138               all_cents = -all_cents;
139     }
140
141     //Uses cstdlib and iostream:
142     void Money::output(ostream& outs)
143     {
144          long positive_cents, dollars, cents;
145          positive_cents = labs(all_cents);
146          dollars = positive_cents / 100;
147          cents = positive_cents % 100;
148
149          if (all_cents < 0)
150               outs << "-$" << dollars << '.';
151          else
152               outs << "$" << dollars << '.';
153
154          if (cents < 10)
155               outs << '0';
156          outs << cents;
157     }
158
159     int digit_to_int(char c)
160     {
161          return (static_cast<int>(c) - static_cast<int>('0'));
162     }
163
```

Sample Dialogue

```
Enter an amount of money: $123.45
Your amount is $123.45
My amount is $10.09
One of us is richer.
$123.45 + $10.09 equals $133.54
```

The following assignment statement converts the two digits that make up the cents part of the input amount to a single integer, which is stored in the local variable `cents`:

```
cents = digit_to_int(digit1) * 10 + digit_to_int(digit2);
```

After this assignment statement is executed, the value of `cents` is the number of cents in the input amount.

The helping function `digit_to_int` takes an argument that is a digit, such as `'3'`, and converts it to the corresponding *int* value, such as 3. We need this helping function because the member function `input` reads the two digits for the number of cents as two values of type *char*, which are stored in the local variables `digit1` and `digit2`. However, once the digits are read into the computer, we want to use them as numbers. Therefore, we use the function `digit_to_int` to convert a digit such as `'3'` to a number such as 3. The definition of the function `digit_to_int` is given in Display 11.3. You can simply take it on faith that this definition does what it is supposed to do and treat the function as a black box. All you need to know is that `digit_to_int('0')` returns 0, `digit_to_int('1')` returns 1, and so forth. However, it is not too difficult to see how this function works, so you may want to read the optional section that follows this one. It explains the implementation of `digit_to_int`.

Once the local variables `dollars` and `cents` are set to the number of dollars and the number of cents in the input amount, it is easy to set the member variable `all_cents`. The following assignment statement sets `all_cents` to the correct number of cents:

```
all_cents = dollars * 100 + cents;
```

However, this always sets `all_cents` to a positive amount. If the amount of money is negative, then the value of `all_cents` must be changed from positive to negative. This is done with the following statement:

```
if (negative)
    all_cents = -all_cents;
```

The member function `output` (Display 11.3) calculates the number of dollars and the number of cents from the value of the member variable `all_cents`. It computes the number of dollars and the number of cents using integer division by 100. For example, if `all_cents` has a value of 995 (cents), then the number of dollars is 995/100, which is 9, and the number of cents is 995%100, which is 95. Thus, $9.95 would be the value output when the value of `all_cents` is 995 (cents).

The definition for the member function `output` needs to make special provisions for outputting negative amounts of money. The result of integer division with negative numbers does not have a standard definition and can vary from one implementation to another. To avoid this problem, we have taken the absolute value of the number in `all_cents` before performing division. To compute the absolute value we use the predefined function `labs`. The function `labs` returns the absolute value of its argument, just like the function `abs`, but `labs` takes an argument of type *long* and returns a value of type *long*. The function `labs` is in the library with header file `cstdlib`, just like the function `abs`. (Some versions of C++ do not include `labs`. If your implementation of C++ does not include `labs`, you can easily define the function for yourself.)

Implementation of `digit_to_int` (*Optional*)

The definition of the function `digit_to_int` from Display 11.3 is reproduced here:

```
int digit_to_int(char c)
{
    return (static_cast<int>(c) - static_cast<int>('0'));
}
```

At first glance, the formula for the value returned may seem a bit strange, but the details are not too complicated. The digit to be converted— for example, `'3'`—is the parameter `c`, and the returned value will turn out to be the corresponding *int* value—in this example, 3. As we pointed out in Chapters 2 and 6, values of type *char* are implemented as numbers. Unfortunately, the number implementing the digit `'3'`, for example, is not the number 3. The type cast *static_cast<int>(c)* produces the number that implements the character `c` and converts this number to the type *int*. This changes `c` from the type *char* to a number of type *int* but, unfortunately, not to the number we want. For example, *static_cast<int>('3')* is not 3, but is some other number. We need to convert *static_cast<int>(c)* to the number corresponding to `c` (for example, `'3'` to 3). So let's see how we must adjust *static_cast<int>(c)* to get the number we want.

We know that the digits are in order. So *static_cast<int>('0')* + 1 is equal to *static_cast<int>('1')*; *static_cast<int>('1')* + 1 is equal to *static_cast* *<int>('2')*; *static_cast<int>('2')* + 1 is equal to *static_cast<int>('3')*, and so forth. Knowing that the digits are in this order is all we need to know in order to see that `digit_to_int` returns the correct value. If `c` is `'0'`, the value returned is

static_cast<int>(c) - static_cast<int>('0')

which is

static_cast<int>('0') - static_cast<int>('0')

So `digit_to_int('0')` returns 0.

Now let's consider what happens when `c` has the value `'1'`. The value returned is then *static_cast<int>(c) - static_cast<int>('0')*, which is *static_cast<int>('1') - static_cast<int>('0')*. That equals (*static_* *cast*<*int*>('0') + 1) - *static_cast*<*int*>('0'), and that, in turn, equals *static_cast*<*int*>('0') - *static_cast*<*int*>('0') + 1. Since *static_cast*<*int*>('0') - *static_cast* <*int*>('0') is 0, this result is 0 + 1, or 1. You can check the other digits, '2' through '9', for yourself; each digit produces a number that is 1 larger than the previous digit.

PITFALL   Leading Zeros in Number Constants

The following are the object declarations given in the main part of the program in Display 11.3:

```
Money your_amount, my_amount(10, 9), our_amount;
```

The two arguments in my_amount(10,9) represent $10.09. Since we normally write cents in the format ".09," you might be tempted to write the object declaration as my_amount(10,09). However, this will cause problems. In mathematics, the numerals 9 and 09 represent the same number. However, some C++ compilers use a leading zero to signal a different kind of numeral, so in C++ the constants 9 and 09 are not necessarily the same number. With some compilers, a leading zero means that the number is written in base 8 rather than base 10. Since base 8 numerals do not use the digit 9, the constant 09 does not make sense in C++. The constants 00 through 07 should work correctly, since they mean the same thing in base 8 and in base 10, but some systems in some contexts will have trouble even with 00 through 07.

The ANSI C++ standard provides that input should default to being interpreted as decimal, regardless of the leading 0. The GNU project C++ compiler, g++, and Microsoft's VC++ compiler do comply with the standard, and so they do not have a problem with leading zeros. Most compiler vendors track the ANSI standard and thus should be compliant with the ANSI C++ standard, and so this problem with leading zeros should eventually go away. You should write a small program to test this on your compiler. ■

SELF-TEST EXERCISES

2. What is the difference between a friend function for a class and a member function for the class?

3. Suppose you wish to add a friend function to the class DayOfYear defined in Display 11.2. This friend function will be named after and will take two arguments of the type DayOfYear. The function returns *true* if the first argument represents a date that comes after the date represented by the second argument; otherwise, the function returns *false*. For example, February 2 comes after January 5. What do you need to add to the definition of the class DayOfYear in Display 11.2?

4. Suppose you wish to add a friend function for subtraction to the class Money defined in Display 11.3. What do you need to add to the description of the class Money that we gave in Display 11.3? The subtraction function should take two arguments of type Money and return a value of type Money whose value is the value of the first argument minus the value of the second argument.

5. Notice the member function output in the class definition of Money given in Display 11.3. In order to write a value of type Money to the screen, you call output with cout as an argument. For example, if purse is an object of type Money, then to output the amount of money in purse to the screen, you write the following in your program:

   `purse.output(cout);`

   It might be nicer not to have to list the stream cout when you send output to the screen.

   Rewrite the class definition for the type Money given in Display 11.3. The only change is that this rewritten version overloads the function name output so that there are two versions of output. One version is just like the one shown in Display 11.3; the other version of output takes no arguments and sends its output to the screen. With this rewritten version of the type Money, the following two calls are equivalent:

   `purse.output(cout);`

   and

   `purse.output();`

   but the second is simpler. Note that since there will be two versions of the function output, you can still send output to a file. If outs is an output file stream that is connected to a file, then the following will output the money in the object purse to the file connected to outs:

   `purse.output(outs);`

6. Notice the definition of the member function input of the class Money given in Display 11.3. If the user enters certain kinds of incorrect input, the function issues an error message and ends the program. For example, if the user omits a dollar sign, the function issues an error message. However, the checks given there do not catch all kinds of incorrect input. For example, negative amounts of money are supposed to be entered in the form –$9.95, but if the user mistakenly enters the amount in the form $–9.95, then the input will not issue an error message and the value of the Money object will be set to an incorrect value. What amount will the member function input read if the user mistakenly enters $–9.95? How might you add additional checks to catch most errors caused by such a misplaced minus sign?

7. The Pitfall section entitled "Leading Zeros in Number Constants" suggests that you write a short program to test whether a leading 0 will cause your compiler to interpret input numbers as base-8 numerals. Write such a program.

The *const* Parameter Modifier

A call-by-reference parameter is more efficient than a call-by-value parameter. A call-by-value parameter is a local variable that is initialized to the value of its argument, so when the function is called there are two copies of the argument. With a call-by-reference parameter, the parameter is just a placeholder that is replaced by the argument, so there is only one copy of the argument. For parameters of simple types, such as *int* or *double*, the difference in efficiency is negligible, but for class parameters the difference in efficiency can sometimes be important. Thus, it can make sense to use a call-by-reference parameter rather than a call-by-value parameter for a class, even if the function does not change the parameter.

If you are using a call-by-reference parameter and your function does not change the value of the parameter, you can mark the parameter so that the compiler knows that the parameter should not be changed. To do so, place the modifier *const* before the parameter type. The parameter is then called a **constant parameter.** For example, consider the class Money defined in Display 11.3. The Money parameters for the friend function add can be made into constant parameters as follows:

```
class Money
{
public:
    friend Money add(const Money& amount1, const Money& amount2);
    //Precondition: amount1 and amount2 have been given values.
    //Returns the sum of the values of amount1 and amount2.
        . . .
```

When you use constant parameters, the modifier *const* must be used in both the function declaration and in the heading of the function definition, so with the change in the class definition above, the function definition for add would begin as follows:

```
Money add(const Money& amount1, const Money& amount2)
{
    . . .
```

The remainder of the function definition would be the same as in Display 11.3.

Constant parameters are a form of automatic error checking. If your function definition contains a mistake that causes an inadvertent change to the constant parameter, then the computer will issue an error message.

The parameter modifier *const* can be used with any kind of parameter; however, it is normally used only for call-by-reference parameters for classes (and occasionally for certain other parameters whose corresponding arguments are large).

Call-by-reference parameters are replaced with arguments when a function is called, and the function call may (or may not) change the value of the argument. When you have a call to a member function, the calling object behaves very much like a call-by-reference parameter. When you have a call to a member function, that function call can change the value of the calling object. For example, consider the following, where the class Money is as in Display 11.3:

const with
member functions

```
Money m;
m.input(cin);
```

When the object m is declared, the value of the member variable all_cents is initialized to 0. The call to the member function input changes the value of the member variable all_cents to a new value determined by what the user types in. Thus, the call m.input(cin) changes the value of m, just as if m were a call-by-reference argument.

The modifier *const* applies to calling objects in the same way that it applies to parameters. If you have a member function that should not change the value of a calling object, you can mark the function with the *const* modifier; the computer will then issue an error message if your function code inadvertently changes the value of the calling object. In the case of a member function, the *const* goes at the end of the function declaration, just before the final semicolon, as shown here:

```
class Money
{
public:
        ...
    void output(ostream& outs) const;
        ...
```

The modifier *const* should be used in both the function declaration and the function definition, so the function definition for output would begin as follows:

```
void Money::output(ostream& outs) const
{
    ...
```

The remainder of the function definition would be the same as in Display 11.3.

PITFALL   Inconsistent Use of *const*

Use of the *const* modifier is an all-or-nothing proposition. If you use *const* for one parameter of a particular type, then you should use it for every other parameter that has that type and that is not changed by the function call; moreover, if the type is a class type, then you should also use the *const* modifier for every member function that does not change the value of its calling object. The reason has to do with function calls within function calls. For example, consider the following definition of the function guarantee:

```
void guarantee(const Money& price)
{
    cout << "If not satisfied, we will pay you\n"
         << "double your money back.\n"
         << "That's a refund of $"
         << (2 * price.get_value()) << endl;
}
```

If you do *not* add the *const* modifier to the function declaration for the member function get_value, then the function guarantee will give an error message on most compilers. The member function get_value does not change the calling object price. However, when the compiler processes the function definition for guarantee, it will think that get_value does (or at least might) change the value of price. This is because when it is translating the function definition for guarantee, all that the compiler knows about the member function get_value is the function declaration for get_value; if the function declaration does not contain a *const*, which tells the compiler that the calling object will not be changed, then the compiler assumes that the calling object will be changed. Thus, if you use the modifier *const* with parameters of type Money, then you should also use *const* with all Money member functions that do not change the value of their calling object. In particular, the function declaration for the member function get_value should include a *const*.

In Display 11.4 we have rewritten the definition of the class Money given in Display 11.3, but this time we have used the *const* modifier where appropriate. The definitions of the member and friend functions would be the same as they are in Display 11.3, except that the modifier *const* must be used in function headings so that the headings match the function declarations shown in Display 11.4.   ■

---

const **Parameter Modifier**

If you place the modifier *const* before the type for a call-by-reference parameter, the parameter is called a **constant parameter.** (The heading of the function definition should also have a *const* so that it matches the function declaration.) When you add the *const*, you are telling the compiler that this parameter should not be changed. If you make a mistake in your definition of the function so that it does change the constant parameter, then the computer will give an error message. Parameters of a class type that are not changed by the function ordinarily should be constant call-by-reference parameters, rather than call-by-value parameters.

(continued)

If a member function does not change the value of its calling object, then you can mark the function by adding the *const* modifier to the function declaration. If you make a mistake in your definition of the function so that it does change the calling object and the function is marked with *const*, then the computer will give an error message. The *const* is placed at the end of the function declaration, just before the final semicolon. The heading of the function definition should also have a *const* so that it matches the function declaration.

EXAMPLE

```
class Sample
{
public:
    Sample();
    friend int compare(const Sample& s1, const Sample& s2);
    void input();
    void output() const;
private:
    int stuff;
    double more_stuff;
};
```

Use of the *const* modifier is an all-or-nothing proposition. You should use the *const* modifier whenever it is appropriate for a class parameter and whenever it is appropriate for a member function of the class. If you do not use *const* every time that it is appropriate for a class, then you should never use it for that class.

DISPLAY 11.4 The Class Money with Constant Parameters *(part 1 of 2)*

```
1    //Class for amounts of money in U.S. currency.
2    class Money
3    {
4    public:
5        friend Money add(const Money& amount1, const Money& amount2);
6        //Precondition: amount1 and amount2 have been given values.
7        //Returns the sum of the values of amount1 and amount2.

8        friend bool equal(const Money& amount1, const Money& amount2);
9        //Precondition: amount1 and amount2 have been given values.
10       //Returns true if amount1 and amount2 have the same value;
11       //otherwise, returns false.

12       Money(long dollars, int cents);
```

(continued)

DISPLAY 11.4   The Class Money with Constant Parameters *(part 2 of 2)*

```
13        //Initializes the object so its value represents an amount with the
14        //dollars and cents given by the arguments. If the amount is negative,
15        //then both dollars and cents must be negative.
16        Money(long dollars);
17        //Initializes the object so its value represents $dollars.00.
18        Money( );
19        //Initializes the object so its value represents $0.00.
20        double get_value( ) const;
21        //Precondition: The calling object has been given a value.
22        //Returns the amount of money recorded in the data of the calling object.
23        void input(istream& ins);
24        //Precondition: If ins is a file input stream, then ins has already been
25        //connected to a file. An amount of money, including a dollar sign, has been
26        //entered in the input stream ins. Notation for negative amounts is -$100.00.
27        //Postcondition: The value of the calling object has been set to
28        //the amount of money read from the input stream ins.
29        void output(ostream& outs) const;
30        //Precondition: If outs is a file output stream, then outs has already been
31        //connected to a file.
32        //Postcondition: A dollar sign and the amount of money recorded
33        //in the calling object have been sent to the output stream outs.
34    private:
35        long all_cents;
36    };
```

 SELF-TEST EXERCISES

8. Give the complete definition of the member function get_value that you would use with the definition of Money given in Display 11.4.

9. Why would it be incorrect to add the modifier *const*, as shown here, to the function declaration for the member function input of the class Money given in Display 11.4?

```
class Money
{
    ...
public:
    void input(istream& ins) const;
    ...
```

10. What are the differences and the similarities between a call-by-value parameter and a call-by-*const*-reference parameter? Function declarations that illustrate these are

```
void call_by_value(int x);
void call_by_const_reference(const int& x);
```

11. Given the following definitions:

```
const int x = 17;
class A
{
public:
    A( );
    A(int x);
    int f( ) const;
    int g(const A& x);
private:
    int i;
};
```

Each of the three *const* keywords is a promise to the compiler that the compiler will enforce. What is the promise in each case?

11.2 OVERLOADING OPERATORS

He's a smooth operator.

LINE FROM A SONG BY SADE (WRITTEN BY SADE ADU AND RAY ST. JOHN)

Earlier in this chapter, we showed you how to make the function add a friend of the class Money and use it to add two objects of type Money (Display 11.3). The function add is adequate for adding objects, but it would be nicer if you could simply use the usual + operator to add values of type Money, as in the last line of the following code:

```
Money total, cost, tax;
cout << "Enter cost and tax: ";
cost.input(cin);
tax.input(cin);
total = cost + tax;
```

instead of having to use the slightly more awkward

```
total = add(cost, tax);
```

Recall that an operator, such as +, is really just a function except that the syntax for how it is used is slightly different from that of an ordinary function. In an ordinary function call, the arguments are placed in parentheses after the function name, as in the following:

```
add(cost, tax)
```

With a (binary) operator, the arguments are placed on either side of the operator, as shown here:

```
cost + tax
```

A function can be overloaded to take arguments of different types. An operator is really a function, so an operator can be overloaded. The way you overload an operator, such as +, is basically the same as the way you overload a function name. In this section we show you how to overload operators in C++.

Overloading Operators

You can overload the operator + (and many other operators) so that it will accept arguments of a class type. The difference between overloading the + operator and defining the function add (given in Display 11.3) involves only a slight change in syntax. The definition of the overloaded operator + is basically the same as the definition of the function add. The only differences are that you use the name + instead of the name add and you precede the + with the keyword *operator*. In Display 11.5 we have rewritten the type Money to include the overloaded operator + and we have embedded the definition in a small demonstration program.

The class Money, as defined in Display 11.5, also overloads the == operator so that == can be used to compare two objects of type Money. If amount1 and amount2 are two objects of type Money, we want the expression

```
amount1 == amount2
```

to return the same value as the following Boolean expression:

```
amount1.all_cents == amount2.all_cents
```

As shown in Display 11.5, this is the value returned by the overloaded operator ==.

You can overload most, but not all, operators. The operator need not be a friend of a class, but you will often want it to be a friend. Check the box entitled "Rules on Overloading Operators" for some technical details on when and how you can overload an operator.

Operator Overloading

A (binary) operator, such as +, -, /, %, and so forth, is simply a function that is called using a different syntax for listing its arguments. With an operator, the arguments are listed before and after the operator; with a function, the arguments are listed in parentheses after the function name. An operator definition is written similarly to a function definition, except that the operator definition includes the reserved word *operator* before the operator name. The predefined operators, such as + and so forth, can be overloaded by giving them a new definition for a class type.

An operator may be a friend of a class although this is not required. An example of overloading the + operator as a friend is given in Display 11.5.

DISPLAY 11.5 **Overloading Operators** *(part 1 of 2)*

```
1    //Program to demonstrate the class Money. (This is an improved version of
2    //the class Money that we gave in Display 11.3 and rewrote in Display 11.4.)
3    #include <iostream>
4    #include <cstdlib>
5    #include <cctype>
6    using namespace std;
7
8    //Class for amounts of money in U.S. currency.
9    class Money
10   {
11   public:
12       friend Money operator +(const Money& amount1, const Money& amount2);
13       //Precondition: amount1 and amount2 have been given values.
14       //Returns the sum of the values of amount1 and amount2.
15
16       friend bool operator ==(const Money& amount1, const Money& amount2);
16       //Precondition: amount1 and amount2 have been given values.
17       //Returns true if amount1 and amount2 have the same value;
18       //otherwise, returns false.
19
19       Money(long dollars, int cents);
20
20       Money(long dollars);
21
21       Money( );
22
22       double get_value( ) const;
23
23       void input(istream& ins);
24       void output(ostream& outs) const;
25   private:
26       long all_cents;
27   };
```

Some comments from Display 11.4 have been omitted to save space in this book, but they should be included in a real program.

<Any extra function declarations from Display 11.3 go here.>

```
28   int main( )
29   {
30       Money cost(1, 50), tax(0, 15), total;
31       total = cost + tax;
32
32       cout << "cost = ";
33       cost.output(cout);
34       cout << endl;
35       cout << "tax = ";
36       tax.output(cout);
37       cout << endl;
38       cout << "total bill = ";
39       total.output(cout);
40       cout << endl;
```

(continued)

DISPLAY 11.5   Overloading Operators *(part 2 of 2)*

```
41          if (cost == tax)
42              cout << "Move to another state.\n";
43          else
44              cout << "Things seem normal.\n";
45          return 0;
46      }
47
48      Money operator +(const Money& amount1, const Money& amount2)
49      {
50          Money temp;
51          temp.all_cents = amount1.all_cents + amount2.all_cents;
52          return temp;
53      }
54
55      bool operator ==(const Money& amount1, const Money& amount2)
56      {
57          return (amount1.all_cents == amount2.all_cents);
58      }
59
```

<The definitions of the member functions are the same as in Display 11.3 except that *const* is added to the function headings in various places so that the function headings match the function declarations in the preceding class definition. No other changes are needed in the member function definitions. The bodies of the member function definitions are identical to those in Display 11.3>

Output

```
cost = $1.50
tax = $0.15
total bill = $1.65
Things seem normal.
```

SELF-TEST EXERCISES

12. What is the difference between a (binary) operator and a function?

13. Suppose you wish to overload the operator < so that it applies to the type Money defined in Display 11.5. What do you need to add to the description of Money given in Display 11.5?

14. Suppose you wish to overload the operator `<=` so that it applies to the type `Money` defined in Display 11.5. What do you need to add to the description of `Money` given in Display 11.5?

15. Is it possible using operator overloading to change the behavior of + on integers? Why or why not?

Rules on Overloading Operators

■ When overloading an operator, at least one argument of the resulting overloaded operator must be of a class type.

■ An overloaded operator can be, but does not have to be, a friend of a class; the operator function may be a member of the class or an ordinary (non-friend) function. (Overloading an operator as a class member is discussed in Appendix 8.)

■ You cannot create a new operator. All you can do is overload existing operators, such as +, -, *, /, %, and so forth.

■ You cannot change the number of arguments that an operator takes. For example, you cannot change % from a binary to a unary operator when you overload %; you cannot change ++ from a unary to a binary operator when you overload it.

■ You cannot change the precedence of an operator. An overloaded operator has the same precedence as the ordinary version of the operator. For example, x*y+z always means (x*y)+z, even if x, y, and z are objects and the operators + and * have been overloaded for the appropriate classes.

■ The following operators cannot be overloaded: the dot operator (.), the scope resolution operator (::), and the operators .* and ?:, which are not discussed in this book.

■ Although the assignment operator = can be overloaded so that the default meaning of = is replaced by a new meaning, this must be done in a different way from what is described here. Overloading = is discussed in the section "Overloading the Assignment Operator" later in this chapter. Some other operators, including [] and ->, also must be overloaded in a way that is different from what is described in this chapter. The operators [] and -> are discussed later in this book.

Constructors for Automatic Type Conversion

If your class definition contains the appropriate constructors, the system will perform certain type conversions automatically. For example, if your program contains the definition of the class `Money` given in Display 11.5, you could use the following in your program:

```
Money base_amount(100, 60), full_amount;
full_amount = base_amount + 25;
full_amount.output(cout);
```

The output will be

```
$125.60
```

The code above may look simple and natural enough, but there is one subtle point. The 25 (in the expression base_amount + 25) is not of the appropriate type. In Display 11.5 we only overloaded the operator + so that it could be used with two values of type Money. We did not overload + so that it could be used with a value of type Money and an integer. The constant 25 is an integer and is not of type Money. The constant 25 can be considered to be of type *int* or of type *long*, but 25 cannot be used as a value of type Money unless the class definition somehow tells the system how to convert an integer to a value of type Money. The only way that the system knows that 25 means $25.00 is that we included a constructor that takes a single argument of type *long*. When the system sees the expression

```
base_amount + 25
```

it first checks to see if the operator + has been overloaded for the combination of a value of type Money and an integer. Since there is no such overloading, the system next looks to see if there is a constructor that takes a single argument that is an integer. If it finds a constructor that takes a single-integer argument, it uses that constructor to convert the integer 25 to a value of type Money. The constructor with one argument of type *long* tells the system how to convert an integer, such as 25, to a value of type Money. The one-argument constructor says that 25 should be converted to an object of type Money whose member variable all_cents is equal to 2500; in other words, the constructor converts 25 to an object of type Money that represents $25.00. (The definition of the constructor is in Display 11.3.)

Note that this type conversion will not work unless there is a suitable constructor. For example, the type Money (Display 11.5) has no constructor that takes an argument of type *double*, so the following is illegal and would produce an error message if you were to put it in a program that declares base_amount and full_amount to be of type Money:

```
full_amount = base_amount + 25.67;
```

To make this use of + legal, you could change the definition of the class Money by adding another constructor. The function declaration for the constructor you need to add is the following:

```
class Money
{
public:
    . . .
```

```
Money(double amount);
//Initializes the object so its value represents $amount.
```
. . .

Writing the definition for this new constructor is Self-Test Exercise 16.

These automatic type conversions (produced by constructors) seem most common and compelling with overloaded numeric operators such as + and −. However, these automatic conversions apply in exactly the same way to arguments for ordinary functions, arguments for member functions, and arguments for other overloaded operators.

 SELF-TEST EXERCISE   myprogramming**lab**

16. Give the definition for the constructor discussed at the end of the previous section. The constructor is to be added to the class Money in Display 11.5. The definition begins as follows:

```
Money::Money(double amount)
{
```

Overloading Unary Operators

In addition to the binary operators, such as + in x+y, there are also unary operators, such as the operator - when it is used to mean negation. In the following statement, the unary operator - is used to set the value of a variable x equal to the negative of the value of the variable y:

```
x = -y;
```

The increment and decrement operators ++ and -- are other examples of unary operators.

You can overload unary operators as well as binary operators. For example, you can redefine the type Money given in Display 11.5 so that it has both a unary and a binary operator version of the subtraction/negation operator -. The redone class definition is given in Display 11.6. Suppose your program contains this class definition and the following code:

```
Money amount1(10), amount2(6), amount3;
```

Then the following sets the value of amount3 to amount1 minus amount2:

```
amount3 = amount1 - amount2;
```

The following will, then, output $4.00 to the screen:

```
amount3.output(cout);
```

On the other hand, the following will set amount3 equal to the negative of amount1:

```
amount3 = -amount1;
```

The following will, then, output -$10.00 to the screen:

```
amount3.output(cout);
```

You can overload the ++ and -- operators in ways similar to the way we overloaded the negation operator in Display 11.6. The overloading definition will apply to the operator when it is used in prefix position, as in ++x and --x. The postfix versions of ++ and --, as in x++ and x--, are handled in a different manner, but we will not discuss these postfix versions. (Hey, you can't learn everything in a first course!)

Overloading >> and <<

<< is an operator
The insertion operator << that we used with cout is a binary operator like the binary operators + or -. For example, consider the following:

```
cout << "Hello out there.\n";
```

The operator is <<, the first operand is the output stream cout, and the second operand is the string value "Hello out there.\n". You can change either of these operands. If fout is an output stream of type ofstream and fout has been connected to a file with a call to open, then you can replace cout with fout and the string will instead be written to the file connected to fout. Of course, you can also replace the string "Hello out there.\n" with another string, a variable, or a number. Since the insertion operator << is an operator, you should be able to overload it just as you overload operators such as + and -. This is true, but there are a few more details to worry about when you overload the input and output operators >> and <<.

Overloading <<
In our previous definitions of the class Money, we used the member function output to output values of type Money (Displays 11.3 through 11.6). This is adequate, but it would be nicer if we could simply use the insertion operator << to output values of type Money as in the following:

```
Money amount(100);
cout << "I have " << amount << " in my purse.\n";
```

instead of having to use the member function output as shown here:

```
Money amount(100);
cout << "I have ";
amount.output(cout);
cout << " in my purse.\n";
```

One problem in overloading the operator << is deciding what value should be returned when << is used in an expression like the following:

```
cout << amount
```

DISPLAY 11.6   Overloading a Unary Operator

```
1      //Class for amounts of money in U.S. currency.
2      class Money
3      {
4      public:
5          friend Money operator +(const Money& amount1, const Money& amount2);

6          friend Money operator -(const Money& amount1, const Money& amount2);
7          //Precondition: amount1 and amount2 have been given values.
8          //Returns amount1 minus amount2.

9          friend Money operator -(const Money& amount);
10         //Precondition: amount has been given a value.
11         //Returns the negative of the value of amount.

12         friendbool operator ==(const Money& amount1, const Money& amount2);

13         Money(long dollars, int cents);

14         Money(long dollars);

15         Money( );

16         double get_value( ) const;

17         void input(istream& ins);
18         void output(ostream& outs) const;
19     private:
20         long all_cents;
21     };
```

> This is an improved version of the class **Money** given in Display 11.5.

> We have omitted the **include** directives and some of the comments, but you should include them in your programs.

<Any additional function declarations as well as the main part of the program go here.>

```
22     Money operator -(const Money& amount1, const Money& amount2)
23     {
24         Money temp;
25         temp.all_cents = amount1.all_cents - amount2.all_cents;
26         return temp;
27     }

28     Money operator -(const Money& amount)
29     {
30         Money temp;
31         temp.all_cents = -amount.all_cents;
32         return temp;
33     }
```

<The other function definitions are the same as in Display 11.5.>

The two operands in this expression are `cout` and `amount`, and evaluating the expression should cause the value of `amount` to be written to the screen. But if `<<` is an operator like `+` or `*`, then the expression above should also return some value. After all, expressions with other operands, such as `n1 + n2`, return values. But what does `cout << amount` return? To obtain the answer to that question, we need to look at a more complicated expression involving `<<`.

Chains of <<

Let's consider the following expression, which involves evaluating a chain of expressions using `<<`:

```
cout << "I have " << amount << " in my purse.\n";
```

If you think of the operator `<<` as being analogous to other operators, such as `+`, then the above should be (and in fact is) equivalent to the following:

```
((cout << "I have ") << amount) << " in my purse.\n";
```

What value should `<<` return in order to make sense of this expression? The first thing evaluated is the subexpression:

```
(cout << "I have ")
```

If things are to work out, then the subexpression had better return `cout` so that the computation can continue as follows:

```
(cout << amount) << " in my purse.\n";
```

And if things are to continue to work out, `(cout << amount)` had better also return `cout` so that the computation can continue as follows:

```
cout << " in my purse.\n";
```

<< returns a stream

This is illustrated in Display 11.7. The operator `<<` should return its first argument, which is a stream of type `ostream`.

Thus, the declaration for the overloaded operator `<<` (to use with the class Money) should be as follows:

```
class Money
{
public:
    . . .
    friend ostream& operator <<(ostream& outs, const
                                    Money& amount);
    //Precondition: If outs is a file output stream, then outs
    //has already been connected to a file.
    //Postcondition: A dollar sign and the amount of money
    //recorded in the calling object have been sent to the output
    //stream outs.
    . . .
```

Once we have overloaded the insertion (output) operator `<<`, we will no longer need the member function `output` and thus can delete `output` from

DISPLAY 11.7   << as an Operator

```
1    cout << "I have " << amount << " in my purse.\n";
2
3    means the same as
4
5    ((cout << "I have ") << amount) << " in my purse.\n";
6
7    and is evaluated as follows:
8
9    First evaluate (cout << "I have "), which returns cout:
10   ((cout << "I have ") << amount) << " in my purse.\n";
11
12                        and the string "I have" is output.
13
14   (cout << amount) << " in my purse.\n";
15
16
17   Then evaluate (cout << amount), which returns cout:
18
19   (cout << amount) << " in my purse.\n";
20
21                   and the value of amount is output.
22
23   cout << " in my purse.\n";
24
25
26   Then evaluate cout << " in my purse.\n", which returns cout:
27
28   cout << " in my purse.\n";
29
30                    and the string "in my purse.\n" is output.
31                              Since there are no more <<
32   cout;                      operators, the process ends.
```

our definition of the class Money. The definition of the overloaded operator <<
is very similar to the member function output. In outline form, the definition
for the overloaded operator is as follows:

```
ostream& operator <<(ostream& outs, const Money& amount)
{
        <This part is the same as the body of Money::output
        that is given in Display 11.3 (except that all_cents
        is replaced with amount.all_cents).>

        return outs;
}
```

<< and >> return
a reference

There is one thing left to explain in the previous function declaration and definition for the overloaded operator <<. What is the meaning of the & in the returned type ostream&? The easiest answer is that *whenever an operator (or a function) returns a stream, you must add an & to the end of the name for the returned type.* That simple rule will allow you to overload the operators << and >>. However, although that is a good working rule that will allow you to write your class definitions and programs, it is not very satisfying. You do not need to know what that & really means, but if we explain it, that will remove some of the mystery from the rule that tells you to add an &.

Returning a
reference

When you add an & to the name of a returned type, you are saying that the operator (or function) returns a *reference*. All the functions and operators we have seen thus far return values. However, if the returned type is a stream, you cannot simply return the value of the stream. In the case of a stream, the value of the stream is an entire file or the keyboard or the screen, and it may not make sense to return those things. Thus, you want to return only the stream itself rather than the value of the stream. When you add an & to the name of a returned type, you are saying that the operator (or function) returns a **reference,** which means that you are returning the object itself, as opposed to the value of the object.

The extraction operator >> is overloaded in a way that is analogous to what we described for the insertion operator <<. However, with the extraction (input) operator >>, the second argument will be the object that receives the input value, so the second parameter must be an ordinary call-by-reference parameter. In outline form, the definition for the overloaded extraction operator >> is as follows:

```
istream& operator >>(istream& ins, Money& amount)
{
    <This part is the same as the body of
    Money::input given in Display 11.3 (except that
    all_cents is replaced with amount.all_cents).>

    return ins;
}
```

The complete definitions of the overloaded operators << and >> are given in Display 11.8, where we have rewritten the class Money yet again. This time we have rewritten the class so that the operators << and >> are overloaded to allow us to use these operators with values of type Money.

Overloading >> and <<

The input and output operators >> and << can be overloaded just like any other operators. The value returned must be the stream. The type for the value returned must have the & symbol added to the end of the type name. The function declarations and beginnings of the function definitions are as shown on the next page. See Display 11.8 for an example.

(continued)

FUNCTION DECLARATIONS

Parameter for the object to receive the input

```
class Class_Name
{                   Parameter for
public:             the stream
    . . .

    friend istream& operator >>(istream& Parameter_1,
                                Class_Name& Parameter_2);

    friend ostream& operator <<(ostream& Parameter_3,
                                const Class_Name&
                                Parameter_4);

    . . .
```

DEFINITIONS

```
istream& operator >>(istream& Parameter_1,
                     Class_Name& Parameter_2)
{
    . . .
}
ostream& operator <<(ostream& Parameter_3,
                     const Class_Name& Parameter_4)
{
    . . .
```

DISPLAY 11.8 Overloading << and >> *(part 1 of 4)*

```
1   //Program to demonstrate the class Money
2   #include <iostream>
3   #include <fstream>
4   #include <cstdlib>
5   #include <cctype>
6   using namespace std;
7
8   //Class for amounts of money in U.S. currency.
9   class Money
10  {
11  public:
12      friend Money operator +(const Money& amount1, const Money& amount2);

13      friend Money operator -(const Money& amount1, const Money& amount2);

14      friend Money operator -(const Money& amount);
```

*This is an improved version of the class **Money** that we gave in Display 11.6.*

Although we have omitted some of the comments from Displays 11.5 and 11.6, you should include them.

(continued)

DISPLAY 11.8 **Overloading << and >>** *(part 2 of 4)*

```
15        friend bool operator ==(const Money& amount1, const Money& amount2);

16        Money(long dollars, int cents);

17        Money(long dollars);

18        Money( );

19    double get_value( ) const;

20        friend istream& operator >>(istream& ins, Money& amount);
21        //Overloads the >> operator so it can be used to input values of type Money.
22        //Notation for inputting negative amounts is as in -$100.00.
23        //Precondition: If ins is a file input stream, then ins has already been
24        //connected to a file.

25        friend ostream& operator <<(ostream& outs, const Money& amount);
26        //Overloads the << operator so it can be used to output values of type Money.
27        //Precedes each output value of type Money with a dollar sign.
28        //Precondition: If outs is a file output stream,
29        //then outs has already been connected to a file.
30    private:
31        long all_cents;
32    };
33    int digit_to_int(char c);
34    //Used in the definition of the overloaded input operator >>.
35    //Precondition: c is one of the digits '0' through '9'.
36    //Returns the integer for the digit; for example, digit_to_int('3') returns 3.
37
38    int main( )
39    {
40        Money amount;
41        ifstream in_stream;
42        ofstream out_stream;
43
44        in_stream.open("infile.dat");
45        if (in_stream.fail( ))
46        {
47            cout << "Input file opening failed.\n";
48            exit(1);
49        }
50
51        out_stream.open("outfile.dat");
52        if (out_stream.fail( ))
53        {
54            cout << "Output file opening failed.\n";
55            exit(1);
56        }
```

(continued)

DISPLAY 11.8 Overloading << and >> *(part 3 of 4)*

```
57
58        in_stream >> amount;
59        out_stream << amount
60                  << " copied from the file infile.dat.\n";
61        cout << amount
62            << " copied from the file infile.dat.\n";
63
64        in_stream.close( );
65        out_stream.close( );
66
67        return 0;
68    }
69    //Uses iostream, cctype, cstdlib:
70    istream& operator >>(istream& ins, Money& amount)
71    {
72        char one_char, decimal_point,
73            digit1, digit2; //digits for the amount of cents
74        long dollars;
75        int cents;
76        bool negative;//set to true if input is negative.

77        ins >> one_char;
78        if (one_char == '-')
79        {
80            negative = true;
81            ins >> one_char; //read '$'
82        }
83        else
84            negative = false;
85        //if input is legal, then one_char == '$'

86        ins >> dollars >> decimal_point >> digit1 >> digit2;

87        if (one_char != '$' || decimal_point != '.'
88            || !isdigit(digit1) || !isdigit(digit2))
89        {
90            cout << "Error illegal form for money input\n";
91            exit(1);
92        }

93        cents = digit_to_int(digit1) * 10 + digit_to_int(digit2);

94        amount.all_cents = dollars * 100 + cents;
95        if (negative)
96            amount.all_cents = -amount.all_cents;
97        return ins;
98    }
99
```

(continued)

DISPLAY 11.8 Overloading << and >> *(part 4 of 4)*

```
100    int digit_to_int(char c)
101    {
102        return ( static_cast<int>(c) - static_cast<int>('0') );
103    }

104    //Uses cstdlib and iostream:
105    ostream& operator <<(ostream& outs, const Money& amount)
106    {
107        long positive_cents, dollars, cents;
108        positive_cents = labs(amount.all_cents);
109        dollars = positive_cents/100;
110        cents = positive_cents%100;
111
112        if (amount.all_cents < 0)
113            outs << "- $" << dollars << '.';
114        else
115            outs << "$" << dollars << '.';
116
117        if (cents < 10)
118            outs << '0';
119        outs << cents;
120
121        return outs;
122    }
123
```

<The definitions of the member functions and other overloaded operators go here. See Displays 11.3, 11.4, 11.5, and 11.6 for the definitions.>

infile.dat	**outfile.dat**
(Not changed by program.)	(After program is run.)
$1.11 $2.22 $3.33	$1.11 copied from the file infile.dat.

Screen Output

$1.11 copied from the file infile.dat.

SELF-TEST EXERCISES   myprogramminglab

17. Here is a definition of a class called `Pairs`. Objects of type `Pairs` can be used in any situation where ordered pairs are needed. Your task is to write implementations of the overloaded operator >> and the overloaded operator << so that objects of class `Pairs` are to be input and output in the form (5,6)(5,-4)(-5,4) or (-5,-6). You need not implement any constructor or other member, and you need not do any input format checking.

```
#include <iostream>
using namespace std;
class Pairs
{
public:
    Pairs( );
    Pairs(int first, int second);
    //other members and friends
    friend istream& operator >>(istream& ins, Pairs& second);
    friend ostream& operator <<(ostream& outs, const Pairs& second);
private:
    int f;
    int s;
};
```

18. Following is the definition for a class called `Percent`. Objects of type `Percent` represent percentages such as 10% or 99%. Give the definitions of the overloaded operators >> and << so that they can be used for input and output with objects of the class `Percent`. Assume that input always consists of an integer followed by the character '%', such as 25%. All percentages are whole numbers and are stored in the *int* member variable named `value`. You do not need to define the other overloaded operators and do not need to define the constructor. You only have to define the overloaded operators >> and <<.

```
#include <iostream>
using namespace std;

class Percent
{
public:
    friend bool operator ==(const Percent& first,
                            const Percent& second);

    friend bool operator <(const Percent& first,
                           const Percent& second);

    Percent();

    Percent(int percent_value);
```

```
        friend istream& operator >>(istream& ins,
                                    Percent& the_object);

        //Overloads the >> operator to input values of type
        //Percent.
        //Precondition: If ins is a file input stream, then ins
        //has already been connected to a file.

        friend ostream& operator <<(ostream& outs,
                                    const Percent& a_percent);
        //Overloads the << operator for output values of type
        //Percent.
        //Precondition: If outs is a file output stream, then
        //outs has already been connected to a file.
private:
        int value;
};
```

11.3 ARRAYS AND CLASSES

You can combine arrays, structures, and classes to form intricately structured types such as arrays of structures, arrays of classes, and classes with arrays as member variables. In this section we discuss a few simple examples to give you an idea of the possibilities.

Arrays of Classes

The base type of an array may be any type, including types that you define, such as structure and class types. If you want each indexed variable to contain items of different types, make the array an array of structures. For example, suppose you want an array to hold ten weather data points, where each data point is a wind velocity and a wind direction (north, south, east, or west). You might use the following type definition and array declaration:

```
struct WindInfo
{
    double velocity; //in miles per hour
    char direction; //'N', 'S', 'E', or 'W'
};

WindInfo data_point[10];
```

To fill the array data_point, you could use the following *for* loop:

```
int i;
for (i = 0; i < 10; i++)
```

```
    {
        cout << "Enter velocity for "
             << i << " numbered data point: ";
        cin >> data_point[i].velocity;
        cout << "Enter direction for that data point"
             << " (N, S, E, or W): ";
        cin >> data_point[i].direction;
    }
```

The way to read an expression such as data_point[i].velocity is left to right and very carefully. First, data_point is an array. So, data_point[i] is the ith indexed variable of this array. An indexed variable of this array is of type WindInfo, which is a structure with two member variables named velocity and direction. So, data_point[i].velocity is the member variable named velocity for the ith array element. Less formally, data_point[i].velocity is the wind velocity for the ith data point. Similarly, data_point[i].direction is the wind direction for the ith data point.

The ten data points in the array data_point can be written to the screen with the following *for* loop:

```
    for (i = 0; i < 10; i++)
        cout << "Wind data point number " << i << ": \n"
             << data_point[i].velocity
             << " miles per hour\n"
             << "direction " << data_point[i].direction
             << endl;
```

Display 11.9 contains the definition for a class called Money. Objects of the class Money are used to represent amounts of money in U.S. currency. The definitions of the member functions, member operations, and friend functions for this class can be found in Displays 11.3 through 11.8 and in the answer to Self-Test Exercise 13. You can have arrays whose base type is the type Money. A simple example is given in Display 11.9. That program reads in a list of five amounts of money and computes how much each amount differs from the largest of the five amounts. Notice that an array whose base type is a class is treated basically the same as any other array. In fact, the program in Display 11.9 is very similar to the program in Display 7.1, except that in Display 11.9 the base type is a class.

When an array of classes is declared, the default constructor is called to initialize the indexed variables, so it is important to have a default constructor for any class that will be the base type of an array. An array of classes is manipulated just like an array with a simple base type like *int* or *double*. For example, the difference between each amount and the largest amount is stored in an array named difference, as follows:

Constructor call

```
    Money difference[5];
    for (i = 0; i < 5; i++)
        difference[i] = max - amount[i];
```

DISPLAY 11.9   **Program Using an Array of Money Objects** *(part 1 of 2)*

```
1    //This is the definition for the class Money.
2    //Values of this type are amounts of money in U.S. currency.
3    #include <iostream>
4    using namespace std;

5    class Money
6    {
7    public:
8        friend Money operator +(const Money& amount1, const Money& amount2);
9        //Returns the sum of the values of amount1 and amount2.

10       friend Money operator -(const Money& amount1, const Money& amount2);
11       //Returns amount1 minus amount2.

12       friend Money operator -(const Money& amount);
13       //Returns the negative of the value of amount.

14       friend bool operator ==(const Money& amount1, const Money& amount2);
15       //Returns true if amount1 and amount2 have the same value; false otherwise.

16       friend bool operator <(const Money& amount1, const Money& amount2);
17       //Returns true if amount1 is less than amount2; false otherwise.

18       Money(long dollars, int cents);
19       //Initializes the object so its value represents an amount with
20       //the dollars and cents given by the arguments. If the amount
21       //is negative, then both dollars and cents should be negative.

22       Money(long dollars);
23       //Initializes the object so its value represents $dollars.00.

24       Money( );
25       //Initializes the object so its value represents $0.00.

26       double get_value( ) const;
27       //Returns the amount of money recorded in the data portion of the calling
28       //object.

29       friend istream& operator >>(istream& ins, Money& amount);
30       //Overloads the >> operator so it can be used to input values of type
31       //Money. Notation for inputting negative amounts is as in - $100.00.
32       //Precondition: If ins is a file input stream, then ins has already been
33       //connected to a file.
34
35       friend ostream& operator <<(ostream& outs, const Money& amount);
36       //Overloads the << operator so it can be used to output values of type
37       //Money. Precedes each output value of type Money with a dollar sign.
38       //Precondition: If outs is a file output stream, then outs has already been
39       //connected to a file.
40   private:
41       long all_cents;
42   };
43
```

(continued)

DISPLAY 11.9 Program Using an Array of Money Objects *(part 2 of 2)*

<The definitions of the member functions and the overloaded operators goes here.>

```
44    //Reads in 5 amounts of money and shows how much each
45    //amount differs from the largest amount.
46    int main( )
47    {
48        Money amount[5], max;
49        int i;

50        cout << "Enter 5 amounts of money:\n";
51        cin >> amount[0];
52        max = amount[0];
53        for (i = 1; i < 5; i++)
54        {
55            cin >> amount[i];
56            if (max < amount[i])
57                max = amount[i];
58            //max is the largest of amount[0], . . ., amount[i].
59        }
60        Money difference[5];
61        for (i = 0; i < 5; i++)
62            difference[i] = max - amount[i];

63        cout << "The highest amount is " << max << endl;
64        cout << "The amounts and their\n"
65            << "differences from the largest are:\n";
66        for (i = 0; i < 5; i++)
67        {
68            cout << amount[i] << " off by "
69                << difference[i] << endl;
70        }

71        return 0;
72    }
```

Sample Dialogue

```
Enter 5 amounts of money:
$5.00 $10.00 $19.99 $20.00 $12.79
The highest amount is $20.00
The amounts and their
differences from the largest are:
$5.00 off by $15.00
$10.00 off by $10.00
$19.99 off by $0.01
$20.00 off by $0.00
$12.79 off by $7.21
```

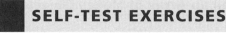

19. Give a type definition for a structure called Score that has two member variables called home_team and opponent. Both member variables are of type *int*. Declare an array called game that is an array with ten elements of type Score. The array game might be used to record the scores of each of ten games for a sports team.

20. Write a program that reads in five amounts of money, doubles each amount, and then writes out the doubled values to the screen. Use one array with Money as the base type. (*Hint:* Use Display 11.9 as a guide, but this program will be simpler than the one in Display 11.9.)

Arrays as Class Members

You can have a structure or class that has an array as a member variable. For example, suppose you are a speed swimmer and want a program to keep track of your practice times for various distances. You can use the structure my_best (of the type Data given next) to record a distance (in meters) and the times (in seconds) for each of ten practice tries swimming that distance:

```
struct Data
{
    double time[10];
    int distance;
};

Data my_best;
```

The structure my_best, declared above, has two member variables: One, named distance, is a variable of type *int* (to record a distance); the other, named time, is an array of ten values of type *double* (to hold times for ten practice tries at the specified distance). To set the distance equal to 20 (meters), you can use the following:

```
my_best.distance = 20;
```

You can set the ten array elements with values from the keyboard as follows:

```
cout << "Enter ten times (in seconds):\n";
for (int i = 0; i < 10; i++)
    cin >> my_best.time[i];
```

The expression my_best.time[i] is read left to right: my_best is a structure; my_best.time is the member variable named time. Since my_best.time is an array, it makes sense to add an index. So, the expression my_best.time[i] is the ith indexed variable of the array my_best.time. If you use a class rather than a structure type, then you can do all your array manipulations with member functions and avoid such confusing expressions. This is illustrated in the following Programming Example.

| **PROGRAMMING EXAMPLE** | **A Class for a Partially Filled Array** |

Display 11.10 shows the definition for a class called TemperatureList, whose objects are lists of temperatures. You might use an object of type TemperatureList in a program that does weather analysis. The list of temperatures is kept in the member variable list, which is an array. Since this array will typically be only partially filled, a second member variable, called size, is used to keep track of how much of the array is used. The value of size is the number of indexed variables of the array list that are being used to store values.

An object of type TemperatureList is declared like an object of any other type. For example, the following declares my_data to be an object of type TemperatureList:

```
TemperatureList my_data;
```

This declaration calls the default constructor with the new object my_data, and so the object my_data is initialized so that the member variable size has the value 0, indicating an empty list.

Once you have declared an object such as my_data, you can add an item to the list of temperatures (that is, to the member array list) with a call to the member function add_temperature as follows:

```
my_data.add_temperature(77);
```

In fact, this is the only way you can add a temperature to the list my_data, since the array list is a private member variable. Notice that when you add an item with a call to the member function add_temperature, the function call first tests to see if the array list is full and adds the value only if the array is not full.

The class TemperatureList is very specialized. The only things you can do with an object of the class TemperatureList are to initialize the list so it is empty, add items to the list, check if the list is full, and output the list. To output the temperatures stored in the object my_data (declared previously), the call would be as follows:

```
cout << my_data;
```

With the class TemperatureList you cannot delete a temperature from the list (array) of temperatures. You can, however, erase the entire list and start over with an empty list by calling the default constructor, as follows:

```
my_data = TemperatureList();
```

The type TemperatureList uses almost no properties of temperatures. You could define a similar class for lists of pressures or lists of distances or lists of any other data expressed as values of type *double*. To save yourself the trouble of defining all these different classes, you could define a single class that represents an arbitrary list of values of type *double* without specifying what the values represent.

DISPLAY 11.10   **Program for a Class with an Array Member** *(part 1 of 2)*

```
1    //This is a definition for the class
2    //Temperaturelist. Values of this type are lists of Fahrenheit temperatures.
3
4    #include <iostream>
5    #include <cstdlib>
6    using namespace std;
7
8    const int MAX_LIST_SIZE = 50;
9
10   class TemperatureList
11   {
12   public:
13       TemperatureList( );
14       //Initializes the object to an empty list.
15
16       void add_temperature(double temperature);
17       //Precondition: The list is not full.
18       //Postcondition: The temperature has been added to the list.
19
20       bool full( ) const;
21       //Returns true if the list is full; false otherwise.
22
23       friend ostream& operator <<(ostream& outs,
24           const TemperatureList& the_object);
25       //Overloads the << operator so it can be used to output values of
26       //type TemperatureList. Temperatures are output one per line.
27       //Precondition: If outs is a file output stream, then outs
28       //has already been connected to a file.
29   private:
30       double list[MAX_LIST_SIZE]; //of temperatures in Fahrenheit
31       int size; //number of array positions filled
32   };
33
34   //This is the implementation for the class TemperatureList.
35
36   TemperatureList::TemperatureList( ) : size(0)
37   {
38       //Body intentionally empty.
39   }
40   void TemperatureList::add_temperature(double temperature)
41   {//Uses iostream and cstdlib:
42       if ( full( ) )
43       {
44           cout << "Error: adding to a full list.\n";
45           exit(1);
46       }
```

(continued)

DISPLAY 11.10 Program for a Class with an Array Member *(part 2 of 2)*

```
47        else
48        {
49            list[size] = temperature;
50            size = size + 1;
51        }
52    }
53    bool TemperatureList::full( ) const
54    {
55        return (size == MAX_LIST_SIZE);
56    }
57    //Uses iostream:
58    ostream& operator <<(ostream& outs, const TemperatureList& the_object)
59    {
60        for (int i = 0; i < the_object.size; i++)
61            outs << the_object.list[i] << " F\n";
62        return outs;
63    }
```

SELF-TEST EXERCISES

myprogramminglab

21. Change the class TemperatureList given in Display 11.10 by adding a member function called get_size, which takes no arguments and returns the number of temperatures on the list.

22. Change the type TemperatureList given in Display 11.10 by adding a member function called get_temperature, which takes one *int* argument that is an integer greater than or equal to 0 and strictly less than MAX_LIST_SIZE. The function returns a value of type *double*, which is the temperature in that position on the list. So, with an argument of 0, get_temperature returns the first temperature; with an argument of 1, it returns the second temperature, and so forth. Assume that get_temperature will not be called with an argument that specifies a location on the list that does not currently contain a temperature.

11.4 CLASSES AND DYNAMIC ARRAYS

With all appliances and means to boot.

WILLIAM SHAKESPEARE, *King Henry IV, Part III*

A dynamic array can have a base type that is a class. A class can have a member variable that is a dynamic array. You can combine the techniques you learned about classes and the techniques you learned about dynamic arrays in just about any way. There are a few more things to worry about when using classes and dynamic arrays, but the basic techniques are the ones that you have already used. Let's start with an example.

PROGRAMMING EXAMPLE   A String Variable Class

In Chapter 8 we showed you how to define array variables to hold C strings. In the previous section you learned how to define dynamic arrays so that the size of the array can be determined when your program is run. In this example we will define a class called StringVar whose objects are string variables. An object of the class StringVar will be implemented using a dynamic array whose size is determined when your program is run. So objects of type StringVar will have all the advantages of dynamic arrays, but they will also have some additional features. We will define StringVar's member functions so that if you try to assign a string that is too long to an object of type StringVar, you will get an error message. The version we define here provides only a small collection of operations for manipulating string objects. In Programming Project 1 you are asked to enhance the class definition by adding more member functions and overloaded operators.

Since you could use the standard class string, as discussed in Chapter 8, you do not really need the class StringVar, but it will be a good exercise to design and code it.

Constructors

The definition for the type StringVar is given in Display 11.11. One constructor for the class StringVar takes a single argument of type *int*. This argument determines the maximum allowable length for a string value stored in the object. A default constructor creates an object with a maximum allowable length of 100. Another constructor takes an array argument that contains a C string of the kind discussed in Chapter 8. Note that this means the argument to this constructor can be a quoted string. This constructor initializes the object so that it can hold any string whose length is less than or equal to the length of its argument, and it initializes the object's string value to a copy of the value of its argument. For the moment, ignore the constructor that is labeled *Copy constructor*. Also ignore the member function named ~StringVar. Although it may look like one, ~StringVar is not a constructor. We will discuss these two new kinds of member functions in later subsections. The meanings of the remaining member functions for the class StringVar are straight forward.

Size of string value

A simple demonstration program is given in Display 11.11. Two objects, your_name and our_name, are declared within the definition of the function conversation. The object your_name can contain any string that is max_name_ size or fewer characters long. The object our_name is initialized to the string value "Borg" and can have its value changed to any other string of length 4 or less.

DISPLAY 11.11   Program Using the StringVar **Class** *(part 1 of 2)*

```
1    //This is the definition for the class StringVar
2    //whose values are strings. An object is declared as follows.
3    //Note that you use (max_size), not [max_size]
4    //StringVar the_object(max_size);
5    //where max_size is the longest string length allowed.
6    #include <iostream>
7    using namespace std;
8
9    class StringVar
10   {
11   public:
12       StringVar(int size);
13       //Initializes the object so it can accept string values up to size
14       //in length. Sets the value of the object equal to the empty string.
15
16       StringVar( );
17       //Initializes the object so it can accept string values of length 100
18       //or less. Sets the value of the object equal to the empty string.
19
20       StringVar(const char a[]);
21       //Precondition: The array a contains characters terminated with '\0'.
22       //Initializes the object so its value is the string stored in a and
23       //so that it can later be set to string values up to strlen(a) in length.
24
25       StringVar(const StringVar& string_object);
26       //Copy constructor.
27
28       ~StringVar( );
29       //Returns all the dynamic memory used by the object to the freestore.
30
31       int length( ) const;
32       //Returns the length of the current string value.
33
33       void input_line(istream& ins);
34       //Precondition: If ins is a file input stream, then ins has been
35       //connected to a file.
36       //Action: The next text in the input stream ins, up to '\n', is copied
37       //to the calling object. If there is not sufficient room, then
38       //only as much as will fit is copied.
39
39       friend ostream& operator <<(ostream& outs, const StringVar& the_string);
40       //Overloads the << operator so it can be used to output values
41       //of type StringVar
42       //Precondition: If outs is a file output stream, then outs
43       //has already been connected to a file.
44
```

(continued)

DISPLAY 11.11   Program Using the StringVar Class *(part 2 of 2)*

```
45    private:
46        char *value; //pointer to dynamic array that holds the string value.
47        int max_length; //declared max length of any string value.
48    };
49
50
51    <The definitions of the member functions and overloaded operators go here>
52
53    //Program to demonstrate use of the class StringVar.
54
55    void conversation(int max_name_size);
56    //Carries on a conversation with the user.
57
58    int main( )
59    {
60        using namespace std;
61        conversation(30);           ◄──────     Memory is returned to the freestore
62        cout << "End of demonstration.\n";        when the function call ends.
63        return 0;
64    }
65
66    //This is only a demonstration function:
67    void conversation(int max_name_size)             Determines the size of the
68    {                                                dynamic array
69        using namespace std;
70
71        StringVar your_name(max_name_size), our_name("Borg");
72
73        cout << "What is your name?\n";
74        your_name.input_line(cin);
75        cout << "We are " << our_name << endl;
76        cout << "We will meet again " << your_name << endl;
77    }
```

Sample Dialogue

```
What is your name?
Kathryn Janeway
We are Borg
We will meet again Kathryn Janeway
End of demonstration
```

As we indicated at the beginning of this subsection, the class StringVar is implemented using a dynamic array. The implementation is shown in Display 11.12. When an object of type StringVar is declared, a constructor is called to initialize the object. The constructor uses the *new* operator to create a new dynamic array of characters for the member variable value. The string value is stored in the array value as an ordinary string value, with '\0' used to mark the end of the string. Notice that the size of this array is not determined until the object is declared, at which point the constructor is called and the argument to the constructor determines the size of the dynamic array. As illustrated in Display 11.11, this argument can be a variable of type *int*. Look at the declaration of the object your_name in the definition of the function conversation. The argument to the constructor is the call-by-value parameter max_name_size. Recall that a call-by-value parameter is a local variable, so max_name_size is a variable. Any *int* variable may be used as the argument to the constructor in this way.

Implementation

The implementation of the member functions length, input_line, and the overloaded output operator << are all straightforward. In the next few subsections we discuss the function ~StringVar and the constructor labeled *Copy constructor*.

Destructors

VideoNote
Arrays of Classes using Dynamic Arrays

There is one problem with dynamic variables. They do not go away unless your program makes a suitable call to *delete*. Even if the dynamic variable was created using a local pointer variable and the local pointer variable goes away at the end of a function call, the dynamic variable will remain unless there is a call to *delete*. If you do not eliminate dynamic variables with calls to *delete*, they will continue to occupy memory space, which may cause your program to abort because it used up all the memory in the freestore. Moreover, if the dynamic variable is embedded in the implementation of a class, the programmer who uses the class does not know about the dynamic variable and cannot be expected to perform the call to *delete*. In fact, since the data members are normally private members, the programmer normally *cannot* access the needed pointer variables and so *cannot* call *delete* with these pointer variables. To handle this problem, C++ has a special kind of member function called a *destructor*.

A **destructor** is a member function that is called automatically when an object of the class passes out of scope. This means that if your program contains a local variable that is an object with a destructor, then when the function call ends, the destructor is called automatically. If the destructor is defined correctly, the destructor calls *delete* to eliminate all the dynamic variables created by the object. This may be done with a single call to *delete* or it may require several calls to *delete*. You might also want your destructor to perform some other cleanup details as well, but returning memory to the freestore is the main job of the destructor.

The member function ~StringVar is the destructor for the class StringVar shown in Display 11.11. Like a constructor, a destructor always has the same name as the class it is a member of, but the destructor has the tilde symbol,~, at the beginning of its name (so you can tell that it is a destructor and not a constructor). Like a constructor, a destructor has no type for the value returned, not even the type *void*. A destructor has no parameters. Thus, a class can have only one destructor; you cannot overload the destructor for a class. Otherwise, a destructor is defined just like any other member function.

Notice the definition of the destructor ~StringVar given in Display 11.12. ~StringVar calls *delete* to eliminate the dynamic array pointed to by the member pointer variable value. Look again at the function conversation in the sample program shown in Display 11.11. The local variables your_name and our_name both create dynamic arrays. If this class did not have a destructor, then after the call to conversation has ended, these dynamic arrays would still be occupying memory, even though they are useless to the program. This would not be a problem here because the sample program ends soon after the call to conversation is completed; but if you wrote a program that made repeated calls to functions like conversation, and if the class StringVar did not have a suitable destructor, then the function calls could consume all the memory in the freestore and your program would then end abnormally.

DISPLAY 11.12   Implementation of StringVar *(part 1 of 2)*

```
1    //This is the implementation of the class StringVar.
2    //The definition for the class StringVar is in Display 11.11.
3    #include <cstdlib>
4    #include <cstddef>
5    #include <cstring>
6
7    //Uses cstddef and cstdlib:
8    StringVar::StringVar(int size) : max_length(size)
9    {
10       value = new char[max_length + 1];//+1 is for '\0'.
11       value[0] = '\0';
12   }
13
14   //Uses cstddef and cstdlib:
15   StringVar::StringVar( ) : max_length(100)
16   {
17       value = new char[max_length + 1];//+1 is for '\0'.
18       value[0] = '\0';
19   }
20
21   //Uses cstring, cstddef, and cstdlib:
22   StringVar::StringVar(const char a[]) : max_length(strlen(a))
23   {
24       value = new char[max_length + 1];//+1 is for '\0'.
```

(continued)

DISPLAY 11.12 **Implementation of** StringVar *(part 2 of 2)*

```
25          strcpy(value, a);
26      }
27      //Uses cstring, cstddef, and cstdlib:
28      StringVar::StringVar(const StringVar& string_object)
29                          : max_length(string_object.length( ))
30      {
31          value = new char[max_length + 1];//+1 is for '\0'.
32          strcpy(value, string_object.value);
33      }
34      StringVar::~StringVar( )
35      {
36          delete [] value;
37      }
38
39      //Uses cstring:
40      int StringVar::length( ) const
41      {
42          return strlen(value);
43      }
44
45      //Uses iostream:
46      void StringVar::input_line(istream& ins)
47      {
48          ins.getline(value, max_length + 1);
49      }
50
51      //Uses iostream:
52      ostream& operator <<(ostream& outs, const StringVar& the_string)
53      {
54          outs << the_string.value;
55          return outs;
56      }
```

Copy constructor (discussed later in this chapter)

Destructor

Destructor

A **destructor** is a member function of a class that is called automatically when an object of the class goes out of scope. Among other things, this means that if an object of the class type is a local variable for a function, then the destructor is automatically called as the last action before the function call ends. Destructors are used to eliminate any dynamic variables that have been created by the object so that the memory occupied by these dynamic variables is returned to the freestore. Destructors may perform other cleanup tasks as well. The name of a destructor must consist of the tilde symbol,~, followed by the name of the class.

PITFALL   Pointers as Call-by-Value Parameters

When a call-by-value parameter is of a pointer type, its behavior can be subtle and troublesome. Consider the function call shown in Display 11.13. The parameter temp in the function sneaky is a call-by-value parameter, and hence it is a local variable. When the function is called, the value of temp is set to the value of the argument p and the function body is executed. Since temp is a local variable, no changes to temp should go outside of the function sneaky. In particular, the value of the pointer variable p should not be changed. Yet the sample dialogue makes it look as if the value of the pointer variable p had changed. Before the call to the function sneaky, the value of *p was 77, and after the call to sneaky the value of *p is 99. What has happened?

DISPLAY 11.13   A Call-by-Value Pointer Parameter *(part 1 of 2)*

```
1    //Program to demonstrate the way call-by-value parameters
2    //behave with pointer arguments.
3    #include <iostream>
4    using namespace std;
5
6    typedef int* IntPointer;
7
8    void sneaky(IntPointer temp);
9
10   int main( )
11   {
12       IntPointer p;
13
14       p = new int;
15       *p = 77;
16       cout << "Before call to function *p == "
17           << *p << endl;
18
19       sneaky(p);
20
21       cout << "After call to function *p == "
22           << *p << endl;
23
24       return 0;
25   }
26
27   void sneaky(IntPointer temp)
28   {
29       *temp = 99;
30       cout << "Inside function call *temp == "
31           << *temp << endl;
32   }
```

(continued)

DISPLAY 11.13   A Call-by-Value Pointer Parameter *(part 2 of 2)*

Sample Dialogue

```
Before call to function *p == 77
Inside function call *temp == 99
After call to function *p == 99
```

The situation is diagrammed in Display 11.14. Although the sample dialogue may make it look as if p were changed, the value of p was not changed by the function call to sneaky. Pointer p has two things associated with it: p's pointer value and the value stored where p points. Now, the value of p is a pointer (that is, a memory address). After the call to sneaky, the variable p contains the same pointer value (that is, the same memory address). The call to sneaky has changed the value of the variable pointed to by p, but it has not changed the value of p itself.

If the parameter type is a class or structure type that has member variables of a pointer type, the same kind of surprising changes can occur with call-by-value arguments of the class type. However, for class types, you can avoid (and control) these surprise changes by defining a *copy constructor*, as described in the next subsection. ■

Copy Constructors

A **copy constructor** is a constructor that has one parameter that is of the same type as the class. The one parameter must be a call-by-reference parameter, and normally the parameter is preceded by the *const* parameter modifier, so it is a constant parameter. In all other respects, a copy constructor is defined in the same way as any other constructor and can be used just like other constructors.

DISPLAY 11.14   The Function Call sneaky(p);

1. Before call to sneaky:

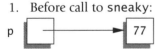

2. Value of p is plugged in for temp:

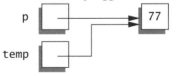

3. Change made to *temp:

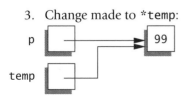

4. After call to sneaky:

For example, a program that uses the class `StringVar` defined in Display 11.11 might contain the following:

```
StringVar line(20), motto("Constructors can help.");
cout << "Enter a string of length 20 or less:\n";
line.input_line(cin);
StringVar temp(line);//Initialized by the copy constructor.
```

The constructor used to initialize each of the three objects of type `StringVar` is determined by the type of the argument given in parentheses after the object's name. The object `line` is initialized with the constructor that has a parameter of type *int*; the object `motto` is initialized by the constructor that has a parameter of type *const char* `a[]`. Similarly, the object `temp` is initialized by the constructor that has one argument of type *const* `StringVar&`. When used in this way, a copy constructor is being used just like any other constructor.

A copy constructor should be defined so that the object being initialized becomes a complete, independent copy of its argument. So, in the declaration

```
StringVar temp(line);
```

the member variable `temp.value` is not simply set to the same value as `line.value`; that would produce two pointers pointing to the same dynamic array. The definition of the copy constructor is shown in Display 11.12. Note that in the definition of the copy constructor, a new dynamic array is created and the contents of one dynamic array are copied to the other dynamic array. Thus, in the previous declaration, `temp` is initialized so that its string value is equal to the string value of `line`, but `temp` has a separate dynamic array. Thus, any change that is made to `temp` has no effect on `line`.

As you have seen, a copy constructor can be used just like any other constructor. A copy constructor is also called automatically in certain other situations. Roughly speaking, whenever C++ needs to make a copy of an object, it automatically calls the copy constructor. In particular, the copy constructor is called automatically in three circumstances: (1) when a class object is declared and is initialized by another object of the same type, (2) when a function returns a value of the class type, and (3) whenever an argument of the class type is "plugged in" for a call-by-value parameter. In this case, the copy constructor defines what is meant by "plugging in."

To see why you need a copy constructor, let's see what would happen if we did not define a copy constructor for the class `StringVar`. *Suppose we did not include the copy constructor in the definition of the class* `StringVar` and suppose we used a call-by-value parameter in a function definition, for example:

```
void show_string(StringVar the_string)
{
    cout << "The string is: "
        << the_string << endl;
}
```

Consider the following code, which includes a function call:

```
StringVar greeting("Hello");
show_string(greeting);
cout << "After call: " << greeting << endl;
```

Assuming there is no copy constructor, things proceed as follows: When the function call is executed, the value of `greeting` is copied to the local variable `the_string`, so `the_string.value` is set equal to `greeting.value`. But these are pointer variables, so during the function call, `the_string.value` and `greeting.value` point to the same dynamic array, as follows:

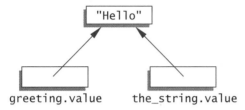

When the function call ends, the destructor for `StringVar` is called to return the memory used by `the_string` to the freestore. The definition of the destructor contains the following statement:

delete [] value;

Since the destructor is called with the object `the_string`, this statement is equivalent to:

delete [] the_string.value;

which changes the picture to the following:

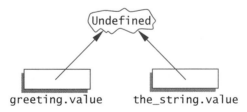

Since `greeting.value` and `the_string.value` point to the same dynamic array, deleting `the_string.value` is the same as deleting `greeting.value`. Thus, `greeting.value` is undefined when the program reaches the statement

```
cout << "After call: " << greeting << endl;
```

This cout statement is therefore undefined. The cout statement may by chance give you the output you want, but sooner or later the fact that `greeting.value` is undefined will produce problems. One major problem occurs when the object `greeting` is a local variable in some function. In this case the destructor will be called with `greeting` when the function call ends. That destructor call will be equivalent to

delete [] greeting.value;

But, as we just saw, the dynamic array pointed to by `greeting.value` has already been deleted once, and now the system is trying to delete it a second time. Calling *delete* twice to delete the same dynamic array (or other variable created with *new*) can produce a serious system error that can cause your program to crash.

That was what would happen if there were no copy constructor. Fortunately, we included a copy constructor in our definition of the class `StringVar`, so the copy constructor is called automatically when the following function call is executed:

```
StringVar greeting("Hello");
show_string(greeting);
```

The copy constructor defines what it means to "plug in" the argument `greeting` for the call-by-value parameter `the_string`, so that now the picture is as follows:

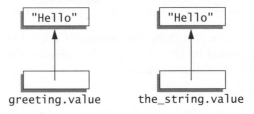

Thus, any change that is made to `the_string.value` has no effect on the argument `greeting`, and there are no problems with the destructor. If the destructor is called for `the_string` and then called for `greeting`, each call to the destructor deletes a different dynamic array.

Returned value

When a function returns a value of a class type, the copy constructor is called automatically to copy the value specified by the return statement. If there is no copy constructor, then problems similar to what we described for value parameters will occur.

When you need a copy constructor

If a class definition involves pointers and dynamically allocated memory using the *new* operator, then you need to include a copy constructor. Classes that do not involve pointers or dynamically allocated memory do not need a copy constructor.

Assignment statements

Contrary to what you might expect, the copy constructor is *not* called when you set one object equal to another using the assignment operator.[2] However, if you do not like what the default assignment operator does, you can redefine the assignment operator in the way described in the subsection entitled "Overloading the Assignment Operator."

---

[2] C++ makes a careful distinction between initialization (the three cases where the copy constructor is called) and assignment. Initialization uses the copy constructor to create a new object; the assignment operator takes an existing object and modifies it so that it is an identical copy (in all but location) of the right-hand side of the assignment.

Copy Constructor

A **copy constructor** is a constructor that has one call-by-reference parameter that is of the same type as the class. The one parameter must be a call-by-reference parameter. Normally, the parameter is also a constant parameter, that is, preceded by the *const* parameter modifier. The copy constructor for a class is called automatically whenever a function returns a value of the class type. The copy constructor is also called automatically whenever an argument is "plugged in" for a call-by-value parameter of the class type. A copy constructor can also be used in the same ways as other constructors.

Any class that uses pointers and the *new* operator should have a copy constructor.

The Big Three

The **copy constructor**, the **=operator**, and the **destructor** are called the **big three** because experts say that if you need to define any of them, then you need to define all three. If any of these is missing, the compiler will create it, but it may not behave as you want. So it pays to define them yourself. The copy constructor and overloaded =operator that the compiler generates for you will work fine if all member variables are of predefined types such as *int* and *double*, but they may misbehave on classes that have class or pointer member variables. For any class that uses pointers and the *new* operator, it is safest to define your own copy constructor, overloaded =, and destructor.

= must be a member

SELF-TEST EXERCISES

23. If a class is named MyClass and it has a constructor, what is the constructor named? If MyClass has a destructor, what is the destructor named?

24. Suppose you change the definition of the destructor in Display 11.12 to the following. How would the sample dialogue in Display 11.11 change?

```
StringVar::~StringVar()
{
    cout << endl
        << "Good-bye cruel world! The short life of\n"
        << "this dynamic array is about to end.\n";
    delete [] value;
}
```

25. The following is the first line of the copy constructor definition for the class `StringVar`. The identifier `StringVar` occurs three times and means something slightly different each time. What does it mean in each of the three cases?

    `StringVar::StringVar(const StringVar& string_object)`

26. Answer these questions about destructors.
    a. What is a destructor and what must the name of a destructor be?
    b. When is a destructor called?
    c. What does a destructor actually do?
    d. What should a destructor do?

Overloading the Assignment Operator

VideoNote
Overloading = and = for
a Class

Suppose `string1` and `string2` are declared as follows:

    `StringVar string1(10), string2(20);`

The class `StringVar` was defined in Displays 11.11 and 11.12. If `string2` has somehow been given a value, then the following assignment statement is defined, but its meaning may not be what you would like it to be:

    `string1 = string2;`

As usual, this predefined version of the assignment statement copies the value of each of the member variables of `string2` to the corresponding member variables of `string1`, so the value of `string1.max_length` is changed to be the same as `string2.max_length` and the value of `string1.value` is changed to be the same as `string2.value`. But this can cause problems with `string1` and probably even cause problems for `string2`.

The member variable `string1.value` contains a pointer, and the assignment statement sets this pointer equal to the same value as `string2.value`. Thus, both `string1.value` and `string2.value` point to the same place in memory. If you change the string value in `string1`, you will therefore also change the string value in `string2`. If you change the string value in `string2`, you will change the string value in `string1`.

In short, the predefined assignment statement does not do what we would like an assignment statement to do with objects of type `StringVar`. Using the predefined version of the assignment operator with the class `StringVar` can only cause problems. The way to fix this is to overload the assignment operator = so that it does what we want it to do with objects of the class `StringVar`.

The assignment operator cannot be overloaded in the way we have overloaded other operators, such as `<<` and `+`. When you overload the assignment operator, it must be a member of the class; it cannot be a friend of the class. To add an overloaded version of the assignment operator to the class `StringVar`, the definition of `StringVar` should be changed to the following:

```
class StringVar
{
public:
    void operator =(const StringVar& right_side);
    //Overloads the assignment operator = to copy a string
    //from one object to another.
    <The rest of the definition of the class can be the same as in
        Display 11.11.>
```

The assignment operator is then used just as you always use the assignment operator. For example, consider the following:

```
string1 = string2;
```

In this call, `string1` is the calling object and `string2` is the argument to the member operator =.

Calling object for =

The definition of the assignment operator can be as follows:

```
//The following is acceptable, but
//we will give a better definition:
void StringVar::operator =(const StringVar& right_side)
{
    int new_length = strlen(right_side.value);
    if ((new_length) > max_length)
        new_length = max_length;

    for (int i = 0; i < new_length; i++)
        value[i] = right_side.value[i];
    value[new_length] = '\0';
}
```

Notice that the length of the string in the object on the right side of the assignment operator is checked. If it is too long to fit in the object on the left side of the assignment operator (which is the calling object), then only as many characters as will fit are copied to the object receiving the string. But suppose you do not want to lose any characters in the copying process. To fit in all the characters, you can create a new, larger dynamic array for the object on the left-hand side of the assignment operator. You might try to redefine the assignment operator as follows:

```
//This version has a bug:
void StringVar::operator =(const StringVar& right_side)
{
    delete [] value;
    int new_length = strlen(right_side.value);
    max_length = new_length;

    value = new char[max_length + 1];

    for (int i = 0; i < new_length; i++)
        value[i] = right_side.value[i];
    value[new_length] = '\0';
}
```

This version has a problem when used in an assignment with the same object on both sides of the assignment operator, like the following:

```
my_string = my_string;
```

When this assignment is executed, the first statement executed is

```
delete [] value;
```

But the calling object is my_string, so this means

```
delete [] my_string.value;
```

So, the string value in my_string is deleted and the pointer my_string.value is undefined. The assignment operator has corrupted the object my_string, and this run of the program is probably ruined.

One way to fix this bug is to first check whether there is sufficient room in the dynamic array member of the object on the left-hand side of the assignment operator and to delete the array only if extra space is needed. Our final definition of the overloaded assignment operator does just such a check:

```
//This is our final version:
void StringVar::operator =(const StringVar& right_side)
{
    int new_length = strlen(right_side.value);
    if (new_length > max_length)
    {
        delete [] value;
        max_length = new_length;
        value = new char[max_length + 1];
    }
    for (int i = 0; i < new_length; i++)
        value[i] = right_side.value[i];
    value[new_length] = '\0';
}
```

For many classes, the obvious definition for overloading the assignment operator does not work correctly when the same object is on both sides of the assignment operator. You should always check this case and be careful to write your definition of the overloaded assignment operator so that it also works in this case.

SELF-TEST EXERCISE

27. a. Explain carefully why no overloaded assignment operator is needed when the only data consists of built-in types.

   b. Same as part (a) for a copy constructor.

   c. Same as part (a) for a destructor.

CHAPTER SUMMARY

■ A **friend** function of a class is an ordinary function except that it has access to the private members of the class, just like the member functions do.

■ If your classes each have a full set of accessor and mutator functions, then the only reason to make a function a friend is to make the definition of the friend function simpler and more efficient, but that is often reason enough.

■ A parameter of a class type that is not changed by the function should normally be a constant parameter.

■ Operators, such as + and ==, can be overloaded so they can be used with objects of a class type that you define.

■ When overloading the >> or << operators, the type returned should be a stream type and must be a reference, which is indicated by appending an & to the name of the returned type.

■ The base type of an array can be a structure or class type. A structure or class can have an array as a member variable.

■ A **destructor** is a special kind of member function for a class. A destructor is called automatically when an object of the class passes out of scope. The main reason for destructors is to return memory to the freestore so the memory can be reused.

■ A **copy constructor** is a constructor that has a single argument that is of the same type as the class. If you define a copy constructor, it will be called automatically whenever a function returns a value of the class type and whenever an argument is "plugged in" for a call-by-value parameter of the class type. Any class that uses pointers and the operator *new* should have a copy constructor.

■ The assignment operator = can be overloaded for a class so that it behaves as you wish for that class. However, it must be overloaded as a member of the class; it cannot be overloaded as a friend. Any class that uses pointers and the operator *new* should overload the assignment operator for use with that class.

Answers to Self-Test Exercises

```
1. bool before(DayOfYear date1, DayOfYear date2)
   {
       return ((date1.get_month() < date2.get_month())
              || (date1.get_month() == date2.get_month()
                 && date1.get_day ( ) < date2.get_day ( )));
   }
```

The previous Boolean expression says that date1 is before date2, provided the month of date1 is before the month of date2 or that the months are the same and the day of date1 is before the day of date2.

2. A friend function and a member function are alike in that they both can use any member of the class (either public or private) in their function definition. However, a friend function is defined and used just like an ordinary function; the dot operator is not used when you call a friend function, and no type qualifier is used when you define a friend function. A member function, on the other hand, is called using an object name and the dot operator. Also, a member function definition includes a type qualifier consisting of the class name and the scope resolution operator ::.

3. The modified definition of the class DayOfYear is shown below. The part in color is new. We have omitted some comments to save space, but all the comments shown in Display 11.2 should be included in this definition.

```
class DayOfYear
{
public:
    friend bool equal(DayOfYear date1, DayOfYear date2);
    friend bool after(DayOfYear date1, DayOfYear date2);
    //Precondition: date1 and date2 have values.
    //Returns true if date1 follows date2 on the calendar;
    //otherwise, returns false.

    DayOfYear(int the_month, int the_day);
    DayOfYear();
    void input();
    void output();
    int get_month();
    int get_day();
private:
    void check_date( );
    int month;
    int day;
};
```

You also must add the following definition of the function after:

```
bool after(DayOfYear date1, DayOfYear date2)
{
    return ((date1.month > date2 month))||
        ((date1.month == date2.month) && (date1.day > date2.day))
}
```

4. The modified definition of the class Money is shown here. The part in color is new. We have omitted some comments to save space, but all the comments shown in Display 11.3 should be included in this definition.

```
class Money
{
public:
    friend Money subtract(Money amount1, Money amount2);
    //Precondition: amount1 and amount2 have values.
    //Returns amount1 minus amount2.

    friend bool equal(Money amount1, Money amount2);
    Money(long dollars, int cents);
    Money(long dollars);
    Money();
    double get_value();
    void input(istream& ins);
    void output(ostream& outs);
private:
    long all_cents;
};
```

You also must add the following definition of the function `subtract`:

```
Money subtract(Money amount1, Money amount2)
{
    Money temp;
    temp.all_cents = amount1.all_cents
                      - amount2.all_cents;
    return temp;
}
```

5. The modified definition of the class Money is shown here. The part in color is new. We have omitted some comments to save space, but all the comments shown in Display 11.3 should be included in this definition.

```
class Money
{
public:
    friend Money add(Money amount1, Money amount2);
    friend bool equal(Money amount1, Money amount2);
    Money(long dollars, int cents);
    Money(long dollars);
    Money();
    double get_value();
    void input(istream& ins);

    void output(ostream& outs);
    //Precondition: If outs is a file output stream, then
    //outs has already been connected to a file.
    //Postcondition: A dollar sign and the amount of money
    //recorded in the calling object has been sent to the
    //output stream outs.
```

```
    void output();
    //Postcondition: A dollar sign and the amount of money
    //recorded in the calling object has been output to the
    //screen.
private:
    long all_cents;
};
```

You also must add the following definition of the function name output. (The old definition of output stays, so that there are two definitions of output.)

```
void Money::output()
{
    output(cout);
}
```

The following longer version of the function definition also works:

```
//Uses cstdlib and iostream
void Money::output()
{
    long positive_cents, dollars, cents;
    positive_cents = labs(all_cents);
    dollars = positive_cents/100;
    cents = positive_cents%100;

    if (all_cents < 0)
        cout << "-$" << dollars << '.';
    else
        cout << "$" << dollars << '.';

    if (cents < 10)
        cout << '0';
    cout << cents;
}
```

You can also overload the member function input so that a call like

```
purse.input();
```

means the same as

```
purse.input(cin);
```

And, of course, you can combine this enhancement with the enhancements from previous Self-Test Exercises to produce one highly improved class Money.

6. If the user enters $-9.95 (instead of -$9.95), the function input will read the '$' as the value of one_char, the -9 as the value of dollars, the '.' as the value of decimal_point, and the '9' and '5' as the values of digit1 and digit2. That means it will set dollars equal to -9 and cents equal

to 95 and so set the amount equal to a value that represents –$9.00 plus 0.95, which is –$8.05. One way to catch this problem is to test if the value of dollars is negative (since the value of dollars should be an absolute value). To do this, rewrite the error message portion as follows:

```
if (one_char != '$' || decimal_point != '.'
       || !isdigit(digit1) || !isdigit(digit2)
       || dollars < 0)    ◄───────────── New
{
    cout << "Error illegal form for money input\n";
    exit(1);
}
```

This code still will not give an error message for incorrect input with zero dollars as in $-0.95. However, with the material we have learned thus far, a test for this case, while certainly possible, would significantly complicate the code and make it harder to read.

7. ```
#include <iostream>
using namespace std;
int main( )
{
    int x;
    cin >> x;
    cout << x << endl;
    return 0;
}
```

If the compiler interprets input with a leading 0 as a base-8 numeral, then with input data 077, the output should be 63. The output should be 77 if the compiler does not interpret data with a leading 0 as indicating base 8.

8. The only change from the version given in Display 11.3 is that the modifier *const* is added to the function heading, so the definition is

```
double Money::get_value() const
{
    return (all_cents * 0.01);
}
```

9. The member function input changes the value of its calling object, and so the compiler will issue an error message if you add the *const* modifier.

10. *Similarities:* Each parameter call protects the caller's argument from change. *Differences:* The call-by-value makes a copy of the caller's argument, so it uses more memory than a call-by-constant-reference.

11. In the *const int* x = 17; declaration, the *const* keyword promises the compiler that code written by the author will not change the value of x.
```

In the *int* f() *const*; declaration, the *const* keyword is a promise to the compiler that code written by the author to implement function f will not change anything in the calling object.

In the int g(const A& x); declaration, the *const* keyword is a promise to the compiler that code written by the class author will not change the argument plugged in for x.

12. The difference between a (binary) operator (such as +, *, /, and so forth) and a function involves the syntax of how they are called. In a function call, the arguments are given in parentheses after the function name. With an operator, the arguments are given before and after the operator. Also, you must use the reserved word *operator* in the declaration and in the definition of an overloaded operator.

13. The modified definition of the class Money is shown here. The part in color is new. We have omitted some comments to save space, but all the comments shown in Display 11.5 should be included in this definition.

```
class Money
{
public:
    friend Money operator +(const Money& amount1,
                            const Money& amount2);
    friend bool operator ==(const Money& amount1,
                            const Money& amount2);
    friend bool operator <(const Money& amount1,
                           const Money& amount2);
    //Precondition: amount1 and amount2 have been given
    //values.
    //Returns true if amount1 is less than amount2;
    //otherwise, returns false.
    Money(long dollars, int cents);
    Money(long dollars);
    Money();
    double get_value() const;
    void input(istream& ins);
    void output(ostream& outs) const;
private:
    long all_cents;
};
```

You also must add the following definition of the overloaded operator <:

```
bool operator <(const Money& amount1,
                const Money& amount2)
{
    return (amount1.all_cents < amount2.all_cents);
}
```

14. The modified definition of the class Money is shown here. The part in color is new. We have omitted some comments to save space, but all the comments shown in Display 11.5 should be included in this definition. We have included the changes from the previous exercises in this answer, since it is natural to use the overloaded < operator in the definition of the overloaded <= operator.

```
class Money
{
public:
    friend Money operator +(const Money& amount1,
                            const Money& amount2);
    friend bool operator ==(const Money& amount1,
                            const Money& amount2);
    friend bool operator <(const Money& amount1,
                           const Money& amount2);
    //Precondition: amount1 and amount2 have been given
    //values.
    //Returns true if amount1 is less than amount2;
    //otherwise, returns false.
    friend bool operator <=(const Money& amount1,
                            const Money& amount2);
    //Precondition: amount1 and amount2 have been given
    //values.
    //Returns true if amount1 is less than or equal to
    //amount2; otherwise, returns false.
    Money(long dollars, int cents);
    Money(long dollars);
    Money();
    double get_value() const;
    void input(istream& ins);
    void output(ostream& outs) const;
private:
    long all_cents;
};
```

You also must add the following definition of the overloaded operator <= (as well as the definition of the overloaded operator < given in the previous exercise):

```
bool operator <=(const Money& amount1,
                 const Money& amount2)
{
    return ((amount1.all_cents < amount2.all_cents)
           ||(amount1.all_cents == amount2.all_cents));
}
```

15. When overloading an operator, at least one of the arguments to the operator must be of a class type. This prevents changing the behavior of + for integers. Actually, this requirement prevents changing the effect of any operator on any built-in type.

16.
```
//Uses cmath (for floor):
Money::Money(double amount)
{
    all_cents = floor(amount * 100);
}
```

This definition simply discards any amount that is less than one cent. For example, it converts 12.34999 to the integer 1234, which represents the amount $12.34. It is possible to define the constructor to instead do other things with any fraction of a cent.

17.
```
istream& operator >>(istream& ins, Pairs& second)
{
    char ch;
    ins >> ch;          //discard initial '('
    ins >> second.f;
    ins >> ch;          //discard comma ','
    ins >> second.s;
    ins >> ch;          //discard final ')'
    return ins;
}

ostream& operator <<(ostream& outs, const Pairs& second)
{
    outs << '(';
    outs << second.f;
    outs << ','; //You might prefer ","
                 //to get an extra space
    outs << second.s;
    outs << ')';
    return outs;
}
```

18.
```
//Uses iostream:
istream& operator >>(istream& ins, Percent& the_object)
{
    char percent_sign;
    ins >> the_object.value;
    ins >> percent_sign;//Discards the % sign.
    return ins;
}

//Uses iostream:
ostream& operator <<(ostream& outs,
    const Percent& a_percent)
{
    outs << a_percent.value << '%';
    return outs;
}
```

19. *struct* Score
    {
        int home_team;
        int opponent;
    };
    Score game[10];

20. //Reads in 5 amounts of money, doubles each amount,
    //and outputs the results.
    #include <iostream>

    <The definitions for the Money class go here>

    int main()
    {
        using namespace std;
        Money amount[5];
        int i;
        cout << "Enter 5 amounts of money:\n";
        for (i = 0; i < 5; i++)
            cin >> amount[i];
        for (i = 0; i < 5; i++)
        amount[i] = amount[i] + amount[i];
        cout << "After doubling, the amounts are:\n";
        for (i = 0; i < 5; i++)
            cout << amount[i] << " ";
        cout << endl;
        return 0;
    }

    (You cannot use 2 * amount[i], since * has not been overloaded for operands of type Money.)

21. See answer 22.

22. This answer combines the answers to this and the previous Self-Test Exercise. The class definition would change to the following. (We have deleted some comments from Display 11.10 to save space, but you should include them in your answer.)

    class TemperatureList
    {
    public:
        TemperatureList();

        int get_size( ) *const*;
        //Returns the number of temperatures on the list.

        void add_temperature(*double* temperature);

        double get_temperature(*int* position) *const*;

```
        //Precondition: 0 <= position < get_size( ).
        //Returns the temperature that was added in position
        //specified. The first temperature that was added is
        //in position 0.

        bool full() const;

        friend ostream& operator <<(ostream& outs,
        const TemperatureList& the_object);
private:
        double list[MAX_LIST_SIZE];//of temperatures in
                                  //Fahrenheit
        int size; //number of array positions filled
};
```

You also need to add the following member function definitions:

```
int TemperatureList::get_size() const
{
        return size;
}

//Uses iostream and cstdlib:
double TemperatureList::get_temperature (int position) const
{
        if ((position >= size) || (position < 0))
        {
            cout << "Error:"
                << " reading an empty list position.\n";
            exit(1);
        }
        else
            return (list[position]);
}
```

23. The *constructor* is named `MyClass`, the same name as the name of the class. The *destructor* is named `~MyClass`.

24. The dialogue would change to the following:

```
What is your name?
Kathryn Janeway
We are Borg
We will meet again Kathryn Janeway
Good-bye cruel world! The short life of
this dynamic array is about to end.
Good-bye cruel world! The short life of
this dynamic array is about to end.
End of demonstration
```

25. The `StringVar` before the `::` is the name of the class. The `StringVar` right after the `::` is the name of the member function. (Remember, a constructor is a member function that has the same name as the class.) The `StringVar` inside the parentheses is the type for the parameter `string_object`.

26. a. A destructor is a member function of a class. A destructor's name always begins with a tilde, `~`, followed by the class name.

    b. A destructor is called when a class object goes out of scope.

    c. A destructor actually does whatever the class author programs it to do!

    d. A destructor is supposed to delete dynamic variables that have been allocated by constructors for the class. Destructors may also do other cleanup tasks.

27. In the case of the assignment operator = and the copy constructor, if there are only built-in types for data, the default copy mechanism is exactly what you want, so the default works fine. In the case of the destructor, no dynamic memory allocation is done (no pointers), so the default do-nothing action is again what you want.

PROGRAMMING PROJECTS

Visit www.myprogramminglab.com to complete many of these Programming Projects online and get instant feedback.   myprogramminglab

1. Modify the definition of the class `Money` shown in Display 11.8 so that all of the following are added:

   a. The operators `<`, `<=`, `>`, and `>=` have each been overloaded to apply to the type `Money`. (*Hint:* See Self-Test Exercise 13.)

   b. The following member function has been added to the class definition. (We show the function declaration as it should appear in the class definition. The definition of the function itself will include the qualifier `Money::`.)

   ```
   Money percent(int percent_figure) const;
   //Returns a percentage of the money amount in the
   //calling object. For example, if percent_figure is 10,
   //then the value returned is 10% of the amount of
   //money represented by the calling object.
   ```

   For example, if `purse` is an object of type `Money` whose value represents the amount $100.10, then the call

   ```
   purse.percent(10);
   ```

   returns 10% of $100.10; that is, it returns a value of type `Money` that represents the amount $10.01.

2. Self-Test Exercise 17 asked you to overload the operator >> and the operator << for a class `Pairs`. Complete and test this exercise. Implement the default constructor and the constructors with one and two *int* parameters. The one-parameter constructor should initialize the first member of the pair; the second member of the pair is to be 0.

   Overload binary operator+ to add pairs according to the rule

   (a, b) + (c, d) = (a + c, b + d)

   Overload operator- analogously.

   Overload operator* on `Pairs` and *int* according to the rule

   (a, b) * c = (a * c, b * c)

   Write a program to test all the member functions and overloaded operators in your class definition.

3. In Chapter 8 we discussed vectors, which are like arrays that can grow in size. Suppose that vectors were not defined in C++. Define a class called `VectorDouble` that is like a class for a vector with base type *double*. Your class `VectorDouble` will have a private member variable for a dynamic array of *double*s. It will also have two member variables of type *int*; one called `max_count` for the size of the dynamic array of *double*s; and one called `count` for the number of array positions currently holding values. (`max_count` is the same as the capacity of a vector; `count` is the same as the size of a vector.)

   If you attempt to add an element (a value of type *double*) to the vector object of the class `VectorDouble` and there is no more room, then a new dynamic array with twice the capacity of the old dynamic array is created and the values of the old dynamic array are copied to the new dynamic array.

   Your class should have all of the following:

   ■ Three constructors: a default constructor that creates a dynamic array for 50 elements, a constructor with one *int* argument for the number of elements in the initial dynamic array, and a copy constructor.

   ■ A destructor.

   ■ A suitable overloading of the assignment operator =.

   ■ A suitable overloading of the equality operator ==. To be equal, the values of `count` and the `count` array elements must be equal, but the values of `max_count` need not be equal.

   ■ Member functions push_back, `capacity`, `size`, `reserve`, and `resize` that behave the same as the member functions of the same names for vectors.

■ Two member functions to give your class the same utility as the square brackets: value_at(i), which returns the value of the ith element in the dynamic array; and change_value_at(d, i), which changes the *double* value at the ith element of the dynamic array to d. Enforce suitable restrictions on the arguments to value_at and change_value_at. (Your class will not work with the square brackets. It can be made to work with square brackets, but we have not covered the material which tells you how to do that.)

4. Write a C++ program containing a class called OperatorDemo with one *integer* type data member. Implement the default constructor and the constructor with one *int* parameter. Overload the * and + operators to multiply and add the data members of two instances of the class Opera-torDemo. Also, overload the - operator to allow subtraction of the data members of two instances of the class OperatorDemo.

Write a program to test all the member functions and overloaded operators in your class definition.

5. Define a class for rational numbers. A rational number is a number that can be represented as the quotient of two integers. For example, 1/2, 3/4, 64/2, and so forth are all rational numbers. (By 1/2, etc., we mean the everyday meaning of the fraction, not the integer division this expression would produce in a C++ program.) Represent rational numbers as two values of type *int*, one for the numerator and one for the denominator. Call the class Rational.

Include a constructor with two arguments that can be used to set the member variables of an object to any legitimate values. Also include a constructor that has only a single parameter of type *int*; call this single parameter whole_number and define the constructor so that the object will be initialized to the rational number whole_number/1. Also include a default constructor that initializes an object to 0 (that is, to 0/1).

Overload the input and output operators >> and <<. Numbers are to be input and output in the form 1/2, 15/32, 300/401, and so forth. Note that the numerator, the denominator, or both may contain a minus sign, so -1/2, 15/32, and -300/-401 are also possible inputs. Overload all of the following operators so that they correctly apply to the type Rational: ==, <, <=, >, >=, +, -, *, and /. Also write a test program to test your class.

(*Hints:* Two rational numbers *a/b* and *c/d* are equal if *a*d* equals *c*b*. If *b* and *d* are *positive* rational numbers, *a/b* is less than *c/d* provided *a*d* is less than *c*b*. You should include a function to normalize the values stored so that, after normalization, the denominator is positive and the numerator and denominator are as small as possible. For example, after normalization 4/-8 would be represented the same as -1/2. You should also write a test program to test your class.)

6. Define a class for complex numbers. A complex number is a number of the form

   a + b * i

   where, for our purposes, *a* and *b* are numbers of type *double*, and *i* is a number that represents the quantity $\sqrt{-1}$. Represent a complex number as two values of type *double*. Name the member variables `real` and `imaginary`. (The variable for the number that is multiplied by *i* is the one called `imaginary`.) Call the class `Complex`.

   Include a constructor with two parameters of type *double* that can be used to set the member variables of an object to any values. Also include a constructor that has only a single parameter of type *double*; call this parameter `real_part` and define the constructor so that the object will be initialized to `real_part+0*i`. Also include a default constructor that initializes an object to 0 (that is, to `0+0*i`). Overload all of the following operators so that they correctly apply to the type `Complex`: ==, +, -, *, >>, and <<. You should write a test program to test your class.

   > (*Hints:* To add or subtract two complex numbers, you add or subtract the two member variables of type *double*. The product of two complex numbers is given by the following formula:
   >
   > $$(a + b{*}i){*}(c + d{*}i) == (a{*}c - b{*}d) + (a{*}d + b{*}c){*}i$$

   In the interface file, you should define a constant *i* as follows:

   const Complex *i*(0, 1);

   This defined constant *i* will be the same as the *i* discussed earlier.

   delete p;

7. Enhance the definition of the class `StringVar` given in Displays 11.11 and 11.12 by adding all of the following:

   - Member function `copy_piece`, which returns a specified substring; member function `one_char`, which returns a specified single character; and member function `set_char`, which changes a specified character

   - An overloaded version of the == operator (note that only the string values have to be equal; the values of `max_length` need not be the same)

   - An overloaded version of + that performs concatenation of strings of type `StringVar`

   - An overloaded version of the extraction operator >> that reads one word (as opposed to `input_line`, which reads a whole line)

If you did the section on overloading the assignment operator, then add it as well. Also write a suitable test program and thoroughly test your class definition.

8. Define a class called `Text` whose objects store lists of words. The class `Text` will be just like the class `StringVar` except that the class `Text` will use a dynamic array with base type `StringVar` rather than base type *char* and will mark the end of the array with a `StringVar` object consisting of a single blank, rather than using `'\0'` as the end marker. Intuitively, an object of the class `Text` represents some text consisting of words separated by blanks. Enforce the restriction that the array elements of type `StringVar` contain no blanks (except for the end marker elements of type `StringVar`).

   Your class `Text` will have member functions corresponding to all the member functions of `StringVar`. The constructor with an argument of type `const char a[]` will initialize the `Text` object in the same way as described below for `input_line`. If the C-string argument contains the new-line symbol `'\n'`, that is considered an error and ends the program with an error message.

   The member function `input_line` will read blank separated strings and store each string in one element of the dynamic array with base type `StringVar`. Multiple blank spaces are treated the same as a single blank space. When outputting an object of the class `Text`, insert one blank between each value of type `StringVar`. You may either assume that no tab symbols are used or you can treat the tab symbols the same as a blank; if this is a class assignment, ask your instructor how you should treat the tab symbol.

   Add the enhancements described in Programming Project 6. The overloaded version of the extraction operator >> will fill only one element of the dynamic array.

9. Using dynamic arrays, implement a polynomial class with polynomial addition, subtraction, and multiplication.

   Discussion: A variable in a polynomial does very little other than act as a placeholder for the coefficients. Hence, the only interesting thing about polynomials is the array of coefficients and the corresponding exponent. Think about the polynomial

   `x*x*x + x + 1`

   One simple way to implement the polynomial class is to use an array of *doubles* to store the coefficients. The index of the array is the exponent of the corresponding term. Where is the term in x*x in the previous example? If a term is missing, then it simply has a zero coefficient.

There are techniques for representing polynomials of high degree with many missing terms. These use so-called sparse polynomial techniques. Unless you already know these techniques, or learn very quickly, don't use them.

Provide a default constructor, a copy constructor, and a parameterized constructor that enable an arbitrary polynomial to be constructed. Also supply an overloaded operator = and a destructor.

Provide these operations:

- polynomial + polynomial
- constant + polynomial
- polynomial + constant
- polynomial - polynomial
- constant - polynomial
- polynomial - constant
- polynomial * polynomial
- constant * polynomial
- polynomial * constant

Supply functions to assign and extract coefficients, indexed by exponent.

Supply a function to evaluate the polynomial at a value of type *double*.

You should decide whether to implement these functions as members, friends, or stand-alone functions.

10. Write a checkbook balancing program. The program will read in the following for all checks that were not cashed as of the last time you balanced your checkbook: the number of each check, the amount of the check, and whether or not it has been cashed. Use an array with a class base type. The class should be a class for a check. There should be three member variables to record the check number, the check amount, and whether or not the check was cashed. The class for a check will have a member variable of type Money (as defined in Display 19) to record the check amount. So, you will have a class used within a class. The class for a check should have accessor and mutator functions as well as constructors and functions for both input and output of a check.

In addition to the checks, the program also reads all the deposits, as well as the old and the new account balance. You may want another array to hold the deposits. The new account balance should be the old balance plus all deposits, minus all checks that have been cashed.

The program outputs the total of the checks cashed, the total of the deposits, what the new balance should be, and how much this figure differs from what the bank says the new balance is. It also outputs two lists of checks: the checks cashed since the last time you balanced your checkbook and the checks still not cashed. Display both lists of checks in sorted order from lowest to highest check number.

If this is a class assignment, ask your instructor if input/output should be done with the keyboard and screen or if it should be done with files. If it is to be done with files, ask your instructor for instructions on file names.

11. Define a class called `List` that can hold a list of values of type *double*. Model your class definition after the class `TemperatureList` given in Display 11.10, but your class `List` will make no reference to temperatures when it outputs values. The values may represent any sort of data items as long as they are of type *double*. Include the additional features specified in Self-Test Exercises 21 and 22. Change the member function names so that they do not refer to temperature.

Add a member function called `get_last` that takes no arguments and returns the last item on the list. The member function `get_last` does not change the list, and it should not be called if the list is empty. Add another member function called `delete_last` that deletes the last element on the list. The member function `delete_last` is a *void* function. Note that when the last element is deleted, the member variable `size` must be adjusted. If `delete_last` is called with an empty list as the calling object, the function call has no effect. Design a program to thoroughly test your definition for the class `List`.

12. Define a class called `StringSet` that will be used to store a set of STL strings. Use an array or a vector to store the strings. Create a constructor that takes as an input parameter an array of strings for the initial values in the set. Then write member functions to add a string to the set, remove a string from the set, clear the entire set, return the number of strings in the set, and output all strings in the set. Overload the + operator so that it returns the union of two `StringSet` objects. Also overload the * operator so that it returns the intersection of two `StringSet` objects. Write a program to test all member functions and overloaded operators in your class.

13. This programming project requires you to complete Programming Project 12 first.

The field of information retrieval is concerned with finding relevant electronic documents based upon a query. For example, given a group of keywords (the query), a search engine retrieves Web pages (documents) and displays them sorted by relevance to the query. This technology requires a way to compare a document with the query to see which is most relevant to the query.

A simple way to make this comparison is to compute the binary cosine coefficient. The coefficient is a value between 0 and 1, where 1 indicates that the query is very similar to the document and 0 indicates that the query has no keywords in common with the document. This approach treats each document as a set of words. For example, given the following sample document:

"Chocolate ice cream, chocolate milk, and chocolate bars are delicious."

This document would be parsed into keywords where case is ignored and punctuation discarded and turned into the set containing the words {chocolate, ice, cream, milk, and, bars, are, delicious}. An identical process is performed on the query to turn it into a set of strings. Once we have a query Q represented as a set of words and a document D represented as a set of words, the similarity between Q and D is computed by:

$$Sim = \frac{|Q \cap D|}{\sqrt{|Q|}\ \sqrt{|D|}}$$

Modify the `StringSet` from Programming Project 12 by adding an additional member function that computes the similarity between the current `StringSet` and an input parameter of type `StringSet`. The `sqrt` function is in the `cmath` library.

Create two text files on your disk named `Document1.txt` and `Document2.txt`. Write some text content of your choice in each file, but make sure that each file contains different content. Next, write a program that allows the user to input from the keyboard a set of strings that represents a query. The program should then compare the query to both text files on the disk and output the similarity to each one using the binary cosine coefficient. Test your program with different queries to see if the similarity metric is working correctly.

14. Write a C++ program containing a dynamic array and array size within a class. The class should have public member functions `countEntry`, `addEntry` and `displayAllEntry`. The `countEntry` function returns the number of elements in the array, `addEntry` can add elements to the array and `displayAllEntry` will display the current content of the array. Also provide appropriate functions for getting and setting specific items in the array. Add a destructor that frees up the memory allocated to the dynamic array. Also, add a copy constructor and overload the assignment operator so that the dynamic array is properly copied from the object on the right-hand side of the assignment to the object on the left-hand side.

15. To combat election fraud, your city is instituting a new voting procedure. The ballot has a letter associated with every selection a voter may make. A sample ballot is shown.

VideoNote
Solution to Programming
Project 11.5

1. VOTE FOR MAYOR
   A. Pincher, Penny   ☐
   B. Dover, Skip   ☐
   C. Perman, Sue   ☐

2. PROPOSITION 17
   D. YES   ☐
   E. NO   ☐

3. MEASURE 1
   F. YES   ☐
   G. NO   ☐

4. MEASURE 2
   H. YES   ☐
   I. NO   ☐

After submitting the ballot, every voter receives a receipt that has a unique ID number and a record of the voting selections. For example, a voter who submits a ballot for Sue Perman, Yes on Proposition 17, No on Measure 1, and Yes on Measure 2 might receive a receipt with

ID 4925 : CDGH

The next day the city posts all votes on its Web page sorted by ID number. This allows a voter to confirm their submission and allows anyone to count the vote totals for themselves. A sample list for the sample ballot is shown.

ID	VOTES
4925	CDGH
4926	AEGH
4927	CDGI
4928	BEGI
4929	ADFH

Write a program that reads the posted voting list from a file and outputs the percent of votes cast for each ballot item. You may assume that the file does not have any header lines. The first line will contain a voter ID and a string representing votes. Define a class named Voter that stores an individual's voting record. The class should have a constructor that takes as input a string of votes (for example, "CDGH"), a voter ID, and accessor function(s) that return the person's ID and vote for a specific question. Store each Voter instance in an array or vector. Your program should iterate over the array to compute and output the percent of votes cast for each candidate, proposition, and measure. It should then prompt the user to enter a voter ID, iterate over the list again to find the object with that ID, and print his or her votes.

16. Write a C++ program containing a class called VectorCollection that will be used to store a collection of vectors whose instances are of type *string*. Write a single parameter constructor that receives an array of strings for initializing values in the collection. Add functions to add instances to the collection, remove instances from the collection, delete all entries from the collection, return the number of strings in the collection, and display the entire collection. Also overload the * operator so that it returns the intersection of two VectorCollection objects. Write a program to test all member functions and overloaded operators in your class.

Next, modify the main function so that instead of creating separate variables for each Movie object, an array of at least four Movie objects is created with sample data. Loop through the array and output the name, MPAA rating, and average rating for each of the four movies.

Separate Compilation and Namespaces 12

From mine own library with volumes that
I prize above my dukedom.

WILLIAM SHAKESPEARE, *The Tempest*

INTRODUCTION

This chapter covers two topics that have to do with how you organize a C++ program into separate parts. Section 12.1 on separate compilation discusses how a C++ program can be distributed across a number of files so that when some parts of the program change, only those parts need to be recompiled. The separate parts can also be more easily reused in other applications.

Section 12.2 discusses namespaces, which we introduced briefly in Chapter 2. Namespaces are a way of allowing you to reuse the names of classes, functions, and other items by qualifying the names to indicate different uses. Namespaces divide your code into sections so that the different sections may reuse the same names with differing meanings. Namespaces allow a kind of local meaning for names that is more general than local variables.

PREREQUISITES

This chapter uses material from Chapters 2 through 6 and 10 through 11.

12.1 SEPARATE COMPILATION

Your "if" is the only peacemaker; much virtue in "if."

WILLIAM SHAKESPEARE, *As You Like It*

C++ has facilities for dividing a program into parts that are kept in separate files, compiled separately, and then linked together when (or just before) the program is run. You can place the definition for a class (and its associated function definitions) in files that are separate from the programs that use the class. That way you can build up a library of classes so that many programs can use the same class. You can compile the class once and then use it in many different programs, just like you use the predefined libraries (such as those with header files iostream and cstdlib). Moreover, you can define the class itself in two files so that the specification of what the class does is separate from how the class is implemented. If your class is defined following the guidelines we have been giving you and you change only the implementation of the class, then you need only recompile the file with the class implementation. The other files, including the files with the programs that use the class, need not be changed or even recompiled. In this section, we tell you how to carry out this separate compilation of classes.

ADTs Reviewed

Recall that an ADT (abstract data type) is a class that has been defined so as to separate the interface and the implementation of the class. All your class definitions should be ADTs. In order to define a class so that it is an ADT, you need to separate the specification of how the class is used by a programmer from the details of how the class is implemented. The separation should be so complete that you can change the implementation without needing to change any program that uses the class in any way. The way to ensure this separation can be summarized in three rules:

1. Make all the member variables private members of the class.

2. Make each of the basic operations for the ADT (the class) either a public member function of the class, a friend function, an ordinary function, or an overloaded operator. Group the class definition and the function and operator declarations together. This group, along with its accompanying comments, is called the **interface** for the ADT. Fully specify how to use each such function or operator in a comment given with the class or with the function or operator declaration.

3. Make the implementation of the basic operations unavailable to the programmer who uses the abstract data type. The **implementation** consists of the function definitions and overloaded operator definitions (along with any helping functions or other additional items these definitions require).

   In C++, the best way to ensure that you follow these rules is to place the interface and the implementation of the ADT class in separate files. As you might guess, the file that contains the interface is often called the **interface file,** and the file that contains the implementation is called the **implementation file.** The exact details of how to set up, compile, and use these files will vary slightly from one version of C++ to another, but the basic scheme is the same in all versions of C++. In particular, the details of what goes into the files are the same in all systems. The only things that vary are what commands you use to compile and link these files. The details about what goes into these files are illustrated in the next Case Study.

   An ADT class has private member variables. Private member variables (and private member functions) present a problem to our basic philosophy of placing the interface and the implementation of an ADT in separate files. The public part of the class definition for an ADT is part of the interface for the ADT, but the private part is part of the implementation. This is a problem because C++ will not allow you to split the class definition across two files. Thus, some sort of compromise is needed. The only sensible compromise, and the one we use, is to place the entire class definition in the interface file. Since a programmer who is using the ADT class cannot use any of the private members of the class, the private members will, in effect, still be hidden from the programmer.

Private members are part of the implementation.

ADT

A data type is called an abstract data type (abbreviated ADT) if the programmers who use the type do not have access to the details of how the values and operations are implemented. All the classes that you define should be ADTs. An ADT class is a class that is defined following good programming practices that separate the interface and implementation of the class. (Any nonmember basic operations for the class such as overloaded operators are considered part of the ADT, even though they may not be officially part of the class definition.)

CASE STUDY *DigitalTime* —A Class Compiled Separately

Display 12.1 contains the interface file for an ADT class called DigitalTime. DigitalTime is a class whose values are times of day, such as 9:30. Only the public members of the class are part of the interface. The private members are part of the implementation, even though they are in the interface file. The label *private*: warns you that these private members are not part of the public interface. Everything that a programmer needs to know in order to use the ADT DigitalTime is explained in the comment at the start of the file and in the comments in the public section of the class definition. This interface tells the programmer how to use the two versions of the member function named advance, the constructors, and the overloaded operators =, >>, and <<. The member function named advance, the overloaded operators, and the assignment statement are the only ways that a programmer can manipulate objects and values of this class. As noted in the comment at the top of the interface file, this ADT class uses 24-hour notation, so, for instance, 1:30 PM is input and output as 13:30. This and the other details you must know in order to effectively use the class DigitalTime are included in the comments given with the member functions.

We have placed the interface in a file named dtime.h. The suffix .h indicates that this is a header file. An interface file is always a header file and therefore always ends with the suffix .h. Any program that uses the class DigitalTime must contain an include directive like the following, which names this file:

```
#include "dtime.h"
```

When you write an include directive, you must indicate whether the header file is a predefined header file that is provided for you or is a header file that you wrote. If the header file is predefined, write the header file name in angular brackets, like <iostream>. If the header file is one that you wrote, then write the header file name in quotes, like "dtime.h". This distinction tells the compiler where to look for the header file. If the header file name is

DISPLAY 12.1   Interface File for `DigitalTime`

```
1    //Header file dtime.h: This is the INTERFACE for the class DigitalTime.
2    //Values of this type are times of day. The values are input and output in
3    //24-hour notation, as in 9:30 for 9:30 AM and 14:45 for 2:45 PM.
4    #include <iostream>
5    using namespace std;                    For the definition of the types
                                            istream and ostream, which
6    class DigitalTime                       are used as parameter types
7    {
8    public:
9        friend bool operator ==(const DigitalTime& time1, const DigitalTime& time2);
10       //Returns true if time1 and time2 represent the same time;
11       //otherwise, returns false.

12       DigitalTime(int the_hour, int the_minute);
13       //Precondition: 0 <= the_hour <= 23 and 0 <= the_minute <= 59.
14       //Initializes the time value to the_hour and the_minute.

15       DigitalTime( );
16       //Initializes the time value to 0:00 (which is midnight).

17       void advance(int minutes_added);
18       //Precondition: The object has a time value.
19       //Postcondition: The time has been changed to minutes_added minutes later.

20       void advance(int hours_added, int minutes_added);
21       //Precondition: The object has a time value.
22       //Postcondition: The time value has been advanced
23       //hours_added hours plus minutes_added minutes.

24       friend istream& operator >>(istream& ins, DigitalTime& the_object);
25       //Overloads the >> operator for input values of type DigitalTime.
26       //Precondition: If ins is a file input stream, then ins has already been
27       //connected to a file.

28       friend ostream& operator <<(ostream& outs, const DigitalTime& the_object);
29       //Overloads the << operator for output values of type DigitalTime.
30       //Precondition: If outs is a file output stream, then outs has already been
31       //connected to a file.
32   private:                               This is part of the implementation.
33       int hour;                          It is not part of the interface.
34       int minute;                        The word private indicates that
35   };                                     this is not part of the public interface.
```

in angular brackets, the compiler looks wherever the predefined header files are kept in your implementation of C++. If the header file name is in quotes, the compiler looks in the current directory or wherever programmer-defined header files are kept on your system.

Any program that uses our `DigitalTime` class must contain the previous include directive that names the header file `dtime.h`. That is enough to allow you to compile the program but is not enough to allow you to run the program. In order to run the program, you must write (and compile) the definitions of the member functions and the overloaded operators. We have placed these function and operator definitions in another file, which is called the **implementation file.** Although it is not required by most compilers, it is traditional to give the interface file and the implementation file the same name. The two files do, however, end in different suffixes. We have placed the interface for our ADT class in the file named `dtime.h` and the implementation for our ADT class in a file named `dtime.cpp`. The suffix you use for the implementation file depends on your version of C++. Use the same suffix for the implementation file as you normally use for files that contain C++ programs. If your program files end in `.cxx`, then you would use `.cxx` in place of `.cpp`. If your program files end in `.CPP`, then your implementation files will end in `.CPP` instead of `.cpp`. We are using `.cpp` since most compilers accept `.cpp` as the suffix for a C++ source code file. The implementation file for our `DigitalTime` ADT class is given in Display 12.2. After we explain how the various files for our ADT interact with each other, we will return to Display 12.2 and discuss the details of the definitions in this implementation file.

In order to use the ADT class `DigitalTime` in a program, the program must contain the include directive

```
#include "dtime.h"
```

Notice that both the implementation file and the program file must contain this include directive that names the interface file. The file that contains the program (that is, the file that contains the main part of the program) is often called the **application file** or **driver file.** Display 12.3 contains an application file with a very simple program that uses and demonstrates the `DigitalTime` ADT class.

Compiling and running the program

The exact details on how you run this complete program, which is contained in three files, depend on what system you are using. However, the basic details are the same for all systems. You must compile the implementation file, and you must compile the application file that contains the main part of your program. You do not compile the interface file, which in this example is the file `dtime.h` given in Display 12.1. You do not need to compile the interface file because the compiler thinks the contents of this interface file are already contained in each of the other two files. Recall that both the implementation file and the application file contain the directive

```
#include "dtime.h"
```

Compiling your program automatically invokes a preprocessor that reads this include directive and replaces it with the text in the file `dtime.h`. Thus, the compiler sees the contents of `dtime.h`, and so the file `dtime.h` does not need to be compiled separately. (In fact, the compiler sees the contents of `dtime.h` twice: once when you compile the implementation file and once when you compile the application file.) This copying of the file `dtime.h` is

DISPLAY 12.2   Implementation File for DigitalTime *(part 1 of 3)*

```
1     //Implementation file dtime.cpp (Your system may require some
2     //suffix other than .cpp): This is the IMPLEMENTATION of the ADT DigitalTime.
3     //The interface for the class DigitalTime is in the header file dtime.h.
4     #include <iostream>
5     #include <cctype>
6     #include <cstdlib>
7     #include "dtime.h"
8     using namespace std;

9     //These FUNCTION DECLARATIONS are for use in the definition of
10    //the overloaded input operator >>:
11    void read_hour(istream& ins, int& the_hour);
12    //Precondition: Next input in the stream ins is a time in 24-hour notation,
13    //like 9:45 or 14:45.
14    //Postcondition: the_hour has been set to the hour part of the time.
15    //The colon has been discarded and the next input to be read is the minute.

16    void read_minute(istream& ins, int& the_minute);
17    //Reads the minute from the stream ins after read_hour has read the hour.

18    int digit_to_int(char c);
19    //Precondition: c is one of the digits '0' through '9'.
20    //Returns the integer for the digit; for example, digit_to_int('3') returns 3.
21    bool operator ==(const DigitalTime& time1, const DigitalTime& time2)
22    {
23        return (time1.hour == time2.hour && time1.minute == time2.minute);
24    }
25    //Uses iostream and cstdlib:
26    DigitalTime::DigitalTime(int the_hour, int the_minute)
27    {
28        if (the_hour< 0 || the_hour> 23 || the_minute< 0 || the_minute> 59)
29        {
30            cout<< "Illegal argument to DigitalTime constructor.";
31            exit(1);
32        }
33
34        else
35        {
36            hour = the_hour;
37            minute = the_minute;
38        }
39    }
40    DigitalTime::DigitalTime( ) : hour(0), minute(0)
41    {
42        //Body intentionally empty.
43    }
44
```

(continued)

DISPLAY 12.2   Implementation File for DigitalTime *(part 2 of 3)*

```
45    void DigitalTime::advance(int minutes_added)
46    {
47        int gross_minutes = minute + minutes_added;
48        minute = gross_minutes % 60;
49
50        int hour_adjustment = gross_minutes / 60;
51        hour = (hour + hour_adjustment) % 24;
52    }
53
54    void DigitalTime::advance(int hours_added,  int minutes_added)
55    {
56        hour = (hour + hours_added) % 24;
57        advance(minutes_added);
58    }
59
60    //Uses iostream:
61    ostream& operator <<(ostream& outs, const DigitalTime& the_object)
62    {
63        outs << the_object.hour<< ':';
64        if (the_object.minute< 10)
65            outs << '0';
66        outs << the_object.minute;
67        return outs;
68    }
69
70    //Uses iostream:
71    istream& operator >>(istream& ins, DigitalTime& the_object)
72    {
73        read_hour(ins, the_object.hour);
74        read_minute(ins, the_object.minute);
75        return ins;
76    }
77
78    int digit_to_int(char c)
79    {
80        return (static_cast <int>(c) - static_cast<int>('0'));
81    }
82
83    //Uses iostream, cctype, and cstdlib:
84    void read_minute(istream& ins, int& the_minute)
85    {
86        char c1, c2;
87        ins >> c1 >> c2;
88
89        if (!(isdigit(c1) && isdigit(c2)))
```

(continued)

DISPLAY 12.2   Implementation File for `DigitalTime` *(part 3 of 3)*

```
90          {
91              cout<< "Error illegal input to read_minute\n";
92              exit(1);
93          }
94
95          the_minute = (digit_to_int(c1) * 10) + digit_to_int(c2);
96
97          if (the_minute< 0 || the_minute> 59)
98          {
99              cout<< "Error illegal input to read_minute\n";
100             exit(1);
101         }
102     }
103
104     //Uses iostream, cctype, and cstdlib:
105     void read_hour(istream& ins, int& the_hour)
106     {
107         char c1, c2;
108         ins >> c1 >> c2;
109         if ( !( isdigit(c1) && (isdigit(c2) || c2 == ':' ) ) )
110         {
111             cout<< "Error illegal input to read_hour\n";
112             exit(1);
113         }
114
115         if (isdigit(c1) && c2 == ':')
116         {
117             the_hour = digit_to_int(c1);
118         }
119         else//(isdigit(c1) && isdigit(c2))
120         {
121             the_hour = (digit_to_int(c1) * 10) + digit_to_int(c2);
122             ins >> c2;//discard ':'
123             if (c2 != ':')
124             {
125                 cout<< "Error illegal input to read_hour\n";
126                 exit(1);
127             }
128         }
129         if (the_hour < 0 || the_hour > 23)
130         {
131             cout<< "Error illegal input to read_hour\n";
132             exit(1);
133         }
134     }
```

DISPLAY 12.3 **Application File Using** DigitalTime

```
1      //Application file timedemo.cpp (your system may require some suffix
2      //other than .cpp): This program demonstrates use of the class DigitalTime.
3      #include <iostream>
4      #include "dtime.h"
5      using namespace std;
6
7      int main( )
8      {
9          DigitalTime clock, old_clock;
10
11         cout<< "Enter the time in 24-hour notation: ";
12         cin>> clock;
13
14         old_clock = clock;
15         clock.advance(15);
16         if (clock == old_clock)
17             cout << "Something is wrong.";
18         cout << "You entered " << old_clock << endl;
19         cout << "15 minutes later the time will be "
20             << clock << endl;
21
22         clock.advance(2, 15);
23         cout << "2 hours and 15 minutes after that\n"
24             << "the time will be "
25             << clock << endl;
26
27         return 0;
28     }
```

Sample Dialogue

```
Enter the time in 24-hour notation: 11:15
You entered 11:15
15 minutes later the time will be 11:30
2 hours and 15 minutes after that
the time will be 13:45
```

only a conceptual copying. The compiler acts as if the contents of dtime.h were copied into each file that has the include directive. However, if you look in that file after it is compiled, you will only find the include directive; you will not find the contents of the file dtime.h.

Once the implementation file and the application file are compiled, you still need to connect these files so that they can work together. This is called

linking the files and is done by a separate utility called a **linker.** The details for how you call the linker depend on what system you are using. After the files are linked, you can run your program. (Often the linking is done automatically as part of the process of running the program.)

This process sounds complicated, but many systems have facilities that manage much of this detail for you automatically or semiautomatically. On any system, the details quickly become routine.

Displays 12.1, 12.2, and 12.3 contain one complete program divided into pieces and placed in three different files. You could instead combine the contents of these three files into one file and then compile and run this one file without all this fuss about include directives and linking separate files. Why bother with three separate files? There are several advantages to dividing your program into separate files. Since you have the definition and the implementation of the class DigitalTime in files separate from the application file, you can use this class in many different programs without needing to rewrite the definition of the class in each of the programs. Moreover, you need to compile the implementation file only once, no matter how many programs use the class DigitalTime. But there are more advantages than that. Since you have separated the interface from the implementation of your DigitalTime ADT class, you can change the implementation file and will not need to change any program that uses the ADT. In fact, you will not even need to recompile the program. If you change the implementation file, you only need to recompile the implementation file and to relink the files. Saving a bit of recompiling time is nice, but the big advantage is not having to rewrite code. You can use the ADT class in many programs without writing the class code into each program. You can change the implementation of the ADT class and you need not rewrite any part of any program that uses the class.

Why separate files?

Defining a Class in Separate Files: A Summary

You can define a class and place the definition of the class and the implementation of its member functions in separate files. You can then compile the class separately from any program that uses the class, and you can use this same class in any number of different programs. The class and the program that uses the class are placed in three files as follows:

1. Put the definition of the class in a header file called the **interface file.** The name of this header file ends in .h. The interface file also contains the declarations for any functions and overloaded operators that define basic operations for the class but that are not listed in the class definition. Include comments that explain how all these functions and operators are used.

(continued)

2. The definitions of all the functions and overloaded operators mentioned in step 1 (whether they are members or friends or neither) are placed in another file called the **implementation file.** This file must contain an include directive that names the interface file described above. This include directive uses quotes around the file name, as in the following example:

```
#include "dtime.h"
```

The interface file and the implementation file traditionally have the same name, but end in different suffixes. The interface file ends in .h. The implementation file ends in the same suffix that you use for files that contain a complete C++ program. The implementation file is compiled separately before it is used in any program.

3. When you want to use the class in a program, place the main part of the program (and any additional function definitions, constant declarations, and so on) in another file called an **application file.** This file also must contain an include directive naming the interface file, as in the following example:

```
#include "dtime.h"
```

The application file is compiled separately from the implementation file. You can write any number of these application files to use with one pair of interface and implementation files. To run an entire program, you must first link the object code that is produced by compiling the application file and the object code that is produced by compiling the implementation file. (On some systems the linking may be done automatically or semiautomatically.)

Implementation details

Now that we have explained how the various files in our ADT class and program are used, let's discuss the implementation of our ADT class (Display 12.2) in more detail. Most of the implementation details are straightforward, but there are two things that merit comment. Notice that the member function name advance is overloaded so that it has two function definitions. Also notice that the definition for the overloaded extraction (input) operator >> uses two "helping functions" called read_hour and read_minute and these two helping functions themselves use a third helping function called digit_to_int. Let's discuss these points.

The class DigitalTime (Displays 12.1 and 12.2) has two member functions called advance. One version takes a single argument, which is an integer giving the number of minutes to advance the time. The other version takes two arguments, one for a number of hours and one for a number of minutes, and advances the time by that number of hours plus that number of minutes. Notice that the definition of the two-argument version of advance includes a call to the one-argument version of advance. Look at the definition of the two-argument version that is given in Display 12.2. First the time is advanced by hours_added hours, and then the single-argument version of advance is used to advance the time by an additional minutes_added minutes. At first this may seem strange, but it is perfectly legal. The two functions named advance are two different functions that, as far as the compiler is concerned, coincidentally happen to have the same name. The situation is no different in this regard than it would be if one of the two versions of the overloaded function advance had been called another_advance.

Now let's discuss the helping functions. The helping functions read_hour and read_minute read the input one character at a time and then convert the input to integer values that are placed in the member variables hour and minute. The functions read_hour and read_minute read the hour and minute one digit at a time, so they are reading values of type *char*. This is more complicated than reading the input as *int* values, but it allows us to perform error checking to see whether the input is correctly formed and to issue an error message if the input is not well formed. These helping functions read_ hour and read_minute use another helping function named digit_to_int, which is the same as the digit_to_int function we used in our definition of the class Money in Displays 11.3. The function digit_to_int converts a digit, such as '3', to a number, such as 3.

Reusable Components

An ADT class developed and coded into separate files is a software component that can be used again and again in a number of different programs. **Reusability,** such as the reusability of these ADT classes, is an important goal to strive for when designing software components. A reusable component saves effort because it does not need to be redesigned, recoded, and retested for every application. A reusable component is also likely to be more reliable than a component that is used only once—for two reasons. First, you can afford to spend more time and effort on a component if it will be used many times. Second, if the component is used again and again, it is tested again and again. Every use of a software component is a test of that component. Using a software component many times in a variety of contexts is one of the best ways to discover any remaining bugs in the software.

Using #ifndef

We have given you a method for placing a program in three files: two for the interface and implementation of a class, and one for the application part of the program. A program can be kept in more than three files. For example, a program might use several classes, and each class might be kept in a separate pair of files.

VideoNote
Avoiding Multiple
Definitions

Suppose you have a program spread across a number of files and more than one file has an include directive for a class interface file such as the following:

```
#include "dtime.h"
```

Under these circumstances, you can have files that include other files, and these other files may in turn include yet other files. This can easily lead to a situation in which a file, in effect, contains the definitions in dtime.h more than once. C++ does not allow you to define a class more than once, even if the repeated definitions are identical. Moreover, if you are using the same header file in many different projects, it becomes close to impossible to keep track of whether you included the class definition more than once. To avoid this problem, C++ provides a way of marking a section of code to say "if you have already included this stuff once before, do not include it again." The way this is done is quite intuitive, although the notation may look a bit weird until you get used to it. We will go through an example, explaining the details as we go.

The following directive "defines" DTIME_H:

```
#define DTIME_H
```

What this means is that the compiler's preprocessor puts DTIME_H on a list to indicate that DTIME_H has been seen. *Defines* is perhaps not the best word for this, since DTIME_H is not defined to mean anything but is merely put on a list. The important point is that you can use another directive to test whether or not DTIME_H has been defined and so test whether or not a section of code has already been processed. You can use any (nonkeyword) identifier in place of DTIME_H, but you will see that there are standard conventions for which identifier you should use.

The following directive tests to see whether or not DTIME_H has been defined:

```
#ifndef DTIME_H
```

If DTIME_H has already been defined, then everything between this directive and the first occurrence of the following directive is skipped:

```
#endif
```

(An equivalent way to state this, which may clarify the way the directives are spelled, is the following: If DTIME_H is *not* defined, then the compiler processes everything up to the next #endif. That *not* is why there is an n in #ifndef. This may lead you to wonder whether there is a #ifdef directive as well as a #ifndef directive. There is, and it has the obvious meaning, but we will have no occasion to use #ifdef.

Now consider the following code:

```
#ifndef DTIME_H
#define DTIME_H
<a class definition>
#endif
```

If this code is in a file named dtime.h, then no matter how many times your program contains

    #include "dtime.h"

the class will be defined only one time.

The first time

    #include "dtime.h"

is processed, the flag DTIME_H is defined and the class is defined. Now, suppose the compiler again encounters

    #include "dtime.h"

When the include directive is processed this second time, the directive

    #ifndef DTIME_H

says to skip everything up to

    #endif

and so the class is not defined again.

In Display 12.4 we have rewritten the header file dtime.h shown in Display 12.1, but this time we used these directives to prevent multiple definitions. With the version of dtime.h shown in Display 12.4, if a file contains the following include directive more than once, the class DigitalTime will still be defined only once:

    #include "dtime.h"

DISPLAY 12.4 Avoiding Multiple Definitions of a Class

```
1    //Header file dtime.h: This is the INTERFACE for the class DigitalTime.
2    //Values of this type are times of day. The values are input and output in
3    //24-hour notation, as in 9:30 for 9:30 AM and 14:45 for 2:45 PM.
4    #ifndef DTIME_H
5    #define DTIME_H
6    #include <iostream>
7    using namespace std;
8    class DigitalTime
9    {
10

    <The definition of the class DigitalTime is the same as in Display 12.1.>

11
12    };
13
14    #endif //DTIME_H
```

You may use some other identifier in place of `DTIME_H`, but the normal convention is to use the name of the file written in all uppercase letters with the underscore used in place of the period. You should follow this convention so that others can more easily read your code and so that you do not have to remember the flag name. This way the flag name is determined automatically and there is nothing arbitrary to remember.

These same directives can be used to skip over code in files other than header files, but we will not have occasion to use these directives except in header files.

■ **PROGRAMMING TIP**   Defining Other Libraries

You need not define a class in order to use separate compilation. If you have a collection of related functions that you want to make into a library of your own design, you can place the function declarations and accompanying comments in a header file and the function definitions in an implementation file, just as we outlined for ADT classes. After that, you can use this library in your programs the same way you would use a class that you placed in separate files.   ■

myprogramminglab   **SELF-TEST EXERCISES**

1. Suppose that you are defining an ADT class and that you then use this class in a program. You want to separate the class and program parts into separate files as described in this chapter. Specify whether each of the following should be placed in the interface file, implementation file, or application file:

   a.   The class definition

   b.   The declaration for a function that is to serve as an ADT operation, but that is neither a member nor a friend of the class

   c.   The declaration for an overloaded operator that is to serve as an ADT operation, but that is neither a member nor a friend of the class

   d.   The definition for a function that is to serve as an ADT operation, but that is neither a member nor a friend of the class

   e.   The definition for a friend function that is to serve as an ADT operation

   f.   The definition for a member function

   g.   The definition for an overloaded operator that is to serve as an ADT operation, but that is neither a member nor a friend of the class

   h.   The definition for an overloaded operator that is to serve as an ADT operation and that is a friend of the class

   i.   The `main` part of your program

2. Which of the following files has a name that ends in .h: the interface file for a class, the implementation file for the class, or the application file that uses the class?

3. When you define a class in separate files, there is an interface file and an implementation file. Which of these files needs to be compiled? (Both? Neither? Only one? If so, which one?)

4. Suppose you define a class in separate files and use the class in a program. Now suppose you change the class implementation file. Which of the following files, if any, need to be recompiled: the interface file, the implementation file, or the application file?

5. Suppose you want to change the implementation of the class DigitalTime given in Displays 12.1 and 12.2. Specifically, you want to change the way the time is recorded. Instead of using the two private variables hour and minute, you want to use a single (private) *int* variable, which will be called minutes. In this new implementation, the private variable minutes will record the time as the number of minutes since the time 0:00 (that is, since midnight). So 1:30 is recorded as 90 minutes, since it is 90 minutes past midnight. Describe how you need to change the interface and implementation files shown in Displays 12.1 and 12.2. You need not write out the files in their entirety; just indicate what items you need to change and how, in a very general way, you would change them.

6. What is the difference between an ADT you define in C++ and a class you define in C++?

12.2 NAMESPACES

What's in a name? That which we call a rose
By any other name would smell as sweet.

WILLIAM SHAKESPEARE, *Romeo and Juliet*

When a program uses different classes and functions written by different programmers, there is a possibility that two programmers will use the same name for two different things. Namespaces are a way to deal with this problem. A namespace is a collection of name definitions, such as class definitions and variable declarations.

Namespaces and *using* Directives

We have already been using the namespace that is named std. The std namespace contains all the names defined in the standard library files (such as `iostream` and `cstdlib`) that you use. For example, when you place the following at the start of a file,

```
#include <iostream>
```

that places all of the name definitions (for names like `cin` and `cout`) into the `std` namespace. Your program does not know about names in the `std` namespace unless you specify that it is using the `std` namespace. So far, the only way we know how to specify the `std` namespace (or any namespace) is with the following sort of *using* directive:

```
using namespace std;
```

A good way to see why you might want to include this *using* directive is to think about why you might want to *not* include it. If you do not include this *using* directive for the namespace `std`, then you can define `cin` and `cout` to have some meaning other than their standard meaning. (Perhaps you want to redefine `cin` and `cout` because you want them to behave a bit differently from the standard versions.) Their standard meaning is in the `std` namespace, and without the *using* directive (or something like it), your code knows nothing about the `std` namespace, and therefore, as far as your code is concerned, the only definitions of `cin` and `cout` are whatever definitions you give them.

Every bit of code you write is in some namespace. If you do not place the code in some specific namespace, then the code is in a namespace known as the **global namespace.** So far, we have not placed any code we wrote in any namespace, so all of our code has been in the global namespace. The global namespace does not have a *using* directive because you are always using the global namespace. You could say that there is always an implicit automatic *using* directive that says you are using the global namespace.

Note that you can be using more than one namespace at the same time. For example, we are always using the global namespace and we are usually using the `std` namespace. What happens if a name is defined in two namespaces and you are using both namespaces? This results in an error (either a compiler error or a run-time error, depending on the exact details). You can have the same name defined in two different namespaces, but if that is true, then you can only use one of those namespaces at a time.[1] However, this does not mean you cannot use the two namespaces in the same program. You can use them each at different times in the same program.

For example, suppose `ns1` and `ns2` are two namespaces, and suppose `my_function` is a *void* function with no arguments that is defined in both namespaces but defined in different ways in the two namespaces. The following is then legal:

---

[1]As you will see later in this chapter, there are ways to use two namespaces at the same time even if they contain the same name, but that is a subtle point that does not yet concern us.

```
{
    using namespace ns1;
    my_function( );
}
{
    using namespace ns2;
    my_function( );
}
```

The first invocation would use the definition of my_function given in the namespace ns1, and the second invocation would use the definition of my_function given in the namespace ns2.

Recall that a block is a list of statements, declarations, and possibly other code, enclosed in braces {}. A *using* directive at the start of a block applies only to that block. So the first *using* directive applies only in the first block, and the second *using* directive applies only in the second block. The usual way of phrasing this is to say that the **scope** of the ns1 namespace is the first block, while the scope of the ns2 namespace is the second block. Note that because of this scope rule, we are able to use two conflicting namespaces in the same program (such as in a program that contains the two blocks we discussed in the previous paragraph).

When you use a *using* directive in a block, it is typically the block consisting of the body of a function definition. If you place a *using* directive at the start of a file (as we have usually done so far), then the *using* directive applies to the entire file. A *using* directive should normally be placed near the start of a file or the start of a block.

Scope Rule for *using* Directives

The scope of a *using* directive is the block in which it appears (more precisely, from the location of the *using* directives to the end of the block). If the *using* directive is outside of all blocks, then it applies to all of the file that follows the *using* directive.

Creating a Namespace

In order to place some code in a namespace, you simply place it in a namespace grouping of the following form:

```
namespace Name_Space_Name
{
    Some_Code
}
```

When you include one of these groupings in your code, you are said to place the names defined in *Some_Code* into the namespace *Name_Space_Name*. These names (really the definitions of these names) can be made available with the *using* directive

```
using namespace Name_Space_Name;
```

For example, the following, taken from Display 12.5, places a function declaration in the namespace savitch1:

```
namespace savitch1
{
    void greeting( );
}
```

If you look again at Display 12.5, you see that the definition of the function greeting is also placed in namespace savitch1. That is done with the following additional namespace grouping:

```
namespace savitch1
{
    void greeting( )
    {
        cout << "Hello from namespace savitch1.\n";
    }
}
```

Note that you can have any number of these namespace groupings for a single namespace. In Display 12.5, we used two namespace groupings for namespace savitch1 and two other groupings for namespace savitch2.

Every name defined in a namespace is available inside the namespace grouping, but the names can be also be made available to code outside of the namespace. That function declaration and function definition in the namespace savitch1 can be made available with the *using* directive

```
using namespace savitch1
```

as illustrated in Display 12.5.

DISPLAY 12.5 Namespace **Demonstration** *(part 1 of 2)*

```
 1    #include <iostream>
 2    using namespace std;
 3
 4    namespace savitch1
 5    {
 6        void greeting( );
 7    }
 8
 9    namespace savitch2
10    {
11        void greeting( );
12    }
```

(continued)

DISPLAY 12.5 **Namespace Demonstration** *(part 2 of 2)*

```
13
14     void big_greeting( );
15
16     int main( )
17     {
18         {
19             using namespace savitch2;
20             greeting( );
21         }
22
23         {
24             using namespace savitch1;
25             greeting( );
26         }
27
28         big_greeting( );
29
30         return 0;
31     }
32
33     namespace savitch1
34     {
35         void greeting( )
36         {
37             cout << "Hello from namespace savitch1.\n";
38         }
39     }
40
41     namespace savitch2
42     {
43         void greeting( )
44         {
45             cout<< "Greetings from namespace savitch2.\n";
46         }
47     }
48
49     void big_greeting( )
50     {
51         cout<< "A Big Global Hello!\n";
52     }
```

Names in this block use definitions in namespaces savitch2, std, *and the global namespace.*

Names in this block use definitions in namespaces savitch1, std, *and the global namespace.*

Names out here use only definitions in namespace std *and the global namespace.*

Sample Dialogue

```
Greetings from namespace savitch2.
Hello from namespace savitch1.
A Big Global Hello!
```

SELF-TEST EXERCISES

7. Consider the program shown in Display 12.5. Could we use the name greeting in place of big_greeting?

8. In Self-Test Exercise 7, we saw that you could *not* add a definition for the following function (to the global namespace):

   void greeting( );

   Can you add a definition for the following function declaration to the global namespace?

   void greeting(*int* how_many);

9. Can a namespace have more than one namespace grouping?

Qualifying Names

Suppose you are faced with the following situation: You have two namespaces, ns1 and ns2. You want to use the function fun1 defined in ns1 and the function fun2 defined in namespace ns2. The complication is that both ns1 and ns2 define a function my_function. (Assume all functions in this discussion take no arguments, so overloading does not apply.) It would not be a good idea to use the following:

```
using namespace ns1;
using namespace ns2;
```

This would provide conflicting definitions for my_function.

What you need is a way to say you are using fun1 in namespace ns1 and fun2 in namespace ns2 and nothing else in the namespaces ns1 and ns2. The following are called *using* **declarations**, and they are your answer:

```
using ns1::fun1;
using ns2::fun2;
```

A *using* declaration of the form

```
using Name_Space::One_Name
```

makes (the definition of) the name *One_Name* from the namespace *Name_Space* available, but does not make any other names in *Name_Space* available.

Note that you have seen the scope resolution operator, ::, before. For example, in Display 12.2 we had the following function definition:

```
void DigitalTime::advance(int hours_added,  int minutes_added)
{
    hour = (hour + hours_added) % 24;
    advance(minutes_added);
}
```

In this case the `::` means that we are defining the function advance for the class `DigitalTime`, as opposed to any other function named advance in any other class. Similarly,

> *using* ns1::fun1;

means we are using the function named fun1 as defined in the namespace ns1, as opposed to any other definition of fun1 in any other namespace.

Now suppose that you intend to use the name fun1 as defined in the namespace ns1, but you intend to use it only one time (or a small number of times). You can then name the function (or other item) using the name of the namespace and the scope resolution operator as in the following:

> ns1::fun1( );

This form is often used when specifying a parameter type. For example, consider

> *int* get_number(std::istream input_stream)
> . . .

In the function get_number, the parameter input_stream is of type istream, where istream is defined as in the std namespace. If this use of the type name istream is the only name you need from the std namespace (or if all the names you need are similarly qualified with std::), then you do *not* need

> *using namespace* std;

A Subtle Point About Namespaces (*Optional*)

There are two differences between a *using* declaration, such as

> *using* std::cout;

and a *using* directive, such as

> *using namespace* std;

The differences are as follows:

1. A *using* declaration (like *using* std::cout;) makes only one name in the namespace available to your code, while a *using* directive (like *using namespace* std;) makes all the names in a namespace available.

2. A *using* declaration introduces a name (like cout) into your code so that no other use of the name can be made. However, a *using* directive only potentially introduces the names in the namespace.

Point 1 is pretty obvious. Point 2 has some subtleties. For example, suppose the namespaces ns1 and ns2 both provide definitions for my_function but have no other name conflicts. Then the following will produce no problems:

```
using namespace ns1;
using namespace ns2;
```

provided that (within the scope of these directives) the conflicting name my_function is never used in your code. On the other hand, the following is illegal, even if the function my_function is never used:

```
using ns1::my_function;
Using ns2::my_function;
```

Sometimes this subtle point can be important, but it does not impinge on most routine code.

SELF-TEST EXERCISES

10. Write the function declaration for a *void* function named wow. The function wow has two parameters, the first of type speed as defined in the speedway namespace and the second of type speed as defined in the indy500 namespace.

11. Consider the following function declarations from the definition of the class Money in Display 11.4.

    ```
    void input(istream& ins);
    void output(ostream& outs) const;
    ```

    Rewrite these function declarations so that they do not need to be preceded by

    ```
    using namespace std;
    ```

    (You do not need to look back at Display 11.4 to do this.)

Unnamed Namespaces

Our definition of the class DigitalTime in Displays 12.1 and 12.2 used three helping functions: digit_to_int, read_hour, and read_minute. These helping functions are part of the implementation for the ADT class DigitalTime, so we placed their definitions in the implementation file (Display 12.2). However, this does not really hide these three functions. We would like these functions to be local to the implementation file for the class DigitalTime. However, as we have done it, they are not. In particular, we cannot define another function with the name digit_to_int (or read_hour or read_minute) in an application program that uses the class DigitalTime. This violates the principle of information hiding. To truly hide these helping functions and make them local to the implementation file for DigitalTime, we need to place them in a special namespace called the *unnamed namespace*.

A **compilation unit** is a file, such as a class implementation file, along with all the files that are #included in the file, such as the interface header file for the class. Every compilation unit has an **unnamed namespace**. A namespace grouping for the unnamed namespace is written in the same way as any other namespace, but no name is given, as in the following example:

```
namespace
{
    void sample_function( )
        .
        .
        .
} //unnamed namespace
```

All the names defined in the unnamed namespace are local to the compilation unit, and thus the names can be reused for something else outside the compilation unit. For example, Displays 12.6 and 12.7 show a rewritten (and our final) version of the interface and implementation file for the class DigitalTime. Note that the helping functions (read_hour, read_minute, and digit_to_int) are all in the unnamed namespace and therefore are local to the compilation unit. As illustrated in Display 12.8, the names in the unnamed namespace can be reused for something else outside the compilation unit. In Display 12.8 the function name read_hour is reused for another different function in the application program.

DISPLAY 12.6   Placing a Class in a Namespace—Header File

```
1     //Header file dtime.h: This is the interface for the class DigitalTime.
2     //Values of this type are times of day. The values are input and output in
3     //24-hour notation, as in 9:30 for 9:30 AM and 14:45 for 2:45 PM.
4
5     #ifndef DTIME_H
6     #define DTIME_H
7
8     #include <iostream>
9     using namespace std;
10
11    namespace dtimesavitch
12    {
13
14        class DigitalTime
15        {
16
          <The definition of the class DigitalTime is the same as in Display 12.1.>
17        };
18    }//end dtimesavitch
19
20    #endif //DTIME_H
```

One grouping for the namespace dtimesavitch. Another grouping for the namespace dtimesavitch is in the implementation file dtime.cpp.

DISPLAY 12.7   Placing a Class in a Namespace—Implementation File *(part 1 of 2)*

```
1   //Implementation file dtime.cpp (your system may require some
2   //suffix other than .cpp): This is the IMPLEMENTATION of the ADT DigitalTime.
3   //The interface for the class DigitalTime is in the header file dtime.h.
4   #include <iostream>
5   #include <cctype>
6   #include <cstdlib>
7   #include "dtime.h"
8   using namespace std;
9                                        One grouping for the unnamed
10  namespace                            namespace
11  {
12      //These function declarations are for use in the definition of
13      //the overloaded input operator >>:
14
15      void read_hour(istream& ins, int& the_hour);
16      //Precondition: Next input in the stream ins is a time in 24-hour notation,
17      //like 9:45 or 14:45.
18      //Postcondition: the_hour has been set to the hour part of the time.
19      //The colon has been discarded and the next input to be read is the minute.
20
21      void read_minute(istream& ins, int& the_minute);
22      //Reads the minute from the stream ins after read_hour has read the hour.
23
24      int digit_to_int(char c);
25      //Precondition: c is one of the digits '0' through '9'.
26      //Returns the integer for the digit; for example, digit_to_int('3')
27      //returns 3.
28  }//unnamed namespace
29
30                                        One grouping for the namespace dtimesavitch.
31  namespace dtimesavitch                Another grouping is in the file dtime.h.
32  {
33      bool operator ==(const DigitalTime& time1, const DigitalTime& time2)
        <The rest of the definition of == is the same as in Display 12.2.>
34
35      DigitalTime::DigitalTime( )
        <The rest of the definition of this constructor is the same as in Display 12.2.>
36
37      DigitalTime::DigitalTime(int the_hour, int the_minute)
        <The rest of the definition of this constructor is the same as in Display 12.2.>
38      void DigitalTime::advance(int minutes_added)
        <The rest of the definition of this advance function is the same as in Display 12.2.>
39
40      void DigitalTime::advance(int hours_added, int minutes_added)
        <The rest of the definition of this advance function is the same as in Display 12.2.>
41
```

(continued)

DISPLAY 12.7   Placing a Class in a Namespace—Implementation File *(part 2 of 2)*

```
42          ostream& operator <<(ostream& outs, const DigitalTime& the_object)
        <The rest of the definition of << is the same as in Display 12.2.>
43
44          //Uses iostream and functions in the unnamed namespace:
45          istream& operator >>(istream& ins, DigitalTime& the_object)
46          {
47              read_hour(ins, the_object.hour);
48              read_minute(ins, the_object.minute);
49              return ins;
50          }
51      } //dtimesavitch
52
53
54      namespace
55      {
56          int digit_to_int(char c)
        <The rest of the definition of digit_to_int is the same as in Display 12.2.>
57
58          void read_minute(istream& ins, int& the_minute)
        <The rest of the definition of read_minute is the same as in Display 12.2.>
59
60          void read_hour(istream& ins, int& the_hour)
        <The rest of the definition of read_hour is the same as in Display 12.2.>
61
62      }//unnamed namespace
```

Functions defined in the unnamed namespace are local to this compilation unit (this file and included files). They can be used anywhere in this file, but have no meaning outside this compilation unit.

Another grouping for the unnamed namespace.

If you look again at the implementation file in Display 12.8, you will see that the helping functions digit_to_int, read_hour, and read_minute are used outside the unnamed namespace without any namespace qualifier. Any name defined in the unnamed namespace can be used without qualification anywhere in the compilation unit. (Of course, this needed to be so, since the unnamed namespace has no name to use for qualifying its names.)

It is interesting to note how unnamed namespaces interact with the C++ rule that you cannot have two definitions of a name (in the same namespace). There is one unnamed namespace in each compilation unit. It is easily possible for compilation units to overlap. For example, both the implementation file for a class and an application program using the class would normally include the header file (interface file) for the class. Thus, the header file is in two compilation units and hence participates in two unnamed namespaces. As dangerous as this sounds, it will normally produce no problems as long as each compilation unit's namespace makes sense when considered by itself. For example, if a name is defined in the unnamed namespace in the header file, it cannot be defined again in the unnamed namespace in either the implementation file or the application file. So, a name conflict is avoided.

DISPLAY 12.8 Placing a Class in a Namespace—Application Program *(part 1 of 2)*

```
1    //This is the application file: timedemo.cpp. This program
2    //demonstrates hiding the helping functions in an unnamed namespace.
3
4    #include <iostream>
5    #include "dtime.h"
6
7    void read_hour(int& the_hour);
8
9    int main( )
10   {
11       using namespace std;
12
13       using namespace dtimesavitch;
14
15       int the_hour;
16       read_hour(the_hour);
17
18       DigitalTime clock(the_hour, 0), old_clock;
19
20       old_clock = clock;
21       clock.advance(15);
22       if (clock == old_clock)
23           cout << "Something is wrong.";
24       cout << "You entered " << old_clock << endl;
25       cout << "15 minutes later, the time will be "
26           << clock; << endl;
27
28       clock.advance(2, 15);
29       cout << "2 hours and 15 minutes after that\n"
30           << "the time will be "
31           << clock; << endl;
32
33       return 0;
34   }
35   void read_hour(int& the_hour)
36   {
37       using namespace std;
38
39       cout << "Let's play a time game.\n"
40           << "Let's pretend the hour has just changed.\n"
41           << "You may write midnight as either 0 or 24,\n"
42           << "but I will always write it as 0.\n"
43           << "Enter the hour as a number (0 to 24): ";
44       cin >> the_hour;
45       if (the_hour == 24)
46           the_hour = 0;
47   }
```

If you place the using directives here, then the program behavior will be the same.

This is a different function **read_hour** than the one in the implementation file **dtime.cpp** (shown in Display 12.7).

(continued)

DISPLAY 12.8   Placing a Class in a Namespace—Application Program *(part 2 of 2)*

Sample Dialogue

```
Let's play a time game.
Let's pretend the hour has just changed.
You may write midnight as either 0 or 24,
but I will always write it as 0.
Enter the hour as a number (0 to 24): 11
You entered 11:00
15 minutes later the time will be 11:15
2 hours and 15 minutes after that
the time will be 13:30
```

■ PROGRAMMING TIP   Choosing a Name for a Namespace

It is a good idea to include your last name or some other unique string in the names of your namespaces so as to reduce the chance that somebody else will use the same namespace name as you do. With multiple programmers writing code for the same project, it is important that namespaces that are meant to be distinct really do have distinct names. Otherwise, you can easily have multiple definitions of the same names in the same scope. That is why we included the name savitch in the namespace dtimesavitch in Display 12.7.   ■

Unnamed Namespace

You can use the **unnamed namespace** to make a definition local to a compilation unit (that is, to a file and its included files). Each compilation unit has one unnamed namespace. All the identifiers defined in the unnamed namespace are local to the compilation unit. You place a definition in the unnamed namespace by placing it in a namespace grouping with no namespace name, as shown in the following:

```
namespace
{
    Definition_1
    Definition_2
        .
        .
        .
    Definition_Last
}
```

You can use any name in the unnamed namespace without a qualifier anyplace in the compilation unit. See Displays 12.6 and 12.7 for a complete example.

PITFALL Confusing the Global Namespace and the Unnamed Namespace

Do not confuse the global namespace with the unnamed namespace. If you do not put a name definition in a namespace grouping, then it is in the global namespace. To put a name definition in the unnamed namespace, you must put it in a namespace grouping that starts as follows, without a name:

```
namespace
{
```

Both names in the global namespace and names in the unnamed namespace may be accessed without a qualifier. However, names in the global namespace have global scope (all the program files), while names in an unnamed namespace are local to a compilation unit.

This confusion between the global namespace and the unnamed namespace does not arise very much in writing code, since there is a tendency to think of names in the global namespace as being "in no namespace," even though that is not technically correct. However, the confusion can easily arise when discussing code. ■

 SELF-TEST EXERCISES

12. Would the program in Display 12.8 behave any differently if you replaced the *using* directive

    ```
    using namespace dtimesavitch;
    ```

    with the following *using* declaration?

    ```
    using dtimesavitch::DigitalTime;
    ```

13. What is the output produced by the following program?

    ```
    #include <iostream>
    using namespace std;

    namespace sally
    {
        void message( );
    }

    namespace
    {
        void message( );
    }

    int main( )
    {
        {
            message( );
    ```

```
            using sally::message;
            message( );
        }

        message( );
        return 0;
    }
    namespace sally
    {
        void message( )
        {
            cout << "Hello from Sally.\n";
        }
    }
    namespace
    {
        void message( )
        {
            cout << "Hello from unnamed.\n";
        }
    }
```

14. In Display 12.7 there are two groupings for the unnamed namespace: one for the helping function declarations and one for the helping function definitions. Can we eliminate the grouping for the helping function declarations? If so, how can we do it?

CHAPTER SUMMARY

- In C++, abstract data types (ADTs) are implemented as classes with all member variables private and with the operations implemented as public member and nonmember functions and overloaded operators.

- You can define an ADT as a class and place the definition of the class and the implementation of its member functions in separate files. You can then compile the ADT class separately from any program that uses it and you can use this same ADT class in any number of different programs.

- A namespace is a collection of name definitions, such as class definitions and variable declarations.

- There are three ways to use a name from a namespace: by making all the names in the namespace available with a *using* directive, by making the single name available by a *using* declaration for the one name, or by qualifying the name with the name of the namespace and the scope resolution operator.

- You place a definition in a namespace by placing it in a namespace grouping for that namespace.

- The unnamed namespace can be used to make a name definition local to a compilation unit.

Answers to Self-Test Exercises

1. Parts (a), (b), and (c) go in the interface file; parts (d) through (h) go in the implementation file. (All the definitions of ADT operations of any sort go in the implementation file.) Part (i) (that is, the main part of your program) goes in the application file.

2. The name of the interface file ends in .h.

3. Only the implementation file needs to be compiled. The interface file does not need to be compiled.

4. Only the implementation file needs to be recompiled. You do, however, need to relink the files.

5. You need to delete the private member variables hour and minute from the interface file shown in Display 12.1 and replace them with the member variable minutes (with an s). You do not need to make any other changes in the interface file. In the implementation file, you need to change the definitions of all the constructors and other member functions, as well as the definitions of the overloaded operators, so that they work for this new way of recording time. (In this case, you do not need to change any of the helping functions read_hour, read_minute, or digit_to_int, but that might not be true for some other class or even some other reimplementation of this class.) For example, the definition of the overloaded operator >> could be changed to the following:

```
istream& operator >>(istream& ins, DigitalTime& the_object)
{
    int input_hour, input_minute;
    read_hour(ins, input_hour);
    read_minute(ins, input_minute);
    the_object.minutes = input_minute + (60 * input_hour);
    return ins;
}
```

You need not change any application files for programs that use the class. However, since the interface file is changed (as well as the implementation file), you will need to recompile any application files, and of course you will need to recompile the implementation file.

6. The short answer is that an ADT is simply a class that you defined following good programming practices of separating the interface from the implementation. Also, when we describe a class as an ADT, we consider the nonmember basic operations such as overloaded operators to be part of the ADT, even though they are not technically speaking part of the C++ class.

7. No. If you replace `big_greeting` with `greeting`, then you will have a definition for the name `greeting` in the global namespace. There are parts of the program where all the name definitions in the namespace `savitch1` and all the name definitions in the global namespace are simultaneously available. In those parts of the program, there would be two distinct definitions for

   void `greeting( );`

8. Yes, the additional definition would cause no problems. This is because overloading is always allowed. When, for example, the namespaces `savitch1` and the global namespace are available, the function name `greeting` would be overloaded. The problem in Self-Test Exercise 7 was that there would sometimes be two definitions of the function name `greeting` with the same parameter lists.

9. Yes, a namespace can have any number of groupings. For example, the following are two groupings for the namespace `savitch1` that appear in Display 12.5:

   ```
   namespace savitch1
   {
       void greeting( );
   }

   namespace savitch1
   {
       void greeting( )
       {
           cout << "Hello from namespace savitch1.\n";
       }
   }
   ```

10. *void* `wow(speedway::speed s1, indy500::speed s2);`

11. *void* `input(std::istream& ins);`

    void `output(std::ostream& outs)` *const*;

12. The program would behave exactly the same.

13. `Hello from unnamed. Hello from Sally. Hello from unnamed.`

14. Yes, you can eliminate the grouping for the helping function declarations, as long as the grouping with the helping function definitions occurs before the helping functions are used. For example, you could remove the namespace with the helping function declarations and move the grouping with the helping function definitions to just before the namespace grouping for the namespace `dtimesavitch`.

PROGRAMMING PROJECTS

Visit www.myprogramminglab.com to complete many of these Programming Projects online and get instant feedback.

1. Add the following member function to the ADT class DigitalTime defined in Displays 12.1 and 12.2:

```
void DigitalTime::interval_since(const DigitalTime& a_previous_time,
     int& hours_in_interval, int& minutes_in_interval) const
```

This function computes the time interval between two values of type DigitalTime. One of the values of type DigitalTime is the object that calls the member function interval_since, and the other value of type DigitalTime is given as the first argument. For example, consider the following code:

```
DigitalTime current(5, 45), previous(2, 30);
int hours, minutes;
current.interval_since(previous, hours, minutes);
cout << "The time interval between " << previous
     << " and " << current << endl
     << "is " << hours << " hours and "
<< minutes << " minutes.\n";
```

In a program that uses your revised version of the DigitalTime ADT, this code should produce the following output:

> The time interval between 2:30 and 5:45
> is 3 hours and 15 minutes.

Allow the time given by the first argument to be later in the day than the time of the calling object. In this case, the time given as the first argument is assumed to be on the previous day. You should also write a program to test this revised ADT class.

2. Do Self-Test Exercise 5 in full detail. Write out the complete ADT class, including interface and implementation files. Also write a program to test your ADT class.

VideoNote
Solution to Programming
Project 12.3

3. Redo Programming Project 1 from Chapter 11, but this time define the Money ADT class in separate files for the interface and implementation so that the implementation can be compiled separately from any application program.

4. Redo Programming Project 2 from Chapter 11, but this time define the Pairs ADT class in separate files for the interface and implementation so that the implementation can be compiled separately from any application program.

5. Redo (or do for the first time) Programming Project 4 from Chapter 11. Define your ADT class in separate files so that it can be compiled separately.

6. Redo (or do for the first time) Programming Project 5 from Chapter 11. Define your ADT class in separate files so that it can be compiled separately.

7. Redo (or do for the first time) Programming Project 12 from Chapter 11. Define your ADT class in separate files so that it can be compiled separately. Put the main function in its own file separate from the ADT files.

8. This Programming Project explores how the unnamed namespace works. Listed below are snippets from a program to perform input validation for a username and password. The code to input and validate the username is in a file separate from the code to input and validate the password.

File `user.cpp`:

```
namespace Authenticate
{
    void inputUserName()
    {
        do
        {
        cout << "Enter your username (8 letters only)"  << endl;
        cin >> username;
        } while (!isValid());
    }
    string getUserName()
    {
        return username;
    }
}
```

Define the username variable and the `isValid()` function in the unnamed namespace so the code will compile. The `isValid()` function should return `true` if username contains exactly eight letters. Generate an appropriate header file for this code.

Repeat the same steps for the file `password.cpp`, placing the `password` variable and the `isValid()` function in the unnamed namespace. In this case, the `isValid()` function should return `true` if the input password has at least eight characters including at least one nonletter:

File `password.cpp`:
```
namespace Authenticate
{
    void inputPassword()
```

```
    {
        do
        {
        cout << "Enter your password (at least 8 characters " <<
                "and at least one nonletter)"  << endl;
        cin >> password;
        } while (!isValid());
    }
    string getPassword()
    {
        return password;
    }
}
```

At this point you should have two functions named isValid(), each in different unnamed namespaces. Place the following main function in an appropriate place. The program should compile and run.

```
int main()
{
    inputUserName();
    inputPassword();
    cout << "Your username is " << getUserName() <<
            " and your password is: " <<
            getPassword() << endl;
    return 0;
}
```

Test the program with several invalid usernames and passwords.

Pointers and Linked Lists 13

If somebody there chanced to be
Who loved me in a manner true
My heart would point him out to me
And I would point him out to you.

GILBERT AND SULLIVAN, *Ruddigore*

INTRODUCTION

A *linked list* is a list constructed using pointers. A linked list is not fixed in size, but can grow and shrink while your program is running. This chapter shows you how to define and manipulate linked lists, which will serve to introduce you to a new way of using pointers.

PREREQUISITES

This chapter uses material from Chapters 2 through 12.

13.1 NODES AND LINKED LISTS

Useful dynamic variables are seldom of a simple type such as *int* or *double*, but are normally of some complex type such as an array, *struct*, or class type. You saw that dynamic variables of an array type can be useful. Dynamic variables of a *struct* or class type can also be useful, but in a different way. Dynamic variables that are either *structs* or classes normally have one or more member variables that are pointer variables which connect them to other dynamic variables. For example, one such structure, which happens to contain a shopping list, is diagrammed in Display 13.1.

Nodes

A structure like the one shown in Display 13.1 consists of items that we have drawn as boxes connected by arrows. The boxes are called **nodes** and the arrows represent pointers. Each of the nodes in Display 13.1 contains a string, an integer, and a pointer that can point to other nodes of the same type. Note that pointers point to the entire node, not to the individual items (such as 10 or "rolls") that are inside the node.

Nodes are implemented in C++ as *structs* or classes. For example, the *struct* type definitions for a node of the type shown in Display 13.1, along with the type definition for a pointer to such nodes, can be as follows:

```
struct ListNode
{
    string item;
```

DISPLAY 13.1 **Nodes and Pointers**

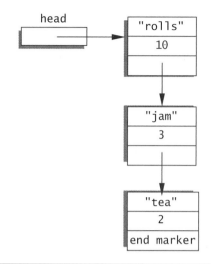

```
        int count;
        ListNode *link;
};
typedef ListNode* ListNodePtr;
```

The order of the type definitions is important. The definition of ListNode must come first, since it is used in the definition of ListNodePtr.

The box labeled head in Display 13.1 is not a node, but is a pointer variable that can point to a node. The pointer variable head is declared as follows:

```
ListNodePtr head;
```

Even though we have ordered the type definitions to avoid some illegal forms of circularity, the definition of the *struct* type ListNode is still blatantly circular. The definition uses the type name ListNode to define the member variable link. There is nothing wrong with this particular circularity, and it is allowed in C++. One indication that this definition is not logically inconsistent is the fact that you can draw pictures, like Display 13.1, that represent such structures.

We now have pointers inside of *structs* and have these pointers pointing to *structs* that contain pointers, and so forth. In such situations the syntax can sometimes get involved, but in all cases the syntax follows those few rules we have described for pointers and *structs*. As an illustration, suppose the declarations are as above, the situation is as diagrammed in Display 13.1, and you want to change the number in the first node from 10 to 12. One way to accomplish this is with the following statement:

```
(*head).count = 12;
```

The expression on the left side of the assignment operator may require a bit of explanation. The variable head is a pointer variable. So, the expression *head is the thing it points to, namely the node (dynamic variable) containing "rolls" and the integer 10. This node, referred to by *head, is a *struct*, and the member variable of this *struct*, which contains a value of type *int*, is called count, and so (*head).count is the name of the *int* variable in the first node. The parentheses around *head are not optional. You want the dereferencing operator * to be performed before the dot operator. However, the dot operator has higher precedence than the dereferencing operator *, and so without the parentheses, the dot operator would be performed first (and that would produce an error). In the next paragraph, we will describe a shortcut notation that can avoid this worry about parentheses.

C++ has an operator that can be used with a pointer to simplify the notation for specifying the members of a *struct* or a class. The **arrow operator** -> combines the actions of a dereferencing operator * and a dot operator to specify a member of a dynamic *struct* or object that is pointed to by a given pointer. For example, the assignment statement above for changing the number in the first node can be written more simply as

```
head->count = 12;
```

This assignment statement and the previous one mean the same thing, but this one is the form normally used.

The string in the first node can be changed from "rolls" to "bagels" with the following statement:

```
head->item = "bagels";
```

The result of these changes to the first node in the list is diagrammed in Display 13.2. Look at the pointer member in the last node in the lists shown in Display 13.2. This last node has the word NULL written where there should be a pointer. In Display 13.1 we filled this position with the phrase "end marker," but "end marker" is not a C++ expression. In C++ programs we use the constant NULL as an end marker to signal the end of a linked list. NULL is a special defined constant that is part of the C++ language (provided as part of the required C++ libraries).

NULL is typically used for two different (but often coinciding) purposes. It is used to give a value to a pointer variable that otherwise would not have any value. This prevents an inadvertent reference to memory, since NULL is not

DISPLAY 13.2   Accessing Node Data

```
head->count = 12;
head->item = "bagels";
```

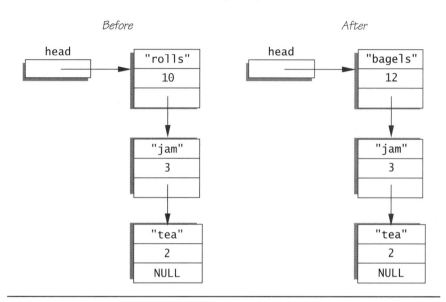

the address of any memory location. The second category of use is that of an end marker. A program can step through the list of nodes as shown in Display 13.2, and when the program reaches the node that contains NULL, it knows that it has come to the end of the list.

The constant NULL is actually the number 0, but we prefer to think of it and spell it as NULL. That makes it clear that you mean this special-purpose value that you can assign to pointer variables. The definition of the identifier NULL is in a number of the standard libraries, such as <iostream> and <cstddef>, so you should use an include directive with either <iostream> or <cstddef> (or other suitable library) when you use NULL. No *using* directive is needed in order to make NULL available to your program code. In particular, it does not require *using namespace* std;, although other things in your code are likely to require something like *using namespace* std;.[1]

NULL is 0

_____

[1] The details are as follows: The definition of NULL is handled by the C++ preprocessor, which replaces NULL with 0. Thus, the compiler never actually sees "NULL" and so there are no namespace issues, and no *using* directive is needed.

The Arrow Operator ->

The arrow operator -> specifies a member of a *struct* (or a member of a class object) that is pointed to by a pointer variable. The syntax is as follows:

```
Pointer_Variable->Member_Name
```

The above refers to a member of the *struct* or object pointed to by the *Pointer_Variable*. Which member it refers to is given by the *Member_Name*.

For example, suppose you have the following definition:

```
struct Record
{
    int number;
    char grade;
};
```

The following creates a dynamic variable of type Record and sets the member variables of the dynamic *struct* variable to 2001 and 'A':

```
Record *p;
p = new Record;
p->number = 2001;
p->grade = 'A';
```

A pointer can be set to NULL using the assignment operator, as in the following, which declares a pointer variable called there and initializes it to NULL:

```
double *there = NULL;
```

The constant NULL can be assigned to a pointer variable of any pointer type.

NULL

NULL is a special constant value that is used to give a value to a pointer variable that would not otherwise have a value. NULL can be assigned to a pointer variable of any type. The identifier NULL is defined in a number of libraries, including the library with header file <cstddef> and the library with header file <iostream>. The constant NULL is actually the number 0, but we prefer to think of it and spell it as NULL.

SELF-TEST EXERCISES

1. Suppose your program contains the following type definitions:

```
struct Box
{
    string name;
    int number;
    Box *next;
};

typedef Box* BoxPtr;
```

What is the output produced by the following code?

```
BoxPtr head;
head = new Box;
head->name = "Sally";
head->number = 18;
cout << (*head).name << endl;
cout << head->name << endl;
cout << (*head).number << endl;
cout << head->number << endl;
```

2. Suppose that your program contains the type definitions and code given in Self-Test Exercise 1. That code creates a node that contains the string "Sally" and the number 18. What code would you add in order to set the value of the member variable next of this node equal to NULL?

3. Suppose that your program contains the type definitions and code given in Self-Test Exercise 1. Assuming that the value of the pointer variable head has not been changed, how can you destroy the dynamic variable pointed to by head and return the memory it uses to the freestore so that it can be reused to create new dynamic variables?

4. Given the following structure definition:

```
struct ListNode
{
    string item;
    int count;
    ListNode *link;
};
ListNode *head = new ListNode;
```

write code to assign the string "Wilbur's brother Orville" to the member item of the node pointed to by head.

Linked Lists

Lists such as those shown in Display 13.2 are called *linked lists.* A **linked list** is a list of nodes in which each node has a member variable that is a pointer that points to the next node in the list. The first node in a linked list is called the **head,** which is why the pointer variable that points to the first node is named head. Note that the pointer named head is not itself the head of the list but only points to the head of the list. The last node has no special name, but it does have a special property. The last node has NULL as the value of its member pointer variable. To test to see whether a node is the last node, you need only test to see if the pointer variable in the node is equal to NULL.

Our goal in this section is to write some basic functions for manipulating linked lists. For variety, and to simplify the notation, we will use a simpler type of node than that used in Display 13.2. These nodes will contain only an integer and a pointer. The node and pointer type definitions that we will use are as follows:

```
struct Node
{
    int data;
    Node *link;
};

typedef Node* NodePtr;
```

As a warm-up exercise, let's see how we might construct the start of a linked list with nodes of this type. We first declare a pointer variable, called head, that will point to the head of our linked list:

```
NodePtr head;
```

To create our first node, we use the operator *new* to create a new dynamic variable that will become the first node in our linked list.

```
head = new Node;
```

We then give values to the member variables of this new node:

```
head->data = 3;
head->link = NULL;
```

Notice that the pointer member of this node is set equal to NULL. That is because this node is the last node in the list (as well as the first node in the list). At this stage, our linked list looks like this:

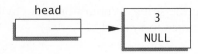

Our one-node list was built in a purely ad hoc way. To have a larger linked list, your program must be able to add nodes in a systematic way. We next describe one simple way to insert nodes in a linked list.

Inserting a Node at the Head of a List

In this subsection we assume that our linked list already contains one or more nodes, and we develop a function to add another node. The first parameter for the insertion function will be a call-by-reference parameter for a pointer variable that points to the head of the linked list, that is, a pointer variable that points to the first node in the linked list. The other parameter will give the number to be stored in the new node. The function declaration for our insertion function is as follows:

```
void head_insert(NodePtr& head, int the_number);
```

Linked Lists as Arguments

You should always keep one pointer variable pointing to the head of a linked list. This pointer variable is a way to name the linked list. When you write a function that takes a linked list as an argument, this pointer (which points to the head of the linked list) can be used as the linked list argument.

To insert a new node into the linked list, our function will use the *new* operator to create a new node. The data is then copied into the new node, and the new node is inserted at the head of the list. When we insert nodes this way, the new node will be the first node in the list (that is, the head node) rather than the last node. Since dynamic variables have no names, we must use a local pointer variable to point to this node. If we call the local pointer variable `temp_ptr`, the new node can be referred to as `*temp_ptr`. The complete process can be summarized as follows:

Pseudocode for head_insert Function

1. Create a new dynamic variable pointed to by `temp_ptr`. (This new dynamic variable is the new node. This new node can be referred to as `*temp_ptr`.)

2. Place the data in this new node.

3. Make the link member of this new node point to the head node (first node) of the original linked list.

4. Make the pointer variable named `head` point to the new node.

Display 13.3 contains a diagram of this algorithm. Steps 2 and 3 in the diagram can be expressed by these C++ assignment statements:

```
temp_ptr->link = head;
head = temp_ptr;
```

The complete function definition is given in Display 13.4.

You will want to allow for the possibility that a list contains nothing. For example, a shopping list might have nothing in it because there is nothing to buy this week. A list with nothing in it is called an **empty list.** A linked list is named by naming a pointer that points to the head of the list, but an empty list has no head node. To specify an empty list, you use the pointer NULL. If the pointer variable head is supposed to point to the head node of a linked list and you want to indicate that the list is empty, then you set the value of head as follows:

```
head = NULL;
```

Whenever you design a function for manipulating a linked list, you should always check to see if it works on the empty list. If it does not, you may be able to add a special case for the empty list. If you cannot design the function to apply to the empty list, then your program must be designed to handle empty lists some other way or to avoid them completely. Fortunately, the empty list can often be treated just like any other list. For example, the function head_insert in Display 13.4 was designed with nonempty lists as the model, but a check will show that it works for the empty list as well.

DISPLAY 13.3 Adding a Node to a Linked List *(part 1 of 2)*

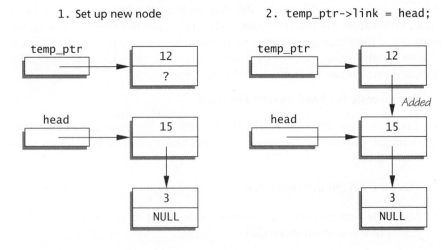

1. Set up new node

2. temp_ptr->link = head;

(continued)

DISPLAY 13.3   Adding a Node to a Linked List *(part 2 of 2)*

3. head = temp_ptr;   4. After function call

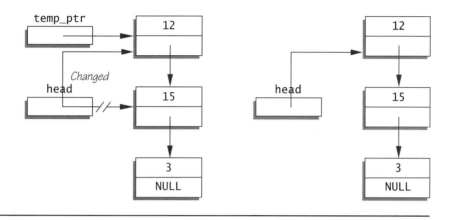

DISPLAY 13.4   Function to Add a Node at the Head of a Linked List

Function Declaration

```
1     struct Node
2     {
3         int data;
4         Node *link;
5     };
6
7     typedef Node* NodePtr;
8
9     void head_insert(NodePtr& head, int the_number);
10    //Precondition: The pointer variable head points to
11    //the head of a linked list.
12    //Postcondition: A new node containing the_number
13    //has been added at the head of the linked list.
```

Function Definition

```
1     void head_insert(NodePtr& head, int the_number)
2     {
3         NodePtr temp_ptr;
4         temp_ptr = new Node;
5
6         temp_ptr->data = the_number;
7
8         temp_ptr->link = head;
9         head = temp_ptr;
10    }
```

PITFALL   Losing Nodes

You might be tempted to write the function definition for `head_insert` (Display 13.4) using the pointer variable `head` to construct the new node, instead of using the local pointer variable `temp_ptr`. If you were to try, you might start the function as follows:

```
head = new Node;
head->data = the_number;
```

At this point the new node is constructed, contains the correct data, and is pointed to by the pointer `head`, all as it is supposed to be. All that is left to do is to attach the rest of the list to this node by setting the pointer member given below so that it points to what was formerly the first node of the list:

```
head->link
```

Display 13.5 shows the situation when the new data value is 12. That illustration reveals the problem. If you were to proceed in this way, there would be nothing pointing to the node containing 15. Since there is no named pointer pointing to it (or to a chain of pointers ending with that node), there is no way the program can reference this node. The node below this node is also lost. A program cannot make a pointer point to either of these nodes, nor can it access the data in these nodes, nor can it do anything else to the nodes. It simply has no way to refer to the nodes.

Such a situation ties up memory for the duration of the program. A program that loses nodes is sometimes said to have a "memory leak." A significant memory leak can result in the program running out of memory, causing abnormal termination. Worse, a memory leak (lost nodes) in an ordinary user's program can cause the operating system to crash. To avoid such lost nodes, the program must always keep some pointer pointing to the head of the list, usually the pointer in a pointer variable like `head`. ■

DISPLAY 13.5   Lost Nodes

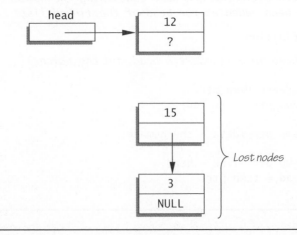

Searching a Linked List

Next we will design a function to search a linked list in order to locate a particular node. We will use the same node type, called Node, that we used in the previous subsections. (The definition of the node and pointer types is given in Display 13.4.) The function we design will have two arguments: for the linked list and the integer we want to locate. The function will return a pointer that points to the first node which contains that integer. If no node contains the integer, the function will return the pointer NULL. This way, our program can test to see whether the integer is on the list by checking to see if the function returns a pointer value that is not equal to NULL. The function declaration and header comment for our function is as follows:

```
NodePtr search(NodePtr head, int target);
//Precondition: The pointer head points to the head of
//a linked list. The pointer variable in the last node
//is NULL. If the list is empty, then head is NULL.
//Returns a pointer that points to the first node that
//contains the target. If no node contains the target,
//the function returns NULL.
```

We will use a local pointer variable, called here, to move through the list looking for the target. The only way to move around a linked list, or any other data structure made up of nodes and pointers, is to follow the pointers. So we will start with here pointing to the first node and move the pointer from node to node following the pointer out of each node. This technique is diagrammed in Display 13.6. Since empty lists present some minor problems that would clutter our discussion, we will at first assume that the linked list contains at least one node. Later we will come back and make sure the algorithm works for the empty list as well. This search technique yields the following algorithm:

Pseudocode for search Function

Make the pointer variable here point to the head node (that is, first node) of the linked list.

```
while (here is not pointing to a node containing target
       and here is not pointing to the last node)
{
    Make here point to the next node in the list.
}
if (the node pointed to by here contains target)
    return here;
else
    return NULL;
```

In order to move the pointer here to the next node, we must think in terms of the named pointers we have available. The next node is the one

DISPLAY 13.6 Searching a Linked List

target *is* 6

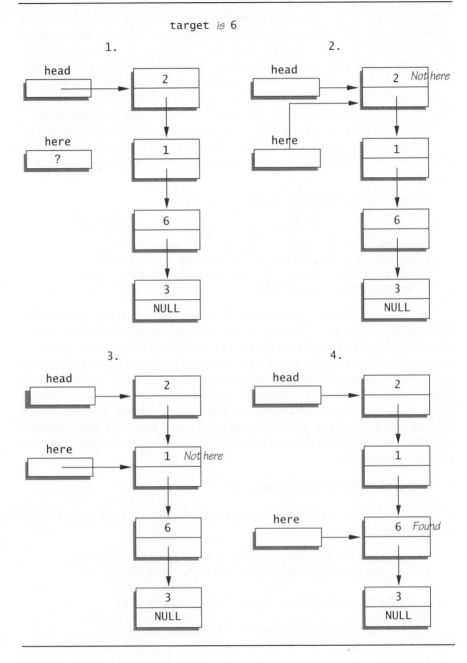

pointed to by the pointer member of the node currently pointed to by here. The pointer member of the node currently pointed to by here is given by the expression

```
here->link
```

To move here to the next node, we want to change here so that it points to the node that is pointed to by the above-named pointer (member) variable. Hence, the following will move the pointer here to the next node in the list:

```
here = here->link;
```

Putting these pieces together yields the following refinement of the algorithm pseudocode:

Preliminary Version of the Code for the search **Function**

```
here = head;

while (here->data != target &&  here->link != NULL)
    here = here->link;

if (here->data == target)
    return here;
else
    return NULL;
```

Notice the Boolean expression in the *while* statement. We test to see if here is not pointing to the last node by testing to see if the member variable here->link is not equal to NULL.

We still must go back and take care of the empty list. If we check our code, we find that there is a problem with the empty list. If the list is empty, then here is equal to NULL and hence the following expressions are undefined:

```
here->data
here->link
```

When here is NULL, it is not pointing to any node, so there is no member named data nor any member named link. Hence, we make a special case of the empty list. The complete function definition is given in Display 13.7.

Pointers as Iterators

An **iterator** is a construct that allows you to cycle through the data items stored in a data structure so that you can perform whatever action you want on each data item. An iterator can be an object of some iterator class or something simpler, such as an array index or a pointer. Pointers provide a simple example of an iterator. In fact, a pointer is the prototypical example of an iterator. The basic ideas can be easily seen in the context of linked lists. You can use a pointer as an iterator by moving through the linked list one node at

DISPLAY 13.7   Function to Locate a Node in a Linked List

Function Declaration

```
1    struct Node
2    {
3        int data;
4        Node *link;
5    };
6
7    typedef Node* NodePtr;
8
9    NodePtr search(NodePtr head, int target);
10   //Precondition: The pointer head points to the head of
11   //a linked list. The pointer variable in the last node
12   //is NULL. If the list is empty, then head is NULL.
13   //Returns a pointer that points to the first node that
14   //contains the target. If no node contains the target,
15   //the function returns NULL.
```

Function Definition

```
1    //Uses cstddef:
2    NodePtr search(NodePtr head, int target)
3    {
4        NodePtr here = head;
5
6        if (here == NULL)
7        {
8            return NULL;                          Empty list case
9        }
10       else
11       {
12           while (here->data != target &&
13                   here->link != NULL)
14               here = here->link;
15
16           if (here->data == target)
17               return here;
18           else
19               return NULL;
20       }
21   }
```

a time starting at the head of the list and cycling through all the nodes in the list. The general outline is as follows:

```
Node_Type *iter;
for (iter = head; iter != NULL; iter = iter->link)
    Do whatever you want with the node pointed to by iter;
```

where *head* is a pointer to the head node of the linked list and *link* is the name of the member variable of a node that points to the next node in the list.

For example, to output the data in all the nodes in a linked list of the kind we have been discussing, you could use

```
NodePtr iter; //Equivalent to: Node *iter;
for (iter = head; iter != NULL; iter = iter->link)
    cout << (iter->data);
```

The definition of Node and NodePtr are given in Display 13.7.

Inserting and Removing Nodes Inside a List

We next design a function to insert a node at a specified place in a linked list. If you want the nodes in some particular order, such as numeric order or alphabetical order, you cannot simply insert the node at the beginning or end of the list. We will therefore design a function to insert a node after a specified node in the linked list. We assume that some other function or program part has correctly placed a pointer called after_me pointing to some node in the linked list. We want the new node to be placed after the node pointed to by after_me, as illustrated in Display 13.8. The same technique works for nodes with any kind of data, but to be concrete, we are using the same type of nodes as in previous subsections. The type definitions are given in Display 13.7. The function declaration for the function we want to define is:

Inserting in the middle of a list

DISPLAY 13.8   Inserting in the Middle of a Linked List

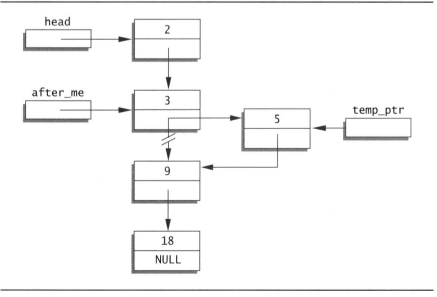

```
void insert(NodePtr after_me, int the_number);
//Precondition: after_me points to a node in a linked list.
//Postcondition: A new node containing the_number
//has been added after the node pointed to by after_me.
```

A new node is set up the same way it was in the function head_insert in Display 13.4. The difference between this function and that one is that we now wish to insert the node not at the head of the list, but after the node pointed to by after_me. The way to do the insertion is shown in Display 13.8 and is expressed as follows in C++ code:

```
//add a link from the new node to the list:
temp_ptr->link = after_me->link;
//add a link from the list to the new node:
after_me->link = temp_ptr;
```

The order of these two assignment statements is critical. In the first assignment we want the pointer value after_me->link *before it is changed*. The complete function is given in Display 13.9.

DISPLAY 13.9 Function to Add a Node in the Middle of a Linked List

Function Declaration

```
1    struct Node
2    {
3        int data;
4        Node *link;
5    };
6
7    typedef Node* NodePtr;
8
9    void insert(NodePtr after_me, int the_number);
10   //Precondition: after_me points to a node in a linked
11   //list.
12   //Postcondition: A new node containing the_number
13   //has been added after the node pointed to by after_me.
```

Function Definition

```
1    void insert(NodePtr after_me, int the_number)
2    {
3        NodePtr temp_ptr;
4        temp_ptr = new Node;
5
6        temp_ptr->data = the_number;
7
8        temp_ptr->link = after_me->link;
9        after_me->link = temp_ptr;
10   }
```

DISPLAY 13.10 Removing a Node

1. Position the pointer discard so that it points to the node to be deleted, and position the pointer before so that it points to the node before the one to be deleted.

2. before->link = discard->link;

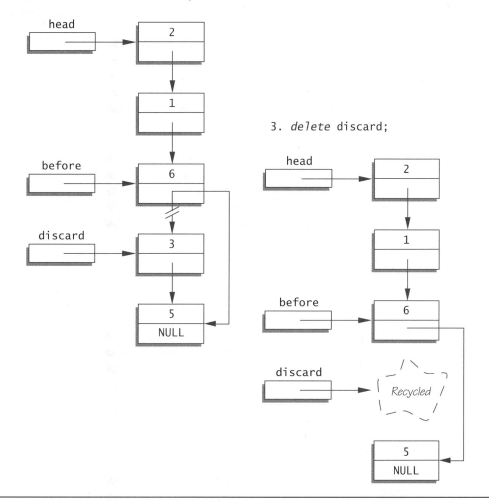

3. *delete* discard;

If you go through the code for the function insert, you will see that it works correctly even if the node pointed to by after_me is the last node in the list. However, insert will not work for inserting a node at the beginning of a linked list. The function head_insert given in Display 13.4 can be used to insert a node at the beginning of a list.

By using the function insert you can maintain a linked list in numerical order or alphabetical order or other ordering. You can "squeeze" a new node into the correct position by simply adjusting two pointers. This is true no matter

Insertion at the ends

Comparison to arrays

how long the linked list is or where in the list you want the new data to go. If you instead used an array, much, and in extreme cases all, of the array would have to be copied in order to make room for a new value in the correct spot. Despite the overhead involved in positioning the pointer after_me, inserting into a linked list is frequently more efficient than inserting into an array.

Removing a node   Removing a node from a linked list is also quite easy. Display 13.10 illustrates the method. Once the pointers before and discard have been positioned, all that is required to remove the node is the following statement:

```
before->link = discard->link;
```

This is sufficient to remove the node from the linked list. However, if you are not using this node for something else, you should destroy it and return the memory it uses to the freestore; you can do this with a call to *delete* as follows:

```
delete discard;
```

PITFALL   Using the Assignment Operator with Dynamic Data Structures

If head1 and head2 are pointer variables and head1 points to the head node of a linked list, the following will make head2 point to the same head node and hence the same linked list:

```
head2 = head1;
```

However, you must remember that there is only one linked list, not two. If you change the linked list pointed to by head1, then you will also change the linked list pointed to by head2, because they are the same linked list.

If head1 points to a linked list and you want head2 to point to a second, identical *copy* of this linked list, the assignment statement above will not work. Instead, you must copy the entire linked list node by node. Alternatively, you can overload the assignment operator = so that it means whatever you want it to mean. Overloading = is discussed in the subsection of Chapter 11 entitled "Overloading the Assignment Operator." ◼

SELF-TEST EXERCISES

5. Write type definitions for the nodes and pointers in a linked list. Call the node type NodeType and call the pointer type PointerType. The linked lists will be lists of letters.

6. A linked list is normally given by giving a pointer that points to the first node in the list, but an empty list has no first node. What pointer value is normally used to represent an empty list?

7. Suppose your program contains the following type definitions and pointer variable declarations:

```
struct Node
{
    double data;
    Node *next;
};

typedef Node* Pointer;
Pointer p1, p2;
```

Suppose p1 points to a node of this type that is on a linked list. Write code that will make p1 point to the next node on this linked list. (The pointer p2 is for the next exercise and has nothing to do with this exercise.)

8. Suppose your program contains type definitions and pointer variable declarations as in Self-Test Exercise 7. Suppose further that p2 points to a node of type Node that is on a linked list and is not the last node on the list. Write code that will delete the node *after* the node pointed to by p2. After this code is executed, the linked list should be the same, except that there will be one less node on the linked list. (*Hint:* You might want to declare another pointer variable to use.)

9. Choose an answer and explain it.

For a large array and large list holding the same type objects, inserting a new object at a known location into the middle of a linked list compared with insertion in an array is

a. More efficient

b. Less efficient

c. About the same

d. Dependent on the size of the two lists

Variations on Linked Lists

In this subsection we give you a hint of the many data structures that can be created using nodes and pointers. We briefly describe two additional data structures, the doubly linked list and the binary tree.

An ordinary linked list allows you to move down the list in only one direction (following the links). A node in a **doubly linked list** has two links, one link that points to the next node and one that points to the previous node. Diagrammatically, a doubly linked list looks like the sample list in Display 13.11.

DISPLAY 13.11   A Doubly Linked List

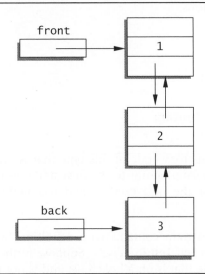

The node class for a doubly linked list could be as follows:

```
struct Node
{
    int data;
    Node *forward_link;
    Node *back_link;
};
```

Rather than a single pointer to the head node, a doubly linked list normally has a pointer to each of the two end nodes. You can call these pointers front and back, although the choice of which is front and which is back is arbitrary. The definitions of constructors and some of the functions in the doubly linked list class will have to change (from the singly linked case) to accommodate the extra link.

A **tree** is a data structure that is structured as shown in Display 13.12. In particular, in a tree you can reach any node from the top (root) node by some path that follows the links. Note that there are no cycles in a tree. If you follow the links, you eventually get to an "end." Note that each node has two links that point to other nodes (or the value NULL). This sort of tree is called a **binary tree**, because each node has exactly two links. There are other kinds of trees with different numbers of links in the nodes, but the binary tree is the most common case.

A tree is not a form of linked list, but does use links (pointers) in ways that are similar to how they are used in linked lists. The definition of the node type for a binary tree is essentially the same as what it is for a doubly linked list, but

DISPLAY 13.12   A Binary Tree

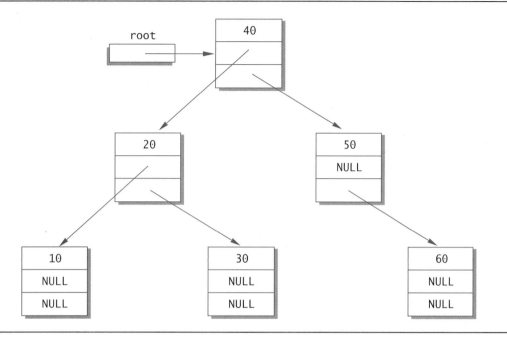

the two links are usually named using some form of the words *left* and *right*. The following is a node type that can be used for constructing a binary tree:

```
struct TreeNode
{
    int data;
    TreeNode *left_link;
    TreeNode *right_link;
};
```

In Display 13.12, the pointer named root points to the **root node** ("top node"). The root node serves a purpose similar to that of the head node in an ordinary linked list (Display 13.10). Any node in the tree can be reached from the root node by following the links.

The term *tree* may seem like a misnomer. The root is at the top of the tree and the branching structure looks more like a root branching structure than a tree branching structure. The secret to the terminology is to turn the picture (Display 13.12) upside down. The picture then does resemble the branching structure of a tree and the root node is where the tree's root would begin. The nodes at the ends of the branches with both link instance variables set to NULL are known as **leaf nodes,** a terminology that may now make some sense.

Although we do not have room to pursue the topic in this book, binary trees can be used to efficiently store and retrieve data.

Linked Lists of Classes

In the preceding examples we created linked lists by using a struct to hold the contents of a node within the list. It is possible to create the same data structures using a class instead of a struct. The logic is identical except the syntax of using and defining a class should be substituted in place of that for a struct.

VideoNote
Walkthrough of Linked Lists of Classes

Displays 13.13 and 13.14 illustrate how to define a Node class. The data variables are declared *private* using the principle of information hiding, and *public* methods have been created to access the data value and next node in the link. Display 13.15 creates a short list of five nodes by inserting new nodes onto the front of the list. The head_insert function is logically identical to the same function defined in Display 13.4 except the constructor defined for the Node class is used to set the data.

DISPLAY 13.13   Interface File for a Node Class

```
1    //This is the header file for Node.h. This is the interface for
2    //a node class that behaves similarly to the struct defined
3    //in Display 13.4
4    namespace linkedlistofclasses
5    {
6        class Node
7        {
8        public:
9            Node( );
10           Node(int value, Node *next);
11           //Constructors to initialize a node
12
13           int getData( ) const;
14           //Retrieve value for this node
15
16           Node *getLink( ) const;
17           //Retrieve next Node in the list
18
19           void setData(int value);
20           //Use to modify the value stored in the list
21
22           void setLink(Node *next);
23           //Use to change the reference to the next node
24
25       private:
26           int data;
27           Node *link;
28       };
29       typedef Node* NodePtr;
30   } //linkedlistofclasses
31   //Node.h
```

DISPLAY 13.14   Implementation File for a Node Class

```
1    //This is the implementation file Node.cpp.
2    //It implements logic for the Node class. The interface
3    //file is in the header file Node.h
4    #include <iostream>
5    #include "Node.h"
6
7    namespace linkedlistofclasses
8    {
9        Node::Node( ) : data(0), link(NULL)
10       {
11           //deliberately empty
12       }
13
14       Node::Node(int value, Node *next) : data(value), link(next)
15       {
16           //deliberately empty
17       }
18
19       //Accessor and Mutator methods follow
20
21       int Node::getData( ) const
22       {
23           return data;
24       }
25
26       Node* Node::getLink( ) const
27       {
28           return link;
29       }
30
31       void Node::setData(int value)
32       {
33           data = value;
34       }
35
36       void Node::setLink(Node *next)
37       {
38           link = next;
39       }
40   } //linkedlistofclasses
41   //Node.cpp
```

DISPLAY 13.15   Program Using the Node Class *(part 1 of 3)*

```
1    //This program demonstrates the creation of a linked list
2    //using the Node class. Five nodes are created, output, then
3    //destroyed.
```

(continued)

DISPLAY 13.15 **Program Using the Node Class** *(part 2 of 3)*

```
4    #include <iostream>
5    #include "Node.h"
6
7    using namespace std;
8    using namespace linkedlistofclasses;
9
10   //This function inserts a new node onto the head of the list
11   //and is a class-based version of the same function defined
12   //in Display 13.4.
13   void head_insert(NodePtr& head, int the_number)
14   {
15       NodePtr temp_ptr;
16       //The constructor sets temp_ptr->link to head and
17       //sets the data value to the_number
18       temp_ptr = new Node(the_number, head);
19       head = temp_ptr;
20   }
21
22   int main()
23   {
24       NodePtr head, tmp;
25
26       //Create a list of nodes 4 -> 3 -> 2 -> 1 -> 0
27       head = new Node(0, NULL);
28       for (int i = 1; i < 5; i++)
29       {
30           head_insert(head, i);
31       }
32       //Iterate through the list and display each value
33       tmp = head;
34       while (tmp != NULL)
35       {
36           cout << tmp->getData() << endl;
37           tmp = tmp->getLink();
38       }
39       //Delete all nodes in the list before exiting
40       //the program.
41       tmp = head;
42       while (tmp != NULL)
43       {
44           NodePtr nodeToDelete = tmp;
45           tmp = tmp->getLink();
46           delete nodeToDelete;
47       }
48       return 0;
49   }
```

(continued)

DISPLAY 13.15   Program Using the Node Class *(part 3 of 3)*

Sample Dialogue

```
4
3
2
1
0
```

13.2 STACKS AND QUEUES

But many who are first now will be last, and many who are last now will be first.

MATTHEW 19:30

Linked lists have many applications. In this section we give two samples of what they can be used for. We use linked lists to give implementations of two data structures known as a *stack* and a *queue*. In this section we always use regular linked lists and not doubly linked lists.

Stacks

A *stack* is a data structure that retrieves data in the reverse of the order in which the data is stored. Suppose you place the letters 'A', 'B', and then 'C' in a stack. When you take these letters out of the stack, they will be removed in the order 'C', 'B', and then 'A'. This use of a stack is diagrammed in Display 13.16. As shown there, you can think of a stack as a hole in the ground. In order to get something out of the stack, you must first remove the items on top of the one you want. For this reason a stack is often called a *last-in/first-out* (LIFO) data structure.

DISPLAY 13.16   A Stack

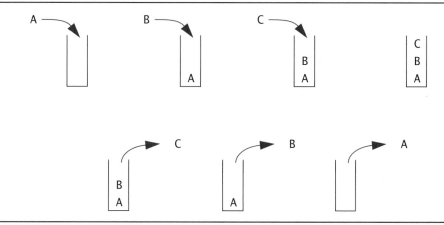

Stacks are used for many language processing tasks. In Chapter 14 we will discuss how the computer system uses a stack to keep track of C++ function calls. However, here we will do only one very simple application. Our goal in this example is to show you how you can use the linked list techniques to implement specific data structures; a stack is one simple example of the use of linked lists. You need not read Chapter 14 to understand this example.

| PROGRAMMING EXAMPLE | A Stack Class |

The interface for our Stack class is given in Display 13.17. This particular stack is used to store data of type *char*. You can define a similar stack to store data of any other type. There are two basic operations you can perform on a stack: adding an item to the stack and removing an item from the stack. Adding an item is called *pushing* the item onto the stack, and so we called the member function that does this push. Removing an item from a stack is called *popping* the item off the stack, and so we called the member function that does this pop.

DISPLAY 13.17 Interface File for a Stack Class *(part 1 of 2)*

```
1    //This is the header file stack.h. This is the interface for the class Stack,
2    //which is a class for a stack of symbols.
3    #ifndef STACK_H
4    #define STACK_H
5    namespace stacksavitch
6    {
7        struct StackFrame
8        {
9            char data;
10           StackFrame *link;
11       };

12       typedef StackFrame* StackFramePtr;

13       class Stack
14       {
15       public:
16           Stack( );
17           //Initializes the object to an empty stack.
18           Stack(const Stack& a_stack);
19           //Copy constructor.

20           ~Stack( );
21           //Destroys the stack and returns all the memory to the freestore.
```

(continued)

DISPLAY 13.17   Interface File for a Stack Class *(part 2 of 2)*

```
22              void push(char the_symbol);
23              //Postcondition: the_symbol has been added to the stack.

24              char pop( );
25              //Precondition: The stack is not empty.
26              //Returns the top symbol on the stack and removes that
27              //top symbol from the stack.

28              bool empty( ) const;
29              //Returns true if the stack is empty. Returns false otherwise.
30          private:
31              StackFramePtr top;
32          };
33      }//stacksavitch

34      #endif //STACK_H
```

The names push and pop derive from another way of visualizing a stack. A stack is analogous to a mechanism that is sometimes used to hold plates in a cafeteria. The mechanism stores plates in a hole in the countertop. There is a spring underneath the plates with its tension adjusted so that only the top plate protrudes above the countertop. If this sort of mechanism were used as a stack data structure, the data would be written on plates (which might violate some health laws, but still makes a good analogy). To add a plate to the stack, you put it on top of the other plates, and the weight of this new plate *pushes* down the spring. When you remove a plate, the plate below it *pops* into view.

Display 13.18 shows a simple program that illustrates how the Stack class is used. This program reads a word one letter at a time and places the letters in a stack. The program then removes the letters one by one and writes them to the screen. Because data is removed from a stack in the reverse of the order in which it enters the stack, the output shows the word written backward.

Application program

DISPLAY 13.18   Program Using the Stack Class *(part 1 of 2)*

```
1      //Program to demonstrate use of the Stack class.
2      #include <iostream>
3      #include "stack.h"
4      using namespace std;
5      using namespace stacksavitch;
6
7      int main( )
8      {
```

(continued)

DISPLAY 13.18 Program Using the Stack Class *(part 2 of 2)*

```
 9       stack s;
10       char next, ans;
11
12       do
13       {
14           cout << "Enter a word: ";
15           cin.get(next);
16           while (next != '\n')
17           {
18               s.push(next);
19               cin.get(next);
20           }
21
22           cout << "Written backward that is: ";
23           while ( ! s.empty( ) )
24           cout << s.pop( );
25           cout << endl;
26
27           cout << "Again?(y/n): ";
28           cin >> ans;
29           cin.ignore(10000, '\n');
30       } while (ans != 'n' && ans != 'N');
31
32       return 0;
33   }
```

<*The* ignore *member of* cin *is discussed in Chapter 8. It discards input remaining on the current input line up to 10,000 characters or until a return is entered. It also discards the return (*'\n'*) at the end of the line.*>

Sample Dialogue

```
Enter a word: straw
Written backward that is: warts
Again?(y/n): y
Enter a word: C++
Written backward that is: ++C
Again?(y/n): n
```

Implementation   As shown in Display 13.19, our Stack class is implemented as a linked list in which the head of the list serves as the top of the stack. The member variable top is a pointer that points to the head of the linked list.

DISPLAY 13.19   Implementation of the Stack **Class** *(part 1 of 2)*

```cpp
1    //This is the implementation file stack.cpp.
2    //This is the implementation of the class Stack.
3    //The interface for the class Stack is in the header file stack.h.
4    #include <iostream>
5    #include <cstddef>
6    #include "stack.h"
7    using namespace std;
8
9    namespace stacksavitch
10   {
11       //Uses cstddef:
12       Stack::Stack( ) : top(NULL)
13       {
14           //Body intentionally empty.
15       }
16
17       Stack::Stack(const Stack& a_stack)
```

         <The definition of the copy constructor is Self-Test Exercise 11.>

```cpp
18       Stack::~Stack( )
19       {
20           char next;
21           while (! empty( ))
22               next = pop( ); //pop calls delete.
23       }
24
25       //Uses cstddef:
26       bool Stack::empty( ) const
27       {
28           return (top == NULL);
29       }
30
31       void Stack::push(char the_symbol)
```

         <The rest of the definition is Self-Test Exercise 10.>

```cpp
32       //Uses iostream:
33       char Stack::pop( )
34       {
35           if (empty( ))
36           {
37               cout << "Error: popping an empty stack.\n";
38               exit(1);
39           }
40
```

(continued)

DISPLAY 13.19 **Implementation of the** Stack **Class** *(part 2 of 2)*

```
41              char result = top->data;
42
43              StackFramePtr temp_ptr;
44              temp_ptr = top;
45              top = top->link;
46
47              delete temp_ptr;
48
49              return result;
50          }
51      }//stacksavitch
```

Writing the definition of the member function push is Self-Test Exercise 10. However, we have already given the algorithm for this task. The code for the push member function is essentially the same as the function head_insert shown in Display 13.4, except that in the member function push we use a pointer named top in place of a pointer named head.

An empty stack is just an empty linked list, so an empty stack is implemented by setting the pointer top equal to NULL. Once you realize that NULL represents the empty stack, the implementations of the default constructor and of the member function empty are obvious.

The definition of the copy constructor is a bit complicated but does not use any techniques we have not already discussed. The details are left to Self-Test Exercise 11.

The pop member function first checks to see if the stack is empty. If the stack is not empty, it proceeds to remove the top character in the stack. It sets the local variable result equal to the top symbol on the stack. That is done as follows:

```
char result = top->data;
```

After the symbol in the top node is saved in the variable result, the pointer top is moved to the next node on the linked list, effectively removing the top node from the list. The pointer top is moved with the following statement:

```
top = top->link;
```

However, before the pointer top is moved, a temporary pointer, called temp_ptr, is positioned so that it points to the node that is about to be removed from the list. The node can then be removed with the following call to *delete*:

```
delete temp_ptr;
```

Each node that is removed from the linked list by the member function pop is destroyed with a call to *delete*. Thus, all that the destructor needs to do is remove each item from the stack with a call to pop. Each node will then have its memory returned to the freestore.

SELF-TEST EXERCISES

10. Give the definition of the member function push of the class Stack described in Display 13.17.

11. Give the definition of the copy constructor for the class Stack described in Display 13.17.

Queues

A stack is a last-in/first-out data structure. Another common data structure is a **queue,** which handles data in a first-in/first-out (FIFO) fashion. A queue behaves exactly the same as a line of people waiting for a bank teller or other service. The people are served in the order they enter the line (the queue). The operation of a queue is diagrammed in Display 13.20.

A queue can be implemented with a linked list in a manner that is similar to our implementation of the Stack class. However, a queue needs a pointer at both the head of the list and at the other the end of the linked list, since action takes place in both locations. It is easier to remove a node from the head of a linked list than from the other end of the linked list. So, our implementation will remove a node from the head of the list (which we will now call the **front** of the list) and we will add nodes to the other end of the list, which we will now call the **back** of the list (or the back of the queue).

Queue

A **queue** is a first-in/first-out data structure; that is, the data items are removed from the queue in the same order that they were added to the queue.

DISPLAY 13.20 A Queue

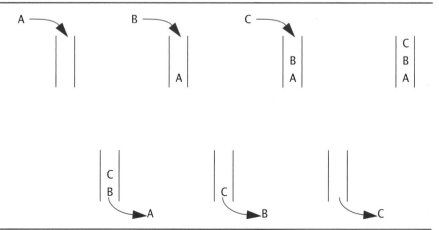

PROGRAMMING EXAMPLE	A Queue Class

The interface for our queue class is given in Display 13.21. This particular queue is used to store data of type *char*. You can define a similar queue to store data of any other type. There are two basic operations you can perform on a queue: adding an item to the end of the queue and removing an item from the front of the queue.

DISPLAY 13.21 Interface File for a Queue Class

```
1    //This is the header file queue.h. This is the interface for the class Queue,
2    //which is a class for a queue of symbols.
3    #ifndef QUEUE_H
4    #define QUEUE_H
5    namespace queuesavitch
6    {
7        struct QueueNode
8        {
9            char data;
10           QueueNode *link;
11       };
12       typedef QueueNode* QueueNodePtr;
13
14       class Queue
15       {
16       public:
17           Queue();
18           //Initializes the object to an empty queue.
19           Queue(const Queue& aQueue);
20           ~Queue();
21           void add(char item);
22           //Postcondition: item has been added to the back of the queue.
23           char remove();
24           //Precondition: The queue is not empty.
25           //Returns the item at the front of the queue and
26           //removes that item from the queue.
27           bool empty() const;
28           //Returns true if the queue is empty. Returns false otherwise.
29       private:
30           QueueNodePtr front; //Points to the head of a linked list.
31                               //Items are removed at the head
32           QueueNodePtr back;  //Points to the node at the other end of the
33                               //linked list. Items are added at this end.
34       };
35   }//queuesavitch
36   #endif //QUEUE_H
```

Display 13.22 shows a simple program that illustrates how the queue class is used. This program reads a word one letter at a time and places the letters in a queue. The program then removes the letters one by one and writes them to the screen. Because data is removed from a queue in the order in which it enters the queue, the output shows the letters in the word in the same order that the user entered them. It is good to contrast this application of a queue with a similar application using a stack that we gave in Display 13.18.

Application program

DISPLAY 13.22   **Program Using the Queue Class** *(part 1 of 2)*

```
1    //Program to demonstrate use of the Queue class.
2    #include <iostream>
3    #include "queue.h"
4    using namespace std;
5    using namespace queuesavitch;
6
7    int main()
8    {
9        Queue q;
10       char next, ans;
11
12       do
13       {
14           cout << "Enter a word: ";
15           cin.get(next);
16           while (next != '\n')
17           {
18               q.add(next);
19               cin.get(next);
20           }
21
22           cout << "You entered:: ";
23           while ( ! q.empty() )
24               cout << q.remove();
25           cout << endl;
26
27           cout << "Again?(y/n): ";
28           cin >> ans;
29           cin.ignore(10000, '\n');
30       } while (ans !='n' && ans != 'N');
31
32       return 0;
33   }
```

<*The* ignore *member of* cin *is discussed in Chapter 8. It discards input remaining on the current input line up to 10,000 characters or until a return is entered. It also discards the return (* '\n' *) at the end of the line.*>

(continued)

DISPLAY 13.22 Program Using the Queue Class *(part 2 of 2)*

Sample Dialogue

```
Enter a word: straw
You entered: straw
Again?(y/n): y
Enter a word: C++
You entered: C++
Again?(y/n): n
```

Implementation As shown in Displays 13.21 and 13.23, our queue class is implemented as a linked list in which the head of the list serves as the front of the queue. The member variable front is a pointer that points to the head of the linked list. Nodes are removed at the head of the linked list. The member variable back is a pointer that points to the node at the other end of the linked list. Nodes are added at this end of the linked list.

An empty queue is just an empty linked list, so an empty queue is implemented by setting the pointers front and back equal to NULL. The rest of the details of the implementation are similar to things we have seen before.

DISPLAY 13.23 Implementation of the Queue Class *(part 1 of 3)*

```
1    //This is the implementation file queue.cpp.
2    //This is the implementation of the class Queue.
3    //The interface for the class Queue is in the header file queue.h.
4    #include <iostream>
5    #include <cstdlib>
6    #include <cstddef>
7    #include "queue.h"
8    using namespace std;
9
10   namespace queuesavitch
11   {
12       //Uses cstddef:
13       Queue::Queue() : front(NULL), back(NULL)
14       {
15           //Intentionally empty.
16       }
17
18       Queue::Queue(const Queue& aQueue)
19               <The definition of the copy constructor is Self-Test Exercise 12.>
```

(continued)

DISPLAY 13.23   Implementation of the Queue Class *(part 2 of 3)*

```
20
21        Queue::~Queue()
22                  <The definition of the destructor is Self-Test Exercise 13.>
23
24        //Uses cstddef:
25        bool Queue::empty() const
26        {
27            return (back == NULL); //front == NULL would also work
28        }
29
30        //Uses cstddef:
31        void Queue::add(char item)
32        {
33            if (empty())
34            {
35                front = new QueueNode;
36                front->data = item;
37                front->link = NULL;
38                back = front;
39            }
40
41            else
42            {
43                QueueNodePtr temp_ptr;
44                temp_ptr = new QueueNode;
45                temp_ptr->data = item;
46                temp_ptr->link = NULL;
47                back->link = temp_ptr;
48                back = temp_ptr;
49            }
50        }
51
52        //Uses cstdlib and iostream:
53        char Queue::remove()
54        {
55            if (empty())
56            {
57                cout << "Error: Removing an item from an empty queue.\n";
58                exit(1);
59            }
60
61            char result = front->data;
62
63            QueueNodePtr discard;
64            discard = front;
65            front = front->link;
```

(continued)

DISPLAY 13.23 **Implementation of the Queue Class** *(part 3 of 3)*

```
66            if (front == NULL) //if you removed the last node
67                back = NULL;
68
69            delete discard;
70
71            return result;
72        }
73    }//queuesavitch
```

myprogramminglab

SELF-TEST EXERCISES

12. Give the definition of the copy constructor for the class Queue described in Display 13.21.

13. Give the definition of the destructor for the class Queue described in Display 13.21.

CHAPTER SUMMARY

■ A node is a *struct* or class object that has one or more member variables that are pointer variables. These nodes can be connected by their member pointer variables to produce data structures that can grow and shrink in size while your program is running.

■ A linked list is a list of nodes in which each node contains a pointer to the next node in the list.

■ The end of a linked list (or other linked data structure) is indicated by setting the pointer member variable equal to NULL.

■ A stack is a first-in/last-out data structure. A stack can be implemented using a linked list.

■ A queue is a first-in/first-out data structure. A queue can be implemented using a linked list.

Answers to Self-Test Exercises

```
1.    Sally
      Sally
      18
      18
```

Note that (*head).name and head->name mean the same thing. Similarly, (*head).number and head->number mean the same thing

2. The best answer is

```
head->next = NULL;
```

However, the following is also correct:

```
(*head).next = NULL;
```

3. *delete* head;

4. head->item = "Wilbur's brother Orville";

5.
```
struct NodeType
{
    char data;
    NodeType *link;
};

typedef NodeType* PointerType;
```

6. The pointer value NULL is used to indicate an empty list.

7. p1 = p1-> next;

8. Pointer discard;
```
discard = p2->next;
//discard now points to the node to be deleted.
p2->next = discard->next;
```

This is sufficient to delete the node from the linked list. However, if you are not using this node for something else, you should destroy the node with a call to *delete* as follows:

delete discard;

9. a. Inserting a new item at a known location into a large linked list is more efficient than inserting into a large array. If you are inserting into a list, you have about five operations, most of which are pointer assignments, regardless of the list size. If you insert into an array, on the average you have to move about half the array entries to insert a data item.

For small lists, the answer is (c), about the same.

10.
```
//Uses cstddef:
void Stack::push(char the_symbol)
{
    StackFramePtr temp_ptr;
    temp_ptr = new StackFrame;
```

```
            temp_ptr->data = the_symbol;

            temp_ptr->link = top;
            top = temp_ptr;
        }

11. //Uses cstddef:
    Stack::Stack(const Stack& a_stack)
    {
        if (a_stack.top == NULL)
            top = NULL;
        else
        {
            StackFramePtr temp = a_stack.top;//temp moves
                //through the nodes from top to bottom of
                //a_stack.
            StackFramePtr end;//Points to end of the new stack.

            end = new StackFrame;
            end->data = temp->data;
            top = end;
            //First node created and filled with data.
            //New nodes are now added AFTER this first node.

            temp = temp->link;
            while (temp != NULL)
            {
                end->link = new StackFrame;
                end = end->link;
                end->data = temp->data;
                temp = temp->link;
            }
            end->link = NULL;
        }
    }

12. //Uses cstddef:
    Queue::Queue(const Queue&aQueue)
    {
        if (aQueue.empty( ))
            front = back = NULL;
        else
        {
            QueueNodePtr temp_ptr_old = aQueue.front;
            //temp_ptr_old moves through the nodes
            //from front to back of aQueue.
            QueueNodePtr temp_ptr_new;
            //temp_ptr_new is used to create new nodes.

            back = new QueueNode;
            back->data = temp_ptr_old->data;
```

```
            back->link = NULL;
            front = back;
            //First node created and filled with data.
            //New nodes are now added AFTER this first node.

            temp_ptr_old = temp_ptr_old->link;
            //temp_ptr_old now points to second
            //node or NULL if there is no second node.

            while (temp_ptr_old != NULL)
            {
                temp_ptr_new = new QueueNode;
                temp_ptr_new->data = temp_ptr_old->data;
                temp_ptr_new->link = NULL;
                back->link = temp_ptr_new;
                back = temp_ptr_new;
                temp_ptr_old = temp_ptr_old->link;
            }
        }
    }
}

13. Queue::~Queue( )
    {
        char next;
        while (! empty( ))
            next = remove( );//remove calls delete.
    }
```

PROGRAMMING PROJECTS

Visit www.myprogramminglab.com to complete many of these Programming Projects `myprogramminglab`
online and get instant feedback.

1. Write a C++ program that contains a linked list and doubles the content of all data parts of each node. Each node of the linked list contains a data part of type *integer*. Note that your function will neither create nor destroy any nodes. It will simply update the content of the nodes. Also provide a mechanism to display the content of the linked list before and after updating the list. Place your function in a suitable test program.

2. Write a C++ program that implements a linked list. The linked list contains items of type *double*. The program contains some member functions which are as follows: a default constructor; a member function named delete_item to delete an item from the list; a test for an empty list that is a Boolean-valued function named empty( ); and a *friend* function overloading the insertion operator <<.

3. Design and implement a class whose objects represent polynomials. The polynomial

$$a_n x^n + a_{n-1} x^{n-1} + \ldots + a_0$$

will be implemented as a linked list. Each node will contain an *int* value for the power of x and an *int* value for the corresponding coefficient. The class operations should include addition, subtraction, multiplication, and evaluation of a polynomial. Overload the operators +, -, and * for addition, subtraction, and multiplication.

Evaluation of a polynomial is implemented as a member function with one argument of type *int*. The evaluation member function returns the value obtained by plugging in its argument for x and performing the indicated operations. Include four constructors: a default constructor, a copy constructor, a constructor with a single argument of type *int* that produces the polynomial that has only one constant term that is equal to the constructor argument, and a constructor with two arguments of type *int* that produces the one-term polynomial whose coefficient and exponent are given by the two arguments. (In the notation above, the polynomial produced by the one-argument constructor is of the simple form consisting of only a_0. The polynomial produced by the two-argument constructor is of the slightly more complicated form $a_n x^n$.) Include a suitable destructor. Include member functions to input and output polynomials.

When the user inputs a polynomial, the user types in the following:

a_nx^n + a_{n-1}x^n-1 + . . . + a_0

However, if a coefficient a_i is zero, the user may omit the term a_ix^i. For example, the polynomial

$$3x^4 + 7x^2 + 5$$

can be input as

3x^4 + 7x^2 + 5

It could also be input as

3x^4 + 0x^3 + 7x^2 + 0x^1 + 5

If a coefficient is negative, a minus sign is used in place of a plus sign, as in the following examples:

3x^5 - 7x^3 + 2x^1 - 8
-7x^4 + 5x^2 + 9

A minus sign at the front of the polynomial, as in the second of the two examples, applies only to the first coefficient; it does not negate the entire polynomial. Polynomials are output in the same format. In the case of output, the terms with zero coefficients are not output.

To simplify input, you can assume that polynomials are always entered one per line and that there will always be a constant term a_0. If there is no constant term, the user enters 0 for the constant term, as in the following:

```
12x^8 + 3x^2 + 0
```

4. In this project you will redo Programming Project 11 from Chapter 1 using a linked list instead of an array. As noted there, this is a linked list of *double* items. This fact may imply changes in some of the member functions. The members are as follows: a default constructor; a member function named add_item to add a *double* to the list; a test for a full list that is a Boolean-valued function named full( ); and a *friend* function overloading the insertion operator <<.

5. A harder version of Programming Project 4 would be to write a class named List, similar to Project 4, but with all the following member functions:

   ■ Default constructor, List();

   ■ *double* List::front();, which returns the first item in the list

   ■ *double* List::back();, which returns the last item in the list

   ■ *double* List::current();, which returns the "current" item

   ■ *void* List::advance();, which advances the item that current() returns

   ■ *void* List::reset(); to make current() return the first item in the list

   ■ *void* List::insert(*double* after_me, *double* insert_me);, which inserts insert_me into the list after after_me and increments the *private*: variable count.

   ■ *int* size();, which returns the number of items in the list

   ■ *friend* istream& *operator* <<(istream& ins, *double* write_me);

The private data members should include the following:

```
node* head;
node* current;
int count;
```

and possibly one more pointer.

You will need the following *struct* (outside the list class) for the linked list nodes:

```
struct node
{
    double item;
    node *next;
};
```

Incremental development is essential to all projects of any size, and this is no exception. Write the definition for the List class, but do not implement any members yet. Place this class definition in a file list.h. Then #include "list.h" in a file that contains int main(){}. Compile your file. This will find syntax errors and many typographical errors that would cause untold difficulty if you attempted to implement members without this check. Then you should implement and compile one member at a time, until you have enough to write test code in your main function.

VideoNote
Solution to Programming
Project 13.6

6. In an ancient land, the beautiful princess Eve had many suitors. She decided on the following procedure to determine which suitor she would marry. First, all of the suitors would be lined up one after the other and assigned numbers. The first suitor would be number 1, the second number 2, and so on up to the last suitor, number n. Starting at the first suitor she would then count three suitors down the line (because of the three letters in her name) and the third suitor would be eliminated from winning her hand and removed from the line. Eve would then continue, counting three more suitors, and eliminate every third suitor. When she reached the end of the line she would continue counting from the beginning.

For example, if there were six suitors then the elimination process would proceed as follows:

123456	initial list of suitors, start counting from 1
12456	suitor 3 eliminated, continue counting from 4
1245	suitor 6 eliminated, continue counting from 1
125	suitor 4 eliminated, continue counting from 5
15	suitor 2 eliminated, continue counting from 5
1	suitor 5 eliminated, 1 is the lucky winner

Write a program that creates a circular linked list of nodes to determine which position you should stand in to marry the princess if there are n suitors. A circular linked list is a linked list where the link field of the last node in the list refers to the node that is the head of the list. Your program should simulate the elimination process by deleting the node that corresponds to the suitor that is eliminated for each step in the process. Consider the possibility that you may need to delete the "head" node in the list.

7. Use a linked list to store the roll number and the computer assigned to each student in a computer laboratory in a college. Each node in the linked

list should contain a roll number and the computer number assigned. If nobody is assigned to a computer, then no entry should exist in the linked list for that computer station. Place your linked list in a suitable test program.

8. Modify or rewrite the Queue class (Display 13.21 through 13.23) to simulate customer arrivals at the Department of Motor Vehicles (DMV) counter. As customers arrive, they are given a ticket number starting at 1 and incrementing with each new customer. When a customer service agent is free, the customer with the next ticket number is called. This system results in a FIFO queue of customers ordered by ticket number. Write a program that implements the queue and simulates customers entering and leaving the queue. Input into the queue should be the ticket number and a timestamp when the ticket was entered into the queue. A ticket and its corresponding timestamp is removed when a customer service agent handles the next customer. Your program should save the length of time the last three customers spent waiting in the queue. Every time a ticket is removed from the queue, update these times and output the average of the last three customers as an estimate of how long it will take until the next customer is handled. If nobody is in the queue, output that the line is empty.

Code to compute a timestamp based on the computer's clock is given below. The time(NULL) function returns the number of seconds since January 1, 1970, on most implementations of C++:

```
#include <ctime>
...
int main()
{
    long seconds;
    seconds = static_cast<long>(time(NULL));
    cout << "Seconds since 1/1/1970: " << seconds << endl;
    return 0;
}
```
Sample execution is shown here:
```
The line is empty.
Enter '1' to simulate a customer's arrival, '2' to help the
next customer, or '3' to quit.
1
Customer 1 entered the queue at time 100000044.
Enter '1' to simulate a customer's arrival, '2' to help the
next customer, or '3' to quit.
1
Customer 2 entered the queue at time 100000049.
Enter '1' to simulate a customer's arrival, '2' to help the
next customer, or '3' to quit.
1
```

```
Customer 3 entered the queue at time 100000055.
Enter '1' to simulate a customer's arrival, '2' to help the
next customer, or '3' to quit.
2
Customer 1 is being helped at time 100000069. Wait time = 25
seconds.
The estimated wait time for customer 2 is 25 seconds.
Enter '1' to simulate a customer's arrival, '2' to help the
next customer, or '3' to quit.
2
Customer 2 is being helped at time 100000076. Wait time = 27
seconds.
The estimated wait time for customer 3 is 26 seconds.
Enter '1' to simulate a customer's arrival, '2' to help the
next customer, or '3' to quit.
1
Customer 4 entered the queue at time 100000080.
Enter '1' to simulate a customer's arrival, '2' to help the
next customer, or '3' to quit.
2
Customer 3 is being helped at time 100000099. Wait time = 44
seconds.
The estimated wait time for customer 4 is 32 seconds.
```

VideoNote
Solution to Programming
Project 13.9

9. The following figure is called a *graph*. The circles are called *nodes*, and the lines are called *edges*. An edge connects two nodes. You can interpret the graph as a maze of rooms and passages. The nodes can be thought of as rooms, and an edge connects one room to another. Note that each node has at most four edges in the graph.

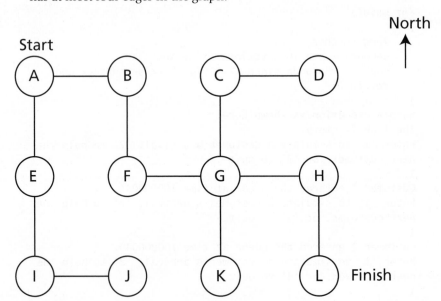

Write a program that implements the maze using nodes and pointers. Each node in the graph will correspond to a node in your code that is implemented in the form of a class or struct. The edges correspond to bidirectional links that point from one node to another. Start the user in node A. The user's goal is to reach the finish in node L. The program should output possible moves in the north, south, east, or west direction. Sample execution is shown here.

```
You are in room A of a maze of twisty little passages, all alike.
You can go (E)ast, (S)outh, or (Q)uit.
E
You are in room B of a maze of twisty little passages, all alike.
You can go (W)est, (S)outh, or (Q)uit.
S
You are in room F of a maze of twisty little passages, all alike.
You can go (E)ast, (N)orth, or (Q)uit.
E
```

10. Reverse Polish Notation (RPN), or postfix notation, is a format to specify mathematical expressions. In RPN, the operator comes after the operands instead of the normal format in which the operator is between the operands (this is called *infix* notation). Starting with an empty stack, a RPN calculator can be implemented with the following rules:

   ■ If a number is input, push it on the stack.

   ■ If "+" is input, then pop the last two operands off the stack, add them, and push the result on the stack.

   ■ If "-" is input then pop value1, pop value2, then push value2-value1 on the stack.

   ■ If "*" is input, then pop the last two operands off the stack, multiply them, and push the result on the stack

   ■ If "/" is input them pop value1, pop value2, then push value2/value1 on the stack

   ■ If "q" is input, then stop inputting values, print out the top of the stack, and exit the program

   Modify the Stack class given in Section 13.2 to store integers instead of characters. Use the modified stack to implement a RPN calculator. Output an appropriate error message if there are not two operands on the stack when given an operator. Here is a sample input and output that is equivalent to ((10 - (2 + 3)) * 2)/5:

```
10
2
3
+
```

(continued)

```
-
2
*
5
/
q
The top of the stack is:  2
```

11. You should complete the Programming Project 10 before attempting this one. Write a program that converts a fully parenthesized mathematical infix expression into an equivalent postfix expression and then evaluates the postfix expression. A fully parenthesized expression is one in which parentheses surround every operator and its operands. Starting with an empty stack of strings to store operators and an empty queue of strings to store the postfix expression, the conversion can be implemented with the following rules:

   ■ If "(" is input, then ignore it.
   ■ If a number is input, then add it to the queue.
   ■ If an operator (either "*", "+", "-", or "/") is input, then push it on the stack.
   ■ If ")" is input, then pop the operator from the stack and add it to the queue.
   ■ If "q" is input, then exit.

   When the final operator is popped from the stack, the queue contains the equivalent postfix expression. Use your solution from Programming Project 10 to evaluate it. You will need to convert a string object to an integer. Use the c_str() function to convert the string to a C string, and then use the atoi function to convert the C string into an integer. Refer to Chapter 8 for details.

   Sample output is shown below for ((10 - (2 + 3)) * 2), which translates to the postfix expression 10 2 3 + - 2 *:

```
(
(
10
-
(
2
+
3
)
)
*
2
)
q
The expression evaluates to 10
```

Recursion 14

After a lecture on cosmology and the structure of the solar system, William James was accosted by a little old lady.

"Your theory that the sun is the center of the solar system, and the earth is a ball which rotates around it has a very convincing ring to it, Mr. James, but it's wrong. I've got a better theory," said the little old lady.

"And what is that, madam?" inquired James politely.

"That we live on a crust of earth which is on the back of a giant turtle."

Not wishing to demolish this absurd little theory by bringing to bear the masses of scientific evidence he had at his command, James decided to gently dissuade his opponent by making her see some of the inadequacies of her position.

"If your theory is correct, madam," he asked, "what does this turtle stand on?"

"You're a very clever man, Mr. James, and that's a very good question," replied the little old lady, "but I have an answer to it. And it is this: the first turtle stands on the back of a second, far larger, turtle, who stands directly under him."

"But what does this second turtle stand on?" persisted James patiently.

To this the little old lady crowed triumphantly. "It's no use, Mr. James—it's turtles all the way down."

J. R. ROSS, *Constraints on Variables in Syntax*

INTRODUCTION

You have encountered a few cases of circular definitions that worked out satisfactorily. The most prominent examples are the definitions of certain C++ statements. For example, the definition of a *while* statement says that it can contain other (smaller) statements. Since one of the possibilities for these smaller statements is another *while* statement, there is a kind of circularity in that definition. The definition of the *while* statement, if written out in complete detail, will contain a reference to *while* statements. In mathematics, this kind of circular definition is called a recursive definition. In C++, a function may be defined in terms of itself in the same way. To put it more precisely, a function definition may contain a call to itself. In such cases, the function is said to be recursive. This chapter discusses recursion in C++ and more generally discusses recursion as a programming and problem-solving technique.

PREREQUISITES

Sections 14.1 and 14.2 use material only from Chapters 2 through 5. Section 14.3 uses material from Chapters 2 through 7 and 10.

14.1 RECURSIVE FUNCTIONS FOR TASKS

I remembered too that night which is at the middle of the Thousand and One Nights when Scheherazade (through a magical oversight of the copyist) begins to relate word for word the story of the Thousand and One Nights, establishing the risk of coming once again to the night when she must repeat it, and thus to infinity.

JORGE LUIS BORGES, *The Garden of Forking Paths*

When you are writing a function to solve a task, one basic design technique is to break the task into subtasks. Sometimes it turns out that at least one of the subtasks is a smaller example of the same task. For example, if the task is to search an array for a particular value, you might divide this into the subtask of searching the first half of the array and the subtask of searching the second half of the array. The subtasks of searching the halves of the array are "smaller" versions of the original task. Whenever one subtask is a smaller version of the original task to be accomplished, you can solve the original task using a recursive function. It takes a little training to easily decompose problems this way, but once you learn the technique, it can be one of the quickest ways to design an algorithm, and, ultimately, a C++ function. We begin with a simple case study to illustrate this technique.

Recursion

In C++, a function definition may contain a call to the function being defined. In such cases, the function is said to be **recursive.**

CASE STUDY   Vertical Numbers

In this case study we design a recursive *void* function that writes numbers to the screen with the digits written vertically, so that, for example, 1984 would be written as

```
1
9
8
4
```

Problem Definition

The declaration and header comment for our function is as follows:

```
void write_vertical(int n);
//Precondition: n >= 0.
//Postcondition: The number n is written to the screen
//vertically with each digit on a separate line.
```

Algorithm Design

One case is very simple. If n, the number to be written out, is only one digit long, then just write out the number. As simple as it is, this case is still important, so let's keep track of it.

Simple Case: If n < 10, then write the number n to the screen.

Now let's consider the more typical case in which the number to be written out consists of more than one digit. Suppose you want to write the number 1234 vertically so that the result is

One way to decompose this task into two subtasks is the following:

1. Output all the digits except the last digit like so:

```
1
2
3
```

2. Output the last digit, which in this example is 4.

Subtask 1 is a smaller version of the original task, so we can implement this subtask with a recursive call. Subtask 2 is just the simple case we listed earlier. Thus, an outline of our algorithm for the function write_vertical with parameter n is given by the following pseudocode:

```
if (n < 10)
{
    cout << n << endl;
}
else //n is two or more digits long:
{
    write_vertical(the number n with the last digit removed);
    cout << the last digit of n << endl;
}
```

Recursive subtask

In order to convert this pseudocode into the code for a C++ function, all we need to do is translate the following two pieces of pseudocode into C++ expressions:

the number n with the last digit removed

and

the last digit of n

These expressions can easily be translated into C++ expressions using the integer division operators / and % as follows:

```
n / 10 //the number n with the last digit removed
n % 10 //the last digit of n
```

For example, 1234 / 10 evaluates to 123, and 1234 % 10 evaluates to 4.

Several factors influenced our selection of the two subtasks we used in this algorithm. One was that we could easily compute the argument for the recursive call to write_vertical (shown in color) that we used in the pseudocode. The number n with the last digit removed is easily computed as n/10. As an alternative, you might have been tempted to divide the subtasks as follows:

1. Output the first digit of n.

2. Output the number n with the first digit removed.

This is a perfectly valid decomposition of the task into subtasks, and it can be implemented recursively. However, it is difficult to calculate the result of removing the first digit from a number, while it is easy to calculate the result of removing the last digit from a number.

Another reason for choosing these sorts of decompositions is that one of the subcases does not involve a recursive call. A successful definition of a recursive function always includes at least one case that does not involve a recursive call (as well as one or more cases that do involve at least one recursive call). This aspect of the recursive algorithm is discussed in the subsections that follow this case study.

Coding

We can now put all the pieces together to produce the recursive function write_vertical shown in Display 14.1. In the next subsection we will explain more details of how recursion works in this example.

DISPLAY 14.1 A Recursive Output Function *(part 1 of 2)*

```
1    //Program to demonstrate the recursive function write_vertical.
2    #include <iostream>
3    using namespace std;
4
5    void write_vertical(int n);
6    //Precondition: n >= 0.
7    //Postcondition: The number n is written to the screen vertically
8    //with each digit on a separate line.
9
10   int main( )
11   {
12       cout<< "write_vertical(3):" <<endl;
13       write_vertical(3);
14
```

(continued)

DISPLAY 14.1   A Recursive Output Function *(part 2 of 2)*

```
15        cout<< "write_vertical(12):" <<endl;
16        write_vertical(12);
17
18        cout<< "write_vertical(123):" <<endl;
19        write_vertical(123);
20
21        return 0;
22    }
23
24    //uses iostream:
25    void write_vertical(int n)
26    {
27        if (n < 10)
28        {
29            cout << n << endl;
30        }
31        else //n is two or more digits long:
32        {
33            write_vertical(n / 10);
34            cout << (n % 10) << endl;
35        }
36    }
```

Sample Dialogue

```
write_vertical(3):
3
write_vertical(12):
1
2
write_vertical(123):
1
2
3
```

Tracing a Recursive Call

Let's see exactly what happens when the following function call is made:

```
write_vertical(123);
```

When this function call is executed, the computer proceeds just as it would with any function call. The argument 123 is substituted for the parameter n in the function definition, and the body of the function is executed. After the substitution of 123 for n, the code to be executed is as follows:

```
if (123 < 10)
{
    cout << 123 << endl;
}
else //n is two or more digits long:
{
    write_vertical(123 / 10);  ◄──────  Computation will
    cout << (123 % 10) << endl;         stop here until the
}                                       recursive call returns.
```

Since 123 is not less than 10, the logical expression in the *if-else* statement is *false*, so the *else* part is executed. However, the *else* part begins with the following function call:

```
write_vertical(n / 10);
```

which (since n is equal to 123) is the call

```
write_vertical(123 / 10);
```

which is equivalent to

```
write_vertical(12);
```

When execution reaches this recursive call, the current function computation is placed in suspended animation and this recursive call is executed. When this recursive call is finished, the execution of the suspended computation will return to this point, and the suspended computation will continue from this point.

The recursive call

```
write_vertical(12);
```

is handled just like any other function call. The argument 12 is substituted for the parameter n and the body of the function is executed. After substituting 12 for n, there are two computations, one suspended and one active, as follows:

```
if (123 < 10)
{
    cou      if (12 < 10)
}        {
else //        cout << 12 << endl;
{        }
    wri      else //n is two or more digits long:
    cou      {
}                write_vertical(12 / 10); ◄── Computation will stop
                 cout << (12 % 10) << endl;   here until the recursive
             }                                call returns.
```

Since 12 is not less than 10, the Boolean expression in the *if-else* statement is *false* and so the *else* part is executed. However, as you already saw, the *else* part begins with a recursive call. The argument for the recursive call is n / 10, which in this case is equivalent to 12 / 10. So this second computation of the function write_vertical is suspended and the following recursive call is executed:

```
write_vertical(12/ 10);
```

which is equivalent to

```
write_vertical(1);
```

At this point there are two suspended computations waiting to resume and the computer begins to execute this new recursive call, which is handled just like all the previous recursive calls. The argument 1 is substituted for the parameter n, and the body of the function is executed. At this point, the computation looks like the following:

```
if (123 < 10)
{
}
el
{

}            if (12 < 10)
             {

             }            if (1 < 10)
             e             {
             {                 cout << 1 << endl;            No recursive call
             }                                              this time
             }            else //n is two or more digits long:
                          {
                              write_vertical(1 / 10);
                              cout << (1 % 10) << endl;
                          }
```

Output the digit 1   When the body of the function is executed this time, something different happens. Since 1 is less than 10, the Boolean expression in the *if-else* statement is *true*, so the statement before the *else* is executed. That statement is simply a cout statement that writes the argument 1 to the screen, and so the call write_vertical(1) writes 1 to the screen and ends without any recursive call.

When the call write_vertical(1) ends, the suspended computation that is waiting for it to end resumes where that suspended computation left off, as shown by the following:

```
if (123 < 10)
{
}
el
{          if (12 < 10)
           {
}              cout << 12 << endl;
           }
           else //n is two or more digits long:
           {
               write_vertical(12 / 10);            Computation
               cout << (12 % 10) << endl;          resumes here.
           }
```

When this suspended computation resumes, it executes a `cout` statement that outputs the value 12 % 10, which is 2. That ends that computation, but there is yet another suspended computation waiting to resume. When this last suspended computation resumes, the situation is as follows:

```
if (123 < 10)
{
    cout << 123 << endl;
}
else //n is two or more digits long:
{
    write_vertical(123 / 10);
    cout << (123 % 10) << endl;  ← Computation
                                    resumes here.
}
```

When this last suspended computation resumes, it outputs the value 123 % 10, which is 3, and the execution of the original function call ends. And, sure enough, the digits 1, 2, and 3 have been written to the screen one per line, in that order.

A Closer Look at Recursion

The definition of the function `write_vertical` uses recursion. Yet we did nothing new or different in evaluating the function call `write_vertical(123)`. We treated it just like any of the function calls we saw in previous chapters. We just substituted the argument 123 for the parameter `n` and then executed the code in the body of the function definition. When we reached the recursive call

```
write_vertical(123 / 10);
```

we simply repeated this process one more time.

The computer keeps track of recursive calls in the following way. When a function is called, the computer plugs in the arguments for the parameter(s) and begins to execute the code. If it should encounter a recursive call, then it temporarily stops its computation. This is because it must know the result of the recursive call before it can proceed. It saves all the information it needs to continue the computation later on and proceeds to evaluate the recursive call. When the recursive call is completed, the computer returns to finish the outer computation.

The C++ language places no restrictions on how recursive calls are used in function definitions. However, in order for a recursive function definition to be useful, it must be designed so that any call of the function must ultimately terminate with some piece of code that does not depend on recursion. The function may call itself, and that recursive call may call the function again.

The process may be repeated any number of times. However, the process will not terminate unless eventually one of the recursive calls does not depend on recursion. The general outline of a successful recursive function definition is as follows:

- One or more cases in which the function accomplishes its task by using recursive calls to accomplish one or more smaller versions of the task.
- One or more cases in which the function accomplishes its task without the use of any recursive calls. These cases without any recursive calls are called **base cases** or **stopping cases.**

Often, an *if-else* statement determines which of the cases will be executed. A typical scenario is for the original function call to execute a case that includes a recursive call. That recursive call may in turn execute a case that requires another recursive call. For some number of times each recursive call produces another recursive call, but eventually one of the stopping cases should apply. *Every call of the function must eventually lead to a stopping case, or else the function call will never end because of an infinite chain of recursive calls.* (In practice, a call that includes an infinite chain of recursive calls will usually terminate abnormally rather than actually running forever.)

The most common way to ensure that a stopping case is eventually reached is to write the function so that some (positive) numeric quantity is decreased on each recursive call and to provide a stopping case for some "small" value. This is how we designed the function write_vertical in Display 14.1. When the function write_vertical is called, that call produces a recursive call with a smaller argument. This continues with each recursive call producing another recursive call until the argument is less than 10. When the argument is less than 10, the function call ends without producing any more recursive calls and the process works its way back to the original call and then ends.

General Form of a Recursive Function Definition

The general outline of a successful recursive function definition is as follows:

- One or more cases that include one or more recursive calls to the function being defined. These recursive calls should solve "smaller" versions of the task performed by the function being defined.

- One or more cases that include no recursive calls. These cases without any recursive calls are called **base cases** or **stopping cases.**

PITFALL   Infinite Recursion

In the example of the function write_vertical discussed in the previous subsections, the series of recursive calls eventually reached a call of the function that did not involve recursion (that is, a stopping case was reached). If, on the other hand, every recursive call produces another recursive call, then a call to the function will, in theory, run forever. This is called **infinite recursion.** In practice, such a function will typically run until the computer runs out of resources and the program terminates abnormally. Phrased another way, a recursive definition should not be "recursive all the way down." Otherwise, like the lady's explanation of the universe given at the start of this chapter, a call to the function will never end, except perhaps in frustration.

Examples of infinite recursion are not hard to come by. The following is a syntactically correct C++ function definition, which might result from an attempt to define an alternative version of the function write_vertical:

```
void new_write_vertical(int n)
{
    new_write_vertical(n / 10);
    cout << (n % 10) << endl;
}
```

If you embed this definition in a program that calls this function, the compiler will translate the function definition to machine code and you can execute the machine code. Moreover, the definition even has a certain reasonableness to it. It says that to output the argument to new_write_vertical, first output all but the last digit and then output the last digit. However, when called, this function will produce an infinite sequence of recursive calls. If you call new_write_vertical(12), that execution will stop to execute the recursive call new_write_vertical (12/10), which is equivalent to new_write_vertical(1). The execution of that recursive call will, in turn, stop to execute the recursive call

```
new_write_vertical(1/10);
```

which is equivalent to

```
new_write_vertical(0);
```

That, in turn, will stop to execute the recursive call new_write_vertical (0/10); which is also equivalent to

```
new_write_vertical(0);
```

and that will produce another recursive call to again execute the same recursive function call new_write_vertical(0); and so on, forever. Since the definition of new_write_vertical has no stopping case, the process will proceed forever (or until the computer runs out of resources). ∎

myprogramminglab

SELF-TEST EXERCISES

1. What is the output of the following program?

```
#include <iostream>
using namespace std;
void cheers(int n);

int main()
{
    cheers(3);
    return 0;
}

void cheers(int n)
{
if (n == 1)
{
        cout << "Hurray\n";
}
else
{
        cout << "Hip ";
        cheers(n - 1);
    }
}
```

2. Write a recursive *void* function that has one parameter which is a positive integer and that writes out that number of asterisks '*' to the screen all on one line.

3. Write a recursive *void* function that has one parameter, which is a positive integer. When called, the function writes its argument to the screen backward. That is, if the argument is 1234, it outputs the following to the screen:

   4321

4. Write a recursive *void* function that takes a single *int* argument n and writes the integers 1, 2, . . ., n.

5. Write a recursive *void* function that takes a single *int* argument n and writes integers n, n-1, . . ., 3, 2, 1. (*Hint:* Notice that you can get from the code for Self-Test Exercise 4 to that for Self-Test Exercise 5, or vice versa, by an exchange of as little as two lines.)

Stacks for Recursion

In order to keep track of recursion, and a number of other things, most computer systems make use of a structure called a *stack*. A **stack** is a very specialized kind of memory structure that is analogous to a stack of paper. In this analogy there is an inexhaustible supply of extra blank sheets of paper. To place some information in the stack, it is written on one of these sheets of paper and placed on top of the stack of papers. To place more information in the stack, a clean sheet of paper is taken, the information is written on it, and this new sheet of paper is placed on top of the stack. In this straightforward way, more and more information may be placed on the stack.

Getting information out of the stack is also accomplished by a very simple procedure. The top sheet of paper can be read, and when it is no longer needed, it is thrown away. There is one complication: Only the top sheet of paper is accessible. In order to read, say, the third sheet from the top, the top two sheets must be thrown away. Since the last sheet that is put on the stack is the first sheet taken off the stack, a stack is often called a **last-in/first-out (LIFO)** memory structure.

Using a stack, the computer can easily keep track of recursion. Whenever a function is called, a new sheet of paper is taken. The function definition is copied onto this sheet of paper, and the arguments are plugged in for the function parameters. Then the computer starts to execute the body of the function definition. When it encounters a recursive call, it stops the computation it is doing on that sheet in order to compute the recursive call. But before computing the recursive call, it saves enough information so that, when it does finally complete the recursive call, it can continue the stopped computation. This saved information is written on a sheet of paper and placed on the stack. A new sheet of paper is used for the recursive call. The computer writes a second copy of the function definition on this new sheet of paper, plugs in the arguments for the function parameters, and starts to execute the recursive call. When it gets to a recursive call within the recursively called copy, it repeats the process of saving information on the stack and using a new sheet of paper for the new recursive call. This process is illustrated in the earlier subsection entitled "Tracing a Recursive Call." Even though we did not call it a stack in that section, the illustrations of computations placed one on top of the other demonstrate the actions of the stack.

VideoNote
Recursion and the Stack

This process continues until some recursive call to the function completes its computation without producing any more recursive calls. When that happens, the computer turns its attention to the top sheet of paper on the stack. This sheet contains the partially completed computation that is waiting for the recursive computation that just ended. So, it is possible to proceed with that suspended computation. When that suspended computation ends, the computer discards that sheet of paper, and the suspended computation that is below it on the stack becomes the computation on top of the stack. The computer turns its attention to the suspended computation that is now on the top of the stack, and so forth. The process continues until the computation on the bottom sheet is completed. Depending on how many recursive calls are made and how the function definition is written, the stack may grow and shrink in any fashion. Notice that the sheets in the stack can only be accessed in a last-in/first-out fashion, but that is exactly what is needed to keep track of recursive calls. Each suspended version is waiting for the completion of the version directly above it on the stack.

Needless to say, computers do not have stacks of paper of this kind. This is just an analogy. The computer uses portions of memory rather than pieces of paper. The contents of one of these portions of memory ("sheets of paper") is called an **activation frame.** These activation frames are handled in the last-in/first-out manner we just discussed. (The activation frames do not contain a complete copy of the function definition, but merely reference a single copy of the function definition. However, an activation frame contains enough information to allow the computer to act as if the frame contained a complete copy of the function definition.)

Stack

A **stack** is a *last-in/first-out* memory structure. The first item referenced or removed from a stack is always the last item entered into the stack. Stacks are used by computers to keep track of recursion (and for other purposes).

PITFALL   Stack Overflow

There is always some limit to the size of the stack. If there is a long chain in which a function makes a recursive call to itself, and that call results in another recursive call, and that call produces yet another recursive call, and so forth, then each recursive call in this chain will cause another activation frame to be placed on the stack. If this chain is too long, then the stack will attempt to grow beyond its limit. This is an error condition known as a **stack overflow.** If you receive an error message that says *stack overflow*, it is likely that some function call has produced an excessively long chain of recursive calls. One common cause of stack overflow is infinite recursion. If a function is recursing infinitely, then it will eventually try to make the stack exceed any stack size limit. ∎

Recursion Versus Iteration

Recursion is not absolutely necessary. In fact, some programming languages do not allow it. Any task that can be accomplished using recursion can also be done in some other way without using recursion. For example, Display 14.2 contains a nonrecursive version of the function given in Display 14.1. The nonrecursive version of a function typically uses a loop (or loops) of some sort in place of recursion. For that reason, the nonrecursive version is usually referred to as an **iterative version.** If the definition of the function write_vertical given in Display 14.1 is replaced by the version given in Display 14.2, then the output will be the same. As is true in this case, a recursive version of a function can sometimes be much simpler than an iterative version.

DISPLAY 14.2   Iterative Version of the Function in Display 14.1

```
1    //Uses iostream:
2    void write_vertical(int n)
3    {
4        int tens_in_n = 1;
5        int left_end_piece = n;
6        while (left_end_piece> 9)
7        {
8            left_end_piece = left_end_piece/10;
9            tens_in_n = tens_in_n * 10;
10       }
11       //tens_in_n is a power of ten that has the same number
12       //of digits as n. For example, if n is 2345, then
13       //tens_in_n is 1000.
14
15       for (int power_of_10 = tens_in_n;
16            power_of_10 > 0; power_of_10 = power_of_10/10)
17       {
18           cout << (n/power_of_10) <<endl;
19           n = n % power_of_10;
20       }
21   }
```

A recursively written function will usually run slower and use more storage than an equivalent iterative version. Although the iterative version of write_vertical given in Display 14.2 looks like it uses more storage and does more computing than the recursive version in Display 14.1, the two versions of write_vertical actually use comparable storage and do comparable amounts of computing. In fact, the recursive version may use more storage and run somewhat slower, because the computer must do a good deal of work manipulating the stack in order to keep track of the recursion. However, since the system does all this for you automatically, using recursion can sometimes make your job as a programmer easier and can sometimes produce code that is easier to understand. As you will see in the examples in this chapter and in the Self-Test Exercises and Programming Projects, sometimes a recursive definition is simpler and clearer; other times, an iterative definition is simpler and clearer.

SELF-TEST EXERCISES

myprogramminglab

6. If your program produces an error message that says *stack overflow*, what is a likely source of the error?

7. Write an iterative version of the function *cheers* defined in Self-Test Exercise 1.

8. Write an iterative version of the function defined in Self-Test Exercise 2.

9. Write an iterative version of the function defined in Self-Test Exercise 3.

10. Trace the recursive solution you made to Self-Test Exercise 4.

11. Trace the recursive solution you made to Self-Test Exercise 5.

14.2 RECURSIVE FUNCTIONS FOR VALUES

To iterate is human, to recurse divine.

ANONYMOUS

General Form for a Recursive Function That Returns a Value

The recursive functions you have seen thus far are all *void* functions, but recursion is not limited to *void* functions. A recursive function can return a value of any type. The technique for designing recursive functions that return a value is basically the same as for *void* functions. An outline for a successful recursive function definition that returns a value is as follows.

- One or more cases in which the value returned is computed in terms of calls to the same function (that is, using recursive calls). As was the case with *void* functions, the arguments for the recursive calls should intuitively be "smaller."
- One or more cases in which the value returned is computed without the use of any recursive calls. These cases without any recursive calls are called **base cases** or **stopping cases** (just as they were with *void* functions).

This technique is illustrated in the next Programming Example.

| **PROGRAMMING EXAMPLE** | Another Powers Function |

In Chapter 4 we introduced the predefined function pow that computes powers. For example, pow(2.0,3.0) returns $2.0^{3.0}$, so the following sets the variable x equal to 8.0:

```
double x = pow(2.0, 3.0);
```

The function pow takes two arguments of type *double* and returns a value of type *double*. Display 14.3 contains a recursive definition for a function that is similar but that works with the type *int* rather than *double*. This new function is called power. For example, the following will set the value of y equal to 8, since 2^3 is 8:

```
int y = power(2, 3);
```

DISPLAY 14.3   The Recursive Function power

```
1    //Program to demonstrate the recursive function power.
2    #include <iostream>
3    #include <cstdlib>
4    using namespace std;

5    int power(int x, int n);
6    //Precondition: n > = 0.
7    //Returns x to the power n.

8    int main( )
9    {
10       for (int n = 0; n < 4; n++)
11           cout << "3 to the power " << n
12                   << " is " << power(3, n) << endl;

13       return 0;
14   }

15   //uses iostream and cstdlib:
16   int power(int x, int n)
17   {
18       if (n < 0)
19       {
20           cout << "Illegal argument to power.\n";
21           exit(1);
22       }

23       if (n > 0)
24           return ( power(x, n - 1) * x);
25       else // n == 0
26           return (1);
27   }
```

Sample Dialogue

```
3 to the power 0 is 1
3 to the power 1 is 3
3 to the power 2 is 9
3 to the power 3 is 27
```

Our main reason for defining the function power is to have a simple example of a recursive function, but there are situations in which the function power would be preferable to the function pow. The function pow returns values of type *double*, which are only approximate quantities. The function power returns values of type *int*, which are exact quantities. In some situations, you might need the additional accuracy provided by the function power.

The definition of the function power is based on the following formula:

x^n is equal to $x^{n-1} * x$

Translating this formula into C++ says that the value returned by power(x,n) should be the same as the value of the expression

```
power(x, n - 1) * x
```

The definition of the function power given in Display 14.3 does return this value for power(x, n), provided n > 0. The case where n is equal to 0 is the stopping case. If n is 0, then power(x,n) simply returns 1 (since x^0 is 1).

Let's see what happens when the function power is called with some sample values. First consider the following simple expression:

```
power(2, 0)
```

When the function is called, the value of x is set equal to 2, the value of n is set equal to 0, and the code in the body of the function definition is executed. Since the value of n is a legal value, the *if-else* statement is executed. Since this value of n is not greater than 0, the *return* statement after the *else* is used, so the function call returns 1. Thus, the following would set the value of y equal to 1:

```
int y = power(2, 0);
```

Now let's look at an example that involves a recursive call. Consider the expression

```
power(2, 1)
```

When the function is called, the value of x is set equal to 2, the value of n is set equal to 1, and the code in the body of the function definition is executed. Since this value of n is greater than 0, the following *return* statement is used to determine the value returned:

```
return ( power(x, n - 1) * x );
```

which in this case is equivalent to

```
return ( power(2, 0) * 2 );
```

At this point the computation of power(2,1) is suspended, a copy of this suspended computation is placed on the stack, and the computer then starts a new function call to compute the value of power(2,0). As you have already seen, the value of power(2,0) is 1. After determining the value of power(2,0), the computer replaces the expression power(2,0) with its value of 1 and resumes the suspended computation. The resumed computation determines the final value for power(2,1) from the *return* statement above as follows:

```
power(2, 0) * 2 is 1 * 2, which is 2.
```

Thus, the final value returned for power(2,1) is 2. The following would therefore set the value of z equal to 2:

```
int z = power(2, 1);
```

Larger numbers for the second argument will produce longer chains of recursive calls. For example, consider the statement

```
cout << power(2, 3);
```

The value of power(2, 3) is calculated as follows:

```
power(2, 3) is power(2, 2) * 2
power(2, 2) is power(2, 1) * 2
power(2, 1) is power(2, 0) * 2
power(2, 0) is 1 (stopping case)
```

When the computer reaches the stopping case, power(2,0), there are three suspended computations. After calculating the value returned for the stopping case, it resumes the most recently suspended computation to determine the value of power(2,1). After that, the computer completes each of the other suspended computations, using each value computed as a value to plug into another suspended computation, until it reaches and completes the computation for the original call, power(2,3). The details of the entire computation are illustrated in Display 14.4.

DISPLAY 14.4 Evaluating the Recursive Function Call *power (2, 3)*

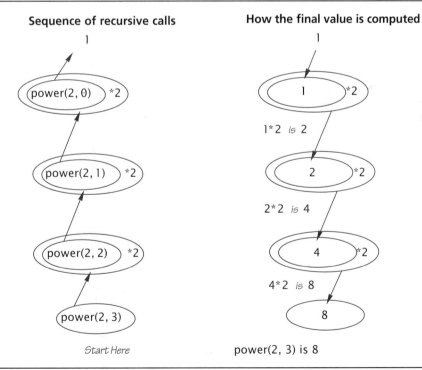

Sequence of recursive calls

How the final value is computed

Start Here

power(2, 3) is 8

SELF-TEST EXERCISES

12. What is the output of the following program?

```cpp
#include <iostream>
using namespace std;
int mystery(int n);
//Precondition n > = 1.

int main()
{
    cout << mystery(3);
    return 0;
}
int mystery(int n)
{
    if (n < = 1)
        return 1;
    else
        return ( mystery(n - 1) + n );
}
```

13. What is the output of the following program? What well-known mathematical function is rose?

```cpp
#include <iostream>
using namespace std;
int rose(int n);
//Precondition: n >= 0.

int main()
{
    cout << rose(4);
    return 0;
}

int rose(int n)
{
    if (n <= 0)
        return 1;
    else
        return ( rose(n - 1) * n );
}
```

14. Redefine the function power so that it also works for negative exponents. In order to do this, you will also have to change the type of the value returned to *double*. The function declaration and header comment for the redefined version of power is as follows:

```cpp
double power(int x, int n);
```

```
//Precondition: If n < 0, then x is not 0.
//Returns x to the power n.
```

(*Hint:* x^{-n} is equal to $1/(x^n)$.)

14.3 THINKING RECURSIVELY

There are two kinds of people in the world: those who divide the world into two kinds of people and those who do not.

ANONYMOUS

Recursive Design Techniques

When defining and using recursive functions you do not want to be continually aware of the stack and the suspended computations. The power of recursion comes from the fact that you can ignore that detail and let the computer do the bookkeeping for you. Consider the example of the function power in Display 14.3. The way to think of the definition of power is as follows:

```
power(x, n) returns power (x, n - 1) * x
```

Since x^n is equal to $x^{n-1} * x$, this is the correct value to return, provided that the computation will always reach a stopping case and will correctly compute the stopping case. So, after checking that the recursive part of the definition is correct, all you need check is that the chain of recursive calls will always reach a stopping case and that the stopping case always returns the correct value.

When you design a recursive function, you need not trace out the entire sequence of recursive calls for the instances of that function in your program. If the function returns a value, all that you need do is confirm that the following three properties are satisfied:

Criteria for functions that return a value

1. There is no infinite recursion. (A recursive call may lead to another recursive call and that may lead to another and so forth, but every such chain of recursive calls eventually reaches a stopping case.)

2. Each stopping case returns the correct value for that case.

3. For the cases that involve recursion: *If* all recursive calls return the correct value, *then* the final value returned by the function is the correct value.

For example, consider the function power in Display 14.3:

1. *There is no infinite recursion:* The second argument to power(x,n) is decreased by 1 in each recursive call, so any chain of recursive calls must eventually reach the case power(x,0), which is the stopping case. Thus, there is no infinite recursion.

2. *Each stopping case returns the correct value for that case*: The only stopping case is power(x,0). A call of the form power(x,0) always returns 1, and the correct value for x^0 is 1. So the stopping case returns the correct value.

3. *For the cases that involve recursion—if all recursive calls return the correct value, then the final value returned by the function is the correct value*: The only case that involves recursion is when n>1. When n>1, power(x,n) returns

power(x, n - 1) * x

To see that this is the correct value to return, note that: *if* power(x,n-1) returns the correct value, *then* power(x,n-1) returns x^{n-1} and so power(x,n) returns

$x^{n-1} * x$, which is x^n

and that is the correct value for power(x,n).

That's all you need to check in order to be sure that the definition of power is correct. (This technique is known as *mathematical induction*, a concept that you may have heard about in a mathematics class. However, you do not need to be familiar with the term in order to use this technique.)

We gave you three criteria to use in checking the correctness of a recursive function that returns a value. Basically, the same rules can be applied to a recursive *void* function. If you show that your recursive *void* function definition satisfies the following three criteria, then you will know that your *void* function performs correctly:

Criteria for *void* functions

1. There is no infinite recursion.

2. Each stopping case performs the correct action for that case.

3. For each of the cases that involve recursion: *If* all recursive calls perform their actions correctly, *then* the entire case performs correctly.

CASE STUDY Binary Search—An Example of Recursive Thinking

In this case study we develop a recursive function that searches an array to find out whether it contains a specified value. For example, the array may contain a list of numbers for credit cards that are no longer valid. A store clerk needs to search the list to see if a customer's card is valid or invalid. In Chapter 7 (Display 7.10) we discussed a simple method for searching an array by simply checking every array element. In this section we will develop a method that is much faster for searching a sorted array.

The indexes of the array a are the integers 0 through final_index. In order to make the task of searching the array easier, we assume that the array is sorted. Hence, we know the following:

```
a[0] <= a[1] <= a[2] <= ... <= a[final_index]
```

When searching an array, you are likely to want to know both whether the value is in the list and, if it is, where it is in the list. For example, if we are searching for a credit card number, then the array index may serve as a record number. Another array indexed by these same indexes may hold a phone number or other information to use for reporting the suspicious card. Hence, if the sought-after value is in the array, we will want our function to tell where that value is in the array.

Problem Definition

We will design our function to use two call-by-reference parameters to return the outcome of the search. One parameter, called found, will be of type *bool*. If the value is found, then found will be set to *true*. If the value is found, then another parameter, called location, will be set to the index of the value found. If we use key to denote the value being searched for, the task to be accomplished can be formulated precisely as follows:

> *Precondition:* a[0] through a[final_index] are sorted in increasing order.

> *Postcondition:* if key is not one of the values a[0] through a[final_ index], then found == *false*; otherwise, a[location] == key and found == *true*.

Algorithm Design

Now let us proceed to produce an algorithm to solve this task. It will help to visualize the problem in very concrete terms. Suppose the list of numbers is so long that it takes a book to list them all. This is in fact how invalid credit card numbers are distributed to stores that do not have access to computers. If you are a clerk and are handed a credit card, you must check to see if it is on the list and hence invalid.

How would you proceed? Open the book to the middle and see if the number is there. If it is not and it is smaller than the middle number, then work backward toward the beginning of the book. If the number is larger than the middle number, you work your way toward the end of the book. This idea produces our first draft of an algorithm:

```
found = false; //so far.
mid = approximate midpoint between 0 and final_index;
if (key == a[mid])
{
    found = true;
    location = mid;
}
else if (key < a[mid])
    search a[0] through a[mid - 1];
else if (key > a[mid])
    search a[mid + 1] through a[final_index];
```

Algorithm—first version

Since the searchings of the shorter lists are smaller versions of the very task we are designing the algorithm to perform, this algorithm naturally lends itself to the use of recursion. The smaller lists can be searched with recursive calls to the algorithm itself.

Our pseudocode is a bit too imprecise to be easily translated into C++ code. The problem has to do with the recursive calls. There are two recursive calls shown:

search a[0] *through* a[mid - 1];

and

search a[mid + 1] *through* a[final_index];

More parameters

To implement these recursive calls, we need two more parameters. A recursive call specifies that a subrange of the array is to be searched. In one case it is the elements indexed by 0 through mid-1. In the other case it is the elements indexed by mid+1 through final_index. The two extra parameters will specify the first and last indexes of the search, so we will call them first and last. Using these parameters for the lowest and highest indexes, instead of 0 and final_index, we can express the pseudocode more precisely as follows:

Algorithm—first refinement

To search a[first] *through* a[last] *do the following:*
found = *false*; //so far.
mid = *approximate midpoint between* first *and* last;
if (key == a[mid])
{
    found = *true*;
    location = mid;
}
else if (key < a[mid])
    search a[first] *through* a[mid - 1];
else if (key > a[mid])
    search a[mid + 1] *through* a[last];

To search the entire array, the algorithm would be executed with first set equal to 0 and last set equal to final_index. The recursive calls will use other values for first and last. For example, the first recursive call would set first equal to 0 and last equal to the calculated value mid-1.

Stopping case algorithm—final version

As with any recursive algorithm, we must ensure that our algorithm ends rather than producing infinite recursion. If the sought-after number is found on the list, then there is no recursive call and the process terminates, but we need some way to detect when the number is not on the list. On each recursive call, the value of first is increased or the value of last is decreased. If they ever pass each other and first actually becomes larger than last, then we will know that there are no more indexes left to check and that the number key is not in the array. If we add this test to our pseudocode, we obtain a complete solution as shown in Display 14.5.

Coding

Now we can routinely translate the pseudocode into C++ code. The result is shown in Display 14.6. The function search is an implementation of the recursive algorithm given in Display 14.5. A diagram of how the function performs on a sample array is given in Display 14.7.

DISPLAY 14.5   Pseudocode for Binary Search

int a[*Some_Size_Value*];

Algorithm to search a[first] through a[last]

```
1    //Precondition:
2    //a[first]<= a[first + 1] <= a[first + 2] <= ... <= a[last]
```

To locate the value key:

```
1    if (first > last) //A stopping case
2        found = false;
3    else
4    {
5        mid = approximate midpoint between first and last;
6        if (key == a[mid]) //A stopping case
7        {
8            found = true;
9            location = mid;
10       }
11       else if key < a[mid] //A case with recursion
12           search a[first] through a[mid - 1];
13       else if key > a[mid] //A case with recursion
14           search a[mid + 1] through a[last];
15   }
```

DISPLAY 14.6   Recursive Function for Binary Search *(part 1 of 2)*

```
1    //Program to demonstrate the recursive function for binary search.
2    #include <iostream>
3    using namespace std;
4    const int ARRAY_SIZE = 10;
5
6
7    void search(const int a[], int first, int last,
8        int key, bool& found, int& location);
9    //Precondition: a[first] through a[last] are sorted in increasing order.
10   //Postcondition: if key is not one of the values a[first] through a[last],
11   //then found == false; otherwise, a[location] == key and found == true.
12
13
14   int main( )
15   {
16       int a[ARRAY_SIZE];
17       constint final_index = ARRAY_SIZE - 1;
18
```

(continued)

DISPLAY 14.6 Recursive Function for Binary Search *(part 2 of 2)*

<This portion of the program contains some code to fill and sort the array a. The exact details are irrelevant to this example.>

```
19          int key, location;
20          bool found;
21          cout << "Enter number to be located: ";
22          cin >> key;
23          search(a, 0, final_index, key, found, location);
24
25          if (found)
26              cout << key << " is in index location "
27                      << location <<endl;
28          else
29              cout << key << " is not in the array." <<endl;
30
31          return 0;
32      }
33      void search(const int a[], int first, int last,
34                              int key, bool& found, int& location)
35      {
36          int mid;
37          if (first > last)
38          {
39              found = false;
40          }
41          else
42          {
43              mid = (first + last)/2;
44
45              if (key == a[mid])
46              {
47                  found = true;
48                  location = mid;
49              }
50              else if (key < a[mid])
51              {
52                  search(a, first, mid -1, key, found, location);
53              }
54              else if (key > a[mid])
55              {
56                  search(a, mid + 1, last, key, found, location);
57              }
58          }
59      }
```

DISPLAY 14.7 **Execution of the Function** search

key is 63

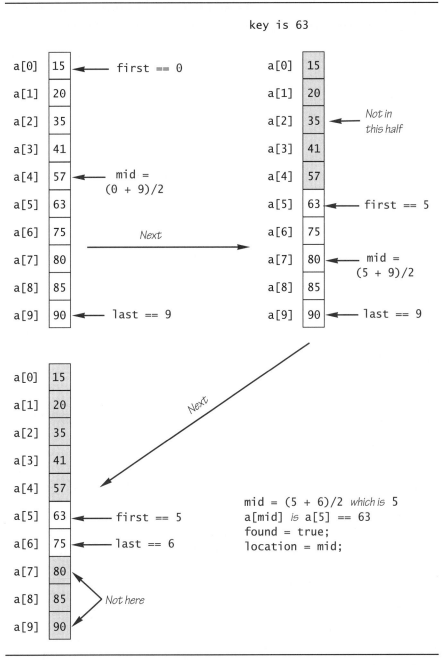

Solve a more
general problem

Notice that the function search solves a more general problem than the original task. Our goal was to design a function to search an entire array. Yet the function will let us search any interval of the array by specifying the index bounds first and last. This is common when designing recursive functions. Frequently, it is necessary to solve a more general problem in order to be able to express the recursive algorithm. In this case, we only wanted the answer in the case where first and last are set equal to 0 and final_index. However, the recursive calls will set them to values other than 0 and final_index.

Checking the Recursion

In the subsection entitled "Recursive Design Techniques," we gave three criteria that you should check to ensure that a recursive *void* function definition is correct. Let's check these three things for the function search given in Display 14.6.

1. *There is no infinite recursion:* On each recursive call, the value of first is increased or the value of last is decreased. If the chain of recursive calls does not end in some other way, then eventually the function will be called with first larger than last, and that is a stopping case.

2. *Each stopping case performs the correct action for that case:* There are two stopping cases: when first > last and when key==a[mid]. Let's consider each case.

   If first > last, there are no array elements between a[first] and a[last], and so key is not in this segment of the array. (Nothing is in this segment of the array!) So, if first > last, the function search correctly sets found equal to *false*.

   If key==a[mid], the algorithm correctly sets found equal to *true* and location equal to mid. Thus, both stopping cases are correct.

3. *For each of the cases that involve recursion, if all recursive calls perform their actions correctly, then the entire case performs correctly:* There are two cases in which there are recursive calls: when key < a[mid] and when key > a[mid]. We need to check each of these two cases.

   First suppose key < a[mid]. In this case, since the array is sorted, we know that if key is anywhere in the array, then key is one of the elements a[first] through a[mid-1]. Thus, the function need only search these elements, which is exactly what the recursive call

   search(a, first, mid - 1, key, found, location);

   does. So if the recursive call is correct, then the entire action is correct.

   Next, suppose key > a[mid]. In this case, since the array is sorted, we know that if key is anywhere in the array, then key is one of the elements a[mid+1] through a[last]. Thus, the function need search only these elements, which is exactly what the recursive call

```
search(a, mid + 1, last, key, found, location);
```

does. So if the recursive call is correct, then the entire action is correct. Thus, in both cases the function performs the correct action (assuming that the recursive calls perform the correct action).

The function `search` passes all three of our tests, so it is a good recursive function definition.

Efficiency

The binary search algorithm is extremely fast compared to an algorithm that simply tries all array elements in order. In the binary search, you eliminate about half the array from consideration right at the start. You then eliminate a quarter, then an eighth of the array, and so forth. These savings add up to a dramatically fast algorithm. For an array of 100 elements, the binary search will never need to compare more than 7array elements to the key. A simple serial search could compare as many as 100 array elements to the key and on the average will compare about 50 array elements to the key. Moreover, the larger the array is, the more dramatic the savings will be. On an array with 1000 elements, the binary search will need to compare only about 10 array elements to the key value, as compared to an average of 500 for the simple serial search algorithm.

An iterative version of the function `search` is given in Display 14.8. On some systems, the iterative version will run more efficiently than the recursive version. The algorithm for the iterative version was derived by mirroring the recursive version. In the iterative version, the local variables `first` and `last` mirror the roles of the parameters in the recursive version, which are also named `first` and `last`. As this example illustrates, it often makes sense to derive a recursive algorithm even if you expect to later convert it to an iterative algorithm.

Iterative version

DISPLAY 14.8   Iterative Version of Binary Search *(part 1 of 2)*

Function Declaration

```
1    void search(const int a[], int low_end, int high_end,
2    int key, bool& found, int& location);
3    //Precondition: a[low_end] through a[high_end] are sorted in increasing
4    //order.
5    //Postcondition: If key is not one of the values a[low_end] through
6    //a[high_end], then found == false; otherwise, a[location] == key and
7    //found == true.
```

Function Definition

```
1    void search(const int a[], int low_end, int high_end,
2        int key, bool& found, int& location)
3    {
4        int first = low_end;
5        int last = high_end;
```

(continued)

DISPLAY 14.8   Iterative Version of Binary Search *(part 2 of 2)*

```
6        int mid;
7
8        found = false; //so far
9        while ( (first <= last) && !(found) )
10       {
11           mid = (first + last)/2;
12           if (key == a[mid])
13           {
14               found = true;
15               location = mid;
16           }
17           else if (key < a[mid])
18           {
19               last = mid -1;
20           }
21           else if (key > a[mid])
22           {
23               first = mid + 1;
24           }
25       }
26   }
```

| PROGRAMMING EXAMPLE   A Recursive Member Function

A member function of a class can be recursive. Member functions can use recursion in the same way that ordinary functions do. Display 14.9 contains an example of a recursive member function. The class BankAccount used in that display is the same as the class named BankAccount that was defined in Display 10.6, except that we have overloaded the member function name update. The first version of update has no arguments and posts one year of simple interest to the bank account balance. The other (new) version of update takes an *int* argument that is some number of years. This member function updates the account by posting the interest for that many years. The new version of update is recursive;has one parameter, called years; and uses the following algorithm:

If the number of years is 1, then *//Stopping case:*
        call the other function named update (the one with no arguments).
If the number of years is greater than 1, then *//Recursive case:*
        make a recursive call to post years-1 worth of interest, and then call the other function called update (the one with no arguments) to post one more year's worth of interest.

DISPLAY 14.9 A Recursive Member Function *(part 1 of 2)*

```
1    //Program to demonstrate the recursive member function update(years).
2    #include <iostream>
3    using namespace std;
4
5    //Class for a bank account:
6    class BankAccount
7    {
8    public:
9        BankAccount(int dollars, int cents, double rate);
10       //Initializes the account balance to $dollars.cents and
11       //initializes the interest rate to rate percent.
12
       BankAccount(int dollars, double rate);
13       //Initializes the account balance to $dollars.00 and
14       //initializes the interest rate to rate percent.
15
       BankAccount( );
16       //Initializes the account balance to $0.00 and
17       //initializes the interest rate to 0.0%.
18       void update( );
19       //Postcondition: One year of simple interest
20       //has been added to the account balance.
21       void update(int years);
22       //Postcondition: Interest for the number of years given has been added to the
23       //account balance. Interest is compounded annually.
24       double get_balance( );
25       //Returns the current account balance.
26       double get_rate( );
27       //Returns the current account interest rate as a percentage.
28       void output(ostream& outs);
29       //Precondition: If outs is a file output stream, then outs has already
30       //been connected to a file.
31       //Postcondition: Balance & interest rate have been written to the stream outs.
32   private:
33       double balance;
34       double interest_rate;
35       double fraction(double percent); //Converts a percentage to a fraction.
36   };
37   int main( )
38   {
39       BankAccount your_account(100, 5);
40       your_account.update(10);
41       cout.setf(ios::fixed);
```

The class **BankAccount** *in this program is an improved version of the class* **BankAccount** *given in Display 10.6.*

Two different functions with the same name

(continued)

DISPLAY 14.9   A Recursive Member Function *(part 2 of 2)*

```
42          cout.setf(ios::showpoint);
43          cout.precision(2);
44          cout << "If you deposit $100.00 at 5% interest, then\n"
45               << "in ten years your account will be worth $"
46               << your_account.get_balance( ) << endl;
47          return 0;
48      }
49
50      void BankAccount::update( )
51      {
52          balance = balance + fraction(interest_rate)*balance;
53      }
54
55      void BankAccount::update(int years)
56      {
57          if (years == 1)
58          {
59              update( );
60          }
61          else if (years > 1)
62          {
63              update(years - 1);
64              update( );
65          }
66      }
```

Overloading (that is, calls to another function with the same name)

Recursive function call

<Definitions of the other member functions are given in Display 10.5 and Display 10.6, but you need not read those definitions in order to understand this example.>

Sample Dialogue

```
If you deposit $100.00 at 5% interest, then
in ten years your account will be worth $162.89
```

It is easy to see that this algorithm produces the desired result by checking the three points given in the subsection entitled "Recursive Design Techniques."

1. *There is no infinite recursion:* Each recursive call reduces the number of years by 1 until the number of years eventually becomes 1, which is the stopping case. So there is no infinite recursion.

2. *Each stopping case performs the correct action for that case:* The one stopping case is when years==1. This case produces the correct action, since it simply calls the other overloaded member function called update, and we checked the correctness of that function in Chapter 10.

3. *For the cases that involve recursion, if all recursive calls perform correctly, then the entire case performs correctly:* The recursive case—that is, years>1—works correctly, because if the recursive call correctly posts years-1 worth of interest, then all that is needed is to post one additional year's worth of interest and the call to the overloaded zero-argument version of update will correctly post one year's worth of interest. Thus, *if* the recursive call performs the correct action, *then* the entire action for the case of years>1 will be correct.

In this example, we have overloaded update so that there are two different   Overloading
functions named update: one that takes no arguments and one that takes a single argument. Do not confuse the calls to the two functions named update. These are two different functions that, as far as the compiler is concerned, just coincidentally happen to have the same name. When the definition of the function update with one argument includes a call to the version of update that takes no arguments, that is not a recursive call. Only the call to the version of update with the *exact* same function declaration is a recursive call. To see what is involved here, note that we could have named the version of update that takes no argument post_one_year(), instead of naming it update(), and then the definition of the recursive version of update would read as follows:

```
void BankAccount::update(int years)
{
    if (years == 1)
    {
        post_one_year();
    }
    else if (years > 1)
    {
        update(years - 1);
        post_one_year();
    }
}
```

Recursion and Overloading

Do not confuse recursion and overloading. When you overload a function name, you are giving two different functions the same name. If the definition of one of these two functions includes a call to the other, that is not recursion. In a recursive function definition, the definition of the function includes a call to the *exact* same function with the *exact same definition,* not to some other function that coincidentally uses the same name. It is not too serious an error if you confuse overloading and recursion, since they are both legal. It is simply a question of getting the terminology straight so that you can communicate clearly with other programmers and so that you understand the underlying processes.

SELF-TEST EXERCISES

15. Write a recursive function definition for the following function:

    ```
    int squares(int n);
    //Precondition: n >= 1
    //Returns the sum of the squares of numbers 1 through n.
    ```

    For example, squares(3) returns 14 because $1^2 + 2^2 + 3^2$ is 14.

16. Write an iterative version of the one-argument member function BankAccount::update(int years) that is described in Display 14.9.

CHAPTER SUMMARY

■ If a problem can be reduced to smaller instances of the same problem, then a recursive solution is likely to be easy to find and implement.

■ A recursive algorithm for a function definition normally contains two kinds of cases: one or more cases that include at least one recursive call and one or more stopping cases in which the problem is solved without any recursive calls.

■ When writing a recursive function definition, always confirm that the function will not produce infinite recursion.

■ When you define a recursive function, use the three criteria given in the subsection "Recursive Design Techniques" to confirm that the function is correct.

■ When you design a recursive function to solve a task, it is often necessary to solve a more general problem than the given task. This may be required to allow for the proper recursive calls, since the smaller problems may not be exactly the same problem as the given task. For example, in the binary search problem, the task was to search an entire array, but the recursive solution is an algorithm to search any portion of the array (either all of it or a part of it).

Answers to Self-Test Exercises

1. Hip Hip Hurray

2. ```
   void stars(int n)
   {
       cout << '*';
       if (n > 1)
           stars(n - 1);
   }
   ```
   ```

The following is also correct but is more complicated:

```cpp
void stars(int n)
{
    if (n <= 1)
    {
        cout << '*';
    }
    else
    {
        stars(n - 1);
        cout << '*';
    }
}
```

3.
```cpp
void backward(int n)
{
    if (n < 10)
    {
        cout << n;
    }
    else
    {
        cout << (n % 10);//write last digit
        backward(n / 10);//write the other digits backward
    }
}
```

4. and 5. The answer to 4 is write_up(int n);. The answer to 5 is write_down(int n);.

```cpp
#include <iostream>
using namespace std;
void write_down(int n)
{
    if (n > = 1)
    {
        cout << n << " ";
        write_down(n - 1);
    }
}

void write_up(int n)
{
    if (n >= 1)
    {
        write_up(n - 1);
        cout << n << " ";
    }
}
```

```
//testing code for both #4 and #5
int main()
{
    cout << "calling write_up(" << 10 << ")\n";
    write_up(10);
    cout << endl;
    cout << "calling write_down(" << 10 << ")\n";
    write_down(10);
    cout << endl;
    return 0;
}
/* Test results
calling write_up(10)
1 2 3 4 5 6 7 8 9 10
calling write_down(10)
10 9 8 7 6 5 4 3 2 1
*/
```

6. An error message that says *stack overflow* is telling you that the computer has attempted to place more activation frames on the stack than are allowed on your system. A likely cause of this error message is infinite recursion.

7.
```
void cheers(int n)
{
    while (n > 1)
    {
        cout << "Hip ";
        n--;
    }
    cout << "Hurray\n";
}
```

8.
```
void stars(int n)
{
    for (int count = 1; count <= n; count++)
        cout << '*';
}
```

9.
```
void backward(int n)
{
    while (n >= 10)
    {
        cout << (n % 10); //write last digit
        n = n / 10; //discard the last digit
    }
    cout << n;
}
```

10. Trace for Exercise 4: If n = 3, the code to be executed is

```
if ( 3 >= 1 )
{
    write_up( 3 - 1 );
    cout << 3 << " ";
}
```

On the next recursion, n = 2; the code to be executed is

```
if ( 2 >= 1 )
{
    write_up( 2 - 1 );
    cout << 2 << " ";
}
```

On the next recursion, n = 1 and the code to be executed is

```
if ( 1 >= 1 )
{
    write_up( 1 - 1 );
    cout << 1 << " ";
}
```

On the final recursion, n = 0 and the code to be executed is

```
if ( 0 >= 1 ) // condition false, body skipped
{
    // skipped
}
```

The recursions unwind; the output (obtained while recursion was winding up) is 1 2 3.

11. Trace for Exercise 5: If n = 3, the code to be executed is

```
if ( 3 >= 1 )
{
    cout << 3 << " ";
    write_down(3 - 1);
}
```

Next recursion, n = 2, the code to be executed is

```
if ( 2 > = 1 )
{
    cout << 2 << " ";
    write_down(2 - 1)
}
```

Next recursion, n = 1, the code to be executed is

```
if ( 1 >= 1 )
```

```
{
    cout << 1 << " ";
    write_down(1 - 1)
}
```

Final recursion, n = 0, and the "*true*" clause is not executed:

```
if (0 >= 1 ) // condition false
{
    // this clause is skipped
}
```

The output is 3 2 1.

12. 6

13. The output is 24. The function is the factorial function, usually written *n!* and defined as follows:

   n! is equal to *n* * (*n* - 1) * (*n* - 2) *...* 1

14. ```
//Uses iostream and cstdlib:
double power(int x, int n)
{
    if (n < 0 && x == 0)
    {
        cout << "Illegal argument to power.\n";
        exit(1);
    }

    if (n < 0)
        return (1/power(x, -n));
    else if (n > 0)
        return (power(x, n - 1)*x);
    else // n == 0
        return (1.0);
}
```

15. ```
int squares(int n)
{
    if (n <= 1)
        return 1;
    else
        return ( squares(n - 1) + n * n );
}
```

16. ```
void BankAccount::update(int years)
{
    for (int count = 1; count <= years; count++)
        update( );
}
```
```

PROGRAMMING PROJECTS

Visit www.myprogramminglab.com to complete many of these Programming Projects online and get instant feedback.   `myprogramminglab`

1. Write a recursive function definition for a function that has one parameter *n* of type *int* and returns the factorial of the given number. See Programming Project 3 in Chapter 5 for the definition of factorial numbers. Embed the function in a program and test it.

2. Write a recursive version of the function `index_of_smallest` that was used in the sorting program in Display 7.12 of Chapter 7. Embed the function in a program and test it.

3. Write a function to find the greatest common divisor of two numbers.

4. Write a program which will use the recursive function `count_prime()` to find the number of prime numbers in between the two arguments given in the function as parameters. The definition of the recursive function is as follows:

   ```
   count_prime(a,b) = 0, ifa>b
   count_prime(a,b) = count_prime(a,b-1) + 1, if b is prime
   count_prime(a,b) = count_prime(a,b-1), otherwise
   ```

   The recursive definition may use a `function prime()` to check if a number is a prime number or not. For example the number of prime numbers from 2 to 7 is 4 i.e., 2, 3, 5 and 7. The range of numbers should be taken from the user.

5. Write a recursive function that has an argument that is an array of characters and two arguments that are bounds on array indexes. The function should reverse the order of those entries in the array whose indexes are between the two bounds. For example, if the array is

   ```
   a[0] == 'A' a[1] == 'B' a[2] == 'C' a[3] == 'D' a[4] == 'E'
   ```

   and the bounds are 1 and 4, then after the function is run the array elements should be

   ```
   a[0] == 'A' a[1] == 'E' a[2] == 'D' a[3] == 'C' a[4] == 'B'
   ```

   Embed the function in a program and test it. After you have fully debugged this function, define another function that takes a single argument which is an array that contains a string value and that reverses the spelling of the string value in the array argument. This function will include a call to the recursive definition you did for the first part of this project. Embed this second function in a program and test it.

6. Write a recursive version of the iterative function of the exponent program in Programming Project 4 of Chapter 5. Embed it in a program and test it.

7. Write a recursive function to sort an array of integers into ascending order using the following idea: Place the smallest element in the first position, then sort the rest of the array by a recursive call. This is a recursive version of the selection sort algorithm discussed in Chapter 7. (*Note:* Simply taking the program from Chapter 7 and plugging in a recursive version of index_of_smallest will not suffice. The function to do the sorting must itself be recursive and not merely use a recursive function.)

8. Towers of Hanoi: There is a story about Buddhist monks who are playing this puzzle with 64 stone disks. The story claims that when the monks finish moving the disks from one post to a second via the third post, time will end.

A stack of *n* disks of decreasing size is placed on one of three posts. The task is to move the disks one at a time from the first post to the second. To do this, any disk can be moved from any post to any other post, subject to the rule that you can never place a larger disk over a smaller disk. The (spare) third post is provided to make the solution possible. Your task is to write a recursive function that describes instructions for a solution to this problem. We don't have graphics available, so you should output a sequence of instructions that will solve the problem.

(*Hint:* If you could move up *n*–1 of the disks from the first post to the third post using the second post as a spare, the last disk could be moved from the first post to the second post. Then by using the same technique (whatever that may be) you can move the *n*–1 disks from the third post to the second post, using the first disk as a spare. There! You have the puzzle solved. You only have to decide what the nonrecursive case is, what the recursive case is, and when to output instructions to move the disks.)

9. The game of "Jump It" consists of a board with *n* positive integers in a row, except for the first column, which always contains 0. These numbers represent the cost to enter each column. Here is a sample game board where *n* is 6:

0	3	80	6	57	10

The object of the game is to move from the first column to the last column with the lowest total cost. The number in each column represents the cost to enter that column. You always start the game in the first column and have two types of moves. You can either move to the adjacent column or jump over the adjacent column to land two columns over. The cost of a game is the sum of the costs of the columns visited.

In the board shown above, there are several ways to get to the end. Starting in the first column, our cost so far is 0. We could jump to 80, then jump to 57, then move to 10 for a total cost of 80 + 57 + 10 = 147.

However, a cheaper path would be to move to 3, jump to 6, then jump to 10, for a total cost of 3 + 6 + 10 = 19.

Write a recursive solution to this problem that computes the lowest cost of the game and outputs this value for an arbitrarily large game board represented as an array. Your program doesn't have to output the actual sequence of jumps, only the lowest cost of this sequence. After making sure that your solution works on small arrays, test it on boards of larger and larger values of n to get a feel for the scalability and efficiency of your solution.

10. Suppose we can buy chocolate bars from the vending machine for $1 each. Inside every chocolate bar is a coupon. We can redeem 7 coupons for 1 chocolate bar from the machine. We would like to know how many chocolate bars can be eaten, including those redeemed via coupon, if we have n dollars.

    For example, if we have $20, then we can initially buy 20 chocolate bars. This gives us 20 coupons. We can redeem 14 coupons for 2 additional chocolate bars. These two additional chocolate bars have 2 more coupons, so we now have a total of 8 coupons when added to the 6 left over from the original purchase. This gives us enough to redeem for 1 final chocolate bar. As a result we now have 23 chocolate bars and 2 leftover coupons.

    Write a recursive solution to this problem that inputs from the user the number of dollars to spend on chocolate bars and outputs how many chocolate bars you can collect after spending all your money and redeeming as many coupons as possible. Your recursive function will be based upon the number of coupons owned.

11. Some problems require finding all permutations (different orderings) of a set of items. For a set of n items $\{ a_1, a_2, a_3, \ldots a_n \}$ there are $n!$ permutations. For example, given the set $\{1, \ 2, \ 3\}$ there are six permutations:

    VideoNote
    Solution to Programming
    Project 14.11

    {3, 2, 1} {2, 3, 1} {2, 1, 3} {3, 1, 2} {1, 3, 2} {1, 2, 3}

    Write a recursive function that generates all the permutations of a set of numbers. The general outline of a solution is given here, but the implementation is up to you. The program will require storing a set of permutations of numbers that you can implement in many ways (for example, linked lists of nodes, linked lists of vectors, arrays, etc.) Your program should call the recursive function with sets of several different sizes, printing the resulting set of permutations for each.

    One solution is to first leave out the n th item in the set. Recursively find all permutations using the set of $(n-1)$ items. If we insert the nth item into each position for all of these permutations, then we get a new set of permutations that includes the *n* th item. The base case is when there is only one item in the set, in which case the solution is simply the permutation with the single item.

For example, consider finding all permutations of {1, 2, 3}. We leave the 3 out and recursively find all permutations of the set {1, 2}. This consists of the permutations:

{1, 2}   {2, 1}

Next we insert the 3 into every position for these permutations. For the first permutation, we insert the 3 in the front, between 1 and 2, and after 2. For the second permutation, we insert the 3 in the front, between 2 and 1, and after 1:

{3, 1, 2} {1, 3, 2} {1, 2, 3} {3, 2, 1} {2, 3, 1} {2, 1, 3}

The resulting six permutations comprise all permutations of the set {1, 2, 3}.

12. Write a program which will perform exponent computation (x^n) using the following recursive definition:

```
fast_power(x,n) = 1, if n is equal to 0
fast_power(x,n) = x*square(fast_power(x, n/2))),  if n is odd
fast_power(x,n) = square(fast_power(x, n/2))),  otherwise
```

Your program can calculate the exponent faster than the conventional "to the power" method. Take the base and the exponent from the user, and be sure to provide proper documentation for the program.

13. Write a program which will find the sum of the natural numbers starting from 1 to any number (given by the user) greater than 1, using the following recursive definition:

```
int sum_rec(int a, int b)
{
    if (a>b) return 0;
    else return (b + sum_rec(a,b-1));
}
```

For example, the sum of the numbers from 1 to 5 is $1 + 2 + 3 + 4 + 5 = 15$.

Inheritance 15

With all appliances and means to boot.

WILLIAM SHAKESPEARE, *King Henry IV, Part III*

INTRODUCTION

Object-oriented programming is a popular and powerful programming technique. Among other things, it provides for a new dimension of abstraction known as *inheritance*. This means that a very general form of a class can be defined and compiled. Later, more specialized versions of that class can be defined and can inherit all the properties of the previous class. Facilities for inheritance are available in all versions of C++.

PREREQUISITES

Section 15.1 uses material from Chapters 2 to 8 and 10 to 12. Sections 15.2 and 15.3 use material from Chapters 9 and 13 in addition to Chapters 2 to 8, 10 to 12, and Section 15.1.

15.1 INHERITANCE BASICS

If there is anything that we wish to change in the child, we should first examine it and see whether it is not something that could better be changed in ourselves.

CARL GUSTAV JUNG, *The Integration of the Personality*

One of the most powerful features of C++ is the use of inheritance to derive one class from another. **Inheritance** is the process by which a new class—known as a **derived class**—is created from another class, called the **base class**. A derived class automatically has all the member variables and functions that the base class has and can have additional member functions and/or additional member variables.

In Chapter 10, we noted that saying that class D is derived from another class B means that class D has all the features of class B and some extra, added features as well. When a class D is derived from a class B, we say that B is the base class and D is the derived class. We also say that D is the **child class** and B is the **parent class.**[1]

---

[1] Some authors speak of a *subclass* D and *superclass* B instead of derived class D and base class B. However, we have found the terms *derived class* and *base class* to be less confusing. We only mention this in an effort to help you to read other texts.

For example, in Chapter 10 we discussed how a CD account is a more specialized version of a savings account. By deriving the class CDAccount from SavingsAccount, we automatically inherit all of the SavingsAccount public functions and variables when we create a CDAccount object. C++ uses inheritance in predefined classes as well. In using streams for file I/O, the predefined class ifstream is derived from the (predefined) class istream by adding member functions such as open and close. The stream cin belongs to the class of all input streams (that is, the class istream), but it does not belong to the class of input-file streams (that is, does not belong to ifstream), partly because it lacks the member functions open and close of the derived class ifstream.

Derived Classes

Suppose we are designing a record-keeping program that has records for salaried employees and hourly employees. There is a natural hierarchy for grouping these classes. These are all classes of people who share the property of being employees.

Employees who are paid an hourly wage are one subset of employees. Another subset consists of employees who are paid a fixed wage each month or each week. Although the program may not need any type corresponding to the set of all employees, thinking in terms of the more general concept of employees can be useful. For example, all employees have names and Social Security numbers, and the member functions for setting and changing names and Social Security numbers will be the same for salaried and hourly employees.

Within C++ you can define a class called Employee that includes all employees, whether salaried or hourly, and then use this class to define classes for hourly employees and salaried employees. Displays 15.1 and 15.2 show one possible definition for the class Employee.

You can have an (undifferentiated) Employee object, but our reason for defining the class Employee is so that we can define derived classes for different kinds of employees. In particular, the function print_check will always have its definition changed in derived classes so that different kinds of employees can have different kinds of checks. This is reflected in the definition of the function print_check for the class Employee (Display 15.2). It makes little sense to print a check for such an (undifferentiated) Employee. We know nothing about this employee's salary details. Consequently, we implemented the function print_check of the class Employee so that the program stops with an error message if print_check is called for a base class Employee object. As you will see, derived classes will have enough information to redefine the function print_check to produce meaningful employee checks.

A class that is derived from the class Employee will automatically have all the member variables of the class Employee (name, ssn, and net_pay). A class that is derived from the class Employee will also have all the member functions of the class Employee, such as print_check, get_name, set_name, and the other member functions listed in Display 15.1. This is usually expressed by

DISPLAY 15.1   Interface for the Base Class Employee

```
1    //This is the header file employee.h.
2    //This is the interface for the class Employee.
3    //This is primarily intended to be used as a base class to derive
4    //classes for different kinds of employees.
5    #ifndef EMPLOYEE_H
6    #define EMPLOYEE_H

7    #include <string>
8    using namespace std;

9    namespace employeessavitch
10   {

11       class Employee
12       {
13       public:
14           Employee( );
15           Employee(string the_name, string the_ssn);
16           string get_name( ) const;
17           string get_ssn( ) const;
18           double get_net_pay( ) const;
19           void set_name(string new_name);
20           void set_ssn(string new_ssn);
21           void set_net_pay(double new_net_pay);
22           void print_check( ) const;
23       private:
24           string name;
25           string ssn;
26           double net_pay;
27       };

28   }//employeessavitch

29   #endif //EMPLOYEE_H
```

saying that the derived class **inherits** the member variables and member functions.

The interface files with the class definitions of two derived classes of the class Employee are given in Displays 15.3 (HourlyEmployee) and 15.4 (SalariedEmployee). We have placed the class Employee and the two derived classes in the same namespace. C++ does not require that they be in the same namespace, but since they are related classes, it makes sense to put them there. We will first discuss the derived class HourlyEmployee given in Display 15.3.

Note that the definition of a derived class begins like any other class definition but adds a colon, the reserved word *public*, and the name of the

DISPLAY 15.2   Implementation for the Base Class Employee *(part 1 of 2)*

```
1    //This is the file: employee.cpp.
2    //This is the implementation for the class Employee.
3    //The interface for the class Employee is in the header file employee.h.
4    #include <string>
5    #include <cstdlib>
6    #include <iostream>
7    #include "employee.h"
8    using namespace std;

9    namespace employeessavitch
10   {
11       Employee::Employee( ) : name("No name yet"), ssn("No number yet"), net_pay(0)
12       {
13           //deliberately empty
14       }

15       Employee::Employee(string the_name, string the_number)
16            : name(the_name), ssn(the_number), net_pay(0)
17       {
18           //deliberately empty
19       }

20       string Employee::get_name( ) const
21       {
22           return name;
23       }

24       string Employee::get_ssn( ) const
25       {
26           return ssn;
27       }
28
29       double Employee::get_net_pay( ) const
30       {
31           return net_pay;
32       }

33       void Employee::set_name(string new_name)
34       {
35           name = new_name;
36       }
37       void Employee::set_ssn(string new_ssn)
38       {
39           ssn = new_ssn;
40       }
```

(continued)

DISPLAY 15.2 Implementation for the Base Class Employee *(part 2 of 2)*

```
41        void Employee::set_net_pay (double new_net_pay)
42        {
43            net_pay = new_net_pay;
44        }

45        void Employee::print_check( ) const
46        {
47            cout << "\nERROR: print_check FUNCTION CALLED FOR AN \n"
48                 << "UNDIFFERENTIATED EMPLOYEE. Aborting the program.\n"
49                 << "Check with the author of the program about this bug.\n";
50            exit(1);
51        }

52    }//employeessavitch
```

DISPLAY 15.3 Interface for the Derived Class HourlyEmployee *(part 1 of 2)*

```
1     //This is the header file hourlyemployee.h.
2     //This is the interface for the class HourlyEmployee.
3     #ifndef HOURLYEMPLOYEE_H
4     #define HOURLYEMPLOYEE_H

5     #include <string>
6     #include "employee.h"

7     using namespace std;
8     namespace employeessavitch
9     {

10        class HourlyEmployee : public Employee
11        {
12        public:
13            HourlyEmployee( );
14            HourlyEmployee(string the_name, string the_ssn,
15                           double the_wage_rate, double the_hours);
16            void set_rate(double new_wage_rate);
17            double get_rate( ) const;
18            void set_hours(double hours_worked);
19            double get_hours( ) const;
```

(continued)

DISPLAY 15.3 Interface for the Derived Class HourlyEmployee *(part 2 of 2)*

```
20              void print_check( );
21          private:
22              double wage_rate;
23              double hours;
24          };

25      }//employeessavitch

26      #endif //HOURLY EMPLOYEE_H
```

> You only list the declaration of an inherited member function if you want to change the definition of the function.

DISPLAY 15.4 Interface for the Derived Class SalariedEmployee

```
1       //This is the header file salariedemployee.h.
2       //This is the interface for the class SalariedEmployee.
3       #ifndef SALARIEDEMPLOYEE_H
4       #define SALARIEDEMPLOYEE_H

5       #include <string>
6       #include "employee.h"

7       using namespace std;

8       namespace employeessavitch
9       {

10          class SalariedEmployee : public Employee
11          {
12          public:
13              SalariedEmployee( );
14              SalariedEmployee (string the_name, string the_ssn,
15                                  double the_weekly_salary);
16              double get_salary( ) const;
17              void set_salary(double new_salary);
18              void print_check( );
19          private:
20              double salary;//weekly
21          };

22      }//employeessavitch

23      #endif //SALARIEDEMPLOYEE_H
```

base class to the first line of the class definition, as in the following (from Display 15.3):

```
class HourlyEmployee : public Employee
{
```

The derived class (such as HourlyEmployee) automatically receives all the member variables and member functions of the base class (such as Employee) and can add additional member variables and member functions.

The definition of the class HourlyEmployee does not mention the member variables name, ssn, and net_pay, but every object of the class HourlyEmployee has member variables named name, ssn, and net_pay. These member variables are inherited from the class Employee. The class HourlyEmployee declares two additional member variables named wage_rate and hours. Thus, every object of the class HourlyEmployee has five member variables named name, ssn, net_pay, wage_rate, and hours. Note that the definition of a derived class (such as HourlyEmployee) only lists the added member variables. The member variables defined in the base class are not mentioned. They are provided automatically to the derived class.

Just as it inherits the member variables of the class Employee, the class HourlyEmployee inherits all the member functions from the class Employee. So, the class HourlyEmployee inherits the member functions get_name, get_ssn, get_net_pay, set_name, set_ssn, set_net_pay, and print_check from the class Employee.

In addition to the inherited member variables and member functions, a derived class can add new member variables and new member functions. The new member variables and the declarations for the new member functions are listed in the class definition. For example, the derived class HourlyEmployee adds the two member variables wage_rate and hours, and it adds the new member functions named set_rate, get_rate, set_hours, and get_hours. This is shown in Display 15.3. Note that you do not give the declarations of the inherited member functions except for those whose definitions you want to change, which is the reason we list only the member function print_check from the base class Employee. For now, do not worry about the details of the constructor definition for the derived class. We will discuss constructors in the next subsection.

In the implementation file for the derived class, such as the implementation of HourlyEmployee in Display 15.5, you give the definitions of all the added member functions. Note that you do not give definitions for the inherited member functions unless the definition of the member function is changed in the derived class, a point we discuss next.

The definition of an inherited member function can be changed in the definition of a derived class so that it has a meaning in the derived class that is different from what it is in the base class. This is called **redefining** the inherited member function. For example, the member function print_check( ) is redefined in the definition of the derived class HourlyEmployee. To redefine a

DISPLAY 15.5 Implementation for the Derived Class HourlyEmployee
                    (part 1 of 2)

```
1    //This is the file: hourlyemployee.cpp
2    //This is the implementation for the class HourlyEmployee.
3    //The interface for the class HourlyEmployee is in
4    //the header file hourlyemployee.h.
5    #include <string>
6    #include <iostream>
7    #include "hourlyemployee.h"
8    using namespace std;

9    namespace employeessavitch
10   {

11       HourlyEmployee::HourlyEmployee( ) : Employee( ), wage_rate(0), hours(0)
12       {
13           //deliberately empty
14       }

15       HourlyEmployee::HourlyEmployee(string the_name, string the_number,
16                                   double the_wage_rate, double the_hours)
17       : Employee(the_name, the_number), wage_rate(the_wage_rate), hours(the_hours)
18       {
19           //deliberately empty
20       }

21       void HourlyEmployee::set_rate(double new_wage_rate)
22       {
23           wage_rate = new_wage_rate;
24       }

25       double HourlyEmployee::get_rate( ) const
26       {
27           return wage_rate;
28       }

29       void HourlyEmployee::set_hours(double hours_worked)
30       {
31           hours = hours_worked;
32       }

33       double HourlyEmployee::get_hours( ) const
34       {
35           return hours;
36       }
```

(continued)

DISPLAY 15.5 **Implementation for the Derived Class** HourlyEmployee
(part 2 of 2)

> We have chosen to set net_pay as part of the print_check function since that is the question. But note that C++ allows us to drop the const in the function print_check when we redefine it in a derived class.

```
37      void HourlyEmployee::print_check( )
38      {
39          set_net_pay (hours * wage_rate);

40          cout << "\n_____\n";
41          cout << "Pay to the order of " << get_name( ) << endl;
42          cout << "The sum of " << get_net_pay( ) << " Dollars\n";
43          cout << "_____\n";
44          cout << "Check Stub: NOT NEGOTIABLE\n";
45          cout << "Employee Number: " << get_ssn( ) << endl;
46          cout << "Hourly Employee. \nHours worked: " << hours
47              << " Rate: " << wage_rate << " Pay: " << get_net_pay( ) << endl;
48          cout << "_____\n";
49      }


50      }//employeessavitch
```

member function definition, simply list it in the class definition and give it a new definition, just as you would do with a member function that is added in the derived class. This is illustrated by the redefined function print_check( ) of the class HourlyEmployee (Displays 15.3 and 15.5).

> **Parent and Child Classes**
>
> When discussing derived classes, it is common to use terminology derived from family relationships. A base class is often called a **parent class.** A derived class is then called a **child class.** This makes the language of inheritance very smooth. For example, we can say that a child class inherits member variables and member functions from its parent class. This analogy is often carried one step further. A class that is a parent of a parent of a parent of another class (or some other number of "parent of" iterations) is often called an **ancestor class.** If class A is an ancestor of class B, then class B is often called a **descendant** of class A.

Inherited Members

A derived class automatically has all the member variables and all the ordinary member functions of the base class. (As discussed later in this chapter, there are some specialized member functions, such as constructors, that are not automatically inherited.) These members from the base class are said to be **inherited.** These inherited member functions and inherited member variables are, with one exception, not mentioned in the definition of the derived class, but they are automatically members of the derived class. As explained in the text, you do mention an inherited member function in the definition of the derived class if you want to change the definition of the inherited member function.

SalariedEmployee is another example of a derived class of the class Employee. The interface for the class SalariedEmployee is given in Display 15.4. An object declared to be of type SalariedEmployee has all the member functions and member variables of Employee and the new members given in the definition of the class SalariedEmployee. This is true even though the class SalariedEmployee lists none of the inherited variables and only lists one function from the class Employee, namely, the function print_check, which will have its definition changed in SalariedEmployee. The class SalariedEmployee, nonetheless, has the three member variables name, ssn, and net_pay, as well as the member variable salary. Notice that you do not have to declare the member variables and member functions of the class Employee, such as name and set_name, in order for a SalariedEmployee to have these members. The class SalariedEmployee gets these inherited members automatically without the programmer doing anything.

Note that the class Employee has all the code that is common to the two classes HourlyEmployee and SalariedEmployee. This saves you the trouble of writing identical code two times, once for the class HourlyEmployee and once for the class SalariedEmployee. Inheritance allows you to reuse the code in the class Employee.

Constructors in Derived Classes

A constructor in a base class is not inherited in the derived class, but you can invoke a constructor of the base class within the definition of a derived class constructor, and that is all you need or normally want. A constructor for a derived class uses a constructor from the base class in a special way. A constructor for the base class initializes all the data inherited from the base class. Thus, a constructor for a derived class begins with an invocation of a constructor for the base class.

There is a special syntax for invoking the base class constructor that is illustrated by the constructor definitions for the class HourlyEmployee given in Display 15.5. In what follows we have reproduced (with minor changes in the line breaks to make it fit the text column) one of the constructor definitions for the class HourlyEmployee taken from that display:

```
HourlyEmployee::HourlyEmployee(string the_name,
        string the_number, double the_wage_rate,
        double the_hours)
    : Employee(the_name, the_number),
                wage_rate(the_wage_rate), hours(the_hours)
{
    //deliberately empty
}
```

The portion after the colon is the initialization section of the constructor definition for the constructor HourlyEmployee::HourlyEmployee. The part Employee(the_name, the_number) is an invocation of the two-argument constructor for the base class Employee. Note that the syntax for invoking the base class constructor is analogous to the syntax used to set member variables: The entry wage_rate(the_wage_rate) sets the value of the member variable wage_rate to the_wage_rate; the entry Employee(the_name, the_number) invokes the base class constructor Employee with the arguments the_name and the_number. Since all the work is done in the initialization section, the body of the constructor definition is empty.

Here we reproduce the other constructor for the class HourlyEmployee from Display 15.5:

```
HourlyEmployee::HourlyEmployee( ) : Employee( ), wage_rate(0),
                hours(0)
{
    //deliberately empty
}
```

In this constructor definition the default (zero-argument) version of the base class constructor is called to initialize the inherited member variables. You should always include an invocation of one of the base class constructors in the initialization section of a derived class constructor.

If a constructor definition for a derived class does not include an invocation of a constructor for the base class, then the default (zero-argument) version of the base class constructor will be invoked automatically. So, the following definition of the default constructor for the class HourlyEmployee (with Employee( ) omitted) is equivalent to the version we just discussed:

```
HourlyEmployee::HourlyEmployee( ) : wage_rate(0), hours(0)
{
    //deliberately empty
}
```

> **An Object of a Derived Class Has More Than One Type**
>
> In everyday experience an hourly employee is an employee. In C++ the same sort of thing holds. Since HourlyEmployee is a derived class of the class Employee, every object of the class HourlyEmployee can be used anywhere an object of the class Employee can be used. In particular, you can use an argument of type HourlyEmployee when a function requires an argument of type Employee. You can assign an object of the class HourlyEmployee to a variable of type Employee. (But be warned: You cannot assign a plain old Employee object to a variable of type HourlyEmployee. After all, an Employee is not necessarily an HourlyEmployee.) Of course, the same remarks apply to any base class and its derived class. You can use an object of a derived class anywhere that an object of its base class is allowed.
>
> More generally, an object of a class type can be used anywhere that an object of any of its ancestor classes can be used. If class Child is derived from class Ancestor and class Grandchild is derived from class Child, then an object of class Grandchild can be used anywhere an object of class Child can be used, and the object of class Grandchild can also be used anywhere that an object of class Ancestor can be used.

However, we prefer to always explicitly include a call to a base class constructor, even if it would be invoked automatically.

A derived class object has all the member variables of the base class. When a derived class constructor is called, these member variables need to be allocated memory and should be initialized. This allocation of memory for the inherited member variables must be done by a constructor for the base class, and the base class constructor is the most convenient place to initialize these inherited member variables. That is why you should always include a call to one of the base class constructors when you define a constructor for a derived class. If you do not include a call to a base class constructor (in the initialization section of the definition of a derived class constructor), then the default (zero-argument) constructor of the base class is called automatically. (If there is no default constructor for the base class, that is an error condition.)

The call to the base class constructor is the first action taken by a derived class constructor. Thus, if class B is derived from class A and class C is derived from class B, then when an object of the class C is created, first a constructor for the class A is called, then a constructor for B is called, and finally the remaining actions of the C constructor are taken.

Constructors in Derived Classes

A derived class does not inherit the constructors of its base class. However, when defining a constructor for the derived class, you can and should include a call to a constructor of the base class (within the initialization section of the constructor definition).

If you do not include a call to a constructor of the base class, then the default (zero-argument) constructor of the base class will automatically be called when the derived class constructor is called.

PITFALL Use of Private Member Variables from the Base Class

An object of the class HourlyEmployee (Displays 15.3 and 15.5) inherits a member variable called name from the class Employee (Displays 15.1 and 15.2). For example, the following code would set the value of the member variable name of the object joe to "Josephine". (This code also sets the member variable ssn to "123-45-6789" and both the wage_rate and hours to 0.)

```
HourlyEmployee joe("Josephine", "123-45-6789", 0, 0);
```

If you want to change joe.name to "Mighty-Joe", you can do so as follows:

```
joe.set_name("Mighty-Joe");
```

But you must be a bit careful about how you manipulate inherited member variables such as name. The member variable name of the class HourlyEmployee was inherited from the class Employee, but the member variable name is a private member variable in the definition of the class Employee. That means that name can be directly accessed only within the definition of a member function in the class Employee. A member variable (or member function) that is private in a base class is not accessible *by name* in the definition of a member function for *any other class, not even in a member function definition of a derived class*. Thus, although the class HourlyEmployee does have a member variable named name (inherited from the base class Employee), it is illegal to directly access the member variable name in the definition of any member function in the class definition of HourlyEmployee.

For example, the following are the first few lines from the body of the member function HourlyEmployee::print_check (taken from Display 15.5):

```
void HourlyEmployee::print_check( )
{
    set_net_pay(hours * wage_rate);

    cout << "\n_____\n";
    cout << "Pay to the order of " << get_name( ) << endl;
    cout << "The sum of " << get_net_pay( ) << " Dollars\n";
```

You might have wondered why we needed to use the member function set_net_pay to set the value of the net_pay member variable. You might be tempted to rewrite the start of the member function definition as follows:

```
void HourlyEmployee::print_check( )
{                                            Illegal use of net_pay
    net_pay = hours * wage_rate;
```

As the comment indicates, this will not work. The member variable net_pay is a private member variable in the class Employee, and although a derived class like HourlyEmployee inherits the variable net_pay, it cannot access it directly. It must use some public member function to access the member variable net_pay. The correct way to accomplish the definition of print_check in the class HourlyEmployee is the way we did it in Display 15.5 (and part of which was displayed earlier).

The fact that name and net_pay are inherited variables that are private in the base class also explains why we needed to use the accessor functions get_name and get_net_pay in the definition of HourlyEmployee::print_check instead of simply using the variable names name and net_pay. You cannot mention a private inherited member variable by name. You must instead use public accessor and mutator member functions (such as get_name and set_name) that were defined in the base class. (Recall that an *accessor function* is a function that allows you to access member variables of a class, and a *mutator function* is one that allows you to change member variables of a class. Accessor and mutator functions were covered in Chapter 10.)

The fact that a private member variable of a base class cannot be accessed in the definition of a member function of a derived class often seems wrong to people. After all, if you are an hourly employee and you want to change your name, nobody says, "Sorry name is a private member variable of the class Employee." After all, if you are an hourly employee, you are also an employee. In Java, this is also true; an object of the class HourlyEmployee is also an object of the class Employee. However, the laws on the use of private member variables and member functions must be as we described, or else their privacy would be compromised. If private member variables of a class were accessible in member function definitions of a derived class, then anytime you wanted to access a private member variable, you could simply create a derived class and access it in a member function of that class, which would mean that all private member variables would be accessible to anybody who wanted to put in a little extra effort. This adversarial scenario illustrates the problem, but the big problem is unintentional errors, not intentional subversion. If private member variables of a class were accessible in member function definitions of a derived class, then the member variables might be changed by mistake or in inappropriate ways. (Remember, accessor and mutator functions can guard against inappropriate changes to member variables.)

We will discuss one possible way to get around this restriction on private member variables of the base class in the subsection entitled "The *protected* Qualifier" a bit later in this chapter. ■

PITFALL   Private Member Functions Are Effectively Not Inherited

As we noted in the previous Pitfall section, a member variable (or member function) that is private in a base class is not directly accessible outside of the interface and implementation of the base class, *not even in a member function definition for a derived class*. Note that private member functions are just like private variables in terms of not being directly available. But in the case of member functions, the restriction is more dramatic. A private variable can be accessed indirectly via an accessor or mutator member function. A private member function is simply not available. It is just as if the private member function were not inherited.

This should not be a problem. Private member functions should just be used as helping functions, and so their use should be limited to the class in which they are defined. If you want a member function to be used as a helping member function in a number of inherited classes, then it is not *just* a helping function, and you should make the member function public. ■

The *protected* Qualifier

As you have seen, you cannot access a private member variable or private member function in the definition or implementation of a derived class. There is a classification of member variables and functions that allows them to be accessed by name in a derived class but not anyplace else, such as in some class that is not a derived class. If you use the qualifier *protected*, rather than *private* or *public*, before a member variable or member function of a class, then for any class or function other than a derived class, the effect is the same as if the member variable were labeled *private*; however, in a derived class the variable can be accessed by name.

For example, consider the class HourlyEmployee that was derived from the base class Employee. We were required to use accessor and mutator member functions to manipulate the inherited member variables in the definition of HourlyEmployee::print_check. If all the private member variables in the class Employee were labeled with the keyword *protected* instead of *private*, the definition of HourlyEmployee::print_check in the derived class Employee could be simplified to the following:

```
void HourlyEmployee::print_check( )
//Only works if the member variables of Employee are marked
//protected instead of private.
{
    net_pay = hours * wage_rate;

    cout << "\n_____\n";
    cout << "Pay to the order of " << name << endl;
```

```
    cout << "The sum of " << net_pay << " Dollars\n";
    cout << "_____\n";
    cout << "Check Stub: NOT NEGOTIABLE\n";
    cout << "Employee Number: " << ssn << endl;
    cout << "Hourly Employee. \nHours worked: " << hours
         << " Rate: " << wage_rate << " Pay: " << net_pay
         << endl;
    cout << "_____\n";

}
```

In the derived class HourlyEmployee, the inherited member variables name, net_pay, and ssn can be accessed by name, provided they are marked as *protected* (as opposed to *private*) in the base class Employee. However, in any class that is not derived from the class Employee, these member variables are treated as if they were marked *private*.

Member variables that are protected in the base class act as though they were also marked *protected* in any derived class. For example, suppose you define a derived class PartTimeHourlyEmployee of the class HourlyEmployee. The class PartTimeHourlyEmployee inherits all the member variables of the class HourlyEmployee, including the member variables that HourlyEmployee inherits from the class Employee. So, the class PartTimeHourlyEmployee will have the member variables net_pay, name, and ssn. If these member variables were marked *protected* in the class Employee, then they can be used by name in the definitions of functions of the class PartTimeHourlyEmployee. Except for derived classes (and derived classes of derived classes, etc.), a member variable that is marked *protected* is treated the same as if it were marked *private*.

We include a discussion of *protected* member variables primarily because you will see them used and should be familiar with them. Many, but not all, programming authorities say it is bad style to use *protected* member variables. They say it compromises the principle of hiding the class implementation and that all member variables should be marked *private*. If all member variables are marked *private*, the inherited member variables cannot be accessed by name in derived class function definitions. However, this is not as bad as its sounds. The inherited *private* member variables can be accessed indirectly by invoking inherited functions that either read or change the *private* inherited variables. Since authorities differ, you will have to make your own decision on whether or not to use protected members.

Protected Members

If you use the qualifier *protected*, rather than *private* or *public*, before a member variable of a class, then for any class or function other than a derived class (or a derived class of a derived class, etc.), the

(continued)

situation is the same as if the member variable were labeled *private*. However, in the definition of a member function of a derived class, the variable can be accessed by name. Similarly, if you use the qualifier *protected* before a member function of a class, then for any class or function other than a derived class (or a derived class of a derived class, etc.), that is the same as if the member function were labeled *private*. However, in the definition of a member function of a derived class the protected function can be used.

Inherited protected members are inherited in the derived class as if they were marked *protected* in the derived class. In other words, if a member is marked as *protected* in a base class, then it can be accessed by name in the definitions of all descendant classes, not just in those classes directly derived from the base class.

SELF-TEST EXERCISES

1. Is the following program legal (assuming appropriate #include and *using* directives are added)?

   ```
   void show_employee_data(const Employee object);

   int main( )
   {
       HourlyEmployee joe("Mighty Joe",
                       "123-45-6789", 20.50, 40);
       SalariedEmployee boss("Mr. Big Shot",
                           "987-65-4321", 10500.50);
       show_employee_data(joe);
       show_employee_data(boss);

       return 0;
   }

   void show_employee_data(const Employee object)
   {
       cout << "Name: " << object.get_name( ) << endl;
       cout << "Social Security Number: "
           << object.get_ssn( ) << endl;
   }
   ```

2. Give a definition for a class SmartBut that is a derived class of the base class Smart, which we reproduce for you here. Do not bother with #include directives or namespace details.

```
class Smart
{
public:
    Smart( );
    void print_answer( ) const;
protected:
    int a;
    int b;
};
```

This class should have an additional data field, crazy, that is of type *bool*, one additional member function that takes no arguments and returns a value of type *bool*, and suitable constructors. The new function is named is_crazy. You do not need to give any implementations, just the class definition.

3. Is the following a legal definition of the member function is_crazy in the derived class SmartBut discussed in Self-Test Exercise 2? Explain your answer. (Remember, the question asks if it is legal, not if it is a sensible definition.)

```
bool SmartBut::is_crazy( ) const
{
    if (a > b)
        return false;
    else
        return true;
}
```

Redefinition of Member Functions

In the definition of the derived class HourlyEmployee (Display 15.3), we gave the declarations for the new member functions set_rate, get_rate, set_hours, and get_hours. We also gave the function declaration for only one of the member functions inherited from the class Employee. The inherited member functions whose function declarations were not given (such as set_name and set_ssn) are inherited unchanged. They have the same definition in the class HourlyEmployee as they do in the base class Employee. When you define a derived class like HourlyEmployee, you list only the function declarations for the inherited member functions whose definitions you want to change to have a different definition in the derived class. If you look at the implementation of the class HourlyEmployee, given in Display 15.5, you will see that we have redefined the inherited member function print_check. The class SalariedEmployee also gives a new definition to the member function print_check, as shown in Display 15.6. Moreover, the two classes give different definitions from each other. The function print_check is **redefined** in the derived classes.

> ### Redefining an Inherited Function
>
> A derived class inherits all the member functions (and member variables as well) that belong to the base class. However, if a derived class requires a different implementation for an inherited member function, the function may be redefined in the derived class. When a member function is redefined, you must list its declaration in the definition of the derived class even though the declaration is the same as in the base class. If you do not wish to redefine a member function that is inherited from the base class, then it is not listed in the definition of the derived class.

DISPLAY 15.6 Implementation for the Derived Class SalariedEmployee
(part 1 of 2)

```
1    //This is the file salariedemployee.cpp.
2    //This is the implementation for the class SalariedEmployee.
3    //The interface for the class SalariedEmployee is in
4    //the header file salariedemployee.h.
5    #include <iostream>
6    #include <string>
7    #include "salariedemployee.h"
8    using namespace std;

9    namespace employeessavitch
10   {
11       SalariedEmployee::SalariedEmployee( ) : Employee( ), salary(0)
12       {
13           //deliberately empty
14       }
15       SalariedEmployee::SalariedEmployee(string the_name, string the_number,
16           double the_weekly_salary)
17                   : Employee(the_name, the_number), salary(the_weekly_salary)
18       {
19           //deliberately empty
20       }

21       double SalariedEmployee::get_salary( ) const
22       {
23           return salary;
24       }

25       void SalariedEmployee::set_salary(double new_salary)
26       {
27           salary = new_salary;
28       }
```

(continued)

DISPLAY 15.6 **Implementation for the Derived Class** SalariedEmployee
(part 2 of 2)

```
29      void SalariedEmployee::print_check( )
30      {
31          set_net_pay(salary);
32          cout << "\n_____\n";
33          cout << "Pay to the order of " << get_name( ) << endl;
34          cout << "The sum of " << get_net_pay( ) << " Dollars\n";
35          cout << "_____\n";
36          cout << "Check Stub NOT NEGOTIABLE \n";

37      void SalariedEmployee::print_check( )
38      {
39          set_net_pay(salary);
40          cout << "\n_____\n";
41          cout << "Pay to the order of " << get_name( ) << endl;
42          cout << "The sum of " << get_net_pay( ) << " Dollars\n";
43          cout << "_____\n";
44          cout << "Check Stub NOT NEGOTIABLE \n";
45          cout << "Employee Number: " << get_ssn( ) << endl;
46          cout << "Salaried Employee. Regular Pay: "
47               << salary << endl;
48          cout << "_____\n";
49      }
50  }//employeessavitch
```

Display 15.7 gives a demonstration program that illustrates the use of the derived classes HourlyEmployee and SalariedEmployee.

DISPLAY 15.7 **Using Derived Classes** *(part 1 of 2)*

```
1      #include <iostream>
2      #include "hourlyemployee.h"
3      #include "salariedemployee.h"
4      using std::cout;
5      using std::endl;
6      using namespace employeessavitch;

7      int main( )
8      {
9          HourlyEmployee joe;
10         joe.set_name("Mighty Joe");
11         joe.set_ssn("123-45-6789");
12         joe.set_rate(20.50);
13         joe.set_hours(40);
```

(continued)

DISPLAY 15.7   Using Derived Classes *(part 2 of 2)*

```
14        cout << "Check for " << joe.get_name( )
15             << " for " << joe.get_hours( ) << " hours.\n";
16        joe.print_check( );
17        cout << endl;

18        SalariedEmployee boss("Mr. Big Shot", "987-65-4321", 10500.50);
19        cout << "Check for " <<boss.get_name( )<< endl;
20        boss.print_check( );
```

> The functions set_name, set_ssn, set_rate, set_hours,
> and get_name *are inherited unchanged from the class* Employee. *The*
> *function* print_check *is redefined. The function* get_hours *was added*
> *to the derived class* HourlyEmployee.

```
21        return 0;
22    }
```

Sample Dialogue

```
Check for Mighty Joe for 40 hours.

_____
Pay to the order of Mighty Joe
The sum of 820 Dollars

_____
Check Stub: NOT NEGOTIABLE
Employee Number: 123-45-6789
Hourly Employee.
Hours worked: 40 Rate: 20.5 Pay: 820

_____
Check for Mr. Big Shot

_____
Pay to the order of Mr. Big Shot
The sum of 10500.5 Dollars

_____
Check Stub NOT NEGOTIABLE
Employee Number: 987-65-4321
Salaried Employee. Regular Pay: 10500.5

_____
```

Redefining Versus Overloading

Do not confuse *redefining* a function definition in a derived class with
overloading a function name. When you redefine a function definition, the
new function definition given in the derived class has the same number and

types of parameters. On the other hand, if the function in the derived class were to have a different number of parameters or a parameter of a different type from the function in the base class, then the derived class would have both functions. That would be overloading. For example, suppose we added a function with the following function declaration to the definition of the class HourlyEmployee:

```
void set_name(string first_name, string last_name);
```

The class HourlyEmployee would have this two-argument function set_name, and it would also inherit the following one-argument function set_name:

```
void set_name(string new_name);
```

The class HourlyEmployee would have two functions named set_name. This would be *overloading* the function name set_name.

On the other hand, both the class Employee and the class HourlyEmployee define a function with the following function declaration:

```
void print_check( );
```

In this case, the class HourlyEmployee has only one function named print_check, but the definition of the function print_check for the class HourlyEmployee is different from its definition for the class Employee. In this case, the function print_check has been *redefined*.

If you get redefining and overloading confused, you do have one consolation. They are both legal. So, it is more important to learn how to use them than it is to learn to distinguish between them. Nonetheless, you should learn the difference.

Signature

A function's **signature** is the function's name with the sequence of types in the parameter list, not including the *const* keyword and not including the ampersand (&). When you overload a function name, the two definitions of the function name must have different signatures using this definition of signature.[2]

If a function has the same name in a derived class as in the base class but has a different signature, that is overloading, not redefinition.

---

[2] Some compilers may allow overloading on the basis of *const* versus no *const*, but you cannot count on this and so should not do it. For this reason, some definitions of *signature* include the *const* modifier, but this is a cloudy issue that is best avoided until you become an expert.

Access to a Redefined Base Function

Suppose you redefine a function so that it has a different definition in the derived class from what it had in the base class. The definition that was given in the base class is not completely lost to the derived class objects. However, if you want to invoke the version of the function given in the base class with an object in the derived class, you need some way to say "use the definition of this function as given in the base class (even though I am an object of the derived class)." The way you say this is to use the scope resolution operator with the name of the base class. An example should clarify the details.

Consider the base class Employee (Display 15.1) and the derived class HourlyEmployee (Display 15.3). The function print_check( ) is defined in both classes. Now suppose you have an object of each class, as in

```
Employee jane_e;
HourlyEmployee sally_h;
```

Then

```
jane_e.print_check( );
```

uses the definition of print_check given in the class Employee, and

```
sally_h.print_check( );
```

uses the definition of print_check given in the class HourlyEmployee.

But, suppose you want to invoke the version of print_check given in the definition of the base class Employee with the derived class object sally_h as the calling object for print_check. You do that as follows:

```
sally_h.Employee::print_check( );
```

Of course, you are unlikely to want to use the version of print_check given in the particular class Employee, but with other classes and other functions, you may occasionally want to use a function definition from a base class with a derived class object. An example is given in Self-Test Exercise 6.

SELF-TEST EXERCISES

4. The class SalariedEmployee inherits both of the functions get_name and print_check (among other things) from the base class Employee, yet only the function declaration for the function print_check is given in the definition of the class SalariedEmployee. Why isn't the function declaration for the function get_name given in the definition of SalariedEmployee?

5. Give a definition for a class TitledEmployee that is a derived class of the base class SalariedEmployee given in Display 15.4. The class

TitledEmployee has one additional member variable of type string called title. It also has two additional member functions: get_title, which takes no arguments and returns a string; and set_title, which is a *void* function that takes one argument of type string. It also redefines the member function set_name. You do not need to give any implementations, just the class definition. However, do give all needed #include directives and all *using namespace* directives. Place the class TitledEmployee in the namespace employeessavitch.

6. Give the definitions of the constructors for the class TitledEmployee that you gave as the answer to Self-Test Exercise 5. Also, give the redefinition of the member function set_name. The function set_name should insert the title into the name. Do not bother with #include directives or namespace details.

15.2 INHERITANCE DETAILS

The devil is in the details.

COMMON SAYING

This section presents some of the more subtle details about inheritance. Most of the topics are relevant only to classes that use dynamic arrays or pointers and other dynamic data.

Functions That Are Not Inherited

As a general rule if Derived is a derived class with base class Base, then all "normal" functions in the class Base are inherited members of the class Derived. However, there are some special functions that are, for all practical purposes, not inherited. We have already seen that, as a practical matter, constructors are not inherited and that private member functions are not inherited. Destructors are also effectively not inherited.

In the case of the copy constructor, it is not inherited, but if you do not define a copy constructor in a derived class (or any class for that matter), C++ will automatically generate a copy constructor for you. However, this default copy constructor simply copies the contents of member variables and does not work correctly for classes with pointers or dynamic data in their member variables. Thus, if your class member variables involve pointers, dynamic arrays, or other dynamic data, then you should define a copy constructor for the class. This applies whether or not the class is a derived class.

The assignment operator = is also not inherited. If the base class Base defines the assignment operator, but the derived class Derived does not define the assignment operator, then the class Derived will have an assignment operator, but it will be the default assignment operator that C++ creates (when you do not define =); it will not have anything to do with the base class assignment operator defined in Base.

It is natural that constructors, destructors, and the assignment operator are not inherited. To correctly perform their tasks, they need information that the base class does not possess. To correctly perform their functions, they need to know about the new member variables introduced in the derived class.

Assignment Operators and Copy Constructors in Derived Classes

Overloaded assignment operators and constructors are not inherited. However, they can be, and in almost all cases must be, used in the definitions of overloaded assignment operators and copy constructors in derived classes.

When overloading the assignment operator in a derived class, you normally use the overloaded assignment operator from the base class. We will present an outline of how the code for doing this is written. To help understand the code outline, remember that an overloaded assignment operator must be defined as a member function of the class.

If Derived is a class derived from Base, then the definition of the overloaded assignment operator for the class Derived would typically begin with something like the following:

```
Derived& Derived::operator =(const Derived& right_side)
{
    Base::operator =(right_side);
```

The first line of code in the body of the definition is a call to the overloaded assignment operator of the Base class. This takes care of the inherited member variables and their data. The definition of the overloaded assignment operator would then go on to set the new member variables that were introduced in the definition of the class Derived.

A similar situation holds for defining the copy constructor in a derived class. If Derived is a class derived from Base, then the definition of the copy constructor for the class Derived would typically use the copy constructor for the class Base to set up the inherited member variables and their data. The code would typically begin with something like the following:

```
Derived::Derived(const Derived& object)
              : Base(object), <probably more initializations>
    {
```

The invocation of the base class copy constructor Base(object) sets up the inherited member variables of the Derived class object being created. Note that since object is of type Derived, it is also of type Base; therefore, object is a legal argument to the copy constructor for the class Base.

Of course, these techniques do not work unless you have a correctly functioning assignment operator and a correctly functioning copy constructor for the base class. This means that the base class definition must include a copy constructor and that either the default automatically created assignment operator must work correctly for the base class or the base class must have a suitable overloaded definition of the assignment operator.

Destructors in Derived Classes

If a base class has a correctly functioning destructor, then it is relatively easy to define a correctly functioning destructor in a class derived from the base class. When the destructor for the derived class is invoked, it automatically invokes the destructor of the base class, so there is no need for the explicit writing of a call to the base class destructor; it always happens automatically. The derived class destructor therefore need only worry about using *delete* on the member variables (and any data they point to) that are added in the derived class. It is the job of the base class destructor to invoke *delete* on the inherited member variables.

If class B is derived from class A and class C is derived from class B, then when an object of the class C goes out of scope, first the destructor for the class C is called, then the destructor for class B is called, and finally the destructor for class A is called. Note that the order in which destructors are called is the reverse of the order in which constructors are called.

▌ SELF-TEST EXERCISES   myprogramminglab

7. You know that an overloaded assignment operator and a copy constructor are not inherited. Does this mean that if you do not define an overloaded assignment operator or a copy constructor for a derived class, then that derived class will have no assignment operator and no copy constructor?

8. Suppose Child is a class derived from the class Parent, and the class Grandchild is a class derived from the class Child. This question is concerned with the constructors and destructors for the three classes Parent, Child, and Grandchild. When a constructor for the class Grandchild is invoked, what constructors are invoked and in what order? When the destructor for the class Grandchild is invoked, what destructors are invoked and in what order?

9. Give the definitions for the member function add_value, the copy constructor, the overloaded assignment operator, and the destructor for the following class. This class is intended to be a class for a partially filled array. The member variable number_used contains the number of array positions currently filled. The other constructor definition is given to help you get started.

```
#include <iostream>
#include <cstdlib>
```

```
using namespace std;

class PartFilledArray
{
public:
    PartFilledArray(int array_size);
    PartFilledArray(const PartFilledArray& object);
    ~PartFilledArray();
    void operator =(const PartFilledArray& right_side);
    void add_value(double new_entry);
    //There would probably be more member functions
    //but they are irrelevant to this exercise.
protected:
    double *a;
    int max_number;
    int number_used;
};
PartFilledArray::PartFilledArray(int array_size)
                : max_number(array_size), number_used(0)
{
    a = new double[max_number];
}
```

(Many authorities would say that the member variables should be private rather than protected. We tend to agree. However, using *protected* makes for a better practice assignment, and you should have some experience with protected variables because some programmers do use them.)

10. Define a class called PartFilledArrayWMax that is a derived class of the class PartFilledArray. The class PartFilledArrayWMax has one additional member variable named max_value that holds the maximum value stored in the array. Define a member accessor function named get_max that returns the maximum value stored in the array. Redefine the member function add_value and define two constructors, one of which has an *int* argument for the maximum number of entries in the array. Also define a copy constructor, an overloaded assignment operator, and a destructor. (A real class would have more member functions, but these will do for an exercise.)

15.3 POLYMORPHISM

I did it my way.

FRANK SINATRA

Polymorphism refers to the ability to associate multiple meanings to one function name. As it has come to be used today, *polymorphism* refers to a very particular way of associating multiple meanings to a single function name. That is, **polymorphism** refers to the ability to associate multiple meanings to one function name by means of a special mechanism known as *late binding*. Polymorphism is one of the key components of a programming philosophy known as *object-oriented programming*. Late binding, and therefore polymorphism, is the topic of this section.

Late Binding

A *virtual function* is one that, in some sense, may be used before it is defined. For example, a graphics program may have several kinds of figures, such as rectangles, circles, ovals, and so forth. Each figure might be an object of a different class. For example, the Rectangle class might have member variables for a height, width, and center point, while the Circle class might have member variables for a center point and a radius. In a well-designed programming project, all of them would probably be descendants of a single parent class called, for example, Figure. Now, suppose you want a function to draw a figure on the screen. To draw a circle, you need different instructions from those you need to draw a rectangle. So, each class needs to have a different function to draw its kind of figure. However, because the functions belong to the classes, they can all be called draw. If r is a Rectangle object and c is a Circle object, then r.draw ( ) and c.draw ( ) can be functions implemented with different code. All this is not news, but now we move on to something new: *virtual functions* defined in the parent class Figure.

Now, the parent class Figure may have functions that apply to all figures. For example, it might have a function called center that moves a figure to the center of the screen by erasing it and then redrawing it in the center of the screen. Figure::center might use the function draw to redraw the figure in the center of the screen. When you think of using the inherited function center with figures of the classes Rectangle and Circle, you begin to see that there are complications here.

To make the point clear and more dramatic, let's suppose the class Figure is already written and in use and at some later time we add a class for a brand-new kind of figure, say, the class Triangle. Now, Triangle can be a derived class of the class Figure, and so the function center will be inherited from the class Figure; thus, the function center should apply to (and perform correctly for!) all Triangles. But there is a complication. The function center uses draw, and the function draw is different for each type of figure. The inherited function center (if nothing special is done) will use the definition of the function draw given in the class Figure, and that function draw does not work correctly for Triangles. We want the inherited function center to use the function Triangle::draw rather than the function Figure::draw. But the class Triangle, and therefore the function Triangle::draw, was not even written when the function center (defined in the class Figure) was written and compiled! How can the function center possibly work correctly for Triangles? The compiler did not know anything about Triangle::draw at the time that `center` was compiled. The answer is that it can apply provided `draw` is a *virtual function*.

When you make a function **virtual**, you are telling the compiler, "I do not know how this function is implemented. Wait until it is used in a program, and then get the implementation from the object instance." The technique of waiting until run-time to determine the implementation of a procedure is called **late binding** or **dynamic binding**. Virtual functions are the way C++ provides late binding. But enough introduction. We need an example to make this come alive (and to teach you how to use virtual functions in your programs). In order to explain the details of virtual functions in C++, we will use a simplified example from an application area other than drawing figures.

Virtual Functions in C++

Suppose you are designing a record-keeping program for an automobile parts store. You want to make the program versatile, but you are not sure you can account for all possible situations. For example, you want to keep track of sales, but you cannot anticipate all types of sales. At first, there will be only regular sales to retail customers who go to the store to buy one particular part. However, later you may want to add sales with discounts, or mail-order sales with a shipping charge. All these sales will be for an item with a basic price and ultimately will produce some bill. For a simple sale, the bill is just the basic price, but if you later add discounts, then some kinds of bills will also depend on the size of the discount. Your program will need to compute daily gross sales, which intuitively should just be the sum of all the individual sales bills. You may also want to calculate the largest and smallest sales of the day or the average sale for the day. All these can be calculated from the individual bills, but the functions for computing the bills will not be added until later, when you decide what types of sales you will be dealing with. To accommodate this, we make the function for computing the bill a virtual function. (For simplicity in this first example, we assume that each sale is for just one item, although with derived classes and virtual functions we could, but will not here, account for sales of multiple items.)

Displays 15.8 and 15.9 contain the interface and implementation for the class `Sale`. All types of sales will be derived classes of the class `Sale`. The class `Sale` corresponds to simple sales of a single item with no added discounts or charges. Notice the reserved word *virtual* in the function declaration for the function `bill` (Display 15.8). Notice (Display 15.9) that the member function `savings` and the overloaded operator < both use the function `bill`. Since `bill` is declared to be a virtual function, we can later define derived classes of the class `Sale` and define their versions of the function `bill`, and the definitions of the member function `savings` and the overloaded operator <, which we gave with the class `Sale`, will use the version of the function `bill` that corresponds to the object of the derived class.

DISPLAY 15.8   Interface for the Base Class Sale

```
1    //This is the header file sale.h.
2    //This is the interface for the class Sale.
3    //Sale is a class for simple sales.
4    #ifndef SALE_H
5    #define SALE_H
6
7    #include <iostream>
8    using namespace std;
9
10   namespace salesavitch
11   {
12
13       class Sale
14       {
15       public:
16           Sale();
17           Sale(double the_price);
18           virtual double bill() const;
19           double savings(const Sale& other) const;
20           //Returns the savings if you buy other instead of the calling object.
21       protected:
22               double price;
23       };
24
25       bool operator <(const Sale& first, const Sale& second);
26       //Compares two sales to see which is larger.
27   }//salesavitch
28
29   #endif // SALE_H
```

DISPLAY 15.9   Implementation of the Base Class Sale *(part 1 of 2)*

```
1    //This is the implementation file: sale.cpp
2    //This is the implementation for the class Sale.
3    //The interface for the class Sale is in
4    //the header file sale.h.
5    #include "sale.h"
6
7    namespace salesavitch
8    {
9        Sale::Sale() : price(0)
10       {}
11
12       Sale::Sale(double the_price) : price(the_price)
13       {}
14
```

(continued)

DISPLAY 15.9   Implementation of the Base Class Sale *(part 2 of 2)*

```
15      double Sale::bill() const
16      {
17          return price;
18      }
19
20      double Sale::savings(const Sale& other) const
21      {
22          return ( bill() - other.bill() );
23      }
24
25      bool operator <(const Sale& first, const Sale& second)
26      {
27          return (first.bill() < second.bill());
28      }
29   }//salesavitch
```

For example, Display 15.10 shows the derived class DiscountSale. Notice that the class DiscountSale requires a different definition for its version of the function bill. Nonetheless, when the member function savings and the overloaded operator < are used with an object of the class DiscountSale, they will use the version of the function definition for bill that was given

DISPLAY 15.10   The Derived Class DiscountSale *(part 1 of 2)*

```
1    //This is the interface for the class DiscountSale.
2    #ifndef DISCOUNTSALE_H
3    #define DISCOUNTSALE_H                  This is the file discountsale.h.
4    #include "sale.h"
5
6    namespace salesavitch
7    {
8        class DiscountSale : public Sale
9        {
10       public:
11           DiscountSale();
12           DiscountSale(double the_price, double the_discount);
13           //Discount is expressed as a percent of the price.
14           virtual double bill() const;    ←
15       protected:
16           double discount;
17       };
18   }//salesavitch
19   #endif //DISCOUNTSALE_H
```

The keyword virtual is not required here, but it is good style to include it.

(continued)

DISPLAY 15.10   The Derived Class DiscountSale *(part 2 of 2)*

```
1    //This is the implementation for the class DiscountSale.
2    #include "discountsale.h"              This is the file discountsale.cpp.
3
4    namespace salesavitch
5    {
6        DiscountSale::DiscountSale() : Sale(), discount(0)
7        {}
8        DiscountSale::DiscountSale(double the_price, double the_discount)
9                  : Sale (the_price), discount(the_discount)
10       {}
11       double DiscountSale::bill ( ) const
12       {
13           double fraction = discount/100;
14           return (1 - fraction)*price;
15       }
16   }//salesavitch
```

with the class DiscountSale. This is indeed a pretty fancy trick for C++ to pull off. Consider the function call d1.savings(d2) for objects d1 and d2 of the class DiscountSale. The definition of the function savings (even for an object of the class DiscountSale) is given in the implementation file for the base class Sale, which was compiled before we ever even thought of the class DiscountSale. Yet, in the function call d1.savings(d2), the line that calls the function bill knows enough to use the definition of the function bill given for the class DiscountSale.

How does this work? In order to write C++ programs, you can just assume it happens by magic, but the real explanation was given in the introduction to this section. When you label a function *virtual*, you are telling the C++ environment, "Wait until this function is used in a program, and then get the implementation corresponding to the calling object."

Display 15.11 gives a sample program that illustrates how the virtual function bill and the functions that use bill work in a complete program.

DISPLAY 15.11   Use of a Virtual Function *(part 1 of 2)*

```
1    //Demonstrates the performance of the virtual function bill.
2    #include <iostream>
3    #include "sale.h" //Not really needed, but safe due to ifndef.
4    #include "discountsale.h"
5    using namespace std;
6    using namespace salesavitch;
7
```

(continued)

DISPLAY 15.11 **Use of a Virtual Function** *(part 2 of 2)*

```
8     int main()
9     {
10        Sale simple(10.00); //One item at $10.00.
11        DiscountSale discount(11.00, 10);//One item at $11.00 at 10% discount.
12
13        cout.setf(ios::fixed);
14        cout.setf(ios::showpoint);
15        cout.precision(2);
16
17        if (discount < simple)
18        {
19            cout << "Discounted item is cheaper.\n";
20            cout << "Savings is $" << simple.savings(discount) << endl;
21        }
22        else
23            cout << "Discounted item is not cheaper.\n";
24
25        return 0;
26    }
```

Sample Dialogue

```
Discounted item is cheaper.
Savings is $0.10
```

There are a number of technical details you need to know in order to use virtual functions in C++. We list them here:

- If a function will have a different definition in a derived class than in the base class and you want it to be a virtual function, you add the keyword *virtual* to the function declaration in the base class. You do not need to add the reserved word *virtual* to the function declaration in the derived class. If a function is virtual in the base class, then it is automatically virtual in the derived class. (However, it is a good idea to label the function declaration in the derived class *virtual*, even though it is not required.)
- The reserved word virtual is added to the function declaration and not to the function definition.
- You do not get a virtual function and the benefits of virtual functions unless you use the keyword *virtual*.

Since virtual functions are so great, why not make all member functions virtual? Almost the only reason for not always using virtual functions is efficiency. The compiler and the run-time environment need to do much more work for virtual functions, and so if you label more member functions *virtual* than you need to, your programs will be less efficient.

Overriding

When a virtual function definition is changed in a derived class, programmers often say the function definition is **overridden.** In the C++ literature, a distinction is sometimes made between the terms *redefined* and *overridden*. Both terms refer to changing the definition of the function in a derived class. If the function is a virtual function, it's called *overriding*. If the function is not a virtual function, it's called *redefining*. This may seem like a silly distinction to you, the programmer, since you do the same thing in both cases, but the two cases are treated differently by the compiler.

Polymorphism

The term **polymorphism** refers to the ability to associate multiple meanings to one function name by means of late binding. Thus, polymorphism, late binding, and virtual functions are really all the same topic.

SELF-TEST EXERCISE

 myprogramminglab

11. Suppose you modify the definitions of the class Sale (Display 15.8) by deleting the reserved word *virtual*. How would that change the output of the program in Display 15.11?

Virtual Functions and Extended Type Compatibility

We will discuss some of the further consequences of declaring a class member function to be *virtual* and do one example that uses some of these features.

C++ is a fairly strongly typed language. This means that the types of items are always checked and an error message is issued if there is a type mismatch, such as a type mismatch between an argument and a formal parameter when there is no conversion that can be automatically invoked. This also means that normally the value assigned to a variable must match the type of the variable, although in a few well-defined cases C++ will perform an automatic type cast (called a *coercion*) so that it appears that you can assign a value of one type to a variable of another type. For example, C++ allows you to assign a value of type *char* or *int* to a variable of type *double*. However, C++ does not allow you to assign a value of type *double* or *float* to a variable of any integer type (*char*, *short*, *int*, *long*).

However, as important as strong typing is, this strong type checking interferes with the very idea of inheritance in object-oriented programming. Suppose you have defined class A and class B and have defined objects of type class A and class B. You cannot always assign between objects of these types. For example, suppose a program or unit contains the following type declarations:

```
class Pet
{
public:
    virtual void print();
    string name;
};

class Dog : public Pet
{
public:
    virtual void print(); //Keyword virtual not needed, but is
            //put here for clarity. (It is also good style!)
    string breed;
};

Dog vdog;
Pet vpet;
```

Now concentrate on the data members, name and breed. (To keep this example simple, we have made the member variables *public*. In a real application, they should be *private* and have functions to manipulate them.)

Anything that is a Dog is also a Pet. It would seem to make sense to allow programs to consider values of type Dog to also be values of type Pet, and hence the following should be allowed:

```
vdog.name = "Tiny";
vdog.breed = "Great Dane";
vpet = vdog;
```

C++ does allow this sort of assignment. You may assign a value, such as the value of vdog, to a variable of a parent type, such as vpet, but you are not allowed to perform the reverse assignment. Although the assignment above is allowed, the value that is assigned to the variable vpet loses its breed field. This is called the **slicing problem.** The following attempted access will produce an error message:

```
cout << vpet.breed; //Illegal: class Pet has no member named breed
```

You can argue that this makes sense, since once a Dog is moved to a variable of type Pet it should be treated like any other Pet and not have properties peculiar to Dogs. This makes for a lively philosophical debate, but it usually just makes for a nuisance when programming. The dog named Tiny is still a Great Dane and we would like to refer to its breed, even if we treated it as a Pet someplace along the line.

Fortunately, C++ does offer us a way to treat a Dog as a Pet without throwing away the name of the breed. To do this, we use pointers to dynamic object instances. Suppose we add the following declarations:

```
Pet *ppet;
Dog *pdog;
```

If we use pointers and dynamic variables, we can treat Tiny as a Pet without losing his breed. The following is allowed:

```
pdog = new Dog;
pdog->name = "Tiny";
pdog->breed = "Great Dane";
ppet = pdog;
```

Moreover, we can still access the breed field of the node pointed to by ppet. Suppose that

```
Dog::print();
```

has been defined as follows:

```
//uses iostream
void Dog::print()
{
    cout << "name: " << name << endl;
    cout << "breed: " << breed << endl;
}
```

The statement

```
ppet->print();
```

will cause the following to be printed on the screen:

```
name: Tiny
breed: Great Dane
```

This is by virtue of the fact that print() is a *virtual* member function. (No pun intended.) We have included test code in Display 15.12.

DISPLAY 15.12 More Inheritance with Virtual Functions *(part 1 of 2)*

```
1    //Program to illustrate use of a virtual function
2    //to defeat the slicing problem.

3    #include <string>
4    #include <iostream>
5    using namespace std;
6
7    class Pet
8    {
9    public:
10       virtual void print();
11       string name;
12   };
13
14    class Dog : public Pet
15   {
16   public:
17       virtual void print(); //Keyword virtual not needed, but put
18                             //here for clarity. (It is also good style!)
19       string breed;
20   };
21
22   int main()
23   {
24       Dog vdog;
25       Pet vpet;
26
27       vdog.name = "Tiny";
28       vdog.breed = "Great Dane";
29       vpet = vdog;
30
31       //vpet.breed; is illegal since class Pet has no member named breed
32
33       Dog *pdog;
34       pdog = new Dog;
35       pdog->name = "Tiny";
36       pdog->breed = "Great Dane";
37
38       Pet *ppet;
39       ppet = pdog;
40       ppet->print(); // These two print the same output:
41       pdog->print(); // name: Tiny breed: Great Dane
42
43       //The following, which accesses member variables directly
44       //rather than via virtual functions, would produce an error:
45       //cout << "name: " << ppet->name << "  breed: "
```

(continued)

DISPLAY 15.12 More Inheritance with Virtual Functions *(part 2 of 2)*

```
46          //     << ppet->breed << endl;
47          //generates an error message: 'class Pet' has no member
48          //named 'breed' .
49          //See Pitfall section "Not Using Virtual Member Functions"
50          //for more discussion on this.
51
52          return 0;
53      }
54
55      void Dog::print()
56      {
57          cout << "name: " << name << endl;
58          cout << "breed: " << breed << endl;
59      }
60
61      void Pet::print()
62      {
63          cout << "name: " << endl;//Note no breed mentioned
64      }
```

Sample Dialogue

```
name: Tiny
breed: Great Dane
name: Tiny
breed: Great Dane
```

PITFALL   The Slicing Problem

Although it is legal to assign a derived class object to a base class variable, assigning a derived class object to a base class object slices off data. Any data members in the derived class object that are not also in the base class will be lost in the assignment, and any member functions that are not defined in the base class are similarly unavailable to the resulting base class object.

If we make the following declarations and assignments:

```
Dog vdog;
Pet vpet;
vdog.name = "Tiny";
vdog.breed = "Great Dane";
vpet = vdog;
```

then vpet cannot be a calling object for a member function introduced in Dog, and the data member, Dog::breed, is lost.   ■

PITFALL   Not Using Virtual Member Functions

In order to get the benefit of the extended type compatibility we discussed earlier, you must use *virtual* member functions. For example, suppose we had not used member functions in the example in Display 15.12. Suppose that in place of

```
ppet->print();
```

we had used the following:

```
cout << "name: " << ppet->name
        << " breed: " << ppet->breed << endl;
```

This code would have precipitated an error message. The reason for this is that the expression

```
*ppet
```

has its type determined by the pointer type of ppet. It is a pointer type for the type Pet, and the type Pet has no field named breed.

But print() was declared *virtual* by the base class, Pet. So, when the compiler sees the call

```
ppet->print();
```

it checks the *virtual* table for classes Pet and Dog and sees that ppet points to an object of type Dog. It therefore uses the code generated for

```
Dog::print(),
```

rather than the code for

```
Pet::print().
```

Object-oriented programming with dynamic variables is a very different way of viewing programming. This can all be bewildering at first. It will help if you keep two simple rules in mind:

1. If the domain type of the pointer p_ancestor is a base class for the domain type of the pointer p_descendant, then the following assignment of pointers is allowed:

    ```
    p_ancestor = p_descendant;
    ```

    Moreover, none of the data members or member functions of the dynamic variable being pointed to by p_descendant will be lost.

2. Although all the extra fields of the dynamic variable are there, you will need *virtual* member functions to access them.

■ PITFALL   Attempting to Compile Class Definitions Without Definitions for Every Virtual Member Function

It is wise to develop incrementally. This means code a little, then test a little, then code a little more, and test a little more, and so forth. However, if you try to compile classes with *virtual* member functions but do not implement each member, you may run into some very hard to understand error messages, even if you do not call the undefined member functions!

If any virtual member functions are not implemented before compiling, then the compilation fails with error messages similar to this: "undefined reference to *Class_Name* virtual table." Even if there is *no derived class* and there is *only one virtual* member, this kind of message still occurs if that function does not have a definition.

What makes the error messages very hard to decipher is that without definitions for the functions declared *virtual*, there may be further error messages complaining about an undefined reference to default constructors, even if these constructors really are already defined.   ■

■ PROGRAMMING TIP   Make Destructors Virtual

It is a good policy to always make destructors virtual, but before we explain why this is a good policy, we need to say a word or two about how destructors and pointers interact and about what it means for a destructor to be virtual.

Consider the following code, where SomeClass is a class with a destructor that is not virtual:

```
SomeClass *p = new SomeClass;
    . . .
delete p;
```

When *delete* is invoked with p, the destructor of the class SomeClass is automatically invoked. Now, let's see what happens when a destructor is marked as *virtual*.

The easiest way to describe how destructors interact with the virtual function mechanism is that destructors are treated as if all destructors had the same name (even though they do not really have the same name). For example, suppose Derived is a derived class of the class Base and suppose the destructor in the class Base is marked *virtual*. Now consider the following code:

```
Base *pBase = new Derived;
    . . .
delete pBase;
```

When *delete* is invoked with pBase, a destructor is called. Since the destructor in the class Base was marked *virtual* and the object pointed to is of type

Derived, the destructor for the class Derived is called (and it in turn calls the destructor for the class Base). If the destructor in the class Base had not been declared as *virtual*, then only the destructor in the class Base would be called.

Another point to keep in mind is that when a destructor is marked as *virtual*, then all destructors of derived classes are automatically virtual (whether or not they are marked *virtual*). Again, this behavior is as if all destructors had the same name (even though they do not).

Now we are ready to explain why all destructors should be virtual. Suppose the class Base has a member variable pB of a pointer type, the constructor for the class Base creates a dynamic variable pointed to by pB, and the destructor for the class Base deletes the dynamic variable pointed to by pB. And suppose the destructor for the class Base is *not* marked *virtual*. Also suppose that the class Derived (which is derived from Base) has a member variable pD of a pointer type, the constructor for the class Derived creates a dynamic variable pointed to by pD, and the destructor for the class Derived deletes the dynamic variable pointed to by pD. Consider the following code:

```
Base *pBase = new Derived;
    . . .
delete pBase;
```

Since the destructor in the base class is not marked *virtual*, only the destructor for the class Base will be invoked. This will return to the freestore the memory for the dynamic variable pointed to by pB, but the memory for the dynamic variable pointed to by pD will never be returned to the freestore (until the program ends).

On the other hand, if the destructor for the base class Base were marked *virtual*, then when *delete* is applied to pBase, the destructor for the class Derived would be invoked (since the object pointed to is of type Derived). The destructor for the class Derive would delete the dynamic variable pointed to by pD and then automatically invoke the destructor for the base class Base, and that would delete the dynamic variable pointed to by pB. So, with the base class destructor marked as *virtual*, all the memory is returned to the freestore. To prepare for eventualities such as these, it is best to always mark destructors as virtual. ■

SELF-TEST EXERCISES

12. Why can't we assign a base class object to a derived class variable?

13. What is the problem with the (legal) assignment of a derived class object to a base class variable?

14. Suppose the base class and the derived class each have a member function with the same signature. When you have a pointer to a base class object

and call a function member through the pointer, discuss what determines which function is actually called—the base class member function or the derived-class function.

CHAPTER SUMMARY

■ Inheritance provides a tool for code reuse by deriving one class from another by adding features to the derived class.

■ Derived class objects inherit all the members of the base class and may add members.

■ Late binding means that the decision of which version of a member function is appropriate is decided at run-time. Virtual functions are what C++ uses to achieve late binding. Polymorphism, late binding, and virtual functions are really all the same topic.

■ A *protected* member in the base class is directly available to a publicly derived class's member functions.

Answers to Self-Test Exercises

1. Yes. You can plug in an object of a derived class for a parameter of the base class type. An HourlyEmployee is an Employee. A SalariedEmployee is an Employee.

2.
```
class SmartBut : public Smart
{
public:
    SmartBut( );
    SmartBut(int new_a, int new_b, bool new_crazy);
    bool is_crazy( ) const;
private:
    bool crazy;
};
```

3. It is legal because a and b are marked *protected* in the base class Smart and so they can be accessed by name in a derived class. If a and b had instead been marked *private*, then this would be illegal.

4. The declaration for the function get_name is not given in the definition of SalariedEmployee because it is not redefined in the class Salaried-Employee. It is inherited unchanged from the base class Employee.

5.
```
#include <iostream>
#include "salariedemployee.h"
using namespace std;
namespace employeessavitch
```

```
    {
        class TitledEmployee : public SalariedEmployee
        {
        public:
            TitledEmployee( );
            TitledEmployee(string the_name, string the_title
                            string the_ssn, double the_salary);
            string get_title( ) const;
            void set_title(string the_title);
            void set_name(string the_name);
        private:
            string title;
        };
    }//employeessavitch
```

6.
```
   namespace employeessavitch
   {
       TitledEmployee::TitledEmployee( )
             : SalariedEmployee( ), title("No title yet")
       {
           //deliberately empty
       }

       TitledEmployee::TitledEmployee(string the_name,
                           string the_title,
                           string the_ssn, double the_salary)
            :SalariedEmployee(the_name,the_ssn,the_salary),
                           title(the_title)
       {
           //deliberately empty
       }

       void TitledEmployee::set_name(string the_name)
       {
           Employee::set_name(title + the_name);
       }
   }//employeessavitch
```

7. No. If you do not define an overloaded assignment operator or a copy constructor for a derived class, then a default assignment operator and a default copy constructor will be defined for the derived class. However, if the class involves pointers, dynamic arrays, or other dynamic data, then it is almost certain that neither the default assignment operator nor the default copy constructor will behave as you want them to.

8. The constructors are called in the following order: first Parent, then Child, and finally Grandchild. The destructors are called in the reverse order: first Grandchild, then Child, and finally Parent.

9.
```
   //Uses iostream and cstdlib:
   void PartFilledArray::add_value(double new_entry)
```

```
{
    if (number_used == max_number)
    {
        cout << "Adding to a full array.\n";
        exit(1);
    }
    else
    {
        a[number_used] = new_entry;
        number_used++;
    }
}
PartFilledArray::PartFilledArray
        (const PartFilledArray& object)
                : max_number(object.max_number),
                    number_used(object.number_used)
{
    a = new double[max_number];

    for (int i = 0; i < number_used; i++)
        a[i] = object.a[i];
}

void PartFilledArray::operator =
                (const PartFilledArray& right_side)
{
    if (right_side.max_number > max_number)
    {
        delete [] a;
        max_number = right_side.max_number;
        a = new double[max_number];
    }
    number_used = right_side.number_used;

    for (int i = 0; i < number_used; i++)
        a[i] = right_side.a[i];
}

PartFilledArray::~PartFilledArray()
{
    delete [] a;
}
```

10.
```
class PartFilledArrayWMax : public PartFilledArray
{
public:
    PartFilledArrayWMax(int array_size);
    PartFilledArrayWMax(const PartFilledArrayWMax& object);
    ~PartFilledArrayWMax();
    void operator= (const PartFilledArrayWMax& right_side);
    void add_value(double new_entry);
    double get_max();
```

```
private:
    double max_value;
};

PartFilledArrayWMax::PartFilledArrayWMax(int array_size)
                             : PartFilledArray(array_size)
{
    //Body intentionally empty.
    //Max_value uninitialized, since there
    //is no suitable default value.
}

/*
Note that the following does not work, because it calls the
default constructor for PartFilledArray, but PartFilledArray
has no default constructor:
PartFilledArrayWMax::PartFilledArrayWMax(int array_size)
             : max_number(array_size), number_used(0)

{
    a = new double[max_number];
}
*/

PartFilledArrayWMax::PartFilledArrayWMax
            (const PartFilledArrayWMax& object)
               : PartFilledArray(object)
{
    if (object.number_used > 0)
    {
        max_value = a[0];
        for (int i = 1; i < number_used; i++)
            if (a[i] > max_value)
                max_value = a[i];
    }//else leave max_value uninitialized
}

//This is equivalent to the default destructor supplied
//by C++, and so this definition can be omitted.
//But, if you omit it, you must also omit the destructor
//declaration from the class definition.
PartFilledArrayWMax::~PartFilledArrayWMax()
{
    //Intentionally empty.
}

void PartFilledArrayWMax::operator =
                (const PartFilledArrayWMax& right_side)
{
    PartFilledArray::operator =(right_side);
    max_value = right_side.max_value;
}
```

```
//Uses iostream and cstdlib:
void PartFilledArrayWMax::add_value(double new_entry)

{
    if (number_used == max_number)
    {
        cout << "Adding to a full array.\n";
        exit(1);
    }
     if ((number_used == 0) || (new_entry > max_value))
        max_value = new_entry;
     a[number_used] = new_entry;
     number_used++;
}

double PartFilledArrayWMax::get_max()
{
    return max_value;
}
```

11. The output would change to

    ```
    Discounted item is not cheaper.
    ```

12. There would be no member to assign to the derived class's added members.

13. Although it is legal to assign a derived class object to a base class variable, this discards the parts of the derived class object that are not members of the base class. This situation is known as the *slicing problem*.

14. If the base class function carries the *virtual* modifier, then the type of the object to which the pointer was initialized determines whose member function is called. If the base class member function does not have the *virtual* modifier, then the type of the pointer determines whose member function is called.

PROGRAMMING PROJECTS

Visit www.myprogramminglab.com to complete many of these Programming Projects online and get instant feedback.   myprogramminglab

1. Write a program that uses the class SalariedEmployee in Display 15.4. Your program is to define a class called Administrator, which is to be derived from the class SalariedEmployee. You are allowed to change *private* in the base class to *protected*. You are to supply the following additional data and function members:

   A member variable of type string that contains the administrator's title (such as Director or Vice President).

A member variable of type string that contains the company area of responsibility (such as Production, Accounting, or Personnel).

A member variable of type string that contains the name of this administrator's immediate supervisor.

A *protected*: member variable of type *double* that holds the administrator's annual salary. It is possible for you to use the existing salary member if you did the change recommended earlier.

A member function called set_supervisor, which changes the supervisor name.

A member function for reading in an administrator's data from the keyboard.

A member function called print, which outputs the object's data to the screen.

An overloading of the member function print_check() with appropriate notations on the check.

2. Update the class Employee of Display 15.1 by adding address and gross_pay data members to the class. Provide corresponding input and display member functions and test all member functions. A user interface with a menu would be a nice touch for your test program.

VideoNote
Solution to Programming
Project 15.3

3. Give the definition of a class named Doctor whose objects are records for a clinic's doctors. This class will be a derived class of the class Salaried-Employee given in Display 15.4. A Doctor record has the doctor's specialty (such as "Pediatrician," "Obstetrician," "General Practitioner," etc., so use type string) and office visit fee (use type *double*). Be sure your class has a reasonable complement of constructors, accessor, and mutator member functions, an overloaded assignment operator, and a copy constructor. Write a driver program to test all your functions.

4. Create a base class called Vehicle that has the manufacturer's name (type string), number of cylinders in the engine (type *int*), and owner (type Person, given below). Then create a class called Truck that is derived from Vehicle and has additional properties: the load capacity in tons (type *double* since it may contain a fractional part) and towing capacity in pounds (type *int*). Be sure your classes have a reasonable complement of constructors, accessor, and mutator member functions, an overloaded assignment operator, and a copy constructor. Write a driver program that tests all your member functions.

The definition of the class Person follows. The implementation of the class is part of this Programming Project.

```
class Person
{
public:
    Person();
    Person(string the_name);
    Person(const Person& the_object);
    string get_name() const;
    Person& operator = (const Person& rt_side);
    friend istream& operator >>(istream& in_stream,
                    Person& person_object);
    friend ostream& operator <<(ostream& out_stream,
                    const Person& person_object);
private:
    string name;
};
```

5. Define a Worker class that is derived from the Employee class in Display 15.1. Define a class called Supervisor that is derived from the Employee class. Be creative when choosing member variables and functions. Write a driver program to test the Worker and Supervisor classes.

6. Give the definition of two classes, Patient and Billing, whose objects are records for a clinic. Patient will be derived from the class Person given in Programming Project 4. A Patient record has the patient's name (inherited from the class Person) and primary physician, of type Doctor defined in Programming Project 4. A Billing object will contain a Patient object, a Doctor object, and an amount due of type *double*. Be sure your classes have a reasonable complement of constructors, accessor, and mutator member functions, an overloaded assignment operator, and a copy constructor. First write a driver program to test all your member functions, and then write a test program that creates at least two patients, at least two doctors, and at least two Billing records, then prints out the total income from the Billing records.

7. Consider a graphics system that has classes for various figures—rectangles, squares, triangles, circles, and so on. For example, a rectangle might have data members for height, width, and center point, while a square and circle might have only a center point and an edge length or radius, respectively. In a well-designed system, these would be derived from a common class, Figure. You are to implement such a system.

    The class Figure is the base class. You should add only Rectangle and Triangle classes derived from Figure. Each class has stubs for member functions erase and draw. Each of these member functions outputs a message telling what function has been called and what the class of the calling object is. Since these are just stubs, they do nothing more than output this message. The member function center calls the erase and draw functions to erase and redraw the figure at the center. Since you have only stubs for erase and draw, center will not do any "centering" but will call the member functions erase and draw. Also add an output message in the member function center that announces that center is being called. The member functions should take no arguments.

There are three parts to this project:

a. Write the class definitions using no virtual functions. Compile and test.
b. Make the base class member functions virtual. Compile and test.
c. Explain the difference in results.

For a real example, you would have to replace the definition of each of these member functions with code to do the actual drawing. You will be asked to do this in Programming Project 8.

Use the following main function for all testing:

```
//This program tests Programming Project 7.
#include <iostream>
#include "figure.h"
#include "rectangle.h"
#include "triangle.h"
using std::cout;

int main( )
{
    Triangle tri;
    tri.draw( );
    cout <<
      "\nDerived class Triangle object calling center( ).\n";
    tri.center( ); //Calls draw and center
    Rectangle rect;
    rect.draw( );
    cout <<
      "\nDerived class Rectangle object calling center().\n";
    rect.center( ); //Calls draw and center
    return 0;
}
```

8. Flesh out Programming Project 7. Give new definitions for the various constructors and the member functions Figure::center, Figure::draw, Figure::erase, Triangle::draw, Triangle::erase, Rectangle::draw, and Rectangle::erase so that the draw functions actually draw figures on the screen by placing the character '*' at suitable locations. For the erase functions, you can simply clear the screen (by outputting blank lines or by doing something more sophisticated). There are a lot of details in this problem, and you will have to make decisions about some of them on your own.

9. Banks have many different types of accounts, often with different rules for fees associated with transactions such as withdrawals. Customers are allowed to transfer funds between accounts incurring the appropriate fees associated with withdrawal of funds from one account.

Write a program with a base class for a bank account and two derived classes (as described below) representing accounts with different rules for withdrawing funds. Also write a function that transfers funds from one account (of any type) to another. A transfer is a withdrawal from one account and a deposit into the other. Since the transfer can be done at any time with any type of account, the withdraw function in the classes must be virtual. Write a main program that creates three accounts (one from each class) and tests the transfer function.

For the classes, create a base class called BankAccount that has the name of the owner of the account (a string) and the balance in the account (*double*) as data members. Include member functions deposit and withdraw (each with a *double* for the amount as an argument) and accessor functions getName and getBalance. Deposit will add the amount to the balance (assuming the amount is nonnegative) and withdraw will subtract the amount from the balance (assuming the amount is nonnegative and less than or equal to the balance). Also create a class called MoneyMarketAccount that is derived from BankAccount. In a MoneyMarketAccount the user gets two free withdrawals in a given period of time (don't worry about the time for this problem). After the free withdrawals have been used, a withdrawal fee of $1.50 is deducted from the balance per withdrawal. Hence, the class must have a data member to keep track of the number of withdrawals. It also must override the withdraw definition. Finally, create a CDAccount class (to model a Certificate of Deposit) derived from BankAccount that in addition to having the name and balance also has an interest rate. CDs incur penalties for early withdrawal of funds. Assume that a withdrawal of funds (any amount) incurs a penalty of 25% of the annual interest earned on the account. Assume the amount withdrawn plus the penalty are deducted from the account balance. Again, the withdraw function must override the one in the base class. For all three classes, the withdraw function should return an integer indicating the status (either ok or insufficient funds for the withdrawal to take place). For the purposes of this exercise, do not worry about other functions and properties of these accounts (such as when and how interest is paid).

10. Radio Frequency IDentification (RFID) chips are small tags that can be placed on a product. They behave like wireless barcodes and can wirelessly broadcast an identification number to a receiver. One application of RFID chips is to use them to aid in the logistics of shipping freight. Consider a shipping container full of items. Without RFID chips, a human has to

manually inventory all of the items in the container to verify the contents. With an RFID chip attached to the shipping container, the RFID chip can electronically broadcast to a human the exact contents of the shipping container without human intervention.

To model this application, write a base class called ShippingContainer that has a container ID number as an integer. Include member functions to set and access the ID number. Add a virtual function called getManifest that returns an empty string. The purpose of this function is to return the contents of the shipping container.

Create a derived class called ManualShippingContainer that represents the manual method of inventorying the container. In this method, a human simply attaches a textual description of all contents of the container. For example, the description might be "4 crates of apples. 10 crates of pears." Add a new class variable of type string to store the manifest. Add a function called setManifest that sets this string. Override the getManifest function so that it returns this string.

Create a second derived class called RFIDShippingContainer that represents the RFID method of inventorying the container. To simulate what the RFID chips would compute, create an add function to simulate adding an item to the container. The class should store a list of all added items (as a string) and their quantity using the data structures of your choice. For example, if the add function were invoked three times as follows:

```
rfidContainer.add("crate of pears"); // Add one crate of pears
rfidContainer.add("crate of apples"); // Add one crate of apples
rfidContainer.add("crate of pears"); // Add one crate of pears
```

At this point, the data structure should be storing a list of two items: crate of apples and crate of pears. The quantity of apples is 1and the quantity of pears is 2. Override the getManifest function so that it returns a string of all items that is built by traversing the list of items. In the example above, the return string would be "2 crate of pears. 1 crate of apples."

Finally, write a main program that creates an array of pointers to six ShippingContainer objects. Instantiate the array with three ManualShippingContainer objects and three RFIDShippingContainer objects. For the ManualShippingContainer objects, you will have to invoke setManifest to set the contents. For the RFIDShippingContainer objects, you will have to invoke add to set the contents (although, if this were real, the contents of the container would "add" themselves via the RFID chips instead of requiring a human to type them in). Finally, write a loop that iterates through all ShippingContainer pointers and outputs each object's manifest along with the shipping container ID.

This is the output that the receiver of the shipping containers would like to see.

You may need to convert an integer into a string. A simple way to do this is illustrated below:

```
#include <sstream>

string intToString(int i)
{
    stringstream converter;
    converter<< i;
    return converter.str();
}
```

11. The goal for this programming project is to create a simple two-dimensional predator-prey simulation. In this simulation the prey are ants and the predators are doodlebugs. These critters live in a world composed of a 20 × 20 grid of cells. Only one critter may occupy a cell at a time. The grid is enclosed, so a critter is not allowed to move off the edges of the world. Time is simulated in time steps. Each critter performs some action every time step.

The ants behave according to the following model:

■ Move. Every time step, randomly try to move up, down, left, or right. If the neighboring cell in the selected direction is occupied or would move the ant off the grid, then the ant stays in the current cell.

■ Breed. If an ant survives for three time steps, then at the end of the time step (that is; after moving) the ant will breed. This is simulated by creating a new ant in an adjacent (up, down, left, or right) cell that is empty. If there is no empty cell available, then no breeding occurs. Once an offspring is produced, an ant cannot produce an offspring until three more time steps have elapsed.

The doodlebugs behave according to the following model:

■ Move. Every time step, if there is an adjacent ant (up, down, left, or right), then the doodlebug will move to that cell and eat the ant. Otherwise, the doodlebug moves according to the same rules as the ant. Note that a doodlebug cannot eat other doodlebugs.

■ Breed. If a doodlebug survives for eight time steps, then at the end of the time step it will spawn off a new doodlebug in the same manner as the ant.

■ Starve. If a doodlebug has not eaten an ant within the last three time steps, then at the end of the third time step it will starve and die. The doodlebug should then be removed from the grid of cells.

During one turn, all the doodlebugs should move before the ants do.

Write a program to implement this simulation and draw the world using ASCII characters of "o" for an ant and "X" for a doodlebug. Create a class named Organism that encapsulates basic data common to both ants and doodlebugs. This class should have a virtual function named move that is defined in the derived classes of Ant and Doodlebug. You may need additional data structures to keep track of which critters have moved.

Initialize the world with 5 doodlebugs and 100 ants. After each time step, prompt the user to press Enter to move to the next time step. You should see a cyclical pattern between the population of predators and prey, although random perturbations may lead to the elimination of one or both species.

VideoNote
Solution to Programming
Project 15.12

12. Listed below is code to play a guessing game. In the game two players attempt to guess a number. Your task is to extend the program with objects that represent either a human player or a computer player. The rand() function requires you include cstdlib (see Appendix 4):

```cpp
bool checkForWin(int guess, int answer)
{
    cout<< "You guessed" << guess << ".";
    if (answer == guess)
    {
        cout<< "You're right! You win!" <<endl;
        return true;
    }
    else if (answer < guess)
            cout<< "Your guess is too high." <<endl;
    else
            cout<< "Your guess is too low." <<endl;
    return false;
}
void play(Player &player1, Player &player2)
{
    int answer = 0, guess = 0;
    answer = rand() % 100;
    bool win = false;
    while (!win)
    {
        cout<< "Player 1's turn to guess." <<endl;
        guess = player1.getGuess();
        win = checkForWin(guess, answer);
        if (win) return;
        cout<< "Player 2's turn to guess." <<endl;
        guess = player2.getGuess();
        win = checkForWin(guess, answer);
    }
}
```

The play function takes as input two Player objects. Define the Player class with a virtual function named getGuess(). The implementation of Player::getGuess() can simply return 0. Next, define a class named HumanPlayer derived from Player. The implementation of HumanPlayer::getGuess() should prompt the user to enter a number and return the value entered from the keyboard. Next, define a class named ComputerPlayer derived from Player. The implementation of ComputerPlayer::getGuess() should randomly select a number between 0 and 99 (see Appendix 4 for information on random number generation). Finally, construct a main function that invokes play(Player &player1, Player &player2) with two instances of a HumanPlayer (human versus human), an instance of a HumanPlayer and ComputerPlayer (human versus computer), and two instances of ComputerPlayer (computer versus computer).

13. A system to store the internally awarded and externally awarded exam marks of a student is required. Design three classes InternalExamMarks, ExternalExamMarks and Student. The class Student inherits both the classes InternalExamMarks and ExternalExamMarks. The student class has data members such as roll number and stream etc. The InternalExamMarks class stores the internally awarded exam marks for two subjects and the ExternalExamMarks class stores the externally awarded exam marks for two subjects. Write a program to model this relationship. Choose member functions to develop this system. Write a driver program to test the Internal ExamMarks, ExternalExamMarks and Student classes.

14. Consider a system where the scheme of evaluation of a student's performance is calculated with different weights given for their performance at sports as well as their exam scores. Develop a class Sports to store the sports details of a student and a class Exam to store the exam details of a student assuming two subjects for each student. Write a class Result to inherit both Sports and Exam classes. Note that the Exam class is derived from the Student class.

Write a program to model this relationship. Choose data members and member functions to develop this system and write a driver program to test the Student, Exam, Sports and Result class.

Exception Handling 16

It's the exception that proves the rule.

COMMON MAXIM *(possibly a corruption of something like: It's the exception that tests the rule.)*

INTRODUCTION

One way to write a program is to first assume that nothing unusual or incorrect will happen. For example, if the program takes an entry off a list, you might assume that the list is not empty. Once you have the program working for the core situation where things always go as planned, you can then add code to take care of the exceptional cases. In C++, there is a way to reflect this approach in your code. Basically, you write your code as if nothing very unusual happens. After that, you use the C++ exception-handling facilities to add code for those unusual cases. Exception handling is commonly used to handle error situations, but perhaps a better way to view exceptions is as a way to handle "exceptional situations." After all, if your code correctly handles an "error," then it no longer is an error.

Perhaps the most important use of exceptions is to deal with functions that have some special case that is handled differently depending on how the function is used. Perhaps the function will be used in many programs, some of which will handle the special case in one way and some of which will handle it in some other way. For example, if there is a division by zero in the function, then it may turn out that for some invocations of the function, the program should end, but for other invocations of the function something else should happen. You will see that such a function can be defined to throw an exception if the special case occurs, and that exception will allow the special case to be handled outside of the function. That way, the special case can be handled differently for different invocations of the function.

In C++, exception handling proceeds as follows: Either some library software or your code provides a mechanism that signals when something unusual happens. This is called *throwing an exception*. At another place in your program, you place the code that deals with the exceptional case. This is called *handling the exception*. This method of programming makes for cleaner code. Of course, we still need to explain the details of how you do this in C++.

PREREQUISITES

With the exception of one subsection that can be skipped, Section 16.1 uses material only from Chapters 2 to 6 and 10 to 11. The Pitfall subsection of Section 16.1 entitled "Exception Specification in Derived Classes" uses material from Chapter 15. This Pitfall subsection can be skipped without loss of continuity.

With the exception of one subsection that can be skipped, Section 16.2 uses material only from Chapters 2 to 8 and 10 to 12 and Section 15.1 of Chapter 15 in addition to Section 16.1. The subsection of Section 16.2 entitled "Testing for Available Memory" uses material from Chapter 15. This subsection can be skipped without loss of continuity.

16.1 EXCEPTION-HANDLING BASICS

Well, the program works for most cases. I didn't know it had to work for that case.

COMPUTER SCIENCE STUDENT, APPEALING A GRADE

Exception handling is meant to be used sparingly and in situations that are more involved than what is reasonable to include in a simple introductory example. So, we will teach you the exception-handling details of C++ by means of simple examples that would not normally use exception handling. This makes a lot of sense for learning about exception handling, but do not forget that these first examples are toy examples, and in practice, you would not use exception handling for anything that simple.

A Toy Example of Exception Handling

For this example, suppose that milk is such an important food in our culture that people almost never run out of it, but still we would like our programs to accommodate the very unlikely situation of running out of milk. The basic code, which assumes we do not run out of milk, might be as follows:

```
cout << "Enter number of donuts:\n";
cin >> donuts;
cout << "Enter number of glasses of milk:\n";
cin >> milk;
dpg = donuts/static_cast<double>(milk);
cout << donuts << " donuts.\n"
     << milk << " glasses of milk.\n"
     << "You have " << dpg
     << " donuts for each glass of milk.\n";
```

If there is no milk, then this code will include a division by zero, which is an error. To take care of the special situation in which we run out of milk, we can add a test for this unusual situation. The complete program with this added test for the special situation is shown in Display 16.1. The program in Display 16.1 does not use exception handling. Now, let's see how this program can be rewritten using the C++ exception-handling facilities.

DISPLAY 16.1 Handling a Special Case Without Exception Handling

```
1    include <iostream>
2    using namespace std;

3    int main()
4    {
5        int donuts, milk;
6        double dpg;
7        cout << "Enter number of donuts:\n";
8        cin >> donuts;
9        cout << "Enter number of glasses of milk:\n";
10       cin >> milk;

11       if (milk <= 0)
12       {
13           cout << donuts << " donuts, and No Milk!\n"
14                << "Go buy some milk.\n";
15       }
16       Else
17       {
18           dpg = donuts/static_cast<double>(milk);
19           cout << donuts << " donuts.\n"
20                << milk << " glasses of milk.\n"
21                << "You have " << dpg
22                << " donuts for each glass of milk.\n";
23       }

24       cout << "End of program.\n";
25       return 0;
26   }
```

Sample Dialogue

```
Enter number of donuts:
12
Enter number of glasses of milk:
0
12 donuts, and No Milk!
Go buy some milk.
End of program.
```

In Display 16.2, we have rewritten the program from Display 16.1 using an exception. This is only a toy example, and you would probably not use an exception in this case. However, it does give us a simple example. Although the program as a whole is not simpler, at least the part between the words *try* and *catch* is cleaner, and this hints at the advantage of using exceptions. Look

DISPLAY 16.2   Same Thing Using Exception Handling *(part 1 of 2)*

```
1    #include <iostream>
2    using namespace std;
3
4    int main()
5    {
6        int donuts, milk;
7        double dpg;
8
9        try
10       {
11           cout << "Enter number of donuts:\n";
12           cin >> donuts;
13           cout << "Enter number of glasses of milk:\n";
14           cin >> milk;
15
16           if (milk <= 0)
17               throw donuts;
18
19           dpg = donuts/static_cast<double>(milk);
20           cout << donuts << " donuts.\n"
21                << milk << " glasses of milk.\n"
22                << "You have " << dpg
23                << " donuts for each glass of milk.\n";
24       }
25       catch(int e)
26       {
27           cout << e << " donuts, and No Milk!\n"
28                << "Go buy some milk.\n";
29       }
30
31       cout << "End of program.\n";
32       return 0;
33   }
```

Sample Dialogue 1

```
Enter number of donuts:
12
Enter number of glasses of milk:
6
12 donuts.
6 glasses of milk.
You have 2 donuts for each glass of milk.
```

(continued)

DISPLAY 16.2   Same Thing Using Exception Handling *(part 2 of 2)*

Sample Dialogue 2

```
Enter number of donuts:
12
Enter number of glasses of milk:
0
12 donuts, and No Milk!
Go buy some milk.
End of program.
```

at the code between the words *try* and *catch*. That code is basically the same as the code in Display 16.1, but rather than the big *if-else* statement (shown in color in Display 16.1) this new program has the following smaller *if* statement (plus some simple nonbranching statements):

```
if (milk <= 0)
    throw donuts;
```

This *if* statement says that if there is no milk, then do something exceptional. That something exceptional is given after the word *catch*. The idea is that the normal situation is handled by the code following the word *try*, and that the code following the word *catch* is used only in exceptional circumstances. We have thus separated the normal case from the exceptional case. In this toy example, this separation does not really buy us too much, but in other situations it will prove to be very helpful. Let's look at the details.

The basic way of handling exceptions in C++ consists of the *try-throw-catch* threesome. A **try block** has the syntax

```
try
{
    Some_Code
}
```

This *try* block contains the code for the basic algorithm that tells the computer what to do when everything goes smoothly. It is called a *try* block because you are not 100 percent sure that all will go smoothly, but you want to "give it a try."

Now if something *does* go wrong, you want to throw an exception, which is a way of indicating that something went wrong. The basic outline, when we add a *throw*, is as follows:

```
try
{
```

```
    Code_To_Try
    Possibly_Throw_An_Exception
    More_Code
}
```

The following is an example of a *try* block with a *throw* statement included (copied from Display 16.2):

```
try
{
    cout << "Enter number of donuts:\n";
    cin >> donuts;
    cout << "Enter number of glasses of milk:\n";
    cin >> milk;
    if (milk <= 0)
        throw donuts;
    dpg = donuts/static_cast<double>(milk);
    cout << donuts << " donuts.\n"
         << milk << " glasses of milk.\n"
         << "You have " << dpg
         << " donuts for each glass of milk.\n";
}
```

The following statement **throws** the *int* value donuts:

```
throw donuts;
```

The value thrown, in this case donuts, is sometimes called an **exception,** and the execution of a *throw* statement is called **throwing an exception.** You can throw a value of any type. In this case, an *int* value is thrown.

---

throw Statement

SYNTAX

```
throw Expression_for_Value_to_Be_Thrown;
```

When the *throw* statement is executed, the execution of the enclosing *try* block is stopped. If the *try* block is followed by a suitable *catch* block, then flow of control is transferred to the *catch* block. A *throw* statement is almost always embedded in a branching statement, such as an *if* statement. The value thrown can be of any type.

EXAMPLE

```
if (milk <= 0)
    throw donuts;
```

As the name suggests, when something is "thrown," something goes from one place to another place. In C++, what goes from one place to another is the flow of control (as well as the value thrown). When an exception is thrown, the code in the surrounding *try* block stops executing and another portion of code, known as a **catch block,** begins execution. This executing of the *catch* block is called catching the exception or handling the exception. When an exception is thrown, it should ultimately be handled by (caught by) some *catch* block. In Display 16.2, the appropriate *catch* block immediately follows the *try* block. We repeat the *catch* block here:

```
catch(int e)
{
    cout << e << " donuts, and No Milk!\n"
        << "Go buy some milk.\n";
}
```

This *catch* block looks very much like a function definition that has a parameter of a type *int*. It is not a function definition, but in some ways, a *catch* block is like a function. It is a separate piece of code that is executed when your program encounters (and executes) the following (within the preceding *try* block):

```
throw Some_int;
```

So, this *throw* statement is similar to a function call, but instead of calling a function, it calls the *catch* block and says to execute the code in the *catch* block. A *catch* block is often referred to as an **exception handler,** which is a term that suggests that a *catch* block has a function-like nature.

What is that identifier e in the following line from a *catch* block?

```
catch(int e)
```

That identifier e looks like a parameter and acts very much like a parameter. So, we will call this e the **catch-block parameter.** (But remember, this does not mean that the *catch* block is a function.) The *catch*-block parameter does two things:

1. The *catch*-block parameter is preceded by a type name that specifies what kind of thrown value the *catch* block can catch.

2. The *catch*-block parameter gives you a name for the thrown value that is caught, so you can write code in the *catch* block that does things with the thrown value that is caught.

We will discuss these two functions of the *catch*-block parameter in reverse order. In this subsection, we will discuss using the *catch*-block parameter as a name for the value that was thrown and is caught. In the subsection entitled "Multiple Throws and Catches," later in this chapter, we will discuss which *catch* block (which exception handler) will process a value that is thrown. Our current example has only one *catch* block. A common name for a *catch*-block parameter is e, but you can use any legal identifier in place of e.

Let's see how the *catch* block in Display 16.2 works. When a value is thrown, execution of the code in the *try* block ends and control passes to the *catch* block (or blocks) that are placed right after the *try* block. The *catch* block from Display 16.2 is reproduced here:

```
catch(int e)
{
    cout << e << " donuts, and No Milk!\n"
        << "Go buy some milk.\n";
}
```

When a value is thrown, the thrown value must be of type *int* in order for this particular *catch* block to apply. In Display 16.2, the value thrown is given by the variable donuts, and since donuts is of type *int*, this *catch* block can catch the value thrown.

Suppose the value of donuts is 12 and the value of milk is 0, as in the second sample dialogue in Display 16.2. Since the value of milk is not positive, the *throw* statement within the *if* statement is executed. In that case, the value of the variable donuts is thrown. When the *catch* block in Display 16.2 catches the value of donuts, the value of donuts is plugged in for the *catch*-block parameter e and the code in the *catch* block is executed, producing the following output:

```
12 donuts, and No Milk!
Go buy some milk.
```

If the value of donuts is positive, the *throw* statement is not executed. In this case, the entire *try* block is executed. After the last statement in the *try* block is executed, the statement after the *catch* block is executed. Note that if no exception is thrown, then the *catch* block is ignored.

This makes it sound like a *try-throw-catch* setup is equivalent to an *if-else* statement. It almost is equivalent, except for the value thrown. A *try-throw-catch* setup is similar to an *if-else* statement *with the added ability to send a message to one of the branches*. This does not sound much different from an *if-else* statement, but it turns out to be a big difference in practice.

To summarize in a more formal tone, a *try* block contains some code that we are assuming includes a *throw* statement. The *throw* statement is normally executed only in exceptional circumstances, but when it is executed, it throws a value of some type. When an exception (a value like donuts in Display 16.2) is thrown, that is the end of the *try* block. All the rest of the code in the *try* block is ignored and control passes to a suitable *catch* block. A *catch* block applies only to an immediately preceding *try* block. If the exception is thrown, then that exception object is plugged in for the *catch*-block parameter, and the statements in the *catch* block are executed. For example, if you look at the dialogues in Display 16.2, you will see that as soon as the user

---

catch-Block Parameter

The _catch_-block parameter is an identifier in the heading of a _catch_ block that serves as a placeholder for an exception (a value) that might be thrown. When a (suitable) value is thrown in the preceding _try_ block, that value is plugged in for the _catch_-block parameter. You can use any legal (nonreserved word) identifier for a _catch_-block parameter.

EXAMPLE

```
catch(int e)
{
    cout << e << " donuts, and No Milk!\n"
        << "Go buy some milk.\n";
}
```

e is the _catch_-block parameter.

---

enters a nonpositive number, the _try_ block stops and the _catch_ block is executed. For now, we will assume that every _try_ block is followed by an appropriate _catch_ block. We will later discuss what happens when there is no appropriate _catch_ block.

Next, we summarize what happens when no exception is thrown in a _try_ block. If no exception (no value) is thrown in the _try_ block, then after the _try_ block is completed, program execution continues with the code after the _catch_ block. In other words, if no exception is thrown, then the _catch_ block is ignored. Most of the time when the program is executed, the _throw_ statement will not be executed, and so in most cases, the code in the _try_ block will run to completion and the code in the _catch_ block will be ignored completely.

---

try-throw-catch

This is the basic mechanism for throwing and catching exceptions. The _throw_ **statement** throws the exception (a value). The _catch_ **block** catches the exception (the value). When an exception is thrown, the _try_ block ends and then the code in the _catch_ block is executed. After the _catch_ block is completed, the code after the _catch_ block(s) is executed (provided the _catch_ block has not ended the program or performed some other special action).

If no exception is thrown in the _try_ block, then after the _try_ block is completed, program execution continues with the code after the _catch_ block(s). (In other words, if no exception is thrown, then the _catch_ block(s) are ignored.)

SYNTAX

```
try
{
    Some_Statements
        < Either some code with a throw statement or a
                function invocation that might throw an
                exception>
    Some_More_Statements
}
catch(Type_Name e)
{
    < Code to be performed if a value of the
      catch-block parameter type is thrown in the
      try block>
}
```

EXAMPLE

See Display 16.2.

SELF-TEST EXERCISES

myprogramminglab

1. What output is produced by the following code?

```
int wait_time = 46;
try
{
    cout << "Try block entered.\n";
    if (wait_time > 30)
        throw wait_time;
    cout << "Leaving try block.\n";
}
catch(int thrown_value)
{
    cout << "Exception thrown with\n"
         << "wait_time equal to " << thrown_value << endl;
}
cout << "After catch block." << endl;
```

2. What would be the output produced by the code in Self-Test Exercise 1 if we make the following change? Change the line

```
int wait_time = 46;
```

to

```
int wait_time = 12;
```

3. In the code given in Self-Test Exercise 1, what is the *throw* statement?

4. What happens when a *throw* statement is executed? This is a general question. Tell what happens in general, not simply what happens in the code in Self-Test Question 1 or some other sample code.

5. In the code given in Self-Test Exercise 1, what is the *try* block?

6. In the code given in Self-Test Exercise 1, what is the *catch* block?

7. In the code given in Self-Test Exercise 1, what is the *catch*-block parameter?

Defining Your Own Exception Classes

A *throw* statement can throw a value of any type. A common thing to do is to define a class whose objects can carry the precise kind of information you want thrown to the *catch* block. An even more important reason for defining a specialized exception class is so that you can have a different type to identify each possible kind of exceptional situation.

An exception class is just a class. What makes it an exception class is how it's used. Still, it pays to take some care in choosing an exception class's name and other details. Display 16.3 contains an example of a program with a programmer-defined exception class. This is just a toy program to illustrate some C++ details about exception handling. It uses much too much machinery for such a simple task, but it is an otherwise uncluttered example of some C++ details.

Notice the *throw* statement, reproduced in what follows:

```
throw NoMilk(donuts);
```

The part NoMilk(donuts) is an invocation of a constructor for the class NoMilk. The constructor takes one *int* argument (in this case donuts) and creates an object of the class NoMilk. That object is then "thrown."

Multiple Throws and Catches

A *try* block can potentially throw any number of exception values, and they can be of differing types. In any one execution of the *try* block, only one exception will be thrown (since a thrown exception ends the execution of the *try* block), but different types of exception values can be thrown on different occasions when the *try* block is executed. Each *catch* block can only catch values of one type, but you can catch exception values of differing types by placing more than one *catch* block after a *try* block. For example, the program in Display 16.4 has two *catch* blocks after its *try* block.

Note that there is no parameter in the *catch* block for DivideByZero. If you do not need a parameter, you can simply list the type with no parameter.

DISPLAY 16.3 Defining Your Own Exception Class

```
1    #include <iostream>
2    using namespace std;
```

This is just a toy example to learn C++ syntax. Do not take it as an example of good typical use of exception handling.

```
3    class NoMilk
4    {
5    public:
6        NoMilk();
7        NoMilk(int how_many);
8        int get_donuts();
9    private:
10       int count;
11   };

12   int main()
13   {
14       int donuts, milk;
15       double dpg;
16       try
17       {
18           cout << "Enter number of donuts:\n";
19           cin >> donuts;
20           cout << "Enter number of glasses of milk:\n";
21           cin >> milk;
22           if (milk <= 0)
23                   throw NoMilk(donuts);
24           dpg = donuts/static_cast<double>(milk);
25           cout << donuts << " donuts.\n"
26               << milk << " glasses of milk.\n"
27               << "You have " << dpg
28               << " donuts for each glass of milk.\n";
29       }
30       catch(NoMilk e)
31       {
32           cout << e.get_donuts() << " donuts, and No Milk!\n"
33               << "Go buy some milk.\n";
34       }
35       cout << "End of program.";
36       return 0;
37   }
38
39   NoMilk::NoMilk()
40   {}
41   NoMilk::NoMilk(int how_many) : count(how_many)
42   {}
43
44   int NoMilk::get_donuts()
45   {
46       return count;
47   }
```

The sample dialogues are the same as in Display 16.2.

DISPLAY 16.4   Catching Multiple Exceptions *(part 1 of 2)*

```
1    #include <iostream>
2    #include <string>
3    using namespace std;
4
5    class NegativeNumber
6    {
7    public:
8        NegativeNumber();
9        NegativeNumber(string take_me_to_your_catch_block);
10       string get_message();
11   private:
12       string message;
13   };
14
15   class DivideByZero
16   {};
17
18   int main()
19   {
20       int jem_hadar, klingons;
21       double portion;
22
23       try
24       {
25           cout << "Enter number of JemHadar warriors:\n";
26           cin >> jem_hadar;
27           if (jem_hadar< 0)
28               throw NegativeNumber("JemHadar");
29
30           cout << "How many Klingon warriors do you have?\n";
31           cin >> klingons;
32           if (klingons< 0)
33               throw NegativeNumber("Klingons");
34           if (klingons != 0)
35               portion = jem_hadar/static_cast<double>(klingons);
36           else
37               throw DivideByZero();
38           cout << "Each Klingon must fight "
39                << portion << " JemHadar.\n";
40       }
41       catch(NegativeNumber e)
42       {
43           cout << "Cannot have a negative number of "
44                << e.get_message() << endl;
45       }
```

> Although not done here, exception classes can have their own interface and implementation files and can be put in a namespace. This is another toy example.

(continued)

DISPLAY 16.4   Catching Multiple Exceptions *(part 2 of 2)*

```
46        catch (DivideByZero)
47        {
48            cout << "Send for help.\n";
49        }
50
51        cout << "End of program.\n";
52        return 0;
53    }
54
55
56    NegativeNumber::NegativeNumber()
57    {}
58
59    NegativeNumber::NegativeNumber(string take_me_to_your_catch_block)
60            : message(take_me_to_your_catch_block)
61    {}
62
63    string NegativeNumber::get_message()
64    {
65        return message;
66    }
```

Sample Dialogue 1

```
Enter number of JemHadar warriors:
1000
How many Klingon warriors do you have?
500
Each Klingon must fight 2.0 JemHadar.
End of program
```

Sample Dialogue 2

```
Enter number of JemHadar warriors:
-10
Cannot have a negative number of JemHadar
End of program.
```

Sample Dialogue 3

```
Enter number of JemHadar warriors:
1000
How many Klingon warriors do you have?
0
Send for help.
End of program.
```

This case is discussed a bit more in the Programming Tip section entitled "Exception Classes Can Be Trivial."

PITFALL   Catch the More Specific Exception First

When catching multiple exceptions, the order of the *catch* blocks can be important. When an exception value is thrown in a *try* block, the following *catch* blocks are tried in order, and the first one that matches the type of the exception thrown is the one that is executed.

For example, the following is a special kind of *catch* block that will catch a thrown value of any type:

```
catch(...)
{
    <Place whatever you want in here>
}
```

The three dots do not stand for something omitted. You actually type in those three dots in your program. This makes a good default *catch* block to place after all other *catch* blocks. For example, we could add it to the *catch* blocks in Display 16.4 as follows:

```
catch(NegativeNumber e)
{
    cout << "Cannot have a negative number of "
        << e.get_message() <<endl;
}
catch(DivideByZero)
{
    cout<< "Send for help.\n";
}
catch(...)
{
    cout << "Unexplained exception.\n";
}
```

However, it only makes sense to place this default *catch* block at the end of a list of *catch* blocks. For example, suppose we instead used:

```
catch(NegativeNumber e)
{
    cout << "Cannot have a negative number of "
        << e.get_message() <<endl;
}
catch(...)
{
    cout << "Unexplained exception.\n";
}
catch(DivideByZero)
```

```
{
    cout << "Send for help.\n";
}
```

With this second ordering, an exception (a thrown value) of type NegativeNumber will be caught by the NegativeNumber *catch* block, as it should be. However, if a value of type DivideByZero were thrown, it would be caught by the block that starts *catch*(...). So, the DivideByZero *catch* block could never be reached. Fortunately, most compilers tell you if you make this sort of mistake. ■

■ PROGRAMMING TIP   Exception Classes Can Be Trivial

Here we reproduce the definition of the exception class DivideByZero from Display 16.4:

```
class DivideByZero
{};
```

This exception class has no member variables and no member functions (other than the default constructor). It has nothing but its name, but that is useful enough. Throwing an object of the class DivideByZero can activate the appropriate *catch* block, as it does in Display 16.4.

When using a trivial exception class, you normally do not have anything you can do with the exception (the thrown value) once it gets to the *catch* block. The exception is just being used to get you to the *catch* block. Thus, you can omit the *catch*-block parameter. (You can omit the *catch*-block parameter anytime you do not need it, whether the exception type is trivial or not.) ■

Throwing an Exception in a Function

Sometimes it makes sense to delay handling an exception. For example, you might have a function with code that throws an exception if there is an attempt to divide by zero, but you may not want to catch the exception in that function. Perhaps some programs that use that function should simply end if the exception is thrown, and other programs that use the function should do something else. So you would not know what to do with the exception if you caught it inside the function. In these cases, it makes sense to not catch the exception in the function definition, but instead to have any program (or other code) that uses the function place the function invocation in a *try* block and catch the exception in a *catch* block that follows that *try* block.

Look at the program in Display 16.5. It has a *try* block, but there is no *throw* statement visible in the *try* block. The statement that does the throwing in that program is

```
if (bottom == 0)
    throw DivideByZero();
```

DISPLAY 16.5 **Throwing an Exception Inside a Function** *(part 1 of 2)*

```
1   #include <iostream>
2   #include <cstdlib>
3   using namespace std;
4
5   class DivideByZero
6   {};
7
8   double safe_divide(int top, int bottom) throw (DivideByZero);
9
10  int main()
11  {
12      int numerator;
13      int denominator;
14      double quotient;
15      cout << "Enter numerator:\n";
16      cin >> numerator;
17      cout << "Enter denominator:\n";
18      cin >> denominator;
19
20      try
21      {
22          quotient = safe_divide(numerator, denominator);
23      }
24      catch(DivideByZero)
25      {
26          cout << "Error: Division by zero!\n"
27              << "Program aborting.\n";
28          exit(0);
29      }
30
31      cout << numerator << "/" << denominator
32          << " = " << quotient <<endl;
33
34      cout << "End of program.\n";
35      return 0;
36  }
37
38
39  double safe_divide(int top, int bottom) throw (DivideByZero)
40  {
41      if (bottom == 0)
42          throw DivideByZero();
43
44      return top/static_cast<double>(bottom);
45  }
```

(continued)

DISPLAY 16.5   Throwing an Exception Inside a Function *(part 2 of 2)*

Sample Dialogue 1

```
Enter numerator:
5
Enter denominator:
10
5/10 = 0.5
End of Program.
```

Sample Dialogue 2

```
Enter numerator:
5
Enter denominator:
0
Error: Division by zero!
Program aborting.
```

This statement is not visible in the *try* block. However, it is in the *try* block in terms of program execution, because it is in the definition of the function `safe_divide` and there is an invocation of `safe_divide` in the *try* block.

Exception Specification

If a function does not catch an exception, it should at least warn programmers that any invocation of the function might possibly throw an exception. If there are exceptions that might be thrown, but not caught, in the function definition, then those exception types should be listed in an **exception specification**, which is illustrated by the following function declaration from Display 16.5:

```
double safe_divide(int top, int bottom) throw (DivideByZero);
```

As illustrated in Display 16.5, the exception specification should appear in both the function declaration and the function definition. If a function has more than one function declaration, then all the function declarations must have identical exception specifications. The exception specification for a function is also sometimes called the **throw list**.

If there is more than one possible exception that can be thrown in the function definition, then the exception types are separated by commas, as illustrated here:

```
void some_function( ) throw (DivideByZero, OtherException);
```

All exception types listed in the exception specification are treated normally. When we say the exception is treated normally, we mean it is treated as we have described before this subsection. In particular, you can place the function invocation in a *try* block followed by a *catch* block to catch that type of exception, and if the function throws the exception (and does not catch it inside the function), then the *catch* block following the *try* block will catch the exception. If there is no exception specification (no throw list) at all (not even an empty one), then it is the same as if all possible exception types were listed in the exception specification; that is, any exception that is thrown is treated normally.

What happens when an exception is thrown in a function but is not listed in the exception specification (and not caught inside the function)? In that case, the program ends. In particular, notice that if an exception is thrown in a function but is not listed in the exception specification (and not caught inside the function), then it will not be caught by any *catch* block, but instead your program will end. Remember, if there is no specification list at all, not even an empty one, then it is the same as if all exceptions were listed in the specification list, and so throwing an exception will not end the program in the way described in this paragraph.

Keep in mind that the exception specification is for exceptions that "get outside" the function. If they do not get outside the function, they do not belong in the exception specification. If they get outside the function, they belong in the exception specification no matter where they originate. If an exception is thrown in a *try* block that is inside a function definition and is caught in a *catch* block inside the function definition, then its type need not be listed in the exception specification. If a function definition includes an invocation of another function and that other function can throw an exception that is not caught, then the type of the exception should be placed in the exception specification.

To say that a function should not throw any exceptions that are not caught inside the function, you use an empty exception specification like so:

```
void some_function( ) throw ( );
```

By way of summary:

```
void some_function( ) throw (DivideByZero, OtherException);
//Exceptions of type DivideByZero or OtherException are
//treated normally. All other exceptions end the program
//if not caught in the function body.

void some_function( ) throw ( );
//Empty exception list; all exceptions end the
//program if thrown but not caught in the function body.

void some_function( );
//All exceptions of all types treated normally.
```

Keep in mind that an object of a derived class[1] is also an object of its base class. So, if D is a derived class of class B and B is in the exception specification, then a thrown object of class D will be treated normally, since it is an object of class B and B is in the exception specification. However, no automatic type conversions are done. If *double* is in the exception specification, that does not account for throwing an *int* value. You would need to include both *int* and *double* in the exception specification.

One final warning: Not all compilers treat the exception specification as they are supposed to. Some compilers essentially treat the exception specification as a comment, and so with those compilers, the exception specification has no effect on your code. This is another reason to place all exceptions that might be thrown by your functions in the exception specification. This way all compilers will treat your exceptions the same way. Of course, you could get the same compiler consistency by not having any exception specification at all, but then your program would not be as well documented and you would not get the extra error checking provided by compilers that do use the exception specification. With a compiler that does process the exception specification, your program will terminate as soon as it throws an exception that you did not anticipate. (Note that this is a run-time behavior, but which run-time behavior you get depends on your compiler.)

Warning!

PITFALL   Exception Specification in Derived Classes

When you redefine or override a function definition in a derived class, it should have the same exception specification as it had in the base class, or it should have an exception specification whose exceptions are a subset of those in the base class exception specification. Put another way, when you redefine or override a function definition, you cannot add any exceptions to the exception specification (but you can delete some exceptions if you want). This makes sense, since an object of the derived class can be used anyplace an object of the base class can be used, and so a redefined or overwritten function must fit any code written for an object of the base class. ■

SELF-TEST EXERCISES

myprogramminglab

8. What is the output produced by the following program?

```
#include <iostream>
using namespace std;
void sample_function(double test) throw (int);
```

_____

[1] If you have not yet learned about derived classes, you can safely ignore the remarks about them.

```
int main()
{
    try
    {
        cout << "Trying.\n";
        sample_function(98.6);
        cout << "Trying after call.\n";
    }
    catch(int)
    {
        cout << "Catching.\n";
    }
    cout << "End of program.\n";
    return 0;
}
void sample_function(double test) throw (int)
{
    cout << "Starting sample_function.\n";
    if (test < 100)
        throw 42;
}
```

9. What is the output produced by the program in Self-Test Exercise 8 if the following change were made to the program? Change

```
sample_function(98.6);
```

in the *try* block to

```
sample_function(212);
```

16.2 PROGRAMMING TECHNIQUES FOR EXCEPTION HANDLING

Only use this in exceptional circumstances.

WARREN PEACE, *The Lieutenant's Tools*

So far, we have shown you lots of code that explains how exception handling works in C++, but we have not yet shown even one example of a program that makes good and realistic use of exception handling. However, now that you know the mechanics of exception handling, this section can go on to explain exception-handling techniques.

When to Throw an Exception

We have given some very simple code in order to illustrate the basic concepts of exception handling. However, our examples were unrealistically simple. A more complicated but better guideline is to separate throwing an exception and catching the exception into separate functions. In most cases, you should include any *throw* statement within a function definition, list the exception in the exception specification for that function, and place the *catch* clause in *a different function*. Thus, the preferred use of the *try-throw-catch* triad is as illustrated here:

```
void functionA() throw (MyException)
{
        .
        .
        .
    throw MyException(<Maybe an argument>);
        .
        .
        .

}
```

Then, in *some other function* (perhaps even some other function in some other file), you have

```
void functionB()
{
        .
        .
        .
    try
    {
        .
        .
        .
      functionA();
        .
        .
        .
    }
    catch(MyException e)
    {
        <Handle exception.>
    }
        .
        .
        .

}
```

Moreover, even this kind of use of a *throw* statement should be reserved for cases in which it is unavoidable. If you can easily handle a problem in some other way, do not throw an exception. Reserve *throw* statements for situations in which the way the exceptional condition is handled depends on how and where the function is used. If the way that the exceptional condition is handled depends on how and where the function is invoked, then the

---

When to Throw an Exception

For the most part, *throw* statements should be used within functions and listed in an exception specification for the function. Moreover, they should be reserved for situations in which the way the exceptional condition is handled depends on how and where the function is used. If the way that the exceptional condition is handled depends on how and where the function is invoked, then the best thing to do is to let the programmer who invokes the function handle the exception. In all other situations, it is almost always preferable to avoid throwing an exception.

---

best thing to do is to let the programmer who invokes the function handle the exception. In all other situations, it is almost always preferable to avoid throwing exceptions.

PITFALL Uncaught Exceptions

Every exception that is thrown by your code should be caught someplace in your code. If an exception is thrown but not caught anywhere, your program will end. ■

PITFALL Nested *try-catch* Blocks

You can place a *try* block and following *catch* blocks inside a larger *try* block or inside a larger *catch* block. In rare cases, this may be useful, but if you are tempted to do this, you should suspect that there is a nicer way to organize your program. It is almost always better to place the inner *try-catch* blocks inside a function definition and place an invocation of the function in the outer *try* or *catch* block (or maybe just eliminate one or more *try* blocks completely).

If you place a *try* block and following *catch* blocks inside a larger *try* block, and an exception is thrown in the inner *try* block but not caught in the inner *try-catch* blocks, then the exception is thrown to the outer *try* block for processing and might be caught there. ■

PITFALL Overuse of Exceptions

Exceptions allow you to write programs whose flow of control is so involved that it is almost impossible to understand the program. Moreover, this is not hard to do. Throwing an exception allows you to transfer flow of control from anyplace in your program to almost anyplace else in your program. In the early days of programming, this sort of unrestricted flow of control was allowed via a construct known as a *goto*. Programming experts now agree that such unrestricted flow of control is very poor programming style. Exceptions allow you to revert to these bad old days of unrestricted flow of control. Exceptions should be used sparingly and only in certain ways. A good rule is the following: If you are tempted to include a *throw* statement, then think about how you might write your program or class definition without this *throw* statement. If you think of an alternative that produces reasonable code, then you probably do not want to include the *throw* statement. ■

Exception Class Hierarchies

VideoNote
The STL Exception Class

It can be very useful to define a hierarchy of exception classes. For example, you might have an `ArithmeticError` exception class and then define an exception class `DivideByZeroError` that is a derived class of `ArithmeticError`. Since a `DivideByZeroError` is an `ArithmeticError`, every *catch* block for an `ArithmeticError` will catch a `DivideByZeroError`. If you list `ArithmeticError` in an exception specification, then you have, in effect, also added `DivideByZeroError` to the exception specification, whether or not you list `DivideByZeroError` by name in the exception specification.

Testing for Available Memory

In Chapter 13, we created new dynamic variables with code such as the following:

```
struct Node
{
    int data;
    Node *link;
};
typedef Node* NodePtr;
    . . .
NodePtr pointer = new Node;
```

This works fine as long as there is sufficient memory available to create the new node. But, what happens if there is not sufficient memory? If there is not sufficient memory to create the node, then a `bad_alloc` exception is thrown. The type `bad_alloc` is part of the C++ language. You do not need to define it.

Since *new* will throw a `bad_alloc` exception when there is not enough memory to create the node, you can check for running out of memory as follows:

```
try
{
    NodePtr pointer = new Node;
}
```

```
catch (bad_alloc)
{
    cout << "Ran out of memory!";
}
```

Of course, you can do other things besides simply giving a warning message, but the details of what you do will depend on your particular programming task.

Rethrowing an Exception

It is legal to throw an exception within a *catch* block. In rare cases, you may want to catch an exception and then, depending on the details, decide to throw the same or a different exception for handling farther up the chain of exception-handling blocks.

▮ SELF-TEST EXERCISES

10. What happens when an exception is never caught?

11. Can you nest a *try* block inside another *try* block?

CHAPTER SUMMARY

- Exception handling allows you to design and code the normal case for your program separately from the code that handles exceptional situations.

- An exception can be thrown in a *try* block. Alternatively, an exception can be thrown in a function definition that does not include a *try* block (or does not include a *catch* block to catch that type of exception). In this case, an invocation of the function can be placed in a *try* block.

- An exception is caught in a *catch* block.

- A *try* block may be followed by more than one *catch* block. In this case, always list the *catch* block for a more specific exception class before the *catch* block for a more general exception class.

- Do not overuse exceptions.

Answers to Self-Test Exercises

```
1. Try block entered.
   Exception thrown with
   wait_time equal to 46
   After catch block.
```

2. ```
   Try block entered.
   Leaving try block.
   After catch block.
   ```

3. *throw* `wait_time;`

   Note that the following is an *if* statement, not a *throw* statement, even though it contains a *throw* statement:

   ```
   if (wait_time> 30)
       throw wait_time;
   ```

4. When a *throw* statement is executed, that is the end of the enclosing *try* block. No other statements in the *try* block are executed, and control passes to the following *catch* block(s). When we say control passes to the following *catch* block, we mean that the value thrown is plugged in for the *catch*-block parameter (if any), and the code in the *catch* block is executed.

5. ```
   try
   {
       cout << "Try block entered.";
       if (wait_time > 30)
           throw (wait_time);
       cout << "Leaving try block.";
   }
   ```

6. ```
   catch(int thrown_value)
   {
       cout << "Exception thrown with\n"
            << "wait_time equal to" << thrown_value << endl;
   }
   ```

7. `thrown_value` is the *catch*-block parameter.

8. ```
   Trying.
   Starting sample_function.
   Catching.
   End of program.
   ```

9. ```
   Trying.
   Starting sample_function.
   Trying after call.
   End of program.
   ```

10. If an exception is not caught anywhere, then your program ends.

11. Yes, you can have a *try* block and corresponding *catch* blocks inside another larger *try* block. However, it would probably be better to place the inner *try* and *catch* blocks in a function definition and place an invocation of the function in the larger *try* block.
   ```

PROGRAMMING PROJECTS

myprogramminglab *Visit www.myprogramminglab.com to complete many of these Programming Projects online and get instant feedback.*

1. Write a program that converts 24-hour time to 12-hour time. The following is a sample dialogue:

```
Enter time in 24-hour notation:
13:07
That is the same as
1:07 PM
Again?(y/n)
y
Enter time in 24-hour notation:
10:15
That is the same as
10:15 AM
Again?(y/n)
y
Enter time in 24-hour notation:
10:65
There is no such time as 10:65
Try again:
Enter time in 24-hour notation:
16:05
That is the same as
4:05 PM
Again?(y/n)
n
End of program
```

You will define an exception class called `TimeFormatMistake`. If the user enters an illegal time, like `10:65` or even gibberish like `8&*68`, then your program will throw and catch a `TimeFormatMistake`.

2. Write a program that converts dates from numerical month/day format to alphabetic month/day (for example, 1/31 or 01/31 corresponds to January 31). The dialogue should be similar to that in Programming Project 1. You will define two exception classes, one called `MonthError` and another called `DayError`. If the user enters anything other than a legal month number (integers from 1 to 12), then your program will throw and catch a `MonthError`. Similarly, if the user enters anything other than a valid day number (integers from 1 to either 29, 30, or 31, depending on the month), then your program will throw and catch a `DayError`. To keep things simple, always allow 29 days for February.

VideoNote
Solution to Programming
Project 16.3

3. Write a program that inputs numeric values from 1 through 10 and outputs a textual histogram of the values using *'s to count the number of occurrences

of each value. The program should first ask the user how many numbers to enter. If the user enters a value that does not consist of all digits or a number outside the range 1 to 10, then an exception should be caught. (*Hint*: Input each number as a string, and then scan through the string to see if it contains all digits. If not, throw an exception. To convert a string str to an integer, use the following code:

```
atoi(str.c_str());
```

The atoi function is described in Chapter 8.) Here is a sample dialogue:

```
How many numbers to enter?
5
Enter number 1L
one
Please enter your number using digits only.  Try again.
Enter number 1:
9
Enter number 2:
3
Enter number 3:
3
Enter number 4:
33
The number must be between 1-10.  Try again.
Enter number 4:
3
Enter number 5:
7

Here is the histogram of values:
1 :
2 :
3 : ***
4 :
5 :
6 :
7 : *
8 :
9 : *
10:
```

4. Define a class named Student with the data members roll, name and marks for two subjects. The objects of this class are like regular arrays but can perform range checking. If s is an object of the class Student, and j is an illegal index, then use of s[j] will cause your program to throw an exception and display a warning message. Note that the illegal index may be negative or out of range of the total number of objects. For both cases, a separate message must be shown.

5. Queues were introduced in Chapter 13. Define a queue class for storing a set of elements of type *char* following the *First In First Out* principle. A queue object should be of fixed size; the size is a parameter to the constructor that creates the queue object. When used in a program, an object of the queue class will throw exceptions in the following situations:

■ Throw a QueueOverflowException if the application program tries to insert data into a queue that is already full

■ Throw a QueueEmptyException if the application program tries to delete data from an empty queue

Write a suitable C++ program to test the scenario described above.

6. (Based on a problem in Stroustrup, *The C++ Programming Language*, 3rd edition) Write a program consisting of functions calling one another to a calling depth of 10. Give each function an argument that specifies the level at which it is to throw an exception. The main function prompts for and receives input that specifies the calling depth (level) at which an exception will be thrown. The main function then calls the first function. The main function catches the exception and displays the level at which the exception was thrown. Don't forget the case where the depth is 0, where main must both throw and catch the exception.

(*Hints:* You could use 10 different functions or 10 copies of the same function that call one another, but don't. Rather, for compact code, use a main function that calls another function that calls itself recursively. Suppose you do this; is the restriction on the calling depth necessary? This can be done without giving the function any additional arguments, but if you cannot do it that way, try adding an additional argument to the function.)

7. In some cases, a class throws an unspecified exception. Develop a class DemoUnspecified that will receive an *int* from the main function in the member function check_value. If the *int* received is a positive integer, it will throw an exception of type Positive class, and if the *int* received is a negative integer, it will throw an exception of type Negative class. For all other cases, the class DemoUnspecified will throw an exception of type Unspecified and accordingly, the program control will be transferred to the corresponding catch block with the Unspecified class as the parameter.

**VideoNote
Solution to Programming
Project 16.8**

8. A function that returns a special error code is often better implemented by throwing an exception instead. This way, the error code cannot be ignored or mistaken for valid data. The following class maintains an account balance.

```
class Account
{
private:
    double balance;
public:
    Account()
    {
        balance = 0;
    }
    Account(double initialDeposit)
    {
        balance = initialDeposit;
    }
    double getBalance()
    {
        return balance;
    }
    // returns new balance or -1 if error
    double deposit(double amount)
    {
        if (amount > 0)
            balance += amount;
        else
            return -1; // Code indicating error
        return balance;
    }
    // returns new balance or -1 if invalid amount
    double withdraw(double amount)
    {
    if ((amount > balance) || (amount < 0))
        return -1;
    else
        balance -= amount;
    return balance;
    }
};
```

Rewrite the class so that it throws appropriate exceptions instead of returning –1 as an error code. Write test code that attempts to withdraw and deposit invalid amounts and catches the exceptions that are thrown.

Templates 17

All men are mortal.
Aristotle is a man.
Therefore, Aristotle is mortal.
All X's are Y.
Z is an X.
Therefore, Z is Y.
All cats are mischievous.
Garfield is a cat.
Therefore, Garfield is mischievous.

A SHORT LESSON ON SYLLOGISMS

INTRODUCTION

This chapter discusses C++ templates. Templates allow you to define functions and classes that have parameters for type names. This will allow you to design functions that can be used with arguments of different types and to define classes that are much more general than those you have seen before this chapter.

PREREQUISITES

Section 17.1 uses material from Chapters 2 through 5 and Sections 7.1, 7.2, and 7.3 of Chapter 7. It does not use any material on classes. Section 17.2 uses material from Chapters 2 through 7 and 10 through 12.

17.1 TEMPLATES FOR ALGORITHM ABSTRACTION

Many of our previous C++ function definitions have an underlying algorithm that is much more general than the algorithm we gave in the function definition. For example, consider the function swap_values, which we first discussed in Chapter 5. For reference, we now repeat the function definition:

```
void swap_values(int& variable1, int& variable2)
{
    int temp;

    temp = variable1;
    variable1 = variable2;
    variable2 = temp;
}
```

Notice that the function swap_values applies only to variables of type *int*. Yet the algorithm given in the function body could just as well be used to swap the values in two variables of type *char*. If we want to also use the function swap_values with variables of type *char*, we can overload the function name by adding the following definition:

```
void swap_values(char& variable1, char& variable2)
{
    char temp;

    temp = variable1;
    variable1 = variable2;
    variable2 = temp;
}
```

But there is something inefficient and unsatisfying about these two definitions of the swap_values function: They are almost identical. The only difference is that one definition uses the type *int* in three places and the other uses the type *char* in the same three places. Proceeding in this way, if we wanted to have the function swap_values apply to pairs of variables of type *double*, we would have to write a third almost identical function definition. If we wanted to apply swap_values to still more types, the number of almost identical function definitions would be even larger. This would require a good deal of typing and would clutter up our code with lots of definitions that look identical. We should be able to say that the following function definition applies to variables of any type:

```
void swap_values(Type_Of_The_Variables& variable1,
                 Type_Of_The_Variables& variable2)
{
    Type_Of_The_Variables temp;

    temp = variable1;
    variable1 = variable2;
    variable2 = temp;
}
```

As we will see, something like this is possible. We can define one function that applies to all types of variables, although the syntax is a bit different from what we have shown above. That syntax is described in the next subsection.

Templates for Functions

Display 17.1 shows a C++ template for the function swap_values. This function template allows you to swap the values of any two variables, of any type, as long as the two variables have the same type. The definition and the function declaration begin with the line

```
template<class T>
```

This is often called the **template prefix,** and it tells the compiler that the definition or function declaration that follows is a **template** and that T is a

type parameter. In this context, the word *class* actually means *type.*[1] As we will see, the type parameter T can be replaced by any type, whether the type is a class or not. Within the body of the function definition, the type parameter T is used just like any other type.

The function template definition is, in effect, a large collection of function definitions. For the function template for swap_values shown in Display 17.1, there is, in effect, one function definition for each possible type name. Each of these definitions is obtained by replacing the type parameter T with a type name. For example, the function definition that follows is obtained by replacing T with the type name *double*:

```
void swap_values(double& variable1, double& variable2)
{

    double temp;

    temp = variable1;
    variable1 = variable2;
    variable2 = temp;
}
```

A template overloads the function name

Another definition for swap_values is obtained by replacing the type parameter T in the function template with the type name *int*. Yet another definition is obtained by replacing the type parameter T with *char*. The one function template shown in Display 17.1 overloads the function name swap_values so that there is a slightly different function definition for every possible type.

The compiler will not literally produce definitions for every possible type for the function name swap_values, but it will behave exactly as if it had produced all those function definitions. A separate definition will be produced for each different type for which you use the template, but not for any types you do not use. Only one definition is generated for a single type regardless of the number of times you use the template for that type. Notice that the function swap_values is called twice in Display 17.1: One time the arguments are of type *int* and the other time the arguments are of type *char*.

Consider the following function call from Display 17.1:

```
swap_values(integer1, integer2);
```

When the C++ compiler gets to this function call, it notices the types of the arguments—in this case *int*—and then it uses the template to produce a

---

[1] In fact, the ANSI standard provides that you may use the keyword *typename* instead of *class* in the template prefix. Although we agree that using *typename* makes more sense than using *class*, the use of *class* is a firmly established tradition, and so we use *class* for the sake of consistency with most other programmers and authors.

DISPLAY 17.1   A Function Template

```
1    //Program to demonstrate a function template.
2    #include <iostream>
3    using namespace std;

4    //Interchanges the values of variable1 and variable2.
5    template<class T>
6    void swap_values(T& variable1, T& variable2)
7    {
8        T temp;
9
10       temp = variable1;
11       variable1 = variable2;
12       variable2 = temp;
13   }

14   int main( )
15   {
16       int integer1 = 1, integer2 = 2;
17       cout << "Original integer values are "
18           << integer1 << " " << integer2 <<endl;
19       swap_values(integer1, integer2);
20       cout << "Swapped integer values are "
21           << integer1 << " " << integer2 <<endl;

22       char symbol1 = 'A', symbol2 = 'B';
23       cout << "Original character values are "
24           << symbol1 << " " << symbol2 <<endl;
25       swap_values(symbol1, symbol2);
26       cout << "Swapped character values are "
27           << symbol1 << " " << symbol2 <<endl;

28       return 0;
29   }
```

Output

```
Original integer values are 1 2
Swapped integer values are 2 1
Original character values are A B
Swapped character values are B A
```

function definition with the type parameter T replaced with the type name
int. Similarly, when the compiler sees the function call

```
swap_values(symbol1, symbol2);
```

it notices the types of the arguments—in this case *char*—and then it uses the template to produce a function definition with the type parameter T replaced with the type name *char*.

Calling a function template

Notice that you need not do anything special when you call a function that is defined with a function template; you call it just as you would any other function. The compiler does all the work of producing the function definition from the function template.

Notice that in Display 17.1 we placed the function template definition before the main part of the program, and we used no template function declaration. A function template may have a function declaration, just like an ordinary function. You may (or may not) be able to place the function declaration and definition for a function template in the same locations that you place function declarations and definitions for ordinary functions. However, many compilers do not support template function declarations and do not support separate compilation of template functions. When these are supported, the details can be messy and can vary from one compiler to another. Your safest strategy is to not use template function declarations and to be sure the function template definition appears in the same file in which it is used and appears before the function template is used.

We said that a function template definition should appear in the same file as the file that uses the template function (that is, the same file as the file that has an invocation of the template function). However, the function template definition can appear via a #include directive. You can give the function template definition in one file and then #include that file in a file that uses the template function. That is the cleanest and safest general strategy. However, even that may not work on some compilers. If it does not work, consult a local expert.

Although we will not be using template function declarations in our code, we will describe them and give examples of them for the benefit of readers whose compilers support the use of these function declarations.

In the function template in Display 17.1, we used the letter T as the parameter for the type. This is traditional but is not required by the C++ language. The type parameter can be any identifier (other than a keyword). T is a good name for the type parameter, but sometimes other names may work better. For example, the function template for swap_values given in Display 17.1 is equivalent to the following:

```
template<class VariableType>
void swap_values(VariableType& variable1,
                 VariableType& variable2)
{
    VariableType temp;

    temp = variable1;
    variable1 = variable2;
    variable2 = temp;
}
```

It is possible to have function templates that have more than one type parameter. For example, a function template with two type parameters named T1 and T2 would begin as follows:

More than one type parameter

```
template<class T1, class T2>
```

However, most function templates require only one type parameter. You cannot have unused template parameters; that is, each template parameter must be used in your template function.

PITFALL   Compiler Complications

VideoNote
Issues Compiling Programs
with Templates

Many compilers do not allow separate compilation of templates, so you may need to include your template definition with your code that uses it. As usual, at least the function declaration must precede any use of the template function.

Your safest strategy is not to use template function declarations and to be sure the function template definition appears in the same file in which it is used and appears before the function template is called. However, the function template definition can appear via a #include directive. You can give the function template definition in one file and then #include that file in a file that uses the template function.

Some C++ compilers have additional special requirements for using templates. If you have trouble compiling your templates, check your manuals or check with a local expert. You may need to set special options or rearrange the way you order the template definitions and the other items in your files. ■

Function Template

The function definition and the function declaration for a function template are each prefaced with the following:

```
template<class Type_Parameter>
```

The function declaration (if used) and definition are the same as any ordinary function declaration and definition, except that the *Type_Parameter* can be used in place of a type.

For example, the following is a function declaration for a function template:

```
template<class T>
void show_stuff(int stuff1, T stuff2, T stuff3);
```

The definition for this function template might be as follows:

```
template<class T>
void show_stuff(int stuff1, T stuff2, T stuff3)
```

(continued)

```
{
    cout << stuff1 << endl
         << stuff2 << endl
         << stuff3 << endl;
}
```

The function template given in this example is equivalent to having one function declaration and one function definition for each possible type name. The type name is substituted for the type parameter (which is T in the example above). For instance, consider the following function call:

```
show_stuff(2, 3.3, 4.4);
```

When this function call is executed, the compiler uses the function definition obtained by replacing T with the type name *double*. A separate definition will be produced for each different type for which you use the template but not for any types you do not use. Only one definition is generated for a specific type regardless of the number of times you use the template.

 myprogramminglab

SELF-TEST EXERCISES

1. Write a function template named `maximum`. The function takes two values of the same type as its arguments and returns the larger of the two arguments (or either value if they are equal). Give both the function declaration and the function definition for the template. You will use the operator < in your definition. Therefore, this function template will apply only to types for which < is defined. Write a comment for the function declaration that explains this restriction.

2. We have used three kinds of absolute value function: `abs`, `labs`, and `fabs`. These functions differ only in the type of their argument. It might be better to have a function template for the absolute value function. Give a function template for an absolute value function called `absolute`. The template will apply only to types for which < is defined, for which the unary negation operator is defined, and for which the constant 0 can be used in a comparison with a value of that type. Thus, the function `absolute` can be called with any of the number types, such as *int*, *long*, and *double*. Give both the function declaration and the function definition for the template.

3. Define or characterize the template facility for C++.

4. In the template prefix

   template<class T>

   what kind of variable is the parameter T?

a. T must be a class.

b. T must not be a class.

c. T can be only types built into the C++ language.

d. T can be any type, whether built into C++ or defined by the programmer.

Algorithm Abstraction

As we saw in our discussion of the swap_values function, there is a very general algorithm for interchanging the value of two variables, and this more general algorithm applies to variables of any type. Using a function template, we were able to express this more general algorithm in C++. This is a very simple example of *algorithm abstraction*. When we say we are using **algorithm abstraction,** we mean that we are expressing our algorithms in a very general way so that we can ignore incidental detail and concentrate on the substantive part of the algorithm. Function templates are one feature of C++ that supports algorithm abstraction.

PROGRAMMING EXAMPLE   A Generic Sorting Function

In Chapter 7 we gave a simple sorting algorithm to sort an array of values of type *int*. The algorithm was realized in C++ code as the function sort, which we gave in Display 7.12. Here we repeat the definition of this function sort:

```
void sort(int a[], int number_used)
{
    int index_of_next_smallest;
    for (int index = 0; index < number_used - 1; index++)
    {//Place the correct value in a[index]:
        index_of_next_smallest =
                index_of_smallest(a, index, number_used);
        swap_values(a[index], a[index_of_next_smallest]);
        //a[0] <= a[1] <=...<= a[index] are the smallest of
        //the original array elements. The rest of the
        //elements are in the remaining positions.
    }
}
```

If you study this definition of the function sort, you will see that the base type of the array is never used in any significant way. If we replace the base type of the array in the function header with the type *double*, then we would obtain a sorting function that applies to arrays of values of type *double*. Of

Helping functions course, we also must adjust the helping functions so they apply to arrays of elements of type *double*. So let's consider the helping functions that are called inside the body of the function sort. The two helping functions are swap_ values and index_of_smallest.

We already saw that swap_values can apply to variables of any type, provided we define it as a function template (as in Display 17.1). Let's see if index_of_smallest depends in any significant way on the base type of the array being sorted. The definition of index_of_smallest is repeated next so you can study its details.

```
int index_of_smallest(const int a[], int start_index,
                        int number_used)
{
    int min = a[start_index];
    int index_of_min = start_index;
    for (int index = start_index + 1;
        index < number_used; index++)
    {
        if (a[index] < min)
        {
            min = a[index];
            index_of_min = index;
            //min is the smallest of a[start_index] through
            //a[index]
        }
    }
    return index_of_min;
}
```

The function index_of_smallest also does not depend in any significant way on the base type of the array. If we replaced the two highlighted instances of the type *int* with the type *double*, then we will have changed the function index_of_smallest so that it applies to arrays whose base type is *double*.

To change the function sort so that it can be used to sort arrays with the base type *double*, we only needed to replace a few instances of the type name *int* with the type name *double*. Moreover, there is nothing special about the type *double*. We can do a similar replacement for many other types. The only thing we need to know about the type is that the operator < is defined for that type. This is the perfect situation for function templates. If we replace a few instances of the type name *int* (in the functions sort and index_of_ smallest) with a type parameter, then the function sort can sort an array of values of any type provided that the values of that type can be compared using the < operator. In Display 17.2 we have written just such a function template.

Notice that the function template sort shown in Display 17.2 can be used with arrays of values that are not numbers. In the demonstration program in Display 17.3, the function template sort is called to sort an array of characters. Characters can be compared using the < operator. Although the exact meaning of the < operator applied to character values may vary somewhat from one

DISPLAY 17.2   A Generic Sorting Function

```
1    //This is file sortfunc.cpp

2    template<class T>
3    void swap_values(T& variable1, T& variable2)
          <The rest of the definition of swap_values is given in Display 17.1.>
4
5    template<class BaseType>
6    int index_of_smallest(const BaseType a[], int start_index, int number_used)
7    {
8        BaseType min = a[start_index];
9        int index_of_min = start_index;
10
11       for (int index = start_index + 1; index < number_used; index++)
12.          if (a[index] < min)
13           {
14               min = a[index];
15               Index_of_min = index;
16               //min is the smallest of a[start_index] through a[index]
17           }
18
19       return index_of_min;
20   }
21
22   template<class BaseType>
23   void sort(BaseType a[], int number_used)
24   {
25   int index_of_next_smallest;
26   for (int index = 0; index < number_used - 1; index++)
27      {//Place the correct value in a[index]:
28              index_of_next_smallest =
29                  index_of_smallest(a, index, number_used);
30              swap_values(a[index], a[index_of_next_smallest]);
31          //a[0] <= a[1] <=...<= a[index] are the smallest of the original array
32          //elements. The rest of the elements are in the remaining positions.
33      }
34   }
```

implementation to another, some things are always true about how < orders the letters of the alphabet. When applied to two uppercase letters, the operator < tests to see if the first comes before the second in alphabetic order. Also, when applied to two lowercase letters, the operator < tests to see if the first comes before the second in alphabetic order. When you mix uppercase and lowercase letters, the situation is not so well behaved, but the program shown in Display 17.3 deals only with uppercase letters. In that program, an array of

DISPLAY 17.3   Using a Generic Sorting Function *(part 1 of 2)*

```
1    //Demonstrates a generic sorting function.
2    #include <iostream>
3    using namespace std;
4
5    //The file sortfunc.cpp defines the following function:
6    //template<class BaseType>
7    //void sort(BaseType a[], int number_used);
8    //Precondition: number_used <= declared size of the array a.
9    //The array elements a[0] through a[number_used - 1] have values.
10   //Postcondition: The values of a[0] through a[number_used - 1] have
11   //been rearranged so that a[0] <= a[1] <= ... <= a[number_used - 1].
12
13   #include "sortfunc.cpp"
14
15   int main( )
16   {
17       int i;
18       int a[10] = {9, 8, 7, 6, 5, 1, 2, 3, 0, 4};
19       cout << "Unsorted integers:\n";
20       for (i = 0; i < 10; i++)
21           cout << a[i] << " ";
22       cout << endl;
23       sort(a, 10);
24       cout << "In sorted order the integers are:\n";
25       for (i = 0; i < 10; i++)
26           cout << a[i] << " ";
27       cout << endl;

28       double b[5] = {5.5, 4.4, 1.1, 3.3, 2.2};
29       cout << "Unsorted doubles:\n";
30       for (i = 0; i < 5; i++)
31           cout << b[i] << " ";
32       cout << endl;
33       sort(b, 5);
34       cout << "In sorted order the doubles are:\n";
35       for (i = 0; i < 5; i++)
36           cout << b[i] << " ";
37       cout << endl;

38       char c[7] = {'G', 'E', 'N', 'E', 'R', 'I', 'C'};
39       cout << "Unsorted characters:\n";
40       for (i = 0; i < 7; i++)
41           cout << c[i] << " ";
42       cout << endl;
```

Many compilers will allow this function declaration to appear as a function declaration and not merely as a comment. However, including the function declaration is not needed, since the definition of the function is in the file `sortfunc.cpp`, and so the definition effectively appears before `main`.

(continued)

DISPLAY 17.3   Using a Generic Sorting Function *(part 2 of 2)*

```
43          sort(c, 7);
44          cout << "In sorted order the characters are:\n";
45          for (i = 0; i < 7; i++)
46              cout << c[i] << " ";
47          cout << endl;
48          return 0;
49      }
```

Output

```
Unsorted integers:
9 8 7 6 5 1 2 3 0 4
In sorted order the integers are:
0 1 2 3 4 5 6 7 8 9
Unsorted doubles:
5.5 4.4 1.1 3.3 2.2
In sorted order the doubles are:
1.1 2.2 3.3 4.4 5.5
Unsorted characters:
G E N E R I C
In sorted order the characters are:
C E E G I N R
```

uppercase letters is sorted into alphabetical order with a call to the function template sort. (The function template sort will even sort an array of objects of a class that you define, provided you overload the < operator to apply to objects of that class.)

■ PROGRAMMING TIP   How to Define Templates

When we defined the function template in Display 17.2, we started with a function that sorts an array of elements of type *int*. We then created a template by replacing the base type of the array with the type parameter T. This is a good general strategy for writing templates. If you want to write a function template, first write a version that is not a template at all but is just an ordinary function. Completely debug the ordinary function and then convert the ordinary function to a template by replacing some type names with a type parameter. There are two advantages to this method. First, when you are defining the ordinary function you are dealing with a much more concrete case, which makes the problem easier to visualize. Second, you have fewer details to check at each stage; when worrying about the algorithm itself, you need not concern yourself with template syntax rules. ■

PITFALL   Using a Template with an Inappropriate Type[2]

You can use a template function with any type for which the code in the function definition makes sense. However, all the code in the template function must make sense and must behave in an appropriate way. For example, you cannot use the swap_values template (Display 17.1) with the type parameter replaced by a type for which the assignment operator does not work at all or does not work "correctly."

As a more concrete example, suppose that your program defines the template function swap_values as in Display 17.1. You cannot add the following to your program:

```
int a[10], b[10];
<some code to fill arrays>
swap_values(a, b);
```

This code will not work, because assignment does not work with array types. ■

SELF-TEST EXERCISES

5. Display 7.10 shows a function called search, which searches an array for a specified integer. Give a function template version of search that can be used to search an array of elements of any type. Give both the function declaration and the function definition for the template. (*Hint:* It is almost identical to the function given in Display 7.10.)

6. In Programming Project 11 of Chapter 4 you were asked to overload the abs function so that the name abs would work with several of the built-in types that had been studied at the time. Compare and contrast function overloading of the abs function with the use of templates for this purpose in Self-Test Exercise 2.

[2] The example in this Pitfall section uses arrays. If you have not yet covered arrays (Chapter 7), you should skip this Pitfall section and return after covering arrays.

17.2 TEMPLATES FOR DATA ABSTRACTION

Equal wealth and equal opportunities of culture . . . have simply made us all members of one class.

EDWARD BELLAMY, *Looking Backward: 2000–1887*

As you saw in the previous section, function definitions can be made more general by using templates. In this section, you will see that templates can also make class definitions more general.

Syntax for Class Templates

The syntax for class templates is basically the same as that for function templates. The following is placed before the template definition:

```
template<class T>
```

The type parameter T is used in the class definition just like any other type. As with function templates, the type parameter T represents a type that can be any type at all; the type parameter does not have to be replaced with a class type. As with function templates, you may use any (nonkeyword) identifier instead of T.

Type parameter

For example, the following is a class template. An object of this class contains a pair of values of type T; if T is *int*, the object values are pairs of integers, if T is *char*, the object values are pairs of characters, and so on.

```
//Class for a pair of values of type T:
template<class T>
class Pair
{
public:
    Pair();

    Pair(T first_value, T second_value);

    void set_element(int position, T value);
    //Precondition: position is 1 or 2.
    //Postcondition:
    //The position indicated has been set to value.

    T get_element(int position) const;
    //Precondition: position is 1 or 2.
    //Returns the value in the position indicated.
private:
    T first;
    T second;
};
```

Once the class template is defined, you can declare objects of this class. The declaration must specify what type is to be filled in for T. For example, the

Declaring objects

following code declares the object score so it can record a pair of integers and declares the object seats so it can record a pair of characters:

```
Pair<int> score;
Pair<char> seats;
```

The objects are then used just like any other objects. For example, the following sets the score to be 3 for the first team and 0 for the second team:

```
score.set_element(1, 3);
score.set_element(2, 0);
```

Defining member functions

The member functions for a class template are defined the same way as member functions for ordinary classes. The only difference is that the member function definitions are themselves templates. For example, the following are appropriate definitions for the member function set_element and for the constructor with two arguments:

```
//Uses iostream and cstdlib:
template<class T>
void Pair<T>::set_element(int position, T value)
{
    if (position == 1)
        first = value;
    else if (position == 2)
        second = value;
    else
    {
        cout << "Error: Illegal pair position.\n";
        exit(1);
    }
}

template<class T>
Pair<T>::Pair(T first_value, T second_value)
        : first(first_value), second(second_value)
{
    //Body intentionally empty.
}
```

Notice that the class name before the scope resolution operator is Pair<T>, not simply Pair.

The name of a class template may be used as the type for a function parameter. For example, the following is a possible declaration for a function with a parameter for a pair of integers:

```
int add_up(const Pair<int>& the_pair);
//Returns the sum of the two integers in the_pair.
```

Class Template Syntax

The class definition and the definitions of the member functions are prefaced with the following:

```
template<class Type_Parameter>
```

The class and member function definitions are then the same as for any ordinary class, except that the *Type_Parameter* can be used in place of a type.

For example, the following is the beginning of a class template definition:

```
template<class T>
class Pair
{
public:
    Pair();
    Pair(T first_value, T second_value);
    void set_element(int position, T value);
        . . .
```

Member functions and overloaded operators are then defined as function templates. For example, the definition of a function definition for the sample class template above could begin as follows:

```
template<class T>
void Pair<T>::set_element(int position, T value)
{
        . . .
```

Note that we specified the type, in this case *int*, that is to be filled in for the type parameter T.

You can even use a class template within a function template. For example, rather than defining the specialized function add_up given above, you could instead define a function template as follows so that the function applies to all kinds of numbers:

```
template<class T>
T add_up(const Pair<T>& the_pair);
//Precondition: The operator + is defined for values of type T.
//Returns the sum of the two values in the_pair.
```

Type Definitions

You can specialize a class template by giving a type argument to the class name, as in the following example:

`Pair<int>`

The specialized class name, like `Pair<int>`, can then be used just like any class name. It can be used to declare objects or to specify the type of a formal parameter.

You can define a new class type name that has the same meaning as a specialized class template name, such as `Pair<int>`. The syntax for such a defined class type name is as follows:

typedef Class_Name*<Type_Argument>* New_Type_Name;

For example:

typedef Pair*<int>* PairOfInt;

The type name `PairOfInt` can then be used to declare objects of type `Pair<int>`, as in the following example:

`PairOfInt pair1, pair2;`

The type name `PairOfInt` can also be used to specify the type of a formal parameter.

PROGRAMMING EXAMPLE   **An Array Class**

Display 17.4 contains the interface for a class template whose objects are lists. Since this class definition is a class template, the lists can be lists of items of any type whatsoever. You can have objects that are lists of values of type *int*, or lists of values of type *double*, or lists of objects of type string, or lists of items of any other type.

Display 17.5 contains a demonstration program that uses this class template. Although this program does not really do anything much, it does illustrate how the class template is used. Once you understand the syntax details, you can use the class template in any program that needs a list of values. Display 17.6 gives the implementation of the class template.

Notice that we have overloaded the insertion operator << so it can be used to output an object of the class template GenericList. To do this, we made the operator << a friend of the class. In order to have a parameter that is of the same type as the class, we used the expression GenericList<ItemType> for the parameter type. When the type parameter is replaced by, for example, the type *int*, this list parameter will be of type GenericList<*int*>.

A friend

DISPLAY 17.4   Interface for the Class Template GenericList *(part 1 of 2)*

```
1    //This is the header file genericlist.h. This is the interface for the
2    //class GenericList. Objects of type GenericList can be a list of items
3    //of any type for which the operators << and = are defined.
4    //All the items on any one list must be of the same type. A list that
5    //can hold up to max items all of type Type_Name is declared as follows:
6    // GenericList<Type_Name>the_object(max);
7    #ifndef GENERICLIST_H
8    #define GENERICLIST_H
9    #include <iostream>
10   using namespace std;
11
12   namespace listsavitch
13   {
14       template<class ItemType>
15       class GenericList
16       {
17       public:
18           GenericList(int max);
19           //Initializes the object to an empty list that can hold up to
20           //max items of type ItemType.
21
22           ~GenericList( );
23           //Returns all the dynamic memory used by the object to the freestore.
24
25           int length( ) const;
26           //Returns the number of items on the list.
27
28           void add(ItemType new_item);
29           //Precondition: The list is not full.
30           //Postcondition: The new_item has been added to the list.
31
32           bool full( ) const;
33           //Returns true if the list is full.
34
```

(continued)

DISPLAY 17.4 **Interface for the Class Template** GenericList *(part 2 of 2)*

```
35            void erase( );
36            //Removes all items from the list so that the list is empty.
37
38            friend ostream& operator<<(ostream& outs,
39                                const GenericList<ItemType>& the_list);
40            //Overloads the << operator so it can be used to output the
41            //contents of the list. The items are output one per line.
42            //Precondition: If outs is a file output stream, then outs has
43            //already been connected to a file.
44        private:
45            ItemType *item; //pointer to the dynamic array that holds the list.
46            int max_length;//max number of items allowed on the list.
47            int current_length;//number of items currently on the list.
48        };
49   }//listsavitch
50   #endif//GENERICLIST_H
```

DISPLAY 17.5 **Program Using the** GenericList **Class Template** *(part 1 of 2)*

```
1    //Program to demonstrate use of the class template GenericList.
2    #include <iostream>
3    #include "genericlist.h"                Since genericlist.cpp is included,
4    #include "genericlist.cpp"              you need compile only this one file (the
5    using namespace std;                    one with the main).
6    using namespace listsavitch;

7    int main( )
8    {
9        GenericList<int> first_list(2);
10       first_list.add(1);
11       first_list.add(2);
12       cout << "first_list = \n"
13            << first_list;

14       GenericList<char> second_list(10);
15       second_list.add('A');
16       second_list.add('B');
17       second_list.add('C');
18       cout << "second_list = \n"
19            << second_list;

20       return 0;
21   }
```

(continued)

DISPLAY 17.5   Program Using the GenericList **Class Template** *(part 2 of 2)*

Output

```
first_list =
1
2
second_list =
A
B
C
```

DISPLAY 17.6   Implementation of GenericList *(part 1 of 3)*

```
1    //This is the implementation file: genericlist.cpp
2    //This is the implementation of the class template named GenericList.
3    //The interface for the class template GenericList is in the
4    //header filegenericlist.h.
5    #ifndef GENERICLIST_CPP
6    #define GENERICLIST_CPP
7    #include <iostream>
8    #include <cstdlib>
9    #include "genericlist.h"//This is not needed when used as we are using this file,
10                    //but the #ifndef in genericlist.h makes it safe.
11   using namespace std;
12
13   namespace listsavitch
14   {
15       //Uses cstdlib:
16       template<class ItemType>
17       GenericList<ItemType>::GenericList(int max): max_length(max),
                                                  current_length(0)
18
19       {
20           item = new ItemType[max];
21       }
22
23       template<class ItemType>
24       GenericList<ItemType>::~GenericList( )
```

(continued)

DISPLAY 17.6 Implementation of GenericList *(part 2 of 3)*

```
25      {
26          delete [] item;
27      }
28
29      template<class ItemType>
30      int GenericList<ItemType>::length( ) const
31      {
32          return (current_length);
33      }
34
35      //Uses iostream and cstdlib:
36      template<class ItemType>
37      void GenericList<ItemType>::add(ItemType new_item)
38      {
39          if ( full( ) )
40          {
41              cout << "Error: adding to a full list.\n";
42              exit(1);
43          }
44          else
45          {
46              Item[current_length] = new_item;
47              current_length = current_length + 1;
48          }
49      }
50
51      template<class ItemType>
52      bool GenericList<ItemType>::full( ) const
53      {
54          return (current_length == max_length);
55      }
56
57      template<class ItemType>
58      void GenericList<ItemType>::erase( )
59      {
60          current_length = 0;
61      }
62
63      //Uses iostream:
64      template<class ItemType>
65      ostream& operator <<(ostream& outs,
                           const GenericList<ItemType>& the_list)
```

(continued)

DISPLAY 17.6   Implementation of GenericList *(part 3 of 3)*

```
66          {
67              for (int i = 0; i < the_list.current_length; i++)
68                  outs << the_list.item[i] << endl;
69
70              return outs;
71          }
72      }//listsavitch
73      #endif// GENERICLIST_CPP Notice that we have enclosed all the template
74              // definitions in #ifndef... #endif.
```

<A note is in order about compiling the code from Displays 17.4, 17.5, and 17.6. A safe solution to the compilation of this code is to #include the template class definition and the template function definitions before use, as we did. In that case, only the file in Display 17.5 needs to be compiled. Be sure that you use the #ifndef #define #endif mechanism to prevent multiple file inclusion of all the files you are going to #include.>

SELF-TEST EXERCISES   myprogramminglab

7. Give the definition for the member function get_element for the class template Pair discussed in the section "Syntax for Class Templates."

8. Give the definition for the constructor with zero arguments for the class template Pair discussed in the section "Syntax for Class Templates."

9. Give the definition of a template class called HeterogeneousPair that is like the class template Pair discussed in the section "Syntax for Class Templates," except that with HeterogeneousPair the first and second positions may store values of different types. Use two type parameters T1 and T2; all items in the first position will be of type T1, and all items in the second position will be of type T2. The single mutator function set_element in the template class Pair should be replaced by two mutator functions called set_first and set_second in the template class HeterogeneousPair. Similarly, the single accessor function get_element in the template class Pair should be replaced by two accessor functions called get_first and get_second in the template class HeterogeneousPair.

10. Is the following true or false?

Friends are used exactly the same for template and nontemplate classes.

CHAPTER SUMMARY

■ Using function templates, you can define functions that have a parameter for a type.

■ Using class templates, you can define a class with a type parameter for sub-parts of the class.

Answers to Self-Test Exercises

1. Function Declaration:

    ```
    template<class T>
    T maximum(T first, T second);
    //Precondition: The operator < is defined for the type T.
    //Returns the maximum of first and second.
    ```

    Definition:

    ```
    template<class T>
    T maximum(T first, T second)
    {
        if (first < second)
            return second;
        else
            return first;
    }
    ```

2. Function Declaration:

    ```
    template<class T>
    T absolute(T value);
    //Precondition: The expressions x < 0 and -x are defined
    //whenever x is of type T.
    //Returns the absolute value of its argument.
    ```

    Definition:

    ```
    template<class T>
    T absolute(T value)
    {
        if (value < 0)
            return -value;
        else
            return value;
    }
    ```

3. Templates provide a facility to allow the definition of functions and classes that have parameters for type names.

4. d. Any type, whether a primitive type (provided by C++) or a type defined by the user (a *class* or *struct* type, an *enum* type, or a defined array type, or *int*, *float*, *double*, etc.).

5. The function declaration and function definition are given here. They are basically identical to those for the versions given in Display 7.10 except that two instances of *int* are changed to BaseType in the parameter list.

Function Declaration:

```
template<class BaseType>
int search(const BaseType a[],
           int number_used, BaseType target);
//Precondition: number_used is <= the declared size of a.
//Also, a[0] through a[number_used-1] have values.
//Returns the first index such that a[index] == target,
//provided there is such an index; otherwise, returns -1.
```

Definition:

```
template<class BaseType>
int search(const BaseType a[], int number_used,
           BaseType target)
{

    int index = 0, found = false;
    while ((!found) && (index < number_used))
    if (target == a[index])
        found = true;
    else
        index++;

    if (found)
        return index;
    else
        return -1;
}
```

6. Function overloading only works for types for which an overloading is provided. Overloading may work for types that automatically convert to some type for which an overloading is provided but may not do what you expect. The template solution will work for any type that is defined at the time of invocation, provided that the requirements for a definition of < are satisfied.

7. ```
   //Uses iostream and cstdlib:
   template<class T>
   T Pair<T>::get_element(int position) const
   {
       if (position == 1)
           return first;
       else if (position == 2)
           return second;
       else
       {
           cout << "Error: Illegal pair position.\n";
           exit(1);
       }
   }
   ```

8. There are no natural candidates for the default initialization values, so this constructor does nothing, but it does allow you to declare (uninitialized) objects without giving any constructor arguments.

   ```
   template<class T>
   Pair<T>::Pair()
   {
   //Do nothing.
   }
   ```

9. ```
   //Class for a pair of values, the first of type T1
   //and the second of type T2:
   template<class T1, class T2>
   class HeterogeneousPair
   {
   public:
       HeterogeneousPair();
       HeterogeneousPair(T1 first_value, T2 second_value);
       void set_first(T1 value);
       void set_second(T2 value);
       T1 get_first() const;
       T2 get_second() const;
   private:
       T1 first;
       T2 second;
   };
   ```

   The member function definitions are as follows:

   ```
   template<class T1, class T2>
   HeterogeneousPair<T1, T2>::HeterogeneousPair( )
   {
   //Do nothing.
   }
   ```

```
template<class T1, class T2>
HeterogeneousPair<T1, T2>::HeterogeneousPair
    (T1 first_value, T2 second_value)
            : first(first_value), second(second_value)
{
    //Body intentionally empty.
}


template<class T1, class T2>
T1 HeterogeneousPair<T1, T2>::get_first() const
{
    return first;
}


template<class T1, class T2>
T2 HeterogeneousPair<T1, T2>::get_second() const
{
    return second;
}


template<class T1, class T2>
void HeterogeneousPair<T1, T2>::set_first(T1 value)
{
    first = value;
}


template<class T1, class T2>
void HeterogeneousPair<T1, T2>::set_second(T2 value)
{
    second = value;
}
```

10. True.

PROGRAMMING PROJECTS

Visit www.myprogramminglab.com to complete many of these Programming Projects online and get instant feedback.   `myprogramminglab`

1. Write a function template for a function that has parameters for a partially filled array and for a value of the base type of the array. If the value is in the partially filled array, then the function returns the index of the first indexed variable that contains the value. If the value is not in the array, the function returns –1. The base type of the array is a type parameter. Notice that you need two parameters to give the partially filled array: one for the array and one for the number of indexed variables used. Also, write a suitable test program to test this function template.

2. Rewrite the definition of the class template GenericList given in Display 17.4 and Display 17.6 so that it is more general. This more general version has the added feature that you can step through the items on the list in order. One item is always the current item. You can ask for the current item, change the current item to the next item, change the current item to the previous item, start at the beginning of the list by making the first item on the list the current item, and ask for the *n*th item on the list. To do this, you will add the following members: an additional member variable that records the position on the list of the current item, a member function that returns the current item as a value, a member function that makes the next item the current item, a member function that makes the previous item the current item, a member function that makes the first item on the list the current item, and a member function that returns the *n*th item on the list given n as an argument. (Number items as in arrays, so that the first item is the 0th item, the next is item number 1, and so forth.)

   Note that there are situations in which some of these function actions are not possible. For example, an empty list has no first item, and there is no item after the last item in any list. Be sure to test for the empty list and handle it appropriately. Be sure to test for the beginning and end of the list and handle these cases appropriately. Write a suitable test program to test this class template.

3. Write a class template to represent a generic *vector*, which is a series of values. A vector can store an array of *int* values or *float* values. Include member functions to perform the following tasks:

   a. To create the vector
   b. To display the content of the vector
   c. To modify the value of a given element
   d. To multiply by a scalar value

4. (This project requires that you know what operator overloading is. Operator overloading is dealt with in Chapter 11. This is an appropriate project only if you have covered Chapter 11.).

   Modify your program from Programming Project 3 so that the program overloads the * operator to find the sum of the product of corresponding elements, of two instances of the vector class.

5. Display 17.3 gives a template function for sorting an array using the selection sort algorithm. Write a similar template function for sorting an array, but this time use the insertion sort algorithm as described in Programming Project 6 of Chapter 7. If you have not already done it, it would be a good idea to first do the nontemplate version; in other words, it would be a good idea to first do Programming Project 6 from Chapter 7.

6. Write a C++ program to define and declare a class template for reading two data items from the keyboard and to find the product of these two data items.

7. Write a C++ program to demonstrate the function template cube to find the cube of a number. The number may be an *integer*, a *floating point* or *double* data type.

8. (This project requires that you know what a queue is and how to use arrays. Queues are covered in Chapter 13; arrays are covered in Chapter 11. This is an appropriate project only if you have covered Chapters 9 and 11.)

    Write a template version of a queue class. Use a type parameter for the type of data that is stored in the queue. Use arrays to allow the queue to grow to hold any number of items.

9. Write a template version of a class that implements a priority queue. Queues are discussed in Chapter 13 and priority queues are discussed in Chapter 18. To summarize, a priority queue is essentially a list of items that is always ordered by priority. Each item that is added to the list requires an associated priority value. For this problem, make the priority an integer where 0 is the highest priority and larger values are lower in priority. Removing an item from the queue removes the item with the highest priority.

    The add function of the priority queue should take a generic type and then an integer priority. In the following example, the generic type is a char and we have added three items to the queue:

```
q.add('X', 10);
q.add('Y', 1);
q.add('Z', 3);
```

    The remove function should return and remove from the priority queue the item that has the highest priority. Given the example above, we would expect the following:

```
cout << q.remove();        // Outputs Y  (priority 1)
cout << q.remove();        // Returns Z  (priority 3)
cout << q.remove();        // Returns X  (priority 10)
```

    Test your queue on data with priorities in various orders (for example, ascending, descending, mixed). You can implement the priority queue by storing the items using a list(s) of your choice (for example, vector, array, linked list, or GenericList described in this chapter) and then performing a linear search for the item with the lowest integer value in the remove function. In future courses you may study a data structure called a heap that affords a more efficient way to implement a priority queue.

VideoNote
Solution to Programming
Project 17.10

10. Write a template-based class that implements a set of items. A set is a collection of items in which no item occurs more than once. Internally, you may represent the set using the data structure of your choice (for example, list, vector, arrays, etc.). However, the class should externally support the following functions:

    a. Add a new item to the set. If the item is already in the set then nothing happens.
    b. Remove an item from the set.
    c. Return the number of items in the set.
    d. Determine if an item is a member of the set.
    e. Return a pointer to a dynamically created array containing each item in the set. The caller of this function is responsible for deallocating the memory.

    Test your class by creating different sets of different data types (for example, strings, integers, or other classes). If you add objects to your set, then you may need to overload the == and != operators for the object's class so your template-based set class can properly determine membership.

11. This project requires that you complete Programming Project 10 from this chapter and Programming Project 11 from Chapter 14. Programming Project 11 asked you to write a program to find all permutations of a set. Modify the program so that it generates permutations given an instance of the template-based set class defined in Programming Project 10. You may wish to also use your template-based set class to help simplify the implementation of the permutation algorithm itself.

    The algorithm requires that you store a set of lists. C++ allows you to create a set of lists with your template-based set class. For example, myset<vector<T> > will define a set containing a vector of type T. Be careful to place a space between the last two >'s, or the compiler may get confused. The code myset<vector<T>> without a space will likely produce a compiler error.

    Your program should print all permutations of sets of several different sizes and comprised of several different types of data (for example, a set of three integers, a set of four strings, or a set of five doubles).

12. In this chapter we used only a single template class type parameter. C++ allows you to specify multiple type parameters. For example, the following code specifies that the class accepts two type parameters:

```
template<class T, class V>
class Example
{
    . . .
}
```

When creating an instance of the class, we must now specify two data types, such as:

```
Example<int, char> demo;
```

Create a `Map` class that maps keys to values. The data type for the keys and values should be specified separately using type parameters. The map forms the basis for a simple database. For example, to map from employee ID numbers to employee names, we might use integers for the data type of the keys and strings for the data type of the names. The class should have functions to:

1. Add a new key/value pair to the map
2. Set an existing key/value pair to a new value given the key
3. Delete a key/value pair from the map given the key
4. Check if a key/value pair exists in the map given the key
5. Retrieve the value for a key/value pair given the key

Use any data type you wish to implement the map. Write a main function that tests the class by exercising all of the functions with sample data.

Standard Template Library 18

Libraries are not made; they grow.

AUGUSTINE BIRRELL

INTRODUCTION

There is a large collection of standard data structures for holding data. Since they are so standard it makes sense to have standard portable implementations for them. The Standard Template Library (STL) includes libraries for such data structures. Included in the STL are implementations of the stack, queue, and many other standard data structures. When discussed in the context of the STL, these data structures are usually called *container classes* because they are used to hold collections of data. In Chapter 8 we presented a preview of the STL by describing the `vector` template class, which is one of the container classes in the STL. In this chapter we will present an overview of some of the basic classes included in the STL. We do not have room to give a comprehensive treatment of the STL here, but we will present enough to get you started using some basic STL container classes.

The STL was developed by Alexander Stepanov and Meng Lee at Hewlett-Packard and was based on research by Stepanov, Lee, and David Musser. It is a collection of libraries written in the C++ language. Although the STL is not part of the core C++ language, it is part of the C++ standard and so any implementation of C++ that conforms to the standard would include the STL. As a practical matter, you can consider the STL to be part of the C++ language.

As its name suggest, the classes in the STL are template classes. A typical container class in the STL has a type parameter for the type of data to be stored in the container class. The STL container classes make extensive use of iterators, which are objects that facilitate cycling through the data in a container. An introduction to the concept of an iterator was given in Section 13.1, where we discussed pointers used as iterators. You will find it helpful to read that section before reading this chapter. If you have not already done so, you should also read Section 8.3, which covers the `vector` template class of the STL.

The STL also includes implementations of many important generic algorithms, such as searching and sorting algorithms. The algorithms are implemented as template functions. After discussing the container classes, we will describe some of these algorithm implementations.

The STL differs from other C++ libraries, such as `<iostream>` for example, in that the classes and algorithms are **generic,** which is another way of saying they are template classes and template functions.

PREREQUISITES

This chapter uses the material from Chapters 2 through 13, 15, and Chapter 17.

18.1 ITERATORS

> *The White Rabbit put on his spectacles. "Where shall I begin, please your Majesty?" he asked.*
>
> *"Begin at the beginning," the King said, very gravely, "And go on till you come to the end: then stop."*
>
> LEWIS CARROLL, *Alice in Wonderland*

Vectors, introduced in Chapter 8, are one of the container template classes in the STL. Iterators are a generalization of pointers. (Chapter 13 includes an introduction to pointers used as iterators.) This section shows you how to use iterators with vectors. Other container template classes, which we introduce in Section 18.2, use iterators in the same way. So, all you learn about iterators in this section will apply across a wide range of containers and does not apply solely to vectors. This reflects one of the basic tenets of the STL philosophy: The semantics, naming, and syntax for iterator usage should be (and are) uniform across different container types. We begin with a review and discussion of the *using* declarations, which we will use extensively when discussing iterators and the STL.

using Declarations

It may help to review the subsection entitled "Qualifying Names" in Chapter 12 before you continue with this subsection and this chapter.

Suppose `my_function` is a function defined in the namespace `my_space`. The following *using* declaration allows you to use the identifier `my_function` and have it mean the versions of `my_function` defined in the namespace `my_space`:

```
using my_space::my_function;
```

Within the scope of this *using* declaration an expression such as `my_function(1,2)` means the same thing as `my_space::my_function(1,2)`; that is, within the scope of this *using* declaration the identifier `my_function` always indicates the version of `my_function` defined in `my_space`, as opposed to any definition of `my_function` defined in any other namespace.

When discussing iterators we will often apply the `::` operator to another level. You will often see expressions such as the following:

```
using std::vector<int>::iterator;
```

In this case, the identifier `iterator` names a type. So within the scope of this *using* directive, the following would be allowed:

```
iterator p;
```

This declares p to be of the type `iterator`. What is the type `iterator`? It is defined in the definition of the class vector<*int*>. Which class vector<*int*>? The one defined in the namespace `std`. (We will fully explain the type `iterator` later. At this point we are concerned only with explaining *using* directives.)

You may object that this is all a big to-do about nothing. There is no class vector<*int*> defined in any namespace other than the namespace `std`. That may or may not be true, but there could be a class named vector<*int*> defined in some other namespace either now or in the future. You may object further that you never heard of defining a type within a class. We have not covered such definitions, but they are possible and they are common in the STL. So, you must know how to use such types, even if you do not define such types.

In summary, consider the *using* directive

```
using std::vector<int>::iterator;
```

Within the scope of this *using* directive the identifier `iterator` means the type named `iterator` that is defined in the class vector<int>, which in turn is defined in the `std` namespace.

Iterator Basics

An **iterator** is a generalization of a pointer, and in fact is typically even implemented using a pointer, but the abstraction of an iterator is designed to spare you the details of the implementation and give you a uniform interface to iterators that is the same across different container classes. Each container class has its own iterator types, just like each data type has its own pointer type. But just as all pointer types behave essentially the same for dynamic variables of their particular data type, so too does each iterator type behave the same, but each iterator is used only with its own container class.

An iterator is not a pointer, but you will not go far wrong if you think of it and use it as if it were a pointer. Like a pointer variable, an iterator variable is located at ("points to") one data entry in the container. You manipulate iterators using the following overloaded operators that apply to iterator objects:

- Prefix and postfix increment operators, ++, for advancing the iterator to the next data item
- Prefix and postfix decrement operators, --, for moving the iterator to the previous data item.
- Equal and unequal operators, == and !=, to test whether two iterators point to the same data location.

- A dereferencing operator, *, so that if p is an iterator variable, then *p gives access to the data located at ("pointed to by") p. This access may be read-only, write-only, or allow both reading and changing of the data, depending on the particular container class.

Not all iterators have all of these operators. However, the vector template class is an example of a container whose iterators have all these operators and more.

A container class has member functions that get the iterator process started. After all, a new iterator variable is not located at ("pointing to") any data in the container. Many container classes, including the vector template class, have the following member functions that return iterator objects (iterator values) that point to special data elements in the data structure:

- c.begin() returns an iterator for the container c that points to the "first" data item in the container c.
- c.end() returns something that can be used to test when an iterator has passed beyond the last data item in a container c. The iterator c.end() is completely analogous to NULL used to test when a pointer has passed the last node in a linked list of the kind discussed in Chapter 13. The iterator c.end() is thus an iterator that is located at no data item, but that is a kind of end marker or sentinel.

For many container classes, these tools allow you to write *for* loops that cycle through all the elements in a container object c, as follows:

```
//p is an iterator variable of the type for the container object c.
for (p = c.begin(); p != c.end(); p++)
    process *p //*p is the current data item.
```

That's the big picture. Now let's look at the details in the concrete setting of the vector template container class.

Display 18.1 illustrates the use of iterators with the vector template class. Keep in mind that each container type in the STL has its own iterator types, although they are all used in the same basic ways. The iterators we want for a vector of *int*s are of type

```
std::vector<int>::iterator
```

Another container class is the list template class. Iterators for lists of *int*s are of type

```
std::list<int>::iterator
```

In the program in Display 18.1, we specialize the type name iterator so that it applies to iterators for vectors of *int*s. The type name iterator that we want in Display 18.1 is defined in the template class vector and so if we specialize the template class vector to *int*s and want the iterator type for vector<*int*>, we want the type

```
std::vector<int>::iterator;
```

DISPLAY 18.1   Iterators Used with a Vector

```
1    //Program to demonstrate STL iterators.
2    #include <iostream>
3    #include <vector>
4    using std::cout;
5    using std::endl;
6    using std::vector;
7    int main()
8    {
9        vector<int> container;
10       for (int i = 1; i <= 4; i++)
11           container.push_back(i);
12       cout << "Here is what is in the container:\n";
13       vector<int>::iterator p;
14       for (p = container.begin(); p != container.end(); p++)
15           cout << *p << " ";
16       cout <<endl;
17       cout << "Setting entries to 0:\n";
18       for (p = container.begin(); p != container.end(); p++)
19           *p = 0;
20
21       cout << "Container now contains:\n";
22       for (p = container.begin(); p != container.end(); p++)
23           cout << *p << " ";
24       cout << endl;
25       return 0;
26   }
```

Sample Dialogue

```
Here is what is in the container:
1 2 3 4
Setting entries to 0:
Container now contains:
0 0 0 0
```

Since the vector definition places the name vector in the std namespace, the entire *using* declaration is

```
using std::vector<int>::iterator;
```

The basic use of iterators with the vector (or any container class) is illustrated by the following lines from Display 18.1:

```
vector<int>::iterator p;
for (p = container.begin(); p != container.end(); p++)
    cout << *p << " ";
```

Recall that `container` is of type `vector<int>`.

A vector v can be thought of as a linear arrangement of its data elements. There is a first data element `v[0]`, a second data element `v[1]`, and so forth. An **iterator** p is an object that can be **located at** one of these elements. (Think of p as pointing to one of these elements.) An iterator can move its location from one element to another element. If p is located at, say, `v[7]`, then p++ moves p so it is located at `v[8]`. This allows an iterator to move through the vector from the first element to the last element, but it needs to find the first element and needs to know when it has seen the last element.

You can tell if an iterator is at the same location as another iterator using the operator ==. Thus, if you have an iterator pointing to the first, last, or other element, you could test another iterator to see if it is located at the first, last, or other element.

If p1 and p2 are two iterators, then the comparison

```
p1 == p2
```

is true when and only when p1 and p2 are located at the same element. (This is analogous to pointers. If p1 and p2 were pointers, this would be true if they pointed to the same thing.) As usual, != is just the negation of == and so

```
p1 != p2
```

is true when p1 and p2 are not located at the same element.

The member function `begin()` is used to position an iterator at the first element in a container. For vectors, and many other container classes, the member function `begin()` returns an iterator located at the first element. (For a vector v the first element is `v[0]`.) Thus,

```
vector<int>::iterator p = v.begin();
```

initializes the iterator variable p to an iterator located at the first element. So, the basic *for* loop for visiting all elements of the vector v is

```
vector<int>::iterator p;
for (p = v.begin(); Boolean_Expression>; p++)
    Action_At_Location p;
```

The desired *Boolean_Expression* for a stopping condition is

```
p == v.end()
```

The member function `end()` returns a sentinel value that can be checked to see if an iterator has passed the last element. If p is located at the last element, then after p++, the test p = v.end() changes from *false* to *true*. So the *for* loop with the correct *Boolean_Expression* is

```
vector<int>::iterator p;
for (p = v.begin(); p != v.end(); p++)
    Action_At_Location p;
```

Note that p != v.end() does not change from *true* to *false* until after p's location has advanced past the last element. So, v.end() is not located at any element. The value v.end() is a special value that serves as a sentinel value. It is not an ordinary iterator, but you can compare v.end() to an iterator using == and !=. The value v.end() is analogous to the value NULL used to mark the end of a linked list of the kind discussed in Chapter 13.

The following *for* loop from Display 18.1 uses this exact technique with the vector named container:

```
vector<int>::iterator p;
for (p = container.begin(); p != container.end(); p++)
    cout << *p << " ";
```

The action taken at the location of the iterator p is

```
cout << *p << " ";
```

The dereferencing operator * is overloaded for STL container iterators so that *p produces the element at location p. In particular, for a vector container, *p produces the element located at the iterator p. So, the cout statement above outputs the element located at the iterator p and the entire *for* loop outputs all the elements in the vector container.

The **dereferencing operator** *p always produces the element located at the iterator p. In some situations, *p produces read-only access, which does not allow you to change the element. In other situations, it gives you access to the element and will let you change the element. For vectors, *p will allow you to change the element located at p, as illustrated by the following *for* loop from Display 18.1:

```
for (p = container.begin(); p != container.end(); p++)
    *p = 0;
```

This *for* loop cycles through all the elements in the vector container and changes all the elements to 0.

PITFALL   Compiler Problems

Some compilers have problems with iterator declarations. You can declare an iterator in different ways. For example, we have been using the following:

```
using std::vector;
    . . .
vector<char>::iterator p;
```

Alternatively, if your code only uses a single type of iterator, you could use the following:

```
using std::vector<char>::iterator;
    . . .
iterator p;
```

Iterator

An iterator is an object that can be used with a container to gain access to elements in the container. An iterator is a generalization of the notion of a pointer, and the operators ==, !=, ++, and -- behave the same for iterators as they do for pointers. The basic outline of how an iterator can cycle through all the elements in a container is

```
STL_Container<type>::iterator p;
for (p = container.begin(); p != container.end(); p++)
    Process_Element_At_Location p;
```

STL_Container is the name of the container class (for example, vector) and type is the data type of the item to be stored. The member function begin() returns an iterator located at the first element. The member function end() returns a value that serves as a sentinel value one location past the last element in the container.

You also could use the following, which is not quite as nice, because it introduces all names from the std namespace to the current declarative region, increasing the likelihood of a name conflict.

```
using namespace std;
    . . .
vector<char>::iterator p;
```

There are other, similar variations. Your compiler should accept any of these alternatives. However, we have found that some compilers will accept only certain of them. If one form does not work with your compiler, try another. ∎

Dereferencing

The dereferencing operator *p when applied to an iterator p produces the element located at the iterator p. For some STL container classes, *p produces read-only access, which does not allow you to change the element. For other STL container classes, it gives you access to the element and will let you change the element.

SELF-TEST EXERCISES

1. If v is a vector, what does v.begin() return? What does v.end() return?

2. If p is an iterator for a vector object v, what is *p?

3. Suppose v is a vector of *int*s. Write a *for* loop that outputs all the elements of v, except for the first element.

Kinds of Iterators

Different containers have different kinds of iterators. Iterators are classified according to the kinds of operations that work on them. Vector iterators are of the most general form; that is, all the operations work with vector iterators. So, we will again use the vector container to illustrate iterators. In this case we use a vector to illustrate the iterator operators of *decrement* and *random access*. Display 18.2 shows another program using a vector object named container and an iterator p.

DISPLAY 18.2 Bidirectional and Random Access Iterator Use *(part 1 of 2)*

```
1    //Program to demonstrate bidirectional and random access iterators.
2    #include <iostream>
3    #include <vector>
4    using std::cout;
5    using std::endl;
6    using std::vector;
7
8    int main()
9    {
10       vector<char> container;
11       container.push_back('A');
12       container.push_back('B');
13       container.push_back('C');
14       container.push_back('D');

15       for (int i = 0; i < 4; i++)
16           cout << "container[" << i << "] == "
17               << container[i] << endl;
18       vector<char>::iterator p = container.begin();
19       cout << "The third entry is " << container[2] << endl;
20       cout << "The third entry is " << p[2] << endl;
21       cout << "The third entry is " << *(p + 2) << endl;

22       cout << "Back to container[0].\n";
23       p = container.begin();
24       cout << "which has value " << *p << endl;
```

Three different notations for the same thing.

This notation is specialized to vectors and arrays.

These two work for any random access iterator.

(continued)

DISPLAY 18.2   Bidirectional and Random Access Iterator Use
(part 2 of 2)

```
25          cout << "Two steps forward and one step back:\n";
26          p++;
27          cout << *p << endl;
28          p++;
29          cout << *p << endl;
30          p--;
31          cout << *p << endl;
32          return 0;
33     }
```

This is the decrement operator. It works for any bidirectional iterator.

Sample Dialogue

```
container[0] == A
container[1] == B
container[2] == C
container[3] == D
The third entry is C
The third entry is C
The third entry is C
Back to container[0].
which has value A
Two steps forward and one step back:
B
C
B
```

The **decrement operator** is used in Display 18.2, where the line containing it is shown in highlight. As you would expect, p-- moves the iterator p to the previous location. The decrement operator -- is the same as the increment operator ++, but it moves the iterator in the opposite direction.

The increment and decrement operators can be used in either prefix (++p) or postfix (p++) notation. In addition to changing p, they also return a value. The details of the value returned are completely analogous to what happens with the increment and decrement operators on *int* variables. In prefix notation, first the variable is changed and the changed value is returned. In postfix notation, the value is returned before the variable is changed. We prefer not to use the increment and decrement operators as expressions that return a value and use them only to change the variable value.

The following lines from Display 18.2 illustrate that with vector iterators you have *random access* to the elements of a vector, such as `container`:

```
vector<char>::iterator p = container.begin();
cout << "The third entry is " << container[2] << endl;
cout << "The third entry is " << p[2] << endl;
cout << "The third entry is " << *(p + 2) << endl;
```

Random access means you can go in one step directly to any particular element. We have already used `container[2]` as a form of random access to a vector. It is simply the square bracket operator that is standard with arrays and vectors. What is new is that you can use this same square bracket notation with an iterator. The expression `p[2]` is a way to obtain access to the element indexed by 2.

The expressions `p[2]` and `*(p + 2)` are completely equivalent. By analogy to pointer arithmetic (see Chapter 9), `(p + 2)` names the location two places beyond p. Since p is at the first (index 0) location in the above code, `(p + 2)` is at the third (index 2) location. The expression `(p + 2)` returns an iterator. The expression `*(p + 2)` dereferences that iterator. Of course, you can replace 2 with a different nonnegative integer to obtain a pointer pointing to a different element.

Be sure to note that neither `p[2]` nor `(p + 2)` changes the value of the iterator in the iterator variable p. The expression `(p + 2)` returns another iterator at another location, but it leaves p where it was. The same thing happens with `p[2]`. Also note that the meaning of `p[2]` and `(p + 2)` depends on the location of the iterator in p. For example, `(p + 2)` means two locations beyond the location of p, wherever that may be.

For example, suppose the previously discussed code from Display 18.2 were replaced with the following (note the added p++):

```
vector<char>::iterator p = container.begin();
p++;
cout << "The third entry is " << container[2] << endl;
cout << "The third entry is " << p[2] << endl;
cout << "The third entry is " << *(p + 2) << endl;
```

The output of these three couts would no longer be

```
The third entry is C
The third entry is C
The third entry is C
```

but would instead be

```
The third entry is C
The third entry is D
The third entry is D
```

The p++ moves p from location 0 to location 1 and so `(p + 2)` is now an iterator at location 3, not location 2. So, `*(p + 2)` and `p[2]` are equivalent to `container[3]`, not `container[2]`.

Kinds of Iterators

Different containers have different kinds of iterators. The following are the main kinds of iterators:

Forward iterators: ++ works on the iterator.

Bidirectional iterators: both ++ and -- work on the iterator.

Random access iterators: ++, --, and random access all work with the iterator.

We now know enough about iterators to make sense of how iterators are classified. The main kinds of iterators are

Forward iterators: ++ works on the iterator.

Bidirectional iterators: both ++ and -- work on the iterator.

Random access iterators: ++, --, and random access all work with the iterator.

Note that these are increasingly strong categories: Every random access iterator is also a bidirectional iterator, and every bidirectional iterator is also a forward iterator. As we will see, different template container classes have different kinds of iterators. The iterators for the vector template class are random access iterators.

Note that the names *forward iterator*, *bidirectional iterator*, and *random access iterator* refer to kinds of iterators, not type names. The actual type names will be something like std::vector<*int*>::iterator, which in this case happens to be a random access iterator.

SELF-TEST EXERCISE   myprogramminglab

4. Suppose the vector v contains the letters 'A', 'B', 'C', and 'D' in that order. What is the output of the following code?

```
vector<char>::iterator i = v.begin();
i++;
cout << *(i + 2) << " ";
i--;
cout << i[2] << " ";
cout << *(i + 2) << " ";
```

Constant and Mutable Iterators

The categories forward iterator, bidirectional iterator, and random access iterator each subdivide into two categories: *constant* and *mutable*, depending on how the dereferencing operator behaves with the iterator. With a **constant iterator** the dereferencing operator produces a read-only version of the element. With a constant iterator p, you can use *p, for example, to assign it to a variable or output it to the screen, but you cannot change the element in the container by, for example, assigning it to *p. With a **mutable iterator p**, *p can be assigned a value and that will change the corresponding element in the container. The vector iterators are mutable, as shown by the following lines from Display 18.1:

```
cout << "Setting entries to 0:\n";
for (p = container.begin(); p != container.end(); p++)
    *p = 0;
```

If a container has only constant iterators, you cannot obtain a mutable iterator for the container. However, if a container has mutable iterators and you want a constant iterator for the container, you can have it. You might want a constant iterator as a kind of error checking if you intend that your code not change the elements in the container. For example, the following will produce a constant iterator for a vector container named container:

```
std::vector<char>::const_iterator p = container.begin();
```

or equivalently

```
using std::vector<char>::const_iterator;
const_iterator p = container.begin();
```

With p declared in this way, the following would produce an error message:

```
*p = 'Z';
```

For example, Display 18.2 would behave exactly the same if you change

```
vector<int>::iterator p;
```

to

```
vector<int>::const_iterator p;
```

However, a similar change would not work in Display 18.1 because of the following line from the program in Display 18.1:

```
*p = 0;
```

Note that const_iterator is a type name, while *constant iterator* is the name of a kind of iterator. However, every iterator of a type named const_iterator will be a constant iterator.

Constant Iterator

A constant iterator is an iterator that does not allow you to change the element at its location.

Reverse Iterators

Sometimes you want to cycle through the elements in a container in reverse order. If you have a container with bidirectional iterators, you might be tempted to try

```
vector<int>::iterator p;
for (p = container.end(); p != container.begin(); p--)
    cout << *p << " ";
```

This code will compile, and you may be able to get something like this to work on some systems, but there is something fundamentally wrong with this: `container.end()` is not a regular iterator, but only a sentinel, and `container.begin()` is not a sentinel.

Fortunately, there is an easy way to do what you want. For a container with bidirectional iterators, there is a way to reverse everything using a kind of iterator known as a **reverse iterator.** The following will work fine:

```
vector<int>::reverse_iterator rp;
for (rp = container.rbegin(); rp != container.rend(); rp++)
    cout << *rp << " ";
```

The member function `rbegin()` returns an iterator located at the last element. The member function `rend()` returns a sentinel that marks the "end" of the elements in the reverse order. Note that for an iterator of type `reverse_iterator`, the increment operator ++ moves backward through the elements. In other words, the meanings of -- and ++ are interchanged. The program in Display 18.3 demonstrates a reverse iterator.

Reverse Iterators

A reverse iterator can be used to cycle through all elements of a container, provided that the container has bidirectional iterators. The general scheme is as follows:

```
STL_Container<type>::reverse_iterator rp;
for (rp = c.rbegin(); rp != c.rend(); rp++)
    Process_At_Location rp;
```

The object c is a container class with bidirectional iterators.

DISPLAY 18.3 Reverse Iterator

```
1    //Program to demonstrate a reverse iterator.
2    #include <iostream>
3    #include <vector>
4    using std::cout;
5    using std::endl;
6    using std::vector;

7    int main()
8    {
9        vector<char> container;

10       container.push_back('A');
11       container.push_back('B');
12       container.push_back('C');
13       cout << "Forward:\n";
14       vector<char>::iterator p;
15       for (p = container.begin(); p != container.end(); p++)
16           cout << *p << " ";
17       cout << endl;
18
19       cout << "Reverse:\n";
20       vector<char>::reverse_iterator rp;
21       for (rp = container.rbegin(); rp != container.rend(); rp++)
22           cout << *rp << " ";
23       cout << endl;

24       return 0;
25   }
```

Sample Dialogue

```
Forward:
A B C
Reverse:
C B A
```

The `reverse_iterator` type also has a constant version, which is named `const_reverse_iterator`.

Other Kinds of Iterators

There are other kinds of iterators that we will not cover in this book. Briefly, two kinds of iterators you may encounter are an **input iterator**, which is essentially a forward iterator that can be used with input streams, and an

output iterator, which is essentially a forward iterator that can be used with output streams. For more details, you will need to consult a more advanced reference.

 SELF-TEST EXERCISES [myprogramminglab]

5. Suppose the vector v contains the letters 'A', 'B', 'C', and 'D' in that order. What is the output of the following code?

```
vector<char>::reverse_iterator i = v.rbegin();
i++;
i++;
cout << *i << " ";
i--;
cout << *i << " ";
```

6. Suppose you want to run the following code, where v is a vector of *int*s:

```
for (p = v.begin(); p != v.end(); p++)
    cout << *p << " ";
```

Which of the following are possible ways to declare p?

```
std::vector<int>::iterator p;
std::vector<int>::const_iterator p;
```

18.2 CONTAINERS

Put all your eggs in one basket and
—WATCH THAT BASKET.

MARK TWAIN, *Pudd'n head Wilson*

The **container classes** of the STL are different kinds of data structures for holding data, such as lists, queues, and stacks. Each is a template class with a parameter for the particular type of data to be stored. So, for example, you can specify a list to be a list of *int*s, or *double*s, or strings, or any class or struct type you wish. Each container template class may have its own specialized accessor and mutator functions for adding data and removing data from the container. Different container classes may have different kinds of iterators. For example, one container class may have bidirectional iterators while another container class may have only forward iterators. However, whenever they are defined the iterator operators and the member functions begin() and end() have the same meaning for all STL container classes.

DISPLAY 18.4 Two Kinds of Lists

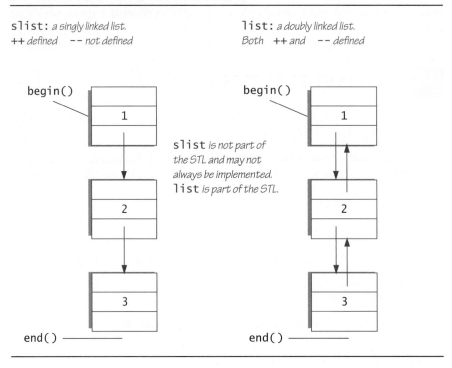

slist: *a singly linked list.*
++ *defined* **−−** *not defined*

list: *a doubly linked list.*
Both **++** *and* **−−** *defined*

begin()

1

slist *is not part of the STL and may not always be implemented.* list *is part of the STL.*

2

3

end()

begin()

1

2

3

end()

Sequential Containers

A sequential container arranges its data items into a list so that there is a first element, a next element, and so forth up to a last element. The linked lists we discussed in Chapter 13 are examples of a kind of list. The lists we discussed in Chapter 13 are sometimes called **singly linked lists** because there is only one link from one location to another. The STL has no container corresponding to such singly linked lists, although some implementations do offer an implementation of them, typically under the name slist. The simplest list that is part of the STL is the **doubly linked list,** which is the template class named list. The difference between these two kinds of lists is illustrated in Display 18.4.

The lists in Display 18.4 contain the three integer values 1, 2, and 3 in that order. The types for the two lists are slist<*int*> and list<*int*>. That display also indicates the location of the iterators begin() and end(). We have not yet told you how you can enter the integers into the lists.

In Display 18.4 we have drawn our singly and doubly linked lists as nodes and pointers of the form discussed in Chapter 14. The STL class list and the nonstandard class slist might (or might not) be implemented in this way.

However, when using the STL template classes, you are shielded from these implementation details. So, you simply think in terms of locations for the data (which may or may not be nodes) and iterators (not pointers). You can think of the arrows in Display 18.4 as indicating the directions for ++ (which is down) and -- (which is up in Display 18.4).

We wanted to present the template class slist to help give a context for the sequential containers. It corresponds to what we discussed most in Chapter 13, and it is the first thing that comes to the mind of most programmers when you mention *linked lists*. However, since the template class slist is not standard, we will discuss it no more. If your implementation offers the template class slist and you want to use it, the details are similar to those we will describe for list, except that the decrement operators -- (prefix and postfix) are not defined for slist.

A simple program using the STL template class list is given in Display 18.5. The function push_back adds an element to the end of the list. Notice that for the list template class, the dereferencing operator gives you access to the data for reading and for changing the data. Also notice that with the list template class and all the template classes and iterators of the STL, all definitions are placed in the std namespace.

DISPLAY 18.5   Using the list Template Class *(part 1 of 2)*

```
1    //Program to demonstrate the STL template class list.
2    #include <iostream>
3    #include <list>
4    using std::cout;
5    using std::endl;
6    using std::list;
7
8    int main()
9    {
10        list<int> list_object;
11
12        for (int i = 1; i <= 3; i++)
13            list_object.push_back(i);
14
15        cout << "List contains:\n";
16        list<int>::iterator iter;
17        for (iter = list_object.begin(); iter != list_object.end(); iter++)
18            cout << *iter << " ";
19        cout << endl;
20
21        cout << "Setting all entries to 0:\n";
```

(continued)

DISPLAY 18.5 Using the list Template Class *(part 2 of 2)*

```
22       for (iter = list_object.begin(); iter != list_object.end(); iter++)
23           *iter = 0;
24
25       cout << "List now contains:\n";
26       for (iter = list_object.begin(); iter != list_object.end(); iter++)
27           cout << *iter << " ";
28       cout << endl;
29
30       return 0;
31   }
```

Sample Dialogue

```
List contains:
1 2 3
Setting all entries to 0:
List now contains:
0 0 0
```

Note that Display 18.5 would compile and run exactly the same if we replace list and list<*int*> with vector and vector<*int*>, respectively. This uniformity of usage is a key part of the STL syntax.

There are, however, differences between a vector and a list container. One of the main differences is that a vector container has random access iterators while a list has only bidirectional iterators. For example, if you start with Display 18.2, which uses random access, and replace all occurrences of vector and vector<*char*> with list and list<*char*>, respectively, and then compile the program, you will get a compiler error. (You will get an error message even if you delete the statements containing container[i] or container[2].)

The basic sequential container template classes of the STL are given in Display 18.6. A sample of some member functions is given in Display 18.7. Other containers, such as stacks and queues, can be obtained from these using techniques discussed in the subsection entitled "Container Adapters stack and queue." All these sequence template classes have a destructor that returns storage for recycling.

Deque, pronounced "d-queue" or "deck," stands for "doubly ended queue." A deque is a kind of super queue. With a queue you add data at one end of the data sequence and remove data from the other end. With a deque

DISPLAY 18.6   STL Basic Sequential Containers

Template Class Name	Iterator Type Names	Kind of Iterators	Library Header File
slist Warning: slist is not part of the STL.	slist<T>::iterator slist<T>::const_iterator	mutable forward constant forward	<slist> Depends on implementation and may not be available.
list	list<T>::iterator list<T>::const_iterator list<T>::reverse_iterator list<T>::const_reverse_iterator	mutable bidirectional constant bidirectional mutable bidirectional constant bidirectional	<list>
vector	vector<T>::iterator vector<T>::const_iterator vector<T>::reverse_iterator vector<T>::const_reverse_iterator	mutable random access constant random access mutable random access constant random access	<vector>
deque	deque<T>::iterator deque<T>::const_iterator deque<T>::reverse_iterator deque<T>::const_reverse_iterator	mutable random access constant random access mutable random access constant random access	<deque>

DISPLAY 18.7   Some Sequential Container Member Functions *(part 1 of 2)*

Member Function (c is a Container Object)	Meaning
c.size()	Returns the number of elements in the container.
c.begin()	Returns an iterator located at the first element in the container.
c.end()	Returns an iterator located one beyond the last element in the container.
c.rbegin()	Returns an iterator located at the last element in the container. Used with reverse_iterator. Not a member of slist.
c.rend()	Returns an iterator located one beyond the first element in the container. Used with reverse_iterator. Not a member of slist.
c.push_back(*Element*)	Insert the *Element* at the end of the sequence. Not a member of slist.

(continued)

DISPLAY 18.7 Some Sequential Container Member Functions *(part 2 of 2)*

c.push_front(*Element*)	Insert the *Element* at the front of the sequence. Not a member of vector.
c.insert(Iterator, *Element*)	Insert a copy of *Element* before the location of *Iterator*.
c.erase(*Iterator*)	Removes the element at location Iterator. Returns an iterator at the location immediately following. Returns c.end() if the last element is removed.
c.clear()	A void function that removes all the elements in the container.
c.front()	Returns a reference to the element in the front of the sequence. Equivalent to *(c.begin()).
c1 == c2	True if c1.size() == c2.size() and each element of c1 is equal to the corresponding element of c2.
c1 != c2	!(c1 == c2)

<All the sequential containers discussed in this section also have a default constructor, a copy constructor, and various other constructors for initializing the container to default or specified elements. Each also has a destructor that returns all storage for recycling and a well-behaved assignment operator.>

you can add data at either end and remove data from either end. The template class deque is a template class for a deque with a parameter for the type of data stored.

Sequential Containers

A sequential container arranges its data items into a list so that there is a first element, a next element, and so forth up to a last element. The sequential container template classes that we have discussed are slist, list, vector, and deque.

PITFALL **Iterators and Removing Elements**

When you add or remove an element to or from a container, that can affect other iterators. In general, there is no guarantee that the iterators will be located at the same element after an addition or deletion. Some containers do, however, guarantee that the iterators will not be moved by additions or deletions, except of course if the iterator is located at an element that is removed.

Of the template classes we have seen so far, `list` and `slist` guarantee that their iterators will not be moved by additions or deletions, except of course if the iterator is located at an element that is removed. The template classes `vector` and `deque` make no such guarantee. ∎

■ PROGRAMMING TIP   Type Definitions in Containers

The STL container classes contain type definitions that can be handy when programming with these classes. We have already seen that STL container classes may contain the type names `iterator`, `const_iterator`, `reverse_iterator`, and `const_reverse_iterator` (and hence must contain their type definitions behind the scenes). There are typically other type definitions as well.

All the template classes we have discussed so far have the defined types `value_type` and `size_type`. The type `value_type` is the type of the elements stored in the container. For example, `list<`*int*`>::value_type` is another name for *int*. Another defined type is `size_type`, which is an unsigned integer type that is the return type for the member function `size`. As we noted in Chapter 8, the `size_type` for the vector template class is *unsigned int*, although most compilers will be happy if you think of the type as just plain *int*. ∎

■ SELF-TEST EXERCISES   myprogramminglab

7. What is a major difference between a `vector` and a `list`?

8. Which of the template classes `slist`, `list`, `vector`, and `deque` have the member function `push_back`?

9. Which of the template classes `slist`, `list`, `vector`, and `deque` have random access iterators?

10. Which of the template classes `slist`, `list`, `vector`, and `deque` can have mutable iterators?

Container Adapters `stack` and `queue`

Container adapters are template classes that are implemented on top of other classes. For example, the `stack` template class is by default implemented on top of the `deque` template class, which means that buried in the implementation of the `stack` is a deque, which is where all the data resides. However, you are shielded from this implementation detail and see a stack as a simple last-in/ first-out data structure.

Other container adapter classes are the queue and priority_queue template classes. Stacks and queues were discussed in Chapter 13. A **priority queue** is like a queue with the additional property that each entry is given a priority when it is added to the queue. If all entries have the same priority, then entries are removed from a priority queue in the same manner as they are removed from a queue. If items have different priorities, the higher-priority items are removed before lower-priority items. We will not be discussing priority queues in any detail, but mention it for those who may be familiar with the concept.

Although an adapter template class has a default container class on top of which it is built, you may choose to specify a different underlying container, for efficiency or other reasons depending on your application. For example, any sequential container may serve as the underlying container for a stack and any sequential container other than vector may serve as the underlying container for a queue. The default underlying data structure is the deque for both the stack and the queue. For a priority_queue, the default underlying container is a vector. If you are happy with the default underlying container type, then a container adapter looks like any other template container class to you. For example, the type name for the stack template class using the default underlying container is stack<*int*> for a stack of *int*s. If you wish to specify that the underlying container is instead the vector template class, you would use stack<*int*, vector<*int*>> as the type name. We will always use the default underlying container.

Warning
If you do specify an underlying container, be warned that you should not place two > symbols in the type expression without a space in between them, or the compiler can be confused. Use stack<*int*, vector<*int*> >, with a space between the last two >'s. Do not use stack<*int*, vector<*int*> >.

The member functions and other details about the stack template class are given in Display 18.8. For the queue template class these details are given in Display 18.9. A simple example of using the stack template class is given in Display 18.10.

DISPLAY 18.8 Stack **Template Class** (*part 1 of 2*)

Stack **Adapter Template Class Details**
Type name stack<T> or stack<T, Underlying_Container> for a stack of elements of type T.
Library header: <stack>, which places the definition in the std namespace.
Defined types: value_type, size_type.
There are no iterators.

(continued)

DISPLAY 18.8   Stack Template Class *(part 2 of 2)*

Sample Member Functions

Member Function (s is a Stack Object.)	Meaning
s.size()	Returns the number of elements in the stack.
s.empty()	Returns *true* if the stack is empty; otherwise returns *false.*
s.top()	Returns a mutable reference to the top member of the stack.
s.push(*Element*)	Inserts a copy of *Element* at the top of the stack.
s.pop()	Removes the top element of the stack. Note that pop is a void function. It does not return the element removed.
s1 == s2	True if s1.size() == s2.size() and each element of s1 is equal to the corresponding element of s2; otherwise returns *false.*

The stack template class also has a default constructor, a copy constructor, as well as a constructor that takes an object of any sequential container class and initializes the stack to the elements in the sequence. It also has a destructor that returns all storage for recycling and a well-behaved assignment operator.

DISPLAY 18.9   Queue Template Class *(part 1 of 2)*

Queue **Adapter Template Class Details**
Type name queue<T> or queue<T, Underlying_Container> for a queue of elements of type T.
For efficiency reasons, the Underlying_Container cannot be a vector type.
Library header: <queue> which places the definition in the std namespace.
Defined types: value_type, size_type.
There are no iterators.

Sample Member Functions

Member Function (q is a Queue Object)	Meaning
q.size()	Returns the number of elements in the queue.
q.empty()	Returns *true* if the queue is empty; otherwise returns *false.*

(continued)

DISPLAY 18.9 Queue **Template Class** *(part 2 of 2)*

q.front()	Returns a mutable reference to the front member of the queue.
q.back()	Returns a mutable reference to the last member of the queue.
q.push(*Element*)	Adds *Element* to the back of the queue.
q.pop()	Removes the front element of the queue. Note that pop is a void function. It does not return the element removed.
q1 == q2	True if q1.size() == q2.size() and each element of q1 is equal to the corresponding element of q2; otherwise returns *false*.

The queue template class also has a default constructor, a copy constructor, as well as a constructor that takes an object of any sequential container class and initializes the stack to the elements in the sequence. It also has a destructor that returns all storage for recycling and a well-behaved assignment operator.

DISPLAY 18.10 **Program Using the** Stack **Template Class** *(part 1 of 2)*

```
1    //Program to demonstrate the use of the stack template class from the STL.
2    #include <iostream>
3    #include stack>
4    using std::cin;
5    using std::cout;
6    using std::endl;
7    using std::stack;
8
9    int main()
10   {
11       stack<char> s;
12
13       cout << "Enter a line of text:\n";
14       char next;
15       cin.get(next);
16       while (next != '\n')
17       {
18           s.push(next);
19           cin.get(next);
20       }
21
22       cout << "Written backward that is:\n";
23       while ( !s.empty() )
24       {
```

(continued)

DISPLAY 18.10   Program Using the Stack Template Class *(part 2 of 2)*

```
25            cout << s.top();
26            s.pop();
27        }
28        cout << endl;
29
30        return 0;
31    }
```

The member function **pop** *removes one element, but does not return that element.* **pop** *is a* **void** *function. So, we needed to use* **top** *to read the element we remove.*

Sample Dialogue

```
Enter a line of text:
straw
Written backward that is:
warts
```

■ SELF-TEST EXERCISES

myprogramminglab

11. What kind of iterators (forward, bidirectional, or random access) does the stack template adapter class have?

12. What kind of iterators (forward, bidirectional, or random access) does the queue template adapter class have?

13. If s is a stack<*char*>, what is the type of the returned value of s.pop()?

Associative Containers set and map

Associative containers are basically very simple databases. They store data, such as structs or any other type of data. Each data item has an associated value known as its **key.** For example, if the data is a struct with an employee's record, the key might be the employee's Social Security number. Items are retrieved on the basis of the key. The key type and the type for data to be stored need not have any relationship to one another, although they often are related. A very simple case is when the each data item is its own key. For example, in a set every element is its own key.

The set template class is, in some sense, the simplest container you can imagine. It stores elements without repetition. The first insertion places an element in the set. Additional insertions after the first have no effect, so no element appears more than once. Each element is its own key; basically, you just add or delete elements and ask if an element is in the set or not. Like all STL classes, the set template class was written with efficiency as a goal. In order to work efficiently, a set object stores its values in sorted order. You can specify the order used for storing elements as follows:

```
set<T, Ordering> s;
```

Ordering should be a well-behaved ordering relation that takes two arguments of type T and returns a *bool* value.[1] T is the type of elements stored. If no ordering is specified, then the ordering is assumed to be the < relational operator. Some basic details about the set template class are given in Display 18.11. A simple example that shows how to use some of the member functions of the template class set is given in Display 18.12.

A **map** is essentially a function given as a set of ordered pairs. For each value first that appears in a pair, there is at most one value second such that the pair (first, second) is in the map. The template class map implements map objects in the STL. For example, if you want to assign a unique number to each string name, you could declare a map object as follows:

```
map<string, int> number_map;
```

For string values known as *keys*, the number_map object can associate a unique *int* value.

An alternate way to think of a map is as an **associative array.** A traditional array maps from a numerical index to a value. For example, a[10] = 5 would store the number 5 at index 10. An associative array allows you to define your own indices using the data type of your choice. For example, numberMap["c++"] = 5 would associate the integer 5 with the string "c++". For convenience, the [] square bracket operator is defined to allow you to use an array-like notation to access a map, although you also can use the insert or find methods if you want.

Like a set object, a map object stores its elements in sorted order by its key values. You can specify the ordering on keys as a third entry in the angular brackets <>. If you do not specify an ordering, a default ordering is used. The restrictions on orderings you can use is the same as those on the orderings allowed for the set template class. Note that the ordering is on key values only. The second type can be any type and need not have anything to do with any ordering. As with the set object, the sorting of the stored entries in a map object is done for reasons of efficiency.

---

[1] The ordering must be a *strict weak ordering*. Most typical orderings used to implement the < operator is strict weak ordering. For those who want the details: A **strict weak ordering** must be: (irreflexive) Ordering(x, x) is always false; (antisymmetric) Ordering(x, y) implies !Ordering(y, x); (transitive) Ordering(x, y) and Ordering(y, z) imply Ordering(x, z); and (transitivity of equivalence) if x is equivalent to y and y is equivalent to z, then x is equivalent to z. Two elements x and y are equivalent if Ordering(x, y) and Ordering(y, x) are both false.

DISPLAY 18.11   set Template Class

set Template Class Details
Type name set<T> or set<T, Ordering> for a set of elements of type
T. The Ordering is used to sort elements for storage. If no Ordering is
given, the ordering used is the binary operator <.

Library header: <set>, which places the definition in the std
namespace.

Defined types include: value_type, size_type.

Iterators: iterator, const_iterator, reverse_iterator, and
const_reverse_iterator. All iterators are bidirectional and those
not including const_ are mutable. begin(), end(), rbegin(), and
rend() have the expected behavior. Adding or deleting elements
does not affect iterators, except for an iterator located at the element
removed.

Sample Member Functions

Member Function (s is a Set Object)	Meaning
s.insert(*Element*)	Inserts a copy of *Element* in the set. If *Element* is already in the set, this has no effect.
s.erase(*Element*)	Removes *Element* from the set. If *Element* is not in the set, this has no effect.
s.find(*Element*)	Returns a mutable iterator located at the copy of *Element* in the set. If *Element* is not in the set, s.end() is returned.
s.erase(*Iterator*)	Erases the element at the location of the *Iterator*.
s.size()	Returns the number of elements in the set.
s.empty()	Returns *true* if the set is empty; otherwise returns *false*.
s1 == s2	Returns *true* if the sets contains the same elements; otherwise returns *false*.

The set template class also has a default constructor, a copy constructor,
as well as other specialized constructors not mentioned here. It also has
a destructor that returns all storage for recycling and a well-behaved
assignment operator.

DISPLAY 18.12   Program Using the set Template Class

```
1    //Program to demonstrate use of the set template class.
2    #include <iostream>
3    #include <set>
4    using std::cout;
5    using std::endl;
6    using std::set;

7    int main()
8    {
9        set<char> s;
10
11       s.insert('A');
12       s.insert('D');
13       s.insert('D');          No matter how many times you add an
14       s.insert('C');          element to a set, the set contains
15       s.insert('C');          only one copy of that element.
16       s.insert('B');
17
18       cout << "The set contains:\n";
19       set<char>::const_iterator p;
20       for (p = s.begin(); p != s.end(); p++)
21           cout << *p << " ";
22       cout << endl;
23
24       cout << "Removing C.\n";
25       s.erase('C');
26       for (p = s.begin(); p != s.end(); p++)
27           cout << *p << " ";
28       cout << endl;
29
30       return 0;
31   }
```

Sample Dialogue

```
The set contains:
A B C D
Removing C.
A B D
```

The easiest way to add and retrieve data from a map is to use the [] operator. Given a map object m, the expression m[key] will return a reference to the data element associated with key. If no entry exists in the map for key, then a new entry will be created with the default value for the data element. For numeric data types, the default value is 0. For objects of type string, the default value is an empty string.

The [] operator can be used to add a new item to the map or to replace an existing entry. For example, the statement m[key] = newData; will create a new association between key and newData. Note that care must be taken to ensure that map entries are not created by mistake. For example, if you execute the statement val = m[key]; with the intention of retrieving the value associated with key but mistakenly enter a value for key that is not already in the map, then a new entry will be made for key with the default value and assigned into val.

Some basic details about the map template class are given in Display 18.13. In order to understand these details, you first need to know something about the pair template class.

The STL template class pair<T1,T2> has objects that are pairs of values such that the first element is of type T1 and the second is of type T2. If aPair is an object of type pair<T1,T2>, then aPair.first is the first element, which is of type T1, and aPair.second is the second element, which is of type T2. The member variables first and second are public member variables, so no accessor or mutator functions are needed.

The header file for the pair template is <utility>. So, to use the pair template class, you need the following, or something like it, in your file:

```
#include <utility>
using std::pair;
```

The map template class uses the pair template class to store the association between the key and a data item. For example, given the definition

```
map<string, int> numberMap;
```

we can add a mapping from "c++" to the number 10 by using a pair object:

```
pair<string, int> toInsert("c++", 10);
numberMap.insert(toInsert);
```

or by using the [] operator:

```
numberMap["c++"] = 10;
```

In either case, when we access this pair using an iterator, iterator->first will refer to the key "c++" while iterator->second will refer to the data value 10. A simple example that shows how to use some of the member functions of the template class map is given in Display 18.14.

We will mention two other associative containers, although we will not give any details about them. The template classes multiset and multimap

DISPLAY 18.13 map **Template Class**

map Template Class Details

Type name map<KeyType, T> or map<KeyType, T, Ordering> for a map that associates ("maps") elements of type KeyType to elements of type T.
The Ordering is used to sort elements by key value for efficient storage.
If no Ordering is given, the ordering used is the binary operator <.

Library header: <map> places the definition in the std namespace.

Defined types include: key_type for the type of the key values, mapped_type for the type of the values mapped to, and size_type. (So, the defined type key_type is simply what we called KeyType earlier.)

Iterators: iterator, const_iterator, reverse_iterator, and const_reverse_iterator. All iterators are bidirectional. Those iterators not including const_ are neither constant nor mutable, but something in between. For example, if p is of type iterator, then you change the key value but not the value of type T. Perhaps it is best, at least at first, to treat all iterators as if they were constant.
begin(), end(), rbegin(), and rend() have the expected behavior. Adding or deleting elements does not affect iterators, except for an iterator located at the element removed.

Sample Member Functions

Member Function (m is a Map Object.)	Meaning
m.insert(*Element*)	Inserts *Element* in the map. *Element* is of type pair<KeyType, T>. Returns a value of type pair<iterator, *bool*>. If the insertion is successful, the second part of the returned pair is true and the iterator is located at the inserted element.
m.erase(*Target_Key*)	Removes the element with the key *Target_Key*.
m.find(*Target_Key*)	Returns an iterator located at the element with key value *Target_Key*. Returns m.end() if there is no such element.
m[*Target_Key*]	Returns a reference to the object associated with the key *Target_Key*. If the map does not already contain such an object, then a default object of type T is inserted and returned.
m.size()	Returns the number of pairs in the map.
m.empty()	Returns *true* if the map is empty; otherwise returns *false*.
m1 == m2	Returns *true* if the maps contains the same pairs; otherwise returns *false*.

The map template class also has a default constructor, a copy constructor, as well as other specialized constructors not mentioned here. It also has a destructor that returns all storage for recycling and a well-behaved assignment operator.

DISPLAY 18.14   Program Using the map Template Class *(part 1 of 2)*

```
1    //Program to demonstrate use of the map template class.
2    #include <iostream>
3    #include <map>
4    #include <string>
5    using std::cout;
6    using std::endl;
7    using std::map;
8    using std::string;

9    int main()
10   {
11       map<string, string> planets;

12       planets["Mercury"] = "Hot planet";
13       planets["Venus"] = "Atmosphere of sulfuric acid";
14       planets["Earth"] = "Home";
15       planets["Mars"] = "The Red Planet";
16       planets["Jupiter"] = "Largest planet in our solar system";
17       planets["Saturn"] = "Has rings";
18       planets["Uranus"] = "Tilts on its side";
19       planets["Neptune"] = "1500 mile-per-hour winds";
20       planets["Pluto"] = "Dwarf planet";
21       cout << "Entry for Mercury - " << planets["Mercury"]
22           << endl << endl;
23       if (planets.find("Mercury") != planets.end())
24           cout << "Mercury is in the map." << endl;
25       if (planets.find("Ceres") == planets.end())
26           cout << "Ceres is not in the map." << endl << endl;
27       cout << "Iterating through all planets: " << endl;
28       map<string, string>::const_iterator iter;
29       for (iter = planets.begin(); iter != planets.end(); iter++)
30       {
31           cout << iter->first << " - " << iter->second << endl;
32       }
33       return 0;
34   }
```

Sample Dialogue

```
Entry for Mercury - Hot planet

Mercury is in the map.
Ceres is not in the map.


Iterating through all planets:
Earth - Home
```

The iterator will output the map in order sorted by the key. In this case the output will be listed alphabetically by planet.

(continued)

DISPLAY 18.14   Program Using the map Template Class *(part 2 of 2)*

```
Jupiter - Largest planet in our solar system
Mars - The Red Planet
Mercury - Hot planet
Neptune - 1500 mile-per-hour winds
Pluto - Dwarf planet
Saturn - Has rings
Uranus - Tilts on its side
Venus - Atmosphere of sulfuric acid
```

are essentially the same as set and map, respectively, except that a multiset allows repetition of elements and a multimap allows multiple values to be associated with each key value.

Efficiency

The STL was designed with efficiency as an important consideration. In fact, the STL implementations strive to be optimally efficient. For example, the set and map elements are stored in sorted order so that algorithms that search for the elements can be more efficient.

Each of the member functions for each of the template classes has a guaranteed maximum running time. These maximum running times are expressed using what is called big-*O* notation, which we discuss in Section 18.3. (Section 18.3 also gives some guaranteed running times for some of the container member functions we have already discussed. These are in the subsection entitled "Container Access Running Times.") When using more advanced references or even later in this chapter, you will be told the guaranteed maximum running times for certain functions.

SELF-TEST EXERCISES

14. How many elements will be in the map mymap after the following code is executed?

    ```
    map<int, string> mymap;
    mymap[5] = "c++";
    cout << mymap[4] << endl;
    ```

15. Can a set have elements of a class type?

16. Suppose s is of the type set<char>. What value is returned by s.find('A') if 'A' is in s? What value is returned if 'A' is not in s?

18.3 GENERIC ALGORITHMS

"Cures consumption, anemia, sexual dysfunction, and all other diseases."

TYPICAL CLAIM BY A TRAVELING SALESMAN OF "SNAKE OIL"

This section covers some basic function templates in the STL. We cannot give you a comprehensive description of them all here, but will present a large enough sample to give you a good feel for what is contained in the STL and to give you sufficient detail to start using these template functions.

These template functions are sometimes called **generic algorithms.** The term *algorithm* is used for a reason. Recall that an algorithm is just a set of instructions for performing a task. An algorithm can be presented in any language, including a programming language like C++. But when using the word *algorithm*, programmers typically have in mind a less formal presentation given in English or pseudocode. As such, it is often thought of as an abstraction of the code defining a function. It gives the important details but not the fine details of the coding. The STL specifies certain details about the algorithms underlying the STL template functions and that is why they are sometimes called generic *algorithms*.

These STL function templates do more than just deliver a value in any way that the implementers wish. The function templates in the STL come with minimum requirements that must be satisfied by their implementations if they are to satisfy the standard. In most cases, they must be implemented with a guaranteed running time. This adds an entirely new dimension to the idea of a function interface. In the STL, the interface not only tells a programmer what the function does and how to use the functions; the interface also tells how rapidly the task will be done. In some cases, the standard even specifies the particular algorithm that is used, although not the exact detail of the coding. Moreover, when it does specify the particular algorithm, it does so because of the known efficiency of the algorithm. The key new point is a specification of an efficiency guarantee for the code. In this chapter we will use the terms *generic algorithm*, *generic function*, and *STL function template* to all mean the same thing.

In order to have some terminology to discuss the efficiency of these template functions or generic algorithms, we first present some background on how the efficiency of algorithms is usually measured.

Running Times and Big-*O* Notation

If you ask a programmer how fast his or her program is, you might expect an answer like "two seconds." However, the speed of a program cannot be given by a single number. A program will typically take a longer amount of time on larger inputs than it will on smaller inputs. You would expect that a program to sort numbers would take less time to sort ten numbers than it would to sort one thousand numbers. Perhaps it takes two seconds to sort ten numbers, but ten seconds to sort one thousand numbers. How, then, should the programmer answer the question, "How fast is your program?"

The programmer would have to give a table of values showing how long the program took for different sizes of input. For example, the table might be as shown in Display 18.15. This table does not give a single time, but instead gives different times for a variety of different input sizes. The table is a description of what is called a **function** in mathematics. Just as a (non-*void*) C++ function takes an argument and returns a value, so too does this function take an argument, which is an input size, and returns a number, which is the time the program takes on an input of that size. If we call this function T, then $T(10)$ is 2 seconds, $T(100)$ is 2.1 seconds, $T(1000)$ is 10 seconds, and $T(10,000)$ is 2.5 minutes. The table is just a sample of some of the values of this function T. The program will take some amount of time on inputs of every size. So although they are not shown in the table, there are also values for $T(1)$, $T(2)$, . . . , $T(101)$, $T(102)$, and so forth. For any positive integer N, $T(N)$ is the amount of time it takes for the program to sort N numbers. The function T is called the **running time** of the program.

So far we have been assuming that this sorting program will take the same amount of time on any list of N numbers. That need not be true. Perhaps it takes much less time if the list is already sorted or almost sorted. In that case, $T(N)$ is defined to be the time taken by the "hardest" list, that is, the time taken on that list of N numbers which makes the program run the longest. This is called the **worst-case running time.** In this chapter *we will always mean worst-case running time* when we give a running time for an algorithm or for some code.

The time taken by a program or algorithm is often given by a formula, such as $4N + 3$, $5N + 4$, or N^2. If the running time $T(N)$ is $5N + 5$, then on inputs of size N the program will run for $5N + 5$ time units.

Following is some code for searching an array a with N elements to determine whether a particular value target is in the array:

```
int i = 0;
bool found = false;
while (( i < N) && !(found))
```

DISPLAY 18.15 Some Values of a Running-Time Function

Input Size	Running Time
10 numbers	2 seconds
100 numbers	2.1 seconds
1000 numbers	10 seconds
10,000 numbers	2.5 minutes

```
if (a[i] == target)
    found = true;
else
    i++;
```

We want to compute some estimate of how long it will take a computer to execute this code. We would like an estimate that does not depend on which computer we use, either because we do not know which computer we will use or because we might use several different computers to run the program at different times. One possibility is to count the number of "steps," but it is not easy to decide what a step is. In this situation the normal thing to do is to count the number of **operations.** The term *operations* is almost as vague as the term *step*, but there is at least some agreement in practice about what qualifies as an operation. Let us say that, for this C++ code, each application of any of the following will count as an operation: =, <, &&, !, [], ==, and ++. The computer must do other things besides carry out these operations, but these seem to be the main things that it is doing and we will assume that they account for the bulk of the time needed to run this code. In fact, our analysis of time will assume that everything else takes no time at all and that the total time for our program to run is equal to the time needed to perform these operations. Although this is an idealization that clearly is not completely true, it turns out that this simplifying assumption works well in practice and so is often made when analyzing a program or algorithm.

Even with our simplifying assumption, we still must consider two cases: Either the value target is in the array or it is not. Let us first consider the case when target is not in the array. The number of operations performed will depend on the number of array elements searched. The operation = is performed two times before the loop is executed. Since we are assuming that target is not in the array, the loop will be executed N times, one for each element of the array. Each time the loop is executed, the following operations are performed: <, &&, !, [], ==, and ++ This adds six operators for each of N loop iterations. Finally, after N iterations, the Boolean expression is again checked and found to be false. This adds a final three operations (<, &&, !).[2] If we tally all these operations, we get a total of $6N + 5$ operations when the target is not in the array. We will leave it as an exercise for you to confirm that if the target is in the array, then the number of operations will be $6N + 5$ *or less*. Thus, the worst-case running time is $T(N) = 6N + 5$ operations for any array of N elements and any value of target.

We just determined that the worst-case running time for our search code is $6N + 5$ operations. But operations is not a traditional unit of time, like nanoseconds, seconds, or minutes. If we want to know how long the algorithm

---

[2] Because of short circuit evaluation, !(found) is not evaluated, so we actually get two, not three operations. However, the important thing is to obtain a good upper bound. If we add in one extra operation that is not significant.

will take on some particular computer, we must know how long it takes that computer to perform one operation. If an operation can be performed in 1 nanosecond, then the time will be $6N + 5$ nanoseconds. If an operation can be performed in 1 second, the time will be $6N + 5$ seconds. If we use a slow computer that takes 10 seconds to perform an operation, the time will be $60N + 50$ seconds. In general, if it takes the computer c nanoseconds to perform one operation, then the actual running time will be approximately $c(6N + 5)$ nanoseconds. (We say *approximately*, since we are making some simplifying assumptions and so the result may not be the absolutely exact running time.) This means that our running time of $6N + 5$ is a very crude estimate. To get the running time expressed in nanoseconds, you must multiply by some constant that depends on the particular computer you are using. Our estimate of $6N + 5$ is only accurate to "within a constant multiple." There is a standard notation for these sorts of estimates and we discuss this notation next.

Estimates on running time, such as the one we just went through, are normally expressed in something called **big-O notation.** (The O is the letter "Oh," not the digit zero.) Suppose we estimate the running time to be, say, $6N + 5$ operations and suppose we know that no matter what the exact running time of each different operation may turn out to be, there will always be some constant factor c such that the real running time is less than or equal to $c(6N + 5)$.

Under these circumstances, we say the code (or program or algorithm) runs in time $O(6N + 5)$. This is usually read as "big-O of $6N + 5$." We need not know what the constant c will be. In fact, it will undoubtedly be different for different computers, but we must know that there is one such c for any reasonable computer system. If the computer is very fast, then the c might be less than 1—say, 0.001. If the computer is very slow, the c might be very large—say, 1000. Moreover, since changing the units, say from nanosecond to second, only involves a constant multiple, there is no need to give any units of time.

Be sure to notice that a big-O estimate is an upper-bound estimate. We always approximate by taking numbers on the high side, rather than the low side, of the true count. Also notice that when performing a big-O estimate, we need not determine a very exact count of the number of operations performed. We only need an estimate that is correct "up to a constant multiple." If our estimate is twice as large as the true number, that is good enough.

An order of magnitude estimate, such as the previous $6N + 5$, contains a parameter for the size of the task solved by the algorithm (or program or piece of code). In our sample case, this parameter N was the number of array elements to be searched. Not surprisingly, it takes longer to search a larger number of array elements than it does to search a smaller number of array elements. Big-O running time estimates are always expressed as a function of the size of the problem. In this chapter all our algorithms will involve a range of values in some container. In all cases N will be the number of elements in that range.

The following is an alternative, pragmatic way to think about big-O estimates:

Look only at the term with the highest exponent and do not pay attention to constant multiples.

For example, all of the following are $O(N^2)$:

$$N^2 + 2N + 1,\ 3N^2 + 7,\ 100N^2 + N$$

All of the following are $O(N^3)$:

$$N^3 + 5N^2 + N + 1,\ 8N^3 + 7,\ 100N^3 + 4N + 1$$

Big-O running-time estimates are admittedly crude, but they do contain some information. They will not distinguish between a running time of $5N + 5$ and a running time of $100N$, but they do let us distinguish between some running times and so determine that some algorithms are faster than others. Look at the graphs in Display 18.16; notice that all the graphs for functions

DISPLAY 18.16 Comparison of Running Times

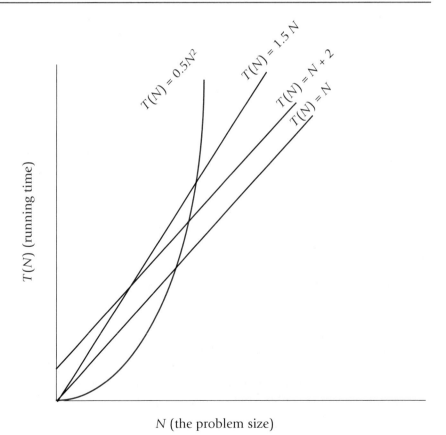

that are $O(N)$ eventually fall below the graph for the function $0.5N^2$. The result is inevitable: An $O(N)$ algorithm will always run faster than any $O(N^2)$ algorithm, provided we use large enough values of N. Although an $O(N^2)$ algorithm could be faster than an $O(N)$ algorithm for the problem size you are handling, programmers have found that in practice $O(N)$ algorithms perform better than $O(N^2)$ algorithms for most practical applications that are intuitively "large." Similar remarks apply to any other two different big-O running times.

Some terminology will help with our descriptions of generic algorithm running times. **Linear running time** means a running time of $T(N) = aN + b$. A linear running time is always an $O(N)$ running time. **Quadratic running time** means a running time with highest term N^2. A quadratic running time is always an $O(N^2)$ running time. We will also occasionally have logarithms in running-time formulas. Those normally are given without any base, since changing the base is just a constant multiple. If you see log N, think log base 2 of N, but it would not be wrong to think log base 10 of N. Logarithms are very slow-growing functions. So, a $O(\log N)$ running time is very fast. Sometimes $\log_2 N$ is written as lg N.

Container Access Running Times

Now that we know about big-O notation, we can express the efficiency of some of the accessing functions for container classes that we discussed in Section 18.2 "Containers." Insertions at the back of a `vector` (`push_back`), the front or back of a `deque` (`push_back` and `push_front`), and anywhere in a `list` (`insert`) are all $O(1)$ (that is, a constant upper bound on the running time that is independent of the size of the container.) Insertion or deletion of an arbitrary element for a `vector` or deque is $O(N)$, where N is the number of elements in the container. For a `set` or `map`, finding (`find`) is $O(\log N)$, where N is the number of elements in the container.

SELF-TEST EXERCISES

17. Show that a running time $T(N) = aN + b$ is an $O(N)$ running time. (*Hint:* The only issue is the $+ b$. Assume N is always at least 1.)

18. Show that for any two bases a and b for logarithms, if a and b are both greater than 1, then there is a constant c such that $\log_a N \le c(\log_b N)$. Thus, there is no need to specify a base in $O(\log N)$. That is, $O(\log_a N)$ and $O(\log_b N)$ mean the same thing.

Nonmodifying Sequence Algorithms

This section describes template functions that operate on containers but do not modify the contents of the container in any way. A good simple and typical example is the generic find function.

The generic find function is similar to the find member function of the set template class but is a different find function; in particular, the generic find function takes more arguments than the find function we discussed when we presented the set template class. The generic find function searches a container to locate a particular element, but the generic find can be used with any of the STL sequential container classes. Display 18.17 shows a sample use of the generic find function used with the class vector<*char*>. The function in Display 18.17 would behave exactly the same if we replaced vector<*char*> with list<*char*> throughout, or if we replaced vector<*char*> with any other sequential container class. That is one of the reasons why the functions are called *generic*. One definition of the find function works for a wide selection of containers.

If the find function does not find the element it is looking for, it returns its second iterator argument, which need not be equal to some end() as it is in Display 18.17. Sample Dialogue 2 shows the situation when find does not find what it is looking for.

DISPLAY 18.17   The Generic find Function *(part 1 of 2)*

```
1   //Program to demonstrate use of the generic find function.
2   #include <iostream>
3   #include <vector>
4   #include <algorithm>
5   using std::cin;
6   using std::cout;
7   using std::endl;
8   using std::vector;
9   using std::find;

10  int main()
11  {
12      vector<char> line;

13      cout << "Enter a line of text:\n";
14      char next;
15      cin.get(next);
16      while (next != '\n')
17      {
18          line.push_back(next);
19          cin.get(next);
20      }
```

(continued)

DISPLAY 18.17   The Generic find Function (*part 2 of 2*)

```
21        vector<char>::const_iterator where;
22        where = find(line.begin(), line.end(), 'e');
23        //where is located at the first occurrence of 'e' in line.

24        vector<char>::const_iterator p;
25        cout << "You entered the following before you entered your first e:\n";
26        for (p = line.begin(); p != where; p++)
27            cout << *p;
28        cout << endl;
29        cout << "You entered the following after that:\n";
30        for (p = where; p != line.end(); p++)
31            cout << *p;
32        cout << endl;

33        cout << "End of demonstration.\n";
34        return 0;
35    }
```

> If **find** *does not find what it is looking for, it returns its second argument.*

Sample Dialogue 1

```
Enter a line of text
A line of text.
You entered the following before you entered your first e:
A lin
You entered the following after that:
e of text.
End of demonstration.
```

Sample Dialogue 2

```
Enter a line of text
I will not!
You entered the following before you entered your first e:
I will not!  ◄─────────────────
You entered the following after that:

End of demonstration.
```

> If **find** *does not find what it is looking for, it returns* **line.end().**

Does find work with absolutely any container classes? No, not quite. To start with, it takes iterators as arguments, and some containers, such as stack, do not have iterators. To use the find function, the container must have iterators, the elements must be stored in a linear sequence so that the

++ operator moves iterators through the container, and the elements must be comparable using ==. In other words, the container must have forward iterators (or some stronger kind of iterators, such as bidirectional iterators).

When presenting generic function templates, we will describe the iterator type parameter by using the name of the required kind of iterator as the type parameter name. So ForwardIterator should be replaced by a type that is a type for some kind of forward iterator, such as the iterator type in a list, vector, or other container template class. Remember, a bidirectional iterator is also a forward iterator, and a random access iterator is also a bidirectional iterator. So the type name ForwardIterator can be used with any iterator type that is a bidirectional or random access iterator type as well as a plain old forward iterator type. In some cases, when we specify ForwardIterator you can use an even simpler iterator kind; namely, an input iterator or output iterator, but since we have not discussed input and output iterators, we do not mention them in our function template declarations.

Remember the names *forward iterator*, *bidirectional iterator*, and *random access iterator* refer to kinds of iterators, not type names. The actual type names will be something like std::vector<*int*>::iterator, which in this case happens to be a random access iterator.

Display 18.18 gives a sample of some nonmodifying generic functions in the STL. The display uses a notation that is common when discussing container iterators. The iterator locations encountered in moving from an iterator first to, but not equal to, an iterator last is called the **range [first, last)**. For example, the following *for* loop outputs all the elements in the range [first, last):

```
for (iterator p = first; p != last; p++)
    cout << *p << endl;
```

Note that when two ranges are given they need not be in the same container or even in the same type of container. For example, for the search function, the ranges [first1, last1) and [first2, last2) may be in the same or different containers.

Range [first, last)

The movement from some iterator first, often container.begin(), up to but not including some location last, often container.end(), is so common it has come to have a special name, **range** [first, last). For example, the following outputs all elements in the range [c.begin(),c.end()), where c is some container object, such as a vector:

```
for (iterator p = c.begin(); p != c.end(); p++)
    cout << *p << endl;
```

DISPLAY 18.18 Some Nonmodifying Generic Functions

> *These all work for forward iterators, which means they also work for bidirectional and random access iterators. (In some cases they even work for other kinds of iterators, which we have not covered in any detail.)*

```
1   template<class ForwardIterator, class T>
2   ForwardIterator find(ForwardIterator first,
3                        ForwardIterator last, const T& target);
4   //Traverses the range [first, last) and returns an iterator located at
5   //the first occurrence of target. Returns second if target is not found.
6   //Time complexity: linear in the size of the range [first, last).

7   template<class ForwardIterator, class T>
8   int³ count(ForwardIterator first, ForwardIterator last, const T& target);
9   //Traverses the range [first, last) and returns the number
10  //of elements equal to target.
11  //Time complexity: linear in the size of the range [first, last).

12  template<class ForwardIterator1, class ForwardIterator2>
13  bool equal(ForwardIterator1 first1, ForwardIterator1 last1,
14             ForwardIterator2 first2);
15  //Returns true if [first1, last1) contains the same elements in the same order as
16  //the first last1-first1 elements starting at first2. Otherwise, returns false.
17  //Time complexity: linear in the size of the range [first, last).
18
19  template<class ForwardIterator1, class ForwardIterator2>
20  ForwardIterator1 search(ForwardIterator1 first1, ForwardIterator1 last1,
21                          ForwardIterator2 first2, ForwardIterator2 last2);
22  //Checks to see if [first2, last2) is a subrange of [first1, last1).
23  //If so, it returns an iterator located in [first1, last1) at the start of
24  //the first match. Returns last1 if a match is not found.
25  //Time complexity: quadratic in the size of the range [first1, last1).

26  template<class ForwardIterator, class T>
27  bool binary_search(ForwardIterator first, ForwardIterator last,
28                     const T& target);
29  //Precondition: The range [first, last) is sorted into ascending order using <.
30  //Uses the binary search algorithm to determine if target is in the range
31  //[first, last).
32  //Time complexity: For random access iterators O(log N). For non-random-access
33  //iterators
34  //linear is N, where N is the size of the range [first, last).
```

---

³ The actual return type is an integer type that we have not discussed, but the returned value should be assignable to a variable of type int.

Notice that there are three search functions in Display 18.18—find, search, and binary_search. The function search searches for a subsequence, while the find and binary_search functions search for a single value. How do you decide whether to use find or binary_search when searching for a single element? One returns an iterator and the other returns just a Boolean value, but that is not the biggest difference. The binary_search function requires that the range being searched be sorted (into ascending order using <) and run in time $O(\log N)$; the find function does not require that the range be sorted but it guarantees only linear time. If you have or can have the elements in sorted order, you can search for them much more quickly by using binary_search.

Note that with the binary_search function you are guaranteed that the implementation will use the binary search algorithm, which was discussed in Chapter 14. The importance of using the binary search algorithm is that it guarantees a very fast running time, $O(\log N)$. If you have not read Chapter 14 and have not otherwise heard of binary search, just think of it as a very efficient search algorithm that requires that the elements be sorted. Those are the only two points about binary search that are relevant to the material in this chapter.

 SELF-TEST EXERCISES

myprogramminglab

19. Replace all occurrences of the identifier vector with the identifier list in Display 18.17. Compile and run the program.

20. Suppose v is an object of the class vector<*int*>. Use the search generic function (Display 18.18) to write some code to determine whether or not v contains the number 42 immediately followed by 43. You need not give a complete program, but do give all necessary include and using directives. (*Hint:* It may help to use a second vector.)

Container Modifying Algorithms

Display 18.19 contains descriptions of some of the generic functions in the STL which change the contents of a container in some way.

Remember that when you add or remove an element to or from a container, that can affect any of the other iterators. There is no guarantee that the iterators will be located at the same element after an addition or deletion unless the container template class makes such a guarantee. Of the template classes we have seen, list and slist guarantee that their iterators will not be moved by additions or deletions, except of course if the iterator is located at an element that is removed. The template classes vector and deque make no such guarantee. Some of the function templates in Display 18.19 guarantee the values of some specific iterators and those guarantees you can, of course, count on, no matter what the container is.

DISPLAY 18.19   Some Modifying Generic Functions

```
1    template<class T>
2    void swap(T& variable1, T& variable2);
3    //Interchanges the values of variable1 and variable2
```

The name of the iterator type parameter tells the kind of iterator for which the function works. Remember that these are minimum iterator requirements. For example, ForwardIterator works for forward iterators, bidirectional iterators, and random access iterators.

```
4    template<class ForwardIterator1, class ForwardIterator2>
5    ForwardIterator2 copy(ForwardIterator1 first1, ForwardIterator1 last1,
6        ForwardIterator2 first2, ForwardIterator2 last2);
7    //Precondition: The ranges [first1, last1) and [first2, last2) are the same size.
8    //Action: Copies the elements at locations [first1, last1) to locations
9    //[first2, last2).
10   //Returns last2.
11   //Time complexity: linear in the size of the range [first1, last1).

12   template<class ForwardIterator, class T>
13   ForwardIterator remove(ForwardIterator first, ForwardIterator last,
14                   const T& target);
15   //Removes those elements equal to target from the range [first, last).
16   //The size of
17   //the container is not changed. The removed values equal to target are
18   //moved to the
19   //end of the range [first, last). There is then an iterator i in this
20   //range such that
21   //all the values not equal to target are in [first, i). This i is returned.
22   //Time complexity: linear in the size of the range [first, last).

23   template<class BidirectionalIterator>
24   void reverse(BidirectionalIterator first, BidirectionalIterator last);
25   //Reverses the order of the elements in the range [first, last).
26   //Time complexity: linear in the size of the range [first, last).

27   template<class RandomAccessIterator>
28   void random_shuffle(RandomAccessIterator first, RandomAccessIterator last);
29   //Uses a pseudorandom number generator to randomly reorder the elements
30   //in the range [first, last).
31   //Time complexity: linear in the size of the range [first, last).
```

SELF-TEST EXERCISES

21. Can you use the random_shuffle template function with a list container?

22. Can you use the copy template function with vector containers, even though copy requires forward iterators and vector has random access iterators?

Set Algorithms

Display 18.20 shows a sample of the generic set operation functions defined in the STL. Note that these generic algorithms assume the containers store their elements in sorted order. The containers set, map, multiset, and multimap do store their elements in sorted order, so all the functions in Display 18.20 apply to these four template class containers. Other containers, such as vector, do not store their elements in sorted order and these functions should not be used with such containers. The reason for requiring that the elements be sorted is so that the algorithms can be more efficient.

DISPLAY 18.20   Set Operations *(part 1 of 2)*

These operations work for sets, maps, multisets, multimaps (and other containers) but do not work for all containers. For example, they do not work for vectors, lists, or deques unless their contents are sorted. For these containers to work, the elements in the container must be stored in sorted order. These operators all work for forward iterators, which means they also work for bidirectional and random access iterators. (In some cases they even work for other kinds of iterators, which we have not covered in any detail.)

```
1    template<class ForwardIterator1, class ForwardIterator2>
2    bool includes(ForwardIterator1 first1, ForwardIterator1 last1,
3                  ForwardIterator2 first2, ForwardIterator2 last2);
4    //Returns true if every element in the range [first2, last2) also occurs in the
5    //range [first1, last1). Otherwise, returns false.
6    //Time complexity: linear in the size of [first1, last1) plus [first2, last2).
7
8    template<class ForwardIterator1, class ForwardIterator2,
9            class ForwardIterator3>
10   void set_union(ForwardIterator1 first1, ForwardIterator1 last1,
11                  ForwardIterator2 first2, ForwardIterator2 last2,
12                                        ForwardIterator3 result);
13   //Creates a sorted union of the two ranges [first1, last1) and [first2, last2).
14   //The union is stored starting at result.
15   //Time complexity: linear in the size of [first1, last1) plus [first2, last2).
16   template<class ForwardIterator1, class ForwardIterator2,
17           class ForwardIterator3>
18   void set_intersection(ForwardIterator1 first1, ForwardIterator1 last1,
19                      ForwardIterator2 first2, ForwardIterator2 last2,
20                                        ForwardIterator3 result);
21   //Creates a sorted intersection of the two ranges [first1, last1) and
22   //[first2, last2).
23   //The intersection is stored starting at result.
24   //Time complexity: linear in the size of [first1, last1) plus [first2, last2).
25
26   template<class ForwardIterator1, class ForwardIterator2,
27           class ForwardIterator3>
```

(continued)

DISPLAY 18.20 **Set Operations** *(part 2 of 2)*

```
28   void set_difference(ForwardIterator1 first1, ForwardIterator1 last1,
29                   ForwardIterator2 first2, ForwardIterator2 last2,
30                                       ForwardIterator3 result);
31   //Creates a sorted set difference of the two ranges [first1, last1) and
32   //[first2, last2).
33   //The difference consists of the elements in the first range that are not in the
34   //second.
35   //The result is stored starting at result.
36   //Time complexity: linear in the size of [first1, last1) plus [first2, last2).
```

 SELF-TEST EXERCISE

23. The mathematics course version of a set does not keep its elements in sorted order and it has a union operator. Why does the set_union template function require that the containers keep their elements in sorted order?

Sorting Algorithms

Display 18.21 gives the declarations and documentation for two template functions, one to sort a range of elements and one to merge two sorted ranges of elements. Note that the sorting function sort guarantees a run time of $O(N \log N)$. Although it is beyond the scope of this book, it can be shown that you cannot write a comparison-based sorting algorithm that is faster than $O(N \log N)$. So this guarantees that the sorting algorithm is as fast as is possible, up to a constant multiple.

DISPLAY 18.21 **Some Generic Sorting Algorithms**

```
1    template<class RandomAccessIterator>
2    void sort(RandomAccessIterator first, RandomAccessIterator last);
3    //Sorts the elements in the range [first, last) into ascending order.
4    //Time complexity: O(N log N), where N is the size of the range [first, last).
5
6    template<class ForwardIterator1,class ForwardIterator2,
7            class ForwardIterator3>
8    void merge(ForwardIterator1 first1, ForwardIterator1 last1,
9                       ForwardIterator2 first2, ForwardIterator2 last2,
10                      ForwardIterator3 result);
11   //Precondition: The ranges [first1, last1) and [first2, last2) are sorted.
12   //Action: Merges the two ranges into a sorted range [result, last3), where
13   //last3 = result + (last1 - first1) + (last2 - first2).
14   //Time complexity: linear in the size of the range [first1, last1)
15   //plus the size of [first2, last2).
```

> Sorting uses the < operator, and so the < operator must be defined. There are other versions, not given here, that allow you to provide the ordering relation. Sorted means sorted into ascending order.

CHAPTER SUMMARY

- An iterator is a generalization of a pointer. Iterators are used to move through the elements in some range of a container. The operations ++, --, and dereferencing * are usually defined for an iterator.

- Container classes with iterators have member functions end() and begin() that return iterator values such that you can process all the data in the container as follows:

  for (p = c.begin(); p != c.end(); p++)
      process *p //*p *is the current data item.*

- The main kinds of iterators are

  Forward iterators: ++ works on the iterator.

  Bidirectional iterators: both ++ and -- work on the iterator.

  Random access iterators: ++, --, and random access all work with the iterator.

- With a constant iterator p, the dereferencing operator *p produces a read-only version of the element. With a mutable iterator p, *p can be assigned a value.

- A bidirectional container has reverse iterators that allow your code to cycle through the elements in the container in reverse order.

- The main container template classes in the STL are list, which has mutable bidirectional iterators, and the template classes vector and deque, both of which have mutable random access iterators.

- stack and queue are container adaptor classes, which means they are built on top of other container classes. A stack is a last-in/first-out container. A queue is a first-in/first-out container.

- The set, map, multiset, and multimap container template classes store their elements in sorted order for efficiency of search algorithms. A set is a simple collection of elements. A map allows storing and retrieving by key values. The multiset class allows repetitions of entries. The multimap class allows a single key to be associated with multiple data items.

- The STL includes template functions to implement generic algorithms with guarantees on their maximum running time.

Answers to Self-Test Exercises

1. v.begin() returns an iterator located at the first element of v. v.end() returns a value that serves as a sentinel value at the end of all the elements of v.

2. *p is the dereferencing operator applied to p. *p is a reference to the element at location p.

3. `vector<int>::iterator p;`

   ```
   for (p = v.begin(), p++; p != v.end(); p++)
       cout << *p << " ";
   ```

4. D C C

5. B C

6. Either would work.

7. A major difference is that a `vector` container has random access iterators whereas a `list` has only bidirectional iterators.

8. All except `slist`.

9. `vector` and `deque`.

10. They all can have mutable iterators.

11. The `stack` template adapter class has no iterators.

12. The `queue` template adapter class has no iterators.

13. No value is returned; `pop` is a `void` function.

14. `mymap` will contain two entries. One is a mapping from 5 to "c++" and the other is a mapping from 4 to the default string, which is blank.

15. Yes they can be of any type, although there is only one type for each `set` object. The type parameter in the template class is the type of elements stored.

16. If `'A'` is in `s`, then `s.find('A')` returns an iterator located at the element `'A'`. If `'A'` is not in `s`, then `s.find('A')` returns `s.end()`.

17. Just note that $aN + b \leq (a + b)N$, as long as $1 \leq N$.

18. This is mathematics, not C++, so = will mean *equals* not assignment.

    First note that $\log_a N = (\log_a b)(\log_b N)$.

    To see this first identity, just note that if you raise a to the power $\log_a N$, you get N, and if you raise a to the power $(\log_a b)(\log_b N)$, you also get N.

    If you set $c = (\log_a b)$, you get $\log_a N = c(\log_b N)$.

19. The programs should run exactly the same.

20.
    ```
    #include <iostream>
    #include <vector>
    #include <algorithm>
    ```

```
using std::cout;
using std::vector;
using std::search;
...
vector<int> target;
target.push_back(42);
target.push_back(43);
vector<int>::const_iterator result = search(v.begin(), v.end(),
                           target.begin(), target.end());
if (result != v.end())
    cout << "Found 42, 43.\n";
else
    cout << "42, 43 not there.\n";
```

21. No, you must have random access iterators, and the `list` template class has only bidirectional iterators.

22. Yes, a random access iterator is also a forward iterator.

23. The `set_union` template function requires that the containers keep their elements in sorted order to allow the function template to be implemented in a more efficient way.

PROGRAMMING PROJECTS

Visit www.myprogramminglab.com to complete many of these Programming Projects online and get instant feedback.   **myprogramminglab**

1. Write a program in which you declare a class `SwapVal` to store values of different data types, read in two *generic* values, and swap them using a generic function. The program must use the generic swap function to swap the numbers and display the results.

2. Write a program that allows the user to enter any number of employee names and their salaries. The program should then display the employee names and salaries according to the ascending order of salaries. Use the template class `vector` and the generic `sort` function from the STL. Note that you will need to define a structure or class type for data consisting of one employee name and salary. You will also need to overload the < operator for this structure or class.

3. A **prime** number is an integer greater than 1 and divisible only by itself and 1. An integer x is **divisible** by an integer y if there is another integer z such that x = y * z. The Greek mathematician Eratosthenes (pronounced: Er-ah-**tos**-thin-eeze) gave an algorithm, called the S*ieve of Eratosthenes*, for finding all prime numbers less than some integer N. The algorithm works like this: Begin with a list of integers 2 through N. The number 2 is the first prime. (It is instructive to consider why this is true.) The *multiples* of 2, that is, 4, 6, 8, etc., are *not prime*. We cross these off the list. Then the first number after 2 that was not crossed off is the next prime. This number is 3. The *multiples*

of 3 are not primes. Cross the multiples of 3 off the list. Note that 6 is already gone, cross off 9, 12 is already gone, cross off 15, etc. The first number not crossed off is the next prime. The algorithm continues on in this fashion until we reach N. All the numbers not crossed off the list are primes.

  a.   Write a program using this algorithm to find all primes less than a user-supplied number N. Use a vector container for the integers. Use an array of *bool* initially set to all *true* to keep track of crossed-off integers. Change the entry to *false* for integers that are crossed off the list.

  b.   Test for N = 10, 30, 100, and 300.

We can improve our solution in several ways:

  c.   The program does not need to go all the way to N. It can stop at N/2. Try this and test your program. N/2 works and is better but is not the smallest number we could use. Argue that to get all the primes between 1 and N the minimum limit is the square root of N.

  d.   Modify your code from part (a) to use the square root of N as an upper limit.

4. Suppose you have a collection of student records. The records are structures of the following type:

```
struct StudentInfo
{
    string name;
    int grade;
};
```

The records are maintained in a vector<StudentInfo>. Write a program that prompts for and fetches data and builds a vector of student records, then sorts the vector by name, calculates the maximum and minimum grades and the class average, then prints this summarizing data along with a class roll with grades. (We aren't interested in who had the maximum and minimum grade, though, just the maximum, minimum, and average statistics.) Test your program.

5. Continuing Programming Project 4, write a function that separates the students in the vector of StudentInfo records into two vectors, one containing records of passing students and one containing records of failing students. (Use a grade of 60 or better for passing.)

You are asked to do this in two ways, and to give some run-time estimates.

  a.   Consider continuing to use a vector. You could generate a second vector of passing students and a third vector of failing students. This keeps duplicate records for at least some of the time, so don't do it that way. You could create a vector of failing students and a test-for-failing function. Then you push_back failing student records, then erase (which is a member function) the failing student records from the original vector. Write the program this way.

b. Consider the efficiency of this solution. You are potentially erasing *O(N)* members from the middle of a vector. You have to move a lot of members in this case. erase from the middle of a vector is an *O(N)* operation. Give a big-*O* estimate of the running time for this program.

c. If you used a list<StudentInfo>, what are the run-times for the erase and insert functions? Consider how the time efficiency of erase for a list affects the run-time for the program. Rewrite this program using a list instead of a vector. Remember that a list provides neither indexing nor random access and its iterators are only bidirectional, not random access.

6. Suppose you have a collection of employee records. The records are structures of the following type:

```
struct EmployeeInfo
{
    string name;
    int empid;
    int salary;
};
```

The records are maintained in a vector named <EmployeeInfo>. Write a program that prompts for and fetches data and builds a vector of employee records, then sorts the vector by name, calculates the maximum and minimum salary and the average salary, then prints this summarizing data along with the employee's id and salary. (We aren't interested only in who had the maximum and minimum salary, though, just the maximum, minimum, and average statistics.) Test your program.

7. In this project you are to create a database of books that are stored using a vector. Keep track of the author, title, and publication date of each book. Your program should have a main menu that allows the user to select from the following: (1) Add a book's author, title, and date; (2) Print an alphabetical list of the books sorted by author; and (3) Quit.

VideoNote
Solution to Programming
Project 18.7

You must use a class to hold the data for each book. This class must hold three string fields: one to hold the author's name, one for the publication date, and another to hold the book's title. Store the entire database of books in a vector in which each vector element is a book class object.

To sort the data, use the generic sort function from the <algorithm> library. Note that this requires you to define the < operator to compare two objects of type Book so that the author field from the two books are compared.

A sample of the input/output behavior might look as follows. Your I/O need not look identical, this is just to give you an idea of the functionality.

```
Select from the following choices:
1.         Add new book
2.         Print listing sorted by author
3.         Quit
1

Enter title:
More Than Human

Enter author:
Sturgeon, Theodore

Enter date:
1953

Select from the following choices:
1.         Add new book
2.         Print listing sorted by author
3.         Quit
1

Enter title:
Problem Solving with C++

Enter author:
Savitch, Walter

Enter date:
2006

Select from the following choices:
1.         Add new book
2.         Print listing sorted by author
3.         Quit
2

The books entered so far, sorted alphabetically by author are:
           Savitch, Walter.  Problem Solving with C++.  2006.
           Sturgeon, Theodore.  More Than Human.  1953.

Select from the following choices:
1.         Add new book
2.         Print listing sorted by author
3.         Quit
1

Enter title:
At Home in the Universe

Enter author:
Kauffman

Enter date:
1996
```

```
Select from the following choices:
1.         Add new book
2.         Print listing sorted by author
3.         Quit
2

The books entered so far, sorted alphabetically by artist are:
           Kauffman, At Home in the Universe, 1996
           Savitch, Walter.  Problem Solving with C++.  2006.
           Sturgeon, Theodore.  More Than Human.  1953.
```

8. Redo or do for the first time Programming Project 11 from Chapter 14, except use the STL set class for all set operations and the STL linked list class to store and manipulate each individual permutation. When creating a set containing lists, make sure to place a space between the last two >'s or the compiler may get confused. For example, set<list<int> > defines a set where elements are linked lists containing elements of type int. The code set<list<int>> without a space will likely produce a compiler error.

9. You have collected a file of movie ratings where each movie is rated from 1 (bad) to 5 (excellent). The first line of the file is a number that identifies how many ratings are in the file. Each rating then consists of two lines: the name of the movie followed by the numeric rating from 1 to 5. Here is a sample rating file with four unique movies and seven ratings:

```
7
Harry Potter and the Order of the Phoenix
4
Harry Potter and the Order of the Phoenix
5
The Bourne Ultimatum
3
Harry Potter and the Order of the Phoenix
4
The Bourne Ultimatum
4
Wall-E
4
Glitter
1
```

Write a program that reads a file in this format, calculates the average rating for each movie, and outputs the average along with the number of reviews. Here is the desired output for the sample data:

```
Glitter: 1 review, average of 1 / 5
Harry Potter and the Order of the Phoenix: 3 reviews, average
of 4.3 / 5
The Bourne Ultimatum: 2 reviews, average of 3.5 / 5
Wall-E: 1 review, average of 4 / 5
```

Use a map or multiple maps to calculate the output. Your map(s) should index from a string representing each movie's name to integers that store the number of reviews for the movie and the sum of the ratings for the movie.

10. Consider a text file of names, with one name per line, that has been compiled from several different sources. A sample follows:

```
Brooke Trout
Dinah Soars
Jed Dye
Brooke Trout
Jed Dye
Paige Turner
```

There are duplicate names in the file. We would like to generate an invitation list but don't want to send multiple invitations to the same person. Write a program that eliminates the duplicate names by using the set template class. Read each name from the file, add it to the set, and then output all names in the set to generate the invitation list without duplicates.

VideoNote
Solution to Programming
Project 18.11

11. Write a program that uses the map template class to compute a histogram of positive numbers entered by the user. The map's key should be the number that is entered, and the value should be a counter of the number of times the key has been entered so far. Use –1 as a sentinel value to signal the end of user input. For example, if the user inputs:

```
5
12
3
5
5
3
21
-1
```

then the program should output the following (not necessarily in this order):

```
The number 3 occurs 2 times.
The number 5 occurs 3 times.
The number 12 occurs 1 times.
The number 21 occurs 1 times.
```

C++ Keywords

The following keywords should not be used for anything other than their pre-defined purposes in the C++ language. In particular, do not use them for variable names or for programmer-defined functions. In addition to the following keywords listed, identifiers containing a double underscore (__) are reserved for use by C++ implementations and standard libraries and should not be used in your programs.

asm	*do*	*inline*	*return*	*typedef*
auto	*double*	*int*	*short*	*typeid*
bool	*dynamic_cast*	*log*	*signed*	*typename*
break	*else*	*long*	*sizeof*	*union*
case	*enum*	*mutable*	*static*	*unsigned*
catch	*explicit*	*namespace*	*static_cast*	*using*
char	*extern*	*new*	*struct*	*virtual*
class	*false*	*operator*	*switch*	*void*
const	*float*	*private*	*template*	*volatile*
const_cast	*for*	*protected*	*this*	*wchar_t*
continue	*friend*	*public*	*throw*	*while*
default	*goto*	*register*	*true*	
delete	*if*	*reinterpret_cast*	*try*	

These alternative representations for operators and punctuation are reserved and also should not be used otherwise.

and &&	*and_eq &=*	*bitand &*	*bitor |*	*compl ~*	*not !*
not_eq !=	*or ||*	*or_eq |=*	*xor ^*	*xor_eq ^=*	

Precedence of Operators

All the operators in a given box have the same precedence. Operators in higher boxes have higher precedence than operators in lower boxes. Unary operators and the assignment operator are executed right to left when operators have the same precedence. For example, x = y = z means x = (y = z). Other operators that have the same precedences are executed left to right. For example, x + y + z means (x + y) + z.

:: scope resolution operator	*Highest precedence (done first)*
. dot operator -> member selection [] array indexing ( ) function call ++ postfix increment operator (placed after the variable) -- postfix decrement operator (placed after the variable)	
++ prefix increment operator (placed before the variable) -- prefix decrement operator (placed before the variable) ! not - unary minus + unary plus * dereference & address of *new* *delete* *delete[]* *sizeof*	
* multiplication / division % remainder (modulo)	
+ addition - subtraction	
<< insertion operator (output) >> extraction operator (input)	
< less than <= less than or equal > greater than >= greater than or equal	
== equal != not equal	
&& and	
|| or	
= assignment += add and assign -= subtract and assign *= multiply and assign /= divide and assign %= modulo and assign	*Lowest precedence (done last)*

The ASCII Character Set

Only the printable characters are shown. Character number 32 is the blank.

32		56	8	80	P	104	h
33	!	57	9	81	Q	105	i
34	"	58	:	82	R	106	j
35	#	59	;	83	S	107	k
36	$	60	<	84	T	108	l
37	%	61	=	85	U	109	m
38	&	62	>	86	V	110	n
39	'	63	?	87	W	111	o
40	(	64	@	88	X	112	p
41	)	65	A	89	Y	113	q
42	*	66	B	90	Z	114	r
43	+	67	C	91	[	115	s
44	,	68	D	92	\	116	t
45	–	69	E	93	]	117	u
46	.	70	F	94	^	118	v
47	/	71	G	95	_	119	w
48	0	72	H	96	'	120	x
49	1	73	I	97	a	121	y
50	2	74	J	98	b	122	z
51	3	75	K	99	c	123	{
52	4	76	L	100	d	124		
53	5	77	M	101	e	125	}
54	6	78	N	102	f	126	~
55	7	79	O	103	g		

Some Library Functions

The following lists are organized according to what the function is used for, rather than what library it is in. The function declaration gives the number and types of arguments as well as the type of the value returned. In most cases, the function declarations give only the type of the parameter and do not give a parameter name. (See the section "Alternate Form for Function Declarations" in Chapter 4 for an explanation of this kind of function declaration.)

Arithmetic Functions

Function Declaration	Description	Header File
`int abs(int);`	Absolute value	cstdlib
`long labs(long);`	Absolute value	cstdlib
`double fabs(double);`	Absolute value	cmath
`double sqrt(double);`	Square root	cmath
`double pow(double, double);`	Returns the first argument raised to the power of the second argument	cmath
`double exp(double);`	Returns e (base of the natural logarithm) to the power of its argument	cmath
`double log(double);`	Natural logarithm (ln)	cmath
`double log10(double);`	Base 10 logarithm	cmath
`double ceil(double);`	Returns the smallest integer that is greater than or equal to its argument	cmath
`double floor(double);`	Returns the largest integer that is less than or equal to its argument	cmath

Input and Output Member Functions

Form of a Function Call	Description	Header File
Stream_Var.open (*External_File_Name*);	Connects the file with the *External_File_ Name* to the stream named by the *Stream_ Var*. The *External_File_Name* is a string value.	fstream
Stream_Var.fail( );	Returns *true* if the previous operation (such as open) on the stream *Stream_Var* has failed.	fstream or iostream
Stream_Var.close( );	Disconnects the stream *Stream_Var* from the file it is connected to.	fstream
Stream_Var.bad( );	Returns *true* if the stream *Stream_Var* is corrupted.	fstream or iostream
Stream_Var.eof( );	Returns *true* if the program has attempted to read beyond the last character in the file connected to the input stream *Stream_Var*. Otherwise, it returns *false*.	fstream or iostream
Stream_Var.get (*Char_Variable*);	Reads one character from the input stream *Stream_Var* and sets the *Char_Variable* equal to this character. Does *not* skip over whitespace.	fstream or iostream
Stream_Var.getline (*String_Var, Max_ Characters* +1);	One line of input from the stream *Stream_ Var* is read, and the resulting string is placed in *String_Var*. If the line is more than *Max_ Characters* long, only the first *Max_Char- acters* are read. The declared size of the *String_Var* should be *Max_Characters* +1 or larger.	fstream or iostream
Stream_Var.peek( );	Reads one character from the input stream *Stream_Var* and returns that character. But the character read is *not* removed from the input stream; the next read will read the same character.	fstream or iostream

Input and Output Member Functions *(continued)*

Form of a Function Call	Description	Header File
Stream_Var.put (*Char_Exp*);	Writes the value of the *Char_Exp* to the output stream *Stream_Var*.	fstream or iostream
Stream_Var.putback (*Char_Exp*);	Places the value of *Char_Exp* in the input stream *Stream_Var* so that that value is the next input value read from the stream. The file connected to the stream is not changed.	fstream or iostream
Stream_Var.precision (*Int_Exp*);	Specifies the number of digits output after the decimal point for floating-point values sent to the output stream *Stream_Var*.	fstream or iostream
Stream_Var.width (*Int_Exp*);	Sets the field width for the next value output to the stream *Stream_Var*.	fstream or iostream
Stream_Var.setf(*Flag*);	Sets flags for formatting output to the stream *Stream_Var*. See Display 6.5 for the list of possible flags.	fstream or iostream
Stream_Var.unsetf(*Flag*);	Unsets flags for formatting output to the stream *Stream_Var*. See Display 6.5 for the list of possible flags.	fstream or iostream

Character Functions

For all of these the actual type of the argument is *int*, but for most purposes you can think of the argument type as *char*. If the value returned is a value of type *int*, you must perform an explicit or implicit typecast to obtain a *char*.

Function Declaration	Description	Header File
bool isalnum(*char*);	Returns *true* if its argument satisfies either isalpha or isdigit. Otherwise, returns *false*.	cctype
bool isalpha(*char*);	Returns *true* if its argument is an upper- or lowercase letter. It may also return *true* for other arguments. The details are implementation dependent. Otherwise, returns *false*.	cctype
bool isdigit(*char*);	Returns *true* if its argument is a digit. Otherwise, returns *false*.	cctype
bool ispunct(*char*);	Returns *true* if its argument is a printable character that does not satisfy isalnum and is not whitespace. (These characters are considered punctuation characters.) Otherwise, returns *false*.	cctype
bool isspace(*char*);	Returns *true* if its argument is a whitespace character (such as blank, tab, or new line). Otherwise, returns *false*.	cctype
bool iscntrl(*char*);	Returns *true* if its argument is a control character. Otherwise, returns *false*.	cctype
bool islower(*char*);	Returns *true* if its argument is a lowercase letter. Otherwise, returns *false*.	cctype
bool isupper(*char*);	Returns *true* if its argument is an uppercase letter. Otherwise, returns *false*.	cctype
int tolower(*char*);	Returns the lowercase version of its argument. If there is no lowercase version, returns its argument unchanged.	cctype
int toupper(*char*);	Returns the uppercase version of its argument. If there is no uppercase version, returns its argument unchanged.	cctype

String Functions

Function Declaration	Description	Header File
`int atoi(const char a[]);`	Converts a string of characters to an integer.	`cstdlib`
`long atol(const char a[]);`	Converts a string of characters to a *long* integer.	`cstdlib`
`double atof(const char a[]);`	Converts a string of characters to a *double*.	`cstdlib`*
`strcat(String_Variable, String_Expression);`	Appends the value of the *String_Expression* to the end of the string in the *String_Variable*.	`cstring`
`strcmp(String_Exp1, String_Exp2)`	Returns *true* if the values of the two string expressions are different; otherwise, returns *false*.†	`cstring`
`strcpy(String_Variable, String_Expression);`	Changes the value of the *String_Variable* to the value of the *String_Expression*.	`cstring`
`strlen(String_Expression)`	Returns the length of the *String_Expression*.	`cstring`
`strncat(String_Variable, String_Expression, Limit);`	Same as strcat except that at most *Limit* characters are appended.	`cstring`
`strncmp(String_Exp1, String_Exp2, Limit)`	Same as strcmp except that at most *Limit* characters are compared.	`cstring`
`strncpy(String_Variable, String_Expression, Limit);`	Same as strcpy except that at most *Limit* characters are copied.	`cstring`
`strstr(String_Expression, Pattern)`	Returns a pointer to the first occurrence of the string *Pattern* in *String_Expression*. Returns the NULL pointer if the *Pattern* is not found.	`cstring`
`strchr(String_Expression, Character)`	Returns a pointer to the first occurrence of the *Character* in *String_Expression*. Returns the NULL pointer if *Character* is not found.	`cstring`
`strrchr(String_Expression, Character)`	Returns a pointer to the last occurrence of the *Character* in *String_Expression*. Returns the NULL pointer if *Character* is not found.	`cstring`

*Some implementations place it in `cmath`.
†Returns an integer that is less than zero, zero, or greater than zero according to whether *String_Exp1* is less than, equal to, or greater than *String_Exp2*, respectively. The ordering is lexicographic ordering.

Random Number Generator

Function Declaration	Description	Header File
`int random(int);`	The call random(n) returns a pseudorandom integer greater than or equal to 0 and less than or equal to n-1. (Not available in all implementations. If not available, then you must use rand.)	`cstdlib`
`int rand();`	The call rand( ) returns a pseudorandom integer greater than or equal to 0 and less than or equal to RAND_MAX. RAND_MAX is a predefined integer constant that is defined in cstdlib. The value of RAND_MAX is implementation dependent but will be at least 32767.	`cstdlib`

`void srand(unsigned int);`
`void srandom(unsigned int);`
 	
(The type `unsigned int` is an integer type that only allows nonnegative values. You can think of the argument type as `int` with the restriction that it must be nonnegative.)
	Reinitializes the random number generator. The argument is the seed. Calling srand multiple times with the same argument will cause rand or random (whichever you use) to produce the same sequence of pseudorandom numbers. If rand or random is called without any previous call to srand, the sequence of numbers produced is the same as if there had been a call to srand with an argument of 1.	`cstdlib`

Trigonometric Functions

These functions use radians, not degrees.

Function Declaration	Description	Header File
double acos(*double*);	Arc cosine	cmath
double asin(*double*);	Arc sine	cmath
double atan(*double*);	Arc tangent	cmath
double cos(*double*);	Cosine	cmath
double cosh(*double*);	Hyperbolic cosine	cmath
double sin(*double*);	Sine	cmath
double sinh(*double*);	Hyperbolic sine	cmath
double tan(*double*);	Tangent	cmath
double tanh(*double*);	Hyperbolic tangent	cmath

Inline Functions

When a member function definition is short, you can give the function definition within the definition of the class. You simply replace the member function declaration with the member function definition; however, since the definition is within the class definition, you do not include the class name and scope resolution operator. For example, the class Pair defined below has inline function definitions for its two constructors and for the member function get_first:

```
class Pair
{
public:
    Pair( ) {}
    Pair(char first_value, char second_value)
        : first(first_value), second(second_value) {}
    char get_first()
    {
        return first;
    }
    ...
private:
    char first;
    char second;
};
```

Note that there is no semicolon needed after the closing brace in an inline function definition, though it is not incorrect to have a semicolon there.

Inline function definitions are treated differently by the compiler and so they usually run more efficiently, although they consume more storage. With an inline function, each function call in your program is replaced by a compiled version of the function definition, so calls to inline functions do not have the overhead of a normal function call.

Overloading the Array Index Square Brackets

You can overload the square brackets, [], for a class so that they can be used with objects of the class. If you want to use [] in an expression on the left-hand side of an assignment operator, then the operator must be defined to return a reference, which is indicated by adding & to the returned type. (This has some similarity to what we discussed for overloading the I/O operators << and >>.) When overloading [], the operator [] *must* be a member function; the overloaded [] *cannot* be a friend operator. (In this regard, [] is overloaded in a way similar to the way in which the assignment operator = is overloaded; overloading = is discussed in the section of Chapter 11 entitled "Overloading the Assignment Operator.")

For example, the following defines a class called Pair whose objects behave like arrays of characters with the two indexes 1 and 2 (*not* 0 and 1):

```
class Pair
{
public:
    Pair();
    Pair(char first_value, char second_value);
    char& operator[](int index);
private:
    char first;
    char second;
};
```

The definition of the member function[] can be as follows:

```
char& Pair::operator[](int index)
{
    if (index == 1)
        return first;
    else if (index == 2)
        return second;
    else
    {
        cout << "Illegal index value.\n";
        exit(1);
    }
}
```

Objects are declared and used as follows:

```
Pair a;
a[1] = 'A';
a[2] = 'B';
cout << a[1] << a[2] << endl;
```

Note that in a[1], a is the calling object and 1 is the argument to the member function [].

When defining member functions for a class, you sometimes want to refer to the calling object. The *this* pointer is a predefined pointer that points to the calling object. For example, consider a class like the following:

```
class Sample
{
public:
    ...
    void show_stuff();
    ...
private:
    int stuff;
    ...
};
```

The following two ways of defining the member function show_stuff are equivalent:

```
void Sample::show_stuff()
{
    cout << stuff;
}
//Not good style, but this illustrates the this pointer:
void Sample::show_stuff()
{
    cout << (this->stuff);
}
```

Notice that *this* is not the name of the calling object, but is the name of a pointer that points to the calling object. The *this* pointer cannot have its value changed; it always points to the calling object.

As the comment before the previous sample use of *this* indicates, you normally have no need for the pointer *this*. However, in a few situations it is handy.

One place where the *this* pointer is commonly used is in overloading the assignment operator =. For example, consider the following class:

Overloading the assignment operator

```
class StringClass
{
public:
    ...
    StringClass& operator =(const StringClass& right_side);
    ...
private:
    char *a;//Dynamic array for a string value ended with '\0.'
};
```

The following definition of the overloaded assignment operator can be used in chains of assignments like

```
s1 = s2 = s3;
```

This chain of assignments means

```
s1 = (s2 = s3);
```

The definition of the overloaded assignment operator uses the *this* pointer to return the object on the left side of the = sign (which is the calling object):

```
//This version does not work in all cases. Also see the next version.
StringClass& StringClass::operator =(const StringClass& right_side)
{
    delete [] a;
    a = new char[strlen(right_side.a) + 1];
    strcpy(a, right_side.a);
    return *this;
}
```

The definition above does have a problem in one case: If the same object occurs on both sides of the assignment operator (like s=s;), then the array member will be deleted. To avoid this problem, you can use the *this* pointer to test this special case as follows:

```
//Final version with bug fixed:
StringClass& StringClass::operator =(
const StringClass& right_side)
{
    if (this == &right_side)
    {
        return *this;
    }
    else
    {
        delete [] a;
        a = new char [strlen(right_side.a) + 1];
        strcpy(a, right_side.a);
        return *this;
    }
}
```

In the section of Chapter 11 entitled "Overloading the Assignment Operator," we overloaded the assignment operator for a string class called StringVar. In that section, we did not need the *this* pointer because we had a member variable called max_length that we could use to test whether or not the same object was used on both sides of the assignment operator =. With the class StringClass discussed above, we have no such alternative because there is only one member variable. In this case, we have essentially no alternative but to use the *this* pointer.

Overloading Operators as Member Operators

In this book we have normally overloaded operators by treating them as friends of the class. For example, in Display 11.5 of Chapter 11 we overloaded the + operator as a friend. We did this by labeling the operator a friend inside the class definition, as follows:

```
//Class for amounts of money in U.S. currency.
class Money
{
public:
    friend Money operator +(const Money& amount1,
                            const Money& amount2);
    . . .
```

We then defined the overloaded operator + outside the class definition (as shown in Display 11.5).

It is also possible to overload the operator + (and other operators) as **member operators**. To overload the + operator as a member operator, the class definition would instead begin as follows:

```
//Class for amounts of money in U.S. currency.
class Money
{
public:
    Money operator +(const Money& amount2);
```

Note that when a binary operator is overloaded as a member operator, there is only one (not two) parameters. The calling object serves as the first parameter. For example, consider the following code:

```
Money cost(1, 50), tax(0, 15), total;
total = cost + tax;
```

When + is overloaded as a member operator, then in the expression cost + tax, the variable cost is the calling object and tax is the one argument to +.

The definition of the member operator + would be as follows:

```
Money Money::operator +(const Money& amount2)
{
    Money temp;
```

```
        temp.all_cents = all_cents + amount2.all_cents;
        return temp;
    }
```

Notice the following line from this member operator definition:

```
    temp.all_cents = all_cents + amount2.all_cents;
```

The first argument to + is an unqualified all_cents, and so it is the member variable all_cents *of the calling object.*

Overloading an operator as a member variable can seem strange at first, but it is easy to get used to the new details. Many experts advocate always overloading operators as member operators rather than as friends. That is more in the spirit of object-oriented programming. However, there is a big disadvantage to overloading a binary operator as a member operator. When you overload a binary operator as a member operator, the two arguments are no longer symmetric. One is a calling object and only the second "argument" is a true argument. This is unaesthetic, but it also has a very practical shortcoming. Any automatic type conversion will only apply to the second argument. So, for example, the following would be legal:

```
    Money base_amount(100, 60), full_amount;
    full_amount = base_amount + 25;
```

This is because Money has a constructor with one argument of type *long,* and so the value 25 will be considered a *long* value that is automatically converted to a value of type Money.

However, if you overload+ as a member operator, then you cannot reverse the two arguments to +. The following is illegal:

```
    full_amount = 25 + base_amount;
```

This is because 25 cannot be a calling object. Conversion of *long* values to type Money works for arguments but not for calling objects.

On the other hand, if you overload + as a friend, then the following is perfectly legal:

```
    full_amount = 25 + base_amount;
```

Index